The Great Debate:

The Need For Constitution Reform

Rodney D. Scott

University of Saint Francis

 Rampant Lion Press
Chicago

Library of Congress Catalog Card Number 99-093525

ISBN: 0-9674298-0-3

    1. United States - Politics and Government.

    2. Includes Bibliography, References, and Index.

First Printing

Rampant Lion Press

Chicago, Illinois, 60626

Contents

Part 3: The Need for Updating the Constitution

Part 4: A Newly Revised Constitution for the Twenty-First Century

Part 5: An Analysis of the Proposed Constitution

Part 6: An Overview

Part 7: Appendix

Part 8: References and Notes

Figures and Charts

Chapter 1

Introduction

How important are Constitutions? There is a progression that moves such discussions. One question will lead to another, then another, and so forth. It becomes like a journey into the mist. At first all that is seen is the fog and spray of the unknown, but by answering that first question it leads a person to another inquiry. With each response you move down the trail. You find that as you move down the path each idea and concept becomes clear. They can be understood. All that is really required is to face the issue and to ask that first question.

These issues start with the simplest of concepts. We have heard the old adage many times, "A journey of a thousand miles starts with the first step." You know that something is not right, there is something within our system of government, or our structure, or how we have developed, that is incorrect. You can see the symptom. It stands before you like a beacon. In the case of the United States government it is voter participation. If you accept the idea that America presents a system of self-government, but the reality is that the people are not voting and they are not participating, what develops is a contradiction. The very minimum level of participation in government is the casting of a ballot. This in itself is not the problem. It is a symptom of a larger problem, one that is far more profound and far more difficult to address.

As you begin to look at the problems that alienate the people from their government, issues such as campaign finances, representation, taxation, bureaucratic processes, regulation, or governmental expenditures you begin to realize that the problem does not always lead back to our elected officials or their policies. The path many times leads back to the American Constitution. There are a collection of items that are either out of date, no longer apply, are no longer being used, are being ignored, or simply do not work. If we concede that our government, and to a lesser extent our society, emerges from the Constitution, then this becomes the issue. The more a person examines the Constitution the more it becomes apparent that this is part of the reason why many feel disinherited by the process.

It is possible for a person to disagree with this assessment, but there is a simple experiment that can be run. An individual needs to obtain a copy of the United States Constitution. You can find one in an almanac, most encyclopedias, on the Internet, in the back of most 7th grade government books, or in the pages of this work. You can invest an hour in Democracy. Read through the document. Everything that does not make sense, that no longer applies, items that are not being followed, issues that generate some dissatisfaction, sections that are unreadable, or even parts in which you feel we can do better—yellow them with a marking pen. When you compete the process look at the document. There is a belief that the average person will have fifteen or eighteen items that have been yellowed. In actuality it may be even more if a person understands how the document has evolved over the years and how it has been interpreted. The message is a simple one—that the American Constitution is in need of updating.

This should not be seen as a great conspiracy. It is not some effort on the part of our elected officials to estrange the people. This is not a matter of fault. It is time. It is two hundred plus years of living, evolving, changing as a people. We are not the same people that we were two hundred years ago. Our culture has changed, our ethnic mix has changed, our tolerance has improved, our technology has advanced, our status on the world stage has changed. What was important for the Founding Fathers may not be that important to us. The size and structure of our government has changed. These adjustments do not always match the Constitution which we follow. In the end if there is an antagonist to be found it is within us.

I recognize that I have reached a point that many others have not, I believe that the United States constitution is out of sync with our government and our society. If we are to have self-government, democracy and logical processes to our system of administration we need to upgrade and modernize our social contract. This is an important issue. A Constitution should be seen not as an icon of the society, but as a social contract. It is an agreement between the people and their government. It becomes more than just adding a new amendment or changing the legislative rules of order. There comes a time that the fabric of the document itself becomes a problem. This can be found in issues of discrimination, contradictions within the text, and lack of clarity on many subjects.

The concern is that our Constitution will become like the Magna Carta and the British uncodified system. Great Britain does have a Constitution, but it is not a written document. It is a product of custom, common law, and government decrees. The declaration that "the British Constitution is whatever Parliament wants it to be" is true. There will come a time that the Constitution will be so far removed from the realities of our society and government that it no longer applies. It becomes a consideration, but not a usable instrument. What will be important are the interpretations that have emerged from the document. For the average citizen the constitution becomes nothing more than a symbol.

This work should not be seen as a condemnation of the American Constitution. The United States constitution has served this nation. Democracy has been advanced, we have gained from the experience, and as a nation we are better because of it. The constitution has been a beacon of light in a dark world of oppression and tyranny. It has withstood the test of time and we have accomplished great things under its umbrella. Within its pages we have expanded the idea of individual rights and these ideas have been duplicated in other Constitutions found around the world. The greatest compliment that can be given to the American Constitution is that it put the concepts of self-government and democracy into play. It stands as one of the most consequential documents of all time and a pathfinder for civil liberty. The only argument that is being made is that the United States constitution is not the last stop in the road toward democratic Arcadia. It is one of the signposts. As a nation, as a people we need from time to time review and examine the nature of our government. Democracy requires it. It is a healthy process and one in which knowledge can be obtained.

There are so many paradoxes in American institutions and society. As a civilization the United States has obtained the pinnacle of enlightenment— harmonious and accomplished in the ways of popular government. America is a society comfortable in its culture, tolerant of others beliefs, and supportive of initiative. We do not stand on ceremony, but we are proud of our traditions and heritage. There is a richness to our diversity, and an informality to our actions. We are a just people, a fair people, one in which vitality and energy is rewarded. We are by nature inquisitive, industrious, and creative. Yet equally, Americans can be pretentious, self-absorbed, and poorly mannered. We are provincial, trapped in our own idiom and what is familiar.

This same paradox exists for our government. It was the United States that for the first time in recorded history set up a structure of self-government, popularly elected, and with civic administration. In the United States, democracy and republican government are very real. There is a link between the people and their elected officials. Our government is aware of the interest of the people and efforts are made to include the masses in the issues of the day. Our government as an institution has been established by the Constitution, based on principles of justice and equal rights. These ideas of democracy and self-government move not only from the national level but permeate throughout state and local governments as well. Yet, in this same environment the people we elect to office can be aloof and unapproachable. While talking about democracy on one hand our leaders finds ways to insulate themselves from the public on the other. The government becomes fearful of change and determined to protect itself at all cost. It is a government driven by money, personal gratification, and influence.

The great question is whether we are a democracy at all, or whether the United States is actually a plutocracy. If it is so, then every word ever spoken about democracy and self-government has been false. It would represent one of the greatest misappropriations of public trust ever created upon man. Ideas of democracy are incompatible with any other form of government, it must exist in its purest form. Any effort to adjust or contaminate the democratic process of government leads quickly to a degenerate form of rule. Democracy must be first and foremost the chief theory behind the promotion of government.

In this work the issue of whether the United States is a plutocracy is not addressed. It becomes a matter of what a person wants to believe. It is democracy that is important, the key issue is to improve the workings of self-government. The questions that need to be asked are how can we have more democracy, how can we build upon the current system to enhance the ideas of popular government? Republican government is a matter of degrees. The system that was put into place by the Founding Fathers of the United States was not the last word in free government. As a people we need to explore ways to refine, upgrade, and modernize our democracy. The question is not whether we are a democracy, but more a matter of how can we have more of it.

When a person begins to examine the inequities and flaws within our government some of the hardest of all questions must be asked. The problem becomes more profound than first imagined. There are a collection of problems in American society and the practical workings of government. All nations have such issues. Conflicts occurring over procedures, policy, leadership, modes of conduct, and even expectations are common. When an individual begins to examine many of these issues of the day, the problem may not be social or a point of policy at all, it may be constitutional. The path to correcting or addressing the predicaments that we find ourselves may not be a matter of procedure, legislation, or even moral conduct, but in the constitution itself. We are a Constitutional government, it stands to reason that if we have problems with our relationship with our government that some of these difficulties will be found within the document.

Just one example can be made with the issue of Campaign Finance Reform. This has been an ongoing problem for decades. To run for political office in the United States is an extremely expensive process that can cost millions of dollars, and the higher the office the more exorbitant the amount. In the 104th Congress, 92 bills were written to address the issue of campaign reform. The introduction of such statues has become a common occurrence with each Congress. Most bills die, but over the years a number have been passed. Regardless of their intentions each has been ineffective. The amount of money needed to run for office has only increased. The amount of time that a candidate requires to solicit funds has increased proportionately as well. Money finds ways to enter the political arena, loopholes abound, and the realities of running for political office overshadow the spirit of any campaign law.[1]

One of the problems is that the Supreme Court has ruled that money is a form of freedom of speech.[2] This is not an illicit concept. Few of us are eager to have the government tell us how we may spend our personal resources. Independent political action committees can be set up, funds can be given to political parties, and money can be diverted to supportive organizations. There are many ways that money can play a part in the system. If there is an honest desire to correct the problem then the trail leads back to the United States Constitution. Any sincere effort to address the problem of Campaign Finance Reform is going to have to take a long hard look at the Constitution itself. There are solutions, but they are found not in restricting campaign financing, but in establishing finite representation. This is but one example, and scores of these types of process problems exist.

This same type of argument can be made for racism. If the position of our society is that race does not make a difference in character, and that the human condition is universal, then our social contract needs to represent that fact. The reality is that the American Constitution was based on the belief that race did matter and that one group of people was superior to another. If we as a people wish to truly make progress in the area of race relations it must start with our Constitution. It is this document that needs to be reconstructed. All other efforts will be false. A Constitution is a prelude for everything else that follows.

This work can actually be seen in two parts. The first is a critique of the United States Constitution and the second is a proposed Constitution. It seems incredibly unjust to criticize an icon of human rectitude and one of the noblest of documents without producing an alternative. The pressure is always on the progressive or the reformer, not only must they show where the current system is flawed, but they must also put forth a valid alternative. The argument is simply that the American Constitution needs to be upgraded and modernized. It is a document written two hundred years ago, in an age and time that few people today understand or can relate. Its utility comes from our interpretation of the document, not by the intent of its drafters or the reality of the words found within the text. As a people we have changed, and our relationship to the document contrasts that of an infant to an adult. We have grown and we have learned from the experience. The question that is being asked is whether it is the correct document for our times and is it possible to have even greater levels of democracy than what we have had in the past?

The proposed Constitution, which is found in this study, is not designed to be a radical document. While clearly the views and concepts are those of the author, it is not remotely believed that this represents the ultimate in constitution writing. The exercise is done to show that a Constitution can be written that enhances democracy and represents a more conspicuous view of what we are as a nation. It should also be understood and recognized that this should not be an activity only for the elites of our society. Those with common sense and a fair understanding of representative government could write such a document. For those that attempt such an activity, they will learn more about the attributes of democratic government and the spirit of American society than from any other process. It is a feat that allows a person to touch the soul of a nation.

It is also possible to view such a proposed Constitution as being presumptuous. The United States Constitution is truly an icon, not only for this country but the world at large. Any effort at replacing such a document could be viewed as arrogant or egotistical. Again, that is not the intent. The theory is that a Constitution should not just be a symbol of democracy. It is more than simple image. A Constitution is a working document, a contract in the most realistic of terms. It needs to set clear boundaries and structures for government. As a document it needs not only to spell out our rights, but secure those entitlements as well. It is a document of law and one of maintenance of a society. As it is with so many items, time does erode, it nibbles away at intent and meaning. The difference lies between having a Constitution that is dynamic, but unaccustomed, compared to one that is venerated, but needs high levels of explanation.

This does not mean there is not an agenda. To write such a document requires that a base be formed. In this case the issue is either democracy or logic. Every issue needs to be placed into the light of these two concepts. By doing so drives the process forward. Each system in our administration, every law passed by our legislative body, each structure of government, and every Article in the Constitution should be tested against this premise. Is it more democratic?

The challenge is the same for each generation, to accept the traditions of democracy while enlarging its tenets. It is more than simply a matter of legislation, or regulation, or executive order. We should not accept only what is given. The demagoguery of the times can distort the actual purpose and the goals. There comes a time in which the foundation itself must be examined, to see if there are any cracks, to see if what was originally designed is still true. Is it enough simply to be vigilant, or must we also press our government for greater levels of "democratic thought and republican government"?

There will be those that view the idea of a new constitution as being an issue of considerable instability. The hope is nearly the reverse. An honest review of our current document will strengthen the nation and enhance it. We will either confirm our current Constitution, accepting it as it was written, or we will adjust it so that it mirrors our prevailing views of self-government. The greater fear is to do nothing. Each person or group will be able to read into the Constitution their own ideas. They will be able to pick from the time frame, find their own phrases, and use those words that they see as most advantageous to their cause. The Supreme Court is not the only entity that can interpret the United States Constitution. It is a process that nourishes extremism. Each Article will be subject to ever increasing levels of interpretation and renderings. Instead of creating clarity, it will heighten confusion. In the end not only will stability be lost, but so will our democracy. The greater the distance between the people and their social contract the greater the chance of conflict or revolt.

The goal of this work is not acceptance of what has been written, but dialog. It is believed that discussion and debate over the scope and character of government is healthy. After the completion of the American Constitution in 1787, and during the time the states began to ratify the document, there was a great debate in our society. It was communal in nature. Newspapers in the thirteen original states published articles condemning or supporting the new Constitution. It was discussed on street corners, across rail fences, in church yards, in apple orchards and town squares. It was a time of defining the nation, and who we were as a people. It not only established a Constitution, but confirmed a system of government. Nothing can be more vitalizing and inspiring for a people. What is actually being advocated is that same type of discussion and deliberation. It may require effort and time, but we would learn a great deal about ourselves and the essence of what we call America.

Even so, this is a work produced in the most troublesome of circumstances and motives. Political treatises are commonly designed to study a universal truth, or explore some point of logic. They are created from constructs of philosophy and analytical reasoning. This is a document which manifested itself out of a deep-seated sense of frustration. Hostility should not be a basis for a system of review. A study into the basic concepts and the nature of a government should not be done in haste, it should be an orderly activity, objective and fair, but there are times in which an attitude of discord does appear. This is reported with regret and the hope that some of this indiscretion can be forgiven.

It is not clear where this frustration manifests itself. Is it the responsibility of the people to speak out on issues of Constitutional reform? Is it a matter of leadership? Should our political or judicial leaders be advocating Constitutional restoration? Regardless, on a personal level the effort does become therapeutic. It forces an individual to exam our government and society. It sets to paper the nature of the problem and possible solutions. Even if the words are never read or heard they have been placed on the doorstep. The effort has been made and it is better to have made the attempt than not.

The sections that follow is an effort to review parts of the United States Constitution to see if the constructs within the document match our contemporary conception of it and if these sections are responsive to issues related to self-government.

Part One: An Accounting

Chapter 2

How Did We Get to This Point?

The issues related to the United States Constitution did not occur in a vacuum. There is a layering effect—years of events, conflicts, personal ambition, the exercise of power, a communal narrative, and the reality of surviving as a nation. There has also been the advancement of human knowledge, the merging of social interest, the establishment of a distinct culture, and the creation of national myths. Each item has changed the American people. Each one has made us something different, but what has continued is this one strand of history.

Articles of Confederation. The story of the American Constitution is not one that starts with the hot summer of 1787 and the Constitutional Convention in Philadelphia. Rather, the seeds of the American Constitution were sown long before—they are found in the Articles of Confederation and the American Revolution. The war of independence represented a Constitutional crisis.[1] While the British had no written document, nor was a specific social compact in place between the home country and the colonies, there was nevertheless an implied understanding. A tenuous agreement not based on fact. The disunity that brought about the Revolution dealt with the conflict between these two points of view on what the implied agreement represented and the relationship each party had to the other. By virtue of this conflict, the nation's founders thought of written prerequisites and constitutions. The other issue dealt with the existing body of laws, which in this case was the Articles of Confederation.

The Articles of Confederation were adopted in 1781 when the Revolutionary War was still in progress, but it had been written many years earlier.[2] Congress had actually created the document at the beginning of the war, but had great difficulty getting it ratified. The Articles were not set up to install democracy; this was a war time document designed more as a working agreement between the different colonies rather than as a social compact. It created a conformity of action. There was a need for a common purpose. The colonies were involved in a life and death struggle with Great Britain. The ideas of the Articles of

Confederation were simple and plain in design. The document was designed purely to maintain a loose Confederation among the thirteen colonies.[3]

Even with its shortcomings the Articles of Confederation did preserve a relationship among the different states. Many individuals did see the Continental Congress as a central government, but others saw it as nothing more than an association, a gentlemen's agreement to meet and discuss issues of common interest. A review of the Articles of Confederation would not necessarily lead to the belief that the document was inept. Congress did have the power to wage war, make peace, borrow money, create a postal system, raise armed forces, and complete treaties. Under the Articles, congress could also settle disputes among the states, and the central government did act as a unifying force. Even so, some major problems surfaced with this document. It lacked provision for a chief executive who could speak for the nation. While the national government did have a President, the term was for one year, and the officeholder remained solidly aligned to his own state. Equally, the continental Congress had no power to enforce the laws they created. There was no judiciary to interpret the law, nor was there a method of protecting property rights. Congress did have the power to make treaties but no way of forcing the states to adhere to these agreements, and in some cases the states were actively engaged in negotiating with foreign powers themselves. Each state was also beginning to issue its own money, and the weak paper currency that was started began to hurt all the governments concerned.

Dominant problems. A focal point of all these issues was national defense; it was believed a strong union would create greater security for all the states.[4] To this end two problems were considered most pressing. The first dealt with the fact that congress could not levy taxes; needed money had to be requested from the states. Such funds were not guaranteed. If the states disapproved of the reasons the central government wished to requisition the money or had budgetary problems of their own or were politically unsupportive of the national government, no revenue was forthcoming. This had become a major problem, and consequently the states were not sending funds to Congress. Money that had been promised was not being delivered and the debt generated by the Revolutionary War was not being paid.

The second problem dealt with commerce. This was a substantial issue. It dealt with not only trade between states but also international exchanges. Foreign nations were beginning to play one state against another, especially in commerce. since congress under the Articles had no power to regulate commerce, the states were beginning to undermine the trade of one another. There was no national consensus. If the Articles of Confederation had stayed in place it is unlikely the United States would have survived. The country would have broken down into individual commonwealths or realigned into different Confederation.

Issues outside of the Articles of Confederation concerned the nation's founders as well. Shay's Rebellion had a sobering effect on all the legislative bodies. When the framers of the Constitution talked about *domestic tranquillity* they meant just that; possible revolts and ongoing conflicts were a real concern. From their view the Articles had developed into a Constitutional crisis that would lead to ever increasing levels of hostility and discord. In turn this would advance into violence, then chaos, and finally tyranny. The people would turn to a strong leader to give them security and stability. While such a leader may accomplish, and even excel, in such a task of creating stability, it would also lead to a loss of liberty. This was an honest concern and a theme the Federalists advanced. An example of the French Revolution and Napoleon can be used to authenticate such a scenario.

The first attempt to correct the Articles of Confederation occurred in 1786 only twelve delegates appeared; hence they were unable to achieve a quorum. Believing it was the last chance for the nation. Madison pressed forward for another convention the following year. This time it would be held in Philadelphia.[5]

The Virginia Plan. Even so, their mandate was quite limited. The delegates who appeared in Philadelphia were to examine the Articles of Confederation, their goal being not to create a new Constitution, but more a matter of revision. Two proposals were brought to the initial sessions by the delegates, the first being the *New Jersey Plan*. It represented an honest effort to reconsider the Articles of Confederation. A number of suggestions in the New Jersey Plan were designed to strengthen the national government and give it more power. The second proposal was called the *Virginia Plan*. A rebuff of the Articles of Confederation, this plan presented a sketch for a new Constitution. Within the first few weeks of the convention the New Jersey Plan was rejected, leaving the delegates little choice but to draft a new national document.[6]

The Virginia Plan became a basis from which to operate. It was a valid concept, supporting a stronger centralized government with taxing powers and a judiciary. Most of the convention dealt with tinkering with this document, either expanding or adjusting the ideas found within it. Some of the key ideas found within the Virginia Plan were a one-term legislature to which the members would be elected for seven years. The design was closely related to the parliamentary system with the chief executive connected to the legislative branch of government. This premise was widely supported and had survived all of the votes within the convention until the last one; even so, this issue was debated. The topic centered on a strong Presidency to rival the monarchs found in other countries. Governor Morris had felt very fervently about this item and campaigned hard for a more forceful executive office. He was given the task of writing the final draft for the executive branch. He added the veto power, a shorter term, and electoral college, which in effect changed the nature of the office. The vote was close but Morris' position appeared in the final draft of the Constitution.[7]

This Executive branch was designed to have the greatest power beyond the domestic scene. The President would have the power to negotiate treaties, appoint ambassadors, and receive diplomats. It would also be the responsibility of the chief executive to appoint government officials and judges to the courts. One of the reasons for the Constitution in the first place was to have more applicable control over foreign affairs. There was no collective interest and the states were beginning to operate purely in their own interest on foreign affairs.[8]

Few controversial issues surrounded the Judicial branch of government. This package moved through he convention with little revision. The only item debated at any length was the nature of the inferior Federal courts, but the delegates recognized the need for a Supreme Court early in the convention process. It passed through the Constitutional Convention unencumbered.

Many of the issues during the convention centered on the legislative branch of government. In fact the core of most discussions surrounded this concept. The biggest problem was the Senate rather than the House of Representatives.

While most of the delegates were willing to concede that the House would be based on the nation's population, the Senate was a different matter. The smaller states demanded equal representation. As much as any issue the success of the Constitutional Convention hinged on this issue. Proposals were many and the debate extensive. The larger states initially wanted the Senate based on population; later that was changed to classes of population. One proposal put forth wanted the Senate to represent the wealth of the states. The greater the affluence of a state, the greater its representation. The smaller states would not budge. In the end each state obtained two Senators for the upper house.

The issue of a Constitution, or any type of social contract, is always a complex one. The number of issues that need to be reviewed, addressed, debated, voted on, accepted, or rejected is almost unlimited. Even items that clearly do not belong within a Constitution have to be critiqued. As a rule the Founders covered a wide range of political and social issues, their effort was complete. In the case of the Philadelphia Constitutional convention fifty-five delegates were present at various times, each with a point of view, each with ideas that needed to be digested. Every issue cannot be won. In the end the only recourse was compromise. The nation's founders relied on compromise as a tool, and the truth is that the document would never have been written without concessions being made by all the parties concerned. It became part of the Constitutional process. In the end not everyone was happy with the new Constitution. Edmund Randolph, George Mason, and Elbridge Gerry refused to sign the final draft. Robert Yates and John Lansing had left the convention on July 10th and Luther Martin on September 4th. They were dissatisfied with the direction the Constitution was taking.

Ratification. At the end of the convention the document was delivered to the individual states for *ratification*. There would be no referendum by the people; the issue would be determined by the state legislatures either within these bodies or by convention. A great national debate occurred, though, between those opposing the new Constitution and its supporters. Those who encouraged passage were called Federalist and those against the document the Anti-Federalist. The terms can be misleading. The American Constitution as it was drafted in 1787 was not Federalist in nature, it may have been more Federal than the Articles of

Confederation, but the states enjoyed considerable power under this Constitution. One consistent view took the opinion that the power of the Federal government emerged from the state governments, a view not much different from the Articles of Confederation.

Through the Anti-Federalist had many concerns, they were never very consolidated in their opposition. At one time or another they had attacked every section of the Constitution. They were insecure about the Federal government's ability to tax or to organize standing armies, as well as the nature of representation, and the power of the executive office. The Anti-Federalist talked about the "consolidated system" of government, which they saw as an eroding of the independence of the states. They also argued against the national government having power to guide commerce. It was noted that a huge bureaucracy would be needed to regulate interstate and foreign commerce. Equally, there was a concern of the national government's ability to control state militias. The federal government could call them up and then transport these troops to any part of the country that they saw fit. The most powerful of all the Anti-Federalist arguments was the need for a Bill of Rights.[9]

Throughout this great debate, which appeared in the various New York newspapers, the Federalist had one advantage. They were united behind their support for a new Constitution. The views of the Anti-Federalist appeared all over the political spectrum. Some disliked the Constitution, but also hated the Articles of Confederation; others wanted a new Constitution but did not support the draft that appeared out of Philadelphia; still others had specific agendas of their own. Several wanted the establishment of a state religion or wanted the government to endorse various types of Christian doctrine. Some Anti-Federalist were political enemies of the delegates to the convention. No matter what was produced, they would have opposed it. The Anti-Federalist who were state leaders were concerned about the loss of esteem for the states. Others felt that old was better than new; and some believed the new Constitution was not democratic enough. This great debate went on for two years until finally the Federalist carried the day and the new Constitution was ratified.[10]

Delaware was the first to ratify, and they did so during the same year that the Constitution was drafted. A number of state legislatures had uncertainties about this new proposal, and years went by before the issue was settled. Rhode Island was the last to ratify the Constitution in 1790. They felt uncomfortable about being such a small state within this grouping of larger bodies. It was lonely after the other states began to treat Rhode Island as a separate nation that it joined the new Union. The chief Constitutional item that appeared from this great debate was the Bill of Rights. Virginia, Massachusetts, New York, and Pennsylvania refused to ratify the new document unless a promise was given that such a listing of rights would be included. The Bill of Rights, and its supporting Amendments, was one of the first topics taken up by the Congress when it met in 1791.

Even upon ratification the Constitution was but an outline.[11] The task was left to the first Congress to fill out the document and make it a working instrument of government. While the Constitution made provisions for an Army and Navy, the reality was that the United Staes military consisted of only 672 men. The Navy did not have one ship. Not one government department was in place. There were no rules of order or procedure for the Federal legislative body. The first session of Congress had to develop and organize the infrastructure of government and with each step they refined the Constitution. At the same time discussions and debates abounded over the details of the document. The power of the Constitution emerged not from the model but from usage. The first Congress laid most of this groundwork.[12]

James Madison. Three individuals share the greatest responsibility for bringing the United States Constitution into existence. The first is James Madison. He alone was active in pressing the leadership of the Continental Congress to address the problems of the Articles of Confederation. At the Constitutional Convention, Virginia delegates were the dominant players in Colonial politics, and Madison knew how to gain support for this project from Virginia's leadership. Once the Convention was in place he had stationed himself near the front of the hall. He was keenly aware of the magnitude of these proceedings and made a conscious effort to be active in the business at hand.

The only comprehensive notes from the delegates came from Madison. It was a major task to outline the events and direction of the convention. Because

Madison had brought the Virginia Plan to Philadelphia, this allowed for a basis from which to operate, and most of the concepts found within the Constitution emerged from this plan. Madison was also active in the debates, discussions, and arguments that surrounded the assembly. He was willing to challenge any delegate, use whatever persuasion he could, test any theory, and deliberate on each issue.

Many refer to James Madison as the Father of the American Constitution. These words can scarcely be refuted. Madison was the one who stopped to see George Washington at Mount Vernon on his way to the convention in Philadelphia. Washington had been elected as a delegate as well but had shown little interest in attending the convention. After the discussion with Madison, Washington appeared at the conference a few days later. Though Washington's attendance may seem a minor event, in fact it had major implications for the nation as a whole.

George Washington. The second person to contribute in bringing the Constitution into existence was George Washington. He truly represented a piece of good fortune for this budding nation. Washington deserves to be called the Father of Our Country. He was not a flashy military commander; at best his military talents were marginal, but he knew that all he had to do was keep an American force in the field and in the end they would win. When Washington chaired the Constitutional Convention in Philadelphia his interaction with the delegates was limited. He gave only one speech. There were no flashes of brilliance, no vivid insights; George Washington simply administrated the convention. As President of the Constitutional Convention he brought his reputation. It was not his force of will that moved the momentous document to completion, but rather his presence. When the task was complete and those outside of the convention hall had a chance to see the document, it had to be taken seriously, if for no other reason than the fact that Washington had helped design it.

Washington's most important role in fashioning the Constitution was not his interaction at the convention, but his involvement as the first President of the United States. He was the perfect person for that office. He brought a sense of competence and integrity no one else could have at that time.

It is easy to criticize Washington's terms in office. As President his actions and political skills were minimal at best. Washington even openly stated that he disliked politics. Even so, it was his demeanor that made the Constitution real. He set the pattern that all other Presidents followed. It was not his performance as Chief Executive that is consequential, but the traditions he set. The greatest act he ever did for his country was not the battles he fought in the Revolutionary War, but the fact that he resisted becoming a monarch and after two terms in office he simply walked away.

The enormous benefit of George Washington's serving as the first President was that he had already made his reputation. His place in history was secure and to some degree Washington had little prove either to himself or to others. He served as President because his nation needed him; that alone was his motivation. Would this same scenario work if individuals such as Aaron Burr, Alexander Hamilton, or John Hancock had been our first President? Each was politically active at this time; both men pursued the Presidency during their lifetimes. Their personalities and mannerisms were much more intense. They had agendas and would have worked toward their goals. What Washington did was establish the Constitution. He developed the relationship between the Executive Branch and the other parts of government. It was important, far more important than anything else he could have done while in office.

John Marshall. The third individual who breathed life into the American Constitution was John Marshall. Appointed to the Supreme Court by John Adams, Marshall quickly became one of the most dominant individuals the court has ever produced. Until the appointment of Marshall the Supreme Court had been seen as feeble.The High Court was beleaguered by constant turnover, indecisiveness, absenteeism, limited personnel, and a lack of leadership.[13] Through a sense of duty and personal will he established the concept of *Judicial Review*. The Constitution became an animate element in the rule of law and became connected to the society as a whole. Marshall raised the American Constitution to a different level and with it the national government.

This is not to say that Marshall was altruistic in his proceedings within the court. Marshall should be seen as the first judicial activist.[14] In his early years he was also heavily engaged in partisan politics. Marshall served in the Adams

Administration as Secretary of State and was deeply involved in Federalist issues. He also had some animosity toward the Jeffersonians and their political agenda. Nonetheless, he spent thirty-four years on the bench and the impression he made is unmistakable. More than any other person Marshall created an independent judiciary.

The difference with John Marshall was that he began to interpret the Constitution and he did so unlike anyone else had ever done. The court's power of judicial review is not listed in the Constitution. It emanated from the general assertions made by Marshall. He expanded meanings, deciphered original intent, and contested the established view of the document. All the while he increased the power and esteem of the High Court. The United States Constitution developed a character under the supervision of Marshall. The Constitution is as much a product of John Marshall as it is of the nation's founders.

Once created the American Constitution settles into an evolutionary process. The document is pressed, converted, and reinvented. Each branch of government leaves a mark or attempts to twist the document to meet a need or serve an official purpose. Of the three branches of government, the Congress and the Judiciary have had the greatest effect on the Constitution. Of course the Executive Office has increased its power and prestige since the establishment of the Constitution. The Imperial Presidency does exist.[15] It is more to the point that Congress has the last word. The Legislative branch is driven by public opinion. Passing laws to gratify the passions of the masses is more prudent that declaring the issue unconstitutional. In turn, there have been many issues that Congress has been able to adjust within the Constitution without the item ever being successfully challenged in the court or going through the amendment process. Even more decided is the Supreme Court. It is their task to interpret the document. With every ruling and the passing of each year the Constitution changes. Small, unpretentious changes, but each one moves the document in a new direction.

Even the most elementary of reviews of the High Court's judgments will note this evolutionary process. One of the first major cases by John Marshall and surely one of the most important was *Marbury v. Madison* (1803).[16] In this case Marshall, as Chief Justice, declared that the Constitution was both law and the supreme law of the land. What the Supreme Court decided in *Marbury v. Madison* was that they could determine what was Constitutional and what was unconstitutional. In any type of conflict between a law passed by any legislature and the Constitution, the Constitution must prevail. This was not something new. Hamilton had hinted about this issue in the *Federalist Papers*, but it was Marshall who made Judicial Review a reality.[17]

With *McCullch v Maryland* in 1819[18] the court established the concept of implied powers. Specifically the court was talking about Congress creating a national bank, an act that represented an implied power. This decision empowered the Constitution beyond the structures of the basic design. The key was that the Constitution could be seen in a far broader sense and to some degree became more flexible. At this point Marshall argues the difference between plain meaning of the Constitution and literal meaning. From this juncture the Supreme Court begins to assess and interpret the document not just form what the Founders said, but what they intended to say.

In 1824 with *Gibbons v. Ogden* [19] the court moved into another area by declaring stronger Federal control over issues of commerce. A steamboat captain named Aaron Ogden from New Jersey had been using interior waterways in New York. The state of New York had created a monopoly and sold these rights to another steamshp line. They were refusing to allow Ogden access to these rivers. John Marshall ruled that the Federal government had jurisdiction over any issue of commerce that involved more than one state. In this case New York could not grant the monopoly. The ability to control business markets and transportation is a formidable tool in the repertoire of governmental powers.

This process was continued with the seating of each High Court. With each ruling the Constitution either became clearer in definition or is some cases moved in a different direction. *Dred Scott v Sanford* (1857), *Plessy v. Ferguson* (1896) , *Northern Securities v. the United States* (1904), *Schenck v. the United States* (1919), *Gitlow v. New York* (1925), *Schechter Poultry Corporation v. the United States* (1935), *Dennis et al. v. the United States* (1951), *Brown v. Board of Education of Topeka* (1954), *Mapp v. Ohio* (1961), *Griswold v. Connecticut* (1965), *Miranda v. Arizona* (1966), *Roe v. Wade* (1973), and *the United States v.*

Nixon (1974) just to name only a few of the cases that changed the Constitution.[20] In each case it became something different, it expanded, it broadened, it evolved.

The Federal history of the United States began with the American Constitution. Each decision adjusted and changed who we are as a people, each ruling moved our history in a different direction. The judgements of the courts transposed the society. Foreign Affairs, Economic Regulations, Treaty Making, Civil Rights, Suffrage, Minority Rights, Labor Reform, equal Protection under the Law, Segregation, War Powers, and Judicial Review: all of these concepts are revised or modified. Our history becomes the history of the Constitution.

The reality is that we reached this point by intervals of time. History has moved forward, each generation adding to the mix, each changing the perception of the American Constitution. We evolved as a people, but the question is whether our social contract has completed this transition intact? When do we look at our social contract and determine if it is still applicable. At what point does it become more than just an issue of connection? How do we reconcile our history with the obligations of constitutional government, or more correctly, when does history dissolve the document into the vastness of time?

Chapter 3

The Paradoxes to the American Constitution

The Preamble. It is odd that the very best thing about the United states Constitution is also the very worst thing about it. To some degree the best part of the American Constitution is the Preamble. It is more than simply an opening statement or an introduction. The Preamble to the Constitution has developed into a creed. It has moved from a collection of goals to a statement about our relationship with government. "We the people…" must be considered among the noblest words ever written. It represents a true turning point for humankind, a juncture from being ruled by peremptory leaders to a place where the people have a say in that leadership. It is unlike anything that has come before it; in fact to find another moment in history that represents the same type of axiom seems impossible. Clearly the Preamble is the essence of the American Constitution.

Having said this however, the problem is that the statement "We the people…" has actually evolved into the doctrine it represents today. The worst feature of the American Constitution is that when that Preamble was written, that creed of "We the people" did not exist. How we see the Preamble today is not even remotely connected to the views from which the statement was written. "We the people…" was a very secular term in the 1780s. It has the distinct meaning of the responsible electorate. "We the people…" did not mean all the people; but rather a select few. No matter how we wish to see the nations' founders, they were trapped by the logical conceptions of their day. It was a world of the elite few, and while the Revolutionary War was fought over many of these public immunities, levels of privilege continued to exist after the war. Revolutionary America was a community that mirrored British society. After all, the United States was a product of British civilization and culture. The British Parliament of the eighteenth century represented not the people but a select group. When the Founders wrote about "We the people…" it was more apt to mean, "We, the literate Caucasian property-owning males." Even on the issue of religion, the word Protestant could be added to the above statement. Not until after the Bill of Rights and the First Amendment were added to the Constitution did this issue become blurred. [1]

This should not be seen as a direct criticism of the framers of the Constitution. Progress is sometimes taken in small steps. They had to function within the world that they knew and with the knowledge available. The greatness of these words is that the masses took the statement to heart. It was taken straightforward, and from the very first moment that it was written it began to blossom. John Hancock, who had a reputation for being bellicose, howled when he first saw the American Constitution, "Who gave them the right to speak for the people!" [2] Of all the items in the Constitution, this is the one that jumped out at him. Instantly there had been change: no longer the playground for the few, government had a different destiny. John Hancock, who was then governor of Massachusetts, knew it. No matter the original meaning of these words, "We the people..." is a symbol for popular government and truly an extraordinary declaration.

Bill of Rights. An essential part of the American Constitution was not even generated by the Convention of 1787 but became an issue after the document was presented to the states. The Bill of Rights, the first ten Amendments to the Constitution, was not even approved by the delegates in Philadelphia. The central points for the drafters of the American Constitution are found within the Preamble. They were concerned about the Union, domestic tranquility, establishment of a valid national court system, the common defense, and the improvements of the general welfare. The core of the document works through each of these issues. A collection of delegates led by George Mason appealed to the convention to include a Bill of Rights. Though Mason had drafted a similar document for the State of Virginia, his document was voted down by the members of the convention in Philadelphia. The position of most of the writers of the Constitution was that these rights did not have to be listed because they are obvious and self-evident. This, however, must be viewed as a weak argument. History has shown that our basic rights have been challenged at many different levels; if not for the Bill of Rights, they would have been diluted. [3]

Not until many of the states refused to ratify the Constitution as it was written did the Bill of Rights begin to take form. The Bill of Rights became one the first items to be addressed within the new Congress; by 1791 these first ten Amendments had been added to the document. Though the achievement of guaranteeing our rights had little to do with the drafters of the Constitution, the credit needs to go to those present who resisted the document.[4]

The Constitution does need to be seen in two parts. The first is the original composition of seven Articles. This is the core of the document. It deals with structure and the physical nature of the three branches of the United States government. The second part is the Bill of Rights. The argument that is being made here is that the second part, the Bill of Rights, is far more important than the Constitution proper. How a bill moves through the legislative branch or the powers given to the President may be important, but the real character of government is how it deals with individual rights. If a government restricts the rights of free speech, searches our homes with impunity, declares a state religion, refuses to allow newspapers to publish, or judges us by the nature of our personal relationships, it influences the people at a fundamental level. In the same context whether seven steps are taken for a piece of legislation to become a law rather than ten is of small significance. It is the Bill of Rights that maintains our freedom.

The Bill of Rights emerged from the experiences of the Revolutionary War and with oppressive government. This section of the Constitution operates from a far more personal level. The emotions and the pain caused by despotic rule can be seen in the Bill of Rights. It took root in a time when these rights were not allowed and personal liberty did not exist.

The Bill of Rights has proved' to be a far more momentous pillar of American society than the basic structure of our government. Yet it was not even included as part of the original work. Nor was this issue simple overlooked. To exclude this issue was an intentional choice. The Founders heard the arguments during the convention of the need for a Bill of Rights. Many of the state constitutions had already involved such an item. In the end the nation's founders chose not to include such a section. It is a sad commentary for a document that champions individual liberty. It is one of the best and worst aspects of the American Constitution. If one rebuke needs to be leveled at the drafter of the

Constiution, it is that they showed so little interest in our individual rights.[5]

Once established in the Constitution, the Bill of Rights championed an incredibly important piece of political philosophy. Even recognizing the writings of John Locke, it was an immense jump to construct a government in which tolerance and human rights played a major role in the nature of government. The first Amendment, which becomes the sounding board of a free people, is rooted in the views of liberality. When a government and the people agree to allow freedom of speech, freedom of assembly, freedom of religion, and the freedom of the press in their society, that requires considerable allowances to be given to one's fellow human beings. The first Amendment becomes unmanageable unless a liberal view of tolerance is acknowledged. More than a step forward in the political progression of human kind, it is true leap. It is one of the most explicit and remarkable documents human beings have ever written, allowing the issue of tolerance to become a point of social and political behavior for the nation.[6]

To examine just the one issue of religion, a great step forward can be seen. Each of the original thirteen colonies was founded for different reasons, each having a different history. Most were centered on points of theology, most were established by a specific religious persuasion. The nation's founders were aware of these differences. Conflicts and wars had been fought in Europe for just such differences. As a point of great compromise and substantial wisdom they agreed to set aside these fundamental beliefs in theology and create a society where religious tolerance was the norm rather than the exception. Of course there were many miscues, and if the Founders had been pressed, most would have conceded that they thought only of Protestant denominations. Still, the basis of religious tolerance was established by the American Constitution.

Yet, this same level of tolerance was not extended to other segments within the society. The franchise was limited, true civil rights were not acknowledged, indeed, bondage was not only allowed, but established within the Constitution.[7] It is easy to recognize the level of social development that had occurred in Colonial America and even to excuse the gaps in tolerance by the Founders, but the paradox remains. How is it possible for the forerunners of our society and of the Constitution to be so enlightened on one side and so woeful on the other? It is this pretense of virtue that shades the American Constitution. It implies something that it is not there. While it is a great document, the Constitution is not perfect. Its design is limited and its principles open to contradiction.

The Constitution can be such an enigma. On the one side the document is designed to protect—to shield the average citizen from the ever-possible abuses of governmental power. It is a defense and the instrument stands as a guardian of liberty. Yet, to understand the American constitution requires not just a reading of the original document, but literally thousands upon thousands of subsequent court cases. It is not a document of ten pages, but one covering volumes and volumes. For the average citizen the document becomes impractical to comprehend; it exists only in the theoretical. Yet for the document to have value it must be understood, not by some, but by all.

An Inconsistency. One of the paradoxes of the Constitution, or at least one of the missed opportunities of the document, is Article IV, Section 4, which reads, "The United States shall guarantee to every state in this Union a republican form of government…" Many have contended that this represented a Bill of Rights when the original draft was submitted to the states. If a person defines a "republican government," then a collection of rights and privileges will emerge. A republican government cannot be enjoyed without outlining the rights of the people. Though our history has been spotty at times in our commitment to personal liberty and to social justice, within the American Constitution there was a clause that could have been used to press such concepts. It was a gift from the nation's founders to future generations, a promise that liberty would be maintained. Yet, this Article was never activated; even when the most abhorrent of civil abuses occurred to parts of the population, no one stepped forward.[8]

Only once was an effort made to use this Article to advance ideas of civil liberty. In the 1880s the Supreme Court heard a case in which a group was attempting to use this Article to press forward issues of female suffrage. The court said that this Article did not apply. No other case ever appeared before the Supreme Court that demanded action on the part of the Federal government toward points of American oppression.

This clause has languished in the Constitution, ignored and unused. It had the power to improve the lives of many people, to enhance our democracy, and to advocate civil liberties. The political will, or the desire for greater levels of democracy, did not exist. It may say more about the nature of our democracy than we would like to admit. It is one thing to say, "I cannot help you because we do not have the authority to do so," and it is another to have that power and to choose not to help. If democracy is to exist, it requires the commitment of many different entities. The most significant is the people, but government also has a role to play and needs to be committed to the process. The tools at hand need to be used. to ensure the rights of all. It is not simply a matter of governing or administration; there is also the obligation to inspire.

Part Two: The Nature of American Democracy

Chapter 4

Federalism

Federalism is a construct of government by which the sovereignty of the nation is divided among the different components. Federalism requires the maintenance of the subregional governmental systems within the larger national sphere. By definition the United States qualifies as a Federalist state. It should be easy, or at least moderately easy to delineate where the differences in responsibility lie. These issues represent political capabilities, simple territorial limits, and still others represent governmental responsibility. Ideally, the greater the division between the parties, the greater the harmony.

Our evolving government. Yet, the form of American Federalism at the beginning of the twenty-first century is not the same as the one the nation's founders envisioned or even constructed in the eighteenth century.[1] We have evolved into something different than the original design. The original design reserved the powers of states and delegated powers of the Federal government. Over the years an adjustment has occurred. This modification has resulted because of a wide range of reasons: the courts, changing views of government, legislative actions, and the needs of the people, to name a few. No matter what the reasons, two systems seem to be in place. On one side is what the Constitution declares as Federalism, and on the other what we have become. It is simply not a perfect match and this is one of the reasons why the issue of *states rights* reappears throughout our history.

Early attempts at union. When the drafters of the United States Constitution were working on the document, they were unsure what type of government they were creating. Their mandate was from the Continental Congress to review some of the obstacles found in the Articles of confederation. This instrument had declared the union little more than "a firm league of friendship."[2] The Founders knew that the new Constitution had to be more than simply a brotherhood of nations, yet the goal was not clearly defined. In fact they had no name for the new government. James Madison wrote years later that they lacked the "technical terms or phrases" to describe the type of government they were creating. The aim was to combine the idea of a nation-state to that of the old style confederation. If they constructed any outline at all, it dealt with the singular view that the Federal government needed to be strictly limited.[3]

After two hundred years America Federalism still is hard to define. Each scholar will advocate a different position. These disputes center on comparing one nation with another. The old Weimar Republic may declare themselves a Federation, but by system and action they may be neither a democratic state nor a Federalist state. Different classifications of Federalism are possible, since the distinction among them has not been properly defined. In any case the goal of the Founders was to create a Federalist system of government with clear lines differentiating the responsibilities of both states and the national government.[4]

Even before the breakdown of the Articles of Confederation cooperation among the thirteen colonies had been at best marginal. The high water mark of Colonial association was of course the American Revolution, though before this time interaction between the states was slight. Benjamin Franklin had attempted to correct this issue by building a greater sense of unity through the Albany Plan of Union in 1754. It was to address topics related to declaring war, forming treaties with the Indians, and regulating some of the outlying areas. Since not one colonial assembly supported the idea, however, the concept was aborted.[5]

Another opportunity to create a more explicit union occurred in 1776. The issue was discussed at length by the first Continental Congress, but because of the urgency of the war the issue was left unsettled. Though support for a union was considerable at that time, no action was taken, and again momentum was lost. Within a few years the states had developed their own Constitutions, and legislative bodies were well entrenched. By the time of the Constitutional Convention in 1787 the old traditional provincial loyalties had again been firmly established. Though the goal of the Founders had been to make some improvements in the relationships among the states, they encountered restrictions and limits to what they were able to accomplish.[6]

Which came first: the nation or the state? The nagging question that has been left behind concerns the fundamental relationship between the

Federal government and the states. Few questions are more important. This issue
helps define who we are as Americans and outlines the nature of our governmental
relationships. It is also the central issue for those who support *states rights* and
why that issue has not been totally resolved. Most of this centers on which came
first. Did the Federal government come into existence first through the Continental
Congress and the Articles of Confederation or did the states come first through
their colonial experience? Stated another way, is the Federal government a product
and design of the collective state governments, or by the act of creating the United
States did we also create the states?[7] On one side of this issue are those who say
that the states did not come into reality until the Federal government was formed.
After all, the colonies existed quite some time before the Continental Congress. As
a political entity a colony functions considerably differently than a state would
within a Federation, or even a Confederation. Only through this collective action of
obtaining independence were the states created.

On the other side of the argument are those who declare that the states
came first. This position notes that when the colonies become independent they
become autonomous. After all, the bond that existed before the Revolution was the
collective relationship with Great Britain. When that association ended so did the
relationship between these bodies. They were free to form new alliances,
affiliations, or unions. In the case of the American colonies they formed a new
national body through the Articles of Confederation. This argument is furthered by
noting that the United States Constitution was ratified by the states. It was also the
states that chose and empowered the delegates to the Constitutional Convention in
1787.[8]

The Scope of American Federalism. This may not be a question that
can easily be resolved. The real question that needs to be asked concerns the
current scope of American Federalism. The argument here is that Federal law
supersedes State law. In another depiction, Congress supersedes the power of the
individual state legislatures. This should not be seen as a surprise. Most people
recognize this to be true and generally feel comfortable with the spirit of this
concept. Initially though, when the American Constitution was established the
direction was to set limits on the power of the Federal government. The authority

of the central government existed only from within the document. The Constitution either had to specifically confer such power onto Congress or be at least an implied power itself. Article I, Section 8, is an effort by the framers of the Constitution to outline the jurisdiction of the Federal government. In turn the Constitution under the Tenth Amendment declared, "The powers not delegated to the United States by the Constitution , nor prohibited by it to the states, are reserved to the states..."

The issue was clear enough. The Constitution outlined as specifically as possible a division between the national government and the states.

In the *Federalist Papers,* time and again, the Federalist attempted to comfort the state legislatures and the concerns of the Anti-Federalists about the new Union. They were arguing that this new government would not be destroying the credibility of the states. Hamilton wrote in *Number 32*: "But as the plan of the convention aims only at a partial union, or consolidation, the state governments would clearly retain all the rights of sovereignty which they before had..." Madison wrote in a similar tone in *Number 39* when he talked about enumerated powers "...to certain enumerated objects only, and to the several states a residuary and inviolable sovereignty over all other objects" In *Number 40* Madison asked if the states should "be regarded as distinct and independent sovereigns." He answered the question by saying, "They are so regarded by the Constitution proposed." [9]

Each state had its own round of discussions and deliberation at the time of ratification on what would be lost to the national government if the Constitution was confirmed. Most of the state legislatures were concerned about the loss of state sovereignty. In Pennsylvania, James Wilson, a delegate to the Constitutional Convention, later declared at his state convention that the goal was to frame a government "composed of thirteen distinct and independent states." This term "thirteen distinct and independent states" became almost a catch phrase for the Federalist. Very similar words were heard at the conventions in Massachusetts, North Carolina, Connecticut, and Virginia. In New York the Federalist Robert Livingston declared, "We have thirteen distinct governments." They shared a consolidated view that the powers of the Federal government did not overshadow the independence of the separate states.[10] The Federalist turned to the Constitution proper and discussed Article 1, Section 8. They noted the precise nature of this segment of the document.

Restrictions and limits of power. The American Constitution should be seen as a document outlining the restrictions and limits to the power of the national government. The Federal government was not to be all-encompassing. This was done not so much as an issue of political philosophy but as a selling point to the states. The powers circumscribed to Congress by the Constitution under Article I, Section 8, include the following:

Paragraph 1.	The power to tax and the nature of the taxation. Uniformity of that taxation.
Paragraph 2.	To borrow money and maintain the debt.
Paragraph 3.	Regulate international and interstate commerce
Paragraph 4.	Code for naturalization and bankruptcy.
Paragraph 5.	The power to coin money. Develop standards for weights and measures.
Paragraph 6.	Punishment for counterfeiting.
Paragraph 7.	Establishing the Post Office.
Paragraph 8.	Copyrights and Patents
Paragraph 9.	Creating a Federal Court System.
Paragraph 10.	Punish pirates and to follow International Law.
Paragraph 11.	Declaration of War Develop procedures for Privateering and Prizes.
Paragraph 12.	Maintenance of an Army.
Paragraph 13.	Maintenance of a Navy.
Paragraph 14.	Regulating the Armed Services.
Paragraph 15.	The power to call up the militia.
Paragraph 16.	Organization of the militia.
Paragraph 17.	Separate jurisdiction over the District of Columbia and Federal property
Paragraph 18.	The ability to execute these powers.

These items are referred to as the *Enumerated Powers*. Section 9 of the Constitution continues by noting the limits on legislative powers. This listing of specific powers of the Federal Government was required at the time to ensure passage of the Constitution. Under the Articles of Confederation the states held most of the power, and the American Constitution represented a shift in this concept. Even so, the framers had to be specific about the powers of the central government if the states were to pass the document.

While the items found within Article I, Section 8, of the Constitution represent the core powers of the Federal government, a few other items represent parts of their responsibilities as well. They include investigative powers, enforcement of voting rights, proposing amendments to the document, appointment of offices, jurisdiction of the Supreme Court, and determining the succession of the Presidency. These items are found throughout the United States Constitution.

Powers herein granted. The key to this whole concept can be noted at the beginning of the Constitution in Article 1, Section 1. It opens with the statement, "All legislative powers herein granted shall be vested in a Congress of the United States..." The critical words are *herein granted*. It declares that specific powers are being given to the Federal government and then continues by noting the scope of those endowments.

When the Bill of Rights was being formulated the states wanted to make sure that the division between the states and Federal government was understood. The states wanted to ensure that they maintained their sovereignty. This was a critical issue. The states had sent to Congress various amendments that they felt needed to be added to the original Constitution. Ninety-six in all were enumerated, most of them dealing with personal rights. Even so, in every case when a legislative body submitted a set of proposed amendments, they included a section guaranteeing the sovereignty of the states. In the end this did appear in the Constitution and is found in the Tenth Amendment in the "reserved powers" section.[11]

Coupled with these declarations is Article VI of the American Constitution. It is generally referred to as the "national supremacy" clause. It reads as follows:

"This Constitution, and the laws of the United States which shall
be made in pursuance thereof; and all treaties made, or which
shall be made; under the authority of the United States, shall be
the supreme law of the land; and the judges in every state shall be
bound thereby, anything in the Constitution or laws of any state
to the contrary notwithstanding."

The concept was that if a state law and a Federal law were in conflict, the Federal
law would prevail. This idea was developed within the framework of the
designated powers of the central government.[12] As an example, if two governments
disagreed over foreign coinage, the Federal government would predominate. Such
an item was within their Constitutional mandate. In the same context, if a legal
issue developed over criminal law within a state, the matter would be outside of the
Federal Constitutional jurisdiction.

Anti-Federalist response. When the Article was first proposed at the
Constitutional Convention little concern was noted, but the Anti-Federalists were
troubled. Many felt this represented the key concept that would undermine state
sovereignty. They were specifically apprehensive about the idea of a "supreme law
of the land." The Federalists attempted to ease their concerns. Hamilton wrote in
the *Federalist Papers*, "Suppose... the federal legislature should attempt to vary
the law of descent in any state, would it not be evident that in making such an
attempt, it had exceeded its jurisdiction and infringed upon that of the state?"

The Federalists saw the issue more as a matter of utility. If a national
government was to emerge, then it needed appropriate authority to manage the
issues to which it was assigned. Congress needed the power to develop laws related
to this authority, and in this area they were supreme. Federal laws were of three
types: the Constitution, Treaties, and Legislative Acts. Any decrees or laws passed
by Congress were still trapped within the framework of the Constitution. In the
end, the Federalist won the day because they had the better arguments and, to some
degree, presented a better case for ratification of the new Constitution.[13]

Personalities and points of philosophy were involved in this debate. The
Anti-Federalists as a rule stood for state's rights and thus were far more concerned

with state sovereignty. In contrast were the Federalists with their interest in building a nationalist state with the sovereignty invested in a centralized government. While both parties may have danced around this central topic, these issues were principal factors in the way each side saw government. The Anti-Federalist emphasized loyalty to their state and the values these states had represented during the Revolutionary War, while clearly the Federalists were looking at the future.

The Federalists saw the Union as having the greater potential for prosperity and eminence. The question could be boiled down to one idea: which body would best be the guardian of the spirit of the Revolution—the states or the national government? Nor did this conflict end with the ratification of the Constitution. To some degree it was but an opening act.

Article VI, supreme law of the land. Article VI presented problems to the Federalist. Its assertion that the national government would be "the supreme law of the land" had little teeth. Hence, the Judiciary Act became one of the first statutes of the new American Congress in 1789. This was passed even before all the states had ratified the Constitution, and even before the Bill of Rights was added. One of the sections of this act declared that if Federal and state law came into conflict, an automatic appeal to the appropriate federal court would be made. Though it may seem outwardly insignificant, this statute guaranteed that all state and national disagreements would be fought on Federal turf.

The stage was now set for John Marshall. As the Chief Justice of the Supreme Court he sat on the bench from 1801 to 1835. Not only did Marshall establish the dominance of the high court, principles of American Constitutional law, and the power of the courts to review legislation, but he was the leading engineer of the Federalist system found in the United States. Through the cases of *McCullock v. Maryland* and *Gibbons v. Ogden*, the superiority of the Federal government was entrenched within the young nation.[14]

The Separatist view. Needless to say, this struggle continued through the early years of our history. John Calhoun, for example, viciously attacked the "supremacy doctrine." He put forth the view that since the states predate the Constitution, and hence their sovereignty could not be "divided or abrogated," the

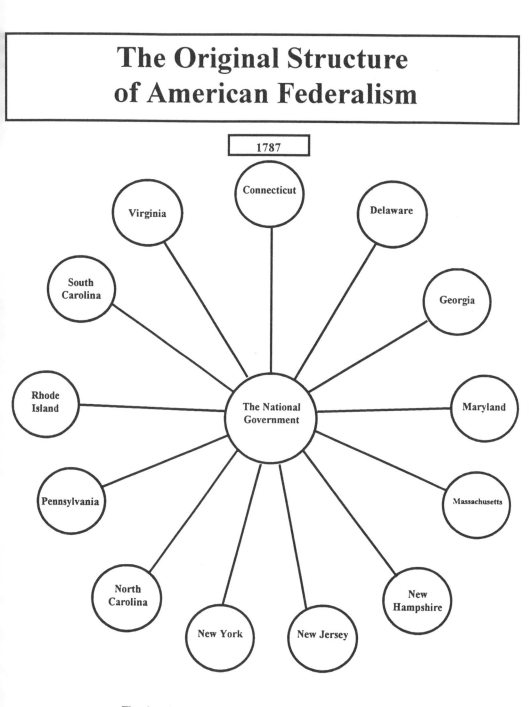

The Original Structure of American Federalism

1787

Connecticut

Virginia

Delaware

South Carolina

Georgia

Rhode Island

The National Government

Maryland

Pennsylvania

Massachusetts

North Carolina

New York

New Jersey

New Hampshire

The view that the American Federal government was but one more governmental body among a number of different governmental entitles.

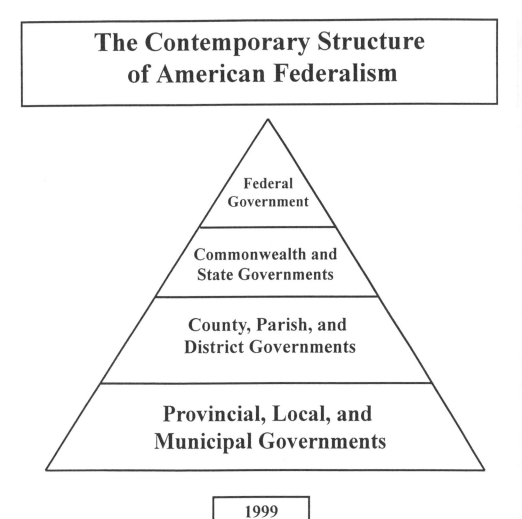

The Contemporary Structure of American Federalism

Federal Government

Commonwealth and State Governments

County, Parish, and District Governments

Provincial, Local, and Municipal Governments

1999

The view that the American Federal government is the foremost governmental body of the nation.

states remained and were completely sovereign. He continued by noting that the Federal government was but an agent of the states. A like debate related to which governmental body had the final say within the Constitution. Those supporting the dominance of the states noted that a convention could always be called to invalidate any Federal statute. In fact, the Constitution itself could be changed by such a process, and so in the end the states were the primary authority.

The controversy ended with the American Civil War. Many of the Constitutional arguments of John Calhoun were used by the separatists as a rationale for withdrawing from the Union. While numerous issues surrounded the Civil War, one of the major problems dealt with the conflict between these two doctrines. By the time the American Civil War had ended, the United States was a Federalist state with a purely dominant central government.[15] The addition of the Fourteenth Amendment to the Constitution seems to be the defining moment in this discussion and it ended the debate over the nature of state sovereignty, or at least not until it flared up briefly during the 1950s and 1960s.

The dominant authority. The reality is that the Federal government is the dominant authority; however, in the United States the national government at times makes an effort to accommodate the wishes of the states. Many Federally generated programs allowed states to use considerable discretion in the administration of these projects. Public works programs, welfare programs, educational programs, a wide collection of social and service related programs -- all have the states playing a major role. At times this concept of a partnership between the Federal and state government is realized. There are even times when the original goal of the nation's founders is allowed to surface, but the question remains. Are the boundaries between the authority of the Federal government and the state governments well defined? More important, if a conflict develops which body has the last word? Notwithstanding the power of the courts, if a dispute arises between two administrative agencies, the Federal government will have its way, at least until the case works its way through the judicial forums.

The argument that is being presented is that the United States should be seen as a pyramid of governments. It is an organizational theory by which the Federal government has the most power and control; the central government sits at the top of the pyramid. The state governments occupy the center level, with the county and city governments at the base. This is a view of government as a hierarchy. The logic of this position can be seen in the fact that the national legislature with great frequency passes laws that the states are required to implement; yet, that same process does not work in reverse. If a state passed a law declaring that the Federal government needed to execute the statute, it would be ignored. There is a downward flow of authority within the bureaucratic institutions of America.

Scores of examples can be used to outline the nature of this power structure, but one seems to be most conspicuous. Originally the states determined the nature of criminal law. Outside of the issue of treason, the national government was not involved in the process of convicting and imprisoning criminals; that was a state function. This is no longer true. Many Federal agencies have been given police powers. An example could be made of a murder case in a metropolitan center. Both the local police and personnel from the Federal Bureau of Investigation arrive. If the FBI declares that the crime is part of their jurisdiction, the local police would have little recourse. Local authorities would be expected to cease all further inquiries and investigations into the case. The commission of the FBI includes espionage, terrorism, sabotage, bank robbery, attacks on governmental officials, civil rights violations, kidnapping, fraud against the government, and authorizing security clearances. There is no system in place for local law enforcement agencies to confirm jurisdiction. In turn if they continued the case without the agreement of the FBI they could be charged with obstruction of justice.

Remembering that the American Constitution would not have come into existence without those initial limits to Federal power. Those who supported the Constitution of 1787 knew that they would have to sell it to their state legislators. It is a rare situation indeed where an individual or a government concedes influence and power. The Constitution had to be supportive of the states, limited in nature, and constructed in such a way that unity represented an enhancement of ascendancy. If it did not, the states would not have ratified the document. The only way this could be done is by limiting the Federal government.

A neutral stance. The effort here is not to take a direct position on the status of American Federalism. A more honest critique can be found in those essays that support either states rights or those that advocate a more centralized tendency for government. Even so, an assertion could be made that if the Constitution were being followed exactly, the United States would be more of a coalition of states rather than a true republic. At some point we have to ask ourselves not only about the current nature of our government, but whether it matches the view of the United States Constitution. What have we evolved into and is it acceptable? Once saying this, citizens need to take note that while this change or movement has taken place in full view of the masses, it has also been done in opposition to our Constitution. The American Constitution was clearly set up to avoid any form of hierarchy or pyramid structure. The remnants of this past system can still be seen in the document. Specific responsibilities were laid out for the Federal government and those of the states. The reality is that we are something else.[16]

When a Constitution is being ignored, regardless of how valid the reason, the document becomes tainted. The only real position that is being advocated is that a Constitution needs to be comprehensible, that any person should be able to pick up the document and get a clear picture of the basic structure of their government, its fundamental powers, and their own rights. With the American Constitution that act is becoming more difficult, and at times, outright confusing.

Chapter 5

The Living Document

Interpretivists. Students of the United States Constitution seem to fall into one of two different camps. One view is that of a living document. This view argues that the American Constitution is an animated document, one that travels from generation to generation, that a universal truth appears in its pages that can withstand the test of time. This set of supporters would be categorized as *interpretivists;* the document becomes a living entity, one that takes on a life of its own. They believe that a concept of an overall judicial philosophy exists. They see the high court maintaining the Constitution by the current system of assessment and review.

Constructionists. The second group are best classified as *constructionists.* Traditional in background, they are far more literal in their approach to the document. This second group resists the idea of implied rights. Nor would they think that ideas have emerged from the document. Instead, they believe that the Constitution says what it means and that the instrument is discredited when additional ideas are attached to it. They view themselves as strict Constitutionalists.

This should not be seen as two academic divisions debating points of philosophy. How we view the Constitution has a profound effect upon how we function in society, how we relate to our government, and how our rights are perpetuated. Not just the words of the document are of value, but how we attach ourselves to those words. The French traveler and writer Alexis de Tocqueville in his most famous passage declared, "There is hardly a political question in the United States which does not sooner or later turn into a judicial one."[1] Tocqueville did strike a cord that represents part of the American personality. The court system is an extension of the Constitution, as is the rest of our government. Everything becomes linked. Which view dominates does make a difference. It becomes critical to how our rights and freedoms are preserved.

Those in support of the concept of a living-document seem to have the more commanding approach. They see the document as an ever-changing and evolving instrument, one in which the meaning expands to include the conditions and climate of the times Under these circumstances the Constitution is constantly experiencing a metamorphosis.[2] On the other side of the debate, if the Constitution is a contract, then it needs to be precise. Reading things into the document not specifically drafted into it can be dangerous.[3] Ironically, both of these ideas are equally valid and equally false. The American Constitution is a living document; it has changed to fit the times. Sometimes it has not been a perfect fit, but the document has adjusted to the ever-changing needs of the people.

In the same context, it is an extremely perilous concept to allow others to interpret items into the Constitution that do not exist. If something needs to be in the document, then it seems fair to request that these be written down. To believe that you have a right when in reality it does not exist could be tragic.

Is the Constitution Forever? The question remains, though, is the Constitution forever? Many questions could be asked about our society that do not elicit easy answers. Not everything has an affirmative or a negative response, for some questions require many shades of gray to answer. The question that is being imposed. however, requires an exact reply. Major implications follow each choice. If one champions the belief that the document will never need to be changed, then the actual wording becomes secondary. What becomes important is the interpretation. The Constitution becomes uncodified. How the Constitution is viewed by the elitist and the masses is all that matters. If a person believes that at some time the Constitution will need to be changed, updated, or replaced, then what appears is a time line. The discussion then turns to a couple hundred years or a couple thousand years. A person may not know the exact date, but they would concede that this process would need to occur at a specified time in the future.

Of course the problem is that when that time does occur, it will be during a Constitutional crisis. Some issue, some unforeseen problem emerges, one in which the profound nature of the document is challenged. To some degree this is what happened during the American Civil War. It represented a Constitutional crisis. The two parties, the North and the South, saw the document very differently. Hundreds of thousands of Americans perished, and when it was over the

Constitution needed to be repaired. Three new amendments were added, in this case the Thirteenth, Fourteenth, and Fifteenth amendments, but cracks still appeared. The words of these amendments were accepted but not the spirit. In the case of the American Civil War these Constitutional changes occurred under force of arms.

Constitutional crises have occurred at times, but instead of reviewing and adjusting the Constitution accordingly, the document has simply been minimized, or a specific section of the document has been demoted. It no longer has the same importance, nor is it viewed in the same way. The meaning becomes blurred. The United States Constitution was viewed differently after the American Civil War than before that conflict. The document that emerged after the Great Depression also was not the same as before that upheaval. A similar argument can be made about the Cold War. In this sense it is a living document; it continues to exist even though the original purpose and concepts are lost.

If a person is willing to accept ongoing changes in perception without changes in text, then the Constitution is forever. While conceding that the Constitution may be amended or changed by consent, the words become subordinate. In this case a new Constitution would never need to be written. The problem, of course, is that the document itself becomes trapped in an age and time that may no longer be relevant. A Constitution deals not only with the general, but also the specific. While many issues will transcend time, others will not. There are issues that represent truths that are self-evident. Two hundred year ago when the Founders of our nation designed the American Constitution, freedom of speech was considered; a thousand years from now if a Constitution is to be reviewed or drafted, the issue of freedom of speech will be discussed. It is that universal. Other issues, however, do not traverse the gap of time. For example, while the Founders had to spent a great deal of time discussing slavery, the issue has been settled, and our society has moved beyond it.

The idea of progress. An argument can be made that humankind is making progress. While we are continually confronted with great issues, great debates, and struggles that test our human insecurities and sense of justice, many of these issues ultimately are resolved. The human race moves on to the next concept, the next stage, and the overall problem of incongruity. If a Constitution is not changed, then those vestiges remain. They represent points of bitterness and pain for many. History becomes baggage dragged from one generation to another.

A Constitution does represent little signposts in the travels of humanity. Clearly how people pictured themselves before the American Constitution compared to after it was established as a document were different. The American Constitution represented the first time in the history of a modem state that power was invested with the people. There is a clear view of what was before and what came after. In this conception Constitutions became rungs of a ladder, each one representing greater levels of democracy, self-government, and tolerance.

The problem of change. The problem is that societies change. Every part of the community and the culture undergoes adjustments: how we interact with our families, our children, the levels of education, how we view our institutions, how we receive information, the nature of relationships, how we earn a living, the problems we face in personal growth or self-esteem. Everything is subject to change. When the American Constitution was developed the United States was a frontier, agricultural, slave economy based on Protestant beliefs and secular ethics. It was geographically specific and culturally Anglo-Saxon. Today the United States is a multiculturally-based society with a mixed economy founded on principles of open markets. The United States is a world leader, militarily powerful, and religiously tolerant. As children are related to their parents we are connected to the past, yet we are not the same as they, we are different persons.

If society and our political institutions continue to change, yet the Constitution remains based in a different era, the meaning of the entire document is lessened. While certain ideas move forward, others do not, The document becomes respected, but underutilized. Even if we accept the idea that the Constitution is a living document, and our society continues to evolve hundreds or thousands of years into the future, what occurs to the document? If this theory is taken to the next level, regardless of the established meaning, a time will come when the document will exist in its original form in the literate equivalence of Latin.

Courage to change. To change a Constitution requires considerable courage from a society, even if it represents little structural, social, or political change. It means that every part of the political and communal life of the nation needs to be examined. It becomes an extremely fundamental act. Such a process can be stressful, self-examinations can be revealing. It forces a nation to look inward. We do not always find what we expect, but there is also something very healthy about the process. It allows the nation to examine those rudimentary concepts of liberty, equality, freedom, and justice.

The last question is whether there is any need for a Constitution at all. With the passage of time and the interpretation and reinterpretation of concepts, it becomes possible to argue that there is little need for a Constitution. Our rights are a matter of interpretation rather than an article of inscription. Our privileges and rights could be maintained within the legislative process. Though Great Britain does not have a document that represents a Constitution, they are a democratic society. While they are a Constitutional Monarchy, their Constitution is uncodified. It should not be discredited, and it does work. The preservation of their democracy and individual rights becomes the responsibility of the legislature. While the average British citizen believes that they have the same civil rights as those found in the American Constitution, this presents two basic problems. Once a Constitution has been established it is impractical, if not impossible, to exclude it. It is like asking someone to return a gift. Second, a Constitution is a contract. Once the contract is firmly incorporated, it becomes impossible to disassociate the parties involved. A new contract could be developed, or an effort could be made to utilize the existing one, but once the relationship is established, it is unfeasible to disconnect the two entities. In this case it is the people and their government. The only way that a separation could occur is for the people to join with another government entirely. In this situation what becomes "forever" is Constitutional government, not necessarily a particular Constitution.

Of course a third option is possible, one that is infrequently discussed. It is not just a matter of accepting the position of the *constructionists* or the *interpretivists*. The third choice deals with periodical reviews, adjustments, and an orderly method of establishing new Constitutions. It is a thin line. One of the goals of a Constitution is to create stability and order to a society. If a Constitution is changed too often, it brings disorder and chaos. Yet, if it is never changed, then the document can do equal harm; it stagnates the society or allows others to determine the meaning of the document. If this third option is neither discussed nor a replacement considered, it is as perilous for a society as to have no Constitution at all.

Without a doubt the American Constitution has served democracy and the concepts of a free people for more than two hundred years. It is and has been a distinguished piece of work, even considering the compromises and miscues found within the document. This one single piece of paper has forged a great nation and created a government founded on the principles of liberty. The question that needs to be asked is, "Can this document truly be forever?" Is it the best that we can aspire to? Is it the limit of democracy?

Chapter 6

The Contract

The Contract is not one concept, but three. *First* is the theory that the American form of government is based on a social contract. *Second* is that the Constitution represents this agreement. *Third* is that as a people we enter into this contract for the common good and the advantages found within society.

Our relationship with our government becomes a contractual arrangement. Government is an extension of this agreement so that we become both governed and ruler. True sovereignty and political authority rest with the people; government as an institution is subordinate. What powers the government possesses have been delegated by the people for the sole purpose of maintaining the public good and the national security. The contract defines the process and makes this interaction possible.[1]

Social Contract. This theme has been so compelling that many, if not most, political philosophers have expanded on the idea and made it analogous with democratic action. It becomes a *social compact*. The relationship between government and the people is described in a written contract. Specific understandings, arrangements, and perceptions can be found, but it is also a concept heavily invested in pure philosophy. Even so, the agreement is binding and enforceable by law. In the case of the United States Constitution, the Supreme Court determines the nature of our compact and how it will be enforced. All contracts, even a social contract must be moral. It cannot be the basis of an illegal or licentious act.

The ancient Greek philosophers saw government as a cycle. It would start with a monarchy, maybe the type of person Plato saw as the philosopher King. The monarch would at first operate within the law: be just to the people and principled. In time the monarchy would become disassociated from the masses and tyrannical. The single ruler would become self-centered and self-seeking. Then the monarchy would be replaced by an aristocratic government. The government would operate in the hands of a few. This type of government would evolve into a very restricted oligarchy with ever-increasing levels of corruption. It would eventually be replaced by a legitimate democracy. It would be based on individual liberty and the promise of governmental self-sufficiency. This type of government, however, would decay into anarchy and lawlessness. The argument being that when the people rule no one rules. It would be replaced by a strong leader, an autocratic individual based on popular ideas. This person would accept the singular title of King and the cycle would begin again. Aristotle put forth the idea that to break this cycle, a Constitution should be established. In this way it could moderate the worst parts of whatever type of government was in place.

Philosophers of government. Most of the philosophers of the seventeenth and eighteenth centuries wrote about the social compact. The nation's founders knew the writings of Locke, Hobbs, Montesquieu, Hume, and Rousseau. While each contributed to the ideas of a social contract, each had a different view of the nature of this agreement. These were concepts that were accepted by the drafters of the Constitution.

John Locke. Locke believed that before the establishment of government we all lived in a "state of nature." In this state we all had perfect freedom. Though we could do whatever we wanted, whenever we wanted to do it, this was inevitably accompanied by disorder and chaos. Everyone had the power to harm or kill everyone else. By entering into a community and inaugurating government, we gained stability and order. What we lost was perfect freedom. Many of our natural rights and privileges we submitted to government. Government and its related extensions are the only entities that can commit legalized violence. John Locke would describe it as surrendering our natural liberty.

Once we unite into this new community it becomes a place of comfort, safe and peaceful in its design. Firmly incorporated by its members, it is established by a social contract. Locke does not talk of a written contract, but rather of an implied contract. It is a contract by proposition and arrangement. The rules of the society are clearly understood by the parties involved. It is a community where government controls but is not equal. The power of the government is still vested with the people, and the idea of government becomes more of a trust. Locke would reject the idea that government had any rights; rather, its existence is determined by its duty to the people. The people have agreed to form this community and, in time, the government. The act of governing was little more than a responsibility.[2]

Thomas Hobbs. Hobbs, who wrote just prior to Locke, rejected the idea of a social compact. He did not want to imply that government was equal to the people. He did support the idea of a "state of nature," but Hobbs painted a far darker picture of humanity. He believed that once we entered into this new arrangement and established our communities, we surrendered all of our rights. What we obtained in return was security. The government and its leaders had power to do whatever they wished as long as they maintained our security. The social contract emerges from the idea that people fear one another or in some situations they collectively fear the sovereign. For Hobbs this compact is more latent, without detail. He would not see the relationship as equal or the people as the dominant entity[3]

Montesquieu. Along with Locke, Charles Louis de Secondat, Baron de Montesquieu was resolutely read by the Founders, especially his ideas of representative government. Montesquieu also wrote about the concept of a social contract. He came to a different set of conclusions than Hobbs. For him there were three categories of law—international law, political law, and civil law. While international law would represent precepts found between nations, civil law was designed to regulate the acts among different individuals. Political law, however, which dealt with the relationship between the state and the masses, represented the social contract. This is the agreement that citizens have made with their government. Political law is the condition under which persons find themselves in this relationship. Also, when the drafters of the Constitution referred to separation of powers as a basis of government, they were quoting Montesquieu.[4]

David Hume. Another thinker who accepted the idea of a social contract was David Hume. He felt governments came into existence because humanity saw the advantages of obedience and command. While at first leaders had to justify their position or consistently prove their leadership ability, over time the relationship and the process became habitual. Monarchies came to power either by conquest or succession. Their subjects acknowledged this process because it was customary, a routine event. The people were in no position to question the system in the first place. The system became reinforced by two elements—an implied consent from God, in which case government became a sacred item and any resistance to it became a point of sacrilege, or by consent of the people through a social contract.

Jean Jacques Rousseau. Another insightful political philosopher is Jean Jacques Rousseau. He wrote about a social contract as well, but his ideas could have been as easily illustrated without the constructs of a contract. Rousseau attacked the idea of giving up our freedom for security. He saw that as a poor bargain.The key was to find a system that not only supported freedom but also protected people from their own human selfishness. The association that was created became the social compact. In Rousseau's contract the people did surrender their rights to the community. He felt nothing of value was lost, and what was gained was the contract. Without the social contract the people lacked equality, legal guarantees, as well as protection from the state. This was the nature of civil liberty. It was a system designed and set up for the people. Rousseau would have argued, "One thing is certain, force is not a basis for legitimacy." In this case government is little more than the instrument of the people.

These were not the only political philosophers who wrote about the concepts of a social contract. Most of the major political thinkers of our times have touched upon these issues, and it is a common theme. Each adds to the body of thought as it relates to a political and social agreement. Jeremy Bentham and Edmund Burke discussed the features of this social contract as well. Each saw the contract from a different perspective. What is most important is not the nature or origins of this social contract but that it be made by equals and well defined. Issues related to power, jurisdiction, limits, and rights need to be agreed upon as a partnership. Within these ideas consent and contract become the same. Government would evolve not to dominate or maintain power, but from an agreement. One of the better stated positions on the topic is from the more recent work of William Graham Sumner, an American author and scholar who wrote the following in 1884:

"Contract, however, is rational—even rationalistic. It is also realistic, cold, and matter-of-fact. A contract relation is based on a sufficient reason, not on custom or prescription. It is not permanent. It endures only so long as the reason for it endures. In a state based on contract, sentiment is out of place in any public or common affairs. It is relegated to the sphere of private and personal relations, where it depends not at all on class types, but on personal acquaintance and personal estimates."[5]

What develops from these philosophical concepts of a social compact is the purer form of a written contract. If the idea of a social contract is accepted, it seems equally valid to place the ideas found within the contract into a written document.

The connection is that the United States Constitution is but an extension of a social contract. It should not be seen as either the beginning of such written agreements or even the last of such transactions. It is but one of a line of such documents—guideposts in the development of humanity. Part of the American Constitution can be found in the Magna Carta (1215), Petition of Rights (1628), Bill of Rights (1689), Act of Settlement (1701), and the Declaration of Independence (1776). These ideas of a social contract have inched their way forward, merging with related ideas of democracy, individual rights, and representative government.

Mayflower Compact. This view of a social contract runs to the core of the American view of government. One of the first purely American documents is the Mayflower Compact of 1620. When the Pilgrims landed in Massachusetts they were not so much a colony as a company. No agreement had been made with the monarchy to establish a colonial state; in fact Plymouth was not even their destination. While it is true that many of the Puritans were interested in religious freedom and were eager to separate themselves from England, their royal charter had nothing to do with those issues. They were part of "The Governor and Company of Massachusetts Bay." They had a corporate charter. To accomplish their goals a covenant was created, in this case the Mayflower Compact, and the members of the company signed it. What some people would see as stockholders, others would see as a populace. While some would view Plymouth Bay as a corporation, others would see it as a municipal government. The line between these two concepts became blurred. The outside world may have seen a company, but the Puritans saw it as a form of self-government. This view of a social contract between government and the people has continued from the Pilgrims. It is an important part of how Americans relate to authority.[6]

A working document. The problem that can develop is that a Constitution can begin to be seen as more than simply a contract. A contract is a little more plainspoken and to the point. As a people, we hear that the Constitution is the highest law in the land, that it stands as a testament to a free people and a symbol to democracy. The Constitution is placed on a plane where it exists as a point of admiration and wonderment. The document becomes an icon of the society and is used as a philosophical emblem to describe all the special distinctions of the society. It is placed at the same level as the national flag, the anthem, and the great seal. While conceding that such symbols are important to a society and a government, this may not be the most acceptable stance for a Constitution.

There is nothing wrong with allowing the Constitution to be a symbol of the nation-state, to allow it to be a representation of the embodiment of the beliefs and spirit of the country. Such images allow us to cope and to work toward ever-increasing ideals of fair play and justice, but there is a difference between recognizing the Constitution as an icon and also realizing that it is a working document.

The British have the same problem with the Magna Carta. When a person is asked about the nature of the Magna Carta the response will generally be that it guarantees basic levels of human rights. The problem is that the Magna Carta had little to do with the ideas of civil liberty. When the charter was signed in 1215 it dealt simply with the rights of the nobles and the monarchy. The masses were still attached to the land and the document confirmed the feudal privileges of the upper classes, but as a symbol of constitutional government, the Magna Carta has become a very powerful entity. The importance of the document is not in what it says, but in what it did. For the first time government entered into a contract with their subjects. It noted that there were limits to the power of the monarchy, and that restrictions could be placed on the ascendancy of government.[7]

To some degree this is also true with the United States Constitution. There is a gap between the written word of the document and its perception in our society. When drafted the Constitution placed numerous constraints on popular government. It allowed slavery and fostered class privilege, but it also represented the first effort at a large self-government. No document before it was as detailed as the American Constitution in outlining the responsibilities of all the parties within the framework of government. The difference is that to honor its achievement may be desirable and worthwhile, but to maintain and declare its utility still another.

A Constitution should be seen as a social contract between the people and their government. It describes the capability of those in authority, creates a level of accountability, and places in writing expectations of all the litigants. A Constitution is a working document. It needs to be clear, understandable, and specific. While social goals are meaningful, even desirable, the core issue of a Constitution is a practical one. It is a working agreement, based on law, and pragmatic in its design.

Of all the practical advantages in having a social contract, the greatest must deal with our own diversity. While each person may declare himself or herself to be an American, each of us has scores of different loyalties. We are each members of differing cultural groupings, religious upbringing, social background, regions of the country, and family traditions. We are loyal to our schools, our gender, our professions, our clubs, our sports teams, our hometowns, and our generation. We each have a favorite automobile, like different kinds of films, read different books, or consume dissimilar brands of soft drinks. We each see the world a little differently and no two people speak quite the same. Yet, we all have in common our social contract, or in this case the Constitution. It binds us together, each to the other. It becomes a connecting force. While each of us may be considerably different than our fellow citizens, those differences are not so immense that they cannot exist under the same set of laws. A Constitution joins us to the whole.

A contract is a special concept with tentative assumptions attached to it. It is a legally enforceable agreement between at least two parties who have outlined specific understandings. These parties have moved into this agreement openly and freely, without intimidation or coercion. Particular responsibilities are inherent with the agreement. These parties consent to undertake or abstain from doing certain acts. In turn the contract can be studied in detail and analyzed. It has two parts, the agreement generated by the separate parties and the obligation, which becomes a point of law. It is this obligation that binds the participants together.

While a Constitution may be a social contract founded more of political philosophy than contract law, it has many of the same qualifications as any other form of a contract. More than any other part it represents a promise. It is not connected to an opinion; it is a promise that requires compliance. This promise becomes the agreement. It is the core of what a social contract is all about and what makes it different from any other administrative document.

The Constitution and Personal Consent. A far more serious question needs to be asked. If the United States Constitution is a contract, and this is a very logical concept, then is it a valid contract? The problem is that an agreement needs to be entered into by all the parties through their consent and without extortion, force, or compulsion. Even allowing for the idea of representative government and majority rule, it still means that large numbers of individuals were forced into accepting the United States Constitution without their permission or agreement.

When the Constitution was drafted, American blacks were not only disenfranchised but were bound to service. The American Constitution stripped large numbers of people of their individual rights and in turn embraced slavery. It cannot be imagined that the black population in the United States would have openly agreed to such an institution as total servitude. Even when the document was changed with the Reconstruction Amendments, the black population was still excluded from the process and the agreement. This same argument can be made for women. They had no say in the nature of the social contract that controls and overrides every part of their lives. Furthermore, the document was ratified by the elitists within the state legislatures. It was at best a minority document. If these issues are conceded, and the concept of a social contract exists; at what point does the Constitution become illegitimate?

What constitutes a breach of contract? The basic promise of government is that it will secure our rights as we enter into this mutual arrangement called community. If the basic ideas of our social contract are not fulfilled, at what point does a breach of contract exist? The problem is that a Constitution is not one promise, not one issue, but many, sometimes even hundreds. If one of these is breached or denied it does not make the whole document invalid, but what about two or three, what about fifteen or twenty? When does a Constitution become disabled? The difficulty faced in trying to change a Constitution is the same as those attempting to change a, monarchy. Once in power, and once established, it becomes extremely difficult to dislodge.

The uncodified Constitution. The phenomena that may occur is that the document may drift from being a codified Constitution to an uncodified one such as that previously mentioned of Great Britain. The concepts of a social contract are found within the legislative body. The Constitution becomes an assortment of enactments, customs, common law, and governmental protocols. This is something very real and should not be seen as contrived. It has formal structure. This uncodified Constitution does exist by agreement and with the support of the people, but it is not a written document. As an element of British law and culture it evolved. It came about not by convention, through council or a plebiscite, but by means of arrangement. It is tangible, but untouchable. The question then becomes this: Is it really so important to have a written Constitution? Would we be any less served by our government if no written social contract existed?[8]

Two problems present themselves. *First*, the process of allowing a written Constitution to dissolve into an uncodified version would take hundreds of years. Meanwhile the people would have no guarantees that their rights would be maintained during the process. *Second*, a written Constitution must be considered superior to an uncodified version. It requires less translation. To adjust, or even amend, a social contract may be one matter, but to change the attributes of the document is clearly something else.

Democracy's chief advantage. At some point, this idea of a social contract must be connected to democratic government. Without a contract the chance of abuse is far greater. Likewise, democracy is not enduring and timeless. Once it is placed into motion there is no reason to believe that it will continue to grow and develop. Great powers are at work against the continuation of democracy, one of which is the people themselves. In a search for greater levels of security the masses assist with the process of reducing popular government. This also occurs as the people drift toward greater levels of affluence and luxury, when it is more important to maintain the status quo than to resist the shift toward authoritarian government. Part of this issue can be found in the ease by which this adjustment can be made, and it is done by tacit consent. Authoritarian regimes create increased levels of order. They manage the affairs of state more pragmatically and possess decisive actions. It is easier to accumulate wealth within them. Democracy on the other hand requires involvement. The people must remain informed, they must help resolve the conflicts of the day, and they need to participate. It can subtract from other interests. Democracy is time consuming, difficult to administer, and may be in its purest form impossible to achieve, but it has one chief advantage. All other forms of government are repressive. If a people are to avoid this pitfall, if they are to resist the retreat back into arbitrary government, the social contract needs to be current, understandable, and consistent.

Chapter 7

Electoral College

It is difficult to be objective about the Electoral College. This is a strictly American concept, not found within the framework of political thought or the governmental structures of other nations. It can be justified only in reference to the untried structures and systems the nation's founders were attempting to develop. Republican government had few past examples of proper procedures or levels of functioning. Most of the ideas the drafters of the Constitution were advocating represented some level of experimentation. Only in this backdrop can the Electoral College be defended.

The presidency. The core issue dealt with how the President of the United States was to be elected. The Virginia Plan had been used by the delegates at the Constitutional Convention in 1787 as a basis for discussion. This plan had supported the idea of a chief executive elected by the legislative assembly. It would have represented a parliamentary design for the new government. The fundamental difference between the parliamentary system and the American form of government is how the chief executive is elected. The issue was debated and the vote close, but in the end a system was proposed whereby the people would be involved at some stage in the process. The issue centered around the ideas of separation of powers and the need for three separate branches of government.[1]

The Founders were also interested in having a chief executive who would parallel the power of the monarchs of Europe. While they would have rejected the idea of a President with absolute power, they did want a chief executive who could at least stand on an equal footing. Though a difficult task, it was thought that if the office was established separately from the legislature, it would appear to be more formidable.

Political parties. The elections would have been far easier, and even workable, if the Founders had conceded the concept of political parties. They worked hard to create a structure of government that could function without these political entities, but it failed. This is one of glaring errors of the Constitution.

By the time John Adams was elected as our second President political parties were firmly entrenched in the American system of government, the only reason political alliances did not occur even earlier is because of the prestige and political will of George Washington. He was opposed to the concept and even warned the country against them. In his Farewell Address in 1796 he attacked their use as "...the baneful effects of the spirit of party."[2] Nonetheless, the Electoral College represented an effort to design a system that did not need political parties.

A buffer. Though the Electoral College also represented a buffer between the people and the chief executive, it was never discussed as such, yet neither was it hidden. Alexander Hamilton in *The Federalist Papers* (68) declared:

> "It was equally desirable that the immediate election should be made by men most capable of analyzing the qualities adapted to the station and acting under circumstances favorable to deliberation, and to a judicious combination of all the reasons and inducements which were proper to govern their choice. A small number of persons, selected by their fellow-citizens from the general mass, will be most likely to possess the information and discernment requisite to so complicated an investigation."[3]

The term Electoral College did not appear until sometime later in American history. Initially, this structure of electing the President did not have a name. The Founders did debate how the President was to be elected, but once the document was completed and sent to the states for ratification, this system had few detractors.

The focus on state politics. One of the reasons the Electoral College was not challenged more aggressively dealt with the environment of the times. As strange as this may sound no mechanisms were in place for Federal elections. Since everything moved through the state structure, little thought was given to it. The mentality of the electorate was focused on state politics, since most of the political loyalty of the period was founded in the individual states. Few were faithful to the United States of America because it hardly existed. The Electoral College was seen as simply one more layer of representative government.[4]

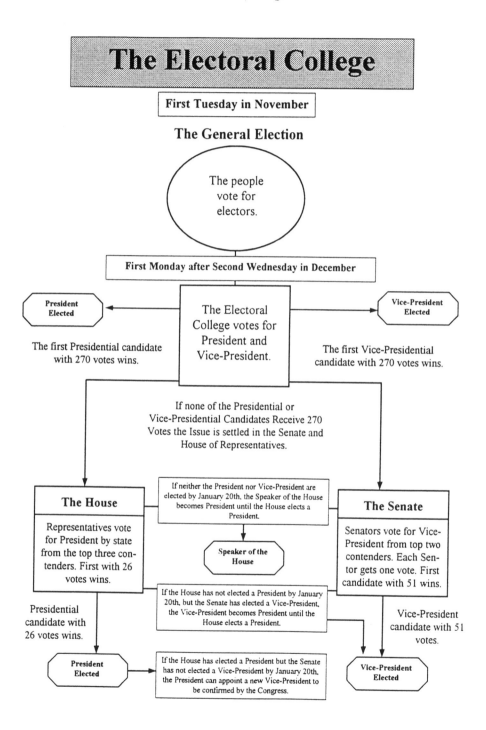

Even so, the Electoral College itself is not structured like a democratic institution. Each state has a little different process for determining who the members of the college will be, but generally they are appointed by the political parties. When the people vote for a given candidate they are actually voting for the party representative to the Electoral College. While party elites have considerable say in who becomes an electoral delegate, the normal process generally starts at the party conventions. Since the parties determine the delegates to the Electoral College, as a rule the members will vote for the candidate who wins the popular vote. Democracy plays little part in the process; the individuals involved are merely loyal party members.[6]

To some degree it is the delegates who won the election. When the people vote for a particular political candidate they are really voting for the party's delegate. The Constitution never made it clear if the delegate had to vote for the candidate with the most votes; in fact if that were the case there would be little need for the Electoral College. The process would be even more superfluous than it is now. Nonetheless currently fifteen states in the Union require by law that their delegates vote only for the presidential candidate chosen by the people or under the direction of the party. This is up from five in the 1940s. While the Supreme Court has not ruled directly on the constitutionality of such laws, generally it is believed that they are unenforceable. Historically, in seven elections one of the members of the Electoral College voted for someone else besides the candidate with the largest popular vote from the member's state. This occurred in 1796, 1824, 1912,1948, 1956, 1960, and 1968.[7]

Who must delegates vote for? In 1968 the Senate wanted to refuse to accept the vote of an unfaithful electoral delegate from North Carolina, the delegate who had voted for George Wallace and Curtis Lemay. Richard Nixon and Spiro Agnew had won the majority of the votes in the North Carolina presidential election. The Senate argued that when delegates were chosen, it was with the understanding that they would vote for the Republican candidate. Voting for someone else represented a breach of trust. In the end the Senate was forced to count the maverick vote because it was agreed that all delegates are free agents.[8]

Criticisms. Criticisms of the Electoral College are many. The college creates odd combinations of events that have little to do with democracy. As has been noted and has occurred many times in our history, individuals have won the Presidency with less than the popular vote, but with a majority of the electoral votes. It is also possible for a person to win the electoral votes and still not be elected President. It can produce a situation in which the House of Representatives would determine who would be President of the United States. Such a situation would be decided along party lines rather than the wishes of the people.[9] This actually happened in 1824.

John Quincy Adams was elected to the Presidency with a popular vote of 105,321 and Andrew Jackson had a popular vote of 155, 872. In this case John Quincy Adams did not even have a majority of the Electoral Votes. He only had 84 votes compared to Jackson's 99. The problem was that Henry Clay and William Crawford also ran that year. Clay had 37 electoral votes and Crawford another 41, but because no one had a majority of the electoral votes, the House of Representatives picked Adams to be President.[10]

Win and still lose. One of the more striking problems with the Electoral College is that a Presidential candidate can win the popular vote and still lose the election. A number of times during the course of American history this has occurred—candidates with fewer popular votes won the election. In 1800 the election of Thomas Jefferson and Aaron Burr ended with an electoral tie. The actual number of popular votes is not clear, but it is generally believed that Aaron Burr won the popular election. When the tied vote reached the House of Representatives, they voted for Jefferson and he became President.[11]

Hayes and Tilden. One of the most controversial elections in American history is the contest between Rutherford B. Hayes and Samuel Tilden in 1876. The official record has Tilden with a popular vote of 4,284,757 and an electoral vote of 184, while Hayes had a popular vote of 4,033,950 and a electoral vote of 185. Historians generally agree that Tilden won the election, but the election results in Oregon, South Carolina, Louisiana, and Florida were disputed and not counted. In an odd joint session of Congress, Rutherford Hayes was declared the President. There is the widespread belief that Republicans agreed to end Reconstruction in the South in exchange for allowing Hayes to be elected.[12]

Harrison and Cleveland. In 1888 the election also showed that it was possible to lose the popular vote and still be elected President. Benjamin Harrison received 5,444,337 votes and Grover Cleveland obtained 5,540,050, but Harrison became President by a distribution of electoral votes of 233 to 168.[13]

Less than fifty percent. In the Presidential elections of 1948, 1960, 1968, 1992, and 1996 the winner received less than fifty percent of the popular vote, but the winning candidate was able to obtain a majority of the electoral votes. In all of these cases the individual with the most popular votes did win, though each had less than a majority. That is because third party or independent candidates split the ballot creating a situation in which no one person won the majority of the total votes.[14]

The television factor. The Electoral College also creates another strictly American eccentricity. Since the invention of the television a tradition has developed by which the viewing public can watch the Presidential returns as they are reported throughout the evening. As each state closes their polls, exit interviews are tallied to determine how the people are voting and which candidate is receiving a majority. The media uses fairly sophisticated systems in this process and their accuracy is quite high. As soon as the winning Presidential candidate is determined for a given state, that information is broadcast to the viewing public. A map of the United States appears, and as the states fall to one Presidential hopeful or the other, each state is illuminated accordingly. A collection of colors may appear as one state after another is categorized. It represents high drama as the candidates work toward the magic number of electoral votes. The problem is that the United States is a large nation with many time zones, meaning that the polls in the western states close later than in the east. As the media map moves across the country, the Presidential contest typically is settled long before the polls close in the western states.

This is not the fault of the broadcast media. What they do is report information. If the Presidential election is over, and a person has been elected to that office, it is well within their responsibility to the public to telecast it. The western states on the other hand have consistently complained that this process diminishes the value of their vote. If the election has already been determined what is the point of voting? While statistically the western states have voted as uniformly as the eastern states, their concern is well founded. If one percent, or even one person. chooses not to vote because from their view the election is over and the outcome has already been affirmed, the process corrupts our democracy.[15]

If we vote because it is one of the obligations and requirements of a free people, then that process needs to be absolute. Any and all votes need to be honored and celebrated. If a system is designed that taints our vote or the nature of our democracy, then that process needs to be examined. It is the Electoral College that devalues our vote, not the media.[16]

Deceptive, misleading, and false. A defense of the Electoral College is difficult, for it is deceptive, misleading, and at the very least false. True democracy is one in which every individual has an opportunity to vote, and the value of that vote is the same as every other person's. The issue should not be that complex. The Electoral College serves little benefit except to tarnish and discolor our democracy.

Chapter 8

One Person, One Vote

At some point a definition of democracy must be determined. The standard view is that a democracy is "majority rule where clear and understood rights exist for the minority." This is a fair statement. It allows for decisions and policies to be determined by majority vote, yet the rights of the minority will not be forfeited. It becomes one of the core ideas of self-government, but without the confirmation of *one person, one vote* the system and the definition becomes unworkable.

Apportionment. The problem has not been how the American people relate to one person, one vote, but how government interacts with the related issue of apportionment or, more correctly, "malapportionment." The issue of malapportionment has been an ongoing problem in American history. There are two parts to this item; the first is fair and equal representation among the states; the second, fair and equal representation within a state. Mostly when this issue has been addressed by the courts or by the general population, it has come in the form of internal state districting. Of course the United States Constitution does allow for inequality within the system. Each state is entitled to one representative in the House and that in itself will create unequal representation. The problem, however, is even more profound and difficult than this one issue. A chronic problem in the United States concerns the nature of our Congressional districts, and this does affect our democracy.

The United States Constitution did not outline a system on how redistricting would occur. It is not even clear that the nation's founders thought in those terms or even reviewed that process. Originally the idea was conceded to the states. What became common was either no action or gerrymandering. Later Congress became involved in redistricting and different types of mechanisms were created. Generally the involvement of Congress only made the issue more confusing.

The idea of reapportionment has never been very popular in the House of Representatives. The whole concept means that if one more Representative is added to a state, one must be taken away from another state. The very process will shift district lines and adversely affect the ability of incumbents to be reelected. If the population of a state has grown and a new district needs to be added, it will change the constituency lines found within all the districts. Similarly, if a district is to be removed from a state, that means that an incumbent is going to lose a job. If there is one issue that elected officials will fight for, it is maintenance of their positions. Nor should we be overly critical. As a rule, most people are not interested in working themselves out of a job, and reapportionment means just that. The United States Congress is a place of compromise; it is part of how business is done. It does not take much of an imagination to develop a scenario in which Representatives are willing to compromise on one piece of legislation in return for no action on redistricting. It would appear far easier, and more politically desirable, to do nothing than to act on the problem.[1]

Equalization of Districts. The problem of equalization of districts has been an ongoing and historical problem. Besides the states' refusals to redistrict or their desire to gerrymander, the simple growth in population creates this problem. As the population grows, it changes the balance in the Congressional districts. Historically, many state districts have not been realigned for sixty years. The idea of *one person, one vote* is damaged by the lopsided nature of the districts when they get out of balance. The examples below are from the 1960s and early 1970s.

State	District	Population	Disparity
Arizona.	Largest district	663,510	3 to 1
	Smallest district	198,236	
Colorado	Largest district	653,954	3 to 1
	Smallest district	195,551	
Connecticut	Largest district	689,555	2 to 1
	Smallest district	317,953	
Georgia	Largest district	823,680	3 to 1
	Smallest district	272,154	

While population shifts create this problem, it is governmental inactions that distorts the meaning of our republic. The value on one person's vote in a larger district is different than what is found in a smaller district.[2]

Regardless of the reasons, Congress has been reluctant to encourage redistricting the House of Representatives. As populations grew and district lines stayed the same, districts within the states became skewed. Throughout our history the Supreme Court was not eager to address the issue. They have seen it as a political issue.

In 1964, this policy did change. At that time the Court ruled that these misaligned state districts were unconstitutional. Internally the states had to have a reasonable level of equality within the districts. The 1964 case came from Atlanta, Georgia, a city with twenty percent of the state's population, but with only ten percent representation. The court's position stated that Article I declared the Representatives would be chosen by the people. They took that to mean *one person, one vote*.[3]

This Atlanta case opened up the floodgates on distracting reform after one hundred years of abuse and nonaction on this issue. While most states went through some form of redistricting during the 1960s, the state governments changed the most. Some state governments required only a quarter of the population to elect a majority in either divisions of the state legislatures. Those that attempted to defend the old system noted the importance of community, historical, and geographical boundaries, or traditional constituencies. The argument against redistricting proved to be ineffectual and change occurred. At this time in American history the body that determines Congressional districts is not so much the legislative branch or the states, but the Judiciary. The court simply felt this needed to be addressed, and they stepped forward.[4]

While nothing within the American Constitution directly states the doctrine of *one person, one vote*, this is a functional part of the election process in most democracies and one the Supreme Court has touched upon.[5] This concept is implied by the very nature of democratic government. As a rule this has been a standard concept and generally is used in describing any form of popular government. As a general principle this idea is found within the United States. Most elections of state, county, and municipal offices are handled in that way. This is also true with Senatorial and Congressional races. The problem is that the United States Presidential elections are handled differently. The system and use of the Electoral College corrupts this fundamental principal of democracy. While electoral votes are assigned to each state, they do not correlate perfectly with each's populations. The value of a person's vote in one state is different from that in another.

A number of methods can compute the true value of an individual's vote. A ratio can be created to represent total population, voting age population, number of registered voters, or actual number of individuals voting in a Presidential race. In each case the statistics will be different, but one clear picture will emerge. The value of each person's vote is determined by the state in which they live. While some states are close to the mean, examples being Arizona, Indiana, and Missouri, in other states the value of a person's vote is badly distorted.

Generally, the smaller the state, the greater the value of a person's vote. In the case of Wyoming the value of an individual vote is three times as great as in Maryland. It is as if a voter in Wyoming is voting as three people or in Alaska as two and a half. Other states such as California, Texas, or New York have a value less than a whole person. In Michigan the Electoral College will change a person's vote so that the real value of that ballot is only .89 of a person.

These same ratios can be used for registered voters. Again the actual value of a person's vote is scattered depending on which state a person lives in. One of the factors that changes the value of a person's vote is how many people actually go to the polls. The more people who vote in a state during the Presidential elections, the less the value of each individual vote. The problem is that the more conscientious the electorate, the less the value of their vote. It can be argued that states such as Oregon, Wisconsin, Washington, and Minnesota which take their voting obligation seriously, are penalized. They register and go to the polls, but instead of this civic responsibility being rewarded, the true worth of their vote is decreased. This occurs because the Electoral College corrupts the significance of our election process.

The difficulty of *one person, one vote* can be applied to the current level of representation as it comes from the states as well. An ever-increasing population

Actual Value of Electoral College Vote By Population

State	Population	Electoral Vote	State Percentage of Total Vote	Actual Percentage of Vote	True Value of Vote
Alabama	4,040,587	9	1.67	1.62	1.03
Alaska	550,043	3	.55	0.22	2.50
Arizona	3,665,228	8	1.48	1.47 ·	1.00
Arkansas	2,350,725	6	1.11	0.94	1.18
California	29,760.02	54	10.03	11.96	0.83
Colorado	3,294,394	8	1.48	1.32	1.12
Connecticut	3,287,116	8	1.48	1.32	1.12
Delaware	666,168	3	0.55	0.26	2.11
District of Columbia	606,900	3	0.55	0.24	2.29
Florida	12,937,926	25	4.64	5.20	0.89
Georgia	6,478,216	13	2.41	2.60	0.92
Hawaii	1,108,229	4	0.74	0.44	1.68
Idaho	1,006,749	4	0.74	0.40	1.85
Illinois	11,430,602	22	4.08	4.59	0.88
Indiana	5,544,159	12	2.23	2.22	1.00
Iowa	2,776,755	7	1.30	1.11	1.17
Kansas	2,477,574	6	1.11	0.99	1.12
Kentucky	3,685,296	8	1.48	1.48	1.00
Louisiana	4,219,973	9	1.67	1.69	0.98
Maine	1,227,928	4	0.74	0.49	1.51
Maryland	4,781,468	10	1.85	1.92	0.96
Massachusetts	6,016,425	12	2.23	2.41	0.92
Michigan	9,295,297	18	3.34	3.73	0.89
Minnesota	4,375,099	10	1.85	1.75	1.05

State	Population	Electoral Vote	State Percentage of Total Vote	Actual Percentage of Vote	True Value of Vote
Mississippi	2,573,216	7	1.30	1.03	1.26
Missouri	5,117,073	11	2.04	2.05	0.99
Montana	799,065	3	0.55	0.32	1.71
Nebraska	1,578,385	5	0.92	0.63	1.46
Nevada	1,201,833	4	0.74	0.48	1.54
New Hampshire	1,109,252	4	0.74	0.44	1.68
New Jersey	7,730,188	15	2.78	3.10	0.89
New Mexico	1,515,069	5	0.92	0.60	1.53
New York	17,990,455	33	6.13	7.23	0.84
North Carolina	6,628,637	14	2.60	2.66	0.97
North Dakota	638,800	3	0.55	0.25	2.20
Ohio	10,847,115	21	3.90	4.36	0.89
Oklahoma	3,145,585	8	1.48	1.26	1.17
Oregon	2,842,321	7	1.30	1.14	1.14
Pennsylvania	11,881,643	23	4.27	4.77	0.89
Rhode Island	1,003,464	4	0.74	0.40	1.85
South Carolina	3,486,703	8	1.48	1.40	1.05
South Dakota	696,004	3	0.55	0.27	2.03
Tennessee	4,877,185	11	2.04	1.96	1.04
Texas	16,986,510	32	5.94	6.82	0.87
Utah	1,722,850	5	0.92	0.69	1.33
Vermont	562,758	3	0.55	0.22	2.50
Virginia	6,187,358	13	2.41	2.48	0.97
Washington	4,866,692	11	2.04	1.95	1.04
West Virginia	1,793,477	5	0.92	0.72	1.27
Wisconsin	4,891,769	11	2.04	1.96	1.04
Wyoming	453,588	3	0.55	0.18	3.05
United States	248,709,873	538	1.00	1.00	1.00

Source: Unite States Bureau of the Census – 1990 Census

Actual Value of Electoral College By Number of Registered Voters

State	Number of Registered Voters	Electoral Vote	State Percentage of Total Vote	Actual Percentage of Vote	True Value of Vote
Alabama	4,040,587	9	1.67	1.62	1.03
Alaska	550,043	3	.55	0.22	2.50
Arizona	3,665,228	8	1.48	1.47	1.00
Arkansas	2,350,725	6	1.11	0.94	1.18
California	29,760.02	54	10.03	11.96	0.83
Colorado	3,294,394	8	1.48	1.32	1.12
Connecticut	3,287,116	8	1.48	1.32	1.12
Delaware	666,168	3	0.55	0.26	2.11
District of Columbia	606,900	3	0.55	0.24	2.29
Florida	12,937,926	25	4.64	5.20	0.89
Georgia	6,478,216	13	2.41	2.60	0.92
Hawaii	1,108,229	4	0.74	0.44	1.68
Idaho	1,006,749	4	0.74	0.40	1.85
Illinois	11,430,602	22	4.08	4.59	0.88
Indiana	5,544,159	12	2.23	2.22	1.00
Iowa	2,776,755	7	1.30	1.11	1.17
Kansas	2,477,574	6	1.11	0.99	1.12
Kentucky	3,685,296	8	1.48	1.48	1.00
Louisiana	4,219,973	9	1.67	1.69	0.98
Maine	1,227,928	4	0.74	0.49	1.51
Maryland	4,781,468	10	1.85	1.92	0.96
Massachusetts	6,016,425	12	2.23	2.41	0.92
Michigan	9,295,297	18	3.34	3.73	0.89
Minnesota	4,375,099	10	1.85	1.75	1.05

State	Number of Registered Voters	Electoral Vote	State Percentage of Total Vote	Actual Percentage of Vote	True Value of Vote
Mississippi	1,352,538	7	1.30	1.14	1.14
Missouri	2,745,231	11	2.04	2.32	0.87
Montana	453,108	3	0.55	0.38	1.44
Nebraska	839,256	5	0.92	0.71	1.29
Nevada	535,095	4	0.74	0.45	1.68
New Hampshire	534,976	4	0.74	0.45	1.64
New Jersey	3,645,488	15	2.78	3.09	0.89
New Mexico	690,900	5	0.92	0.58	1.58
New York	7,724,232	33	6.13	6.54	0.93
North Carolina	3,168,288	14	2.60	2.68	0.97
North Dakota	411,453	3	0.55	0.34	1.61
Ohio	5,266,192	21	3.90	4.46	0.87
Oklahoma	1,529,850	8	1.48	1.29	1.14
Oregon	1,678,643	7	1.30	1.42	0.95
Pennsylvania	5,303,356	23	4.27	4.49	0.95
Rhode Island	468,018	4	0.74	0.39	1.89
South Carolina	1,630,048	8	1.48	1.38	1.07
South Dakota	373,230	3	0.55	0.31	1.77
Tennessee	2,456,272	11	2.04	2.08	0.98
Texas	7,543,988	32	5.94	6.39	0.92
Utah	731,214	5	0.92	0.61	1.50
Vermont	305,424	3	0.55	0.25	2.20
Virginia	2,856,000	13	2.41	2.42	0.99
Washington	2,621,232	11	2.04	2.22	0.91
West Virginia	848,768	5	0.92	0.71	1.29
Wisconsin	2,808,536	11	2.04	2.38	0.85
Wyoming	229,770	3	0.55	0.19	2.89
Registered Voters	117,966,00	538	1.00	1.00	1.00

accompanied by a static number of Representatives to the House requires a major shift in a state's population base to change the Federal representation ratio. A net gain of at least half a million citizens would be needed for a state to gain a single Representative. With the large numbers of people now being represented by one House member and the ever-increasing ratio, a huge gap appears with the number of people each Representative must serve.[8]

The gap can be quite large. At the two extremes are Montana and Wyoming. The State of Montana has about forty-five percent less representation than the State of Wyoming. The greater the differences, the less time, and ultimately the less representation, elected officials can give their constituents. Each percentage point does affect the nature of republican government and impairs the concept of *one person, one vote.*

There is nothing within the United States Constitution that guarantees *one person one vote* elections. In fact the opposite is correct. The Constitution, as a deliberate act, sets up a system by which Presidential elections are determined by delegates. These delegates of the Electoral College actually decide who will be President. The argument that is being made is that the popular vote is the true vote of the people. The Electoral Vote is deceptive. True democracy is one in which every individual has an opportunity to vote, and the value of that vote is the same as the next person's. Again, it is not complex. In the end the only valid system either for an election or democratic action is to be invested in the concept of *one person, one vote.* Any other form or structure contaminates the ideas of self-government.

Chapter 9

What Represents the Economy?

One of the issues within the American Constitution that has the most profound effect upon our society and that currently is not being followed is Article 1, Section 10. The American Constitution describes legal tender and, to a secondary degree, what represents the economy:

> No state shall enter into any treaty, alliance, or confederation; grant letters of marque and reprisal; coin money; emit bills of credit; make anything but gold and silver coin a tender in payment of debts...

The gold and silver standard. This last issue is most notable. For the nation's founders what represented legal tender was gold and silver. To some degree this was the only option. In the fledgling world of the 1700s the concepts of what represented economy were restricted.

At the time of the creation of the Federal government the financial needs of the people were extremely limited. Most items or products that a person needed for survival were constructed within the family, or at the very least within the community. If something essential fell outside their ability to fabricate themselves, barter was generally used. Only as a last method of exchange were coins used. For a long period of time during the Colonial era tobacco represented economy and was used as a medium of exchange.[1] Shortly before or shortly after the Revolutionary War, many of the individual colonies had produced small quantities of copper coins, each with a different value and weight. The most universal money in Colonial America was foreign. The British had laws that restricted sending currency to the Americas; thus, most coins that appeared were clandestinely brought in or quite limited. The most common coins were the *Spanish milled dollar or pieces of eight.* As these were being manufactured in Spanish America, a sizable number of them appeared in the Colonies. When the framers of the

Constitution discussed the powers of Congress in Article 1, Section 8, and they stated their right "to coin money, regulation the value thereof, and of foreign coin..." this is exactly what they were noting.

The Mint. Even with the creation of the United States the situation changed only marginally. When the United State Mint was established it was seen as the central part of what represented the nation's economy. Anyone with gold or silver bullion brought it to the facility for processing. The bullion was returned to the individual in the form of coins. Through the process of *seigniorage,* the Federal government was able to generate a profit.[2] The Mint had a shaky start. Only a small number of coins were manufactured at the beginning. The first coins produced by the Mint were *half dismes..* Though dated 1794 they likely were created the following year. It is said that George Washington supplied the first silver for these coins.

For the Founders gold and silver depicted legal tender. The problem today is that neither gold nor silver represents the economy in modern society, nor even in the world economy. With a few exceptions, most countries of the world base their economy on the *value of the nation.* This is true in the United States. Generally this is done through a centralized banking system. In the U.S. we use the Federal Reserve; money is produced and distributed as needed. It is a complex system. To some degree the value of our money is determined by comparing its value to the value of other national currencies or the simple demand for it.[3]

Outside the confines of the military, the Federal Reserve is the most powerful governmental entity.[4] Their power was not created in one massive edict; rather, it occurred in small steps over a period of time. The Federal Reserve was created in 1913. It came into being as a response to the financial crises that had plagued the nation through most of our history, especially during the Panic of 1907 and the depression that followed. Banking crises were common with each leading to some type of monetary collapse. Shortly after the events of 1907, a Congressional commission was created to look into the problem. Through their effort the Federal Reserve Act was passed that created this body.[5]

James Laurence Laughlin with the support of the New York City banking interest pressed the issue of banking reform. Laughlin had waged a number of political-financial battles in the past and had been supportive of the "sound money" programs of the 1890s, seeing many of them to volition. The efforts of Laughlin and the eastern banking community helped bring the Federal Reserve into existence. While the new system did bring stability and a judicious financial structure to the economic process, it was also a predilection toward the New York financiers and bankers.[6]

The Fed was first established with a board of seven members: five of whom were Presidential appointments, also the Secretary of the Treasury and the Comptroller of the Currency. The term of office was ten years and staggered. Their positions were secure and removal from office a difficult process. They were entrusted with the responsibility of supervising the Reserve Banks and interacting with Congress on economic matters. The Federal Reserve had limited power to direct the banking community or to determine the discount rate.[7]

During the Great Depression the role of the Federal Reserve changed. Congress passed the Banking Act of 1935. Power was centralized with the Board of Governors, all Presidential appointees, and the term was changed to fourteen years. Now given control over the discount rate, the Federal Reserve gave approval for any change. They also had power over Federal securities, in both how they were bought and sold.

A new entity at that time was created called the Federal Open Market Committee, which had a separate body. It was made up of seven governors, the President of the Federal Reserve Bank of New York, and four other Reserve bank presidents. Except for the New York Federal Reserve President, the other bank presidents rotate on the committee. Additional powers were given to the Federal Reserve in the control of holding companies, mergers, deposits, securities, and relationships with international banks.[8]

Currently the Federal Reserve has twelve district banks. They are located in Atlanta, Boston, Chicago, Cleveland, Dallas, Kansas City, Minneapolis, New York, Philadelphia, Richmond, Saint Louis, and San Francisco. While all national banks must be members of the Federal Reserve System, state banks may choose to become members if they wish. Member banks buy stock in the Federal Reserve bank in their district. In return they get a stock dividend and a vote for the district president. The member banks are considered owners of the Federal Reserve, but this should not be misinterpreted, Ownership does not mean control. The Federal Reserve does set an independent monetary policy and one in which the overall economy is considered. Each Federal Reserve bank has a separate board of directors, which falls into different categories. The first two classes are voted on by the member banks, while the last class of directors is appointed by the Board of Governors. Each bank is answerable to the Board of Governors. Additional powers were given the Federal Reserve in 1969. The Credit Control Act was passed, allowing the Federal Reserve additional control of consumer credit and credit cards.[9]

How effective has the Fed been? Opinions vary widely about how effective the Federal Reserve has been in maintaining its commission. Some scholars have placed part of the blame for the Great Depression on the Federal Reserve. After all the Fed had at least partial responsibility for the economy during that time. Yet the Depression of the 1930s needs to be seen as a world depression of which the United States was but a part. Also, the authority that the Federal Reserve had in directing the economy was considerably less at the beginning of the depression than at the end. Critics can point to specific cases where the policies of the Federal Reserve have actually been a destabilizing force. Other critics resist the idea of micromanaging the economy and feel that more established, capitalistic forces should be allowed to play themselves out.[10]

Positive elements of the Fed. The Federal Reserve has had their own dilemmas. This body was unable to control the high rate of inflation during the 1970s, but even so, the overall record of the Federal Reserve is a positive one.[11] Taken as a whole the economy of the United States over the last fifty years has been stable. The money supply has been well managed and for the last twenty years inflation has been under control. The Federal Reserve is one of the few governmental entities that makes money for the U.S. Treasury. The Federal Reserve returns about 18 billion dollars a year back to the government as profit. Thus the Federal Reserve needs to be seen for what it is: an exclusive semi-governmental corporation designed to manage the American economy in a discreet, if not in a particularly diverse, way by persistent applications to control some of the more intoxicating effects of the Capitalist system.

Powers of the Fed. While conceding that the Federal Reserve is not some great evil, it is nevertheless an extremely powerful body. While the Federal Reserve has the potential power to disrupt and destroy the very fabric of our society, equally, it has the power to enhance and create great wealth for the nation. A governmental body that can generate money and control the financial health of the nation must be seen as formidable. Some individuals even refer to it as the fourth branch of government. The policy makers within the Federal Reserve have the ability to move the economy in any direction they see fit. Moreover, it is done outside the controls of Congress or the Executive branch of government. There is a thin line between allowing the Federal Reserve the independence to create a stable economy, the goal of this body, and the inability to be subject to any level of oversight or supervision. While Congress would argue that they do have oversight control, the reality is that the Legislative branch of government does stand on the fringe of our monetary policy. The question returns to the Constitution. "Should the Federal Reserve be a Constitutional entity?"

Some have noted this discrepancy with the American Constitution. Their position is that the United States needs to return to the gold standard, which closely relates to the views found within the Constitution. They feel uncomfortable with the idea of money not being connected to a precious metal and instead the only factor determining how money is generated is by the nation's need.[12]

The other side of this issue deals with the massive size of the United States and the huge size of our economy. The world's supply of gold and silver is now insufficient to maintain this type of national economy under the conditions found two hundred years ago. Even if such a system was instituted and all were to return to the gold standard, it would need to be prorated. The issue becomes even more complex when it is noted that we are actually part of a far larger economic sphere. The United States is a major player in this world economy. Many nations around the world use American currency as a second economy running parallel to their own, and in other cases American currency is the chief form of exchange.

The Fed and the Constitution. The Constitution has given Congress the power to regulate commerce and to determine the value of our currency, at least in regulating the economy. That task, however, since has been delegated to the Federal Reserve. While there is nothing corrupt or deceptive about this organization, it also is not really a governmental agency; rather, it is a private corporation, owned by the banks that use their services, and it is a self-funding body. The Federal Reserve is at best an anomaly of governmental functions. Congress will receive testimony and reports from the officers of the Federal Reserve but feed no information into the process. If there is one criticism that can be leveled at the Federal Reserve it deals with the fact it is a non-bureaucratic entity masquerading as a governmental department. It is simply too important and too powerful not to be placed within the Constitution.

Through most of American history we were on a de facto gold standard, in part because of the Constitution and in part because Congress set the value between gold and silver. The issue became a point of focus during the Presidential elections of 1896; then gold and silver interest competed for dominance, and the gold faction won out.[13] Through this struggle precious metal and the economy became combined, at least throughout the first part of the twentieth century.

Changing standards of currency. The Currency Act of 1900, sometimes called the Gold Standard Act, officially placed the United States on the gold standard.[14] Franklin Roosevelt took the United States off the gold standard in 1933. This precious metal was removed from circulation under the Gold Reserve Act of 1934, eliminating the convertibility of currency into this item. In 1971 all dependence on gold was removed. Silver was removed from circulation in 1965 because the value of these metals on the open market was greater than its monetary worth. It was reaching the point where these coins could be melted down for a profit.

Without being derogatory, there are reasons why the United States and most countries in the world are off the gold standard, but that still does not justify ignoring the requirement found within the Constitution. If the Constitution needs to be changed, and the reason is valid enough, the issues need to be presented accordingly. The people will recognize the logic of such adjustments. We are simply in error passing legislation that ignores our supreme body of laws.

Bills of credit. What creates discord is the gap that exists between the direction of the Constitution and our current modern economy. The Constitution declared that gold and silver represented legal tender for the purpose of paying debts. At this point no gold or silver are in circulation. They have been replaced with Federal Reserve *bills of credit,* which must be seen as a transgression of Article I, Section 10. This part of the Constitution was aimed at the states, declaring that they were not allowed to issue bills of credit. It would seem odd, though, if the states would have been willing to give up issuing bills of credit, only to allow the Federal government the power to create this form of money. In any case our currency at present is not backed by either gold or silver. [15]

The Supreme Court has taken up the issue of paper money as legal tender in the past. During the American Civil War Congress had passed an act that paper notes issued on the credit of the United States had legal tender. Even though the high court had a number of opportunities to rule on the issue earlier, it was not until 1870 that a decision was passed down. In *Hepburn v. Griswold* the Legal Tender Act was declared unconstitutional.[16] The main issue of whether paper money was legitimate was evaded. A year later two more legal tender cases reached the Supreme Court. In *Parker v. Davis and Knox v. Lee* the court stated that Congress did have the power to control the nation's currency and that the government did have the power to issue paper money as legal tender.[17]

The problem with what represents the economy in our contemporary society and how the founding fathers saw economy is badly out of sync with the Constitution. In the case of the Federal Reserve it is simply easier for Congress to create a new semi-governmental entity, give it substantial power, and ignore the Constitution than it is to amend it. When the Constitution is disregarded, even if it is one issue, it taints the entire document. There is always the possibility that one of our rights will no longer be seen as politically feasible, that social or domestic pressure will demand that a specific right be abandoned. If such an act is possible then the Constitution has no value. If the document is begin ignored it has no purpose. It should stand as a defense against improper actions by government of the majority.

Chapter 10

Delegation of Congressional Responsibilities

Though the Constitution clearly defines duties to be performed by each branch of the United States Government, portions of its work, nevertheless, are delegated to other, non-elected entities. This delegation of responsibilities has become a lively point of debate concerning the Federal government, and especially the United States Congress. Delegation takes place in a number of forms, only one of which is the process of creating large regulatory agencies. These agencies or departments are placed into the Executive branch of government, and in turn they create law through their original mandate While the Federal Reserve must be seen as the most important of the charges that Congress has delegated, it is by no means the most prolific in creating law. Agencies such as the Environmental Protection Agency, the Securities and Exchange Commission, and the Occupational Safety and Health Review Commission as examples continually generate regulations that have the power of legislation. The question is whether this process of delegation is unconstitutional.

The First Article of the United States Constitution states, "All legislative powers herein granted shall be vested in a Congress..." It is a simple enough statement. The view of the nation's founders and their intent was for the Legislative branch of government, in this case the House of Representatives and the Senate, to develop the laws of the nation. To do so was not unduly complex and for more than the first 150 years of our history this procedure worked well. Congress as a lawmaking body created enactments subject to review and veto by the President. A number of events changed this process. The most consequential was the increase in the size of the Federal bureaucracy, especially as it related to the outcomes of the Great Depression. Government took a more active role in the lives of the population and the nation's institutions. This can be noted by the number of regulatory bodies constructed and the power they have been given since the New Deal era.

The case for delegation. While it is possible to make a positive argument for delegation, and many do see this process as valid.[1] Some believe that by allowing governmental agencies greater freedom of action, those delegated the task can stand beyond the political arena and be more objective in the regulations that are created. After all, Congress is a political body, far more subject to the caprices of public opinion and special interest.

This argument continues that those regulatory agencies can better appraise the needs of all parties concerned and in a far more analytical environment. Another point is that regulatory bodies can operate far more quickly to potential problems. Congress is a very deliberate body and urgency is not its greatest strength. Besides this, the United States government has become enormous. It is functionally impossible to expect Congress to possess the degree of understanding and detail needed to create laws that impartially relate to very specific concepts. They neither have the time nor knowledge to properly micromanage society. Delegation has become a method by which government can oversee activities and administer national interest with a cohesiveness that could not be done in any other fashion.[2]

Furthermore, the argument is put forth that Congress in fact created these regulatory agencies, which in itself is a legislative process. Congress through its investigative powers and through the committee system continue to monitor these departments. While Congress may have delegated their direct role in creating legislation, they do continue to supervise these governmental bodies at some level. The contention is that Congress no longer becomes a legislative entity, but more of a general policy-making body. While parts of the above statements may be debated, the general assumptions seem to be fair. After all, Congress still has the power to eliminate a given agency and reestablish its own authority over the legislative process. "What Congress has given, Congress can take away;" the responsibility still remains with the Legislative branch.

When the Executive branch legislates. Problems do exist, though, the first of which is the process of delegation itself. The entire procedure places the legislative role of Congress squarely into the lap of the Executive branch. The President as administrator of the Federal bureaucracy has considerable say in the direction of these agencies. Similarly, the President appoints the Cabinet members and departmental heads. Under these conditions the Chief Executive takes on part of the responsibility of the Legislative branch, a function clearly beyond the scope of the Constitution and the intent of its Founders.

While Presidents may face some condemnation from the public for the actions of the departments within their administrations, they are able to use the same tactic as Congress. The President can declare that an unpopular regulation is a product of the Federal bureaucracy. The Chief Executive will shift blame to the bureaucrat or back to Congress. If this same item had come through the Legislative process, the President would have to sign the bill. The Chief Executive would then become part of the process and would have to accept part of the responsibility for the piece of legislation. Through the regulatory process it is easy to deflect public ferment over any given issue.[3]

Roosevelt versus the Supreme Court. Aware of this shift in legislative powers, the Supreme Court has sent mixed messages on this topic. Until the Great Depression, the position of the High Court stated that Congress was not allowed to delegate their authority. The first such case on delegation was *Field v. Clark* (1892). The position had remained that Congress cannot delegate legislative power to the President.[4] This case and those related to the transfer of power were never settled on the issue of delegation alone. They were found to be Constitutional either because of limitations of the act or the act was considered to be reasonable. This doctrine continued at least up until the New Deal programs. The chief conflict that developed between Franklin Roosevelt and the Supreme Court during the Great Depression centered on this issue of delegation.

This conflict proved to be long and protracted. As Roosevelt was attempting to establish New Deal programs, he found himself at loggerheads, with the courts over these ideas. The National Recovery Administration was created to help facilitate a wide range of projects and legislative acts designed to relieve the people from the economic ravages of the Depression. The Social Security Act and the Wagner Act passed during this era as did a collection of other socially directed governmental programs. At the beginning of the New Deal the Supreme Court found most of these Acts unconstitutional.[5] Three cases in particular dealt with delegation: *Panama Refined Company v. Ryan, A.L.A. Schechter Poultry* against government.[6] While politically it has been argued that they were concerned about "creeping socialism," the position the court was taking on these cases was that Congress was improperly delegating its authority. The focal point for the Court was the separation of powers within the Constitution.[7]

Roosevelt and Congress were unsure of how to proceed. Not only were they doubtful that such a Constitutional amendment could be passed, they were not even certain how it should be written. The tactic that developed was to "bully" the Supreme Court. Through intimidation and public opinion Roosevelt was able to change the view of the Supreme Court. He threatened to pack the High Court with more than the nine justices. The coercion must have worked because by 1937 the Supreme Court had changed directions on some of its earlier positions and had allowed most of the important New Deal legislation to survive. By the time the dust had settled, the High Court had conceded delegation as an acceptable process of government.

Other factors made this issue complicated. One of the principles of administrative law is *delegatus non potest delgare*.[8] In this position a person or an organization delegated a responsibility has been given decision-making power. Under this arrangement that authority cannot be delegated to another. A delegate cannot delegate, especially if delegating represents a substantial change in expectation. If this argument is applied to the American government, then the actual power of the state is invested with the people. They alone have sovereignty and authority within a democratic nation. The people have delegated their supremacy to their representative, making Congress a surrogate of the people through the idea of an election. If the concept of *delegatus non potest delgare is* applied, then Congress cannot delegate their responsibilities unless it has been explicitly authorized. The concept is clearly an expectation that Congress will legislate and govern.[9]

This idea is connected to part one of Locke's theses. Government cannot abdicate their responsibility, nor can they delegate their responsibility. This is especially true if it is imposed by the Constitution.

"The legislative cannot transfer the power of making laws to other hands; for it being a delegated power from the people, they who have it cannot pass it over to others. The people alone can appoint the form of the commonwealth, which is by constituting the legislative and appointing in whose hands that shall be. And when the people have said, we will submit to rules and be governed by laws made by such men, and in such forms, nobody else can say other men shall make laws for them; nor can the people be bound by any laws but such as are enacted by those whom they have chosen and authorized to make laws for them. The power of the legislative, being derived from the people by a positive voluntary grant and institution, can be no other than what the positive grant conveyed, which being only to make laws, and not to make legislators, the legislative can have no power to transfer their authority of making laws and represent a repudiation."[10]

There is an expectation that the Legislative branch of government will legislate.

The idea of delegation. A similar idea can be found within contract law. If it is agreed that the Constitution is a social contract then certain performances must be maintained. Here again a number of concepts come to the surface. If one part has delegated responsibility to a third party, it could imply an unwillingness to perform a given function. If it were ruled that this were the case, then the contract could be null and void. It could represent a repudiation.[11] The whole idea of delegation is that, while one person may be sanctioned to act on the behalf of another, the real power and authority has not changed. The representative exists as a proxy and at the discretion of the appointee. They can still interact with a delegate. When a third party appears in this picture it becomes more difficult for the real authority to interact with them. Further is the question of accountability and whether the third party actually is accountable. Is the third party responsible to the original delegate, the group from which that party has subcontracted and the one paying their wages, or are they responsible to the true authority, which in this case is the people. The point is that the electorate can interact with their chosen officials, but they do not have that same capability concerning a civil servant.[12]

A related issue to contract law is applicability. For a contract to be valid there cannot be a fundamental change of circumstances. Major changes in the conditions, circumstances, or reasons why the contract was put into place invalidate the contract as no longer germane or appropriate. Only a strange and compelling set of conditions would lead a Federal judge to nullify the United States Constitution, the rationale being that circumstances of the original agreement had in essence changed. Many issues still remain related to contract law that have pertinent ramifications to our social compact.

Fundamental flaw of delegation. Regardless whether either of these issues of administrative law or contract law applies to the United States Constitution, a fundamental flaw appears to surface in the reason why delegation occurs. Delegation allows Congress to hide from their responsibilities and to shift blame. One of the most basic concepts of government is that for every action there is a reaction. A regulation may help some but harm others. It is the essence of government. Through the use of delegation Congress can dissociate themselves from governmental deeds. If a department commits an act that the people support, then Congress can take the credit; after all they created the body. If a governmental agency commits an act that is unpopular with the majority of the electorate, then Congress can blame the bureaucracy. For them it is a win-win situation. The only point is whether it is "good government."

What is created is a contradiction. How is it possible to have a separation of power and also delegate? Even the entrusting on one piece of legislation or allowing one law to come into existence through another branch of government dissolves the original thesis of the drafters of the Constitution.[13]

Accountability. In the end this may not be an issue that is directly unconstitutional or even ignores a requirement of the document, but it does slip along the edge. Large nations create large bureaucracies, but the idea of delegation as it is currently being used by Congress does operate beyond the intent of the nation's founders. It would be difficult to explain to them how this part of the Constitution evolved. The problem is actually very basic. It simply does not allow for accountability. While accountability may not be a Constitutional issue, it certainly is a qualified one. What is the point of electing individuals to public office if they do not accept accountability for their actions?

Chapter 11

What Congress Has Given Away

The nation's founders did make an effort at outlining the powers and responsibilities of each of the three branches of government. As a rule they were explicit and comprehensive. The responsibility of Congress was to legislate, the Executive branch was to administer, and the Federal Courts were to settle disputes. In the most general sense this is still true. Even so, the United States Congress seems to have either given away or delegated a collection of powers to other parties. In and of itself this should not be seen as a negative. It is not totally clear that such actions are outside the scope of their powers, but it is important to understand what is being given away.

Jurisdiction of the Courts. When the United States Constitution was first drafted, the Founders attempted to outline the jurisdiction of the Supreme Court. This was not something automatically resolved within the document and it was left incomplete. It was agreed that Congress would have the power to determine the jurisdiction of the Federal Courts. There was a collection of reasons. Again, one of the motivations was that the Constitution needed to be ratified by the states. An all powerful Supreme Court would have not been very palatable to the state legislatures. Equally, the founding fathers wanted to have a counterbalance to an imperious court. What was created was a system by which the legislative branch of government held the key to the types of cases the Federal courts could hear. Article III, Section 2, reads as follows:

> "In all cases affecting ambassadors, other public ministers and consuls, and those in which a state shall be party, the Supreme Court shall have original jurisdiction. In all other cases before mentioned, the Supreme Court shall have appellate jurisdiction, both as a law and fact, with such exceptions, and under such regulations as the Congress shall make."

The reality is that Congress has the power to determine the jurisdiction of the

Supreme Court. If Congress disapproved of the direction the Court was taking on issues representing criminal prosecutions, homosexuality, school prayer, abortion, discrimination, privacy rights, police powers, or any number of other items, they had the power to withdraw the Court's ability to hear those cases. Jurisdiction is an important element to any legal body. If the court does not have jurisdiction to review the case, then they cannot proceed.[1]

Part of this process of determining jurisdiction began with the *Judiciary Act of 1789*, which was one of the first acts of Congress. The core of the Supreme Courts appellate powers were bestowed upon the courts at that time. With some restrictions, the Supreme Court was able to review the rulings of the lower Federal Courts. Mostly this dealt with civil, not criminal cases. The most important appellate jurisdiction the high court had was over state judicial actions. This Judiciary Act allowed the Supreme Court to judge the validity of state statutes that were in conflict with Federal law, the ascendant powers of treaties, conflicts between the states, state imposed restrictions of basic rights, and overall Constitutionality of most Federal laws.[2]

Even so, the jurisdiction issue was never complete until the *Judges' Act of 1925*. At that time Congress conceded virtually total authority to the Court to determine what cases they could hear.[3] Currently the decision to review a case or not rests with the High Court.

Congress has withdrawn jurisdiction. In a few incidents in United States history an attempt was made to restrict the Supreme Court's jurisdiction under Article III. The most noted one occurred during Reconstruction. Near the beginning of the American Civil War, President Lincoln withdrew the rights of habeas corpus. This was allowed under the Constitution during a time of rebellion. Lincoln felt this was needed to hold individuals known to be sympathetic to the Southern cause but against whom clear charges could not be brought. On the heels of this was the Habeas Corpus Act of 1863. By 1866 a case had reached the Supreme Court involving an antiwar activist from Indiana who had been tried by a military court for disloyalty and had been sentenced to death. The High Court ruled that the trial was unconstitutional, that military tribunals were not valid in areas where civilian courts were still operating. They ruled that the waiving of the rights of habeas corpus in areas that were not in rebellion was also improper.[4]

This case had angered Congress. The suspension of habeas corpus was still attached to Reconstruction laws. A writ of habeas corpus was not valid in the American South and Congress was not eager to change this situation. A number of cases were working their way through the court system involving this issue. By this time the South was no longer in revolt and Congress was concerned that the Supreme Court would declare these Reconstruction laws unconstitutional. In an effort to exclude the Court from the process, Congress withdrew jurisdiction to hear habeas corpus cases. The Supreme Court, noting that it no longer had authority, removed itself from all cases involving this subject matter.[5]

Currently Congress has conceded the issue of appellate jurisdiction to the courts. This is an important and complex issue. The legislative branch of the Federal government still has the power to determine the jurisdiction of the High Court. If Congress wished, they could decide which items the Supreme Court could hear or not hear. It would be possible for the Legislative branch to reduce our individual rights, and then disallow the Courts to hear these cases. The concept of addressing grievances through the courts would be lost. On the reserve side, the contemporary system allows the Supreme Court a free hand in choosing which cases they think are most worthy. The only real limitation is what types of cases are brought before the Federal courts and, later, what types of cases are brought to the High Court on appeal.

In this situation, the greater power to do harm must lie with Congress. They are by far the more political of the two bodies. One of the purposes of the Supreme Court is to review and check the constitutionality of the laws passed by our governmental entities. The Courts are set up to survey the actions of government. If the courts are no longer able to do this, then every issue relating to personal liberty could be in jeopardy. While Congress has correctly abandoned this power and deferred it to the Courts, this still represents a design flaw in the Constitution. If Judicial Review is one of the cornerstones of our democracy, and it is, then there should not be any limitations to that process. At this point the nation is operating by the "good will" of Congress. A study of history will reveal great moments of enlightenment and humanity; proportionately, stories of enormous evil and despotism can be found. The future will represent those same concepts. It is probably not in the best interest of a free people to leave this kind of issue unresolved.

Who can legislate. Of all the items that the United States Congress has given away, the most important must be the ability to legislate. It is not that Congress has given this power away as much as it is being shared by other elements of government. While Congress maintains that power and still enacts laws with great frequency, so do the other branches of government. The issue of delegation feeds into the concept of legislation.

The ability of governmental agencies and the bureaucracy to regulate represents a form of law. Regulation becomes legislation and carries all the power that legislative acts represent. It is enforceable, penalties exist for noncompliance, and it denotes a level of control. Regulation, like legislation, establishes codes of behaviors and specific courses of actions.

This problem is even further magnified when the High Court attempts to review or judge the Constitutionality of a piece of legislation. If the Court attempts to concentrate on the spirit of the original Constitution or the intent of the nation's founders, there is no logical way of connecting regulation with the document. The Court must rely on past decisions, former interpretation, common law, and the current realities of our society to make judgments. There is nothing within the Constitution that allows the Federal government the power to address social welfare issues or working conditions. Yet, those issues are regulated everyday and the majority of the population accepts this situation as a matter of course.[6]

Similarly, the court begins to legislate; this occurs through the process *judicial activism.* The Supreme Court begins to accept responsibilities for parts of society for which Congress either refuses to act or seems unwilling to act. Court decisions undertake the appearance of legislative orders or an enactment. The Court no longer interprets the law, but embarks on a different path of steering the nation and managing the affairs of state. It generates rules, procedures, and programs that need to be followed, The Court becomes technocratic and in a real sense they govern. The problem with this process has also been that it is undemocratic. Federal judges are appointed for life and their values should not supersede those of elected officials. If fault must be found with this system, it should not be aimed at the Courts. In many ways the Court is only filling a void left by Congress.[7]

This same type of conflict between what is viewed as the nature of legislation can also be found within the concept of Executive Orders. These have become a common practice for American Presidents. During the course of our history more than 12,000 numbered Executive Orders have been proclaimed with estimates of actually 50,000 total. They come in a wide range of forms. Many of these orders represent directives for the military. As Commander in Chief, the President can oversee operations found within the armed services. Abraham Lincoln's Emancipation Proclamation was little more than an Executive Order. It was not backed by legislation, yet the implications of that document had far-reaching social, political, and military ramifications. In fact many of the major political and military events of the American Civil War occurred by Executive Order. Lincoln drafted soldiers into the army by decree, he called up state militias and organized the volunteer regiments, he blockaded the Southern ports, he seized railroads, he pressed former slaves into work gangs, and he spent money that had not been authorized by Congress. While Congress later confirmed these acts by legislation, all were initially generated by Executive Order.[8]

The precedent was started with George Washington over what must be viewed as one of the most logical and mundane of reasons. Washington declared the United States a neutral nation, and he did so by Presidential decree. Congress accepted this concept and was supportive of the action. Isolationism and neutrality were a part of the American fundamental principles at the birth of our country. The act was seen more as a statement of fact and of who we were, rather than a piece of legislation. Yet, within the framework of international law and international relationships, neutrality is very specific. It has distinctions all its own and requirements that are coupled with this declaration. The idea of Executive Orders was established and each President from that time forward has issued orders on different topics.[9]

What makes Executive Orders so perplexing is the variation in these different decrees. Some of them are truly administrative in character, well within the responsibilities of the chief executive. Others seem to be clearly unconstitutional. John Kennedy created a governmental agency, the Peace Corps, by executive order. Later, appropriate legislation came from Congress through budgetary considerations for foreign aid. The most troublesome of all these executive orders came from President Harry Truman. In 1951, during the Korean War, the United Steelworkers of American were on the verge of a strike against the steel companies. Truman ordered the steel mills seized by executive order and to be operated by the Federal government.[10] The Supreme Court finally intervened and declared the act unconstitutional, noting that Congress had the power to commit such an act, but not the President. A more recent event occurred with Jimmy Carter. In an effort to expedite the release of the American hostages in Iran in 1980, Carter suspended all financial litigation against that country by Executive Order. This act proved to be a quagmire of intergovernmental proceedings and problems, to say nothing about the whole theory of due process.[11]

Equally, there is the concept of Executive Agreement. In this case the President has entered into an agreement with a foreign power over an item of mutual concern. These are more than simply governmental protocols. They have the interworkings of a treaty, but without the consent of the Senate. The most notable of these was the Lend-Lease Agreement between Franklin Roosevelt and Winston Churchill just prior to the United States entry into World War II. The United States gave the United Kingdom fifty destroyers, along with an assortment of other pieces of military equipment, in exchange for some Caribbean naval bases.[12] This Executive Agreement had created considerable fervor in Congress, especially among the isolationists. The United States did not need the bases and the agreement was obviously designed to assist Great Britain militarily. It had all the shape and structure of a treaty, but it had not been submitted to the Senate for ratification. Besides the Constitutional question, the transaction was outside of the law. Congress had passed legislation strictly forbidding this type of action.

Again, issues relating to Executive Orders or Executive Agreements stand outside of the American Constitution. They are not inherent to the document and the activity resembles legislative acts. It is Congress that holds this authority. While the nation's founders may have been determined to set up a government with clearly defined areas of responsibility, that concept has been corrupted. In fact the drafters of the Constitution may have stretched the issue too far originally, but if there is one concept that should be absolute it is the power of the legislative branch to legislative. If they lose that one piece of authority what becomes of the validity of that body?

There is one sphere in which these three ideas of Constitution, delegation, and legislative power collide. Of all the concepts found within the American Constitution, it is odd that this one element would be the post office. It is all things and none. It is strange to believe that such an inert subdivision of government has the potential of representing a major Constitutional crisis.

The United States Post Office was one of those entities that was enhanced by the Constitution. At the time of its conception the Post Office had been an item of exuberant pride for the new nation. Benjamin Franklin was the first Post Master General and he was as revered as George Washington among his compatriots. [13] As much as any item the mails represented a unifying force. Most Americans would never go to the national capital, few had ever met their Senator, even the coinage was more apt to be foreign than to have Liberty stamped on it, but there was one physical presence of the Federal government. It was the post office. Everyone knew the local postmaster. He was either the mayor, or ran the inn, or was one of the town's merchants. A letter was treated with great sanctity. It was personal. A loved one or a friend was communicating from a great distance. The post office was also a statement to the world community, for only modern nations had a postal system.

As the nation grew so did the post office department. As the nation's population increased so did the volume of mail. With each new technology a new method of delivering the mail was devised. Business discovered uses for the postal system. It became more than simply a delivery system for personal letters. Postcards, bills, advertisements, parcel post, magazines, books, and catalogs each added to the magnitude of the operation. The United States Post Office was processing billions of pieces of mail each year. At one point, the majority of the civil servants for the country were employed by the post office and this department was also becoming a drain on the nation's treasury. By 1970 Congress was ready to try something different. [14]

Richard Nixon signed into law the Postal Reorganization Act of 1970. The old Post Office Department became the United States Postal Service. It was a government owned and operated company placed under the executive branch. The goal was to develop the Postal Service into a self-supporting program. The cost of services from this new entity would come from those who used the business. An eleven-member board is appointed by the President and approved by the Senate. The board chooses the Post Master General. A separate Postal Rate Commission of five members determines the cost of postage.[15]

Currently the United States Postal Service enjoys a monopoly on first class mail. Without continuation of that exclusive possession, the mails would no doubt dissolve as the entity we know today, but the Postal Service is besieged on two fronts. Competing business concerns come in a wide range of forms—everything from parcel post companies to electronic mail. Each firm attempts to slice into the market share of the postal service. The second group is Congress itself. A large number of elected officials believe that the Post Office should be privatized. It is argued that as a nongovernmental corporation it would become more efficient and would be able to compete more effectively without governmental interference or obstruction.

Privatization is not something new. Some have encouraged a privatization of a number of governmental entities, everything from the weather bureaus to air traffic controllers to the Federal prison system. Each has its supporters and detractors, but the Postal Service is something different. Unlike other governmental agencies the Post Office is a Constitutional item. While it may be agreed that Congress may delegate this responsibility to some other body, even one designed to make a profit, in the end the accountability is still theirs. If the Postal Service was sold to a private group of investors this still would not discharge the government of its responsibility to this agency or reduce their risk. The process would serve no useful purpose. The problem is that the Postal Service would still remain a Constitutional element.[16]

The problem, of course, is not whether the postal service should be a governmental entity or not. The issue is whether it should be a Constitutional one. Two hundred years ago the answer would have been yes, but today the issue is far more complex. Having the post office as a part of the Constitution limits choices. Equally, if Congress ignores the issue and moves forward regardless of the Article 1, Section 8, Paragraph 7, it rips at the fabric of our social contract. The larger issue is not whether Congress has the power to delegate or even if it is in the best interest of the nation for them to bestow these governmental functions to others; the problem is whether it is being done with the fundamental support and understanding of the people. The Constitution is a diagram of expected levels of functioning and areas of responsibility. If the supreme law of the land is being manipulated or rearranged without a complete consensus, then it discredits the entire relationship between the masses and their government.

Chapter 12

How Important Is Efficiency?

One of the most common statements heard about the United States Constitution and its relationship to the American government is that the nation's founders did not want a system that was efficient. Historians generally accepted the idea that when the Founders met at the Constitutional Convention in 1787, they universally agreed that they wanted a government with separation of powers. They were keenly aware of the types of abuses that could be leveled at the masses when power was centrally located. They wanted to set up a government where no one person or group held all the authority. They knew from the very start this would create an inefficient government.

This inefficiency can be found in a collection of different concepts and procedures. The Legislative branch of government is empowered to make laws, but the Executive branch can veto them. The President can appoint department heads, but the Senate must ratify the nominations. The office of the chief executive can negotiate an international treaty, only to have the Senate reject it. In turn the Senate can pass a bill unanimously, but if the House of Representatives does not even take up the measure, it dies. A bill can move through both Houses of government, be signed by the President, and then the Federal Courts system can make it null and void. The Federal Courts can convict people of treason and the President can pardon them. Appropriation bills must start in the House of Representatives, but it is the Executive branch that administers the expenditures. This is part of the system; it is designed to be laborious and at times awkward. For the nation's founders the ideas of separation of powers represented a safeguard of our liberties.

It must be conceded that separation of power does have the desired effect; power is not placed in the hands of one person or group. Equally, it creates a system that is highly ineffective at times. This inefficiency creates situations in which accountability and responsibility are lost. When the Executive branch and the Legislative body disagree over the budget, and because of this inaction governmental services cease, which party is responsible for the impasse? In the end it is the Founding Fathers. They created this system. They did not see ineffectiveness as a negative for government.

This may have been more acceptable when the Federal government consisted of sixty-five lawmakers, four department secretaries, a President, a handful of judges, and a small number of office clerks. The Federal government currently consists of hundreds of different agencies, departments, bureaus, and organizations. The national budget hovers around $700 billion dollars. Millions of people are employed by the Federal government. This massive bureaucracy feeds off the actions of our elected officials. If they function in an inefficient manner, it bleeds through the entire system. It multiplies itself. When the people talk about the ineptitude of a governmental regulation or the exorbitant amount of money spent on a piece of equipment or the pure weight of governmental paperwork, it all represents ineffective government. Leadership comes from the top. If the highest posts in government are set up to be unproductive or impotent, how can we expect less from the entire system?

Impounded funds. One of these areas of inefficiency can be found in the concept of impounded funds. One of the conflicts that can develop between the Legislative and Executive branches of government deals with the expenditure of funds. The way the system should function is that the Congress generates a budget and then allocates expenditures to cover various parts of the budget. Next the Treasury Department is ordered to cover these outlays, and the Executive branch of government administrates the process seeing that the wishes of Congress are accomplished. The reality is that the Executive branch is involved in the process at many different levels, and if the President simply contests how the money is being spent and for which programs, it is possible to manipulate the accounting. At the most extreme point, the President can refuse to pay the money and impound the funds.

Thomas Jefferson was the first President to refuse to spend money appropriated by Congress. The Legislative branch had allotted funds to increase the size of the Navy shortly after the XYZ Affair and during a low point of Franco-American relations. After the purchase of Louisiana many of the points of contention between the two nations had lessened. Jefferson felt the new ships were not needed and prohibited the expenditure. In this case Congress relented. It created a precedent though, one that has played itself out between most of the Presidents and Congress.

Presidents and Congress collide. One of the most stormy clashes occurred between Congress and Andrew Jackson. The legislative branch had allotted funds to pay for the wages of those who carried the mails or rode the post routes. Jackson felt it was excessive and refused to pay the amount authorized. When this case reached the Supreme Court, Jackson was forced to pay the money. In all of these impoundment cases when they are settled by the courts, the tidings invariably favor Congress. The decisions are based purely on the single Constitutional issue of which branch writes appropriation measures, but none of this has stopped Presidents from acting with a different agenda. Harry Truman, Dwight Eisenhower, and John Kennedy all had impounded funds. Mostly over what they saw as excessive defense expenditures. The worst cases dealt with Richard Nixon. Not only was he active in impounding funds, but he refused to release financing for any program that fell outside of the budget generated by his office. It must be remembered that Presidential budgets are merely suggestions or, more correctly, requests.

Impoundment Control Act becomes law. The situation with Richard Nixon freezing expenditures had become so acute that Congress passed the Impoundment Control Act of 1974. President Nixon signed it only because he was so heavily engaged in the Watergate scandal at the time. The Impoundment Control Act is a strange piece of legislation because it attempts to set up a Congressional veto on executive misdeeds. It also requests that Congress be notified if the President terminates a program or delays payment. As it is with so many legislated acts aimed at the Executive Branch it is never clear what the reprimand would be if the President terminates a program or delays payment. The frustration is that appropriations and the expenditure of funds is clearly the responsibility of the Legislative branch. The power of the purse is a key element of democracy. While these issues generally come down to pure politics, the bigger issue is effective government. This is a system that paralyzes, rather than encourages collaboration.[1]

The issue of the budget has created numerous other problems. Congress has never been very efficient at producing a budget. It is one of the weak points of the national governmental process. The reasons are many. It can deal with the size of the federal bureaucracy, basic politics, how information is obtained, the power of the committee chairs, outside pressure groups, the legislative process, and private agendas. Congress has attempted to set a budgetary schedule and timetable. The Budget Act of 1974 attempted to set up timetables for the budget process. While the idea was a valid one, disagreement over priorities continued to persist. Since enacting the law Congress has only met its own deadline three times. What replaces the appropriation process is a system called continuing resolution. Money is funneled into governmental agencies and departments automatically. It is an effort to keep the government running, since it is done without the proper allotment of expenditures.[2]

This lack of budgetary efficiency is one of the chief reasons why the Federal government has not been able to balance the budget.[3] Inefficiency is not penalized, yet there can be rewards on the other end of the process. By creating chaos and inaction it is possible to get designated pet projects funded. Compromise as a political tool can only occur at the end of the procedure. A certain level of immediacy is needed before compromise can be considered.

One of the by-products of governmental inefficiency is "pork." In an effort to obtain special consideration or financial programs for their home districts, Representatives and Senators apply many tactics. They will stall legislation, manipulate the process, and concede special "pork barrel" projects to other legislators. In their zeal to take care of their own, the legislative process is corrupted. Issues that are important to the whole country are compromised to the interest of but a few and disproportionately these few receive greater benefit of America's wealth than others.

Self-generating inefficiency can be found in the way amendments are added to a piece of legislation. Both Representatives and Senators may attempt to add an amendment to a bill at various times in its travels. Many of them are rejected, but others stay with the bill as it moves through committees, to the assembly floor, and on to the Conference Committee. Many of these amendments have nothing to do with the piece of legislation and are simply unrelated. Some are considered expendable. They are applied as "bargaining chips," items that will be yielded in the hope of securing others. The problem is that each of these amendments must be reviewed, each must be digested, and this retards the whole process.

These issues of productivity seem to collide when a bill reaches the Conference Committee. The leadership of both the Senate and the House of Representatives may help draft a piece of legislation that is identical at the start, but by the time the legislation reaches the Conference Committee they are no longer similar. In fact the goals of the law may have been forfeited by the process. The Conference Committee will attempt to blend the two measures, but it is an imperfect system. Whatever is done in the joint committee between the two chambers will change the legislation.

The highest level of ineffective government must be the filibuster. The House has strict rules that limit debate. The Senate on the other hand sees unrestricted debate as a tradition. The accepted reasoning has been that filibusters help moderate radical legislation, create an open debate on topics, and protect minority rights. The reality is that it is a tool of special interest, abridges social progress, and undermines the effectiveness of the body. The rules of closure of debate are such that considerable organization and time are required to mount an opposition to a filibuster. The use of this strategy to block legislation has been increasing. In all of the nineteenth century only 23 filibusters manifested themselves; between the years 1970 to 1994 there were 191.[4] Because of the workload of Senators and the demands on their time even the threat of a filibuster can kill a piece of legislation. The reality is that to get a bill passed in the Senate requires support of three-fifths of the membership of the upper house. This is the level at which debate can be suspended.[5]

Some contend that the filibuster does no harm, that it is part of the "deliberate nature" of the legislative process, and especially for the Senate. The argument would continue by noting that there are individual situations in which the filibuster has caused damage, but the greater good rests with this procedure. Regardless how strongly a person feels about this debate, it nevertheless becomes an ineffective part of government. It also slants the political process toward a select few in the Senate, giving them greater power than what the founding father's had envisioned.

These same types of ineffective processes can be found throughout the structure of government. Many of them are little issues, small in nature, but each contributing to the whole. When an election is held on the first Tuesday in November, but the position is not filled until January, this creates a gap in effectiveness. This is even more pronounced if an individual has lost in the primaries and is not removed from office for almost a year. An example would be an official who has lost her or his bid in March to be reelected, but would serve until January when the new official takes office. Human nature is such that it is doubtful that the incumbents would give the people their best work during the intervening months. It becomes one more part of ineffective government.

The American people seem to relish the idea of voting into office conflicting political parties. Such seems to be the great silent conspiracy of the American electorate. If one political party controls the legislative branch of government and the other the Presidency, this will formulate into a stalemate. The Chief Executive has no power to generate bills, and could never get them passed in a hostile Congress. In turn the legislature is unable to enact laws beyond the veto of the President. What occurs is that progressive government comes to an end. Even the pretense of efficiency does not exist. The national government condenses into a platform for party politics, each blaming the other, each focusing on public opinion, each spurting the platitudes of their causes. It becomes at times even more than inefficient, it becomes irresponsible.

What constitutes representation? A disagreement also exists over what represents interaction with the people. One of the key elements to republican government is representation. The concept is one in which our elected officials exchange ideas with the population. By arrangement and consent, a course of action is manifested. The problem is that a political campaign does not represent this type of interchange. The argument is that political campaigns represent a projection of the candidate, but not dialogue. It is set up to determine leadership, which is not the same as procuring unanimity of action. When political campaigns become continuous, then the heart of representative government is lost. What is also lost is efficiency. Many of the issues dealing with government can be extremely complex and require considerable study. If the focus is one of elections, then the task of government is slighted. The view is one in which no matter how effective or knowledgeable an elected official may be, if the lawmaker is not elected it is all meaningless.

The question does return to the same idea. The nation's founders were concerned that not having separation of powers would lead to tyranny and the abuse of government. We have had separation of governmental powers for two hundred years, yet in numerous points in history abusive American government still exists. Examples of social injustices, discrimination, and oppression still abound. Equally, most of the Constitutional governments around of the world do not have the degree of separation of powers as does the United States, yet most, if not all, function well. Tasks are completed, issues are addressed, and while all such democratic governments are political in nature, efficiency is not totally forfeited.

Chapter 13

The Ratio

Since the Constitution is a document that is subject to interpretation, the fundamental purpose of the Supreme Court is to interpret the Constitution and to see that it is appropriately applied. Human behavior, and societies in general, are complex. In our development as a nation, new and different twists occur to the numerous situations in which we have found ourselves. Each case that has ever been before the Supreme Court is a story, each with two points of view, both with two versions of the story. As each one of these cases is interpreted, the theories of Constitutional law are advanced. These interpretations are required because we are constantly changing. Such changes occur in our individual behaviors, our relationship to government, our technology, our association with our institutions, and our view of the world. Through the court system each one has to be evaluated and compared to the basic premise of the Constitution.

The United States Constitution itself creates an atmosphere requiring interpretation. The Ninth Amendment to the Constitution indicates additional rights not listed in the document, *implied rights.* While such a statement may seem ambiguous or misleading it is nonetheless true. A listing of all of our rights becomes an impractical task. Such an exercise also traps a person between the two logical concepts of the *greater good,* noting that society and people as an aggregate have rights as well as the equally important concept of individual rights. The best that can be hoped for is a balance, and it becomes the responsibility of the Supreme Court to find that level of equilibrium within the Constitution.[1]

Other interpretative voices. While the Supreme Court must be viewed as the most dominant voice, it is not the only voice. Members of the Legislative branch and the Executive branch are reading the same document. They are also making judgments about the Constitution; each attempts to move the document in a direction in which they feel most comfortable, each with their own point of view. Into this mix is placed the people, struggling with their individual lives and trying to make sense of the world in which they find themselves. They too can interpret the Constitution, but their voice is the muffled sound of the multitude.

Into this sea of interpretation is placed one line in the United States Constitution. The first Article of the document states a requirement for representation. "The number of Representatives shall not exceed one for every thirty thousand..." While each generation has taken various views of this statement, currently Congress has interpreted that this provision limits the ratio between the electorate and their representatives to no more than one representative per thirty thousand citizens. This line of reasoning, however, may be false; it could as easily mean the maximum—that one to thirty thousand is the ratio and that any effort to represent more citizens by the same House member is unconstitutional.

A Constitution is not a nebulous, undefinable entity. While accepting the concept that certain ideas will always need to be interpreted, an issue the Founders recognized, other items are clear and precise. Those items that must be accurate are those that deal with structure. In the case of the Senate the number and representation of this body was clearly outlined. Each state is allotted two Senators, and originally they were elected by the state legislatures. Similarly, that same level of finite arrangement must be made for the House of Representatives.

The 1 to 30,000 ratio. Three reasons lead us to believe that the 1 to 30,000 ratio was a permanent Constitutional element. *First,* when the inaugural Congress met in 1791 an effort was made to follow the 1 to 30,000 rule. The House of Representatives started out with 65 members. It was not perfect because each state was guaranteed one Representative regardless of how small the population, but the Constitution fixed what the first level of representation would be. New York would have six, Massachusetts eight, Delaware one, and so forth. These numbers were outlined because a census needed to be taken to determine the actual level of representation. For the first few decades a valid effort was made to follow the Constitution and maintain the 1 to 30,000 ratio. At the first Congress, representation was set at 1 to 30,000; an additional House member was allotted to a state for a fraction above fifty percent.

The *second* reason deals with *The Federalist Papers* and the correspondence of the drafters of the Constitution during this time. Nothing in these papers would lead a person to believe that only a fixed ratio was being established in the Constitution. Throughout *The Federalist Papers* either the word ratio is used or the term one to thirty thousand. An example would be Madison's discussion of representation:

> "Within three years a census is to be taken, when the number may be augmented to one for every thirty thousand inhabitants, and within every successive period of ten years the census is to be renewed, and augmentations may continue to be made under the above limitation."[2]

Nothing in these documents points to a permanent number of Representatives.

Early struggles with the ratio. The *third* reason deals with how Congress was attempting to address the issue of 1 to 30,000 rule. They were still struggling with the ratio during most of the first session of Congress. One of the understandings that was made with the state legislatures concerning passage of the United States Constitution was the incorporation of a Bill of Rights. The first ten amendments represent this agreement and compromise. One of the first acts of Congress was to draft the Bill of Rights and send it to the states for ratification in 1791. While ten amendments were passed by the state assemblies, twelve Articles actually had been sent out. One of the two that was not passed by the states dealt with pay increases for members of Congress. It is curious to note that this amendment was actually passed two hundred years later and became the Twenty-Seventh Amendment to the Constitution. The Amendment to the Bill of Rights that was not passed by the states attempted to address the ratio of representation within the House. It reads:

> "After the first enumeration required by the first article of the Constitution, there shall be one Representative for every thirty thousand, until the number shall amount to one hundred, after which the proportion shall be so regulated by Congress, that there shall be not less than one hundred Representatives, nor less than one Representative for every forty thousand persons, until

Expanding Levels of Representation

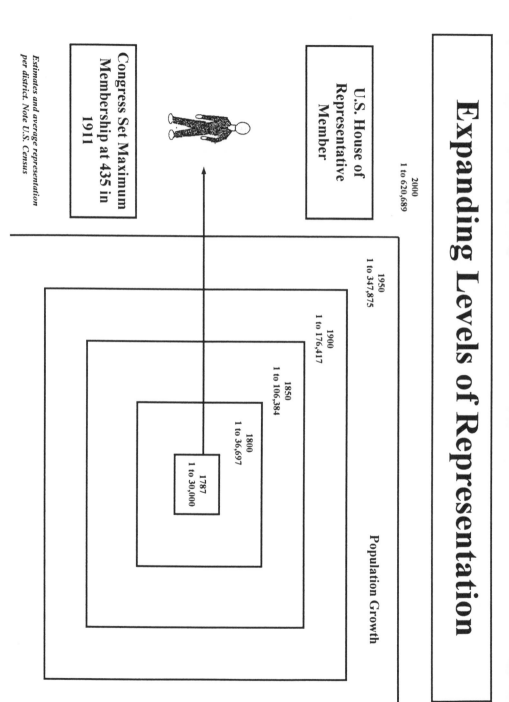

U.S. House of
Representative
Member

Congress Set Maximum
Membership at 435 in
1911

Estimates and average representation
per district. Note U.S. Census

Population Growth

2000
1 to 620,689

1950
1 to 347,875

1900
1 to 176,417

1850
1 to 106,384

1800
1 to 36,697

1787
1 to 30,000

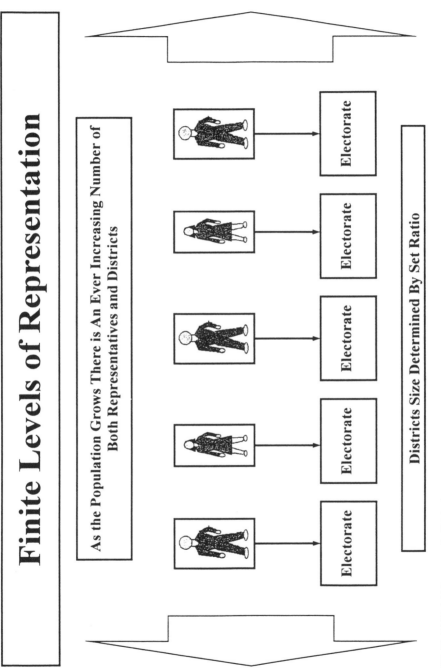

Finite Levels of Representation

As the Population Grows There is An Ever Increasing Number of Both Representatives and Districts

Electorate

Electorate

Electorate

Electorate

Electorate

Districts Size Determined By Set Ratio

This Model Woyuld Represent the Original Direction of the Founding Fathers.

the number of Representatives shall amount to two hundred; after which the proportion shall be so regulated by Congress, that there shall not be less than two hundred Representatives, or more than one Representative for every fifty thousand persons."

Of course this part of the Bill of Rights was not ratified by three-fourths of the states. The indication, though, is that Congress still recognized that the ratio for representation was finite. Part of this Amendment dealt with the Anti-Federalist's concerns about too few Representatives in Congress, but the core item attempted to cover the nature of our representation.

Since the Amendment was not passed by the state legislatures Congress again changed the representation ratio. By 1792 the ratio was fixed at one Representative to every 33,000 citizens with the fractions being disregarded. In 1800 the ratio appeared as 1 to 33,000, but some districts were functioning with more than 40,000 citizens.

Reapportionment and redistricting. The chief dilemma never seemed to be an unwillingness of Congress to observe the 1 to 30,000 rule; the problem was the related concept of reapportionment and redistricting. Originally the belief was widespread that the states would determine what would be the Congressional boundaries for each district. It was never a perfect system and at times the Representatives attempted to assist the process, but interest in redistricting was never high. Whatever plan was drawn up always seemed to contain some level of fractional representation. It led to furious debates and seemingly no proper way to allot such representation. Even in the early years of our republic the Representatives were keenly aware of where their political support lay. Whenever the boundaries were adjusted the political makeup of the district changed. Such activities were never enthusiastically supported. The process was always political and because the people that had the power to make decisions on this issue were either political appointees or elected office holders objectivity was never realized. This problem continued until the 1960s when the Federal Court system became involved and the courts started to force changes in reapportionment.

The paradoxes. As this issue developed and began to be called by a name, it was referred to as the paradoxes, actually two paradoxes in number. The first was called the *Population Paradox*. As the population increased so did the membership of the House of Representatives. Even in the early stages of United States history a concern was expressed with infinite growth of the House. The second item was the *Alabama Paradox*. Observing that while the national population grew and the State of Alabama had an expanding population, the size of their state delegation to the Federal Government was decreasing. By 1830 the ratio was getting out of balance and the number was 1 to 47,700. This occurred even when the number of House members increased to 240.

The Vinton method. By 1850 an effort was made to fix the number of Representatives for the House. The goal was to abandon the idea of a fixed ratio and to keep the House at one established number. This concept was called the Vinton method, after Representative Samuel Vinton of Ohio. Under this new formula the House would remain constant and the population had to be divided between the existing membership. An agreement was made to add additional Representatives as new states were added to the union.[3]

Even this new system proved to be difficult to maintain but new bargains were hard to construct.[4] The American Civil War created even greater upheaval for this provision of the Constitution. The 1860 census was not complete when states began to secede from the Union. The total number of Representatives dropped in the House as the Confederate States formed a new government. The chaos and convulsions the nation faced during the Civil War and during the Reconstruction period were so monumental that the idea of a ratio seemed insignificant in comparison.

By 1867 the process of readmitting the Southern states to the Union had begun, but these delegations were seen as *carpetbaggers,* and few saw these Representatives as permanent. Four new states were added to the Union during the 1860s, changing the makeup of the House. The franchise of the black population also created confusion over the issue of representation. Not until 1877 did Reconstruction end, and by that time the population base of the nation had changed considerably.

The issue of a ratio was mostly ignored through the last, half of the eighteenth century. Some argued that a fixed level of representation would make the assembly "unwieldy." People argued that a fixed ratio could not be maintained. In 1911 Congress set the size of the House of Representatives at 435. Then in 1941 another law was passed by Congress that helped define apportionments.[5] A complicated mathematical formula was developed to cover the issue of representation that guaranteed each state at least one Representative and some level of equal proportions in the House.[6]

Oddly, when the Constitution was first submitted for ratification the issue was not too many Representatives in the House, but too few. A chief concern of the Anti-Federalists during the debate that followed the creation of the Constitution was that the one to thirty thousand rule seemed too large a number. They wanted the ratio reduced even further. Their position dealt with the fact that only 65 Representatives would comprise the house, of which 33 would constitute a quorum, and only 17 would be needed to pass a piece of legislation. In turn, 14 would represent a quorum in the Senate and a majority would be eight Senators. Twenty-five people were needed to pass a bill. Couple that number with the Presidency and the most insidious of laws could be enacted only by a handful of individuals.

Representatives in mass. Using the United States 1990 Census as a point of reference 248,709,873 people reside in this country. If the one to thirty thousand ratio were used 8,290 would be members in the House of Representatives. Under the current system of government and location the process would be cumbersome. That many members of the House of Representatives would require a different method of operation and practice.

One of the chief problems is not unwieldiness, but simply architectural limitations. This is one of the reasons the fixed number was deserted. It is physically impossible to place 8,290 Congresspersons into the Capitol Building and give each a desk. When the United States Capitol Building was first constructed it seemed huge, especially considering the number of people who operated out of it. Currently 435 elected officials are in the House, but they also employ thousands of Workers. On any given day hundreds can move through the facility, each working on various tasks. Architecture is a problem but is not the complete story.

One view suggests that if the House of Representatives had continued to maintain a fixed ratio, Congress would have begun to look more like an ongoing convention rather than a legislative body. Political parties would have become even more dominant in the way government functioned. Of course the issue is not that simple; political parties currently play a major role in the running of government and of Congress. Large assemblage systems are still able to get work done and accomplish the tasks at hand. These situations fall back onto leadership. The effectiveness of the leadership is what moves issues forward regardless of the size of the body.

Arguments for permanent numbers. The argument that Congress made in creating this permanent arrangement was that the Constitution gave them the power to set this optimum number by the fact they can regulate their own body. This argument continued by noting two areas of the document. Article I, Section 4, states as follows:

> "The times, places, and manner of holding elections for Senators and Representatives shall be prescribed in each state by the legislature thereof, but the Congress may at any time by law make or alter such regulations, except as to the places of choosing the Senators."

The original concept of this provision dealt with the way elections would be held, but Congress has attempted to declare that it also includes their ability to regulate the total number of Representatives. The second item was found in Article 1, Section 5, "Each House may determine the rules of its proceedings..." The contention was that the American Constitution gave each legislative body the ability to determine its own rules of order and procedures. Of course the one to thirty thousand ratio does not deal with this kind of arrangement. When Congress made the change to 435 Representatives, the issue was never challenged, either by the people through public opinion or in the courts. The reason was simple enough; there was not a valid alternative. It was not a battle that most people felt a need to fight.

The difficulty is that within the Constitution certain items are clearly spelled out while others allow room to deviate. The nation's founders felt that Congress should determine its own rules of order. An assembly needs the freedom to create its structures and systems of processing work. This issue was debated at the Constitutional Convention in 1787 and in *The Federalist Papers,* and it was agreed that latitude was needed. The Legislative branch needs some room to maneuver, especially in determining its own rules of order. Similarly, other items are far more finite. They are specific in their wording and intent. When the Constitution declares that "The Senate of the United States shall be composed of two Senators from each state...", it would be unthinkable to change such a composition by an Act of Congress. If the Federal government passed a law declaring that we were to have only one Senator from each state, such a transaction would be seen as unconstitutional.

This same argument can be made about the one in thirty thousand requirement. This Article is very specific and little interpretation is needed, especially when it is recognized that initially an effort was made to follow it. The key word in this section is not the one in thirty thousand—it is "exceed." This term sets distinct boundaries. It becomes far more of a directive, rather then a variable when that word is added.

This is also the reason a census was attached to the American Constitution. This provision required a fairly accurate count on the United States population. In our modern society we use the census for determining governmental services and to a lesser degree representation, but the original idea of a census was to help with the one in thirty thousand rule.

Regardless how manageable the one to thirty thousand provision may be, some powerful arguments have been raised in its favor. Central to the American form of democracy is representative government. If the United States is a representative government, then the greater the level of representation the better. If an elected official is required to convey the views and the wishes of the people in their district, it would seem to be far easier to do so at 30,000 than at half a million. Again, using the 1990 U.S. census the ratio is closer to 571,000 to one. This hits home as one of the standard complaints about our Representatives and

Average Number Citizens Represented Per House Member by State

Rank	State	Population	Rank	State	Population
1	Montana	870,000	26	Washington	603,444
2	Nevada	765,000	27	Virginia	601,636
3	South Dakota	729,000	28	North Carolina	599,583
4	Delaware	717,000	29	Michigan	596,813
5	Arizona	703,000	30	Hawaii	593,500
6	Georgia	654,636	31	Missouri	591,556
7	Utah	650,333	32	Illinois	591,500
8	Kentucky	643,333	33	Ohio	586,895
9	Kansas	641,250	34	New York	585,032
10	North Dakota	641,000	35	Vermont	585,000
11	Maryland	630,250	36	Tennessee	584,000
12	Oregon	628,200	37	Idaho	581,500
13	Colorado	624,500	38	Indiana	580,300
14	Texas	624,133	39	Minnesota	576,250
15	Arkansas	621,000	40	Pennsylvania	574,857
16	Maine	620,500	41	New Hampshire	574,000
17	Louisiana	620,286	42	Wisconsin	569,222
18	Florida	615,913	43	Iowa	568,400
19	South Carolina	612,167	44	New Mexico	561,667
20	New Jersey	611,154	45	Oklahoma	546,333
21	West Virginia	609,333	46	Connecticut	545,833
22	Alabama	607,571	47	Nebraska	545,667
23	California	607,481	48	Mississippi	539,400
24	Massachusetts	607,400	49	Rhode Island	495,000
25	Alaska	604,000	50	Wyoming	480,000

The District of Columbia has no representation.

whether or not they are approachable. Even the most conscientious of our House members is going to have an easier time representing 30,000 citizens than half a million.

The position is simple enough. How is it possible to represent a group of people, in this case the electorate, unless you interact with them? The greater the number, the more difficult it will be to understand the will of the people. As it currently stands the people that our Representatives hear from are only those assertive enough to contact them. It would be those who write a letter, send a wire, transmit an E-mail message, or pick up a telephone. Even then it is selective. Generally those that make the effort are focused on one issue. How do Representatives truly know the position of all the people unless they exchange information on a far more personal and wider level?

Mass Media. As the nation's population increases, our Representatives are forced to use other methods of interacting with the people. During political campaigns candidates must use television, newspapers, and radio to get their message across. The media can be expensive; the cost can represent millions of dollars. The candidates see little choice; it is the only way they can reach the mass of voters they need, but for the electorate it feels artificial. In turn the cost of reaching such large numbers of people also has a negative effect. Individuals willing to give enormous amounts of money are solicited. Politics is not a philanthropic activity. People who give money to a candidate expect something in return. It may be nothing more than that fifteen minutes of time to express their position. As a point of human nature people work toward their own best interest, hence it is not much of an exaggeration to believe that those who give large amounts of money to a political organization expect some level of future consideration. If we had smaller districts it might be more difficult to administer the legislative assembly, but elections would be more personable and less expensive.[7]

The process also becomes a one way concourse. The larger the number of people that are being represented the more difficult it is to read the mood and disposition of the people. While the media can be used to get the message of the candidate across to the voters, it occurs only during selective times and can not be used effectively in all situations. The more complex the issue, the less likely the issue will be properly portrayed or even heard. What is used to understand the attitude of the electorate are polls. By their very process they can be skewed and can give a false reading of the general position of the masses. There are few substitutes to meeting a person on their front porch face to face.

Cautions about a "natural aristocracy." One of the issues that permeated the great debate that followed the Constitutional Convention in Philadelphia dealt with the type of people who would serve in our Legislative branch of government. Concern was expressed over what was viewed as a "natural aristocracy." Both the Federalist and the Anti-Federalist held similar beliefs about this concept. They differed only in how such an entity could be created or came into being. In all societies certain individuals rise to the top of their particular profession, in this case civil government. Knowledge, skill, persistence, commitment, luck—all play a part. The concern is that if you add exclusive relationships, political influence, and wealth into this mix it distorts the office and changes the political system. While there are always elites, in fact organizations cannot function without them, this is different from those who represent only a certain group or class. A truly aristocratic individual may hold views counter to those of the masses. Thus, if a nation is to be a representative government, then the views of the people need to be properly postulated. The problem is that with the ever-increasing ratio of representation, the possibility of a "natural aristocracy" becomes ever more likely. The views of the rich and the powerful are more prone to be heard than any other group.

This issue becomes even more clouded when the staff of the House of Representatives is added to the discussion. The United States Office of Personnel Management lists 12,954 employees of the House of Representatives. Each member has between twelve and fifteen employees and those involved with major committees have even more. The actual number of personal staff employees is 7,569. It has to be conceded that a Representative's staff also helps with representing the district. In fact most of the time when a citizen contacts their House member with a problem it will be a handled by a staff member. It is unlikely if you telephone your Representative that you will be able to talk with him or her directly. An entire debate can center around the type of representation we are receiving from our elected officials. It is possible to rationalize that the staff of House members are in fact insulating our representatives from the people. In any case why have a staff member in a position of representing the people when an elected official would better serve the needs of the masses and of the republic?[8]

Two main choices. The real issue may not even be the ratio of representation, but returns to the central theme of democracy, or more correctly how can democracy be best achieved. The issue is not a stable factor, it is impossible to maintain democracy at one fixed level. The issue can be found drifting between two political concepts, democracy and authoritarianism. If we do nothing as a nation we will still move in one direction or the other. Democracy requires that we consistently evaluate and adjust the nature of our power structure. Not to do so places that process in the hands of chance or even worse into the hands of a select few. If the issue is one of democracy, or ever-increasing levels of democracy, which system represents a purer form of republican government? Is it better to have an ever-increasing size of the national assembly or an ever-increasing size of the number of people being represented by an elected official? These are the two main choices. While there may be other options, such as limiting the size of the electorate or stabilizing the population, they seem to be even less manageable. In the case of state governors, senators, county commissioners, and even mayors the level of representation is an ever-expanding number, so this is not an unusual phenomenon. But is it in the best interest of the people to have all segments of government function under this scheme.[9]

Our growing population. Regardless, the population of the United States is growing. It continues to expand through immigration and births. On one hand if we maintained the one to thirty thousand ratio, the total of number of Representatives continues to increase making such a legislative body more difficult to manage. On the other side if we maintain the lower house with 435 members, the total number of people they are forced to represent becomes ever larger. With each passing year the time that a Representative is allowed to spend with even one member of the electorate becomes meager. In the final analysis we are forced to decide which one of the directions is most appropriate, which of these two ideas feel most comfortable.

It is possible for a person to support either side of this issue, but the initial discussion dealt with the United States Constitution. Is the original Article in the Constitution being followed or has the one in thirty thousand ratio been changed? If the item has been changed did that change occur Constitutionally? There are two ways that the Constitution can be modified, one is through the amendment process and the other is by a state generated Constitutional Convention. The argument that is being represented here is that the change in this ratio did not occur Constitutionally, but legislatively. It represents an item that is simply not being followed.

Erosion of representative government. Traditionally the House has been the most democratic of all our national bodies. It originally was the only one of the four national power bases directly voted on by the people and even today it is the body closest aligned to the people. The goal of the Founders was for the Senate to represent the states and the House of Representatives to represent the people. This may be one of the most important issues concerning our relationship with our government. The cornerstone of our democracy is representative government, and the reality is that very issue is beginning to erode away. During the American Revolution the struggle centered on the concept of "No taxation without representation." In modern America what we have is "Taxation with ever decreasing levels of representation."

Chapter 14

The Art of Ignoring the Constitution

All countries face national crises, events so powerful that the very nature of the nation-state is in jeopardy. They come in all types, patterns and dispositions. They can represent an economic catastrophe, war, civil unrest, or a collection of a thousand other events that can change history. Each of these events will adjust the society and the people within. The psyche of the nation will emerge with these great events, and the people will be able to mark time by the extreme danger found within these experiences.

Yet, ideally a Constitution should supersede events. A Constitution should exist as a guide during times of monumental unrest. It becomes an anchor by which the nation can weather such storms. If a Constitution is to be changed it must be done in the full light of day and every voice needs to be heard. It should be a very deliberate act, consistent with the values and beliefs of the people.

Sedition and World War I. The difficulty for Americans is that the Constitution has been ignored at times. The list of such occurrences is considerable and every generation has had to wrestle with the spirit of the Constitution and the national events that have overtaken it. One of the most substantial of all these Constitutional violations must be the Sedition Act of 1918. Along with the Espionage Act of 1917 and the Trading-with-the-Enemy Act of 1917, these three statutes allowed the government powers far in excess of the limits placed on it within our social contract.

These were acts that reduced freedom and restricted the personal liberty found with our Constitution. Congress felt that these powers were needed to focus the nation on the single issue of victory during World War I. The language of these Acts was very broad and allowed for considerable freedom of action on the part of government. The Sedition Act of 1918 was passed in a deliberate attempt to silence domestic critics of the war. This was an Act that for all practical purposes eliminated freedom of expression in the United States during this time frame. Certain offenses were punishable by a heavy fine or imprisonment for twenty years. The following were included:

> ...uttering, printing, writing, or publishing any disloyal, profane,
> scurrilous, or abusive language intended to cause contempt, scorn,
> contumely or disrepute as regards the form of government of the
> United States, or the Constitution, or the flag, or the uniform of the
> Army or Navy, or any language intended to incite resistance to the
> United States or to promote the cause of its enemies; urging any
> curtailment of production or anything necessary to the prosecution
> of the war with intent to hinder its prosecution; advocating,
> teaching, defending, or suggesting the doing of any of these acts;
> and words or acts supporting or favoring the cause of any country
> at war with the United States, or opposing the cause of the United
> States therein.[1]

Under Title XII of the Espionage Act the Post Office was allowed to refuse to deliver mail to any individual or business suspected of being in violation of the Act. It functioned at the optimum level of censorship. Mail would then be returned to the sender stamped "Mail to this address undeliverable under the Espionage Act." Without due process the reputation and the honor of American citizens were destroyed.[2]

Under these three pieces of legislation the United States government was able to shut down all foreign language newspapers and presses. Even the publishing of small foreign language pamphlets was affected. It was expected that any individual wanting to print a foreign language material had to submit to the Post Office a literal translation of all items within the work, especially if it dealt with the war or the govermuent.[3]

As with most Constitutional issues these Acts were challenged in the court system. The Supreme Court upheld those convictions that reached the high court. Anarchists were specifically seen as subversive. The Supreme Court upheld the conviction of five anarchists sentenced for passing out pamphlets opposing the war. During the course of the war hundreds of people were arrested and jailed because they had challenged the loss of their civil liberty.

The famous American socialist Eugene Debs was arrested and charged under the Sedition Act. The Justice Department had agents following Debs around the country listening to his speeches. The indictment occurred because of a speech he made in Canton, Ohio. The charges centered around his public and verbal "utterances."[4]

One of the most notorious cases during this time was *Abrams v. the U.S.* Jacob Abrams was a leftist Jewish immigrant. He was charged under the Sedition Act of throwing Yiddish leaflets out of a factory window into a New York City street. The documents had attacked President Wilson and American intervention in Russia. In this case the issue had nothing to do with the war against Germany. In a highly prejudicial ruling a lower court found him guilty. A wide range of Constitutional guarantees were not allowed Abrams during his trial, yet the Supreme Court in reviewing the case upheld the verdict.[5]

The Red Scare. These same type of Constitutional abuses continued after World War I. Immigrants, mostly from the eastern and southern parts of Europe, were streaming into the United States. This occurred at unparalleled levels. They brought with them not only their own culture but an evolving political ideology as well. At the same time there was also considerable national anxiety over the ever-expanding labor movement. Many saw it as a form of radicalism. Protestant Anglo-American culture felt besieged. The response to these social changes was radical in its own right. From 1919 to 1921 the United States entered a period known as the Red Scare.[6]

Individuals were still being charged under the Sedition Act even though the war was over. An intense social prejudice developed in America. This hysteria did find its way into governmental circles and appeared in various forms of repression. It was even possible for second generation Americans born into families of Eastern European origin to find themselves being deported from the United States. These types of issues strain at the fabric of the American Constitution. They represent a retort that is clearly outside of the spirit of our social contract and the defense of civil liberties noted within the document.

W.W. II Japanese-American detainment. Events such as war seem to place the Constitution in the greatest level of jeopardy. One of the more glaring times that the Constitution was ignored was during World War II. In this case it was not the Legislative branch nor any governmental agency that disregarded the Constitution but rather the Executive branch. President Roosevelt ordered the internment of thousands of Japanese Americans at the beginning of the war.

The Supreme Court would not give any relief. If there is one censure that needs to be applied to the Supreme Court, it is their decisions concerning Japanese-Americans during this military conflict. Their position represented little more than an abandonment of the American Constitution. The reality of that statement can be found in Executive Order 9066.

During World War II the United States government placed Japanese-American citizens in relocation camps. This was done without due process of law and clearly beyond the canons of the Constitution. The event exemplifies more of a point of American prejudice than a national security need. In the end these citizens were stripped of their estates and property. They were held against their will. The eagerness of the Supreme Court to abandon the Constitution can be found in *Hirabayashi v. United States (1943)*, *Yasui v. United States* (1943), and *Korematsu v. United States* (1944).[7] From a lenient point of view, this event must be seen as one of the darkest of days for our republic and the Constitution.

Changing the Constitution through the legislative process. Changing the Constitution should be a very premeditated act. An amendment system is now in place to facilitate such needs, but this has not always been used. Congress at times has changed the Constitution by the legislative process. One example deals with a section in the Fourteenth Amendment. It prevented former Southern rebels from holding political office after the American Civil War. While the Amendment specifically addressed individuals who had held Federal and state governmental offices before the war and hence had violated their oath by becoming active in the Southern cause, it also included a section far more general: "[anyone who] shall have engaged in insurrection or rebellion against the same, or given aid or comfort to the enemies thereof" found themselves also excluded from holding public office. It is fair to say that the majority of the Caucasian population living in the American South during the Civil War supported the goals of the rebellion. This part of the Constitution clearly was designed to punish, and, if taken literally, would have eliminated a large portion of the Southern population from holding political office, both within the Federal and State levels.

The Amnesty Act of 1872. Congress dealt with this by passing the Amnesty Act of 1872, which in reality canceled this clause of the Fourteenth Amendment. No groups or individuals either in the South or North felt strongly enough about this law to challenge the legislation in court. With each passing year the issue became even less notable or even applicable. This is an item that should not have been placed in the document originally. The motivation and intention clearly stand outside the reasons why we have Constitutions; nevertheless, once in place, it is inappropriate for the Legislative branch of government to modify the supreme law of the land by an act of Congress. If that is so, then we have little need for either a Constitution or an amendment process. Few items are more meaningful or dangerous than the idea of having the Constitution changed by legislation. The Constitution is too important a document to allow such indiscretions to exist.

The Treasury ignores the Constitution. Theodore Roosevelt had appointed Leslie Shaw Secretary of the Treasury after the assassination of William McKinley. At the beginning of the 1900s it was common practice for the Treasury to deposit internal revenue receipts into the national bank, but they had to keep custom receipts in the department offices. This represented about forty percent of the total revenues of the country. This was being done because of a provision in the United States Constitution that stated revenues must flow from the Treasury Department. Article I, Section 9, reads, "No money shall be drawn from the Treasury, but in consequence of appropriations made by law; and a regular statement and account of receipts and expenditures of all public money shall be published from time to time." This was interpreted to mean that money flowed into the Treasury from taxes and flowed out of the Treasury by legislative appropriations. In turn some level of accounting was required.

By 1903 Shaw was depositing all revenue receipts into the national bank. Once in the bank these funds were being moved to other financial institutions and subtreasuries. Shaw was receiving criticism for this action; many felt the financial apparatus that was being set up was unconstitutional. They argued that this was money being drawn from the Treasury. Shaw took a different position and created a new policy. He declared that the national bank was a department of the Treasury and that the money was only being transferred. He also reasoned that the national bank's deposits were part of the Treasury as well. This change in the system occurred by departmental and administrative policy.[8]

This issue should not be seen as a major condemnation. There was no effort to defraud. What Shaw did was change the governmental structure on how revenue was handled. At worst it was an administrative change, but the problem was the American Constitution. When the Founders of the nation wrote the Constitution there was no national bank. They clearly wanted a system in which money left the Treasury only by legislative action. Now a third party had access to the nation's financial resources. It represents the same type of Constitutional issues that occurred during the Jacksonian Era.

The Line Item Veto. It is possible to argue that *Pork Barrel* politics represents an internal flaw within our structure of government and correcting the problem is obstructed by the Constitution. Powerful committee chairpersons are able to move forward with pet projects, especially for their own home districts. Back room congressional compromises lead to connecting of frivolous or exclusive amendments to meaningful bills. These are generally narrow or self-seeking pieces of legislation. They benefit only a few and normally these bills would not pass if they stood alone. Such politics has been around almost since the beginning of our republic. Congress has been aware of this governmental defect for a long time and to their credit the Line Item Veto was an attempt to rectify the problem.

The United States Congress and the Executive branch of government have been wrestling with the idea of a *Line Item Veto* for some time. The structure of the United States Constitution allows the Chief Executive to veto a bill. There were those that felt if the President can veto a piece of legislation, why not part of it. In this case the Supreme Court found this type of veto as unconstitutional. The process showed that Congress was aware of the problem, but Constitutionally it was different to correct. Occasionally, ignoring the Constitution is not so much a matter of efficiency, or even crisis-motivation, as it is a test of the Supreme Court.

Chapter 15

The District of Columbia

When the nation's founders wrote the American Constitution, many compromises and disagreements were part of the process. Some delegates refused to attend, others left the convention early, several delegates were political rivals and did not trust each other. Certain delegates refused to sign the document for specific reasons. Most of Hamilton's ideas were rejected early in the convention and he took little part in the process afterwards. This does not mean the environment was combative or confrontational, only that everyone had a point of view. A sizable number of state governmental officials felt the convention in Philadelphia was operating outside of the original commission. Moreover, a handful of people still felt that the Articles of Confederation could be saved. The Constitutional Convention in 1787 was not a place of total harmony. Our Founders were polite, but a Constitutional Convention is not a place for refinement. It was a time and place in which ideas, arguments, and views needed to be heard. After all, the delegates were discussing the very essence of their government and their society. At times it was a place of great passion.

The idea of a national capital. Even if the view of discord is accepted one issue did represent considerable consensus. When the drafters of the Constitution reviewed the ideas of a national capital as a district from which government could function, a high level of conformity was evident. This consensus represented a universal feeling of optimism and pride. A location for a national capital meant the creation of something permanent. For the first time the conflicts of the colonial period, the Revolution, and the disagreements over the Articles of Confederation would be placed behind the nation. A capital represents a point of stability and growth, especially for the Federalists. Their views were far more national in scope; hence a Federal capital represented this idea. For most of the delegates to the convention of 1787 the vision must have been marvelous.

A national district. Early in the Constitutional Convention the delegates agreed that the national government needed to have its own district, not just a capital. They believed that a true separation was needed between the states and the Federal government. The capital if stationed in one of the states proper would create an awkward arrangement. Both New York State and Pennsylvania wanted the new seat of government, but some individuals felt it would represent an unfair political advantage to the state that was awarded the capital. Still others saw the placement of a national capital in their state as a disadvantage. They noted the difficulty of operating the affairs of state within a metropolitan area also being used for commerce. Others felt that a state government might find ways to embarrass a national government operating within their borders.[1] None of these discussions had much sway. The delegates to the Constitutional Convention and to the first Federal Congress remained focused on a district. Article I, Section 8, of the Constitution declared this intent:

> To exercise exclusive legislation in all cases whatsoever, over such District (not exceeding ten miles square) as may by cession of particular states, and the acceptance of Congress, become the seat of the government of the United States, and to exercise like authority over all places purchased by the consent of the legislature of the state in which the same shall be for the erection of forts, magazines, arsenals, dockyards, and other needful buildings.

They recognized that the Federal government may need other facilities, especially those related to defense, but their principal interest was in a national capital.

Location. The first Congress met on March 3rd in 1789 in the Federal Hall in New York. The House of Representatives met downstairs and the Senate upstairs. Within a year Congress had moved to Philadelphia, which became the home of the national government for the next ten years. George Washington had helped pick out the site for the new capital. The location was agreed upon early in the process. The new capital should be built along the Potomac River. While parts of the site were marshy, overall it was a good location. The Potomac was navigable up to this point and would accommodate large ships. Further, it was a central location within the country. Nearby Virginia, also a well-developed state, presented advantages for placing the district nearby. Part of this ten-mile square piece of land was purchased, and both Virginia and Maryland conceded territory. By 1800 the District of Columbia was developed enough for Congress to move to their new home.[2]

The new District. When Congress met in the new district for the first time, it met in a truly undeveloped community. Not all the government buildings had been erected; some were still under construction, while many governmental entities had to share space with other bodies. Housing was a chronic shortage. The first members of Congress had to live in boarding houses and private homes. Yet, one advantage outweighed those of any other location in the country; Congress had the power and authority to legislate all the laws for the District of Columbia. They were a power unto themselves, at least in this one little provincial community.

The district grows. As the nation grew, so did the district. A city emerged and was named after the father of our country. Governmental departments were added and new buildings were constructed to house these agencies. Memorials were built to honor our leaders, our achievements, and the countless thousands of individuals who helped create this nation. People came from different parts of the country seeking services, favors, or employment. The village grew into a town and the town into a city. Today the District of Columbia is a vast metropolitan center with scores of hospital facilities, schools, universities, transportation terminals, shopping malls, and churches. Beyond all of this growth it is still a "company town," and the chief employer is the Federal government.

Attempts at change. Some efforts over the years have been made to change the method and systems of administration of the district. The first notable step was to return the land originally granted to the district by Virginia. This was done by the Federal government in 1846. In 1878 a three-member commission was created to manage the affairs of the city.[3] These three officers were appointed by the President and functioned as overseers to the ever-increasing population.

Another change occurred in 1961 when the Twenty-Third Amendment to the Constitution was passed. This allowed the citizens of the District of Columbia to vote for the President and Vice-President of the United States. This was the first time the people of the District were permitted to participate in national elections. The district was given three electoral votes. In 1967 a new reorganization plan was put into place for the city of Washington. Now with one commissioner and nine city council members, it nevertheless is still controlled by the Federal government. Three years later the House of Representatives gave the district one delegate, though the delegate was not allowed to vote in the assembly. The first true city government for more than a hundred years occurred in 1974.[4] The citizens of Washington were able to vote for a mayor and a thirteen-member city council This new body does have some taxing powers, but it can be vetoed by the Federal government. Congress still has final approval of all city budgets.

Governmental reforms and restrictions. Over the years a wide range of activists and civic-minded individuals have attempted to make the district more democratic and to encourage good government. Reforms generally fell into a number of different categories. One direction was to focus on improving municipal government, others were interested in civil rights, and still others were engaged in encouraging statehood. Though some of the goals of these groups have conflicted, as a rule there was considerable crossover. Inadequate city administrations and resistance from Congress made any progress extremely difficult. By 1995 Washington entered into a new era when Congress created a five-member Financial Control Board to oversee the city's government. Invested with total control over the city's operations, the board can remove any city appointee. A step backward came in the following year when the Control Board eliminated the elected school broad for the district. At this point most of the reform measures are dead. The interests of the citizens of Washington seem to be returning toward more functional needs such as basic city services and security.

The District of Columbia was one of those ideas that did not make the transition from conception to reality very well. Though it was a good idea in the Eighteenth Century, it is a bad idea for the Twenty-First Century. It is not difficult to imagine individuals like Jefferson or Madison viewing the district as a college campus—collections of governmental buildings, parks and open spaces, long walkways, and tree-lined streets where the nation's leaders could meet to, discuss the topics of the day. The future of the country could be contemplated within an

Arcadian setting. Washington has grown into a large urban city, with all the advantages and disadvantages such a metropolitan center would portray.

A dichotomy forms. Not only has the size of Washington, D.C. grown but also the size of the Federal bureaucracy. The sheer number of people needed to run the mass of governmental services and agencies would have astonished the nation's founders. Washington, D.C. has become a strange mix of politically aware, highly educated individuals living within the network of governmental interest or programs on the one hand, while a second group of camp followers are seen as attendants and retinues to the city itself. The one group becomes a part of the Federal complex, feeding off of the customs and services of government, while this second group simply calls the city their home. It is by any measure an eccentric situation that does not speak well of America.

The final word in the administration of the city falls upon Congress. Hence, committees have been set up that help supervise the District. One of the problems is· that the members of Congress who determine how the city is managed or allocate funds to it are not well connected to the municipality. In many cases the Congressperson or Senator may live in the suburbs, beyond the "beltway," and only commute into the capital. In turn, their constituents are in their home districts. The people of Washington, D.C., become subordinate. Voters and their elected officials maintain a direct relationship, for if elected officials do not maintain the interests of their constituents, they will eventually be voted out of office. This same type of association does not exist in the case of Washington. In fact, the voters in the outlying districts are pressuring their Representatives to spend less Federal money, to balance the budget. Since the people of the district have no say in the appropriations for their city and no true vote in Congress, the city suffers.[5]

Disadvantages to the residents. This underfunding of city services can be seen in a wide range of situations. If the city of Washington is compared to other locations of the same size, considerable differences stand out. The police in the city have limited equipment. Welfare or support programs for the residents are modeled after Federal directives. This lack of funding can be seen in every part. of city operation. What makes it so strange is that the citizens of Washington are burdened with some of the highest taxes in the country.[6] The chief disadvantage of the city of Washington is that other urban areas of this size are connected to state governments. The relationship between the large metropolitan areas of the country and the states they exist within are different. They benefit from programs set up to help urban centers. Furthermore the elected bodies and the state representatives are connected to these voters.

The financial problems for the city have been ongoing. One difficulty is that all the revenues generated by local taxes have to be paid into the national treasury. The United States Treasury will then supplement these funds and return them to the district. The problem is that if the city administration or city council passes an ordinance or acts in a way that Congress does not approve, they withhold the funds. This occurred in the 1980s over a number of items, one of which dealt with abortion. Congress did not support the district's policies on abortion and money was withheld.

Jurisdictional disputes. An illustration of how dysfunctional the District of Columbia can be is noted by the number of police officers found within its borders. Sixty different law enforcement agencies have jurisdiction within the district. Some of these police forces are connected to specific departments or agencies, others are related to county or municipal governments, and still others are national. When a crime occurs in the district the question arises about which agencies will show up; jurisdictional disputes are common.[7]

Bad administration may be one problem, since such items can be adjusted and changed internally, but bad government is another. Washington becomes a contradiction to the whole nature of how we see our government. The United States is a *representative democracy*. This system has been fine tuned and adjusted over the years, but it is a fundamental part of how we interact with government. When we elect other individuals to manage the affairs of state, they do so in the name of the people. This is a foundation of American democracy and how we see our government. If we deny one person representation it taints our system of government and our freedoms. In the case of Washington more than 600,000 people in the district lack the same level of representation as everyone else in the country. They have no Senators, and their one Representative has no Constitutional right to exist. This person is allowed to vote in committee but not on the floor. It symbolizes appeasement more than democracy. This one issue exemplifies the very worst our Federal government has to offer. Representation is not an option; it is a requirement of republican government.[8]

It is not even clear that the nation's founders expected the district to exist without representation. Madison wrote in *The Federalist Papers* (43):

> "...the state will no doubt provide in the compact for the rights and the consent of the citizens inhabiting it; as the inhabitants will find sufficient inducements of interest to become willing parties to the cession; as they will have had their voice in the election of the government which is to exercise authority over them."[9]

This statement implies something else. While the states would have no authority in the Federal governmental district, the people living in the area would still be represented by the states.

Statehood. Various efforts have been instituted to make the District of Columbia a state, or at least have representation as a state. In 1978 an amendment was passed by Congress giving Washington both Congressional and Electoral College representation. The state governments showed little interest in allowing the district these levels of equal identity. Sixteen states passed the amendment before it died after seven years. This proposed amendment had read as follows:

> Article I, Section 1. For purposes of representation in the Congress, election of the President and Vice President, and article V of this Constitution, the District constituting the seat of government of the United States shall be treated as though it were a State.

> Section. 2. The exercise of the rights and powers conferred under this article shall be by the people of the District constituting the seat of government, and as shall be provided by the Congress.

Section. 3. The twenty-third article of amendment to the Constitution of the United States is hereby repealed.

Section. 4. This article shall be inoperative, unless it shall have been ratified as an amendment to the Constitution by the legislatures of three-fourths of the several States within seven years from the date of its submission.[10]

One of the complaints leveled at this proposed amendment dealt with what many saw as the creation of a super-state. The issue centered not on representation or even if the District of Columbia should be a state, but how it would be administrated. The rights and privilege of this state would be "by the people." While this may seem forthright and democratic, others noted that such a provision would add rights to the district that other states do not possess. The district would not be subject to the Electoral College nor would the amendment process for the district be the same as other sections of the country.[11]

The statehood issue has mostly been generated by the residents of Washington and was motivated by the most honest of concerns. This political effort was made to correct the inequality in the system. A statehood party was created in the district in 1969 and it proved to be a very active organization. The goal from the very beginning was to pursue actual statehood. Even after Congress had passed the proposed amendment to the Constitution concerning statehood, activists were still attempting to gain support from the district itself. By the early 1980s they had gathered enough signatures on a petition to place the issue before the inhabitants in the district. It passed by a sixty percent margin. In January 1982 a convention was begun to draft a Constitution for the district and to continue to petition the Federal government for statehood. This Constitution was completed near the end of the year and many attacked it for being too radical. It had little support among the city government employees or the core of the Washington city council members; nonetheless, it was marginally passed by the voters.

While progress was being made, a parallel set of events detracted from the effort. The mayor was arrested on illegal drug charges. Momentum was lost and support from Congress dwindled. A set of "shadow" delegates were to be elected to assist with this process, but these elections were repeatedly postponed. By 1990 this process was complete, but by then the original amendment sent to the states was dead. Currently the disposition of statehood for the district rests in Congressional committees, where may be found a number of supporters, but also some powerful detractors. The work that had been done in the 1970s and 1980s on this issue had not proved to be fruitful, and little enthusiasm remains to reinstitute the fight.[12]

Though legislation has been introduced that endorses the idea of returning the district back to Maryland, supporters were unable to work its way through Congress. At one point the governor of Maryland had openly supported the idea, but his position was criticized as some form of domestic hegemony. What this shows is that the Federal government and our elected officials are aware of the inequality of the prevailing system. There simply is neither the direction nor political will to move forward at present.

In the end there is a totality that goes with republican government. One cannot possibly justify democracy for some and reject it for others. The District of Columbia has become an apparition that haunts our society and eats away at our ideals of liberty. We have long since determined that there is no such thing as separate but equal. Duel systems require a blind eye and considerable demagoguery. In this case Washington as a governmental enclave cannot be legitimized; it simply falls short of our own views of representative government. If there was ever a cause that called out, "No taxation without representation," it is the District of Columbia.

Chapter 16

Native Americans

If a Constitution is designed to recognize the manner of republican government, amplify democracy, and maintain human rights, our relationship with Native Americans must be seen as our darkest, most horrid secret. It simply cannot be connected. It is as if the United States exists in two different worlds: one world of Constitutional equalitarianism and another world of half truths, public duality, and opprobrium. It is neither Constitutional nor just, but merely convenient.

Of all the issues that are connected to the United States Constitution the most obfuscated must be the interrelationship with Native Americans. This interrelationship has been an appendage without word or form, an association founded more on dominance than advocacy or mutual support.

Adversaries and opponents. This relationship with the native population within the boundaries of the United States can be broken down into four different stages, the first of which actually could be viewed as the most honest and equal. The two entities were adversaries and opponents for the same territory. While it must be conceded that there were times of peace, even cooperation, the majority of the time before the American Constitution and shortly thereafter must be seen as one of occupation, military conflict, hostility, and even genocide.

Since the nation's founders did not see the American Indians as citizens, ongoing antagonism characterized their interactions as a rule. One of the reasons for the American Revolution revolved around the conduct of, and the association with, the native populations. In 1763 the British monarchy declared the area between the Appalachian Mountains and the Mississippi River as Indian Territory that needed to be reserved for the indigenous population. This never set well with the colonial societies' belief that this region was needed for westward expansion. Many of the colonial charters stretched to the Mississippi, which implied a continuation of their territorial boundary. The British in turn justified their declaration on purely humanitarian grounds, stating they had an equal responsibility to the Native Americans as to the colonial inhabitants. In a royal proclamation King George the Third declared his intent:

"to conciliate the affection of the Indian nations, by every act of strict justice, and by affording them his royal protection from any encroachments on the lands they have reserved to themselves, for their hunting grounds and for their own support and habitation."[1]

The colonials saw this issue completely differently.[2] When the Declaration of Independence was written by Thomas Jefferson, he listed grievances the colonists had against the crown. One of the most noted was the strife between these two warring camps. Jefferson wrote in the Declaration of Independence of "...the merciless Indian savages, whose known rule of warfare is an undistinguished destruction of all ages, sexes, and conditions." This is not a very conciliatory tone, and it also outlines the underlining animosity the colonials had toward the native population.

By the time the nation's founders began to write the United States Constitution, large numbers of pioneers were moving into the regions beyond the Appalachians. The views of the drafters of the Constitution remained hostile. Hamilton wrote in the *Federalist Papers* (24):

"[we have] a constant necessity for keeping small garrisons on our Western frontier. No person can doubt that these will continue to be indispensable, if it should only be against the ravages and depredations of the Indians."[3]

In reviewing the structure of the Federal government, the rights of the people, and those basic concepts of liberty, the Native Americans were considered outside of these discussions. They were not citizens of the United States, but menacing outsiders.

The Founders were aware that they were headed toward a social and political abyss on the status of the native tribes. James Madison in reviewing issues of trade noted the problem of Indian status.

"What description of Indians are to be deemed members of a

State **is** not yet settled, and has been a question of frequent perplexity and contention in the federal councils. And how the trade with Indians, though not members of a State, yet residing within its legislative jurisdiction can be regulated by an external authority, without so far intruding on the internal rights of legislation, is absolutely incomprehensible."[4]

The reality was that the spirit of the American Constitution and the political realities of this situation were not compatible.

Initially the Constitution saw the Native Americans as equals to any other foreign power. The Indian tribes were considered sovereign nations and treaties were negotiated accordingly. A system was established within the Constitution on how treaties would come into existence. The Executive branch was responsible for negotiating such items, generally through their agents, and the treaty would be ratified by the Senate. How fair or just these treaties were is a matter of substantial debate; frequently tactics of bribery, force, and threats were used to move agreements forward. Even when the documents were signed, many Indians did not fully understand the English text. Nonetheless the process and the relationship became a matter of treaty.[5]

Isolation. By the beginnings of the nineteenth century and through the preponderance of that period, a second stage had developed. The outcome of these successive military conflicts with the Indian tribes was no longer in question. Anglo-American culture was spreading across the continent. The native population and their tribal organizations were either destroyed, absorbed, or placed on reservations. Even so the Indians continued to be seen as separate entities. Treaties were negotiated as if they were foreign countries and reservations were created as an extension of the non-Indian prejudice. The goal of the reservation system was simply to remove the native population from the majority of the land and place them in enclaves separate from the general population. It was rather fundamental. Once inside these zones the Indians were free to function independently of the remainder of the society, at least that was the promise.[6] Native Americans stood outside of the Constitution. They had no civil rights and little representation within the greater sphere of the nation-state. Moreover, only the Constitutional process of making treaties applied to the native populations.

The Supreme Court in 1831 attempted to define the relationship between the native tribes and the United States. In *Cherokee Nation v. Georgia,* the Marshall court declared that American Indians were part of a "domestic dependent nation." They were neither a state nor a foreign nation. The reality of this ruling was that Native Americans had no standing in the federal courts. In any case the court's interaction was insignificant; both the states and the federal government basically ignored such decisions concerning the Indians. The realities of the nineteenth century Indian hostilities and wars overshadowed such pronouncements.[7]

Treaties. By 1871, the United States Congress had stopping making treaties with the native tribes. The end to treaty negotiations, and even the appearance of treaty compliance, represents a major shift in governmental attitude, Treaties represent a special point of International Law. In fact part of the development of International Law emerged out of issues related to treaties. International Law, like Legislative Law, is a developing concept. How it was applied, viewed, or adapted has changed over the years, but it existed in the eighteenth century and the nation's founders were aware that treaties superseded the United States Constitution. By the nineteenth and twentieth century the issue of treaties had been so refined that no state could modify or change a treaty and its stipulations except by agreement of both parties. It was understood that this process needed to be open and fairly negotiated. Ideally treaties needed to be secured by peaceful means. In 1880 under *Hauenstein v. Lynham* the court ruled that the "treaty making clause of the Constitution is retroactive as well as prospective." Every treaty made by the United States is above the Constitution and laws of any individual state. If a law of either a state or Federal legislative body is contrary to a treaty that law would be invalid.[8]

Congress was taking a different position, or at least as it related to Native Americans. One of the terms found within International Law is *rebus sic stantibus.* This concept states that if the original provisions of a treaty are no longer valid or if the original circumstance under which the treaty was drafted has substantially changed, then the terms of the treaty can be viewed as no longer binding.[9] This is the general argument that the United States government used to end treaties and treaty obligations with the Native Americans.

Of course none of this was ever challenged at the international level. Under normal conditions this should have been an ongoing process. Generally treaties, like contracts or agreements, experience *conceptual decay*. Sections become less workable over time and some indigenous group would constantly be bargaining with the government. Treaties had reached the point in International Law at which their principles had become well established and they represent a point of equality between the two parties. The main reason that treaty processes and negotiations came to an end with the native tribes was because it simply was not in the best interest of the United States government to continue such proceedings.

Assimilation. By the end of the Eighteenth Century a new stage of American and Indian relationships had emerged. This was a period of unlimited Federal authority. The United States Congress had broad powers to legislate the nature of this relationship toward the tribes and to control internal components within the reservations. The government passed laws concerning tribal lands, property, and social involvement. Congress attempted to control interactions between the native and non-Indian populations, and to define this relationship. During this time the Native Americans truly became wards of the state.

This new stage did symbolize a major shift in governmental policy toward the native populations. Instead of seeing them as non-citizens and sovereign, the goal had become one of assimilation. The cornerstone of this policy can be found in the *General Allotment Act of 1887*.[10] The object was to give each Indian on the reservations a degree of land ownership. A head of the household received 160 acres and each minor received 40 acres. This household allotment was later lowered to 80 acres. Originally this land would remain in trust for twenty-five years, but the Burke Act of 1906 allowed some transfer of Indian lands.

The Allotment Act changed the reservation system and the way non-Indians interacted with the native population. Up until this time the Indian reservation had a specific purpose and was supervised by the Federal government. The reservation was designed to house the indigenous people of the area. Now the Native

Americans could sell their property to non-Indians and transfer title. Many Indians sold their land and left the reservation. Others through fraud, keen negotiations, poorly designed contracts, foreclosure, or tax sales lost their property. In 1887, 138 million acres of land were in the possession of Native Americans; by 1934 acreage declined to 52 million acres. The Indian Reorganization Act of 1934 reversed the process and revitalized the concept of tribalism.[11]

Tribal, federal, state, and local government collide. One of the problems is that remnants of the Allotment Act can still be found on the reservations and within Indian Territory. During the Allotment period a sizable number of non-Indians purchased acreage and now live on the reservations or Federally designated Indian lands. This has created a bizarre set of circumstances where tribal, Federal, state, and local government collide. The Non-Indians vote in state elections, but the Native Americans do not. The Indians of the reservations as a rule distrust state governments, but the non-Indians look toward the states for support. The reservations have established tribal governments that have grown and increased their authority over these territories. Non-Indians own much of this land, but they find themselves subject to ordinances passed by tribal governments. In turn non-Indians are not allowed to participate in these tribal governments. They are based on heredity, culture, and even in some cases theocratic principles. Without being overly critical, tribal governments develop their own form of racial discrimination. Non-Indians cannot run for elected office nor are they part of the tribal electorate. They have no say in the decision-making process. Tribal governments become exclusive. Likewise, these reservation governments have become legitimate political bodies. They are supported within the United States Congress and the Federal court system.

Indian Reorganization Act. A new stage began with the Indian Reorganization Act of 1934.[12] The current relationship with Native Americans is far more complex. It is an elaborate system of property rights, legislated civil liberties, tribal governments, and double standards. Native Americans are able to express themselves and to work within the system toward their own advantage. They interact with government and pursue those benefits for which they are entitled. The native populations are able to use the court systems, lobbying groups, and governmental agencies to promote those issues they see as important. It is by no means a perfect system, but one the Federal and tribal governments seem to accept.[13]

What makes this system so confusing is the number of different associations or groups that have a distinct relationship with the Federal government. In 1988 the Federal government acknowledged 507 *"Indian Entities"* in the United States, each of which has some type of special relationship with the national government. These represent either tribes, reservations, bands, groups, villages, pueblos, or various associations. Of all these different groups, 299 are Indian reservations. Some of these bodies are officially approved Indian organizations established by Federal law; others are traditional Indian organizations recognized without a formal grant by the government, still others are officially approved bodies outside of Federal law but regulated within governmental agencies. Each in some way is entitled to governmental services and special cultural consideration. It is at best awkward and at worst a segregating process.[14]

In the same vein none of the reservations function or operate in the same way. The Navajo are by far the largest reservation with a very integrated tribal system. They currently have about 16 million acres in parts of three states: Arizona, Utah, and New Mexico. The Navajo have a well-established tribal government, internal law enforcement system, and judiciary. They were the first reservation to set up a college and a newspaper. The Navajo have developed a stable economy within the reservation based on lumber, mining, and farming. The Navajo, along with the Apache, Papago, Yavapai, Pima, and the Hopi reservations make up thirty-eight percent of Arizona.

On the other side are reservations such as the Narragansett in Rhode Island, the Wampanoag in Massachusetts, and the Poarch Creek in Alabama. These reservations have a few thousand acres between them, and are well integrated into the local districts. Through intermarriages and close association with the general population the makeup of the tribal units has changed.

Similarly, some reservations maintain individually owned land, tribal land, and Federally owned land all mixed within the same territory. Each reservation differs by the customs found within the tribes and the history that created them.

No two Indian reservations are the same and no two seem to have the same relationship with the Federal government.

Legal landmarks. In each of these stages a collection of Federal laws and Supreme Court rulings mark change in our relationships. Many of these tribal governments have also set up tribal courts. They have grown in importance and authority. A new body of law has developed in the United States called Indian Law. Founded on *tribalism*, it is cross-referenced between Federal treaty obligations, Supreme Court rulings, Indian custom, and tribal law.[15] It has become a set of community laws based squarely within the framework of the reservation system.

The one fundamental difference in Indian law from other categories of law is that the emphasis is on tribal social structure and community. The individual is a secondary concern. Both non-Indians and Native Americans living on these reservations may be subject to the tribal legal process; American Constitutional guarantees, however, do not exist. These are important points. Tribal courts have ever-increasing caseloads and their significance to the reservation system cannot be overstated. Yet, there is no appellate process, nor do issues of due process or equal protection under the law apply. These courts are set up to support tribal interests.

The complexity of this situation becomes even more profound when an effort is made to connect reservations and tribal governments to the Constitution. One of the purposes of the United States Constitution is to recognize the nature of Federal governmental sovereignty, especially within the framework of the nation-state. As well, state governments have established sovereignty within the Constitution. If tribal governments are seen within the scope of eighteenth century treaties, they do have sovereignty, but confusion arises about the attributes of this sovereignty within twentieth-century law. At the very least there has been a retrogression in the relationship between the Native Americans and the Federal government. The whole issue of Indian sovereignty has been violated. In fact it has been violated to the point that it no longer even has the characteristic of a standard form of sovereignty. Yet, in defense of American Indians, this transgression of their sovereignty has been done unilaterally and without their consent.

This overlapping of governmental accountability is what makes this system so obtuse. While Federal law and policy prevail on the Indian reservations, conflict between state and tribal governments are common. Issues related to tenure of land, timber harvesting, mineral rights, tax exemptions, contract law, health care, education, licensures, police powers, zoning laws, self-determination, and hunting and fishing rights continue to surface. Even within the Federal government and its agencies problems of autonomy have been ongoing. Items related to tax laws, civil rights laws, environmental law, public works programs, and agencies with the power to regulate have been points of friction. An example can be made of the tax codes. As a rule, state authority and taxes are not allowed on Indian reservations, but state taxes on tobacco and liquor have been permitted by the courts. Similarly, "hidden taxes" on an item that is passed between a wholesaler and a retail merchant is not. While Indians living on the reservation do not have to pay state taxes, an employee of the Federal government living on a reservation does. Concurrently, many reservations have begun to develop their own tax systems. They have started to tax a multitude of services and activities found within their territory.

Taxes within the Indian communities. This issue of taxes has become an enigma within Indian community structure. It is a source of considerable disharmony on both sides of the reservation lines. In 1958 the Federal courts ruled in *Barto v. Oglala* that the Sioux tribes were able to develop a separate tax system. This decision has not only confirmed the taxing power of tribal governments, but also has adjusted the system of taxation in a discriminatory fashion: a different set of regulations and tax codes apply to Native Americans than to non-Indians.

The current system and the relationships among the native population of the United States living on reservations is difficult to justify, at least within the level of our contemporary Constitutional development. None of the concepts found within the American Constitution seem to work very well when they are applied to the original inhabitants of North America. The system becomes an odd mixture of good will, historical guilt, seclusion, maltreatment, and cultural bias. This problem is even more confounding when it is recognized that individuals on both sides of this dilemma are invested in the status quo. Many Native Americans, instead of resisting the dual on the other hand are trapped by the "original sin." Any effort to address the issue of reservations or the special relationship with Native Americans, forces the national government to face four hundred years of cultural destruction.

The conundrum of Native Americans and U.S. citizenship. All these issues could in some way be Constitutionally justified except for one problem: American Indians are United States citizens.[16] Although in 1924 they were officially granted the same rights and privileges as all other Americans, now a dual system has been created. The states have no jurisdiction over the reservations.[17] Native Americans maintain their United States citizenship while on the reservation, but they have no direct state citizenship. The problem becomes similar to the one found in the District of Columbia. As citizens they have no representation. There are no Senators or members of the House of Representatives to oversee the welfare of the reservations. The Federal government accepts that responsibility, while the states in some cases are actually adversaries of these special arrangements. Not only is the concept of representative government not applied to Native Americans living on reservations, in some cases they are surrounded by unfriendly state governments. State governments are major components of our Constitutional processes and when they are removed, the level of representative government for the individual is reduced.[18]

Equal but separate? This returns us to the same idea of *equal but separate*. Through most of the first half of the twentieth century, the concept of equal but separate was promoted by those seeking segregation of the races. The Supreme Court ruled that concept a fallacy.[19] It is impossible to devise a system equal in every way that creates simultaneously a division between two groups of people. It simply is impossible to erect a system that is perfectly equal, but disconnected. The problem becomes even more compounded when non-Indians who own property on the reservations are included in this discussion. They too begin to suffer under this dual structure and standard. The same dilemma of equal but separate applies to them. They become cultural outcasts within their own communities. At the moment that Native Americans became citizens, whatever justification had been found for the reservation system became invalid. Furthermore, it became a corrupting element and a blight on every part of American democracy.

If some effort is made to place the issue of "ethnic purity" or heredity into this controversy, it begins to collapse under its own weight. The reality is that large numbers of non-Indians have Native American blood in them and likewise large numbers of Indians are from mixed ancestry as well. What is "Native American" becomes a matter of personal perception. A person's cultural background should not be a point of consideration for special living arrangements or programs.

The dual system. It is far easier to note that the dual system found on Indian reservations is unjust and beyond the spirit of the United States Constitution than to find workable solutions. This is an extremely complex problem with social and political repercussions moving beyond even the Constitution. The questions that are being asked have no easy answers. In fact the questions become almost limitless. Is a philosophy of conquest being followed? If it does exist, is this a doctrine the United States wishes to embrace? Is it allowable to have United States citizenship without a state citizenship? Is it possible to disavow your state citizenship and still live within its borders? Can the Federal government create enclaves where equal protection under the law does not exist? Can community governments be established within local metropolitan centers that set up additional taxing systems? How does ancestry relate to citizenship? The list, of course, could be endless. The most important of these questions may actually deal with policy. What is the policy of the United States government toward Native Americans? Equally, what is the position of Native Americans toward the majority of the population?

We come down to two general policy areas, one of assimilation and the other of isolation. If the goal is to assimilate the native population so that it operates within the mainstream of American society, then the reservation system has a paralyzing effect. If the goal is isolation then the reservation system has become badly polluted.[20] Resistance to any type of adjustment in the reservation system will not simply be a political question, but more importantly a cultural one. This contention will manifest itself on both sides of the reservation boundary marker.[21] While historically, reservations represented the worst possible land with the most insignificant of resources, they did serve one advantage—they allowed Native Americans to maintain a resemblance of their cultural heritage. This is not to be discounted. Defining who we are as individuals is as important as any issue in our society. Culture is more important than governmental ideology, but once saying this, it must be understood that the real responsibility of maintaining a culture is the people. Culture represents a collection of beliefs, rites, understandings, attitudes, and behaviors. It adjusts how we see ourselves, how we learn, how we view our community, how we relate to art, and how we associate with others. Culture becomes the total essential quality of our being. This is not a place for government. No government is omnipotent enough to sustain a culture. It is something that comes from the heart. The responsibility of maintaining a culture will always rest with the individual and the community.

In this process we must clearly understand that we are beyond fault. Enough shame and dishonor abounds with these issues to stretch into eternity. A Constitutional process of government implies that there is a singularity of action. That each person within the country is united by the document and that there is an equality of design.

While allowing for our diversity, we must reach an agreement that we are one people. The goal is not to destroy an individual society, but to find ways to improve our democracy. The only saving grace is that it does not have to happen immediately. A system can be set up so that it becomes a process with distinct goals and signposts to mark the journey. In the past the Native population had no say in the process. They were dictated to from without. If democracy is to endure every voice must be heard.

Chapter 17

The Vice-Presidency: Is It Needed?

The Vice-President for Woodrow Wilson, Thomas R. Marshall, was one of the more colorful characters of his time. He worked his way up through state politics and finally to the Vice-Presidency. Marshall seems to have been one of these individuals at the right place at the right time, and most of his success in the political arena dealt with timing. Nonetheless he served Wilson for eight years as his Vice-President and did as well at this job as most. Once he was asked about the position of Vice-Presidency and Marshall's comment was, "The only job of the Vice-President is to knock on the door of the White House and inquire as to the health of the President."

Constitutional jobs of the Vice-President. Of course that is not totally true. The Constitution gives the Vice-President a few tasks. The Vice-President is President of the Senate. The office has no power to introduce legislation, but the Vice-President can vote when there is a tie on the Senate floor. The United States Senate does have its own leadership, and all the political parties have leaders, leaving the Vice-President no real management role in the Senate. As a rule the Vice-President is seen as an extension of the views of the President; thus, during those rare opportunities when there is a chance to vote on a piece of legislation, the Vice-President will follow the lead of the Chief Executive. Generally that would be done after some level of consultation. The primary job of the Vice-President is to succeed the President if the President is ill, disabled, or dies.

Even the responsibility of breaking a tie in the Senate is futile. The miles of the Senate are such that all tie votes are recorded as nonpassage of the measure. If the Vice-President opposes the bill and votes accordingly; or if he or she were not in the chamber and did not vote at all, the outcome would be the same. Only when the Vice-President breaks a tie by voting in the affirmative does the issue matter. What makes the issue even more complex is that the Vice-President's office is in the White House, not the Capitol Building. If a tie vote occurs it is unlikely that the

Vice-President would even be in the Senate. Hence, only with important pieces of legislation and a reasonable expectation of a tie vote would the Vice-President be present. In two hundred years of American history only 223 times has a tied vote been a factor in the Senate. In only a handful of these cases did the Vice-President's vote actually become meaningful.[1]

The Vice-Presidency and the nation's founders. How the nation's founders saw the position of Vice-President is not totally clear. Thomas Jefferson was the second Vice-President and he referred to it as an "innocuous post." Surely that is a true statement. The position is at best harmless; however, a number of other considerations seem to be at work. The first is simply how organizations and governmental bodies are structured. The drafters of the Constitution were aware of how state governments were organized. Most had been active in state legislatures. Since the states had a governor and a lieutenant governor, the idea of a President and a Vice-President seemed logical. Most civic organizations or groups would establish a President and Vice-President as a formula for the hierarchy of their associations. This is as true today as it was in the past. It is a process of little more than the assigning of responsibility. The creation of the position of Vice-President could be seen as a continuation of existing patterns of the time.

Another possible view is that the post of Vice-President was designed as a "consolation prize." It was a gift for those who ran for the Presidency but did not obtain the position. The original idea was to set up a Constitutional system and structure of government that did not need political parties, or at least that was the goal. Those who sought the office of chief executive would run independently. Under Article II, Section 1, of the American Constitution each elector would cast two votes, but it was never proposed that one vote would be for the President and one for the Vice-President. The person with the most votes became President of the United States and the person with the second most ended up being the Vice-President, consequently the idea of the "consolation prize." It did not work out that way; the election in 1800 between Thomas Jefferson, Aaron Burr, John Adams, and Alexander Hamilton froze the process. The election ended up in Congress where the process was deadlocked. Weeks passed before Congress could agree on a President. The Twelfth Amendment to the Constitution changed the system on how the electors voted, eliminating the original design flaw, but it also reduced the necessity of a Vice-President. After the Twelfth Amendment the position became even more obscure, not that the job has ever been indispensable.

When Hamilton attempted to make a case for the position of Vice-President, he argued that if succession to the Presidency came out of the Senate, as a point of reference, then those individuals in the Senate who were interested or predisposed to the Executive office would politically shelter the ideas of the President. This would be done in such a way as to curry favor from the Executive branch. The problem of course is that this type of political maneuvering occurs regardless of a Vice-Presidency. Hamilton also felt the "Vice-President may occasionally become a substitute for the President." This does happen from time to time. There are state functions, dinners, funerals, and presentations that the Vice-President will attend in the name of the President, though these types of activities have also been done by members of the President's family as well as members of the Cabinet.

By no means were the drafters of the Constitution uniform in their support for the office of Vice-President. George Mason felt that placing the Vice-President in the Senate encroached on their rights and privileges as a legislative body. The issue can become confusing when it is remembered that the Vice-President is a member of the Executive branch, but the chief responsibility of the office is in the Legislative branch. The delegates generally agreed that if the Presidency of the Senate were taken from the Vice-President, there would be no job at all for this office. James Madison in his *Notes of Debates in the Federal Convention* recorded the views of Hugh Williamson. He simply said that "such an office as Vice-President was not wanted."[2]

Terms with no Vice-President. A number of Presidents have operated without Vice-Presidents. This generally occurred when a President died in office or in one case resigned, John Tyler spent almost a complete term without a Vice-President. William Harrison had died only a month into his term and Tyler finished it. Tyler was the first Vice-President to succeed to the office. At the time it created a minor Constitutional crisis. The question that was raised was whether he was a President or a Vice-President, with the title of Acting President. Today this does not sound like much of a concern, but in 1841 it had become an issue. The core of the question was whether Tyler would be able to pursue an independent agenda or if he were merely a regent. When John Tyler took the oath of office for the President, he began to work toward his own governmental policies. He set the precedent. Millard Filmore, Andrew Johnson, and Chester Arthur had no Vice-Presidents. Presidents such as Theodore Roosevelt, Calvin Coolidge, Harry Truman, Lyndon Johnson, Richard Nixon, and Gerald Ford spent part of their time in office without a Vice-President.[3]

In the original document the Constitution made no provision for replacing a Vice-President. While some believed it would be appropriate for the new President to appoint someone, others believed the nation needed to wait until the next election to have a Vice-President. This issue was never resolved until the Twenty-Fifth Amendment was approved in 1967. It created a rather complex system of determining succession. The problem of course has never been death. Without sounding too impertinent, we see that death of a President as a rather clear indicator that it is time for the Vice-President to step forward. The problem comes when the president is ill or disabled. Twice during our history Presidents have been so incapacitated that they were unable to perform even the most basic of tasks. James Garfield, who was shot by an assassin, lingered for eighty days before dying of his wounds. Also, Woodrow Wilson had a stroke in the latter part of his Presidency. He continued in office for sixteen months. It is generally believed that his wife assumed the administrative duties for the last part of his term in office.

The Twenty-Fifth Amendment develops a system by which the President determines if he or she is able to continue the duties of office. If the chief executive is too ill or disabled, a declaration is put into writing, and the Vice-President undertakes the job of President. What makes this Amendment awkward is the process by which the President resumes the duties of office. Again the intent must be put into writing, stating that the President is fit, The Vice-President, who is now the President, and the Cabinet must agree. If they disagree the issue is turned over to the Senate where they decide by a two-thirds vote. It is sincerely hoped that this element of the Constitution never has to be implemented. It will be a dark day for the republic. We can easily imagine a scenario galvanized by claims and counterclaims, of medical reports, political conspiracies, and public disgust. It would be the ultimate of media events.

The Twenty-Fifth Amendment. The closest that the United States ever had to allowing a Vice-president to function as a President is with Dwight Eisenhower. He had a heart attack while in office and for a period of time Richard Nixon took over many of his duties. At one point there was even concern that Eisenhower would not be able to return to the business at hand. but he recovered and resumed the activities of the office. One of the reasons for the Twenty-Fifth Amendment dealt with the experiences of the Executive Office during the Eisenhower adniinistration.[4]

The Twenty-Fifth Amendment also changed another item in the Constitution. It allowed for a new Vice-President to be appointed. In this situation the new President appoints an individual to fill the vacancy. The nominee would be confirmed by a majority in both Houses of Congress, and would become the Vice-President. This is as workable as any system, but it is not exceedingly democratic. While this process may be as democratic as appointments of Federal judges, members of the Supreme Court, officials of regulatory agencies, or even the replacement of Senators or Representatives who leave office, it still remains that the people have no say.

The problem is that this situation can produce a chief executive who has never been elected by the people. Even recognizing the buffer that is created by the Electoral College, the people are not involved in this process at any level. This is what occurred with Gerald Ford. Vice-President Spiro Agnew was forced to resign his office in 1973. Agnew pleaded no contest to charges of tax evasion and receipt of illegal money from Baltimore building contractors. Gerald Ford was then appointed to the position by Richard Nixon. He was then confirmed by the rules set out in the Twenty-Fifth Amendment to the Constitution. When Nixon later was forced to resign because of the Watergate scandal in 1974, Ford became President of the United States.

A double standard. Of all the issues that face a society and a free government this type of predicament may be minor, but it alludes to a dual system or standard. It creates undemocratic opportunities. In science is a belief that the more complexity or the more exceptions found within a theory or natural law, the greater the likelihood that theory is incorrect. This may also be true for Constitutional government. When systems are created that are highly complex with multiple levels of contingency it become counterproductive for democracy. There exists a greater opportunity for mischief.

The role of the Vice-President has changed over the years. Recent Presidents have made an effort to include the Vice-President in more of the governmental processes. This occurred with Richard Nixon and Dwight Eisenhower. Nixon was allowed to sit in on Cabinet meetings, discussions with Presidential advisers, and he even chaired a number of governmental commissions. Contemporary Vice-Presidents have been more visible- they are involved in policy meetings, travel, and assist with the political management of the Executive office. This was not always the case. In the past many Vice-Presidents simply went home. They spent the better part of their time in office not even in Washington, but in their home states.

Selection of the Vice-President. The difficulty is that regardless how skilled an administrator a Vice-President may be, this is not the reason the person was chosen as a running mate. In fact this is one of the least important considerations. When a Vice-President is chosen by a Presidential candidate the election is still in question. All issues become political by nature. Vice-Presidents are picked because they represent some level of balance. If one candidate is too conservative, they select a running mate from the liberal wing of the party. If one candidate is from the East, they choose someone from the West. Vice-Presidents are chosen because they know the right people or because they are not offensive to anyone. They are selected because they are good campaigners or are excellent with a phrase or point of wit. They are picked because they are attractive, are from a particular specific age group, served in a war, have been loyal to the party, or have religious denomination, are in a specific age group, served in a war, have been loyal to the party, or have membership in certain organizations. Management skills have little to do with why Vice-Presidents are chosen. It is the most political of occupations in a world of political professions.

The office of Vice-President is only remotely connected to the people. The individual who has won the party's nomination picks her or his running mate.

This has not always been the case but in modern times this is the method by which the position is advanced. Persons chosen to be the candidate for President by the party have worked for that distinction. They have moved about the country, campaigned on the issues, raised money, interacted with the people at some level, and in the end won enough delegates to the party convention to get elected. The Vice-Presidents on the other hand have not committed themselves to this same examination. They are a product of the system, rather than a contestant.

Once in office the Vice-Presidency becomes an elected office. The President cannot remove a Vice-President. The Senate has no power to discharge this person as President of their assembly as well. The office is held to the same standard as the President of the United States and can only be impeached for "High Crimes and Misdemeanors." Even so, this is hardly a concern. Vice-Presidents either operate at the discretion of the chief executive or they do nothing. There is simply not a great deal of substance to the job.

Perks of the office. The actual price tag to this job is not clear. The Vice-President can utilize the financial resources of many different agencies and branches of government, taking advantage of the budgets found in each of these departments. Because of this the total expenditure for the office can be ambiguous. The Vice-President receives an annual salary $115,000 of dollars a year. The position comes with an official residence, the value of which is not listed in budgetary considerations, but its operating expenses are listed in the Federal budget. The estimate for 1996 was $287,000, in 1997 it was $324,000, and the proposed operating expenses for the Vice-President's mansion for 1998 is $334,000 dollars. The Vice-President has a staff and the use of various motor vehicles. This has been budgeted at $3,280,000 a year. This office has printing privileges and travel expenses that are not directly related to the Vice-President's own budget. Items such as materials, supplies, communication equipment, security, retirement benefits, and health care also cost the taxpayer. When equipment for the Vice-President is upgraded, these items may appear in other departmental budgets. Many of these costs are ongoing. Even when a Vice-President is out of office, special services and benefits are allotted them. While the numbers are at best an estimate, it is believed that the office of the Vice-President costs the United States government, and ultimately the people, about twenty-five million dollars a year.[5]

Is the position of Vice-President valid? At some point the question about the validity of the Vice-Presidential position needs to be asked. Within the framework of representative government are two types of positions, the first of which is elected. It is argued that these elected officials are responsible to the people. Their actions are reviewed, monitored, and subject to modification by the will of the masses. The second group is appointed. This group in theory serves at the pleasure of those who have appointed them.

Even the Federal judges, which do not fit into either of these categories very well, still can face some level of recall. The position of Vice-President on the other hand is elected but exists without a constituency. The Vice-President serves through the good will of the President but cannot be removed by the chief executive. The person holding this office cannot move forward on his or her own agenda, yet when they do speak it is viewed as an extension of the Executive branch, which may or may not be true. They are part of the administration but the Vice-President is also independent of that branch. In truth the Vice-President is not responsible to the President of the United States, the Congress, or the Federal court system, and only in the most liberal of senses are they responsible to the people. Most modern Vice-Presidents are generally eager to do additional jobs within the administration. They are political creatures and many are seeking still higher offices. They wish to remain visible; however, if they just went home and refused all interactions with the government, this would not be contrary to the job nor would they be subject to official charges of insubordination. Their own function within the government is to succeed the President or break a tie in the Senate. Additional levels of productivity are not within their job description or within the Constitution. Even if an effort were made to impeach the Vice-President for inactivity this would hardly be seen as outside of their job description. Regardless of the criteria used the position of the Vice-Presidency is basically contrived. Some Vice-Presidents have remained active and productive. They have served the Executive branch and the American people, but each job that was given the Vice-President could have been done by some one else without a loss in efficiency, and probably at much less cost. The true test of any position within a system of administration is whether it is "good government." The problem is that the concept of a Vice-Presidency does not withstand the ultimate test; it is simply not "good government."

Chapter 18

Sections Not Being Followed

A number of items in the American Constitution are simply no longer being followed. While a few of these are minor and several are even a matter of interpretation, clearly these articles have long since reached the point at which they need to be redefined within the document.

Extradition. One example is Article IV, Section 2, which reads as follows:

> A person charged in any state with treason, felony, or other crime, who shall flee from justice, and be found in another state, shall, on demand of the executive authority of the state from which he fled, be delivered up, to be removed to the state having jurisdiction of the crime.

Most of this is rather explicit. The issue deals with *extradition*. This is a common practice within the criminal justice system. If a person has committed a crime in one state and flees to another, it is customary and proper for that individual to be returned to the original state to face these charges. The nature of the law needs to supersede the boundaries of the state. The problem here is the word "shall." Ruling that the word "shall" does not apply, the courts have inserted the word "may." While nothing is fundamentally wrong with "may," it allows some discretion on the part of judges, attorney generals, and even governors to review concepts related to *probable cause*, reasonable grounds for assuming a charge to be well founded. The reality is that, depending on the circumstances, some states will refuse to give up a fugitive. This in itself is not a concern. The problem is that there is a big difference between *may* and *shall*. The word *shall* does not give any room to maneuver. The expectation is that the individual accused of a crime will be delivered up, and this will be done without question. In the case of *may* it becomes discretionary or optional.

The first case that the Supreme Court heard on extradition was *Kentucky v. Dennison.* In this situation the governor of Ohio had refused to give up a fugitive. While the court ruled that the state governor did have a duty to deliver up the accused, it also noted that the court had no power to force compliance. This created a situation in which subsequent governors have refused to give up fugitives for various reasons, including this idea of *may* as opposed to *shall.*[1]

While it may seem odd to argue over the words *shall* and *may,* two discrete concepts are represented by these different assertions. While *shall* is more definite; becoming a pledge to act or requirement, may is far more general and becomes little more than a request. As simple as this clause of the Constitution may be, it strikes at the common theme—the document needs to be updated, and this provision needs to be written properly.

Privateering and letters of marque. Article 1, Section 8, in the Constitution gives Congress the powers both to declare war and to grant *letters of marque.* This is a rather specialized term referring to the use of *Privateers.* One of the common practices of the European monarchs during times of war was to issue letters of marque. If a private citizen owned a large sailing ship and it was properly armed, the monarchy could authorize the citizen to sail against the enemies of the nation. These Privateers would be entitled to prize money and some of the spoils of war.[2] The difference between being a Privateer and a Pirate is slim. The one is *freelance* and the other is operating with the consent of a government. It recalls a time when Henry Morgan sailed from Jamaica toward the Spanish Main a century earlier, but these practices were still active during the last half of the eighteenth century. During the American Revolution the Continental Congress and the individual states issued 1,700 letters of marque.[3] When the nation's founders wrote the Constitution, they made provisions for this element of eighteenth century warfare.

International Law and letters of marquis. The problem is that International Law moved beyond the use of letters of marque. The Declaration of Paris in 1856 outlawed the use of Privateers. This Declaration proved to be one of the legal canons of International Law, especially Maritime Law. While the United States never signed the protocol, it has nevertheless, become a part of American foreign policy. Thus while issuing letters of marque still may be Constitutional for the United States, to do so is now against International Law.[4]

The larger issue is whether the United States government may declare to the nations of the world that Privateering is wrong, thus aligning the military might of our nation against such activities, while within our own Constitution the deed would be legal. This discrepancy sends mixed messages to the world community: while we support International Law and the rule of law between nations, conflicting concepts remain in the Constitution. Our highest law of the land continues to endorse acts forbidden by these international understandings.

Racial discrimination. Another item within the Fourteenth Amendment to the United States Constitution requires some review as well, an item that has never been used. The Fourteenth Amendment of the American Constitution is one of the most powerful portions of the document. Many students of the Constitution refer to the amendment as a second American Revolution. Along with the two other Reconstructionist Amendments, the Thirteenth and Fifteenth, the Fourteenth did profoundly affect our society. Section Two of the Amendment reads as follows:

> Representatives shall be apportioned among the several states according to their respective numbers, counting the whole number of persons in each state, excluding Indians not taxed. But when the right to vote at any election for the choice of electors for President and Vice-President of the United States, Representatives in Congress, the executive and judicial officers of a state, or the members of the legislature thereof, is denied to any of the male inhabitants of such state, being twenty-one years of age, and citizens of the United States, or in any way abridged, except for participation in rebellion, or other crime, the basis of representation therein shall be reduced in the proportion which the number of such male citizens shall bear to the whole of male citizens twenty-one years of age in such state.

Due process. The Fourteenth Amendment to the Constitution granted citizenship to the black slaves and established a *due process* clause for the states as well as the Federal government, but this second section has a different meaning. Not only was this Amendment conceding that blacks would be allowed to vote, but if they were not allowed, there would be a punishment. Many legal scholars argue that this section of the Constitution was superseded by the Fifteenth Amendment, which clearly granted the recently freed slaves the franchise. The difference between these two amendments is that the Fourteenth has *teeth*. If the vote was not extended to the black populations by the individual states, action could be taken.[5]

Of course the great tragedy is that this Section of the Constitution was not used. The United States spent another hundred years attempting to reconcile the direction of the Fourteenth Amendment and the transgressions of racial discrimination. Not only was this Article not followed, its power was eroded, and the promise that was given to a portion of our population was not kept.[6]

As with many items within the Constitution we now have moved beyond this point. Though the need to follow this section is no longer sufficient, we can only speculate about how such an item would have been placed into operation or how such an item would have been applied. If half of the black population of a state were denied the right the vote, what would be penalized? Would an equal number of white votes not be counted? What would occur if Native Americans attempted to vote? What happens if persons were not going to vote anyway? What segment of the state's voting population would be used, or would it be fair to eliminate all Republican votes or focus only on Democratic votes? Who would determine the number of votes that needed to be discounted? A list of problems related to implementing this section of the Constitution would be almost endless. The only regret is that it was not tried at least once. It may have made a difference at some other alternate level of our society, especially to counter those forces invested in *Jim Crow*.

Right of trial by jury. A problem arises as well with the Seventh Amendment to the Constitution, which states as follows:

> In suits at common law where the value in controversy shall
> exceed twenty dollars, that right of trial by jury shall be

preserved, and no fact tried by a jury shall be otherwise reexamined in any court of the United States than according to the rules of the common law.

The difficulty, of course, is the twenty dollars. This Amendment declares that if a suit is brought against another in a common law court and the value of the item in question is more than twenty dollars, a party may demand a trial by jury. This section of the Constitution may have been workable or even practical in the 1790s, but time has corrupted this Amendment. For the average individual on the American frontier at the end of the eighteenth century, twenty dollars was a considerable sum. Most families would have been lucky to see a hundred dollars a year. The United States Mint did not even produce a twenty-dollar gold piece until 1849, and that year they only made one. Time and inflation have deteriorated the value of our money. Again, this was not some nefarious plan on the part of government or the power elites. It simply happened.

To bring suit in the United States Federal court a declared value of $75,000 must be established, and this has nothing to do with a jury trial; it is a matter of just bringing the suit to the court. What has occurred is that this Amendment is being ignored. To operate under these provisions, or to change them, became impractical. If a new Amendment was drafted to correct this article it would be irrational to put forth another sum of money. Seventy-five thousand dollars in the future may seem as equally silly as twenty dollars does now. If the Amendment were simply eliminated it may be seen as politically inappropriate. After all the Seventh Amendment to the United States Constitution is part of the Bill of Rights. To step forward and declare that a part of the Bill of Rights needs to be eliminated may not be a politically sound move.

Can we decide not to follow the Constitution? What occurs is part of the Seventh Amendment to the Constitution is disregarded. The states can justify inaction on this section of the Constitution because originally it was not directed at them but only applied to the Federal courts. Likewise, the Federal courts will not take up the issue. They recognize that if such an item was followed the mechanics of their job would become unmanageable. Most legal theorists will simply discard this section of the *Bill of Rights* as being too confining. In the end it is written off as being unimportant. The problem is that while a jury trial for twenty dollars is frivolous, this gives rise to a bigger concern. Is the Constitution a document that can be ignored? If a precedent is established that sections of the Constitution do not have to be followed, what actions in the future will precipitate other articles to be ignored? The Constitution will always need some level both of interpretation and maybe even exclusion. The one is a matter of point of view while the other is far more caustic.

Chapter 19

Sections No Longer Needed in the Constitution

A few clauses in the United States Constitution contain valid concepts once important to the well being of the nation yet no longer have significance within its framework. Over the years these Articles have simply become supplementary, beyond what is required or sufficient. While at one point in our history they may have been intensely meaningful, nevertheless because of either court rulings or expansion of other Articles or Amendments, they have become nonessential.

The contract clause. One example is the contract clause in Article I, Section 10, where the Constitution forbids the states, not the Federal government, from "[passing] any ...law impairing the obligation of contracts." While this Article has little present-day significance, it played a major part in our Constitutional history and the overall development of American society. When the nation's founders had placed this item in the Constitution, it is universally believed that the provision dealt with private contracts or contracts between individuals.[1] Those who designed the document wanted to make sure that the states did not have the power to absolve debtors of their contracted financial obligations. Likewise, the Constitution gives Congress the power to determine the jurisdiction and define the scope of the nation's bankruptcy laws. The drafters of the Constitution had lived through the convulsions of the Revolutionary period. During the war, contracts were written, promises were made, and agreements were signed, but by the end of the conflict not all of these bargains were being kept. Typically the states were leading the way in either *nullifying* contractual agreements or refusing to support such contracts in the courts, especially if they were made with individuals from another part of the country.[2]

The concept was a valid one. The genuineness of contracts must be maintained if the nation is to grow and prosper. Since Federal government in fact had the responsibility of regulating commerce, it seems proper to allow the national government the equal responsibility of deciding the nature of contracts.[3]

What occurred was that this whole idea took a different turn. The Marshall Court interpreted the contract clause to also include state grants. The position that Marshall had taken on the issue was that state grants become implied contracts, and, once given, a grant becomes an enforceable contract.

State grants as contracts. This process of seeing the state grants as contracts started with the landmark case of *Fletcher v. Peck* (1810).[4] Through a fraudulent grant, the Georgia legislature had given land speculators the better part of what is now Alabama and Mississippi. By the time the Supreme Court had heard the case the public lands had been resold, but an effort was still under way to recover part of the loss incurred in the deal. Some of the Georgia lawmakers had been bribed; however, the court, while conceding the process had been fraudulent, refused to take any action to declare the grant was a contract and one that needed to be honored.[5]

The Marshall Court expanded the contract clause even further in the case of *Dartmouth College v. Woodward* (1819).[6] In this situation the private college of Dartmouth in New Hampshire had become a public institution. Originally the college had a royal charter setting up how the trustees were to be chosen and how they were to function. The state legislature changed the name of the college, how trustees were selected, and their numbers. It provided a state-appointed board of governors with veto power to oversee the trustees. The Supreme Court declared that the original charter represented a contract and the state had overstepped its authority.

The Marshall Court used the contract clause to move the court in an irremediable direction with *New Jersey v. Wilson* (1812),[7] and *Sturges v. Crowninshield* (1819)[8] as well. Under these rulings contracts were seen as outside of the legislative process and could even affect taxing powers of the states. Building upon these early rulings, a full forty percent of all the cases heard by the Supreme Court during the first hundred years of the Constitution dealt with the contract clause. In seventy-five cases state laws were held to be unconstitutional by this standard. The contract clause was the reason that half of all state legislation during this period was declared unconstitutional. Yet, only ten percent of these cases dealt with private contracts. Most of these decisions returned to the Marshall interpretations. A casual reading of the Constitution may miss its importance, but the contract clause must be seen as one of the major elements of the document at least through the first half of its history.

The real problem with the contract clause has not been how the court or the Constitution reacts to this section between two private citizens or firms, but how the state as an institution deals with contracts. Government is set apart from other social activities. It exists at a different level and for different reasons. The ideas related to contracts and those of government are not a perfect match. All governments have an assortment of responsibilities to the public. They include maintenance of the society, overall stability, the general welfare, good government, health and safety of the community, fair play, and justice. These are very general terms, but they cannot be negotiated away. They run to the very heart of why we have governments. These issues fall outside the framework of contracts.

As it is with many topics within the United States Constitution, the Supreme Court began to change their view of the contract clause. Subsequent high courts started to recognize that government had a public responsibility outside the contract clause, and the rulings of the court changed accordingly. One of the turning points came with *Fertilizing Co. v. Hyde Park* (1878)[9] The Supreme Court ruled that regardless of the nature of a contract, the state still cannot bargain away its police powers. It is too fundamental a part of the nature of government. This was especially true in this situation where no such provision was even noted in the contract; conflict had developed about the original contract to operate a fertilizing company within the city limits and a later ordinance that prohibited the movement of malodorous material through the streets.

The death blow to the all-powerful contract clause came with *Home Building and Loan Association v. Blaisdell* (1934).[10] Many Great Depression era banks and loan companies foreclosed on mortgages. Mortgages must be viewed as one of the purest forms of a private contract with the core concept being the repayment of debt. Minnesota had passed a law allowing for a two-year moratorium on foreclosures. The Supreme Court upheld the Minnesota law noting that it was only temporary and the conditions under which it was passed represented a national emergency. This position allows for considerable latitude.

Contracts now become subjective and connected to the public good.

Since 1934 a number of contract clause cases have reached the high court, but the significance and consequence of these cases have lessened. The court is now using a three-prong assertion in reviewing such litigation. The first point is whether a contractual right had been harmed. Second, if it is agreed there was a harm. was there a legitimate public reason that the contract needed to be regulated? Last, was the modification to the contract directly related to these concerns and justified accordingly? The burden of proof falls upon the complainant who must now show there was no abundant reason for the legislation. It becomes a very demanding test. The issue is that the state has a responsibility to the public good and a protective power associated with this responsibility. It is fairly easy to make this type of connection with almost any form of legislation.[11]

While the Federal Courts will surely continue to hear contract clause cases as a separate Constitutional issue, the court has little real, authoritative power. The contract clause becomes little more than a simple category of law. Listing of such a subject in the Constitution has no more significance than inscribing that the court is also responsible for classifications of statutes dealing with Criminal Law, Estate Law, Corporate Law, Environmental Law, Civil Law, Labor Law, Family Law, Maritime Law, Public Law, Commercial Law, Administrative Law, Case Law, or Copyright Law. Contract Law has become but one more division and hardly worth special notation. What makes it most redundant is the issue of due process. As this concept has developed in the judicial system and as a point of political philosophy, the need to have Contract Law singled out has diminished.

The Eleventh Amendment: who sues whom? Another part of the United States Constitution that is similar to the contract clause is the Eleventh Amendment. At one time the concept and the reasons for this Amendment were important, but within the framework of modern Constitutional law it has become meaningless or, more correctly, impotent. The first item attached to the Constitution after the Bill of Rights, it is easy to see this Amendment as a political design rather than a Constitutional issue from the vantage point of two hundred years. Of all the Articles within the document it is also the most reactionary. Congress had been angered by a citizen of South Carolina who sued the state of

Georgia in the Federal court system. Though the reasons for the original suit in *Chisholm v. Georgia* were minor, for Congress it was anything but minor.[12] Though outwardly the issue may seem purely jurisdictional, it became a political issue founded on *states' rights*. While Congress had the power to limit jurisdiction of the Court, the nation's founders determined that a stronger method had to be used to address this concern. By 1794 the Eleventh Amendment to the Constitution was passed and incorporated into the document. It reads as follows:

> The Judicial power of the United States shall not be construed to extend to any suit in law or equity, commenced or prosecuted against one of the United States by citizens of another state, or by citizens or subjects of any foreign state.

The goal of the Amendment was to stop the Federal courts from hearing cases directly affecting state performance or actions. The central issue dealt with maintaining states' sovereignty. They resisted encroachment by what they viewed as an unduly powerful Federal government and judiciary. Since the Eleventh Amendment passed, the states cannot be sued by a citizen of another state or foreign nation without permission of the state in question and only then in their own courts. Without critiquing the concept of whether or not a state would ever allow a suit, the goal was to limit the ability of complainants to sue the states. The Supreme Court has expanded the concept of the Eleventh Amendment to include a state's own citizens as well. This was done even though nothing within the language of the Amendment would exclude such proceedings.[13]

The problem is that even with these restrictions issues may be brought to bear in many ways without directly suing the states. The Eleventh Amendment has had no effect on criminal cases. These cases are seen not as prosecution, or even trials, but as "reviews." The Supreme Court is well within their jurisdiction to review cases already commenced. This Amendment also has no effect upon one state suing another state; it is acceptable within the framework of the Amendment. A state, however, may bring suit against a citizen. If this should happen the case could be heard by the Federal courts upon appeal. The prospect exists of bringing an injunction against a state governmental official and declaring that the official is operating unconstitutionally. In this situation administration of a policy or piece of legislation is being challenged and not the state proper. In *class action suits* large groups of people will use the Federal courts to address a social issue, which may in part be the result of state actions.[14]

If inmates file suit in the Federal courts to call attention to overcrowding in state prisons, the state is actually being sued by the prisoners, though it is not labeled as such. Inmates would be able to bring forth a *class action suit* or injunction against the state's department of prisons asking the Federal courts to review the situation. The inmates would argue that they are not receiving equal protection under the law or that their condition represents *cruel and unusual punishment*. It would become a Constitutional issue. Although the state is actually responsible for the conditions under which the convicts are being housed, the state administrator or department will be sued. This is the type of manipulating or dodging of the Eleventh Amendment that takes place.

Rights of foreigners. The Eleventh Amendment to the Constitution also restricts foreign citizens who wish to sue the states. Regardless of the aliens' status, however, they still maintain their Constitutional rights as long as they are on American soil. A foreign citizen may access the Federal court system and can use it in the same way as a United States citizen. Foreign citizens have the added advantage of using international courts and tribunals as well. As the world has changed, these bodies have increased in practice and authority. They are influential judicial bodies that affect both national and state governments. The Eleventh Amendment to the Constitution would be meaningless in such international forums.[15]

The Eleventh Amendment may be still in force and it may be a conclusive part of the Constitution. Attorneys may even have to consider this section of the Constitution when they write up their motions, but in practice it is little more than a "speed bump" in Constitutional Law. Every action or piece of legislation created by the state governments can in fact be channeled into the Federal courts. Some method can be found to circumnavigate the Eleventh Amendment.

Treason. The drafters of the United States Constitution spent a fair amount of time reviewing the concept of treason. In spite of the fact that a complete section of the Constitution is taken up by this one issue, the issue seems overstated. Certainly a few individuals have committed treason against our nation. Clearly Benedict Arnold was a traitor to his country and history can show other examples. The problem is that treason is a nebulous concept; it implies a betrayal of trust. To know if persons are treasonous requires looking into their hearts, or more correctly, engaging in mind reading.

Treason generally is subsumed under some other crime. In the case of Benedict Arnold, not only did he betray his oath, but he attempted to turn over the fort at West Point to the British for money and position. The argument being made here is that the crime alone would be sufficient grounds to prosecute the person. The other point is whether treason is a Constitutional or criminal issue. If it is a trespass against the law, is it the place of the Constitution to list criminal offenses and punishments?

Treason can also confuse the issue. John Brown was convicted of treason, but the real criminal act was seizing a Federal Armory at Harper's Ferry. The act of trying John Brown for treason simply made him a martyr. Regardless of the nature of his cause, taking firearms from a Federal Armory is stealing. When someone kills his neighbors because they hold a different political view—that is still murder. The list of criminal charges against John Brown would have been extensive. The charge of treason allows the accused greater credibility than they may deserve. It implies a political motive that may or may not be true.[17]

The issue of treason in the United States Constitution has the appearance of being sensational or dramatic. It is as if the drafters of the Constitution wanted to make sure that everyone takes the document seriously. When the Constitution was written, few purely American traditions had been established. Hence the ideas of treason were still connected to the British concept.[18] For the British government and the monarchy, treason was an extremely desolate act. The punishment required that the convicted person be disemboweled and while still alive have the intestines burned. Their head would then be cut off and the body quartered. For those citizens who came up from the colonial period, this vision of treason must have still been active. The Americans were aware of the penalty bestowed upon the Irish when they were accused of treason by the British. The nation's founders were seditionist, revolutionaries, and rebels who fought against the established order. They slept with treason. While the issue may not have been discussed at every turn. they must have been keenly aware of the nature of their own acts and the reality that now they had to govern a nation of treasonous citizens.[19]

If the Federal government has the power to prosecute an individual for the crime of treason, it is evident that it has authority, power, and control. If individuals attack the United States with the goal of overthrowing the government, the full weight and resources of the nation-state will come to bear against them. The point is that governments and the nation-state will be able to defend themselves, with or without having an Article in the Constitution outlining treason.

Restrictions on the military. The Founders also had an ongoing concern, or even fear, of a standing army.[20] These were issues founded on the colonial experience with the British in North America through the last part of the eighteenth century. The drafters of the United States Constitution wanted to place restrictions on the military and chief executive's ability to direct the armed forces of the country. This was done in a number of ways, but mostly through the idea of placing responsibility for the army into the hands of both the Executive and Legislative branches of government. One of their ideas was to develop a rule that military appropriations could not be passed for longer than two years. In this way Congress would have control of the "purse strings." If the President or the military itself were operating improperly, the Legislature could withdraw support by not passing the funds needed to maintain the army. This was listed as one of the powers of Congress in Article I, Section 8.

Alexander Hamilton noted the position of the drafters of the Constitution in *The Federalist Papers* (26):

> "The legislature of the United States will be obliged by the
> provision, once at least in every two years, to deliberate upon the
> propriety of keeping a military force on foot; to come to a new
> resolution on the point; and to declare their sense of the matter by

a formal vote in the face of their constituents."[21]

The world has changed considerably from the time that the nation's founders wrote this section of the Constitution.

It is possible to believe that they saw the role of the military differently than what has transpired two hundred years later. They felt there would be times when no standing army would be needed, and when there was a need, the process of bringing up troops would be very deliberate. The armed forces would meet the needs of a particular event or serve the crisis at hand and then again fall into desuetude. The needs of a modern society dictate a different course of action.

The United States Armed Forces represent an established institution. It is ongoing and continuous. Military planners look far into the future to analyze types of conflicts and expected engagements. Equipment, tactics, training, organization, and maintenance are forecast beyond the environment of the day. The United States military even during peacetime represents two million service personnel, not counting civilians attached to the armed forces in various ways. The image of military operations that the Founders envisioned has long since passed into history. The budgetary process that Congress uses to sustain the military has little connection to the idea of two-year appropriations.[22]

While each year the nation's armed forces have a firmly incorporated budget and the cost of maintaining the military is funded accordingly, many other programs or projects run beyond the two-year appropriation structure. Congress may order many new weapon projects that stretch out for years, meaning that the money for such programs may need to be budgeted for a sizable span of time. Even if Congress is passing appropriation measures each year for such weapon systems, the original contract with the supplier would have recognized the time needed to develop and produce the hardware in question. This same type of situation can occur in ongoing military research programs. The idea of two-year appropriations for the military becomes unworkable.[23]

Two-year military assessments is one of those topics in the Constitution that no longer matches at the end of the twentieth century. The problem is not the views of the nation's founders, nor is it a point of fault with our current legislators. It deals with the reality of our modern society. The Constitution's stipulated two-year review to assess further need for a military has no relevance to the way these funds are appropriated. This is true whether the idea is judged politically, militarily, or even economically; it becomes an appendage to the Constitution that is either politely worked around or softly ignored.

Chapter 20

Sections That Are Confusing or Contradictory

A few Articles within the United States Constitution are outright confusing or contradictory. A prime example of this category can be found in Article 11, Section 4, the section that outlines under what conditions the President can be impeached:

> [the President] shall be removed from office on impeachment for, and conviction of, treason, bribery, or other high crimes and misdemeanors.

While it is easy to place a definition on treason and bribery, the problem has always been high crimes and misdemeanors. "High crimes and misdemeanors" is actually a term that appeared out of English Law. It is used sporadically in some British texts relating to governmental law and pertains to responsibilities of high-ranking governmental officials. The terms covered such malfeasances as corruption, neglect of duty, abuse of power, misappropriation of funds, or transgressions on the legislative process. For the designers of the American Constitution this catch phrase doubtless made sense.[1]

What is an impeachable offense? The difficulty is that each one of the above concepts such as corruption, embezzlement, neglect of duty, abuse of power, or infringement on legislative authority is a matter of considerable interpretation as well. One person's corruption may be another person's code of conduct. Equally, one person's abuse of power may be another person's proficiency. While these definitions may be easier to determine in the secular world, in the political arena of government they may prove more daunting.

Misdemeanors. This issue can be even more confusing when an explication of *misdemeanor* is attempted. The English would have defined the term as meaning little more than a common crime or misdeed.[2] A difference has developed between how the British and Americans see the word, but in both cases it is viewed as a minor offense. In American legal circles the definition is far more exact. It deals with a category of crimes of less significance than a felony, generally punishable by a fine or jail time of less than a year. The loose classification of misdemeanor would be more acceptable if the document making the description was not the Constitution. The Constitution is considered the highest law of the land and one could argue that such a document should not be vague in its usage of legal terms.

Actually the nation's founders may have been unconcerned about the reasons for removing a President from office. Little was said on the topic by the individuals present at the Constitutional Convention in 1787. Their focus was on the larger issue of impeachment, or whether a President could be forcibly removed from office at all. The reasons are of secondary concern. The terminology "high crimes and misdemeanors" is so nebulous that any issue could be subject to impeachment. After all, it is Congress that is able to define the term and to move forward with the impeachment process. When Gerald Ford served in Congress he made the statement, "An impeachable offense is whatever a majority of the House of Representatives considers it to be." This is as true a declaration as can be made on the topic.[3]

Impeachment is an inconclusive process, little more than an accusation. The House of Representatives issues an indictment and the Senate tries the President. Yet, all that is being determined is whether the chief executive is to be removed from office. If found guilty the impeached President would be disqualified from holding public office in the future, but no direct punishment is connected to the impeachment. The person is simply expelled from the Presidency. The courts may or may not take up the issue. While the criminal justice system would be allowed to prosecute a President who has been impeached, there is no guarantee that the legal system would pursue such an item.

Impeachment of Andrew Johnson. When Andrew Johnson was impeached by the House and tried in the Senate, the issue had little to do with crime but rather with policy. A Tennessee resident, Johnson had little enthusiasm for the Reconstruction policies of the Congress after the American Civil War. Considerable conflict developed between Johnson and the Legislative branch during this time. Congress used the pretense that discharging a member of his Cabinet was outside the powers of the Presidency. In this case the reasons were of small importance. The United States Congress had a specific agenda and wished to move forward with these ideas.The President was seen as an obstacle to these policies, and because of it an (unsuccessful) effort was made to remove him. [4]

Breech of public trust. The nation's founders were attempting to note that there were situations in which a public official would need to be removed from office. The idea concerned a breech of public trust, but the exact conditions and circumstances were never detailed. While clearly the issue is not "high crimes and misdemeanors," and people may even concede that point, such crimes have nothing to do with the real meaning of Article II, Section 4. Still, the Article is confusing. The American Constitution would be better served and far more accurate if it said, "Congress may impeach the President for whatever reason they wish." Attempting to outline standards that do not apply presents a masquerade. Any Article in the Constitution that creates confusion or in some cases bewilderment can shelter vindictive minds.

Speedy trial by jury. Confusing ideas are also to be found within the Sixth Amendment. Outwardly this is an important Amendment. The rights are valid to any democratic society, but they are also becoming disheveled in their application. The Sixth Amendment declares,

> ...in all criminal prosecutions the accused shall enjoy the right to a speedy and public trial, by an impartial jury of the state and district wherein the crime shall have been committed...

The key element within this Amendment is a speedy trial. This is hardly a measurable term. What is speed to one person is possibly lethargy to another. A deliberate and expeditious legal process from the court's perspective may not be for the masses or for the accused.[5] The issue is simply embarrassing in its practice. It is not an uncommon situation for an individual to wait two years for trial. The Supreme Court has even ruled in one case that a difference of five years between the indictment and the actual trial was not a breach of the Sixth Amendment.[6]

The United States Congress attempted to address this problem by passing the Speedy Trial Act of 1974. An effort to place some time limits on prosecutions and trials, the law nevertheless has not proved to be very effective. The law states that within thirty days of an arrest or summons, charges need to be filed. If no grand jury has met in the district during this session an extension can be obtained. An arraignment must occur within ten days of filing of the charges, and at that time a guilty or not guilty plea would be entered. A trial is then to take place within sixty days of the arraignment. In the case of a mistrial or a new trial such an event should happen within sixty days as well. In a situation where a new trial has been ordered, upon appeal an extension can be given up to 180 days, especially if locating all the witnesses is difficult. Exceptions are noted. If a number of pretrial hearings or mental competency examinations are called for, the actual trial could be postponed. Even with such delays the goal of the Speedy Trial Act was to ensure that such prosecutions occur within 180 days.

A provision in the Act of 1974 also required that reports be given to Congress about the changes and influence of this piece of legislation on the court system. Many concerns were raised when the original Act was passed by Congress. A collection of voices were heard, fearful that justice would be impaired by such an Act. An effort was to be made to follow the legislation and see whether the Speedy Trial Act was accomplishing its stated purpose. What occurred was the Speedy Trial Act Amendment of 1979. The new piece of legislation extended some of the times and allowed for a wider range of reasons why a trial could be delayed, including delays in different forms of examination, delays resulting from trials with other defendants, delays resulting from interlocutory appeals, delays on hearing a pretrial motion, delays caused by transferring a case, delays caused when the accused is transported to another district or from a hospital, delays that may occur when plea agreements are being considered, or delays resulting from obtaining an attorney. Within the 1979 Act was a catch-all clause that changed the entire spirit of what Congress was attempting to do with the original Speedy Trial Act. Such a trial could be ignored in such circumstances as these (ii):

Whether the case is so unusual or so complex, due to the number of defendants, the nature of the prosecution, or the existence of novel questions of fact or law, that it is unreasonable to expect adequate preparation for pretrial proceedings or for the trial itself within the time limits established by the section. (18 USC 3161 Amended)

What this allows is for the judicial system to determine the nature of such delays. If the time set out in the Speedy Trial Act are not being met, the courts can return to this section for relief.

In both of these Acts a fundamental problem surfaces. If Congress thought the court system was not abiding by this law, their only recourse would be to bring a legal petition to court and file suit. The courts would be expected to hear a case about the courts. There is something about such a process that is very incompatible and contradictory. It is like asking a collection of businesspeople to rule on a case about the presumption of selling. No other option is offered; it is the courts that maintain the law. In America all grievances end up in the courts eventually, but in this case the courts would not be the best medium to review the issue of compliance with the law.

Courts and the legal system have an assortment of complaints about the process and concepts of a "speedy trial." The courts counter by noting the size of their workload, the number of cases processed, the complexity of criminal litigation, the number of different parties involved, and how elaborate the law has become. Each case involves not only a time, but a cost as well. All of this has to be balanced within a system that is adversarial in nature and working against itself. In some cases the defense attorney wants a speedy trial. In other cases the defense is actually working for delays and finding obstacles to slow the process. This can also be said about the prosecuting attorney, depending on the situation. The mandates of the Sixth Amendment are of marginal concern in these cases. The goals of both sides in these proceedings may run counter to the idea of a speedy trial.

The penalty for noncompliance. Another dilemma the court faces over the issue of a speedy trial is the penalty for noncompliance. For the defense there is no penalty. They can delay the process at every step, at every opportunity, and there is no disadvantage for them. They can function with impunity. The least that could happen is that the judge orders the trial to proceed, in which case the defense attorney has lost nothing. On the other side, the prosecuting attorney faces only one serious repercussion: the possibility that the charges could be dismissed.[7] This possibility is unlikely. Outrage from the public over the release of an alleged criminal could hive a negative effect that could vibrate throughout the legal system. Justice is far better served by having the trial, regardless of the length of time needed to prepare the case.

The guarantee of a speedy trial could be a point of contention for the judge as well. Many judges face elections, and even if they do not, anger from the public can appear in other forms, the most serious of which would be an overall disrespect for the judicial process. The penalty for noncompliance of this article in the Constitution is far greater than the strict adherence to it. For the officers of the court the idea of a speedy trial is on the peripheral of their concerns.

In all fairness the states do a far better job of maintaining the concepts of a speedy trial than the Federal Court System. In the state courts a person can file a motion to secure a speedy trial. While exceptions do occur, the states are more apt to move forward with a speedy trial, and this concept is also a common element found with state Constitutions.

The Sixth Amendment: public trial. Connected to the Six Amendment is the idea of a *public trial*. Throughout most of American history this received little analysis. Courthouses around the country were constructed so that a gallery was included in the courtroom and a percentage of the population could witness the proceedings. The process was basic in its design and well within the spirit of the Constitution. What has changed this issue is the capacity of the broadcast media to enter the courtroom and transmit the proceedings around the world. At what point does a public trial become a media event? A balance needs to be maintained between allowing the people access to the workings of the court, so that the concepts of a *star chamber* do not appear, and assuring that the accused receives a fair trial. It is safe to say that in criminal prosecutions the people are interested in two basic outcomes. They want security in their community and they want results. They want a fair trial, not one decided on a technicality. If there is a trial, fairly argued, complete in its procedures, and found in favor of the defendant, that also represents a result.[8]

In the United Kingdom they have come to a different conclusion on dealing with this idea of a public trial. The media is allowed to report and follow a story up to the point at which an indictment is obtained. After that juncture the news media may continue to follow the process, but they are not allowed to print or broadcast the story. After a verdict is reached the media can then publish stories about the crime and the proceedings. This gap in reporting is created to ensure that a fair trial is given to the defendant. While this type of process may run counter to the traditions of American society, the concern that is being addressed is an appropriate one. The reality is that the media itself changes the administration of the court proceedings. The key is to have a public trial so that government does not use the court system as a form of repression and, equally, to allow the courts to function in such a way that they are not influenced by the emotions of the day.

Defining a public trial. The problem may be that a public trial and one observed by the public are two different matters. What may be needed is a better definition of public trial, especially within the Constitution. As the process stands no two court systems take the same position on the openness of a trial. Some limit the number of people in the gallery, others broadcast the proceedings across the air waves, while others will televise but restrict what the cameras can show. Still others develop a lottery system to limit the number that can sit in the gallery, especially in high profile cases.

Further, at what point does the process create instant celebrities? While that may not be a concern for the judges or the attorneys, the question may be a far deeper concern for the witnesses and the jurors. At what point does the requirements of a public trial begin to diminish the purpose of the proceedings and the rights of the accused become lost in the process? These are not easy questions and the answers may not be found within these pages, but one point needs to be made. What made sense for the nation's founders, even something as valid as a public trial, may require adjustment after two hundred years of usage, especially after such items are connected to the capacity of our technology.

Where will a trial be? The last item in the Sixth Amendment that has also undergone changes over the last two centuries is the location of the trial in the "...district wherein the crime shall have been committed." The drafters of the Bill of Rights saw these districts as established by law, with defined boundaries and a judge assigned to that district. They felt it was in the best interest of both the accused and the people to hold the trial in the location where the alleged crime took place. A connection would be made between the event and the serving of justice. What we have learned from the judicial process over the years is that sometimes a *change of venue is* needed. The emotions in a community may be running so high that it will be impossible to find an impartial jury. Similarly, the jurors live in the community; an unpopular decision on their part may find themselves ostracized from their own family and friends. The goal of any prosecution is to have objective witnesses; this also can be difficult to obtain if community emotions are running high. A change of venue is a valid concept. The courts need this added tool to ensure that a fair trial occurs, but the Constitution does not seem to be open to that concept. The spirit of the document is for a trial to be held in the district from which the crime was committed.

The problem is that a change of venue had no precedent in the eighteenth century. While judges may have excused themselves if they felt they might be prejudiced in a case, the idea of moving a trial to another district, or another state, would have been unheard of and outside the ideas of accepted justice. In fact the argument would have run counter to the concepts of changing a venue. The people had a right to see that justice was done and the laws were carried out. The point is that conditions and circumstances have been modified. Every time a judge grants a change of venue, as logical as that decision may be, it conflicts with the nature and intent of the United States Constitution.

Punishment. The greatest test of all the perplexities of the American Constitution is the idea of *cruel and unusual punishment.* It is the one item in the document that pleads for a consistent definition In all fairness efforts have been made to define the concept. The current view of the courts is that it represents "unnecessary or wanton infliction of pain" or an item that is "grossly disproportional to the severity of the crime." While recognizing that the above statements are an impartial explanation of "cruel and unusual punishment," they are also limited and subjected to an abundant amount of interpretation.

Origin of cruel and unusual punishment. The origin of the idea of "cruel and unusual punishment" can be found both in the Magna Carta of 1215 and the English Bill of Rights of 1688. With the English Bill of Rights an honest effort was made to curtail what was viewed as barbaric punishments. Cruel punishments included a wide range of issues such as beheading, burning, whipping, disemboweling, quartering, branding, or the slitting of nostrils. They also were interested in eliminating the use of stocks, dunking stools, thumbscrews, and the rack. There were even those who believed that parading an individual through the streets to their execution represented a "cruel and unusual punishment." The Founders were aware of the British efforts to limit the types of punishment and to set the penalty to a crime. Up until the English Bill of Rights, punishment was commonly determined by the victim or the victim's family. More times than not it represented the purest form of vengeance. The effort was to move the issue of punishment beyond the concept of retaliation toward an officially authorized set of rules.

Through the better part of American history the Eighth Amendment played only a minor role in Constitutional deliberation by the courts. From time to time an issue would be raised, but it represented a small percent of the overall caseload of the Supreme Court. This was equally true with the state courts. All of the State Constitutions had a similar provision in their body of laws. Toward the last half of the twentieth century that all changed. The social philosophy of the nation began to shift. What was seen as acceptable punishment or behavior on the part of the legal authorities in the past was now being challenged in the courts as *cruel and unusual*. This clause was also becoming connected to two basic issues: capital punishment and prison conditions.

At present it is impossible to discuss cruel and unusual punishment without also having a dialogue about the death penalty. Typically in an appeal process on the death penalty cases, a motion is presented declaring the Eighth Amendment has been violated. It has become a standard within the criminal justice system. The reason that it is used with such frequency is that at times the courts are responsive. Enough precedents have been set to continue to encourage defense lawyers. In the same context, attorneys on both sides of the aisle feel strongly that cruel and unusual punishment indeed does apply to capital punishment cases. Many of these are passionate enough to challenge the issue at every opportunity.[9]

The Penal System. Second is the penal system and the conditions under which prisoners are housed. Some facilities are badly in need of repair, overcrowded, poorly staffed, and filthy. A substandard diet or archaic conditions are found within some penitentiaries. The argument is that such situations represent cruel and unusual punishment. The court system has never been overly supportive, but the Federal court system has stepped into the controversy in some cases, especially in prison overcrowding.

Cruel punishment, unusual punishment. The High Court has taken a very narrow interpretation of cruel and unusual punishment. How restricted this view can be is seen in *Ingraham v. Wright* (1977). The position of the Supreme Court was that cruel and unusual punishment only dealt with individuals convicted of a crime and subsequently incarcerated. When an effort was made to expand the issue to mental health patients in *Youngberg v. Romero* (1982) or to a person waiting for a trial such as *Bell v. Wolfish* (1979) the Court declared the issue did not apply.[10]

The chief problem remains, what represents cruel and unusual punishment? This is still a matter of considerable interpretation. While the Supreme Court may be the last word, each person who reads the Constitution may develop a different perception. It is the type of clause that breeds confusion, and as much as any issue in the document it becomes an abstraction.

Part of the dilemma may be that two distinct ideas are being expressed in one phase and they are not very well connected. Without sounding overly simplistic, one issue is what represents cruel punishment and the other is what represents *unusual* punishment. There is no reason why these two concepts should be tied together; they symbolize two entirely different elements. What is actually being said with cruel punishment is that as a people we should not torture those who are being held. A definition of what exemplifies physical torture can be readily obtained.

Likewise, unusual punishment falls into a different category. The theory has been that criminal punishments need to be codified and legislated; this way the penalty fits the crime. There is nothing intrinsically evil about "unusual." In fact, an argument could be made in favor of allowing courts greater flexibility in determining the appropriate punishment. This may be especially true with adolescents and such versatility could be advantageous.

Regardless, *cruel and unusual punishment* does delineate into a point of interpretation, and again, the view of one person may not be any more valid than another.

Chapter 21

Is the American Constitution Discriminatory?

Quite a number of sections in the American Constitution contradict who we are now as a people and what we have become as a nation. Some individuals would argue that these items are minor or have been addressed in accompanying Amendments. To some degree this argument may be true. The problem is that preceding acts of discrimination and prejudice reverberate from the past; they echo throughout the document as hateful reminders of what we were. The American Constitution becomes an antithesis. Instead of the document outlining our rights, the responsibilities of governments, or what we see as important, it ties us to the past in the most painful way. It becomes a blemish. It forces us to drag around baggage that has no place in modern society and issues that we have long since resolved.

Three-fifths of a white man. One such item is the issue that a black person counts as three-fifths of a white person or stated another way "what is the value of a black man?" Of course the American Constitution does not say that explicitly. What it says is this:

> ... the whole number of free persons, including those bound to
> service for a term of years, and excluding Indians not taxed, three
> fifths of all other persons.

The nation's founders were addressing the issue of representation according to population figures in the House of Representatives, and they were clever enough not to use the word slavery. During the Constitutional Convention the Southern states wanted the black slaves counted as part of their overall population, but without rights or privilege in the Constitution. Many of the Northern states felt the blacks should either be freed or not counted at all. The compromise was three-fifths. The Founders when discussing the topic would not use the word slavery, the terminology of the day was "legally held," The Thirteenth, Fourteenth, and

Fifteenth Amendments of the Constitution later changed the concept and eliminated slavery from the document, but the traces remain.

The visible marks of this idea continue, especially when a person considers that the core of the Thirteenth, Fourteenth, and Fifteenth Amendments to the Constitution were ignored for the better part of a hundred years.[1] Those with evil intent, motivated by discrimination and personal bias use the Constitution as proof to confirm their own bigotry. A black man is three-fifths of a white man. No matter how it is explained away or minimized it hangs on the Constitution like a shroud.

We all have a personal legacy. We have stories about our family, of our own individual heritage, who we are as persons. We are all connected to the past. At some point many of us search for links between the past and the future. We study our genealogy and attempt to find those who have preceded us. It becomes an opportunity to hear our own personal narrative. A Constitution represents a part of who we are, not only as a collective group or as a nation, but also individually. The American Constitution is not simply a piece of paper; it helps define our separate identities as well.

A metaphor can be developed about a ten-year-old black child who begins the process of finding out about himself. He has heard from a classmate that a black person is only three-fifths of a white person and that the statement is part of the Constitution. At some point this black child takes the document to his parents and a discussion occurs about its meaning. Even if it is honestly explained that this is not who we are as a people, that the concept was used differently and represented a different time, the wrong message can be conveyed. A seed is planted. If the nation's founders were great human beings, knowledgeable, and honorable in their actions, and they have declared that a black man is three-fifths of a white person, is it possible it could be true? Self-doubt, distrust, suspicion, antipathy become the norm. It creates a division where none should be.

As a nation we need to remember the barbarity of slavery and to understand our own history, but certain items need to be placed squarely in the past— ingredients of the Constitution that have no part in our modern society. The American Constitution is forcing us to drag around items that are false; it binds us to events in which we had no say and were not involved. It taints our democracy and forces us to defend meaningless parts of the document. If there is one thing that a Constitution should do, it should unite a people, not separate them.

The need for gender inclusive language. This same problem can be seen in the Constitution's description of the Presidency. Article II of the American Constitution discusses the role of the Executive branch of government. Most of the Article is straightforward and at least sets the parameters of the office. In its description only the masculine pronoun is used: "He shall hold his office..." or "The President shall, at stated times, receive for his services..." While it is most noticeable with the Presidency, throughout the document whenever a specific office is listed, the sentence structure and grammar depicts the male gender. There is a reason for this, and without sounding flippant, it is because that is what they meant. The nation's founders would have thought it ridiculous for a woman to hold a political office, let alone the Presidency. They lived in a time when women could not vote, had no property rights, and in every sense of the word were extensions of their husbands.[2]

In our current society we see such concepts as archaic. Women are entitled to the same rights and privileges as their male counterparts. If a woman wishes to run for the highest office in the land she has a legitimate right to do so; such issues go without saying. Within the political process equality of resolution exists. It is believed, and at least hoped, that women and men would be subjected to the same standards and essential qualifications. Woman are equal and the political rights are the same. As a people we are in conflict with the spirit of our own Constitution.[3]

This same argument can be used with a ten-year old female as it would for the black child. By either interest or a class assignment she has been reading the American Constitution. During this process she notes that all the pronouns are male. She approaches her mother and asks her the simple question, "Can a woman become President?" Her mother spends a half hour outlining the changes in our society and explaining that the document no longer means what it says. The mother will note that regardless of the views of our Founders we have evolved to a different social plane. She will do a good job, and she will have convinced this ten-year old that the perspective has changed—until she talks to the ten-year old boys in her class. They have read the same document and spotted the same inequality.

What is viewed as teasing, play, and banter is far more profound. It is the beginning of a process of gender hierarchy. The actions of these ten-year old boys may be founded on human behavior, culture, or some form of sexual identity, but it cuts away at the confidence of the female who must endure the tormenting. While conceding that sexual bantering has existed since the dawn of humanity, there is no place for it within the political environment. Each person, no matter what gender, needs to believe that no avenue of governmental involvement or service is closed to them. The Constitution should not be used as an instrument of social superiority.[4]

Age Discrimination. This internal bias and discrimination in the Constitution can also be seen in the limits placed on individuals running for political office. Arbitrary set ages have been established at which a person can become a Representative, Senator, or President. In the case of the American Constitution the President must be thirty-five years old, a Senator thirty, and a member of the House of Representatives twenty-five. While the discrimination laws in America are far more focused on the elderly, a prejudice against a person because of their youth is just as intolerable. The point being that age discrimination, regardless of the order in which it is arranged, is wrong.

While many individuals may question the life experiences and skills of a twenty-year old running for President, in the end it is the responsibility of the electorate to make the decision on a candidate's qualifications. There are issues that are important to a Constitution, that represent the fundamental principles of the nation, but a Constitution should not attempt to limit human potential.

Full participation by naturalized citizens. An equal concern arises concerning the Presidency. The United States Constitution states that only an American-born citizen can become chief executive. While few Americans may think about this issue, the question is whether it is discriminatory. United States law and policy states that it is wrong to differentiate one group of people from another. It is wrong to discriminate against persons because of the their national origin. This Article of the Constitution sets up two systems of citizenship, indigenous citizens and naturalized citizens. This may be true by process, but once citizenship is obtained is it proper to make that distinction? It becomes an issue of trust. It is telling our nationalized citizens that regardless of their status they cannot obtain the highest office in the land, and it further brings into question their loyalty and even their honor. Again, in a democracy the electorate should make that decision. The controlling issue should be merit. Presidential hopefuls need to be judged on character and administrative skill, not their accents.

A rock of discrimination. These concerns become like a big rock. Everywhere we go we carry around this rock. When we talk with someone, we stand there holding this rock. At night when we sleep the rock is in bed with us. When someone asks us, "Why are you carrying around this rock?" The only defense is that this is our rock and this is what we do. These issues of discrimination belong in the past. They belong to history. They should not be forgotten; they need to be remembered and understood for the pain that they caused, but as a people we need to move forward. We must unshackle ourselves from this rock and leave intolerance behind.

Discrimination haunts America. Discrimination holds us back from being a truly great nation. It runs from the past into the future, sweeping the nation along with the current. It festers and can never be explained. The American Constitution was based on discrimination; some of the intent was hidden, others plainly outlined. If we are ever to place these issues behind us, we must start anew and place them squarely in the past.

The language is what brings the concepts and ideas within the Constitution to life. It is the material that ties and connects the document to the realities of our lives. Something as simple as a pronoun can affect each individual. To recognize how important such an item is, a person needs only to remove all of the masculine pronouns from the United States Constitution. The exercise will cause the document to degenerate before one's very eyes with no glimpse of its intent or value.

Chapter 22

Militias

Great Britain was a world power in the eighteenth century. They were as much a world power after the American Revolution as they were before and they were not the only colonial empire in North America. The Spanish, the Portuguese, the Dutch, the French, and even the Russians had possessions in the new world. The two major antagonists were the English and the French; they had been fighting wars dating back to the Norman invasion. The political intrigues and military maneuvering were as constant as the whims of their monarchs. The French and Indian War had changed the balance of power in the New World, but Britain's European rivals still maintained subject states in the Americas.

British troops in America. As a point of colonial authority and as a world power the British maintained troops in North America. The British saw themselves as protectors; after all they had spent years fighting the French for control of the area, and from a global view potential European enemies were still in the region. Over time the colonists had developed a different theory. They felt they were capable of defending themselves. They saw the British army more as an occupying force than a guardian of their interest.

British troop abuses. As the tension increased between the American colonies and the mother country, the British standing army played a major role. In the end, one of the reasons for the American Revolution dealt with the abuses of British troops. The logic the British government used to tax the American colonies centered around military considerations. The huge debt the British government was maintaining resulted in part from the French and Indian War. It occurred in part as a result of the British effort to protect the colonies. They also needed the money to help support the garrisoning of troops in the New World, and the British reasoned that the colonists should help pay for their own defense. It became a primary point of contention, increasing colonial anger toward the soldiers.

The British troops, and especially the officers, saw the colonists as little more than chattel and functioned accordingly. As was the case with most nation-states of the time, the army had police powers. The army could arrest and hold members of the civilian population. During this period the British troops would search homes, confiscate property, and hold people without trial. Able to operate in the colonies without serious restrictions, the British military did so with impunity.

Quartering of troops. One of the standard complaints the colonists had toward the British was the housing of troops in private homes. It brought about such animosity that it appeared in the American Constitution as the Third Amendment. It was seen as an arrogant act. Even soldiers of the lowest ranks functioned in colonial homes not as guests, but as overlords.

Every colonial town and community had their own citizens under arms. Their original intent was a rapid response to possible Indian attacks rather than as an opposition to the British, but colonials saw these militias as their own military organizations. As a rule they could be quickly assembled, and while never heavily armed, they could assemble a sizable number of men at any one time.

When the Revolutionary War broke out a colonial army was raised, but the substructure of the American army always contained a large number of local militias. The militias had met the British at Lexington and Concord. The militias won the battle of Saratoga. The militias kept an American presence alive in the South after the British destroyed all the colonial armies. The militia fought in every major battle in the Revolution. While their military prowess may be in question and their fighting skill always suspect, their commitment to the Revolutionary spirit was hardly an issue. In the end the militias played a significant part in the American victory.[1]

By the time the Founders had set out to create the Constitution, their apprehension and concerns toward a standing army were still vivid. From their view, standing armies were an organization that detracted from personal liberty, and they were expensive. In lieu of the distance between the European powers and the original thirteen states there was also the question of public necessity. This does not mean that the drafters of the Constitution did not allow for such potentiality. Rather, a collection of articles in the Constitution relate to the military, everything from who is commander in chief, how war is declared, appropriations of funds, and the regulation of the armed services, but the militias were also part of this mix. They were seen as an established part of America's defense.

The Militia Act of 1792 set out the basic principles for the militia and their organization. Both the states and the national government were supportive of this military body, both for different reasons. The Federal government recognized that in the field of foreign affairs the projection of military might was an important part of international preeminence. Regardless of how effective the militia might be, they did represent a part of America's total military strength. The states were supportive of the militia because it maintained some level of state autonomy and control. Initially the goal was for all able-bodied white males between the ages of 18 and 45 to serve in the state militias. They were required to provide their own equipment and firearms. For many reasons the state militias fell into decay and few inducements existed to maintain these military forces.

During the American Civil War a type of militia appeared called the Volunteer. While organized from specific districts and helped from wealthy individuals with their inaugural formation, the state and national governments maintained these units upon deployment. After the war, militias did fall from favor and almost ceased to exist. The fear of Indian attacks or even external invasion seemed remote. It was only because of the labor movement that militias were again mustered into service and reinstituted. In the 1880s labor strikes were seen as a form of civil unrest and a riotous act by most state governments. Militias were used as a police power aligned to the state. As the nation moved into the twentieth century, additional usage was found in assisting with natural disasters as well as supporting the traditional armed forces. In 1933 the term militia was officially changed to National Guard and as a military body it was incorporated into the regular army.[2]

Militias in the Constitution. As a Constitutional element the militia is well defined. One of the powers granted the new government under the Constitution was the ability to call up the militias. Article I, Section 8 reads as follows:

To provide for calling forth the militia to execute the laws of the union, suppress insurrections and repel invasions.

It cannot be believed that the Founders of the Constitution felt that the militia would be enough in itself to defend the nation, but in the same account militias were viewed in a positive sense and widely supported. In the end the militias became a Constitutional entity and were permanently fixed in the document. The Second Amendment to the Constitution says as much about militias as it does the right to bear arms. It can actually be argued that the provision says more about civilian armed forces than it does about firearms.

We encounter a problem in attempting to apply these concepts of eighteenth century frontier America and the Founders' views of militias to what is found at the beginning of the twenty-first century. Currently in the United States numerous paramilitary forces are set up as militias. These are bodies that emerge from separate communities, motivated in defense of their communal interest, and invested with conservative philosophies. While many of these militias are focused on a single issue such as the right to bear arms, the problem is more complex. They see their existence as a Constitutional one. A distrust has developed between these twenty-first century militias and the Federal government. Without making the issue overly simplistic, these militias would argue that they are an extension of the *minuteman* of the Revolutionary War; hence any effort to restrict their existence by the part of the Federal government constitutes a form of tyranny. The logic travels in such a way that if the Federal government wishes to circumscribe militias, then the control of the Federal government has fallen into the hands of a despotic leadership. After all, the Constitution is the guarantor of our rights. If the Federal government through its agencies is resisting these militias, then the whole Constitution is in jeopardy.

On the other side, the Federal government invested with the responsibility of maintaining domestic harmony looks at these militias as radicals, potentially violent, and at the very least nonconformist. Many of these militias function outside the framework of mainstream politics, support discriminatory concepts, are racially motivated, and are outright antagonistic to the government. Many of these groups are heavily armed and carry weapons clearly designed for military purposes rather then sportsmanship.

The National Guard. The Federal government would also argue that the National Guard is the true contemporary of the colonial militias. While financially controlled by the Federal government, the command structure of the National Guard leads to the state governors. The contention is that the National Guard is supported by the political state and its government. It is a product of the government and hence better connected to the Constitution. Yet, the vision that the Founders had of militias is far closer aligned to the community-based, self-directed paramilitary forces found in some local communities of the country.

The issue of the National Guard does bring up some interesting questions. Few nations in the world have a military structure similar to that found in the United States. The closest comparison may be Switzerland. The United States has a standing army, the Reserves, and then the National Guard. The command structure of the National Guard represents an extreme oddity. As a military body they have a dual loyalty. The rank of soldiers parallels the other branches of the armed forces. In every major war the United States has been involved in, National Guard troops have participated at some level. They are responsible for the defense of the nation as a whole, but are set up as a state operation. The state governors can call up the Guard and use them as they see fit. This is a duality that is hard to explain, but one with which Americans seems to feel comfortable.

The reason that the National Guard functions in this dual world is because of the Constitution. In the Constitution this duality was created, and part of these issues return to the original idea of state sovereignty. It seems acceptable to allow the Guard to serve this double function, to live as both a Federal and state entity, but the National Guard must also be seen as one part of the equation. They are one variant of this theme called militias. From the view of the drafters of the Constitution the Guard must be seen as an established militia, but they may not be the only body that can claim part of that title.[3]

Many people in the United States hardly think about the Constitution. They have never read it, and it exists for them primarily as an image. They accept the American Constitution as a general philosophy, as a point of perspective. Other people read the Constitution and view every word in the most literal sense. If the

Constitution says that "A well regulated militia being necessary to the security of a free state...," they see that as fact. Those who wish to restrict militias are in turn resisting a free state. The truth always seems to lie somewhere in the center, but these two positions are hard to reconcile.

This disagreement is extremely profound and has the inherent possibility of great violence. The Constitution is not specific about the regulations that can be placed on militias. There is no way of telling at this point which community-based militias are functioning within concepts of the Constitution and which stand outside of the Constitution. Though there are paramilitary forces within the United States that enthusiastically support the destruction of the Federal government, this is not the type of militia force that the Founders had envisioned. This represents a Constitutional crisis. If these groups continue to see themselves as defenders of the Constitution while the Federal government, which is a creation of the Constitution, sees these militias as fanatics, the chances of armed conflict are considerable.[4]

This single issue may have the greatest potential for destruction of our society. The further the gap that exists between the United States Constitution and the original intent, the greater the chance of hostility. As various groups read the document and note the discrepancies, the conclusion they may reach is that government is acting in a conspiratorial manner. It becomes more than simply the sections related to militias and the use of firearms, but the document as a whole. If that issue cannot be reconciled, at what point does the armed defense of the Constitution and our society become a necessity? It develops into an enormous trap for all the parties concerned.

Chapter 23

The Primaries

Political primaries are not connected to the United States Constitution. Any effort to associate primaries with the Constitution is fundamentally flawed. It is far more of a political or party function. The nation's founders were working toward a system of government that did not require political parties, let alone primaries. Of course this proved to be impossible and, to some degree, naive. By the time George Washington had left office political parties were well established and had become a mainstay of the American political process. In this one case the problem with the United States Constitution is not what it says about such a political structure, but more correctly the fact that it says nothing.

Political parties and primaries are not inherently deceptive or wrong; in fact, the opposite is true. Democracies require political parties. They represent a collection of communal ideas. A party becomes a place where individuals with shared beliefs can meet and work toward joint concepts. Political parties represent a more democratic process than the vision the Founders had of the American government.

Equally, the election process has been criticized for being too accommodating to the existing political parties. While this is a valid reproach, primaries may be a part of the democratic process. A two-party system may be the end result of long-term democratic actions. What may be more important is that the existing parties be open enough for new ideas and social concepts to have an honest hearing within these institutions.

Third parties. While primaries should be seen as a party function, most primary systems are not very accommodating to third parties. The difficulty is that a third party needs to be certified by the state to be on the ballot. Each state determines its own laws on political parties and how they can be established. The individuals making these rules are well entrenched in one of the two major political organizations. Regardless of its philosophical base, a new political party still represents competition for the existing parties.

Third parties also have an internal flaw. They are generally centered on one individual's personality. A political candidate has not found the existing political parties supportive of her or his views, and an effort is made to create a third party to propel the person's ideas forward. The process is initially centered on the personality of one person.

The other reason for implementing a new political party is the conviction found within a single issue. The process is driven by one idea. It has become so important to the followers of this point of philosophy that an effort is made to create a new political party to press the issue into the mainstream of society.

Third parties have the rudimentary problem of obtaining success. Some level of attainment or accomplishment is required to maintain the party faithful. If power is never achieved or there is no possibility of success, then third parties like most enterprises will wither and die. If the third party is a one-issue entity and if they become successful, then more than likely one of the major parties will adopt the issue as its own. Those that are founded on the charisma of one person have the added problem of time. Pressure from the opposition and media will change the perception of this leader. Without political success the third-party candidate will be seen as politically eccentric.

Those who support third parties criticize the American political party system for not representing true choices. They would argue that both of the two major political parties are the same. They would continue by noting that both of the established parties represent "property" or the status quo. While this may be true, the system is still designed so that the people can participate. It may require a degree of activism, but the people still could involve themselves and adjust the makeup of the proceedings. In the end the two-party system may be a metabolic part of democracy.

The two-party system. Political parties should be seen as having a dual purpose. On one side they are avenues for political candidates to reach elected office. Through the party individuals are elected and personal political ascendancy is obtained. The second part is the review of issues. Ideas still need to get an honest hearing within these bodies. Political parties are an important part of the democratic process though. They drive the social and political change of the country. They need to be open enough to accept new ideas and allow candidates to function, but have substance enough so that the masses can understand the philosophical base from which the party operates.

Democratic Party Delegates For Primaries in 1992

Date	State	Method	Delegates
February 10	Iowa	Caucus	59
February 18	New Hampshire	Primary	24
February 23	Maine	Caucus	31
February 25	South Dakota	Primary	21
March 3	Colorado	Primary	58
	Georgia	Primary	96
	Maryland	Primary	85
	Idaho	Caucus	26
	Minnesota	Caucus	92
	Utah	Caucus	29
	Washington	Caucus	84
	American Samoa	Caucus	5
March 5	North Dakota	Caucus	22
March 7	South Carolina	Primary	54
	Arizona	Caucus	49
	Wyoming	Caucus	19
	Democrats Abroad	Caucus	9
March 8	Nevada	Caucus	27
March 10	Florida	Primary	167
	Louisiana	Primary	75
	Massachusetts	Primary	119
	Mississippi	Primary	46
	Oklahoma	Primary	58
	Rhode Island	Primary	29
	Tennessee	Primary	85
	Texas	Primary	232
	Delaware	Caucus	21
	Hawaii	Caucus	28
	Missouri	Caucus	92
March 17	Illinois	Primary	195
	Michigan	Primary	159
March 24	Connecticut	Primary	66
March 28	Virgin Islands	Caucus	5

Democratic Party Delegates For Primaries in 1992

Date	State	Method	Delegates
March 31	Vermont	Caucus	21
April 2	Arkansas	Caucus	18
April 5	Puerto Rico	Primary	58
April 7	Kansas	Primary	44
	Minnesota	Primary	92
	New York	Primary	290
	Wisconsin	Primary	94
April 11	Virginia	Caucus	97
May 3	Guam	Caucus	4
May 5	District Columbia	Primary	31
	Indiana	Primary	93
	North Carolina	Primary	99
May 12	Nebraska	Primary	33
	West Virginia	Primary	41
May 19	Oregon	Primary	57
	Washington	Primary	84
May 26	Arkansas	Primary	48
	Idaho	Primary	26
	Kentucky	Primary	64
June 2	Alabama	Primary	67
	California	Primary	406
	Montana	Primary	24
	New Jersey	Primary	126
	New Mexico	Primary	34
	Ohio	Primary	178
	North Dakota	Primary	22

Republican Party Delegates For Primaries in 1992

Date	State	Method	Delegates
November 1-30, 1990	Arizona	Caucus	37
March 1-31, 1991	South Carolina	Caucus	26
January 1-31	Hawaii	Caucus	14
January 1 - May 31	Delaware	Caucus	19
January 1 - March 30	Maine	Caucus	22
January 1 - February 15	Nevada	Caucus	21
February 10	Iowa	Caucus	23
February 18	New Hampshire	Primary	23
February 25	South Dakota	Primary	21
March 3	Colorado	Primary	37
	Maryland	Primary	42
	Minnesota	Caucus	32
March 10	Florida	Primary	97
	Georgia	Primary	52
	Louisiana	Primary	38
	Massachusetts	Primary	38
	Mississippi	Primary	32
	Oklahoma	Primary	34
	Rhode Island	Primary	15
	Tennessee	Primary	45
	Texas	Primary	121
March 17	Illinois	Primary	85
	Michigan	Primary	72
March 24	Connecticut	Primary	35

Republican Party Delegates For Primaries in 1992

Date	State	Method	Delegates
April 1 - May 31	Virginia	Caucus	33
April 7	Kansas	Primary	30
	New York	Primary	100
	Wisconsin	Primary	35
April 20	Utah	Caucus	27
April 28	Pennsylvania	Primary	35
May 1-31	Pennsylvania	State Convention	
May 2	Wyoming	Convention	9
May 5	District Columbia	Primary	14
	Indiana	Primary	51
	North Carolina	Primary	57
	Ohio	Primary	83
May 12	Nebraska	Primary	24
	West Virginia	Primary	18
May 19	Oregon	Primary	23
	Washington	Primary	35
May 26	Arkansas	Primary	27
	Idaho	Primary	18
	Kentucky	Primary	35
	Virginia	Convention	21
June 2	Alabama	Primary	38
	California	Primary	201
	Montana	Primary	20
	New Jersey	Primary	60
	New Mexico	Primary	25
June 9	North Dakota	Primary	17

It can also be argued that the two-party system is too open, that the party itself will give a candidate only marginal support. If a person is going to run for a political office, he or she needs to bring staff and money to the process or there is little hope of staging a successful political campaign. Political parties in the United States are but convergences for the interpersonal process of elections. This is simply one of the items the Founders misjudged.

One national candidate. The American President is the only nationally elected position, at least if the Vice-President is seen as a nonissue. All the states, and the electorate found within, vote for the chief executive. Each state has a different primary system, level of participation, and structure of usage, but all assist with the process of electing a President. For each state to have its own system of primaries is fair and should be seen as impartial within their own political structure, but problems arise when these individual primaries are placed in the national spectrum.

Two problems. Two parts of the primary process are out of sync with democratic actions; both are so well connected that separating them may be impossible. One issue deals with the overall length of the election season and the other item is the date of each state primary. The length of time involved creates problems with cost of a campaign and where candidates must place most of their effort. The longer the campaign the more money that needs to be generated.

The second problem deals with the choices given the voters. With such long campaigns and primaries staggered over the course of a year, candidates begin to drop out before the process is complete. This eliminates choices and options for the electorate in many states. Whereas at the beginning of the campaign year in February hundreds of aspiring Presidential candidates may be in the race, some ten of whom may be serious contenders; by June when the last primary is held only a couple are likely to be still on the ballot, and by then the issues have long since been settled. What happens is that a large body of the American voters have no say in who will run for President from their political party. At least at the national level the primaries are meaningless. A part of American democracy is being disallowed to a large component of the population.

Democratic party system. The first listing in this chapter represents the Democratic Party's nominating process for President and the dates of each state's elections or caucuses. The example is for 1992. Every election year would have minor changes depending on state legislative actions or the calendar, but this list is consistent with most Presidential election years.

Republican party candidate selection. The Republican list for party primaries is similar. Again, the example is for 1992. The process does start earlier and a few different nominating systems are in place.[1]

While the primary season for both Democrats and Republicans differs slightly, the fundamental problem still exists. The issue of who will lead the party has been determined months in advance of many late scheduled state primaries.[2]

Using the same example of 1992, of the top political candidates within both parties, only four still had active campaigns after May 1st. On the Democratic side Paul Tsongas, Lawrence Douglas Wilder, Tom Harkin, and Bob Kerrey had all dropped out of the race before April (Tsongas had withdrawn on March 19th and Kerrey on March 5th). For all practical purposes Bill Clinton had won the party nomination after "Super Tuesday" on March 10th. Only Jerry Brown saw the Democratic Presidential campaign to the end. The Republican side differed little. George Bush as the incumbent was able to use his office to move forward with his campaign. While Buchanan pressed Bush in the primaries and did stay in the race to the end, Bush had won the nomination by March 10th. What occurs after March is an effort in futility. Neither the parties nor the electorate in those states with balloting after March 10 had any say in who would be their Presidential candidate. This issue is even magnified further considering that in the first primary in New Hampshire it is not uncommon for two hundred people to be on the ballot.[3]

No easy solutions. This is a difficult discussion because there are no easy solutions. In fact political primaries were created in an effort to make the process more democratic. Historically candidates were chosen within party state conventions. These were the times of the smoke-filled rooms, party bosses, and party machines controlling the process. If an individual wished to run for political office she or he needed to be supported by the party or at least sanctioned by the party. The political primaries became a method by which the average citizen, while not overly active in party politics but loyal and faithful to the party, would have a say in the process. As a rule this is true. The primaries give more people a voice in the process. At the local and state levels primaries represent a greater level of democracy than what has preceded it. The main problem is the Presidential primaries.

Primaries should not be seen as some auxiliary part of the American political process. In many ways primaries are more important than the general election because in the primaries a candidate must face a collection of challenges. More than one person may be running for the office. The party that is out of power will commonly field a wider slate of potential Presidential participants. This creates an environment of issues rather than simply brazen attacks on the opposite political party. Many unknowns in the political primaries force the candidates to manage their campaigns in a definable fashion. Equally, the candidate in the primaries is not just looking for support within the electorate, but from the party elitists and major financial contributors, many of whom may still be sitting on the sidelines waiting for the dust to clear. Primaries are a very integral part of American political process and government.

Under the current system each state can determine the time, date, and type of primaries it will incorporate; however, there is no order to the process. Some states use elections, some caucuses, and a few still have some delegates chosen at the state political conventions. Each state uses a different system and method of operation. How a person's name appears on the state ballot varies widely. In some cases a person must petition the party and declare himself or herself a candidate through the local party. In some cases the state places the name on the ballot if the national media recognizes the candidate as a genuine contender. In some states the state legislature determines the rules for the primaries and in other states the political parties determine the majority of the rules. In some elections the winner gets all the delegates for the state, in other cases it is proportionate, and this is not always exact. Another difference concerns who may vote in the primaries. In some states all registered voters are allowed to vote for whatever political party they wish and can declare their party of choice at the polls. In other states individuals must register with a given party and can only vote for candidates from within the party they have declared. Some states even have both election primaries and caucuses operating at the same time.

None of this in itself is undemocratic. Each state has the right to determine how delegates are picked for the national party conventions. The primary season officially starts in February and ends in June. Traditionally New Hampshire has kicked off the Presidential campaign and the election year. If a person is to vote or participate in a caucus, that act needs to have meaning. It becomes an exercise in democracy. If a person's vote has no significance, then it detracts from the entire election process. What is happening is that in the latter part of the primary season the electorate has no say in who will represent the party as their Presidential candidate. In most cases by the time the primaries have reached those states with elections in May or June, the Presidential primaries are over. The majority of the candidates have dropped out and one candidate has emerged with a preponderance of the delegates. This means that a number of states, and their citizens, had no part in the election process.

Without being overly critical of New Hampshire, this state has enjoyed the distinction of being the state that inaugurates the Presidential election year. It has made a deliberate effort to maintain itself as the first political primary. When other states have attempted to establish a primary election date similar to New Hampshire's, they have moved their date back even further. This act then increases the overall election year. The better part of the American Presidential campaign will run from January to November. This problem is not arbitrary in nature, but it does create an election process that is tiresome and lengthy.[4]

A lengthy and tiring process. The length of the political campaign in the United States is actually even more pronounced than the January to November time frame. Arthur Hadley, the journalist, has noted that there is also an "invisible primary." Individuals seeking the Presidency will begin to look for support and test the waters long before the political primaries begin. This "invisible primary" will start the day after the general election is completed and the beginning of the first primary. Possible candidates are looking for political support, reviewing options, discussing the issue with their family, and determining their financial resources. Political campaigns, especially within the duration of American political campaigns, require considerable stamina. This is a time in which potential contestants can judge their own personal staying power.[5]

Regardless of the type of process designed the system will still be political. Politics is a strange combination of maneuvering, intrigue, and desire. It has nothing to do with wisdom, principles, efficiency, fair play, or even good government. It is by its own nature emotional and conflicting. We know of no ideal system of determining who will run for office. Some believe that the United States needs to go to a national primary for Presidential elections.[6] This in itself is flawed. Such a national primary would create a media event. Image and money would replace substance and issues. Regional campaigns could develop, splitting the parties and the nation. Political parties would be even less of a factor in the elective process of the nation. This idea of regional campaigns has even been proposed, but has not been ardently embraced.[7]

Yet, two problems remain. One is the collection of people who stand outside the system, not because they chose not to participate, but because the system eliminates any opportunity they may have to involve themselves. The second problem is length. While this is not autocratic in character or design, it does reduce participation by being so fatiguing. Again, there are no easy solutions. To solve these types of problems in American democracy would require an adjustment in the attributes of our political structure.

Chapter 24

How Readable Should a Constitution Be?

One of the questions that can be asked about a Constitution is how clear or how readable is the document? This may seem like an odd question, but Constitutions seem to be trapped in two different worlds. These two competing ideas are not easily reconciled.

The first of these deals with the law. A Constitution is considered the supreme law of the land. By its very nature it is a legal document. Designed to function within the framework of the judiciary system, points of law emerge from the text.

Specific concepts when written require specific words. Examples are numerous, one of which would be *eminent domain.* The government has the right to take privately owned land and convert it to public use after just compensation has been made. A *Bill of Attainder* is a legislative act designed to punish without a judicial trial or *ex post facto law*, which attempts to be retroactive, especially in criminal cases. Other legal terms would be *reprieve, writ of habeas corpus, emolument,* or *extradition*, all of which have very strict legal meanings. Points of law flow from these words and how they are used determine the freedoms and rights found in a Constitution.

Simple readability or legal vernacular? On the other side of this issue is the simple readability of the document. Should it be designed purely in the legal vernacular or should it be composed in such a way that the common person can read it, and, even more importantly, understand it. We hear about how the average newspaper is published so that an individual with a sixth-grade education can read it. Is that concept equally valid for a Constitution? A Constitution is designed for the benefit of the common person as much as it is for the elites of a society. Should not the language represent those most in need of Constitutional rights? John Marshall, the jurist, even believed that opinions of the high court should be written so that the public could read them.[1]

This issue is an extremely difficult one. The reality is that both of these ideas are logical and sound. A Constitution must be both of these; it needs to be legal in definition and composition but readable enough that most people can read the document and comprehend its meaning. There is a place for "legalese," but surely a Constitution is too important a document to be purely statutory.

Of the fifty-five delegates to the convention in Philadelphia thirty-four were lawyers. The terminology is somewhat different than what we use today. Generally it dealt with individuals who had studied some law, even if they were not practicing. Though they took a bar examination, it was far different from what is found in modern society, and the level of complexity has increased. What was most important was membership in the bar association. Less then half had attended college, most education of the day having come from contrasting systems of religious schooling or self-education. Of the total number forty-six had been or were part of state legislatures. Ten of the delegates had worked on state Constitutions. These were educated men of the day and who were not overly concerned about the process of writing the document. Each was capable of writing a Constitution. Most of the process came down to deliberation on key phrases or words.

The nation's founders did a fair job of meeting this dual requirement. In some areas of the Constitution wording is more direct than in others. In the First Article of the Constitution one of the sections reads as follows:

> The times, places, and manner of holding elections for Senators
> and Representatives, shall be prescribed in each state by the
> legislature thereof...

This is an honest example of the wording found in the document and as a rule it is readable. Where the American Constitution finds itself wanting is not in the wording, but in the phraseology.

Two hundred years of language change. In certain sections of the document eighteenth-century language does not translate well into the expressions of modern America. When the drafters were discussing treason they declared,

> ...but no attainder of treason shall work corruption of blood...

What is being said is *under penalty of death,* but this phase does not transcend two centuries of time very well. Equally confusing can be the terms found in Article IV of the Constitution.

> Full faith and credits shall be given in each state to the public acts, records, and judicial proceedings of every other state. And Congress may by general laws prescribe the manner in which such acts, records, and proceedings shall be proved, and the effect thereof.

For the layperson this Article may make no sense at all. What this section acknowledges is that if a person obtains a court judgment in one state and the liable person moves to another state, there is no need to sue them a second time. The second state is obligated to respect the judgment of the first. Once the "Full Faith Clause" is explained, it seems a reasonable and valid concept. Many such items exist in the Constitution; they have become dated and require explanation.

The greatest of all these bewilderments is Article II, Section 1, of the United States Constitution. Here the drafters of the document are explaining how Presidential elections will work:

> Each state shall appoint, in such manner as the Legislature thereof may direct, a number of electors, equal to the whole number of Senators and Representatives to which the State may be entitled in the Congress: but no Senator or Representative, or person holding an office of trust or profit under the United States, shall be appointed an elector. The electors shall meet in their respective states, and vote by ballot for two persons, of whom one at least shall not be an inhabitant of the same state with themselves. And they shall make a list of all the persons voted for, and of the number of votes for each; which list they shall sign and certify, and transmit sealed to the seat of the government of the United States, directed to the President of the Senate. The President of the Senate shall, in the presence of the Senate and House of Representatives, open all the certificates, and the votes shall then

be counted. The person having the greatest number of votes shall be the President, if such number be a majority of the whole number of electors appointed; and if there be more than one who have such majority, and have an equal number of votes, then the House of Representatives shall immediately choose by ballot one of them for President; and if no person have a majority, then from the five highest on the list the said House shall in like manner choose the President. But in choosing the President, the votes shall be taken by States, the representation from each state having one vote; a quorum for this purpose shall consist of a member or members from two thirds of the states, and a majority of all the states shall be necessary to a choice. In every case, after the choice of the President, the person having the greatest number of votes of the electors shall be the Vice President. But if there should remain two or more who have equal votes, the Senate shall choose from them by ballot the Vice President.

The problem may deal more with the complexity of the system than the actual readability of this Article. Without sounding overly critical, this section of the Constitution fails at most standards of intelligible methodology. It must have been as confusing for the average citizen of the 1780s as it is today. What is even more confounding, if not embarrassing, it did not work and the Twelfth Amendment to the Constitution was passed to correct the deficiency. It reads as follows:

The electors shall meet in their respective states and vote by ballot for President and Vice-President, one of whom, at least, shall not be an inhabitant of the same state with themselves; they shall name in their ballots the person voted for as President, and in distinct ballots the person voted for as Vice-President, and they shall make distinct lists of all persons voted for as President, and of all persons voted for as Vice-President, and of the number of votes for each, which lists they shall sign and certify, and transmit sealed to the seat of the Government of the United States, directed to the President of the Senate. The President of the Senate shall, in the presence of the Senate and House of Representatives, open all the certificates and the votes shall then be counted. The person having the greatest number of votes for President, shall be the President, if such number be a majority of the whole number of Electors appointed; and if no person have such majority, then from the persons having the highest numbers not exceeding three on the list of those voted for as President, the House of Representatives shall choose immediately, by ballot, the President. But in choosing the President, the votes shall be taken by states, the representation from each state having one vote; a quorum for this purpose shall consist of a member or members from two-thirds of the states, and a majority of all the states shall be necessary to a choice. And if the House of Representatives shall not choose a President whenever the right of choice shall devolve upon them, before the fourth day of March next following, then the Vice-President shall act as President, as in the case of the death or other constitutional disability of the President. The person having the greatest number of votes as Vice-President, shall be the Vice-President, if such number be a majority of the whole number of electors appointed, and if no person have a majority, then from the two highest numbers on the list, the Senate shall choose the Vice-President; a quorum for the purpose shall consist of two-thirds of the whole number of Senators, and a majority of the whole number shall be necessary to a choice. But no person constitutionally ineligible to the office of President shall be eligible to that of Vice-President of the United States.

While this Amendment did correct the shortfalls of Article II, especially those problems that were found in the election of 1800, it was not any clearer about how the Electoral College operated. Normally when Amendments are added to the Constitution what parts of the document are being changed is rather distinct. In this case, however, it can be confusing about which section of the Constitution the

Twelfth Amendment adjusts.

Indians not taxed. One other item seems unable to find a home. The United States Constitution lists how representation would be determined. Free persons, people "bound to service," which are indentured servants, and "three fifths of all other Persons," which are black slaves are named, but there is another category. This is "Indians not taxed." This statement requires considerable explanation. A major complaint about the Articles of Confederation was that the national government was not receiving any income from the states. Congress had no power to tax, meaning all revenues needed to be obtained from the state governments. Under the Articles themselves, the states were required to pay into the national treasury by a ratio based on the value of all the land in the states. They were also required to conduct a survey of all the land and buildings within their boundaries. This was not done and no such inventory was ever completed. In an effort to obtain funds, Congress attempted to pass the Revenue Act of 1783, which taxed individuals. The wording of this bill made note of "free inhabitants and three-fifths of all other persons, excluding Indians not taxed." Under the Articles of Confederation all the states had to agree or the bill was not passed. The Revenue Act was not ratified; in fact by 1786, New York was refusing to accept any new tax laws from the national government. By the time the delegates to the Constitutional Convention reached Philadelphia all were aware of these events, and the wording in the legislation. In the section under representation the idea was copied and agreed upon. In the case of the Indian population if they were "civilized" and would have been taxed under the 1783 Act, then they would be counted as part of the states' representation. If they were "uncivilized," they were not. Of course this is confusing and has no meaning today. It is not clear who would have determined how civilized an Indian was or was not. The Fourteenth Amendment to the Constitution, which changed the scope of governmental representation, said nothing about Native Americans. While they were born in the United States, they were not considered American citizens, and the discussions during the Reconstruction period were aimed at black Americans.

A secondary issue is attached to the idea of "Indians not taxed." It is also an acknowledgment of previously negotiated treaties with the native population. While tribes did each have their own set of agreements with the Federal government, some of them very specific, this item confirmed parts of these treaties. In some of these treaties the tax issue was covered.

The statement "excluding Indians not taxed" was one of those phrases of the times. Everyone knew and understood its meaning, but two hundred years later it was completely lost. Circumstances change and time does cloud memories.

Taxes, direct and indirect. Another topic in the United States Constitution that had been confusing through most of our history is direct and indirect taxes. In the First Article of the Constitution a section notes that

> ...direct taxes shall be apportioned among the several states which
> may be included within this union...

The goal had been to allow the national government to develop a direct tax as it related to the population of each state. This seems to be confirmed by Section 8 of the same Article, which outlines legislative authority. "The Congress shall have the power to lay and collect taxes, duties, imports, and excises..." The purpose of this section of the Constitution gave the government the authority to have a direct tax, but not an indirect tax. The indirect tax concept came from Article I, Section 9, which reads as follows:

> No capitation, or other direct tax shall be laid unless in proportion
> to the census or enumeration herein before directed to be taken.

The term capitation is generally conceded to mean a fixed amount per individual. The problem is that a direct tax and an indirect tax both could be designed to be a fixed amount of money and established in relationship to the population.

The Founders were confused over this issue as well; after all it appears twice in the document. The issue of taxation surfaced early in the Constitutional Convention with little debate. Most the of the discussion dealt with the related concept of how apportionment would be devised. Near the end of the convention Rufus King, one of the Massachusetts delegates, stepped forward. Madison recorded in his notes that King asked, "What was the precise meaning of direct taxation?"[2] A hush must have fallen over the hall because no one answered.

During the Constitutional Convention a committee was set up to refine the document. This committee connected taxation with the census, noting that all capitation tax should be proportional to the population. Three days before the Philadelphia convention was to come to an end, George Read from Delaware made a motion that the words "or other direct tax" be added to the text. It was seconded and approved without debate. This expression made the content far more nebulous. While the intent of the drafters of the Constitution was to make a distinction between a direct tax and an indirect tax, the words "or other direct tax" shaded the whole issue and allowed many different interpretations of its meaning.[3]

During the great debate that followed between the Federalists and the Anti-Federalists, the issue had only a cursory examination. In *The Federalist Papers* both Hamilton and Madison discussed the issue of a direct tax as if an overall consensus on the topic existed and as if their readers were familiar with the main points that were being presented. Few people may have been concerned about the issue of taxation. In frontier America it was difficult to tax the people directly in the first place. Most of the revenue generated by the Federal government in the early years of our history came from import duties.

Not surprisingly, the Supreme Court was soon faced with a case asking for an interpretation on the idea of a direct tax. This occurred in 1796 with *Hylton v. United States*.[4] The case dealt with a tax on horse carriages. While the high court found the tax Constitutional, there was considerable confusion on the part of the justices. Samuel Chase believed that it would be possible for a tax to be both direct and indirect. Justice William Paterson, who was at the Constitutional Convention as a delegate from New Jersey, felt that a direct tax could only be placed on land or people.

By the end of the nineteenth century the financial needs of the Federal government were growing. A number of different forms of taxation appeared from Congress in an effort to deepen the budgetary base of the Federal government. These new tax laws found themselves being challenged in the court system. In 1895 the Supreme Court found the new income tax law unconstitutional. Many scholars argued at the time, and still do, that the American Constitution in its original form gave the Federal government power to tax income, but part of the problem relates back to the confusion generated in this section of the document. The most honest method of correcting these obstacles was to write an amendment to the Constitution. In 1913 the Sixteenth Amendment was added. While this Amendment did refine the discussion of taxation, the issue still can be found in four different sections of the document.

Today we have a more comprehensive view of direct and indirect taxes. A modern definition of a direct tax would be on income or property. This is a tax levied directly on the taxpayer and the tax is very evident. An indirect tax would be noted as a sales tax or a value-added tax. Here goods and services, rather then property or individuals, are being taxed. In the business world indirect taxes are passed on to consumers in the form of higher prices for the products they buy.

The only real problem is that vestiges of the original wording on taxes are scattered throughout the Constitution. It is also confusing because the framers' initial goal of drawing a distinction between direct and indirect taxes still can be found in our social contract. Again, this issue returns to the idea of readability. Government should have the power to tax. If government is to be responsible for our defense and the general welfare they will need money to perpetuate these concepts, but taxation is also a flash point for rebellion. During the American Revolution the cry was "no taxation without representation." The tax issue had brought about the Boston Tea Party and was one of the major concepts in play during of the Revolutionary War. The issue simply needs to be clear.

Life, limb, and double jeopardy. One of the terms found in the United States Constitution is "life and limb." This phrase is connected to the Fifth Amendment, which covers many of the rights of the accused and includes the idea of *double jeopardy*. It actually reads, "...nor shall any person be subject for the same offense to be twice put in jeopardy of life and limb..." While it is easy to extract the notion of double jeopardy from this statement, and while not common, the expression of "life and limb" can also be heard in modern society. The difficulty is that for the drafters of the Constitution the term was much more literal.[5]

Throughout the greater part of English history punishments for various crimes were far more severe than today. Disemboweling, beheading, and quartering were punishments that a person might have faced if found guilty of numerous offenses against the state. The term *life and limb* refers to these types of penalties. Currently American justice would see the removal of a foot or an arm as "cruel and unusual punishment." This was not a prevailing punishment in colonial America and it is equally doubtful the Founders would have been supportive of these types of infliction, but the statement does lead a person in the wrong direction. It implies that the removal of a limb by the state is allowable. This is an issue that can be confusing and reduces the readability of the document.

Other little oddities. The United States Constitution seems to be full of little oddities that have not traveled well across the expanse of time. It is not a matter of poor insight, incompetence, or expertise in writing the document, but simply time itself. While it may seem fastidious, the question could be asked about the United States Air Force.

The Constitution outlines Congressional responsibility of the armed forces, but it does not refer to the military in the more general term. The document is specific. It states, "To provide and maintain a navy" or "To make rules for the government and regulation of the land and naval forces." Of course the Founders would have conceded the maintenance of an Air Force under these provisions, but that is not what it says. The Federal government and the Judiciary would argue that the spirit of the document is such that it includes the creation of additional branches of the armed forces. A counter-argument would be that those powerful and dominant parts of the Federal government need to be placed in the Constitution. While there are five branches to our armed services, the United States Air Force actually takes up half the military budget. This needs to be represented in some way in the document. While many would argue the issue is a minor one, the air force is as valid a concept as the army or navy; the problem of course is something else. The air force is capable of independent action and has a unique mission. It should not be excluded from the Constitution, especially if the document is going to inscribe specific branches of military service. The real problem is that the whole document is dated. The nation's founders talked about an army and navy because that was all they knew and these represented their only choices.

Cross-referencing the document. One problem of clarity within the Constitution may be found in its Amendments. While amending is a valid part of the Constitutional process, reworking or changing the document and still leaving the original text in place can be detracting. The twenty-seven Amendments of the United States Constitution are actually a small number considering two hundred years of history and the social changes the nation has undertaken. Yet, many of the Amendments have superseded other parts of the document; examples can be found in the Fourteenth, Sixteenth, and Seventeenth Amendments. The uppermost cross-referencing Amendments, though, has to be the Eighteenth and the Twenty-First.

The problem? Not readable. The problem is that the United States Constitution is not very readable. Originally the goal was to make the greater part of the document obvious to the reader. The educated segments of the population at the time of the construction of the Constitution would have been able to work through the language. George Dallas, the Vice-President under James Polk, had commented about the Constitution in the first half of the nineteenth century. He said, "The Constitution in its words is plain and intelligible, and it is meant for the homebred, unsophisticated understanding of our fellow citizens." The dilemma is that one hundred fifty years later this is no longer true.

Chapter 25

The Process of Interpreting

The reality is that no matter how hard a person or a group works at eliminating ambiguities in a Constitution, some inconsistent elements will remain. If an effort were made to list every right that a free people had under every situation, the volumes of material would be equal to the known knowledge of the human race. Without exaggeration or embellishment, it is impossible to list every right humanity may be entitled to within its relationship with government. When James Madison was working on the original Bill of Rights, at one point he had nine amendments with 42 separate rights and the list was still developing. The state legislatures and ratifying state conventions also made up lists of rights to be submitted to Congress. These included ninety-six different rights, of which only thirty-five were on Madison's roster. In the end twenty-six rights appeared in the United States Constitution. At some point these personal privileges, interests, claims, or rights needed to be interpreted. It also needs to be conceded that some rights emerge from existing ones. In the end we need someone, or some group, to help us make sense of these social and governmental interactions.[1]

Beyond legitimate rights. The problem is that the issue is more than simply a matter of our lawful rights. The great Constitutional conflict lies between the concepts of individual rights and the rights of society as a whole. The greater good and the rights of society must be taken into account. It represents a shell from which all of our personal rights can function, though compromises are needed. The rights of the community at times can come into conflict with the rights of the individual. This process of interpreting the limits and nature of our rights has fallen on the Federal Court system and the Supreme Court in particular. It has become the responsibility of the Supreme Court to interpret the nature of our rights and how they correlate with communal rights for self-preservation.

Obviously the mandate of the Supreme Court lies within the Constitution. Their responsibilities of interpreting our rights and the nature of our government has fallen to the high court and their guide is the Constitution. As a rule the Federal court system does an excellent job at absorbing the meanings of the Constitution and applying it to the conditions that have been presented to them. Even so, the role of interpreter becomes more complex as time advances. Certain issues move easily from one generation to another. The idea of freedom of speech in the twenty-first century will not be fundamentally different from how the drafters of the Constitution saw it. While the Supreme Court has had opportunities to interpret the meaning of this clause, the concept rings as true today as it did two hundred years ago. In the same Amendment is the concept of freedom of assembly. For the nation's founders this issue was rather straightforward. If the people wished to gather, meet, or discuss any issue, that was their right and the Constitution supported this activity. Government was not to interfere. Two hundred years later a collection of restrictions have been attached to the concept of assembly. The authorities have a say in the date, time, and place that large gatherings can be held. Differing restrictions apply depending on whether the event is inside or outside. In many cases a permit is required from the local governmental bodies. These changes have occurred through the interpretation process of the courts.

Implied rights or powers. These issues of interpreting the American Constitution become even more complex when the issue of implied powers or implied rights is discussed. The First Amendment to the United States Constitution lists four separate rights: freedom of speech, freedom of religion, freedom of assembly, and freedom of the press. Traditionally these rights were seen as a collection of four separate ideas. During the twentieth century the Supreme Court has begun to see the First Amendment as a set of "Preferred Freedoms." Collectively these four ideas merge to form rights not specifically found in the text of the document, ideas such as freedom of expression, rights of association, freedom of thought, and rights of conscience. The First Amendment becomes an arrangement or matrix for a collection of interpersonal rights. While this position is logical and the Supreme Court has used this idea effectively to expand democratic freedoms, it is not specific to the document. It creates a new category of individual rights that could be called *interpreted rights*.

This same concept can be seen in the Ninth Amendment to the Constitution. Many argue that the Ninth Amendment is little more than a "technical" clause reinforcing the first eight Amendments to the Constitution. The Federal Courts have rarely sighted the Ninth Amendment when making their rulings. Even so, the Amendment is distinct; it notes that the citizens of the country are entitled to rights not listed in the Constitution. It points to the idea that there are *implied rights*. With or without the use of the Ninth Amendment, the Supreme Court has upheld the idea of implied rights.

The nature of interpretation. The mixing together of time and interpretation issues yields some odd combinations. Without stating a position on the characteristics of either of these Constitutional issues, an example can be made of freedom of the press and the right to bear arms. The Supreme Court has consistently held that freedom of the press applies as well to both radio and television broadcasting. These two communication mediums are protected under our First Amendment rights, their only differences being those of technology. The Founders did not know the applications of physics that make broadcast media possible, but the courts have expanded the Constitution to include these types of technology. It is the nature of interpretation.

Using this same argument on the Second Amendment, new technologies have been disallowed. When the Founders talked about the right to bear arms, they thought of a smooth-bore, flintlock musket or a Kentucky long rifle. As our technology has progressed so has the efficiency and lethality of our weaponry. Without commenting on whether a citizen should be allowed to build and own nuclear weapons, there is a dual standard. The high court has confirmed restrictions placed on this technology. The only real point is that technology, and sometimes simply higher levels of knowledge, requires greater levels of interpretation by the court. The further we distance ourselves from the past, the more our technology will change, and the more interpretation we will need.

The Constitution as a tool. Surely the Constitution is best seen, not as pronouncements set in concrete, but as a tool. Though the courts are its chief implementers, the Constitution is also designed to be used by the people. If the document is clear, comprehensible, and legible, the process becomes far more "user friendly." If the document is vague and obscure the value of this tool can be lost.

Past experience, existing law, and the objectives set out by the Constitution have made it clear that the courts have done a better job at maintaining our rights than either the Executive or Legislative branches of government. Though courts are never perfect, history has clearly fallen on the side of the courts. To some degree that is the purpose of the court systems; they are invested with the power to maintain the Constitution and our civil liberties. Yet, there is a flaw. Time corrodes and wears away the original intent. The greater the distance between the past and the present the greater the need for interpretation. At some point we begin to interpret the interpretations and someone else is explaining to us the nature of our rights. Some may argue this is a component of common law, but a Constitution needs to be more precise. While it is the fundamental law of the nation-state, a Constitution is also a covenant.[2]

Some would contend that we do not need an amendment process to the Constitution because the Supreme Court functions as an ongoing Constitutional Convention. While this statement carries considerable truth, still if our constitutional history has reached a point when our court system has become architects rather than administrators of the law, something is extremely wrong with the process.

Reversals. This issue is most notable when a list is made of the court rulings that have not only fluctuated across a spectrum of a given concept, but clearly represent reversals. While this may not be as common as the public may believe, still many examples can be cited. They represent stark differences. The court during one session of time would take a given position on an issue and then later reverse their decision and move in the opposite direction.

One of the most renowned of all the Supreme Court cases was *Plessy v. Ferguson.*[3] While this must be seen as an important case, it was only one of a collection of cases during the late nineteenth century and early twentieth century that established a governmental policy of discrimination. It was curiously combined with the belief that separate was equal. Court rulings such as *Williams v. Mississippi,* and *Berea College v. Kentucky* helped cement discrimination and the repression that went along with it. Between 1900 and 1920 the infamous Jim Crow laws became firmly entrenched in America and in the South particularly. The process of racial distinctions became institutional, at least until the Supreme Court began to reverse the process in the middle of the twentieth century.

This occurred with *Brown v. Board of Education in 1954.*[4] Chief Justice Warren looked at the same issue of segregation and came to a different conclusion. The Supreme Court noted that separate can never be equal. The court wrote that "in the field of public education the doctrine of separate but equal has no place. Separate educational facilities are inherently unequal."[5] In *Bolling v. Sharpe* the high court made a similar decision about the District of Columbia.[6] From this point forward not only was the direction of America's educational systems changed but so was the view of racial discrimination. The court moved beyond the singular issue of education and in time began to apply this doctrine to other social topics, especially after the 1964 Civil Rights Act. The issue remains though. The position of the court was opposite of *Plessy v Ferguson*, and in the sixty years between these two decisions the Constitution had not been altered on this topic.

Commercial laws. Another area of contrasting Supreme Court rulings deals with what is called "Old Swifty." In the early years of our history the high court had taken a position supportive of economic growth and business expansion. Even so, each state in the Union had developed a separate set of commercial laws. Interstate companies were finding themselves ever more frustrated by the multitude of state business statutes they had to deal with and understand. With *Swift v. Tyson* the court embraced the view that common law would bring consistency to commercial law.[7] After *Swift v. Tyson* interstate businesses found Federal courts more willing to champion concepts related to a national marketplace. They were less rigid and more willing to find the right common law precedent that would support the view of a national marketplace.

Old Swifty did have a spotted past, but it nevertheless helped the United States develop a national economy. It allowed the courts considerable flexibility in determining commercial cases. For nearly a hundred years the Supreme Court followed this interpretation. It came to an end with *Erie Railroad Company v. Tompkins*.[8] What had occurred was that the states had become more uniform in their commercial laws over the years, as corporations had become ever-increasingly more skilled at manipulating the legal system. Even when state courts were obviously the most appropriate forum for bringing a suit, a way was found to bring the issue before the pro-business Federal courts. In the case *Erie Railroad Company v. Tompkins* the court was able to deflect *Swift v. Tyson*. The new ruling curtailed the position of earlier courts. The Supreme Court declared that, unless specifically noted, "there is no federal general common law."[9] Again, this symbolizes a major reversal of what the Constitution represented in the past."

Women's Rights. The most obvious of all the Supreme Court's invalidations of past positions must be seen in cases concerning women's rights. One of the first court decisions on the status of women came with *Griswold v. Penniman* in 1818.[10] The court ruled that a husband had all rights to a woman's personal property, even those items she brought into a marriage.

> "He acquires an absolute property in her chattels personal in possession."[11]

In the early years of our republic the courts must be viewed as unsympathetic to the concept of women's rights. Even as late as 1948 the high court was endorsing gender inequalities within the law. With *Goesaert v. Cleary* the Supreme Court noted that legislation that drew a distinction between the sexes was constitutional.[12]

The first crack in this granite subterfuge came with *Reed v. Reed* in 1971.[13] At the time the high court noted no special consideration attached to this ruling, but it did represent a change in direction. When a statute in the State of Idaho gave preference to males over females as estate administrators, the Supreme Court ruled that government did not have the power to classify individuals by sex. This ruling designated a major change in the position of the court. The process continued with three related cases. Utah had a law stating that a parent was required to support a son until the age of twenty-one and a daughter until the age of eighteen. In *Stanton v. Stanton* the court declared that this represented sex discrimination.[14] The court was developing a new criterion for gender issues. A similar item was addressed with *Craig v. Boren.*[15] A statute in Oklahoma allowed woman to buy and drink beer at age eighteen, but males had to wait until they were twenty-one. This law was struck down as was *Kirchberg v. Feenstra* in 1981. This last case dealt with the old Louisiana "head and master" law. It noted that husbands had the unilateral right to dispose of joint property.[16]

The court generally refers to "equal protection under the law" provisions in the Constitution when addressing women's issues, but this is not the same position they had taken in the past. The only change in the United States Constitution was with the Nineteenth Amendment giving women the right to vote. This adjustment in the view of the court was consistent with the changing mores of the nation. We had become something else, but that does not address the bigger issue of Constitutional integrity.

One of the most curious cases ever handed down by the Supreme Court did not deal with a reversal as such, even though this was a type of reversal of an earlier ruling. During the better part of the 1960s the Supreme Court was elucidating the establishment clause of the Constitution. It represented a confirmation of the separation of church and state. One of the landmark decisions of the time was *Flast v. Cohen.*[17] It stated that taxpayers could challenge spending programs to religious schools in the court system, but government involvement in such items signified a violation of the First Amendment. By 1982 the court was moving in a slightly different direction. The Department of Health, Education, and Welfare (HEW) had given to Valley Forge Christian College a small piece of land and the attached buildings. These were properties for which the Federal government had no use. Through their accounting system they were able to write off the transfer of title so that Valley Forge did not have to pay for the property. A taxpayer group sued, noting the real value of the land and buildings was about half a million dollars. The court ruled, however, that, while the governmental act was unconstitutional, the taxpayer group had no *standing*. It continued by noting that in a situation like this no one would ever have *standing*. Without projecting too much into this one case and recognizing the logic of allowing Valley Forge to have this property, it is odd to believe that there are cases in conflict with the Constitution, yet they can never be corrected except through the "consciences of our government officials."[18]

These are not the only issues on which the Supreme Court has reversed decisions in our history. Legal matters related to monopolies, legislative delegation, state sovereignty, labor organizing, status of territories, voting rights, immigration, police powers, contract law, and minority rights each have seen different courts take totally different positions on related concepts or issues. If there is a criticism to this process it should not be totally aimed at the Supreme Court. It can be argued that two impartial and unbiased individuals each can see an issue from a different point of view. As a people we are as much responsible for the changes in interpretation as is the court. The far larger problem is that the Constitution itself loses credibility. The document needs to stand for something. It needs to be the anchor for society. This cannot be done if the processes of interpreting are inconsistent, and this is true even if the points of reversal occur over hundreds of years.

Change in the direction of the nation or related social issues needs to be represented in our Constitution. This is one of the advantages of periodical assessments and even the drafting of a new Constitution. It allows these reversals to be consigned to other documents, in another time and place. The reality is that all Constitutions experience various degrees of interpretation. The problem is not one or two annulments of past court decisions, but fifty or sixty.

Part Three: The Need for Updating the Constitution

Chapter 26

How Nations Decline

It is a rare nation or civilization that collapses virtually overnight. Most nation-states go through a protracted period of decline and disintegration. The sense of what is the nation-state is lost not in one day, one week, or even one year, but over centuries. Consider the real extinction of the Roman Empire; it came not at the hands of invading Germanic tribes, but rather at the hands of brokers who cut up Roman buildings for their granite and marble centuries later. They used the stone to construct newer architectural monuments for a society that saw themselves connected to Rome only through the fact that they occupied the same ground. While history may judge the end of the Roman Empire with the last emperor to hold the title, that is no more correct than to pick the last battle fought or the last ceremony performed under Roman law. The reality is that often nations do decline, civilizations fall from grace.[1] Of the thirty or so great civilization that have dotted the landscape of human existence, only one endures today, and its appearance on the world stage has been brief. It has existed only for two hundred years.

Loss of Faith. Historians are able from the vantage point of time to analyze the process and judge such passages in their entirety. While every civilization has a different story and a different set of events leading to its dissolution, certain consistent themes do run through the process of decay. The most important of all these concepts deals with the loss of faith in the nation's institutions. This represents more than simply government. It is possible for a civilization to boast a manageable government, ability to administer justice and services, as well as knowledgeable leaders, but the nation could still decline. This same government could have an ample military, well trained, properly organized, with modern equipment, and yet without fighting a battle the state could still collapse. The decline and fall of a nation may have nothing to do with government; it may be the other institutions within the society that have fragmented. The problem could have been that the nation was unable to maintain a competent merchant class or that new economic conditions appeared. A new religion or religious cult may have swept across the region destroying the existing theology and the regime that was attached to it. It is possible that educational institutions were no longer able to defend the status quo and new political doctrines were created that did not fit the old codes. Regardless, the issue returns to the idea that the people had lost faith in their institutions and new entities were generated to replace what was seen as no longer valid.

The theory that is being presented is that one observes a merging of history, traditions, and heritage. As these three emerge they begin to originate a separate mythology. At first it is accepted by the people; they embrace the myths that are part of their society. It is seen as a meaningful part of their culture, but there comes a time in which this myth is seen for what it is: it became fiction. What is being supplied to the people by their leaders and their institutions is no longer accepted. A universal loss of faith pervades the society, its institutions, and its government. At this point nations decline. The people are searching for philosophies to fill the gap that has been created and in time they will find competing ideas to replace what they have lost.

Seeds of Destruction. The reality is that causes that bring about the end of a dominion are found not in the present or the future, but in the past. The seeds of destruction are sown by the very history that creates the nation-state. Our own history will betray us. It will become both more accurate and more vague. It will disconnect persons from their society and the nation that shields them.

As the people begin to assess their own national historical events, and as time expands, situations become combined. World War II becomes but an extension of World War I, and they are no longer seen as separate events. Equally, the War of 1812 begins to be seen as part of the American Revolution. The end of America's War of Independence becomes 1815, not 1783. The people and historians alike begin to view events in the context of an era, not specific episodes of the country's history. Likewise, the nation's founding fathers become not just the individuals who served at the Constitutional Convention in Philadelphia, but the membership grows. Samuel Adams and John Hancock are added because they were active in the revolutionary causes of the period. Thomas Jefferson becomes a founder of the nation because of the Declaration of Independence and his service to the nation during that time. Paul Revere, Nathan Hale, and Crispus Attucks also receive promotions. The line becomes even thinner when the populace starts to see Abraham Lincoln as a Founder. Through his leadership freedom was extended to components of society that had been previously unempowered. Being the nation's founder becomes attached to the idea of advancing freedom. In another hundred years history begins to see Franklin Roosevelt at this level. The issue is no longer connected to the Constitution but becomes an item of status. The concept does change and the masses begin to see being a nation's founder as a rank. Being a member signifies that the individual has helped maintain and worked toward American liberty, but it is no longer connected to an event in history.

Tainted by history. On the other side of the issue is the idea that history actually becomes more accurate. We begin to look at historical personalities from many different directions. Not only do we judge persons by their achievements or a specific event, but by their character, behavior, and moral actions. We begin to look beyond their deeds. We analyze their lives and fine-tune their conduct. History makes an individual not only withstand the criticism of their own times, but also those of the future. George Armstrong Custer was seen as a great hero in the late nineteenth century, but future generations of Americans refused to accept this standing. He has come to symbolize wanton ambition, egotistical behavior and oppression. Douglas MacArthur, John Kennedy, and Charles Lindbergh, each a champion of their times, have been tainted by history. The personality of the United States owes a great deal to Thomas Jefferson. He wrote about those issues that are strictly American and each of us have become a part of his ideology. Yet, Jefferson through the eyes of history has been tarnished. He was an individual who lived beyond his means and only because of his status was he able to keep his creditors at bay. There is strong reason to believe that he was involved in propagation with his slaves.[2] Even if such a statement cannot be proved, the keeping of black slaves and the maintaining of overseers while at the same time advocating personal liberty speaks to a darker side. There are even those who have questioned the nature of Jefferson's religious beliefs and his political enemies have attempted to discredit him repeatedly on this issue.[3] These considerations have little to do with his overall contributions to American democracy, but each criticism of his moral conduct defiles his wisdom and his political courage.

In the end individuals do contribute to their own historical tarnishment. Thomas Jefferson was a prolific writer who covered many topics well. Yet, some of his views were not only wrong but outright damaging. Jefferson viewed blacks, for example, as a distinct race, different and separate from the white populations.[4]

> "Comparing them by their faculties of memory, reason, and imagination, it appears to me that in memory they are equal to the whites: in reason much inferior, as I think one could scarcely be found capable of tracing and comprehending the investigation of Euclid; and that in imagination they are dull, tasteless, and anomalous."
>
> "His imagination is wild and extravagant, escapes incessantly from every restraint of reason and taste, and in the course of its vagaries leaves a tract of thought as incoherent and eccentric as is the course of a meteor through the sky. His subjects should often have led him to a process of sober reasoning; yet we find him always substituting sentiment for demonstration."
>
> "I advance it, therefore, as a suspicion only, that the blacks, whether originally a distinct race, or made distinct by time and circumstances, are inferior to the whites in the endowments both of body and mind."[5]

The contradiction is that Americans have seen Jefferson in the most enlightened manner. He is an individual of enormous logic and insight, but the above statements taint his image.

What occurs for the common person centuries later is that these events become disassociated. These are stories about the rich, the powerful, and those overwhelmed by the episodes of their times, but such narratives have nothing to do with the present. They add little to a person's existence. They become historical events pressed into epochs that an average person can no longer relate to or understand. For the average citizen history becomes mythical. Instead of viewing the nation's founders as designers or thinkers, they become legends. Descriptions that are untrue or have no association with the real events begin to be seen as fact. While these tales may be more interesting than the authentic stories, at some point the truth emerges. Everything becomes discredited. The base from which the institution was founded becomes corrupted and the masses begin to lose faith in their national institutions.[6]

As a country begins to decay what becomes important to the citizens is not their national history but a person's separate heritage. Genealogy becomes the source that grounds the individual. Their loyalty is based not on the nation's institutions but on their fidelity to their family. Heritage stretches outward. It moves beyond what is seen as the nation-state. It cuts into the past and creates a continuum for an exclusive allegiance, unique to each individual. We become part of locations, times, and people who no longer exist. Heritage is different in the fact that it does not have to make the past comprehensible.[7] The only institution that becomes important is the family. It is the focus and all other institutions are either rejected or are seen in a far more discriminating fashion.

History can be easily misinterpreted, distorted, or trivialized. This occurs in part because someone is trying to make a point. The elites and our leaders use history for their own purpose—to stretch a point—it becomes self-serving. What is used is not the total history, but only one small part, a half truth. The purpose of the historical example is connected to a current policy that may have little to do with events noted. It becomes misguided and even at times vindictive. History develops into a tool, or more correctly, a weapon, and what is truly important about a nation's chronicles are lost.[8]

History can be controversial. Two individuals can read and study the same material and reach different conclusions. Each may base their theory on logical, rational ideas, but both cannot be right. History can be controversial because we do not want to hear the full truth. We are not eager to hear of the self-indulgent motives of our national heroes. We are not eager to hear those views that run counter to our brief system. History forces us to look at issues in different ways. In time we are forced to see the views of the Indians at Wounded Knee, the Spanish in the annexed territories of the American Southwest, or the starving immigrants who fed the Industrial Revolution in the Northeast. History propels us toward compromise. In so doing it carves away at the political and social base from which we operate. This is not the problem with heritage. It is far safer.

Traditions define a nation. What becomes important about heritage is the traditions that are attached to them—not just the personal stories that are being passed down from generation to generation, but traditions and customs as well. These traditions affect the attitude and amenities of the civilization. They become more than just family traditions. They move throughout the society and into every institution. Tradition more than history defines a nation.

Yet, within these very traditions are seeds of destruction. All nations have traditions and rites. They are important to a society and how they view themselves, but at some point they can begin to work against the survival of the nation or the civilization. On one side traditions create a conformity and sameness for the country, it bonds the society in a way no other issue can; but on the other side it resists change. What is seen as a harmony of beliefs manifests itself in decay. The society becomes inert.

The fall of the Ottoman Empire. An example can be made of the Ottoman Empire. Once they were the most dominant military-economic-social power in the world. By the clever use of diplomatic pressure, royal marriages, financial coercion, and pure military prowess the Ottomans had grown to be a great power in the seventeenth century. They found themselves at the summit in the field of mathematics, literature, astronomy, history, poetry, and medicine. The Ottoman Empire and the Arab world sheltered the great classical works of western civilization and in time returned them to the mainstream of western thought. At the high water mark of Ottoman power they were an effective military presence, controlling an empire that stretched across North Africa, into southeastern Europe, and back across to the Euphrates. They were rulers of most of the Arab world and a sizable part of southern Europe, maintaining their power by military might. The Janissaries made up part of their fighting force and were the dominant military units of their time. The military was also one of the first nations to use a cannon effectively. Called the Bombard, it was the terror weapon of its day.

A huge bulky device, over eighteen feet long and mounted on a carriage, the Bombard was then pulled by oxen. It was difficult to load and hard to aim, but once discharged it could bring down the walls of even the most heavily defended fortress, and for hundreds of years this piece of equipment served the Ottoman army. At its peak the military forces of the Ottomans could drag the Bombard into place and cities would surrender before a shot was fired. Its success had created a mystique and the use of the weapon became part of the traditions of the Ottoman military. Even when social and military reforms were instituted within the Ottoman Empire, the Bombard lived on. Battles were fought and territory lost. When Napoleon invaded Egypt at the end of the eighteenth century the Bombard was still in use. Of course it was no match for the horse artillery of that era. As a military device it had become ineffectual by then, but as a tradition of the Ottoman military it still had great importance. The point is that traditions, while important, freeze a people in a time and place that may not be in their best interest.

Tradition and change. Traditions can make change impossible. They eliminate choices. These customs become part of the belief system of the nation. They are interdependent with every other part of the society and are interwoven into the foundations of the nation. These traditions make a nation; they create one voice from the people, but they also hinder new ideas and concepts. Traditions produce a level of comfort, while at the same time breeding apathy. Apathy goes hand and hand with the loss of faith in our institutions. The problem is far more difficult than any other element of society. While it is easy to say that traditions need to be examined from time to time and to do so represents a healthy mechanism for a society, the reality is that traditions become part of our personality. It is equal to asking a person to change a behavior or part of their demeanor. While people are able to change their behaviors, it is never an easy process. It is who we are as persons and to change may mean that we become something else.

No matter how powerful the tradition, at some point it will come into question. Part of the society will refuse to adjust or change; another part will see change as mandatory. It will tear at the fabric of the nation. Essentially this is what happened with slavery. More than just an economic element of the American South, it had become a tradition and part of the lifestyle of the upper classes. The nation-state almost ceased to exist.

The prediction for America in upcoming years may be firearms. A component of the traditions of the United States, firearms connect us to our forebears and help define ourselves as a people. Nevertheless, the needs of a modem society no longer match with those of frontier America. The division is very real, especially as two parts of our society begin to see themselves very differently.

What destroys a nation-state? The belief that a nation-state can be destroyed by force of arms is false. While one military force may be more powerful than another, and one nation's army may occupy another, that has little to do with the desolation of the country. If one nation occupies another, one of three things will occur. One is that the conquered nation will be *assimilated* into the victorious nation. The culture of the vanquished nation with be subverted and they will accept the new order as their own. The second option is that the triumphant army will *be absorbed*. This occurred with the Mongol tribes. The Mongol hoards of the Thirteenth Century had conquered large sections of Asia and Asia Minor, but the civilization of these nomadic people did not survive; rather, the survivors were the nations that they overran. This could also be said about Norman England. While the Normans were Scandinavian in origin, they were culturally aligned to the French of the Eleventh Century, yet the national culture that emerged three centuries later was far more related to the Germanic Anglo-Saxons.

The third choice is that the subjugated nation *overthrows* the conqueror. The situation becomes unmanageable and they withdraw. Sometimes it is done with great fanfare and in other cases with great bloodshed, but in the end they leave. Even if the dominating country commits genocide, the nation-state was not destroyed by force of arms, but by a horrid criminal act.

It is possible for a nation-state to be destroyed by a political union. This may not be a negative process and the loss of faith occurred not by betrayal of trust but because of logical admonition. A choice has been to given the people and their leaders. There is an adjustment in perception, minor at first, but over time new institutions are established with this union. There is still a loss of faith in the old institutions, but it takes place as a process of political integration.

It is possible to create a new governmental body through the process of political integration and still maintain their status. What represents the nation-state is not just the governmental regime or even governmental processes. All the institutions must be taken into consideration. In the case of Scotland it existed through occupation, war, and oppression. Though Scotland has no government, its borders are firm and a clear understanding remains of what is Scottish. This also could be said about Texas in the United States. Those born into that society have a different bearing than many citizens of other states. In the end, countries are not destroyed through military conquest; only the people within the nation can destroy it.

While history must be recorded, written, taught, and at the very least understood, it must not be celebrated as a path to the future. We need to take the same critical eye when we look at history as when we look at science or physics. Human activities are never founded on one purpose or objective. We move in a given direction for a multitude of reasons. Traditions, on the other hand, are connected to one path. They are the product of agreement, conformity, and in a real way the goal becomes one of harmony. While traditions are of great importance in maintaining the sense of community, they are also equally significant in the decline and destruction of the society at large and, more importantly, the nation-state.

Nations do decline and fall by crisis, but the problem is that many of these crises cannot be easily discovered. A nation-state can be in a crisis and not even be aware of it, like a cancer that grows undetected. Years later when the historian will look at the events and the situation leading to the collapse of the civilization, the root causes will be studied and analyzed. Ideas and hypotheses will be put forward. Groups of scholars will debate the issues and argue the results. The job of the historian takes on the appearance of an autopsy. Yet, the reason for the decline and fall of all great nations is the same: *the citizens have lost faith in the fundamental principles of their institutions.*[9]

Looking back on the American Revolution, this loss of faith brought about the revolt. Before the 1760s the colonists had seen themselves as British. This widely accepted attitude rooted their government and the colonial political body in basic principles of liberty. All assumed that this liberty was unique in the world, and they were a part of an English world that shared this inherent right. Even though there was no formal Constitution for the British masses, the colonists believed that the concept existed. It was central to their ideas of liberty. They began to see the actions of the British government as a betrayal of their perception of "constitution." For many their basic understanding of the crisis of 1776 dealt with how the British had broken faith with the traditional view of their social contract and the concepts related to it.[10]

Unequivocally, monumental events do not destroy nations. They are shattered from within. They are destroyed by that one corrupt official who goes undiscovered, or the one telephone call from a citizen that is not returned, or the one personal meal charged back to the governmental expense account. It is the speech without substance and the predictability of the rhetoric. It is the one handwritten letter with a tear stain near the corner that receives a form letter in return. It is the one person standing in the docket demanding justice while two attorneys argue over protocol. It is the requirement and compliance to a law that benefits only the privileged and is understood by few. Yet, most important, it is the pitch of a word not spoken, but universally understood. It becomes a nod or a look when the name of a governmental official is heard, even if the only other person present is a stranger. To survive, all governments and nations require only this: a faith and belief that society is fair and just. A people must have faith in their institutions. When that is lost it is little more than a matter of writing the last page.

Chapter 27

Periodic Assessments of the Constitution

When the nation's founders met in Philadelphia in 1787 they truly were headed into uncharted waters. Never in human history had this type of popular government been attempted. The republics of ancient Greece were small. These city-states had populations of such small numbers that male members of society could meet in the town square or the rotunda and discuss the issues of the day. At the end of the Revolutionary War the United State's population had reached three million people; nothing had ever been attempted on such a grand scale before. In the truest sense of the word the American government was an experiment. The reality is that fighting for liberty and winning the military struggle is an entirely different matter from setting up a government to maintain and represent those ideas.

Deficiencies of the Articles. This same type of argument can be made about the Articles of Confederation. As with most governmental structures and systems a certain amount of experimentation exists. Some ideas worked and others did not. The grievances that the Founders had against the Articles of Confederation dealt in large part with the ineptitude of the document as a whole. The nation's debt was not being paid, the states had developed conflicting economic interests, the unity of the country was dwindling because of territorial claims, and the states were becoming singular political entities.

The United States Constitution was an honest effort to correct these deficiencies. This is not to say that the Articles of Confederation were a total failure. As a people we learned something from the process, we gained from the experience. The Articles did set up a Congress and created a national body. There was an agreement. We had as assemblage where national issues could be debated, and it did represent the United States on an international level. The problem was that the Articles lacked any level of sophistication and did not meet the needs of the larger collective.

The Convention in Philadelphia: An Assessment. The point is that the Convention in Philadelphia represented an assessment. An evaluation was made of the Articles of Confederation, and they were determined to be no longer workable; hence, the Founders drafted a new Constitution. Of course the process was not simple, but the leaders of the day were able to recognize the need, and they moved forward to address the problem.

When the Founders had established the American Constitution they had a multitude of concerns. They also had a vision about what the nation would be and how government would function. Again, putting these programs and constructs into place and breathing life into them, is one matter, but at what point does a nation actually step back, take a deep breath, and evaluate the process? When do we appraise the system to determine what worked and what did not? As individuals, as a nation, we learn from the experience. The United States Constitution has been in place for more than two hundred years. We have gained from this travel through time. As a people we now have something that the nation's founders did not have: we have experience with democracy.

The importance of periodic evaluations cannot be overstressed. We gain knowledge and wisdom from the process. We learn. If that information is never applied it becomes worthless. We can easily forget that people have sacrificed for the knowledge we have gained about our democracy, some with their very lives. It seems heinous never to review what has been accumulated.

One of the great contradictions in the establishment of America is the attitude of our leadership. On the one side are individuals drafting a Constitution based on popular beliefs in free government, creating a government grounded on compromise, minority rights, and participation by the people. Yet, in the same breath there is a distrust of the people. Certain delegates to the Constitutional Convention believed that the "people" were licentious, lawless, avaricious, and selfish. They saw only the negative characteristics that exist in all of us and expanded these concepts to include all people, especially the lower classes. Shay's Rebellion had a very sobering effect on the delegates at the Constitutional Convention. They were aware of the violence and loss of life that had occurred in this insurrection. It is fair to say that the drafters of the Constitution were concerned about the vices of mob rule. To counter their anxiety they produced a government with many safeguards against the intemperate nature of the masses. Also no exact method for producing a democracy had been devised. They were not even clear if the people would be able to manage the affairs of representative government. In the truest sense it was an experiment into the possibilities of self-rule.

It may be possible to argue that the American form of government initially was an experiment. Even thirty years after the Constitution was written, maybe fifty years; but at some point it stops becoming an experiment. The people and their leaders have learned the basic lessons of democracy. They have grown into the roles delineated by representative government. Two hundred years later these safegurads are still in place. When do we take the training wheels off? When are we able to walk ourselves to school; when is it no longer appropriate to set a curfew? The American people are better at democracy than any other nation in the world. We have been practicing democracy longer. We have made some mistakes. It is even fair to say we have regrets, but we have learned. Evaluations allow us an opportunity to check our progress and correct the inequities.

Checks and Balances. The same discussion can occur with *checks and balances.* The nation's founders were focused on checks and balances. They were fearful of centralized governments. Madison thought the separation of governmental power and the diversity of the government factions would work against personal aggrandizement. This was a common position of the times. What have we learned over the last two hundred years? Were their concerns well founded or has our system of government created uncertainty of its own? Is it possible to maintain a system of *checks and balances,* but with one less layer? Are there too many *checks and balances* or not enough? If the people had greater power would we need as many counteracts? The problem is that each separation of power creates an obstacle and with each obstacle there is inefficiency. Each one of these impediments costs time and money. How many *checks and balances* are really needed? Through the process of assessment we can look at other governments around the world to see what other democracies have tried, how such procedures changed their societies, what has worked, and what has not.

What is most bizarre about this question is that Congress has moved away from many of the *checks and balances* found within the Federal government. The United States Constitution gives Congress the central power to legislate. The Executive branch is designed to administer. In recent years Congress has delegated some of their own responsibilities to the Executive branch and to some degree to other governmental agencies. Congress is entitled to this prerogative. Mostly these are areas of national security or international trade. The reason deals with timeliness or proficiency of action. Yet, when this is done the concept of *checks and balances* changes. Congress should not delegate their responsibilities. Within the Constitution this is their area of accountability. On the other side of the argument is effectiveness. If the chief executive is able to manage a given issue more effectively, and Congress recognizes this, should they not be able to delegate that responsibility?

It is far better to correct those parts of the Constitution that need to be changed rather than find ways to undermine the spirit of the Constitution. Assessments regardless of the forms they may take, allow for review of the differences between what the Constitution says and what is actually being done.

Limited government.   An issue that seems to be connected to the American form of government is the idea of *limited government.* The phrase is commonly heard when describing our system of administration. This is the view that there are restrictions and parameters under which government must function. It is the idea that our national government is not all powerful, that the rights of the individual must be offset by the legitimate needs of government. Is that true? does the government have limited power? An argument could be made that the United States government has the same amount of power over its citizens as any other government, even autocratic governments. This does not mean there are no differences, the chief of which is that power is not centralized. Democracies are more open and function under greater levels of scrutiny. Yet, if consensus among all three branches of government is reached, their power is unlimited. The law or the Constitution is of little significance, for action on the part of government would be unimpeded. The only choice for the people is to wait for the next election or force of arms, both of these would have little effect on the philosophy of limited government.

This same type of discussion can occur with the Presidency. The nation's founders decided that they wanted a strong executive. A system was designed in which the Presidency had considerable power in international affairs, administration of government, control over the military, appointment of the judiciary, establishment of department heads, and the ability to veto. None of these issues are fundamentally wrong. Most world leaders have similar powers, but at what point are these ideas assessed? Do we ever as a people appraise the structure and the system itself?

Each year when we go to the polls to vote, we are evaluating the people in our government, but the real need may not be the people but structure. As some point we need to access the system itself. Even if we elect the best people imaginable into offices of leadership, if the structure and processes of government are confounded and vexing, it still will not work.

Big verses small states. A driving force that took a great deal of time at the Constitutional Convention in 1787 was the open conflict between big and small states. It was by far the most important and dominant issue at the convention, centering around how representation would be determined. Pennsylvania, Massachusetts, and Virginia comprised nearly half the nation's population. Smaller states were understandably concerned that their interests would be suffocated if they entered into a union with these larger states. This is one of the reasons why the United States has a bicameral form of government, why every state is guaranteed at least three electoral votes, and why concepts of state sovereignty were so crucial.

The question that needs to be asked is whether this is still true. Are the smaller states still concerned about being dominated by larger states? Are these concerns still justified? The point is that much has changed. Two hundred years ago the issue was the relationship between the different states; it all centered on how the states interacted with one another. One could argue that currently the issue is the relationship between the Federal government and the individual states. Most states are not overly concerned about what one state is doing or not doing; most of the concerns that the states have are with the Federal bureaucracy. The issue may not be what three states are the most powerful, but what three Federal agencies are the most formidable. If periodic assessments are never done, there is no way of knowing if the original premises are still correct.

War powers. An area of overlapping responsibility within the branches of government is the war powers. Within the United States Constitution, Congress has been given the power to declare war and equally the chief executive has been given the power to command the military. These two issues come into conflict regularly. Rarely in the last half of the twentieth century has a Presidency not had some type of disagreement with Congress over the power to wage war. The difficulty is that the President as commander in chief has the authority to order troops and equipment to any part of the world where the need may arise. The chief executive has the power to deploy. In fact, if the President was unable to marshal troops and deploy them, the title of commander in chief would be meaningless. This act alone will put service personnel in harm's way. The President may be operating in the best interest of the nation. Through a show of force the goal may even be to reduce the possibility of hostilities, but these soldiers could be fired upon and casualties might occur.

The position of Congress is that they are the only body that can declare war and, by delineation, wage war. While there may be degrees of armed conflict, if American troops have been fired upon, military service personnel have been killed, and hostilities are ongoing, then this must be a war. The position of Congress, however, is that unless they have been consulted and support the action, there can be no war.

The reality is that the United States has been involved in military conflicts throughout the twentieth century, most of which were undeclared wars. Each President has pointed to the Constitution to justify his actions and each Congress in turn has emphasized their Constitutional powers to engage in war. The dilemma is that both are right. Each branch of government is arguing the correctness of the Constitution; each branch indeed has the power it proclaims. The difficulty is the constitution itself. The nation's founders did not recognize the uncertainty that these two issues would create. Within eighteenth century American politics with its international affairs, characteristics of world order, and methods of fighting military conflicts, this division made sense. Two hundred years later the problem becomes glaring, baggage that is hauled about by generation after generation. The issue is never resolved because of the reality of what the Constitution says.

The United States Congress did pass the War Powers Act in 1973. While this piece of legislation has merit and may be helpful in cases of continuing, protracted war, the document at best must be seen as another salvo in the ongoing conflict between these two branches of government over this issue. The Supreme Court has not ruled on this issue and whether it ever would is unclear. The Court may view the conflict as a political issue and would be hard-pressed on this question in any event. It would have to determine which part of the Constitution is more important; a task that could scarcely be done without the flip of a coin.

The only way that the war powers issue could ever be properly addressed would be through an adjustment in the United States Constitution. While both branches of government may be willing to struggle over the true nature of the war power issue, they would be unwilling to rectify the issue Constitutionally. The reason is that both Congress and the Presidency currently have this power. While it may overlap, both believe they have the power to wage war. Any effort to review the issue through the Constitution would require compromise, and in the end, one of the parties would have less of a voice. As a separate issue this problem can never be fixed; it could only be addressed as part of a larger package.

Constitutions, like governments, should be goal directed. These are not documents designed to simply make us feel good. Specific goals need to be recognized and carried through. How are we to know if our goals are even being met if evaluations are not being done? One of the goals of the American Constitution was republican government. It is one of the most basic of all our established concepts—government by the people. The Founders created many exceptions and buffers, but the foundation was definitely laid. It is clear that the direction of the United States Constitution was to form a democratic system of administration. Is that being done? The question is an honest one, not meant to insult or condemn. How can we know for sure that our goals are being met unless some type of evaluation is periodically completed and at some point the entire system, our government, and the Constitution is assessed?

Businesses as self-evaluators. Businesses are the best institutions at self-evaluation. The goal is profit and businesses are continuously assessing. Paradigms are created and placed into motion. Information is placed into the system, flows through the arrangement, and comes out the other side. Whether the business is a service, manufactures a product, or deals with information does not matter. Regardless of the end result, at some point the procedure needs to be appraised. Is it efficient, does the system do what it was designed to do, is it able to stand on its own merits? A system should not be in place simply because business has always been done that way. Some level of justification is required, even if it is nothing more than custom. At least the reason is understood. We should not be led to believe that we have the best procedures or structure of government when no evidence of evaluation tells us one way or the other. Such evaluations force us to be honest with ourselves.

The United States has the longest-standing Constitution in the history of mankind, but it is not the only one. Of the 200 plus nations in the world 160 have Constitutions. The majority of these documents are changed periodically. From 1970 to 1983, of the 160 Constitutions, 101 experienced major adjustments.[1] While the United States can argue that our Constitution has had the greatest endurance, this same stability can be problematic. Few Constitutional issues ever get resolved. They reappear and are repackaged, but the Constitution limits workable options. An example can be made of the death penalty. Regardless of the position a person may take, it becomes a Constitutional issue and crisis when half the Supreme Court caseload begins to focus on this one item.[2]

These types of discussions lead in directions we are not normally comfortable with considering. Is the German constitution superior to the American Constitution? In 1949 the Federal Republic of Germany had drafted a new Constitution. It had been written by a consultative assembly formed by representatives of the eleven provinces in West Germany. It was a concentrated process but one in which had moved forward promptly. The great advantage they had was the abundance of past efforts at Constitution writing and Constitutional miscues found around the world. They borrowed heavily from the United States and read hundreds of other such efforts. In the end they created a document that was not only distinctively German, but was solidly invested in democracy. It proved to be superior. Not because they were more competent, or more proficient, but because they had the advantage of looking into the past and judging their effort by what had come before it. In the most global sense, there was an assessment of Constitutional thought and mechanics.

Constitutions are not supposed to be overhauled daily. The court systems are designed to maintain the document, to fine-tune it, but at intervals the entire document needs to be evaluated, each part, each section, each word. Without periodical assessments we are forcing our children and our grandchildren to fight the same battles that we have fought. A problem is never resolved, it is simply passed over or retraced. Only by making this type of an assessment will be able to keep our democracy fresh and our rights secure.

Chapter 28

Philosophy and Perspective

With any document of this magnitude a specific set of philosophies and concepts is needed that moves the document forward. These philosophies bring consistency and accuracy to the work. While these ideals may be difficult to obtain, especially in reference to the needs of society or the obligations to public order, they need to be stated for they represent the common thread that moves through a Constitution and the reasoning on how Articles were determined.

A new juncture of political thought. Writing a constitution requires that a person move to a different level of political perspective. Those issues of secular politics that may have served a person well in the past may not at this new juncture. It is no longer a matter of conservative or liberal thought or positions from the political right or the left. The discussion moves to a plane where governmental structure, basic human rights, and social context are the key elements. Secular politics is far more practical. It generally revolves around the allotments of the governmental pie and how large of a slice is given to each group.

A Constitution functions from a higher ground and a different set of rules apply. Once individuals begin to consider their basic social contract, what has worked politically for them in the past may no longer be valid. It is possible that a person may be conservative in governmental policies, but as soon as they move into the domain of constitutional philosophy they may find themselves advocating progressive concepts. After all the United States Constitution in reality is a liberal document.[1]

Their attitudes and philosophy will change as persons move into the realm of Constitutional thought. A conservative may be as determined as anyone to defend freedom of speech, and in turn, a liberal may be equally supportive of police powers. The old standards will no longer apply.

Surprisingly, standard views of political orientation become unimportant when a person moves to this higher plane of Constitutional philosophy. Liberal or Conservative are contemporary concepts that change with time. They adjust according to the expediency of the age or the social controversy of the day. An example of this can be found in the liberalism of the nineteenth century, which resembles twentieth century conservative thought. In reality every citizen will fluctuate with his political views depending on the issue. At one time they may advocate levels of conservatism, or the status quo, and at other times argue points of social change and progressiveness. When individuals are forced to look at their social contract the issue is far more philosophical than political. It embodies the fundamental principles of the nation. A Constitution is not simply a listing of rules, laws, and practices. It is a document that states not only who we are as a people, but also what we would like to become. By addressing the issue of Constitutions we truly have an opportunity to state what is important and what we find virtuous in ourselves.

The Process. This process should be seen in three parts. *First* is some effort to understand the American political psyche and how it relates to the Constitution. The *second* is a review of some of the philosophical concepts that the nation's founders thought were consequential. There is a reflective base to the American Constitution. Many of these ideas are still active today and part of the subconscious of the nation. The *third* part is the base from which the Proposed Constitution has been written. In many ways the philosophy of the document is as important as the actual structure. The true spirit of the document can be found from within the logical concepts of the text.

One item needs to be noted in reviewing the conduct and beliefs of the nation's founders. Even the term philosophy has changed and developed over the last two hundred years. For the drafters of the American Constitution the idea of philosophy was not a singular element. It included what we would see as separate disciplines today—ethics, psychology, sociology, reason, political science, common sense, theology, and the nature and limits of knowledge and reality (epistemology), were seen in the larger text of philosophy. Divisions in these fields were not well defined. If an effort is made to connect modern-day intellectual trends or philosophical truths to the understandings of the founders of our republic, the gap becomes even more conspicuous. An example would be discussions in idealism, materialism, absolutism, pragmatism, empiricism, or existentialism as points of philosophy. For our Founders their view of philosophy was far more purposeful.

The Founder's ideology. In many ways the views of the nation's founders were not so much points of philosophy as ideology. They were interested not in some interminable truth as much as governmental function and the aspirations of the people. It was more a matter of doctrine. They placed forth given premises as an exercise in logic and came to a given conclusion. Constitutional thought developed from their ideological activities. An example of this concept can be seen in the pamphlets they produced. Designed to be consumed by the masses, these pamphlets represented the rhetoric of the day. These writings were geared toward the ambitions of the colonies. Through the debates and rebuttals of these pamphleteers American ideology and, to a lesser degree philosophy, developed.[2]

Liberty. One of the hardest elements to describe in the American conscious is *liberty*. The nation's founders believed in it and supported the concept. It is found within their exchange of letters, their speeches, and the articles they wrote for newspapers. Both the Federalist and Anti-Federalist used the word liberty freely. It was used to explain why we needed a Constitutional government and was the standard by which each Article in the document was submitted. Yet, to find a true definition of liberty may simply be unfeasible. It is a term readily adhered to, universally accepted, profoundly supported, and proportionately misunderstood.

As a point of philosophy it is impossible to find two individuals who have the same definition for the word Liberty. Even among the nation's founders this was true. Liberty becomes little more than social convention. It is a statement without substance, a condition without fact, or an attitude without action. Though we are all a product of the American Revolution and the liberty invested in the Bill of Rights, it is not a product of political philosophy. It is a cherished eloquence of our society. If liberty is to become an issue of philosophy it is a weak one only because it is without a proper definition. It is issued more as an allegation of faith.[3]

Once saying this, and conceding the truth of the above statement, each person is invested with an individual liberty. It could be described as a natural right.[4] A like example can be found within the issue of theology. Through our own belief system, logic, and understanding of the world around us, we come to some personal agreement about issues related to religion. Regardless of the church a person attends or the creed followed, it is a personal matter. So it is with liberty. Each of us applies our own definition to the word; it becomes part of our own belief system. To remove it, to declare that it has no meaning is to slander the view of individual freedom.

The American Constitution did not walk into existence fully mature and functional. It was a matter of individuals, ideas, and events filling it out. The substance of the document began to appear as political parties started to interact and create momentum. The first two political parties developed their own personalities and goals to reflected the political philosophy of the times. John Adams, Alexander Hamilton, and John Marshall exemplified the thinking of the Federalists. On the other side were the Jeffersonians. Without oversimplifying the differences between these two parties, their views can be seen in two basic concepts—freedom and equality.

Freedom and equality. Embedded in the American consciousness are these twin ideals. While equality and freedom may represent prevailing imagery for the nation's founders and for our society at large, the reality is that these concepts endure without substance. What is even more disconcerting is that these two views are diametrically opposed. Freedom implies the ability to act independently and with a personal will, while equality represents a sameness, being at the same level or condition with others. The problem is that the more freedom a person strives for and obtains, the less equality exists between individuals. In the same context the greater the equality, the more restrictions that are placed on an individual's freedom. While the Declaration of Independence is a document founded on principles of equality, the American Constitution is founded on freedom. If these ideas are viewed as goals, then they become contradictory. Even so, they need to be discussed because both equality and freedom are important parts of the American psyche. The most that can be hoped for is a level of balance, one found more in the ebb and flow of specific issues or judicial rulings than with a critical study.

For Thomas Jefferson the more important of these two ideas was equality. It can be seen in his writings on public education, political participation, and economic justice. Jefferson was concerned about what he saw as the vice, ignorance, and poverty found in large cities. For him the greater virtue was incorporated in an agrarian society. Within his political philosophy the farmer was "the most precious part of the state" and equality established liberty.[5]

On the other side of Jefferson's provincial philosophy stand the Federalist.

Their image for America was that of a dynamic, forceful, energetic nation. A society in such freedom could correlate into economic expansion and growth. One of their chief standard-bearers was Alexander Hamilton. He had the clearest vision of what needed to be accomplished. Hamilton brought the Federalist views into focus and gave body to the political party that developed from these concepts. Hamilton placed these views before the public in the Federalist papers and Hamilton moved the northern states into action and gave them a political direction. While he may not have had the eloquence of Thomas Jefferson, his views are no less complete. He stands as the counterweight to the equalitarian philosophy of Jefferson, and for Hamilton the more important of the two concepts is freedom.

While Jefferson was more apt to expound the virtues of John Locke, Hamilton seemed to be more aligned with Thomas Hobbes. In the *Leviathan* Hobbes noted that the national states should not be limited in their functions. Police powers, keeping of the peace, governmental regulation, and planning are positive terms. These ideas promote the general prosperity of the nation. For the Federalists the Constitution was a practical matter. They used whatever philosophical theory was available to defend their position or deflect those who assailed the new document.[6] A national state was seen as more important than allowing the masses to be consumed by their own passions. If freedom was to be maintained it was more likely to occur in a powerful national state than in an uncomplicated bucolic society limited in its understandings and options.

Federalist papers. *The Federalist Papers* proved to be an excellent medium for Hamilton to express his views. Parts of both Locke and Hobbes can be found in Hamilton's writings, especially in natural law, natural rights and the social contract.[7] Hamilton's focus on national power and authority can be seen in his articles on military authority (No. 29), the capacity to tax (No. 30), the general power of the President (No. 67), appointment powers (No. 68), veto power (No. 75), and judicial supremacy (No. 81). Hamilton was a Federalist. His philosophy was based on the ideas that a dominant national body would guarantee freedom, and equally, prosperity would help ensure that freedom.[8]

The nation's founders and white supremacy. These issues of equality and freedom lead to the harshest statement about the drafters of the Constitution. As part of their belief system and as a political concept they felt that blacks were inferior to whites. This view can also be stretched to all non-Caucasians, but it was black men and women who were enslaved. No matter how the issue is covered or reshaped the nation's founders believed in white superiority. This is not something contrived. Regardless of the wording found in the United States Constitution the message remains clear. The nation's founders saw the black population as subservient, even those who resisted slavery maintained this position. It is as much a part of their basic philosophy as their opposition to a monarchy.

This points up another conflict. How is it possible that the American Constitution denotes a systematic view of segregation and is equally viewed as a document embedded in tolerance? It is another inconsistency with the document. The reality is that it is true. Both of these philosophies can be detected in the Constitution. The reasoning may only be found within the pragmatism of the nation's founders and the difference between the original text and the amendments that followed. The Bill of Rights cemented this view. Once the Bill of Rights was placed in the Constitution the overall effect was to create a more tolerant society.

The whole concept of tolerance may have been fundamentally different for the nation's founders than for us today. The word tolerance comes from the Latin word *tolero,* which means to tolerate, to put up with, or more to the point to endure. A contemporary view of toleration is more a matter of respecting the actions and beliefs of others. It is a recognition that other individuals or groups can hold opinions different from our own. This is not the same as indulging.[9]

Tolerance and John Locke. The philosopher who most affected the founding fathers was John Locke. The issue of tolerance does echo throughout his works. Locke believed that forbearance was a requirement of civil and constitutional government. He felt that to accept any other position would be a step backward for humanity.[10] Of course when the American Constitution was first created it lacked considerably in tolerance. Only with age did this philosophical issue begin to take root. Even Locke, while arguing for points of tolerance, found himself restating issues of accepted religious dogma of his time. We are a people founded on the principles of equality, individual freedom, and tolerance; it is part of our personality. To state any other position would be a denial of who we are and to stand in opposition to one of our fundamental creeds. Yet, our view of tolerance may not be the same as those of the drafters of the Constitution.

A failed philosophy. If there is one eternal element in democratic societies it is politics. Politics flows through democratic governments like sunshine on a cloudless day. It is both the oil that lubricates the machinery of government and the dirt that clogs the gears. The nation's founders spent an enormous amount of time attempting to develop a system of government in which politics did not exist. Though it became a political philosophy, it was one of their failures. In the end democratic governments cannot exist without politics, but the Nation's founders still tried. In the end the drifters of the American Constitution should be commended for their attempt, but the effort should be seen as little more than a form of alchemy. If it is to be viewed as a point of philosophy it should be seen as a failed one.

While many criticisms can be leveled at political parties they offer one great advantage. They are more apt to house ideology than the single candidate or even the special interest group. The party is where ideas are brought, debated, and discussed. It is never a perfect match, but as a forum for debate the political parties serve democracy better than any other medium. The opposite of the political party is the singular personality. The individual that moves into the political arena and by inclination, charisma, and their own force of character brings forth their own candidacy. They are motivated not by ideology, but self-interest and passion. It is difficult to develop a point of political philosophy from such a base. Yet, this is what the nation's founders were attempting to do. They wanted to create a system of government where the leadership was determined by personality rather than party doctrine.

Restricted government. Not too distant is the concept of a restricted government. As every American school child knows, the issue of checks and balances was of primary consideration for the designers of the American Constitution.[11] What at first must be seen as a system of logic, developed into a point of philosophy for the authors of the Constitution. They were fearful of centralized power and authoritarian governments. This does not mean that power totally rested with the people. It was more a matter of spreading the power across the base of the ruling elites. This issue of *checks and balances* became more of a systematic method of operation. It is found throughout the existing Constitution in every order and construct of the document.[12]

The great dilemma of the separation of powers is that it runs counter to accountability and efficacy. There is nothing destructive or corrupt in giving individuals in power the capacity to work toward those agendas or policies that they favored during their elections. Nothing is more sinister than expecting progress on a given social problem, voting people into office who have declared they are going to work on a given problem, but not allowing them the tools or the ability to accomplish these goals. This is one of the reasons why Constitutions are so important. They outline an accepted level of performance. They fix a consistent set of rules and establish a forum from which to operate and then allow the political process to give it direction and action. The process need not be so cumbersome that achievement of goals is overly complex and difficult. Those in power need to have the power to accomplish the task at hand. In turn, the people will know who is responsible for such action and programs. Blame, if that is an appropriate word, needs to be easily fixed.[13]

A Constitutional process and democracy by its very nature creates *checks and balances*. It requires that decisions be made in an open forum, with steps that need to be taken to achieve passage of a piece of legislation described and the participants needed to complete the job. The argument is not one in which responsibility is more important than *checks and balances*, but one in which responsibility is clearly understood and accepted. By the election of our leaders and the invested power of the Constitution, individuals are able to move forward and address the concerns of the nation-state.

Other forms of *checks and balances* besides those found within governmental structure may be found. We must accept the idea that there are ruling elites in our society, but they should be competing elites. The fact that elites can have conflicting views and motives represents a positive element of government. The real impediment to a healthy government is when the elites speak with one voice. Equally, there are competing interests and groups. Those who support the views of a pluralist society would argue that this represents a form of *checks and balances*.[14]

In any case, the real checks and balances for any government should come from the people. We need to have avenues by which we can easily access government and have our views heard. It is this power that will bring unpropitious government back into line.

Representative government. Modern democracies are able to function because of the apparatus of representative government. It is not so much a point of philosophy as a tool. Regardless if we are discussing a new Constitution or an old one we are still trapped by this mechanism. The reality is that the vast majority of the population is involved in the daily activities of their lives. The time required to keep informed about the inter-workings of government or the making of laws is beyond our individual ability. It has become, even in its simplest of forms, a major undertaking. Only a true activist can make that kind of commitment in time and energy. The process falls back onto the concepts of representative government.

This was a central theme of Montesquieu, a philosopher the nation's founders popularized. He supported the election of representatives, especially for large nations. Montesquieu, while a champion of representative government, felt that once elected the national leaders should be free to make their own decisions without interference or involvement by the people. He argued to do otherwise would mean the representatives would have no will of their own. What is important about this issue is not whether it is correct or not, but that it is a philosophy that the nation's founders accepted.

Competing ideas of representation. The pitfall is that there are two competing ideas. One is that a representative should represent. They are elected by the people to exemplify their views; to do anything else means that they are not truly representing the will of the people. The second issue is a dual requirement to lead. While having access to a wider range of information, a representative is also elected to lead the nation in the most appropriate direction. Despite the conflict between these two ideas, representative government is a philosophy of the American Constitution.

Most of what we view as democracy hinges on the concept of representative government. The United States is too large a nation to meet collectively. The *town meeting* may still have a place, but is unworkable with large populations. The only way that democratic governments can operate is through the conduits of elected officials, and by definition it becomes a republican form of government. Of all the structures, systems, procedures, or applications of government the one that must be the most absolute and flawless is the arrangement of representation. If this link is broken between the people and their government, nothing else matters. The government can be perfect in design, economically stable, resolute in purpose, and unbiased to all, but if the people feel that they have no part in the process then that government is as despotic as any that have preceded it. Representative government requires interaction, it must be ongoing and continuous. The moment that elected officials isolate themselves from the people autocratic government begins.

Philosophy by its nature is malleable; two knowledgeable individuals can look at the same event or concept, and come to two different conclusions. Philosophies can be nebulous and abstract. The reality though is that items move from the abstract to the concrete. A building starts as an image and becomes a proposal. These ideas are put onto paper, drawings are made, labor is supplied, materials are combined, and what was once an abstraction becomes a reality. Philosophies are little more than ideas, and the process that creates buildings also creates Constitutions. The inspiration for the American Constitution was a popular government set up on principles of freedom, equality, and law. Once stated though these ideas need to have substance. The value of the American Constitution is not in its concepts but in its utility. Through practice and use, it becomes valuable.

Proposed Constitution. Once saying this, certain issues and philosophies found within the proposed Constitution must be noted. Accepting the dominance of one conception over another allows the document to reach a level of substance. Controversy or discord will spring up. Many paths lead to the same point, but a standard is needed by which each Article is submitted, a litmus test of Constitutional considerations. It becomes a process of comparative thought. This issue is found in contrasting the current system of usage to proposed changes or adjustments. For example this text recommends not just democracy, but more democracy than we currently have in our society. If a collection of ideas or theories are presented for a given Article, the one with the highest level of democracy would be suggested or incorporated into the new Constitution.

This document rejects the idea that democracy is an ongoing experiment in America. Americans have proved a thousand fold their willingness and understanding of democratic values and concepts. Democracy allows for avenues of participation in the inter-workings of government and its related bureaucracy. The people are keenly aware of what democracy means and how it functions. While they may criticize the technocratic nature of our government, the use of regulations, the roles of our leaders, the size of our bureaucratic systems, or administrative impediments, the philosophy of democracy is not only intact but supported by the masses. Our democratic processes are not in jeopardy. America has moved beyond the experimental stage. The people have proved that greater, and even more complex levels of democratic involvement are warranted.

Government by the people. Sometimes we forget how powerful democracies can be. As a point of political philosophy democracy is simply government by the people. The goal of this Proposed Constitution is not so much an issue of redefining democracy as in restating it. It is an exercise in either direct rule by the people or through their representatives. The primary source of all political power is founded from the will of the masses. It is a principle of majority rule, with clearly understood rights of the minority. Again, when a multitude of issues present themselves, the greatest level of democracy should prevail. It is more than just having respect for those institutions that have preceded us. Ever-increasing levels of democracy are not only the goal but the aspiration of humanity. It may need to be reviewed and corrected from time to time, the masses may need education to assist with their understanding, and there will always be charismatic leaders who step forward for given causes, but that leadership must be established within the essential concepts of self-government.

Only democracies need Constitutions. A social contract stating that the people have no entitlement and should not expect to involve themselves in the governmental process would be nefarious. While all political power is invested in the people, we delegate our power to elected representatives that speak on our behalf. Ideally these representatives operate in the best interest of the masses. It is an acceptable and cooperative way to run the affairs of government. What remains and what must be understood is the link. If there is not an established and valid link between the people and their representatives then the whole system is no longer legitimate.

Even so, while accepting these principles of representative government, situations may arise where the interest of the people and government clash. The goals of government and the masses can be different. This type of disagreement simply occur on the style of leadership, the perks given to our representatives, or it may be something more profound such as a military conflict. The philosophy and the spirit of the democracy remains with the people. They should always have the last word in the process.

One last item about democracy—it should not be seen as all or nothing. It is not like a light bulb, turned either on or off. It is a matter of degrees, a spectrum. A given republic may fall at one point along the scale, some being more democratic than others. A new Constitution should move the government and nation forward. While it may be impossible to define the maximum or perfect level of democracy, the journey is still a valid one. With each generation, each new regime, each new Constitution a forward marker should be reached. Some argue that we are not a democratic state; we are an evolving democratic nation. It is not even clear that humankind as a species can ever reach a point of faultless democracy, but that does not mean that we do not work toward that goal. If there is one truly American experience it is this ascent.

Political integration. One of the philosophies rarely discussed and scarcely understood is the issue of political integration. The United States is a product of a Union. We are a Union. Our strength as a nation, the military power we project, the economic capacity of the nation, and resources behind our educational systems are all enhanced by this one concept. It is our Union that makes us resolute and potent as a nation. This point of political philosophy is so readily accepted by both the masses and the ruling elitists in our society that the question is never addressed. There are no conflicts, no counter movements, no literature demanding change, but without doubt it is a driving and animated force within the framework of American government. Without political integration we would be but a shadow of the nation we represent. As an issue of philosophy it appears only once in the American Constitution. "...in order to form a more perfect union...," but it is by far the most powerful axiom in the document and one all future Constitutions must recognize.

A theme that runs through the proposed Constitution is the importance of healthy institutions. A point of philosophy that may not be fully understood but that is critical to the well being of the nation-state is the balance that is found within the different institutions. In part it returns to how Socrates saw society. His view was that society was but a sum of its parts. For him it represented three institutions or classes; the monarchy or ruling elites, the military or soldier-guardians, and the artisan or merchant class.[15] These were the core of society and its most fundamental parts. This philosophy can be extended to modern society within our own institutions of (1) government, (2) family, (3) the military, (4) business, (5) church, (6) the media, (7) education, (8) labor, and (9) foundations. A form of checks and balances can be found within the backdrop of how these institutions relate to one another. The greater the democracy the greater these institutions are in balance. Despotism can be found in those societies where one institution or a few dominate the others. A Constitution must take this essential principle into account and allow each of our institutions not only to survive—but to thrive.

Justice. The one fundamental goal in drafting a new Constitution must be justice. It matters not if the definition of justice is a balance of our institutions, equal protection under the law, or basic standards of conduct. No matter how elusive this idea may be, both society and the law must strive for justice. It becomes a primary reason why we have society. Again, the problem is that true justice may be little more than the destination. There are exceptions and contradictions in this Proposed Constitution as there are in the American Constitution. The hope, and the goal, should be a reduction of these exemptions and political anomalies. Every exception that is found in a Constitution represents an injustice, and the fewer these items the better. A Constitution is a collective part of the law. There is only one purpose for the law and that is justice; all other items are subservient.

If justice cannot be found in a society, then what is created is hypocrisy. If one great evil can be associated with government, it is a pretense of virtue. Dual standards are inadmissible and harmful within any society. Rules simply need to apply to all individuals equally and honestly. The great hypocrisy with the creation of the American Constitution was slavery. In the past the United States Congress has passed laws that affected other institutions in society, but not themselves. While this was a common practice with labor law and issues related to discrimination, it becomes sanctimonious. The continued existence of the Electoral College is another form of hypocrisy. To state that our chief executive is directly elected by the people and then shield the process by use of the Electoral College seems pretentious. It becomes little more than propaganda. Hypocrisy taints the scope of democracy and places significant limitations on the concepts of freedom.

This Proposed Constitution presents a particular view of government. Government does not represent a great evil. It aids us collectively in doing what we cannot do individually. It builds roads, bridges, highways, and aqueducts. As an entity, it speaks for us with a common voice in the world community. It protects the weak and frail. It helps educate and creates a set of laws we all must follow. Government is neither good nor bad. It matters little if government is big or small. This does not mean that systems and structures cannot be set up to make the process more energetic and effective, but government is not corrupt. Good people, properly elected, with insight and animation will always serve the goals of the society better than the perfectly engineered bureaucracy. The real purpose of a Constitution is not to protect us from offensive government, but to protect us from the wicked among us. Madison was right, "If men were angels, no government would be necessary."[16]

Security. One of the standard issues of why we have government, and to a lesser degree Constitutions, is security. There is hardly a philosopher who, at some point in writing, did not address the issue of security. The theory is that people enter into their social compact for mutual protection. Through the collective spirit of government we are able to defend ourselves, our families, and our property. This has always been a strong argument and the reason is that there is no valid alternative. Neutrality is not a defense against aggression. The only fundamental problems are those that hide behind the issue of security. They press forward their own agendas by covering themselves with the disguise of protecting society. The military-industrial-complex will always seek higher levels of security than are needed. The issue becomes a matter of degree. Even so, security is an important part of why we have government. All governments must protect. If they do not they are without validity. The problem is more a matter of how much security we want, need, or can afford. This question becomes a political question.

Measurability. Another principle of a good Constitution is whether it is measurable. Generalities serve no purpose. We all support "good government," but what is the measure of an honorable government? The point is that Articles in a Constitution need to be clearly defined and understood. If elections are to be held on a given day, then without exception or compromise, the election is to be held on that date. If levels of ethical behavior are required from our elected officials, then specific rules dictating ethical conduct must be incorporated into the document. If the people expect fair treatment from positions of authority, then the nature of that treatment needs to be comprehensible and consistent. The more vague the Constitution, or the more vague it becomes, the easier it will be for individuals to use deception to move forward on their own agendas. It is not in the interest of good government to interpret issues in a borderless fashion. A good Constitution is one that is straightforward and conclusive.

Character and public service. Creating a Constitution does incorporate some general ideas that are not found in the document itself—ideas that may be important, even mandatory, but cannot be easily described. They become buried in the structure. The configuration of the document aims to develop the type of person or character needed for the job at hand. The question with American politics has always been; why does an individual, well educated and knowledgeable, run for public office? Why would an individual spend millions of dollars for a job that pays only in the thousands? Even allowing for points of ideology and social change, the influence that one person may have from within the system may be marginal. The large sums of money may be better served in direct support of the programs that the political candidate wishes to endorse. If an argument is made that the motive is public service, then why do so many barriers develop between the people and their elected official? Why is it when part of the constituency telephones a member of Congress, they end up talking to their staff? Why is it that access is determined by campaign contributions?

The most important of these questions concerns what type of person or character we want in our political officials. Is there a way to design into the structure of government systems that would create or parallel the type of personalities we want from our public servants? This is an extremely difficult undertaking and by its very nature may be flawed or impossible to achieve, but it seems at least appropriate to consider these ideas when drafting a Constitution.

What type of personality currently drifts toward politics as a profession? It would be unfair to believe that some positive elements did not exist. As with police work or social work, individuals who run for political office believe that they can make a difference. They believe that their political ideas will improve the nation and benefit the people. Their well meaning intentions may be compromised by the reality of politics and what is required to get reelected, but they continue to work toward the overall betterment of the people. Another type of office seeker will focus more on single issues or represent a specific group. They see some point of injustice or some great wrong in society and aim to correct this problem. All other issues are secondary. They see their constituency as those who support their ideas and beliefs. The problem is that their patronage may not even be in their home district, but much more national. Another group is propelled into politics for a far more personal reason. Their character is far more narcissistic; individuals that are attracted by the limelight. They may find that their oratory skills were able to move the masses; they find that they have the skills to manipulate the media, and they move through the political system playing the part that is required. This does not mean that only this last group has an ego. Any individual who runs for political office has an ego. It is the extreme case that is most dubious, individuals that are characterized by their own grandiosity. They are captivated by politics because of the glamour.

This last group can be the most detracting. While they may possess the personality and the temperament for politics, this may not directly relate well to their representative role within government. A structure needs to be developed by which the alluring effects of politics are removed, and the political environment is one of ideas and public service. This is an extremely difficult process. From a very general sense the only way to achieve such a goal is to have a greater participation by the masses. The gap is that government is a matter of administration and politics is a matter of seduction. They do not connect very well.

Changing the Constitution. In writing a new Constitution one of the issues that comes to the surface is how diverse the changes will be. The fact that a new social contract is being written represents change; it is certain that changes go with the process. Yet, clear-cut reasons why such an adjustment is needed must be made. It cannot be helter-skelter. If the Constitution were to be changed so that each state had three or four Senators, it would not serve any valid purpose. There is no reason to make such a change and there is no logic behind it. This is even true with how long a person serves in an office. The reality is that it matters little if a mayor of a town serves a term in office of two, four, or six years. The assertion centers on little more than a degree. Sound minds can make a valid argument for each of those intervals, but many such immaterial issues represent themselves in writing a

Constitution. They need to be seen as inconsequential.

Machiavelli. There is one last haunting view when discussing the philosophical text of the American Constitution. It is generally believed that the nation's founders were well read and were familiar with the works of Plato, Locke, Hobbes, Voltaire, and Montesquieu. Partial discussions of these reflective thinkers can be found in their correspondence. In reading through their writings and letters there seems to be one philosopher that was rarely noted—Niccolo Machiavelli. His absence seems conspicuous and some level of discussion would seem to have been in order, even if it was a rejection of Machiavelli's views. His works would have been equally available.[17]

Machiavelli would have taken a far darker view of the human personality and condition. He would have seen the masses as being focused on self-interest, indulgence, and worst of all apathy. He would have argued that the lower classes have to be managed rather than included in government. The conjecture, which may be an unfair one, concerns how much of the restrictions and limitations the drafters of the Constitution placed on democratic government were a product of Machiavelli's views of human behavior. This issue does become a concern. When the founding fathers developed our system of government with limitations on direct participation by the masses was this a Machiavellian philosophy?

Even if it were true that humans are depraved, it would make no difference. Government is not created to serve the elites, the rich, or the powerful. It is a construct for all the people and the masses must be brought into the process. It is no more correct to believe that the people are motivated by their own compulsions and gratification than that they are not. The issue is unmistakable. If you want people to act responsibly, then you give them responsibility. The jury system can be used as an example of how well the people do with responsibility. While many avoid this obligation and find ways to excuse themselves from serving, once chosen to sit on a jury the average citizen displays complete creditability and reliability Once seated she or he takes the responsibility very seriously.

A new Constitution must remove this blurred line of intent. A Constitution exists to help the people manage the affairs of government. It is the simplest of all concepts, and when someone argues a different point of view the objective is to limit self-government and the power of the people.

Chapter 29

Past Efforts at Constitutional Reform

In the nation's past a number of efforts have been made to address social inequality or perplexity in the United States Constitution. The amendment process is the first, and probably the easiest, of several avenues. Each year in Congress numerous amendments are proposed to the Constitution, and in the course of our history thousands of such amendments have been filed. Each focuses on a specific issue or problem, including everything from campaign finance reform, the Electoral College, abortion, school prayer, and term limits. In Congress alone more than 10, 900 amendments have been filed.[1]

Six additional amendments not ratified. Besides the twenty-seven amendments added to the Constitution, six others were passed by the Congress but failed to be ratified by three-fourths of the states as required. One such amendment was part of the original Bill of Rights submitted to Congress in 1792. Actually twelve Articles of the Bill of Rights were submitted to the states for ratification. Oddly, one of these Articles was finally approved two hundred years later and became the Twenty-Seventh Amendment to the Constitution. The other Article has languished in Amendment purgatory. It dealt with the representative ratio, an issue that still has not been properly addressed. This Amendment was an attempt to fix the representative ratio by allowing one Representative to 50,000 persons with at least a minimum of two hundred members in the House of Representatives.[2]

Another Amendment was drafted and sent to the states in 1810 relating to nobility, titles, and receiving annuities from foreign powers. It stated that any individual who accepted such titles, offices, honors, or money from another nation without permission from Congress would lose US citizenship.[3]

The third such unratified amendment, referred to as the Corwin Amendment, occurred in 1861. Congress had passed the Constitutional modification forbidding them from interfering with or abolishing the institution of slavery. President Buchanan signed this amendment, though his signature was not a requirement, a fact that seems odd considering the nature of the Amendment.

Even Lincoln offered support for this Amendment.[4]

An Amendment to the Constitution that dealt with child labor passed Congress and was sent to the states in 1926. The goal was for Congress to decide what represented child labor and to restrict its usage. Twenty-eight states passed the Amendment, but this still left the Amendment several votes short of passage.

The Equal Rights Amendment was another revision to the Constitution that did not quite clear the states. Though passed by Congress in 1972 with the object of ensuring equal rights for women, by the time this Article reached the states the issue had become a matter of male and female roles in society.[5] In the end not only did this Amendment fail to pass, but some states assemblies voted down the Amendment after it had been passed in an earlier legislative session.

This brings up another Constitutional question. The last such Article passed by Congress and sent to the states for ratification dealt with the District of Columbia. If this Amendment had been passed the District would have been treated as a state and the people within the District would have been entitled to equal representation similar to any other state.[6] The reasons for nonpassage are many, but it is generally believed the states did not feel comfortable with the demands that this new state would place upon the Federal government.

The flash point. The general indication is that amendments represent just a minor modification to the Constitution. After all only one issue is being addressed. The reality is that they are far more profound. They are the flash point of our society and government. The real essence of democracy is found hovering over these issues rather than the day-to-day business of government. The number and type can be used to examine the health of the nation. The clamor for amendments, their type, and frequency may be more important than those actually passed. They tell a great deal about a nation.

Methods of changing the Constitution. While all of the twenty-seven Amendments to the United States Constitution have emerged from Congress, a second method of changing the document can be employed: the state conventions. While the states have the power to call for a convention to address issues or amendments, many criticize this technique. They are concerned that the mandate for a convention could not be set in advance. Others note that such a system is untried and this presents pitfalls in itself, while still others are fearful of a runaway convention eliminating individual rights. Most of these concerns center on control issues by established ruling entities, and their apprehensions are unjustified. It is no more likely that a new Constitutional Convention would strip away individual liberties than the one in 1787. It symbolizes little more than institutional paranoia.

The great advantage of a Constitutional Convention is not the event itself, but the leverage it can bring against Congress. The Federal government and its many branches have interests that are unique unto their own. A movement to limit terms for members of Congress has gained numerous supporters. Yet, people have a natural tendency not to restrict or eliminate their own jobs. Congress has not unconditionally embraced this concept. If such a program or amendment ever came into existence it would be as a product of massive outside pressure. A state's Constitutional Convention process could represent this type of pressure.

Election reform. This type of urging on the part of the various groups is what brought about the Seventeenth Amendment in 1913. The Senate recognized that if this body were directly elected by the people, many of their membership would not survive politically. The "good old boy" network that was common within the states would no longer be valid if Senators had to run for general election. The amendment met with considerable resistance. Calls for a convention are what moved the issue along and helped ensure passage of this amendment.[8]

Another Constitutional reform comes in the mode of scholarly research or review. Scores of individuals have advocated various Constitutional adjustments at different levels. Noting the flaws within the current system, many have suggested changes. The process becomes political, especially if a person attempts to bring such ideas into the forefront of the public awareness. Most of these suggestions are made in the broadest sense. The United States Constitution is one of the most written about documents in the world. It is difficult to critique the work without drawing some conclusion, analysis, or criticism about at least one section of the document. Those who have written about Constitutional modification and reform come from many walks of life and a complete list would be rather extensive.[9]

Of course, such listings of reformers or Constitutional advocates is limited and represents only a sampling of those interested in Constitutional amelioration.

Even the jurist and great commentator of the United States Constitution, Joseph Story, had suggested changes in the document. He felt that cabinet officers should be members of Congress.[10] Woodrow Wilson also wrote about adjustments that needed to be made in our social contract. He had brought a wide range of experiences to his examination. Wilson was not only a political scientist but an attorney, a college professor, an administrator, and finally President of the United States.[11]

Arguing verses writing a new Constitution. There is a clear difference between arguing that we need a new Constitution, or an adjustment to the old one, and actually writing a new social contract. Arguing for a new Constitution without giving details is far more abstract. To write a new document requires less theoretical and more particulars. The level of criticism can be considerably different and the effort requires a distinct set of objectives. If a person writes a new Constitution, it also becomes a formal proposal. It is placed at the highest level of social and political analysis. Recognizing the explicit scrutiny and the level of controversy that a new Constitution would have to undergo, a number of authors have attempted the process. Steven Boyd reviewed about ten such documents in his work *Alternative Constitutions for the United States.* John Vile believes that there may be even more such efforts.[12] Such items do have a place, even if it is nothing more than to show that such an effort is possible.

Past Proposed Constitutions. Very few proposed Constitutions for the United States actually reach the public eye or obtain publication. It seems odd in the fact that there is an incomparably high level of scholarly and social interest in the Constitution, but it is not translated into the next step which would be to draft a new social contract. Even so, there have been a few that have made the effort.

William Wedgwood. One of the earliest such works was by William Wedgwood. He was active in the Whig Party and the City University of New York. His Constitution, published in 1861, was a direct effort to address many of the political and public issues of the day. Wedgwood recognized that the American Civil War represented a Constitutional crisis, and his response was to write a new document, one designed to rectify the powerful social issues of that day. He advocated the abolition of slavery and supported education reform.[13]

Victoria C. Woodhull. Another Constitution was written by Victoria C. Woodhull. Truly an electrifying individual of her time, Woodhull was a suffragette and an ally of Susan B. Anthony ideals. A newspaper publisher, Woodhull ran for President of the United States in 1872. Part of her platform was the advocacy of a new Constitution. She also felt that uniform Constitutions were important for all the states. Woodhull was seen as a radical of her times, if for no other reason than because of her position on free love, but her chief goal was to address social inequalities within our society, both in gender and in race.

James West. In the 1890s three Constitutions appeared in print. One such document was generated by James West, an attorney who had served as the prosecuting attorney for Springfield, Missouri. A populist by nature, he was resentful of trusts and banking power. One of his goals was to limit the financial intrigues found within Congress. Always interested in politics, West published his new Constitution early in his career and three years before he was admitted to the bar in 1893.[14]

Frederick Upham Adams. A second Constitution during this time was produced by Frederick Upham Adams. A newspaper writer and reporter, Adams had taken a different approach in writing his document. It was included in a novel he wrote called *President John Smith*.[15] A best-seller in its day, the novel proved to be popular with the public. It described the election process of the chief character, John Smith, and the implementation of the new Constitution. The scope of the new social contract was majority rights and the belief that the masses became more active in the political process by being able to vote on the critical issues facing government and society. Within this novel was found Adam's new Constitution.

Henry Morris. A similar approach was taken by author Henry Morris. His novel, published in 1898, was titled *Waiting for the Signal*.[16] Morris took a far darker direction with his work, focusing on governmental corruption and a time of revolutionary change. The intent of his Constitution was far more socialist in nature. The document goes into great detail on tax regulations, even to the point of listing tax rates.

Eustace Reynolds. A pamphlet was published in 1915 by Eustace Reynolds. Very little is known about Reynolds whose booklet does not seem to have enjoyed a wide readership. She preserved the majority sections of the 1787 Constitution wishing only to add segments encouraging antiwar provisions. The main changes in Reynold's Constitution was the connecting of the American Constitution to international legislative assembles, including a world court. The goal seemed to be to make the Constitution more universal in scope.[17]

Hugh Hamilton. Another Constitution was published in 1938 by Hugh Hamilton. While little is know about him, his chief concern seems to be social justice. Hamilton did place forth one interesting idea. He felt that whenever the Supreme Court struck down a piece of legislation, they also had to outline why the item was declared unconstitutional and what type of wording or amendment would be needed to make the item valid.[18]

Thomas Upham. A few years later Thomas Upham wrote a new Constitution that was published in 1941. A Boston playwright, Upham focused his document on the obligations of citizenship and addressed many of the social problems of the day. Though democratic, Upham was also an isolationist who wanted to prohibit residence abroad, restrict foreign trade, and mandate trading balances.[19]

Rex Tugwell. The most famous new Constitution came from Rexford Tugwell, an economics professor who had worked in the Roosevelt Administration. Tugwell was a spokeperson for the "New Dealers," and had helped to develop many of the social welfare programs of his era. He felt that the United States Constitution no longer reflected the realities of our society. Tugwell was a technocrat and his Constitution reflected this concept. He felt society needed planning, especially economic planning.[20]

Lelard Baldwin. Another academician who wrote a new Constitution in the 1970s was Lelard Baldwin. A librarian, administrator, and historian, he was chiefly concerned that both state and federal governments were no longer able to perform their Constitutional function. Baldwin supported a unicameral legislative body and a decentralized political system. Baldwin's work must be seen as a valid effort at Constitutional reform, though it received little public attention.[21]

Common elements. A comparison of these works is not easy, since each was written in different times and with divergent intents. Even so, all maintained

Legislative, Executive and Judicial branches of government. All but one continue to call the chief executive President. That the chief executive officer would be commander in chief of the armed forces and have the power to appoint individuals to governmental positions seems to be a consensus of the reformers. The President is also responsible for the conduct of foreign affairs and the implementation of the laws of the nation. Beyond this point issues become more varied. In only six cases is the President chosen by popular election. Terms of office vary considerably, from as little as four to as much as ten years. The Legislative branch of government seems to have even greater divergence. Terms of office range from one to six years, and in two cases there are term limits. All the Constitutions outline membership requirements and in one document financial worth stipulations are laid out. Additionally, representation varies. There is a range from 1 to 30,000 up to 1 to 500,000, though not all of these Constitutions state a ratio for representation. All of these Constitutions maintain some form of judiciary. The differences lie in less weighty matters—the terms of office, age requirements, and the number of justices. In one of the Constitutions there is a system of electing jurists to the Supreme Court. Most of the issues deal with structure.

The greatest disparity between these documents seems to be in jurisdiction. This becomes even more complex when the lower Federal courts are considered. Each of these proposed Constitutions seem to take a different view on who has the last say.

Individual rights are consistently mentioned. Items related to trial by jury, freedom of speech, and unreasonable search and seizures are likewise uniformly found in these Constitutions. While they may not all list the same rights, nevertheless a package of personal rights is found within the work. If one common theme is found in all these documents it is that power is invested with the people. This may appear in many forms, but it is articulated as a common purpose of Constitutions.

If all these Constitutions share a common problem, it is that the crisis of the times seeps into the documents. It is possible to judge the document from within the time it was written, whether it be the populist movement of the late nineteenth century, the socialist movement of the early twentieth century, or the suffrage movement. Policy is subject to change, but if such issues are placed in a Constitution they become more than simple policy. The Constitution becomes a durable social and political system. Along with the Article or statement comes a list of patterns of behavior and ethical conduct. It is no longer a policy but a method of interaction and relationships.

Those who write new Constitutions do send a message—a view that there is a chronic and unstable condition to the current document. The larger the number that are published and the greater the intensity of the debate, the more the need for a new Constitution. New Constitutions do become a signal. They represent something very different from an amendment or the amendment process. The prediction is that the number and diversity of such efforts will only increase in the future. It seems unavoidable.

Steven Boyd in his examination of different Constitutions developed to replace our current document noted how extremist such a position can be. He wrote the following:

> "Proponents of a new constitution face an enormous task and their proposals are doubly radical. They are by definition 'radical,' for they propose a course of action incompatible with both the amending provisions of the Constitution of 1787 and the notion of change through interpretation. And they are radical in terms of the profound political and social changes their constitutions envision."[22]

Boyd noted that such efforts are generally assigned to the "intelligentsia." While they may have importance to the marketplace of ideas, they exist outside the mainstream of political concepts and propositions.

The issue of a new Constitution is a radical concept. Boyd is correct. It does fall outside the process of normal political objectives and the management of Constitutional order, but there exists on the other side of this issue an equally powerful and perspicacious statement by Thomas Jefferson. In the elequance that is common is Jefferson's writings he noted:

"I am not an advocate for frequent changes in laws and Constitutions, but laws and institutions must go hand in hand with the progress of the human mind. As that becomes more developed, more enlightened, as new discoveries are made, new truths discovered and manners and opinions change, with the change of circumstances, institutions must advance also to keep pace with the times. We might as well require a man to wear still the coat which fitted him when a boy as civilized society to remain ever under the regime of their barbarous ancestors."[23]

The truth lies somewhere in the middle. The issue is never one in which others have tried and failed, or even that you have tried and failed; it is the effort that is most important.

Part Four: A Newly Revised Constitution for the Twenty-First Century

Chapter 30

Problems Not Addressed in the Proposed Constitution

In this Proposed Constitution certain problems are not addressed while others appear to have no valid or appropriate solutions. One such item is *policy making* on the part of the court system. The courts are well within their authority to declare that a course of action or procedure of government is unconstitutional. It is another matter entirely to declare an issue unconstitutional while also moving a step further by putting forth remedies to those problems.

Affirmative Duties. Yet the Federal court system has done just that to a wide range of problems. The courts have been aggressive in changing the conditions within prisons, school systems, mental health institutions, and hospitals. They have mandated what procedures will be followed and the amount of money to be spent on various social programs. The courts have redesigned school districts and Congressional districts. Referring to this process as an "affirmative duty" they have connected the process to the Constitution. This is more than prohibiting improper actions on the part of government; this is a hands-on approach to social change.

If the Federal courts are to be criticized for this type of judicial action, then part of the blame must also be shouldered by Congress or the state governments. *Judicial Activism* are generally problems for which the government and its political bodies are unwilling to accept a leadership role. Nonetheless, the nation's founders would have rejected this function outright or have been astonished by such judicial practices. Nor is any easy way out of this dilemma likely. As much as any governmental body, the courts exist to persevere the issues of basic human justice. Most of these affirmative duties fall into this category. Both the American Legislative and Executive branches are trapped in the concept of majority rule and special interests. Their course of actions are dictated by what is politically expedient. It is up to the courts to pursue issues of justice, even if it is outside the structure of the Constitution.

Heads of Government and State. Another issue not addressed in the

Proposed Constitution that represents a major project flaw is the dual issue of Head of State and the Head of Government. While the United States Constitution does not address this issue directly, over time and usage the President has become both the Head of State and the Head of Government. In most democracies around the world this is not the case, and especially in the parliamentary system where the two responsibilities are split between two persons. This issue of heads of state and government should not be seen as a minor problem. It is a major defect of the United States Constitution and, because it was not solved, a major problem with the Proposed Constitution.

The argument against the Chief Executive serving as both Head of Government and Head of State is that the arrangement creates too much power into the hands of one individual. The President is an elected official with the job of administering the government. It is a hands-on, daily activity that is political and exclusive. We allow our Presidents to act in a biased, self-seeking manner because they were elected with a given agenda and are united to a given political party. A Head of State is a different matter. The Head of State speaks for all the people with the most lofty intent. They embody the essence of what is the nation-state. The office is a symbol equal to the flag or the national anthem. Hence, the justification of allowing one person, especially a political entity, to externalize everything that represents the spirit of the country seems to be a deficiency in the system.

In the case of Great Britain the Head of Government is the Prime Minister and the Head of State is the reigning monarch. For the British this has proved to be a valid system. The monarchy exists at the fringe of government with no power or control over its operations. Appropriately the monarchy becomes the symbol of the nation-state. In the United States by contrast the mere mention of allowing a monarch a toehold into our society would be seen as repugnant. It stands in opposition of everything America has achieved. Another standard is to allow one set of balloting for a President and another for a Prime Minister. In this case the President would serve the more ceremonial position of Head of State. The problem with either system is that both create an additional governmental layer. While conceded that the Head of State is an important position within government, an appraisal of the added costs is also a valid consideration. Nor are the cost benefits for a separate Head of State clear.

The problem of having both positions nestled with the same person is that a division is no longer drawn between these two concepts. If an individual or group stands in opposition to the Chief Executive it is no longer a political issue, but a national one. The leader becomes not simply an executive officer of a party, but the symbol of the nation-state. To be in conflict with the Head of State becomes little more than heresy. It becomes unpatriotic and the individual finds herself or himself in opposition to the very principles of the country.

One is not apt to find an easy way through this predicament. If it is not otherwise stated in the Constitution, the chief executive will annex both jobs. If two separate positions are fabricated they represent an additional cost and a collateral function of government. At least for this proposed Constitution the issue has not been solved.

Double Jeopardy. Another issue that does not seem to have been correctly addressed with this new Constitution concerns double jeopardy. For the nation's founders this issue of double jeopardy was very clear. An individual could not be tried for the same offense twice. From a historical standpoint criminal statutes were far more limited and the choices less noticeable. As example, the jurist of the eighteenth century had a far clearer picture of what represented murder than today's jurist. The three distinctions were murder, self-defense, or an accident. In our contemporary society degrees of murder are several and we even define subcategories such as manslaughter or wrongful death.

Currently a person can be tried in criminal court and, regardless of the verdict, have the same issue brought before a civil court. While the standards may be different and the purpose of the two-court system dissimilar, for the individual placed in this situation it can feel like double jeopardy.

The real problem is not criminal or civil court, but state and Federal courts. It is magnified when state and Federal courts, and their different statutes, are taken into account. A person might feasibly be charged in a state court for murder and in a Federal court for civil rights violations. The same person can appear in two different locations, before two different judges, and with the same evidence being submitted, yet be seen as two distinct cases. These same examples could be used with a state murder case and a Federal racketeering charge. Such instances become a process of diluting the concept of double jeopardy and the safeguard that it designates.

Double jeopardy is an important issue. The defense that Constitutions represent is to oppose self-serving governments. It is not so much the knock in the middle of the night that we must be fearful of, but more the endless stream of subpoenas and writs. It will take a toll as readily as the punishment to the flesh.

This issue was not addressed in the Proposed Constitution. While double jeopardy appears in the document, so would the collection of state and Federal statutes. It becomes another issue that sill needs to be resolved.

Chapter 31

Why A New Constitution

At first glance it may seem arrogant and egotistical for an individual to write a new Constitution for the United States. The American Constitution after all is an icon of our nation and a symbol of democracy. Around the world nations have looked toward the United States Constitution not only as a system for popular government, but have accepted large parts of the document for their own Constitutions. It has been praised, modeled, respected, and revered. It is the pillar of our government and thread that binds our society. These issues are conceded. The American Constitution regardless of its flaws is a great document. It has served not only the United States but mankind. There is far more good in that document than bad, but once saying this it is also believed that we can do better.

As for any level of personal talent in Constitutional writing no such mastery is implied. In fact the Proposed Constitution that is being presented is more of an exercise into the possibilities of Constitutional options. While it is conceded that the Proposed Constitution is the preference of the originator, it is also a personal choice. Any individual or group of people given the responsibility of designing a Constitution would come up with different variations of the theme. This Proposed Constitution is not the last word in Constitution writing. An alternative needs to be written. It allows for comparisons between the two documents and helps generate a debate as to the nature of Constitutional government.

Another reason why this Proposed Constitution was written deals with hypocrisy. It seems incredibly unjust to criticize a document, especially the image of democracy that the American Constitution represents, without equally putting forth an alternative. There must be a willingness to accept equal criticism. It becomes a point of fairness and integrity. The pressure is always on the Progressive for they must not only articulate the problem or flaw in the current system but put forth a valid alternative as well.

To write a new Constitution can also be seen as a teaching aid. There is no better way of understanding the difficulties and problems related to writing a Constitution than by writing one. There is no substitute. Each one of the dilemmas the Founding Fathers faced becomes far more real when that same road is traveled. The drafting of a new Constitution requires the asking of the same questions about many of the same issues. A respect is developed for the process and it sheds light on items which normally would not be understood. It represents an act, and contemplation, few would comprehend without entering into such procedures. History can be helpful in understanding constitutional systems, but by experiencing the process gives an individual an entirely different outlook.

The greatest trap that any institution can fall into is the inability to determine what is best to keep and what needs to be discarded. Old is not always better than new, nor is new always better than old. The trick is in the skill of knowing when it is best to move on, or defend the status quo. Something that is unchanging will limit options and choices. The people will never experience the cornucopia that life has to offer. In the same text, if change is ongoing and constant it creates of society without roots or stability. It becomes a society without a birthright. The key is in knowing when it is best to modify the existing system. In the end the test has to be growth. While change may be inconvenient, and at times hard, if we gain from the process, in the end we have grown from the experience then it is worth the effort. There are two problems. One is that we will not know the outcome until it has been completed, and second, we are constantly changing regardless if we want to or not. Heraclitus, the Greek Philosopher, wrote, "Change alone is Unchanging." To apply these issues to the American Constitution, the document is changing but under the current system we have no input.

Another issue which should be addressed is the symbol that it would represent. A new Constitution would denote a new beginning, a sign post in the history of our nation. It would be possible to place events on one side of this marker or the other. This is what we were and this is what we are now. There are elements of American character that belong in a different place and time, items of the most dark of intent, and the lower forms of human behavior. A new constitution would allow us an opportunity to adjust our own views of how we see ourselves.

One view does need to be expressed. The more prevailing and current the constitution, the less likelihood of governmental abuse. Government wields great power and it is our social contract that checks this authority. Power is the most pervasive of all the addictions. The only defense for the people is to build firm structures of government, document our rights, and keep the activities of our leader in the light of day. It is a Constitution that will best protect the people from any betrayal or misuse of power. An interesting statement was one made by Eric Hoffer. He noted, "Those in possession of absolute power can not only prophesy and make their prophecies come true, but they can also lie and make their lies come true."[1] We must be vigilant. There is always a risk, but the greater risk falls on the side of doing nothing. There is nothing wrong with trusting our national leaders and our government, but it should be done with the Constitution in our back pocket.

Proposed Constitution for the United States of America

PREAMBLE.

We the people, in order to form a more perfect union, enhance democracy, maintain our liberties, promote the general welfare, provide for the common defense, commission for a stable society, and verify axioms of law do hereby ordain and establish this Constitution.

ARTICLE 1.

Continuation of Obligations

The document presented heretofore shall be considered a continuation of the rights and responsibilities of the current Constitution and all testaments presented before it. In those cases where points of Constitutional law have been firmly established and clearly understood by the people, those doctrines shall remain in force and ongoing. Only when a specific adjustment has been noted within this document should a new arrangement be promoted. All debts, contracts, agreements, treaties, obligations, covenants, and conventions shall remain in force.

Congress

ARTICLE 2.

Parameters of Congress

The legislative powers of the Federal government shall consist of two houses with an upper and lower chamber. The process shall be by parliamentary design with the House of Representatives denoting the lower house and the Senate denoting the upper house. A session of Congress shall run from January 2nd to November 15th of each year.

ARTICLE 3.

Record Keeping

A record shall be published and given general circulation, with exception to only those areas or proceedings held in secret. Debates and deliberations in both Houses shall be public.

ARTICLE 4.
Congressional Rules

Section 1. Congressional Rules. Both Houses of Congress shall determine their own rules of order, procedure, and quorum. The House of Representatives and the Senate each shall choose its own officers and leaders. Each body of Congress shall judge the election, returns, and qualifications of its own members. Congress shall determine its own rules for censure and expulsion of its membership.

Section 2. Membership Rules. An individual may not be a member of both Houses simultaneously.

Section 3. Compensation. The Representatives and Senators shall be compensated for their services and work as prescribed by law. Such compensation shall be taken from the Treasury. No member of Congress shall be employed for pay outside of their respective bodies without written permission from their legislative leadership and only when no conflict of interest applies. Rules related to honorariums shall be determined by each legislative chamber. All changes in compensation of either House's membership shall not take effect until after a general election.

Section 4. Ancillary positions. Both Houses of Congress shall have a sergeant at arms, an administrative clerk, and a chaplain. The administrative clerk shall accept petitions and letters from the public, and assist with the record keeping of the legislative process. The public shall have open and free access to the office of administrative clerk. The administrative clerks shall be civil servants. The sergeant at arms shall be appointed by the leadership of each assembly. The sergeant at arms shall be responsible for the compliance of Congressional rules, the guardianship of the elected officials, and the maintenance of all legislative equipment.

Section 5. Residency. Members of Congress must live in the State from which they are elected.

Section 6. Consistency of the Law. It is the responsibility of Congress to faithfully execute the laws of the Federal government and to hold such laws as honorable and complete.

ARTICLE 5.

Open Sessions

Debates and committee hearings in both houses of Congress shall be open to the public, unless two-thirds of the respected body votes to close the assemblies due to the need for a secret process. Written and electronic communication between members of the government or between elected officials or both shall be considered privileged communication.

ARTICLE 6.

House of Representatives

Section 1. Selection of Representatives. The House of Representatives shall be selected for office by direct popular election. Districts shall be maintained with a state in a uniform fashion without concern for bias or partiality. One Representative shall be elected for every 77,000 per count by population. A Representative must be eighteen years of age and a citizen of the Union. Each Representative shall have one vote.

Section 2. Power to Legislate. The power to legislate shall rest with the House of Representatives and the people. All bills, appropriations, amendments, and Federal charters shall be generated by the House. A bill that shall have passed the House with a vote of fifty percent shall be sent to the Senate for action. Bills returned from the Senate with no action taken or bills the Senate vetoed may pass the House of Representatives with a vote of two-thirds. Such a bill would then become law. The House will have three weeks to override a Senate veto, not counting the holiday break, or the issue will be considered expired. Any member of the House of Representatives may submit a bill for action to the administrative clerk. A bill must receive three readings before it can be passed by the House.

Section 3. Power to Investigate. The House of Representatives shall have the power to investigate and subpoena individuals and pursue issues of public accounting. They may also request that the Senate perform separate governmental investigations or participate equally in such undertakings within the House or both.

Section 4. Facility. The House of Representatives shall not be viewed as having a permanent residence or structure from which to operate. Each member shall operate from the member's home district. Day to day interactions and governmental duties shall be performed by teleconferencing. The Representatives may meet either in committee or in the assemblage according to this method. As seen fit by House leadership, specific meetings may be held to take confidential or sealed information. All equipment and items of technology needed for these interactions shall be at the expense and maintenance of the government. Once a year the House of Representatives shall meet in full association to review consequential business and issues. These sessions shall last no longer than two weeks. The location of these congresses shall be at the direction of the House leadership.

Section 5. Change of Session. The House of Representatives shall assemble in full session within ten days after a general election, at which time an oath of office will be administered. This assemblage shall not be viewed as part of the yearly two-week congress, but one of instruction and review of procedure.

Section 6. House Immunity. Members of the House of Representatives shall have *public immunity*. While members are not exempt from arrest, lawsuits, criminal penalties, civil action, and fines, law enforcement agencies shall not take into confinement members of the House. Issues related to infractions and misdemeanors shall be forwarded to the sergeant at arms for processing and resolution. Issues related to felonies and capital offenses shall be processed provincially, but the member of the House may not be taken into custody until a conviction is secured or the individual's membership has been terminated either by election or censure.

Section 7. Power to Borrow. The House of Representatives shall have the power to borrow money on the credit of the Union.

Section 8. Proxy Vote and Certification Codes. A member of the House of Representatives may not vote by proxy, either in committee or in assemblage. The use of legislative voting certification codes by another party shall be considered a capital crime. Any member of the House who willfully and consciously gives such voting certification codes to another party shall be subjected to expulsion from the House as classified by law and regulated by the House of Representative's code of ethics.

Section 9. Appropriation. All legislation generated by the House of Representatives and sent to the Senate for ratification shall include specific and detailed funding sources. No money may be drawn from the Treasury without the passage of an appropriation bill.

Section 10. Legislative Violations. The House of Representatives shall pass no bill of attainder or ex post facto laws.

ARTICLE 7.
The Senate

Section 1. Composition. The Senate shall consist of two members from each State in the Union. They will be chosen by direct election of the people. Their election shall run concurrently with the elections of each respective State governor and a term of office shall be four years. A member of the Senate must be eighteen years of age. Each Senator shall have one vote and must be a citizen of the Union.

Section 2. The Senate. The Senate shall review and vote on legislation submitted to it by the House of Representatives. It may write recommendations, but not amend. A vote of fifty percent represents passage by the Senate. A bill needs to be acted upon within sixty days of reaching the Senate or is considered vetoed. The sixty-day time frame shall not include the holiday period between November fifteenth and the first Monday after Congress reconvenes.

Section 3. Senate Rules. The Senate shall determine its own rules of order, procedure, and quorum. The Senate will choose its own officers and leaders. The Senate shall judge the election, returns, and qualifications of its own members. The Senate shall develop its own Codes of Ethics, censure its own members, and create procedures for removal of those members in violation of such ethical standards.

Section 4. Investigation and Review. The Senate shall have the power to investigate and call hearings. They have the power to subpoena and address issues of public accounting. They may begin such investigation without House permission or direction. Such investigation shall be straightforward and goals clearly defined. All subsequent findings shall be noted and published.

Section 5. Treaty Ratification. All international treaties shall be submitted to the Senate for approval. Passage requires a two-thirds vote by the Senators present. The Senate shall have ninety days to review and vote on such treaties or the measure shall be considered vetoed. No recourse of action is allowed by the House and no treaty may be passed into law without Senate consent. Treaties may be resubmitted for ratification.

Section 6. Ambassadorship Ratification. Appointments and nominations for ambassadorships or diplomatic representatives shall be approved by the Senate. Such approval shall be by a vote of fifty percent.

Section 7. Court Ratification. The Senate shall review the qualification and eligibility of those individuals appointed by the Prime Minister to hold judgeships. This would include the Supreme Court, all Federal courts, and the Chief Justice of the Supreme Court. Approval would be by a vote of fifty percent.

Section 8. Cabinet and Administrative ratification. Appointments of ministers to governmental posts or to the cabinet shall be approved by the Senate. Such approval shall be by a vote of fifty percent.

Section 9. Sanctioned Territory Ratification. Independent sovereign states may petition the Senate for support under the Sanctioned Territory section of this document. This function is an autonomous power of the Senate. The Senate may ratify such arrangement by a vote of fifty percent.

Section 10. Senate Immunity. No member of the Senate may be arrested, or served with a warrant in the chambers of that body. Nor may any member of the Senate be served with such a warrant or detained while traveling to or from the Senate. No member of the Senate shall be held accountable in any other forum or subsequent hearing for any type of communication made within that body.

Section 11. Residence. The Senate shall meet in a permanent structure determined by its leadership.

Prime Minister

ARTICLE 8

Prime Minister

Section 1. Prime Minister as Executive Officer. The Prime Minister shall be considered the highest officer in the land and the executive officer of the government.

Section 2. Election of Prime Minister. The Prime Minister shall be elected by members of the House of Representatives. There is no established period of time for that office, except that the total time in the position shall not reach more than ten years. An election may be held at any time that the majority in the House requests such a balloting for the position. No debate is required. A period of one week shall be allowed for transition. The new Prime Minister shall accept the oath of office seven days from the vote. House votes on the Prime Minister shall not be allowed during the holiday period unless the Prime Minister is gravely ill or shall have died. A Prime Minister must be at least eighteen years of age.

Section 3. Head of Government. The Prime Minister shall be the Head of Government.

Section 4. Foreign Relationships. The office of the Prime Minister shall represent the Federal Government in all relationships with foreign states. This office shall have the power to negotiate treaties, administrate agreements generated by international law, and represent the government in all customary functions. The Prime Minister shall be able to receive, accredit, and dismiss foreign envoys.

Section 5. Appointment of the Cabinet. The Prime Minister shall appoint members to the cabinet with review and confirmation by the Senate.

Section 6. Prime Minister Status. The Prime Minister must be a member of the House of Representatives and may not hold the position unless the person has run for direct election and won a seat. At all times the Prime Minister retains voting rights within the House of Representatives. The Prime Minister shall have a remuneration level separate from other members of the House. The Prime Minister may appoint a representative to oversee her or his duties in the person's home district while the responsibilities of office are being performed. Such a representative may be chosen without administrative or governmental approval.

Section 7. Commander in Chief. The Prime Minister shall be Commander in Chief of the armed forces.

Section 8. Executive Function. The Prime Minister shall be responsible for all executive functions within the government. Within the framework of the Constitution and established by law, the size of the governmental departments and agencies shall be the responsibility of the Prime Minister. All regulatory functions of the executive government's operations become the responsibility of the Prime Minister.

Section 9. Question and Answer Period. At the request of one-tenth of the membership of the House of Representatives, the Prime Minister shall appear in person if the House is meeting with full membership or electronically if they are not and address concerns related to the administration of the government. This shall occur within three days of the request. The opposition political parties shall be given one hour to ask questions of the Prime Minister. These question-and-answer periods shall be allowed twice a month and not during the holiday period. The House leadership may be substituted only if the Prime Minister is out of the country. Additional rules may be set by the House of Representatives.

     Section 10. Pardons. The Prime Minister has the power to pardon and grant reprieves, except in the case of impeachment.

     Section 11. The Prime Minister shall have a permanent residence.

     Section 12. The power of the Prime Minister shall remain in force during periods of the general election, but new legislation may not be initiated nor new appointments made to offices.

     Section 13. Immunity. The Prime Minster shall be immune from private damage suits for any official activity carried out while in office.

Propositions

ARTICLE 9.

Proposition and Initiatives

     The people shall have the power to draft legislation separate from Congress. A petition must be signed by fifteen percent of the registered voters of a state and verified by the state Attorney General. Such petitions shall be needed from two-thirds of the states and such wording on all the petitions shall be the same. Each signature on the petition must have a date. The petition must reach the Office of the Administrative Clerk within five years of that date or the signature becomes invalid. The petitions shall be given to the clerk of the House of Representatives and the item shall be placed on the ballot of the next general election. If the Initiative is passed in the next two general elections by a vote of fifty percent it shall become law. Such legislative processes cannot be used to amend the Constitution.

Cabinet

ARTICLE 10.

Cabinet

Section 1. Cabinet Officials. The Cabinet shall consist of the Prime Minister and those officers by departments. The Prime Minister shall be the director and principal minister. All Cabinet posts shall be held by civilians. The Cabinet officers shall assist and oversee governmental departments, administer those departments, encourage legislation related to their departments, assist with the budget, and be responsible for the performance of their departments. Cabinet officers and all appointed members of the government shall serve at the discretion of the Prime Minister.

Section 2. Cabinet Membership Requirements. Cabinet Ministers may or may not be chosen from within the government. Any members of the House of Representatives or the Senate who become Cabinet officers must resign the elected and legislative positions.

Section 3. Appointments. The Prime Minister shall appoint the Cabinet Ministers, and they shall be confirmed by the Senate by a vote of fifty percent.

Section 4. Administrative Modification. When a vacancy has occurred in the position of Prime Minister, the Cabinet shall resign en masse. In such cases the Cabinet officers shall continue to function until superseded.

ARTICLE 11.

Regulations

Cabinet Officers shall be accountable for and have responsibility for the regulatory processes within their department. Regulations generated by each governmental department or agency shall be submitted to the House for action and if passed will become law. Cabinet Ministers shall be responsible for all contracts made within their departments.

Government Duties and Powers

ARTICLE 12.

Priority

Federal law takes precedence over state law unless especially noted in the Constitution, but the Federal government may delegate, concede, or defer to the states any legislative responsibility.

ARTICLE 13.

Declaration of War

Section 1. Power to Declare War. The power to declare war rests with Congress. The Prime Minister shall present to Congress such a resolution declaring the necessity for war and listing such grievance against a foreign power. A declaration of war requires passage by both houses of Congress with a vote of fifty percent and may be submitted simultaneously to both Houses. A declaration of war may only be requested against another sovereign nation.

Section 2. Military Conflicts. If at any time the Prime Minister commits armed forces to a conflict absent of a declaration of war, a written notice must be sent to the House of Representatives indicating the circumstances of these hostilities. The Prime Minister shall note the scope and duration of these hostilities. As long as military forces are in the theater of operations of this conflict, the Prime Minister must submit reports to the Congress every two months. In the absence of a declaration of war the House of Representatives may choose to end the involvement in such conflicts. This may be done by a vote of fifty percent. The Prime Minister will then have sixty days to cease military operations; the House may grant extensions at their discretion.

Section 3. Means of Production. Emergency war powers that command control of the means of production or financial resources of the nation can only occur under a declaration of war.

ARTICLE 14.

Budget

Section 1. Mandatory Balanced Budget. The House of Representatives is mandated to balance the budget every year. This shall be supervised by the Senate and confirmed by the General Accounting Office. At any time it is viewed that the budget is not balanced general elections must be called.

Section 2. Budget Exception. The budget need not be balanced under a Declaration of War.

Section 3. General Accounting Office. The General Accounting Office shall be a Constitutional body. Each year the General Accounting Office shall submit an annual report on the Federal government noting the economic, institutional, and social health of the nation. The department shall have independence in pursuing budgetary information and in reviewing contracts and service agreements. The General Accounting Office shall be made up of civil servants and may not be converted to appointed positions. Both the House of Representatives and the Senate may request reports on specific topics from the General Accounting Office. Congress shall pass no laws restricting the General Accounting Office in its ability to obtain information for its reports, but a special numbered accounting category may assist for security-related projects.

ARTICLE 15.
Redistricting

The General Accounting Office shall be responsible for adjusting the Congressional districts. After each census the General Accounting Office shall make an inventory of the House districts. Boundary modifications needed to maintain the ratio between population and representation shall be made at that time.

ARTICLE 16.
Language

The official language of the Federal government shall be English.

ARTICLE 17.
Taxation

Congress has the power to tax. Congress also has the power to legislate custom duties and restrict importation of commodities.

ARTICLE 18.
Freedom of Information

Federal governmental agencies shall be required to release records to the public upon request, unless such information is exempt. When information is requested by the public and an exemption is noted, the reason for the denial shall be clearly signified. No document may have an exempt status longer than fifty years. Federal governmental bodies and agencies shall be required to open their meetings to the public, unless an exemption has been granted by the legislative process. All governmental meetings where the public is allowed to attend shall be announced seven days in advance.

ARTICLE 19.
Treaties

No treaty shall be in force longer than ninety-nine years. Acts of Union shall not be considered treaties.

ARTICLE 20.
Census

Once every ten years a national census shall be taken at the expense of the Federal Government.

ARTICLE 21.
Commerce

Section 1. Power to Regulate. Congress shall have the power to regulate interstate, intrastate, and international commerce emulating from within or connected to the Union. Congress has the authority to create monopolies and grant trusts. Corporations or enterprises obtained by the Federal government by default, bankruptcy, or legal action shall be privatized within one year.

Section 2. Bankruptcy Laws. The Federal government shall be responsible for determining the bankruptcy laws of the nation.

Section 3. Copyrights, Patents, and Trademarks. The Federal government shall be responsible for the issuing of copyrights, patents, and the registration of trademarks.

Section 4. Weights and Measures. The Federal government shall have the power to determine a uniform system of weights and measures.

Political Process

ARTICLE 22.
Political Parties

Section 1. Recognition of Political Parties. With the clear understanding that political parties represent the establishment of the political will of the people, political parties shall be recognized within the framework of this Constitution. To obtain placement on the national ballot for a given district, three percent of the registered voters must sign a petition stating their desire to have that party's name represented within. The political party candidates shall be chosen by convention, election, or caucus. Political parties shall operate within the scope of democratic concepts, freedom of association, fixed procedures, and rules of law. Any political party that does not obtain five percent of the popular vote in the general election will be said to have "lost status." They will then have two general elections to gain five percent of the vote or be removed from the ballot. A political party may then be reinstated by petition of the three-percent rule.

Section 2. Public Accounting. Political parties must adhere to public accounting of all funds obtained and resources provided to that organization.

Section 3. Party Platform. Party Platforms must be developed by all political parties clearly stating the goals, policies, aims, and nature of the political organization. These platforms need to be easily available to citizens upon request.

Section 4. Party Interplay. Laws may not be developed that restrict the use or progress of political parties or their interaction with the people.

Section 5. Party Access. Each person is equally eligible to run for political office; parties shall allow equal access to all individuals to the process.

ARTICLE 23.

Elections

Section 1. Free Elections. Elections shall be open and free. It shall be considered the minimum level of involvement of the people in their government and the maintenance of a democratic society.

Section 2. General Elections. General elections for members of the House of Representatives shall be held at the time that the body has been dissolved. This has occurred when the Prime Minister submits an application for new elections to the leader of the House, the General Accounting Office has declared Constitutional provisions have not been met, or when a motion of "No Confidence" has been passed by the House. From the date of passage of the motion or the submission of the application, general elections shall be held on the first Saturday after six weeks from that measurement. General elections must be held once every five years, which is determined from the date of the last election.

Section 3. Election Dispute. Disputes arising from the general election shall be reviewed and adjudicated by the House of Representatives. Equally, the Senate shall arbitrate disputes arising from Senatorial races and outcomes.

Section 4. Parallel Elections. The election of each State's two Senators shall parallel the occurrence of the election of their individual state governor. The dates, procedures, and times of such elections shall be determined by each State in accordance with their laws and Constitution.

Section 5. Election Financial Responsibility. The state governments shall be financially responsible for all elections from which state or local offices are being filled. The Federal government shall be financially responsible for all general elections.

ARTICLE 24.

Voting

Section 1. Voting shall be viewed as the formal expression of the will of the people in their preference for a candidate or their support for a proposition. Universal suffrage shall exist, with the view of one person, one vote. Any citizen over the age of eighteen years may vote. Voting is seen as a right and not a privilege. The government may not restrict, limit, or abridge voting rights. An individual may cast their vote from a polling location or by mail. A person may exercise their vote regardless of circumstance or condition.

Section 2. Secret Ballot. Voting shall be by secret ballot.

Section 3. Special Elections. If a member of the House of Representatives resigns, retires, or is expelled from that body, a special election shall be held in that district with the same rules that would apply to a general election held in that State. If a member of the Senate resigns, retires, or is expelled from that body, the term shall be completed by appointment by the state's governor. If fifty percent of the registered voters of a district request a recall of a member of the House of Representatives and it is confirmed by petition submitted to the state's Attorney General, a special election shall be held in that district under the same rules as a general election. If fifty percent of the registered voters of a State request a recall of a member of the Senate and it is confirmed by petition submitted to the State's

Attorney General, the recall drive shall be deemed successful. The governor of that State shall have ten days to appoint a new Senator to complete the term. In all recall cases the State Attorney General shall have thirty days to confirm petition signatures and to issue a verification.

Judicial System

ARTICLE 25.

Judiciary

Section 1. Judicial Review. With invested interest in the people a judicial system shall be developed for concluding the rights, privileges, and immunities of its citizens through judicial review. The court system shall consist of a Supreme Court, a Court of Appeals, and district courts. The role of the judicial system is to confirm the rule of law. By use or denial, the courts shall issue renderings and decisions based on law, treaty, or Constitution.

Section 2. Jurisdiction. The Supreme Court shall be the highest court in the land. Jurisdiction rests with the Supreme Court. No appellate restrictions may be applied to the Federal Court System.

Section 3. Appointment. The Supreme Court shall consist of nine members. Open positions shall be filled by appointment from the Prime Minister and confirmed by the Senate. There shall be a Chief Justice and eight Associate Justices. The Chief Justice shall be appointed by the Prime Minister and be chosen from the existing Justices with confirmation by the Senate. Decisions shall be made by a majority vote.

Section 4. Affiliation and Impeachment. Judges of the Supreme Court and all Federal Courts shall be appointed for life. A sitting judge may be removed from their position only by impeachment. The House of Representatives may impeach with a fifty percent vote. The writ would be then sent to the Senate. An impeachment trial would be held by the full Senate, with a two-thirds vote needed for a recall of an appointment. Accused parties may retain and secure counsel.

Section 5. Quorum. No business may be transacted or judgments made by the Supreme Court without a quorum.

Section 6. Counsel. Upon request the Chief Justice of the Supreme Court may be called upon to counsel both the House of Representatives and the Senate on legislation not yet passed. Written and oral briefs may be given to Congress addressing concerns or the Constitutionality of a given piece of legislation. Such judicial interaction shall not be considered legally binding or represent rulings of the Supreme Court. The Chief Justice may refuse such request, or delegate the brief to another Justice. A refusal must be submitted to Congress in writing.

ARTICLE 26.
Order of Authority

The order of authority of law shall be properly resolved as international treaties, the Federal Constitution, acts of Congress, state constitutions, state statutory law, codified law, and common law.

ARTICLE 27.
Litigation.

Judicial power within the Union shall not be constructed or restricted in such a way to deny individuals, groups, or government the ability to bring litigation against another party. Nor may restrictions be placed on one section of government bringing suit against another, nor one state bringing forth legal proceedings against another state, nor the ability of the states to petition the courts adversely against the Federal government. Foreign citizens are without standing in state courts.

Rights

ARTICLE 28.
Equal Protection Under the Law

The law shall provide equal protection to all individuals existing under the Constitution and its statutes. All citizens are equal under the law

ARTICLE 29.
Freedom of Expression

The right to free expression is confirmed. Individuals have the right to express themselves through their opinions, speech, writing, and pictures.

ARTICLE 30.

Freedom of the Press

With the understanding that a free and open press represents a cornerstone of a democratic society, Congress shall pass no laws abridging the freedom of the press. This shall be viewed as the media in all its related forms.

ARTICLE 31.

Freedom of the Exchange of Ideas

In a free and open society, an exchange of ideas and views should be viewed as paramount. Laws forbidding the interchange, commerce, or inspection of ideas is not allowed. This shall include areas of academic, scientific, and religious tutelage.

ARTICLE 32.

Freedom of Religion

Freedom of religion, creed, or conscience is confirmed. Congress shall pass no laws restricting the rights of individuals to practice their religion.

ARTICLE 33.

Freedom of Assembly

The people have the right to assemble peacefully, without prior notification or authorization. Statutes governing open-air meetings and gatherings may be written by the States with the goal of not abbreviating the right of assembly.

ARTICLE 34.

Freedom of Association

The people have the right to form groups, clubs, and societies. Such associations may represent religious, cultural, economic, professional, social, or political interest, but not be inclusive thereof. Such associations may not conflict with criminal statutes where such organizations are designed for unlawful activities.

ARTICLE 35.

Right to Privacy

Each citizen has the right to develop her/his own personality insofar that it does not violate the rights of others, transgress on the prohibitions of the Constitution, or violate moral standards as they would be found apart from the home environment. The privacy of letters, journals, post, and telecommunications is guaranteed; only by court order on an individual basis and conforming to "probable cause," of illegal activity may this right be infringed.

ARTICLE 36.

Freedom to Petition

The people have the right to petition the government for redress of grievances. Such petitions may be done within a group or individually. Such written petitions may be addressed to Congress or specific agencies or departments.

ARTICLE 37.

Property Rights

The people shall have a right to own property. These rights shall be defined by law within the responsibilities of property ownership. Private property may be taken for public use, but only with just compensation and due process. Both the Federal and state governments have the right of eminent domain.

ARTICLE 38.

Freedom of Movement

Citizens have the right to move freely within the boundaries of the nation-state or to live legally in any State or locale. This shall be with exception to dangers of epidemics, to deal with natural disasters, catastrophe, accidents, or the protection of the young.

ARTICLE 39.

Discrimination

Congress shall pass no laws that discriminate against an individual or group because of race, creed, color, gender, age, national origin, economic status, physical capacity, handicaps, or sexual orientation. Such differences are viewed as being conceptional to the values, beliefs, and practices of a free people. Minority groups shall not receive unequal treatment or oppression under the law.

ARTICLE 40.
Emancipation

All individuals shall be emancipated at the age of eighteen.

ARTICLE 41.
Inherent Rights

All persons are born equally free and have certain natural, inherent, and inalienable rights. Among these are the rights of liberty, life, acquiring possessions, being productive, and seeking happiness and security.

Judicial Entitlements

ARTICLE 42.
Search and Seizures

The people have a right to be secure from unreasonable searches and seizures of their persons, papers, homes, effects, and property. Warrants shall be specific to the person, place, or items to be searched, and the person or items to be seized. At all times "probable cause"of illegal activity regulations must to adhered to and written warrants shall describe the "probable cause" supported under oath and affirmation.

ARTICLE 43.
Due Process

Section 1. Guarantee of Due Process. No person shall be deprived of life, liberty, or property without due process under the law, nor shall any person be denied equal protection under the law. Nor shall private property be taken for public use without just compensation. Due Process shall exist both at the Federal and state levels.

Section 2. Legal Affirmation. No person shall be required or compelled to testify against himself or herself in a criminal case or be a witness against him or herself.

Section 3. Double Jeopardy. No person shall be placed in jeopardy twice for the same offense. Nor may a person be charged with different degrees of the same offense. Nor may an individual be charged or tried for an offense, or a degree of an offense, greater than the one of which the person has been convicted.

Section 4. Rights of the Accused. Accused persons are free to remain silent and to be warned that anything they say may be used against them in a court of law. They have a right to an attorney and an attorney can be present during questioning. An attorney will be provided if the accused cannot afford one; and the accused can terminate questioning at any time. At the time of arrest accused persons must be informed of the nature of the charges against them and the reasons they are being held.

Section 5. Writ of Habeas Corpus. The right and writ of habeas corpus shall not be suspended except under written decree by the Prime Minister or under a Declaration of War. If the Prime Minister withholds the right of habeas corpus, the written decree must state the specific reason and have a set period of time.

Section 6. Trial by Jury. All persons accused of a felony crime shall be entitled to a trial by jury. Such juries shall be impartially seated and fairly chosen. State and Federal governments shall determine the size and characteristic of juries within their respective court systems.

Section 7. Judicial Rights. In all criminal cases a person shall be entitled to be confronted by their accusers, witnesses, and points of evidence. They are entitled to cross-examine such individuals. The accused has a right to be represented by counsel. The accused may present their own witnesses and items of evidence. An accused person has the right to have testimony interpreted to them in a language that they understand.

Section 8. Arraignments and Bail. All persons accused of a crime shall be entitled to an arraignment to determine bail. Such bail shall be reasonable and codified to the crime in question. Accused parties shall be required to show financial responsibility and post sureties. Bail may be denied to individuals with a high risk of flight, poor connections to the community, conviction of two or more felonies, or unwilling to place their financial resources before the court.

Section 9. Grand Jury. No person shall be held to answer for a capital offense unless on a presentment or indictment of a grand jury. A grand jury shall not be composed of less than twelve citizens and must reside in the county from which the grand jury has convened. The finding of an indictment by a grand jury shall be prescribed by law, but such concurrence shall not be by less than a majority.

Section 10. Prompt and Public Trial. Any individual charged with a criminal offense shall have the option of requesting a "speedy trial." The accused must submit the request in writing and the trial must be held within sixty days of this application. The prosecution may ask for a delay, but it can only be granted by an appellate court. All accused persons shall be entitled to a public trial.

ARTICLE 44.
Torture

No person may be subject to the infliction of physical pain as a means of punishment or coercion. No such instruments, device, tool, or material may be used on an individual being held by the authorities or government.

ARTICLE 45.
Capital Punishment

Capital punishment is abolished.

ARTICLE 46.
Imprisonment for Debt

No person shall be imprisoned for debt in any civil action.

ARTICLE 47.
Victim's Rights

It is recognized that victims of violent crime have rights equal to or greater than those accused of criminal offenses. They have the right to be treated respectfully and with dignity throughout the criminal process. They have the right to be reasonably protected from the accused. They have the right to be notified of all court proceedings, the right to attend such proceedings, and a right to make a statement at sentencing. Victims of violent crime have a right to restitution from convicted persons of such crimes. They have a right to confer with the prosecution.

They have a right to appear at all ensuing proceedings dealing with changes in the convicted person's condition or circumstance and to be notified of any such changes or proceedings.

Awards

ARTICLE 48.

Awards and Titles

The Federal government shall not grant titles of nobility. Individuals, either within the government or from without, shall be entitled to receive awards, decoration, distinctions, scholarships, titles, or prizes from another foreign power or official. No privilege shall accompany any such awards, titles, or distinctions. No such award, title, or distinction shall be valid beyond the lifetime of the individual who received it.

Education

ARTICLE 49.

Education

All children from the age of six through seventeen years shall be entitled to an education.

ARTICLE 50.

Academic Freedom

Academic freedom is guaranteed in all colleges and universities within the Union that receive Federal funding.

Economy

ARTICLE 51.

Federal Reserve

Section 1. Function of the Federal Reserve. The responsibility of maintaining the nation's money supply and a stable economy shall fall on the Federal Reserve System, the Federal Reserve Banks, and their Board of Governors. The "worth of the nation" shall be the determining basis for the economy. The

Federal Reserve shall direct the Mint and the Bureau of Engraving about levels of production and the money needs of the nation. The Mint and the Bureau of Engraving shall be departments found within the Federal Reserve System.

Section 2. Ownership. Private ownership of the Federal Reserve shall be disallowed.

Section 3. Appointment of Officers. The twelve member Board of Governors of the Federal Reserve and the directors of the individual Federal Reserve Banks shall be appointed by the Prime Minister and approved by a fifty percent vote of the Senate. Their terms of office shall be for eight years with a staggered appointment rate with three appointments every two years. No Board of Governor or Federal Reserve Director shall maintain their position longer than sixteen years.

Section 4. Economic Policy. The Federal Reserve shall not be subservient to Congress, and shall be allowed to pursue an independent economic policy within the framework of its mandate. Federal Reserve Board of Governors and Federal Reserve Bank Directors may be removed from their positions only by impeachment. The meetings of the Federal Reserve shall have exempt status but may be open to the public at the discretion of the Chairperson.

Section 5. Expenses. The expenses of the Federal Reserve System shall be maintained from within the Federal Budget. All income, profit, or seigniorage, from debits and credits, shall be returned to the Federal Treasury.

Military

ARTICLE 52.
Subordinate Power

The Armed Forces of the United States, in all of its variations, shall be subordinate to the civilian government.

ARTICLE 53.
Military Conscription

Military conscription shall only be allowed under a Declaration of War against another foreign state. Under such conditions, all individuals over the age of eighteen, shall be subject to conscription. A person refusing the use of arms on the grounds of conscience shall be subject to alternative service, the duration of which may not be in excess of time served under general military conscription.

ARTICLE 54.
Military Judicial Systems

Section 1. Separate Military Judicial Systems. The armed forces of the Union shall be entitled to a separate judicial system independent of civilian processes with detached rules of evidence, representation, and use of juries and judges. Individuals accused of a crime within the military shall be allowed rights of due process. Appeals may be made to the Federal courts.

Section 2. Restriction of Freedoms. Those individuals serving in the armed forces, or substitute service, shall be subjected to restrictions on their basic rights of freedom of expression and the rights of mobility. All other rights shall remain in force.

Section 3. Rite of Enlistment. Instruction of such changes in procedure, military law, and restrictions on basic rights shall be given to all new recruits upon entry into the armed forces.

ARTICLE 55.
Quartering of Soldiers

No member of the armed forces shall be housed in private dwellings during peacetime. Only under a Declaration of War may such quartering of military personnel occur and then only if written permission is obtained by both the resident and owner of such property.

State Directives

ARTICLE 56.
State Legitimacy

Each state within the union shall have a right to exist within established borders. States have a right to tax their citizens. The Federal government may not tax the basic governmental functions of the states. States are secure in their ability to legislate.

ARTICLE 57.

Militias

It shall be the responsibility of the individual States to charter militias within their borders. The States shall be responsible for laws related to the practice and use of firearms. The Federal government shall not infringe upon the States' power to encourage, regulate, or satisfy such items within their boundary.

ARTICLE 58.

Legal Counselors

It shall be the responsibility of the individual states to create legislation regulating, and the codification of the cost of legal actions, originating of legal documents, and services generated by officers of the court.

ARTICLE 59.

Privileges and Immunities

The citizens of each state shall be entitled to all the privileges and immunities of citizens in the several states. Equally, extradition for a felony or capital crime shall be universally accepted.

ARTICLE 60.

Rite of Passage

It shall be the responsibility of the individual States to charter organizations, associations, and affiliates in the education of the young to accept the rights and accountabilities of adulthood. This shall be viewed as a Rite of Passage. Issues relating to ethics, expectations of adulthood, noble human interaction, and managing personal affairs shall be addressed. Titles shall be awarded and rituals performed. A State may not discriminate in the issuance of its charters to the civic, cultural, moral, or conscientious base from which an organization operates, but it may revoke a charter for the lack of commitment to ethical standards and educational criteria.

ARTICLE 61.

Public School Districts

The individual States shall administer and determine public school districts. Financial considerations shall be equal and fair to each district.

ARTICLE 62.

Reciprocity in Judicial Acts

Full Faith and Credit shall be given in each state to the public acts, accounts, records, and judicial proceedings of every other state. Congress may pass laws pertaining to these proceedings and to assist with these amenities.

Family

ARTICLE 63.

Responsibility to the Young

It is the natural right of parents to care for, support, and direct the upbringing of their children. This right is seen as primary, but the state has an equal responsibility to supervise this exercise.

ARTICLE 64.

Tutelage

Families shall have a right to educate their own children, to assist with the direction of that education by others, and to help foster educational programs within academic facilities.

ARTICLE 65.

Child Information

Parents shall be privileged to all information generated on behalf of or for the welfare of their child. Parents shall have access to documents, charts, test results, claims, papers, and records produced on behalf of the child by institutions, professionals, or agencies. Such access shall be prescribed by law but subject to limited conditions.

Labor

ARTICLE 66.

Right to Labor Representation

Employees of a company, organization, agency, or association that pays wages shall be entitled to vote on labor representation within the framework of existing labor law and legislation. Labor Unions have a legally protected right to organize and to negotiate collective-bargaining agreements. Neither a company nor its personnel may discriminate or intimidate individuals seeking such certification. Only the military shall be exempt from labor laws and organizations.

ARTICLE 67.
Child Labor

Congress shall have the power to limit, regulate, and prohibit the labor of persons under the age of eighteen years.

Territory

ARTICLE 68.
District of Columbia

The District of Columbia shall be abolished. All lands within the District shall be returned to either Maryland or Virginia in accordance with the original land grants. The Federal government shall be entitled to maintenance and usage of those areas deemed in the public good in agreement with other national properties found within other states and territories.

ARTICLE 69.
Union

Section 1. The National Union. The national Union shall consist of the individual states and territories bound together for a common purpose, security, mutual support, and the advocacy of democratic behavior. All rights not listed or resolved within this Constitution revert to the States. The Federal government shall respect the diversity of the individual State and regard such diversity as a national resource.

Section 2. State Autonomy. A State shall be an internally autonomous territory, determined by treaty and association, within the federation of States. It shall have a separate legitimacy and government. All States shall be Constitutionally based and derive their political authority from the people. A State is considered a reciprocal part of the Union, not convertible or subject to modification. Once confirmed a State may not leave the Union accept at a point of Constitutional substitution at two hundred year intervals.

Section 3. Commonwealth. A commonwealth shall be a self-governing, autonomous political unit voluntarily associated with the Union. The rights and privileges of its citizens shall be the same as those associated with the Union and its States. At the discretion of its citizens, plebiscites may be held to determine statehood, independence, or maintenance of the status quo. Such a change in status may not be contested by the Federal government. Federal law shall apply to commonwealths. They shall not be able to vote in national elections or receive representation at the national level. To have commonwealth status the territory must have a population of 150,000 people or more.

Section 4. Protectorate. A *protectorate* is a territory administered by governmental departments. A protectorate may or may not be a Trust. A reservation set aside for Native Americans shall be a protectorate and subject to Treaty.

Section 5. Sanctioned Territory. A *sanctioned territory* shall be an independent sovereign nation that through their own legislative process requests association with the Union and is confirmed by a fifty percent vote of the Senate. Such a sanctioned territory shall have its military demobilized and its foreign policy shall be subordinate to Congress. Such territories shall maintain an independent monetary system and governmental processes. The goal of such relationships shall be to enhance democracy through the stabilization of the society, economy, and governmental functions. The Federal government shall have no financial obligation to the dominion but shall have a responsibility to maintain the territorial integrity of this sovereign state. Within ten years a plebiscite shall be submitted to the people of that sanctioned territory to determine status, and every ten years thereafter if the people of that nation vote to continue to be a sanctioned territory. If commonwealth status is requested by the people of such a sanctioned territory, it must be passed by both houses of Congress.

Modification and Termination

ARTICLE 70.

Amendments to the Constitution

Any member of the House of Representatives may submit an amendment to the Constitution with the same rules related to legislative action. Such amendments must pass the House of Representatives by a two-thirds vote and the Senate by fifty percent. Such amendments shall then be sent to the States for ratification. The Amendment must pass in two-thirds of the States before it becomes enacted. The states shall have seven years to review and ratify all such Amendments.

ARTICLE 71.

Constitutional Conventions

If a call for a Constitutional Convention passes in three-fourths of the States a Constitutional Conference shall be held. The Convention shall be entitled to amend the Constitution, restructure the document, or draft a new Constitution.

ARTICLE 72.

Ratification of the Constitution

This Constitution shall be in full force and empowered upon the vote of two-thirds of the States in the Union. Such a vote shall be held by referendum of the people.

ARTICLE 73.

Discharge

The execution and performance of this Constitution shall not remain in force beyond two hundred years after ratification. At the end of that time it shall become null and void.

Part Five: An Analysis of the Proposed Constitution

Chapter 33
Commentary

Preamble

It is doubtful that a more distinct and noble statement has ever been made than the Preamble to the American Constitution. Never in the history of man have three words carried more weight and had greater significance, *"We the people..."* Civilization, and man as a species, can mark the Preamble of the American Constitution as one of the great steps forward in humanity. It was a declaration that from this point forward the people would have a say in government. There would be at least one cluster of people in the world that would band together and rule as one. It is such a magnificent concept, and written with such honest simplicity. There is nothing that could be written that could move beyond this method of measurement. It is more than a statement of political will, but a beginning narrative of a unique people.

In the Preamble that has been written in this proposed Constitution there is no pretense of greatness. It is clearly recognized the any effort to write a corresponding Preamble to the American Constitution would be pale in comparison. It is by definition matchless.

Once saying this a Preamble does have a purpose. It should outline the aspirations of the document and the general goals being represented. The Founding Fathers wanted to create a more stable union, insure domestic harmony, secure our borders, enhance economic prosperity, and maintain liberty. The Preamble sets these goals into motion. It becomes a matter of stating what is important for the society and the direction the nation wishes to go.

Article 1. Continuation of Obligations

The Proposed Constitution should not been seen as a radical document. The goal and the focus is a continuation of Constitutional government. While this proposal examines many adjustments and changes of direction, they should be seen neither as an elimination of our responsibilities as a nation-state, nor of accepted points of law, nor of our liabilities to one another. This is true whether in reference to domestic issues or international treaties. Even if the United States had no

Constitution at all we would still have a considerable list of obligations to our own people as well as the other nations of the world. The document needs to be seen as ongoing and connected.

For two hundred years the United States has been accumulating a Constitutional history. Many Constitutional issues already have been debated, resisted, contested, challenged, and eventually established. To reinvest time, energy, and money to repeat this process would be foolish for the nation. By far the core of the Proposed Constitution falls within the framework of existing Constitutional law. It is in essence the same.

The act of changing a Constitution, however, does not exempt a nation from past commitments. We are still the same nation. We have incurred debts; we have made promises to our people, signed contracts and made agreements. All of these were made in good faith. They need to be protected and all the parties need to be reassured.

Article 2. Congress

In writing a new Constitution the first issue that a person confronts is structure. In some ways structure has little to do with democracy or good government. It can be interpreted as nothing more than how a bill moves from point A to point B or how decisions are made within a given assembly or where the centers of power rest. Other components within democracy are far more important but difficult to design into a Constitution. Examples would be the ideas of a loyal opposition or judicial supervision of our rights. Once saying this, structure is a critical problem if for no other reason than how the people view their own government. If the structure is founded on democratic ideas and procedures, the people will see the body as an extension of egalitarian beliefs. If the structure instead becomes so restrictive or cumbersome that alternative ideas cannot surface, the nature of government will seem detached and aloof. This issue remains important in designing a governmental structure that allows for accessibility without creating too many buffers to our representatives.

Even if it were possible to develop a perfect forum for the exchange of ideas and views, then place within this assembly persons of unconscionable nature, the whole process would be corrupted. It is individuals who lead other individuals. It is people who maltreat, injure, and harm—not structure. This argument can be seen in the reverse with Plato's advocacy of a "philosopher king." The problem will remain. In the end a structure will have to be developed that allows for the expression of ideas, is democratic in nature, and is one in which all the parties concerned are invested.

A great advantage at this juncture of history is the abundance of democratic governments and systems that are found in the world community. We live in a time when democracy has taken root and is flourishing. History is dotted with democratic bodies that have collapsed and died while others have brought about true government of the people. The nation's founders were at a serious disadvantage on this issue. They lived at a time when republican forms of government did not exist. It is said that "we all walk backwards into the future" and so it was with the nation's founders. They knew what had been given to them in the past, especially the concepts of an absolute monarchy, but it is not clear that they understood the true implication of a democratic society. They designed a government and configured it according to the best ideas of the day. They used the best of the options available to them at the time. It was in every sense of the word an experiment. Two hundred years later we have learned from the process that some parts are worth keeping while others represent nothing more than unnecessary baggage. We have a great sense of what democracy exemplifies at this point in our history—far more that we did at its beginning and we should use this knowledge in a constructive manner.

If an effort is made to examine the nature and structure of all the democracies in the world, a few points become evident. While each nation in the world has its own traditions and mechanisms of government, at the broadest sense these discussions of structure fall into two general categories. At each end of the spectrum of democracy is one of these two configurations—the American Presidential System or the Parliamentary System. Both systems, and both structures, represent democracy. Both systems have advantages and disadvantages. The key to any such proposal is which system represents the greatest benefits and improvements to the society as a whole.

A brief review of these two systems of governments does appear to be appropriate. Two core areas of structure invite examination: how laws are passed and how elections occur. In the United States at the Federal level are three branches

of government—the Executive branch, the Legislative, and the Judiciary. The key
for the designers of the American Constitution was a balance of power whereby
each governmental entity checked the power of the other, each debating the merits
of a piece of legislation, each having an opportunity to critique a new law.

American Presidential System. Ideally Congress is the sole source of
legislation. A bill can only be introduced in the House of Representatives or the
Senate. An individual member will write the piece of legislation and send it to the
clerk of the respective assemblage. A legislator may request that other members of
their body sign onto their bill, the idea being that the more lawmakers supporting a
bill the, greater chance it will be processed and passed through the system. The
clerk will assign the bill a number and title. In this process, called *the first reading,*
the clerk will then send the bill to a House or Senate committee. The type of law
being proposed would determine which Committee would receive it. If the
chairperson or a majority of the Committee members oppose the bill they will *table*
it, allowing it to die. If they are supportive a hearing will be scheduled. They will
deliberate, discuss, offer amendments, and then vote on it. If a committee has
recommended passage it will be sent back to the clerk. The *second reading* occurs
when the clerk reads the measure to the full body. Members will debate the issue,
again offering amendments and recommendations. At the *third reading* the bill's
number is placed before the legislature for a vote. This is done by either a voice
vote or by roll call. If the bill passes it will then move to the other chamber of
Congress for consideration.

To become law a bill must pass both houses of Congress. If differences
remain or amendments have been added, the bill will go to a conference committee
with members from both houses. It is rare for a bill not to end up in a conference
committee. Concessions are made and differences ironed out. The final version then
returns to the appropriate chamber where it is again voted on. If passed, it will then
be sent to the President.

If signed the bill becomes a law. A bill is vetoed when the President does not
sign the legislation and returns the bill to Congress with listed objections. Once
returned both houses can pass the bill by a two-thirds vote, which overrides the
veto. The last word rests with Congress.

Of course the above inventory of events represents the sanitary view of how a bill is passed within the Federal government. Without criticizing the process, the reality may be something different. Committee chairpersons wield considerable power. They determine which bills receive hearings and which die in committee. The President also may support a bill and add his considerable influence to move a piece of legislation through Congress. It is even possible for a bill to move directly to the floor for debate or appear from a committee with a negative recommendation. The reality is that Congress is a highly political creature, a chasm of political intrigue where compromise and bureaucratic maneuvering are seen as desirable skills. This is not a great evil; it is more a matter of conceding the physical existence of politics.

Even without including special interest groups and lobbyists into the mix, the process of passing a bill in Congress is complex, laborious, and overwhelming. If the goal of the nation's founders was to create a system of exhaustive deliberation, they did so. It is a labyrinth of deal making and consideration. The question that needs to be asked is whether the structure we have is meeting the interest of all concerned.

The Parliamentary System. On the other end of the democratic spectrum is the parliamentary system with its many variations. Each nation that has developed an assembly based on this model has added its own traditions and proceedings. Most have evolved from the British example and from their colonial experiences rather than from an independent set of circumstances; yet, it still remains that the most democratic nations in the world have a parliamentary system. When nations were given choices, the consensus has been toward this model. An example can be made of the numerous countries that emerged after World War II with new governments and constitutions. Even so, we should not judge a model as being the best simply because it is the most numerous,

In the British House of Commons bills are generated by the political party in power. Major bills or those deemed controversial are drafted by the Cabinet with support from the Prime Minister. When a bill appears from the Cabinet this is considered *the first reading*. The commonly held view is that the members of Parliament do not legislate as much as they legitimize the process. While bills are deviated and discussed by the House it is not the practice to offer amendments from the floor. A *second reading* occurs on the floor of Parliament, and the bill, with some exceptions, will be sent to a *Standing Committee*. The committee will report on the bill, with or without amendments. A third reading and debate follows. The piece of legislation will then be voted on, but party discipline is a crucial part of the parliamentary process and the issue is rarely defeated. Such a reversal could lead to a *No Confidence Vote*, which would bring down the government and force new elections.

Once the bill is passed by the House of Commons it is sent to the House of Lords where a similar process occurs. If both Houses agree, and it is extremely rare for this not to happen, then the bill receives the *Royal Assent*. The Monarch does have a veto power and could refuse assent, but that has not occurred since 1707. A system does exist in which if the House of Lords voted down a bill, the House of Commons could override their vote. It requires that the identical bill be passed twice in two successive sessions. The *second reading* must occur within the first year and the *third reading* in the second year with one year separating.

When the parliamentary process and the congressional process may look mechanically different, both fulfill similar functions. In both cases political parties play a major role. With the support of the major political party, regardless of the system, passage of a bill is virtually assured. In both systems leadership plays a major role. As with most organizations and assemblages certain key players can dominate the process. It is difficult, if not impossible, to design a system in which individuals neither are given leadership responsibilities nor choose to step forward of their volition. Both are systems of administration. Management skill is required to move a bill through the system. The reality is that both structures are more alike than different, and this deals more with human nature than structure. In both systems the people have access to their government, both have an established form of representative government, and both use free and open forums in which to conduct business.

A structure of government could possibly be created that combines these two concepts, but such an effort would manifest some odd consequences and would no doubt increase the time needed for elections. It would be hard to justify. Any such effort would be difficult to explain, and the logic for creating such a system would have limited support. In the end it would be "very hard to sell." There is no overriding reason to have a mutation of these two structures of government. Rather, it is best to list the advantages and disadvantages of both the Parliamentary System and the Presidential System. Such an exercise should be helpful in determining the benefits and desirability of both structures.

Advantages of the Parliamentary System

1. Length of political campaigns. In the parliamentary system elections are handled in a short period of time, generally within six weeks. The theory is that the electorate is able to digest the issues and make a decision concerning the candidates in an appropriate amount of time. By contrast the American system requires months, if not years, and contributes to voter apathy. With the parliamentary system it is not clear when the next election will be held, and so the parties must remain vigilant. The length of time also has an effect on the work being done by our elected officials. If they are out campaigning, they are not providing the time to the job for which they were originally elected.

2. The cost of political campaigns. The length of time involved in elections has a direct relationship to the amount of money needed to get selected. The more time involved in an election, the more financial resources are needed. The most expensive campaign in the United States is for president. Since in the parliamentary system the party chooses the chief executive, that money is saved. Money has a very corrupting influence. The less money involved in the political process the better.

3. Ease of changing the chief executive. The United States Constitution has four separate Articles or Amendments that attempt to address the issue of secession. In the end the process is cumbersome. In the parliamentary system should the chief executive become ill, incapacitated, or die, the ruling party simply votes on a new prime minister. This same procedure can be used in cases of scandal. If the chief executive becomes connected in inappropriate behaviors, corruption, or some level of depravity, he or she can quickly be replaced. This process also eliminates the need for a vice-president.

4. Accountability. Under the parliamentary system the ruling party has more power but also more accountability. If their policies prove to be unsuitable to the people it is clear who must accept responsibility.

5. Friction between the Executive and Legislative branches. This problem can be found in parts of the American governmental structure. It is not uncommon for the Congress and the Executive branch of government to be controlled by different parties. It is a system that creates gridlock and manifests itself into pure party politics. Instead of working toward valid goals for the society, government becomes involved in brinkmanship and political exploitation. Another example can be found in the concept of war powers. Both the American President and Congress have military powers; because of this, conflict can occur. In the parliamentary system the chief executive and the legislature are part of the same party. They share the same policy.

6. Improved party system. Regardless how political parties are perceived they are the keepers of ideology and beliefs. If ideas are to be more important than personalities, then the parliamentary design for government is preferred. In this system it is the party that moves forward with the political and social conceptions of a government. It is a structure of government that forces people to look at the ideas of the party far more closely than the individual candidate.

7. Legislative involvement. In the American system of government, the President is the administrator of the Federal bureaucracy but has no Constitutional participation in the programs of policies generated by Congress. This is most acute with budgetary considerations. As the administrator the chief executive may see needs not understood by Congress and equally the legislature may have a different administrative agenda than the President. In the parliamentary system the process becomes one. The Prime Minister is part of the legislative branch. The budgetary process becomes better defined.

8. Cabinet functions. In the American structure cabinet officers are insulated from the Legislative branch of government by their chief executive. While Congress has the power to investigate and review politics, it becomes a negative process, especially if different political parties are operating. In the parliamentary model the cabinet officers are more involved in designing and setting up pieces of legislation they need for their departments. It also creates a system by which regulations can be channeled through parliament so that they become laws.

9. Elections connected to issues. While not always the case, if a "no confidence" has brought about an election, it is because the government has not been able to establish an agreed-upon course of action. This allows for greater information from the people. Through their vote they are able to express their point of view and help the government steer in a given direction.

10. One person, one vote. The parliamentary system eliminates the abnormality found within the American Presidential system on how votes are counted and determined. There is no longer a need for the Electoral College.

11. Legislative consistency. The issue of delegation of legislative responsibility is no longer an issue. Actions of the prime minister, the cabinet, the legislative committees, and the bureaucracy all must pass through parliament. While not eliminating the concept of "pork" or special interest, it is reduced because of the nature of the power structure,

12. Immediacy of action. During points of crisis the parliamentary model is better able to determine a course of action and pursue it. The process becomes less political. It is easier to conclude a consensus within the government and declare a policy. At least in foreign affairs the result is less perception of inconsistency.

13. The power of incumbency. With the electorate more focused on party platforms, party philosophy, and issues, the candidate is less of an issue. Being an incumbent has less sway with the voters.

14. Primaries. The system of choosing a candidate becomes more of a party function, and those individuals interested in having a say in the process will need to be more active. Primaries are less awkward with a considerable reduction in cost.

15. Character and personality. In the American system of government the President is both head of state and head of government. Issues related to the "Imperial Presidency" are founded in the idea of executive supremacy. The chief executive is able to operate from a position of loftiness that may not be appropriate. Though the Prime Minister may wield power equal to that of the American President, the position is seen much more as a governmental entity.

16. Leadership. In the Parliamentary System able leadership is a requirement. If the ruling party is to stay in power, they must maintain party discipline, which requires decisive leadership. The Prime Minister must understand how to get things done and work within the legislative process. Generally individuals with experience in government and party practice will surface to become Prime Minister.

17. Eliminates the need for Impeachment. In the American Presidential System the chief executive can be removed from office for "High Crimes and Misdemeanor." It is a difficult definition to interpret. In the Parliamentary System the chief executive is removed from office when they become an embarrassment to the party. This will occur far sooner than a trial on the Senate floor. The court system is then free to pursue any legal issues that may exist.

18. Improvement in the budgetary process. The American system of drafting a budget and passing it into law is an extremely laborious procedure. It is a system that breeds "pork" and supports special interest. While the President can suggest a budget, they have no real power to allot expenditures. Yet, it is the Executive Branch that must administer the departments and their budgets. In the Parliamentary System the budgetary process is streamlined with far more focus on the needs of the people.

Advantages of the American Presidential System

1. Deliberation. The process of moving a piece of legislature forward is far more time-consuming in the American presidential system. This forces a high level of deliberation. There is less likelihood of overreacting to a crisis. Both sides of the issue will be able to receive a hearing and the likelihood of minority opinions being heard is greater.

2. Compromise. One of the greatest strengths of the American presidential system is the process of compromise. It is a requirement of this model. Individuals of different parties may come together to promote a bill or resist a policy. A settlement of differences occurs through this process of granting concessions.

3. Separation of power. The American structure of government is designed so that the three branches of government must play off one another. Each have different responsibilities with assigned tasks. Power is distributed across the political spectrum. Action and augmentation require that the different power bases concede the same issue.

4. Election of the chief executive. The chief negative of the parliamentary model is that there is no direct link between the people and the Prime Minister. The majority party determines who will be the chief executive. Even with the buffers created by the American system of election the people feel as if they are selecting the President.

5. State and district loyalty. American elected officials are most apt to see themselves connected to the general philosophies of their home districts and states than in other models. Part of it represents the American form of Federalism and part because party discipline is not as pronounced. Nonetheless state and district loyalty is far more definite.

6. Introduction of bills. In the parliamentary structure most bills emerge from the leadership of the body. Individual members would encourage the leadership to promote a piece of legislation. In the American system a representative can introduce a proposed law and campaign accordingly for its passage using the system at large. In the Parliamentary system the passage of bills can take on the appearance of a rubber stamp.

Of course the greatest advantage of the American presidential system is that the people are familiar with its usage. A new structure of government would have to be learned and it would represent a major change. It becomes a social process as much as a governmental adjustment. In the same context an adaptation of the parliamentary model would align our government to the other world democracies. Events and processes of other nations would be better understood by our people.

The new Constitution being advocated is a shift toward the parliamentary system. If the goal is more democracy, then the parliamentary system has an advantage. It does correct a collection of problems currently found in the American structure of government. In working through the logic and attempting to do a comparative study of the two systems the advantages of the Parliamentary system are not immense. Even so, the advantages and benefits are enough to encourage the change. The difference is not legislative. The chief advantage deals with the difference between the American President and the Prime Minister. As this document has unfolded, those differences have been noted.

This Article also addresses the time in which Congress would meet. When the nation's founders developed their vision of the Federal government, they did not picture a legislature that needed to be in session continuously. They were obliged to

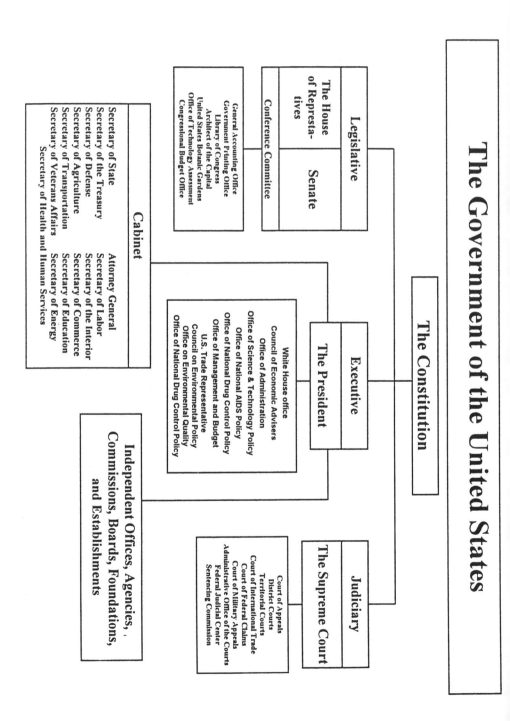

The Government of the United States

The Constitution

Legislative

The House of Representatives — **Senate**

Conference Committee

General Accounting Office
Government Printing Office
Library of Congress
Architect of the Capital
United States Botanic Gardens
Office of Technology Assessment
Congressional Budget Office

Executive

The President

White House office
Council of Economic Advisers
Office of Administration
Office of Science & Technology Policy
Office of National AIDS Policy
Office of National Drug Control Policy
Office of Management and Budget
U.S. Trade Representative
Council on Environmental Policy
Office on Environmental Quality
Office of National Drug Control Policy

Cabinet

Secretary of State
Secretary of the Treasury
Secretary of Defense
Secretary of Agriculture
Secretary of Transportation
Secretary of Veterans Affairs
Secretary of Health and Human Services

Attorney General
Secretary of Labor
Secretary of the Interior
Secretary of Commerce
Secretary of Education
Secretary of Energy

Independent Offices, Agencies, Commissions, Boards, Foundations, and Establishments

Judiciary

The Supreme Court

Court of Appeals
District Courts
Territorial Courts
Court of International Trade
Court of Federal Claims
Court of Military Appeals
Administrative Office of the Courts
Federal Judicial Center
Sentencing Commission

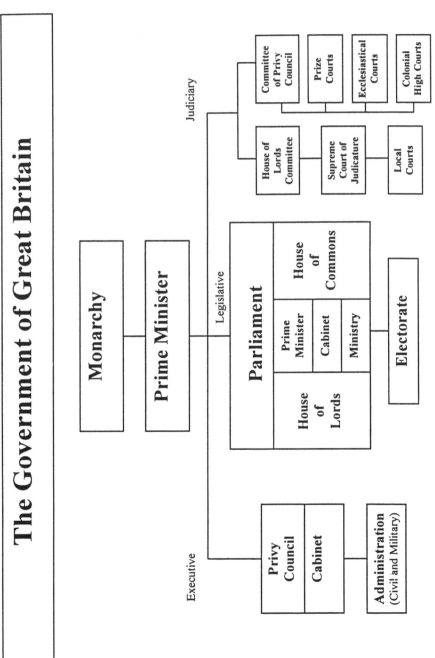

The Government of Great Britain

Monarchy

Prime Minister

Executive

Privy Council

Cabinet

Administration (Civil and Military)

Legislative

Parliament

House of Lords

Prime Minister

Cabinet

Ministry

House of Commons

Electorate

Judiciary

House of Lords Committee

Supreme Court of Judicature

Local Courts

Committee of Privy Council

Prize Courts

Ecclesiastical Courts

Colonial High Courts

G. Jacobsen and M. Lipman, *Political Science*, *(New York 1979)* travel great distances. Further, the capital did not initially have the physical structure, either in housing or governmental buildings to support an ongoing session. The drafters of the American Constitution did not see the need for Congress to be constantly meeting. They anticipated that the legislators would meet for a few months, work through the business at hand, and return to their home districts, repeating the cycle as needed.

At the beginning of the twenty-first century government exists at a different plane. Government is an ongoing process. Sessions meet throughout the better part of the year. A set time is appropriate and should be required. In the case of this Proposed Constitution, Congress would meet from January second until November fifteenth, which is well within range of the current calendar.

Article 3. Record Keeping

The nation's founders saw the publication of a record of Congress as an important part of the structure of government. Currently the *Congressional Quarterly* has been fulfilling that obligation. Such official record keeping is important; hence a continuation of the current system seems germane. While the information represented may be imperfect it still exemplifies a base. Likewise Congress needs to have some level of discretion. Times may come when issues of national security may demand that Congress will need the ability to limit information. Even so, the spirit of any republican government must be openness and a publication of its proceedings. This is an important part of self-government.

Article 4, Section 1. Congressional Rules

Who should make the rules for the legislative body? All such assemblies require rules of order and procedure. One might conceivably outline in great detail the procedures of Congress—everything from who is allowed to speak to how long a speech may last, how bills are amended, how they are to be numbered, or the format required. The effort would be considerable and should be seen as beyond the scope of a Constitution. The only fair and proper course is to allow the members who must exist within these procedures to set the order.

Likewise both Houses of Congress should develop and vote on their own leadership within the assembly. While such leadership may translate into party

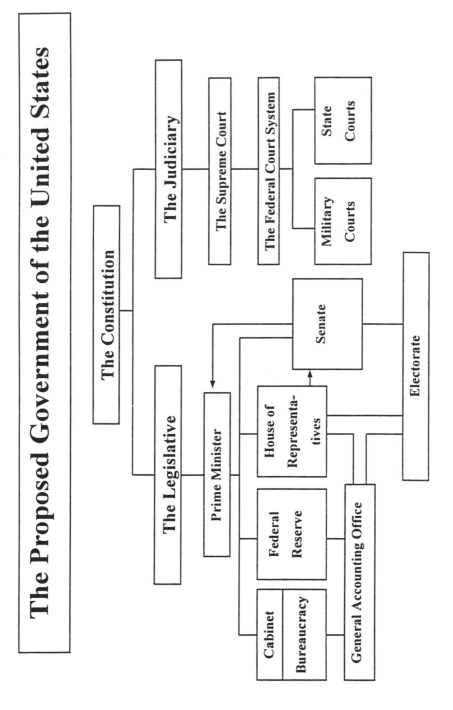

The Proposed Government of the United States

leadership, the administration of the assembly needs to be defined. The political party with the greatest number in Congress would determine how business will be conducted. This issue may have little to do with democracy but is more a matter of simple convenience and utility.

The issue that may be most controversial deals with Congress defining their own rules of censure and expulsion. The better question to be asked is whether it is proper to have an organization—any organization—police itself. The truth of the matter is that law still takes precedence. Nothing within this document will allow a member of Congress to commit a criminal offense and not be prosecuted. The issue deals more with ethical conduct. The group that has the greatest say and the greatest knowledge of what represents unprincipled behavior will be the membership of that body. These rules of censure will not be secret. It will be reasonably clear if the House of Representatives and the Senate are following their own rules.

Another issue related to censure and expulsion of members of Congress concerns the sergeant-at-arms. This position becomes a Constitutional position in the Proposed Constitution. Specific tasks and duties are required of the sergeant-at-arms, and both Houses have such a position. This office will be responsible for making sure that the rules of the assembly are being followed, including ethical conduct. The sergeant-at-arms will not set the policy; Congress would have that right, but once the rules were in place the sergeant-at-arms would be charged with seeing that they were followed.

The sergeant-at-arms would function in a protective manner. Currently within both Houses of Congress there are ethics committees. Chief of their assortment of duties is to review behaviors and conduct of its members. Appointing the sergeant-at-arms as the permanent chairperson of these committees seems befitting. From such a position the sergeant-at-arms would be better able to view, initiate, and follow through with these types of related concerns. If the sergeant-at-arms is responsible for order within the body itself, this seems like a logical next step.

Regardless of how these issues are viewed the real determining factor is the electorate. If they see an individual functioning outside the scope of ethical conduct, good government, or simply manners, they will vote her or him out. In the end the matter returns to the issue of trusting the people.

Article 4, Section 2. Membership

"An individual may not be a member of both Houses simultaneously." If this issue were not addressed it would be possible for a person to be elected to the House of Representatives and then be appointed to the Senate by a governor. A number of different scenarios are possible. It would be hard to imagine a person wanting to be a member of both Houses at the same time; the workload would be unmanageable. Nevertheless if no provision is made for such a set of circumstances it could occur. Even if a person held one of those offices for only a short time, the system would not be very satisfactory for all the parties concerned.

Article 4, Section 3. Compensation

The members of Congress need to be compensated for work they do on behalf of the people. Congress, through the legislative process, has one advantage over any other organization, company, or institution—they are able to set their own wages. The problem is that all of the other options are not very realistic or manageable. If salary amounts were set within a Constitution, the levels would be depressed within a decade. A Constitutional amendment to allow Congress a wage increase would also be required. If their wages connected to some type of rate or scale, economic situations in the future could make such percentages unworkable. It would be equally impractical for a governmental agency to handle Congressional wages. In truth members of Congress need to be paid a fair wage and in the end it will be done through the legislative process. What is important for the masses is for them to be aware of the level of compensation. The people need to be watchful and make note of the economic value of the job. A more significant issue may not be earnings but expenses. Citizens need to be aware of what expenses are being allowed and what those costs represent.

One of the reasons that Senators and Congresspersons need to be paid well is to avoid impropriety. Even with the best of intentions unusual situations may occur. Money can corrupt. It is far better to pay our representatives what is fair, and move on, than to believe that some type of savings would occur by reducing salaries of the membership. The people do expect something in return, and that is "good government."

Once accepting the concept that members of the government need to be paid well it is also hoped that the individual wage would be decreased. Under the Proposed Constitution the members of the House of Representatives would be based in their home communities whereas under the current system members of the House must maintain two residences—one in their own districts and one in Washington, D.C. This by any stretch of the imagination can be costly, and in the end the taxpayer is covering the expense. It is doubtful that this would represent any real savings in Federal reimbursements. The goal is not so much the reduction of wages as improvement in representative government and democracy.

Despite what our representatives are paid, it is important for the electorate to be aware or involved at some point. Congress would have the power to legislate their own wages but such increases would not go into effect until after a general election. This will give the masses an opportunity to review the issue and see how strongly they feel about it. If it is a major topic the ballot will mimic that concern.

The most vital of all these issues is to make sure that the elected officials of our government do not compromise their positions or be seen in situations that would represent a conflict of interest. These are the type of issues that would be worked out by the ethics committees and instruction would be given to the membership. Generally these conflicts of interest occur when a Senator or Congressperson accepts other responsibilities outside his or her elected position. If a member of Congress sat on the board of an international conglomerate, regardless of intentions, there would be an implied conflict of interest and these situations need to be avoided.

Even so, there may be circumstances when it is proper for a member of the Congress to work outside of established duties. An example may be to teach a class at one of the local universities. A person who is working within the framework of government and has the skills to be elected does have something to say, and it seems proper to allow them to pass on such information to others. Many times this is a matter of passing on one's life experiences. The system should not be so restrictive as to disallow positive levels of human interaction and involvement. The issue is who is to determine what represents a conflict of interest. The Proposed Constitution would cede the issue to the leadership of each body. Permission would be granted or rejected from that level.

Article 4, Section 4. Ancillary Positions

Two positions become part of the Constitution that are administrative in nature. Both of these jobs are necessary to the mechanics of the system. The first one is the *administrative clerk*. This is more than one person or one job; it is an office or department within the legislative process. The administrative clerk handles the bills as they are created by the members of the House of Representatives. They assign numbers and direct the bills to the proper committee. The status of any bill can be determined by contacting the administrative clerk or reviewing it through an Internet posting. The office would also list how individuals voted on a given measure and that information would be available to the public. Most of this would be a matter of record keeping.

The public would be allowed as much contact with the office of the Administrative Clerk as the members of each assembly. They too may have interest in the status of a specific bill or the results. These issues do not have to be complex; such information could be readily available on the electronic postings and updated consistently.

The administrative clerk would also be the location for individuals to present petitions. This could come in many forms. The office could be used as a clearing house for general concerns about government, whether they be in the form of a petition or simply a letter. This office would be the location where *referendums or propositions* would begin their journey to the ballot boxes of the nation. *Certified proposition petitions* would be sent to the administrative clerk for processing. The clerks would be able to assist citizens on how such referendums could be developed and postulated.

The other Constitutionally directed position becomes the *sergeant-at-arms*. More than a ceremonial position, the sergeant-at-arms would be expected to keep order in the Senate. The House of Representatives no longer would have a permanent structure from which to operate. The sergeant-at-arms would have the responsibility to maintain the computers, equipment, and service agreements required to keep Congress in place and operating. If a representative were having problems with equipment, or needed instruction, the sergeant-at-arms and the corresponding department would help keep the system functioning.

The sergeant-at-arms would also have responsibilities concerning ethical conduct of the Congressional membership. Reports of concerns could be submitted to the sergeant-at-arms for follow-up and review. It is possible, and hoped, that the sergeant-at-arms would have an established seat on all ethical committees.

The issue that seemed to be the most difficult to resolve is whether the sergeant-at-arms should be an appointed position or a civil servant. An argument can be made for either type of status. While the advantage is slight in either case, it was thought that an appointed sergeant-at-arms would be more in tune with the service needs of the Representatives and their equipment. The sergeant-at-arms must supply reliable service to the body or that person could be easily replaced.

While the sergeant-at-arms should not have police powers, the person would have some responsibility is maintaining the safety of the Representatives. If a citizen were engaged in an alleged activity of criminal behavior against a member of Congress, and local authorities were unable or unwilling to review such concerns, then the sergeant-at-arms could be contracted to assist with security. This could be done in concert with other governmental agencies.

Traditionally a chaplain has been a functional part of the United States Congress since its beginnings. Like the clerk and sergeant-at-arms the position becomes Constitutional, but no duties are assigned. The concept of separation of church and state is extremely valid; nothing is implied otherwise. It becomes more a matter of conceding the obvious. It is hoped that the position is subject to some level of rotation with numerous religious groups.

Article 4, Section 5. Residency

It seems odd even to have to state that a Representative or a Senator must live in the state from which they were elected. If this item were not in a Constitution a collection of abuses would be feasible. It would be possible to create a scenario in which a lame duck governor appointed the chairperson of the national party to be state Senator. The party official would have no ties to the state in question. Both the new Senator and governor would recognize that they would not have to run for reelection. The action would represent nothing more than returning a past favor or securing senatorial retirement pay.

It seems only fair to all the parties concerned to have their elected officials live in that state from which they were either appointed or voted on. It ties individuals to a given area, and in the most real sense, they become spokespersons for those given sections of the nation. It seems so basic, yet this is one of the most fundamental ideas of a large democratic nation.

Another equally important issue that is not discussed or included deals with requiring Representatives to live only in their own districts. This becomes less manageable under the Proposed Constitution since the districts will not be as large. It could be possible that through gerrymandering or even normal growth in the population an individual from a given district could find a home outside the elected district, perhaps by no more than a city block. Allowing voters to determine if they want a Representative who lives outside of their district seems appropriate. This type of information would come out in the election campaign. If the issue becomes a major concern for the electorate this would be portrayed in the final vote.

Article 4, Section 6. Consistency of the Law

Not only is the matter of making laws an issue; there is also the matter of who is to enforce the laws of the land. In this case it is Congress. With the Proposed Constitution the Prime Minister and Congress have the dual responsibility to make sure that the laws are followed. This power is invested in those individuals who need to exercise that authority, and again that returns to Congress.

A key concept for Congress, as well as the masses, is to understand that no one is above the law. It is improper, unfair, and immoral to pass laws that do not encompass everyone. To pass a law that exempts one group or favors one institution over another is wrong. The greatest level of balance in society is simply a matter of treating everyone fairly and the same. The exceptions that are found in a society should be institutional deviations, not individual exemptions.

There are always individuals willing to participate in a principled "civil disobedience." Such issues are very much a part of the democratic process. Laws do change, but until that occurs, laws need to be enforced and someone needs to be accountable for that function. In this case it is Congress.

The key to this Article is that it gives the Federal government police powers.

Article 5. Open Sessions

Government needs to be open, visible, and observable. This is the best way to maintain a free society. We do live in a different age than our nation's founders; we have the ability to use our technology to examine and watch the inter-workings of government. We need to use that technology. It will give us a window into the nature of how we are governed and the scope of representative democracy.

Exceptions always seem to occur, in this case the issue of national security. There is a difference between allowing the citizens of a nation to hear everything, and also allowing possible adversaries to hear everything. Discretion at times is needed. The reality is that we do not live in a world free of malevolence, trepidation, or hatred. One of the most basic and primal functions of government is security. John Locke and Thomas Hobbs would argue that this is one of the basic reasons we have government in the first place. Without debating that issue, security is important and we need to allow our government to perform that duty.

A related issue is that the process of government needs to be open, which would include both the Congressional assemblies and committees. Currently within our technology and satellite communications we are capable of setting up programs in which every function of government can be viewed by the public. This is well within our concepts of democracy and good government. Not that every such operation is either interesting or exciting. Government can be tedious, but that is not the point. Government needs to be a public process.

There is a difference between observing our legislative process and allowing this to become a barrier to the system. Our elected officials still need to be able to conduct the affairs of state, regardless of the form it may take. If a member of Congress is interacting with a member of the Cabinet as an example, such conversations should be considered privileged communications. Such freedom allows for a frank discussion of the topics at hand. It should be seen as a tool of the legislative process and should give a level of confidentiality to the system and reduce some impediments to the decision-making process.

Equally all letters and electrically charged communications should also be seen as private. Being able to view government is not the same as becoming involved at the microscopic level. We all husband our privacy and we need to allow our national leaders that same right.

Article 6, Section 1. The House of Representatives

All members of the House of Representatives will have participated in direct elections. This is not fundamentally different from what has occurred in the House for the last two hundred years. It is the same throughout the democratic world. Individuals run for political office, debates occur, ideas are exchanged, some more civilized than others, but in the end an election is held and the person with the majority of the votes wins. The districts will be established with the state boundaries. A district's configuration should not differ widely in size or makeup as it relates to the population, nor should the intent be to give one political group or party an advantage over another.

One of the points that is most troublesome within the current American Constitution is the *one in thirty thousand rule.* The nation's founders had set up the Constitution so that one member of the House of Representatives would represent thirty thousand people. A clear argument is being presented. It is a statement noting that such a ratio is finite. Regardless how this idea has been reworked, the original idea was to have infinite representation, the idea being that the fewer people whom are represented by an elected official—the more democratic. A direct correlation exists between the total number of individuals that a Representative must serve and the level of democracy. In the view of the nation's founders that finite ratio was one to thirty thousand.

This was also during a time when government played little part in the lives of its citizens. No governmental agencies were assigned to social improvement or to enhance the quality of life. Rarely would a citizen approach a Representative requesting assistance with a bureaucratic problem. This was also during a time when traveling within a district was more difficult. Yet, one in thirty thousand seemed proper and applicable to the developing form of the American Constitution.

In modern times Representatives have become more than simple delegates for the citizenship; they have become ombudsmen. It would be hard to imagine that the nation's founders had expected the citizens to vote on a Representative just so that members of Congress would hire someone else to represent them. To some degree that is just what is occurring. There are reasons why so many feel that our elected officials are aloof and detached. It deals with the fact that there are only so many hours in the day. The relationship between government and the people has been distorted by the sheer numbers.

The Proposed Constitution that is being represented herein returns to this finite concept, but instead of accepting the one in thirty thousand ratio, a ratio of one to seventy-seven thousand is being offered. There are two reasons. The first is that modern conveniences of travel and also telecommunications allow for representation at a higher level. The second is that this is the same ratio used by the British for their members of the House of Commons. It has proved to work well and it allows for satisfactory representation without overwhelming the Representative.

Using the 1990 United States census of 248,709,873 and dividing by 77,000 there would be 3,230 members of the House of Representatives. The number does become relative. Some people may argue that the total number is too large. Comparing to the one to thirty thousand ratio, the total number of Representatives needed would be 8,290. Using that system the number may seem too small. The numbers are not the real issues though. The one issue is representative government and how it interacts with democracy. On the other side is the ongoing problem of architecture. With the elimination of the need for an assembly and the change to the parliamentary system, the issue should be manageable.

What needs to be remembered in this discussion is the number of staff members assigned to each Representative. The average Representative has between 12 to 15 staff members. They play a large part in representing the district, but they also insulate our public officials. We should not think in terms of 435 members of the house, but 12,000 employees that are attached to this assembly. Even with 4,000 elected House members, with support staff it should not equal 12,000. In the end the issue deals with leadership. It matters little if you are attempting to manage 3,230 or 435 individuals, guidance and management would be the key.

There is an added benefit in allowing representation to be a finite number. The issue of campaign finance reform becomes lessened. During a general election if a Congressperson has 77,000 people in her or his district of which about half would be registered voters, a candidate for office actually would be able to shake the hand of every voter in the district. If election hopefuls have a one-on-one style campaign the need for large amounts of money diminishes. Political campaigns become more personable and less financial.

The nation's founders placed within the American Constitution a collection of ages from which a person may run for political office. In the case of a Representative it is twenty-five years of age. A Senator must be thirty, and the President of the United States needs to be thirty-five years old. In all of these cases the ages are contrived. There is no special significance to being thirty or thirty-five years old. It all deals with human personality and character. Maturity is impossible to measure. If there is one piece of philosophy that this document champions it is that government should not develop systems that limit human potential.

Throughout the Proposed Constitution the age at which individuals are allowed to run for political office is eighteen years. This is the age at which a person may vote. This is the same age at which a person must accept the responsibilities of citizenship. It is the same age at which an individual becomes emancipated. A clear boundary is important; a time when the society bestows upon an individual the liberties of the land but in return expects a defense of those liberties. A person becomes an equal partner in that defense. If that is so, then there should not be an age limit from which a person may run for political office.

There is an added concern about investing young people in the elective process. It is not so much a matter of enticing younger people to run for office as it is not creating barriers for them to do so. The system should be such that anyone can run for an elected position, regardless of background, experience, or even age. We criticize the youth of America for voting in such small numbers, yet the political system does not allow their participation at all its levels.

As it is with most situations the real limitation to running for an elected office is the people. If the voters feel that a person is too young, it will be represented at the ballot. If it is not an issue for the electorate, then it should not be an issue for the Constitution.

Article 6, Section 2. Power to Legislate

Within this proposed system of government the chief focus becomes the House of Representatives. They have the greatest contact with the people. Within this model the core activities of government emerge from the House. If there is to be a government of the people, the assembly with the greatest involvement with the masses should have the greatest say. The House should be the main focus. It becomes the responsibility of the House of Representatives to generate bills and to some degree set the agenda for the nation. This is a major change in what the American government has experienced in the past. It is believed that under this system the towns and communities of the country will become connected to their Representatives in ways that have not been seen before.

The biggest advantage in allowing one House to generate bills is that it streamlines government. It eliminates the need for a conference committee to work out differences in bills, it reduces the time that a bill may linger in the system, and it gives one House the responsibility to legislate. The Senate becomes much more of an overseer to the process. Again, it returns to the idea of allowing government to do its job. There are still checks and balances in the system, but it is also clear who is responsible. If something is not done properly or correctly, if the interest of the people are not met, then culpability can be easily fixed.

The issue for the Senate is that there is a reduction in the power for that body. While they still have many responsibilities to the democracy, they no longer can generate a bill. This would be a point of contention for many groups and organizations. The giving up of power is one of the most agonizing and ominous of any process. It becomes almost incompatible with human nature, but clearly the shift of that power is back to the people. The Representatives, living in their home districts, will have a greater feel for the needs of the people than Senators connected to the states and the national capital.

There is a process to be followed. A bill is generated by the House of Representatives, works its way through committee, and is voted on by that assemblage. It is then sent to the Senate. The Senate would have a period of time to review the measure and vote on it. If they passed it by fifty percent, the bill would be sent back to the House and the Prime Minister would sign it. At that point the bill would become law. The Senate of course could reject the piece of legislation; they have the power of veto. The House of Representatives would then have to pass the measure by two-thirds for the bill to become law.

The issue of the three readings is an accepted part of the legislative process of both the parliamentary system and the American presidential system of government. It allows for review and examination of a bill. The readings also allow time for a bill to be inspected and for an investigation to occur. It eliminates the possibility of instant legislation. It is a subtle but important part of the legislative process.

Article 6, Section 3. Power to Investigate

The House of Representatives needs to have the power to investigate and gather information on any topic. In part it deals with the ability of Congress to make informed decisions. There may also be times when the House may need to investigate criminal wrongdoing. This issue is connected to the fact that Congress is responsible to make sure the laws of the land are followed. The tools of the inquest and the subpoena must be open to them.

While the Senate has the same power to investigate any issue they see as pertinent to the well being of either society or government, other issues may require the involvement of members from both Houses. To allow for such interaction seems appropriate. It will be possible for a bi-level committee to research and investigate a given problem or topic.

Article 6, Section 4. Facility

One of the core concepts of this Proposed Constitution is the shift of the House of Representatives from an established, structured body to one expressed in the form of a *virtual assembly* or a national governmental network. Members of the House of Representatives will be based in the home districts, and the connection to the national assembly will be by the use of telecommunication and teleconferencing. The question is a candid one. Is it more democratic to base our representatives in our communities, or is it better to have them based at a national capital? This is a very fundamental question and the answer will lead in a direction not normally considered. The argument is that democracy would be better served if our elected officials remained in their districts. The next question is how that can be done. This returns us to our technology and the advancements we have had in the field of telecommunications. Maybe as little as ten years ago such an electronic structure would not have been realistic, but our technology has moved to the point that such a system is not only possible, but desirable.

With the use of computers, miniature cameras, speaker phones, printers, visual imaging machines, electronic communication systems, satellites dishes, and conventional telephone lines, it has become possible to connect an individual to the larger body. Through the use of computers a matrix can be created that becomes the assembly. In those cases when it is needed, codes and cryptograms have been developed that make electronic communication virtually indecipherable. The cost would be marginal, especially when considering the expenditure of having Representatives exist outside of their districts. The cost of maintaining permanent buildings, staff, and equipment is considerable. Most of this would no longer be needed. As well, the members of the House would not have the problem of maintaining two residences.

The advantage for the population is that their Representatives would be living in their communities. Contact and interaction would be less restrictive. Concerns or issues could be addressed by personal contact. The process becomes more distinctive and in the end more democratic. The populace would see their Representatives at the basketball game, at the grocery store, or at a town meeting. The whole issue of our Representatives being distant or aloof would begin to disappear.

It is also possible that local government officials would be better served by requiring members of the House to live in the districts. Individuals on city councils, county planning boards, school boards, mayors, and even elected state officials would have greater contact with their Representatives. It would be possible for members of government to attend city council meetings or Parent Teacher Association meetings (PTA). In turn they would be better connected to their own local party and its organization. By being involved and participating at the local level, even if it is nothing more then observing, the Representative would have a better feel for the problems at the local level.

Here is a conception of how the system would work. Some members of the House of Representatives would have an office separate from their residence. They would be able to use a party headquarters, a room in a City-County government building, or maybe simply rented office space. It would be a matter of what they felt most comfortable, but others would operate out of their own homes. Within a section of their house a place would be set aside for the business of government. They would need space for their equipment, screens, and computers. There would be a desk from which to work, and from that location representative government would originate.

Those who would come to see the Representative would meet with her or him in their living room. The sanctity of a person's home will bring about a different environment. Truly, government would be operating at a level unequaled since the beginning of the American experience. Even if there were conflicting views on an issue, the atmosphere and forum would be far more personable.

If congressional representatives were operating out of their own homes, the issue of lobbyists and special interests would also be seen in a different light. If long rows of luxury automobiles are lined up in front of a Representative's house, the neighbors will know. We are all members of a collection of interest groups; this should not all be seen as a negative. Lobbyists in a very real sense pass on valid pieces of information and knowledge to our Representatives. It is part of the political system. As it is done now our representatives have contact with lobbyists outside the view of the electorate. Regardless of the system employed, special interest will find a way to get their message to our Representatives. Yet, from a community-based system the effect is not the same; positions of dominance currently enjoyed would no longer be feasible were Congress not nestled in one location.

There will be times when the House of Representatives will meet in full session. It will give the members an opportunity to interact and review similar business, and a chance to meet with people on a personal basis. There is no reason why such meetings would need to be held in Washington, D.C.; in fact they could be held in any large convention center throughout the country. It would be possible that one year the House would meet in Seattle, the next year Philadelphia, the following year Oklahoma City. Government would become more woven into the mainstream of American life.

Clearly, these yearly meetings would take on the atmosphere of a convention. It is hoped that some business of government would take place, and that there are advantages to having Congress meet in full session. The political parties surely would be able to take advantage of these meetings. Even so, many of the events of such sessions would be for general consumption. These sessions and meetings will allow the media an opportunity to interview the membership at a central location. It will allow an opportunity for special interests and lobbyists to interact with the House and make their pitches. It is very possible that for a two-week period these sessions could become more carnival than governmental. Even so, the direction is one of balance. Day-to-day interaction in the home district will be far more exclusive. These sessions will give the House membership a chance to talk to individuals experiencing the same types of problems and under the very same conditions. It becomes a point of mutual support. All of this would be done at the government's expense.

Lack of a permanent location for the House of Representatives and the ability to vote from remote areas would change the arrangement of voting on House measures. If a vote has been called or scheduled for a piece of legislation, it would be possible to have the votes come in through the course of a twenty-four hour period. Through the use of laptop computers and modems, votes could be entered from any place in the world. Congresspersons could be out of their districts, either on recreation or doing the business of government, and still be able to interact, debate, and vote on issues within the assembly.

The need for a twenty-four hour voting period may be obligatory because of the different time zones. Currently the United States cuts across six time zones with a five hour variation. Some type of accommodation would have to be made. Sections of the day's activities could be taped and reviewed before voting. It is possible that a member in Hawaii might have to be up at five in the morning to participate in a committee hearing. The trade-off is that they will not have to travel 5,000 miles to get back home.

While members of the House would be based out of their districts, they still would be allowed mobility. This would even be expected. While Congresspersons would not be expected to meet with lobbyist outside their districts, they could still give speeches and pursue different levels of investigations. Depending on the committee assignments, the leadership may request personal gatherings to take sealed information. The spirit of the new system would be such that while House members would be allowed free access to the nation as a whole, it would be possible for a woman to be both a Congressperson and a mother. No matter what she would not be away from her four year old for very long.

Article 7, Section 1. Senate Functions Maintained

The Senate of the United States will still maintain many of its current functions, and the scope of its duties will remain uniform. A number of fundamental changes, however, will be made, the chief of which is that the Senate will no longer originate legislation. They will still be responsible to confirm appointments at all levels of government, including the Supreme Court. The Senate will also be expected to approve or reject all treaties. In the legislative process the Senate will become the chief form of *checks and balances* and will have the power to veto measures sent to them. The major difference is that the Senate will no longer be to able to set the national agenda. What they will do is more a matter of endorsing the direction set out by the House of Representatives.

The primary point that the Proposed Constitution would like to address is the connection between state and Federal government. When the nation's founders first established the American Constitution, the Senators were elected by the state legislators. The standard criticism was that the Senate was a "rich man's club." The hope concerning the Seventeenth Amendment to the United States Constitution was that it would associate and reconnect the Senate with the masses. While the Amendment does establish a greater sense of democracy, it is doubtful that its entire spirit was reached. The office of Senator still requires considerable wealth and the objective of keeping the Senators connected to the states has been lost.

To be a Senator in the nineteenth century required considerable affluence; hence, the system developed many abuses. The Senators knew that their true constituents were the state legislators, and in fact to some degree Senate action was crafted to represent this relationship. The problem is that the states do have interests. The American Constitution as much as any document was designed to allow the bicameral system to represent two distinct concepts. The House of Representatives was to represent the people and the Senate the states. The problem with the Senate is that while each state is given two Senators, the connection with the people is not well defined. It is possible to argue that the Senate has become most attentive to their financial sponsors that assist with their political campaigns. Both the people and the states are a secondary concern.

An effort is made in the Proposed Constitution to reconnect the Senate to the states by letting the Senators run for office at the same times as their state governors. A strong Senatorial slate should help the state officials running for office. In turn the appeal of the gubernatorial race would assist the Senators. At the very least the Senators will need to be more aware of state governmental issues and obstacles. The political parties will focus more on a slate rather than individual candidacy.

The other issue that has emerged recently in American politics and has taken on considerable acceleration is *term limits*. A strong argument can be made for both sides of this issue. On one side is the concept that our elected officials should not be professional politicians and that public service should not be a career in itself. On the other side of the controversy is the view that experience in government does count, that the greater the knowledge, the greater the capacity to serve the people. Those opposing term limits note that the final word is always the people's. If they disapprove of how the system operates, they would vote these officials out of office. Of course this is an extremely complex issue. What is being proposed in this new Constitution is simply letting the Senators run for office more frequently. Instead of facing election every six years the number has been reduced to four. This would give the masses an increased opportunity to review the record and contribution the Senators were making to their constituents.

The issue that gets tangled in the process is the staggering of the Senatorial elections. While the issue may be a minor one, the greater continuity would be found in letting one Senator run for office opposite his or her counterpart, alternating them every two years. The problem is aligning the Senate races with the gubernatorial races. Here the preferred concept is seen as better connecting the United States Senate to the states, which will mean that both Senators will run for office at the same time.

The only real criteria for running for office will be that a Senatorial candidate must be eighteen years old and a citizen. Any and all other issues would be sorted out by the electorate.

Article 7, Section 2. Legislative Responsibility

The Senate does become a different type of body with their chief responsibility to review legislation. The changes force them to address the implications of the legislation that is sent to them. The Senate must also act on and return all legislation. They would be given sixty days to debate and discuss the measure, but at some point they either would have to pass the law or veto it.

Filibusters would no longer have the same effect on a piece of legislation. At some time the issue would have to be voted on regardless of the views of its protractors.

Instead of the President, the Senate would have the power to veto. A situation may develop in which a piece of legislation is sent to the Senate in early November, and before it can be acted upon, the holiday break occurs. No time is accrued. The bill will simply wait until after the break and then the clock will start again. If the Senate felt insufficient time remained to review a measure, they could simply vote it down. The House could then either attempt to pass it by a two-thirds vote or resubmit it to the Senate.

The Senate would be allowed, and to some degree expected, to write reviews and list recommendations to a bill. Such critiques could be helpful and even desirable. The objective is for the Senate to become advisory and contemplative. They become overseers to the process. Their power becomes a matter of influence and statesmanship. They can encourage and support, but not direct. In part this deals with the use of the parliamentary system, but, more important, the House of Representatives is seen as having the greatest link to the people.

Article 7, Section 3. Senate Rules

The group that knows the most about the Senate are the members of the Senate. While a Constitution may outline the basic responsibilities of the job, the detail becomes a matter for the Senate to work out. They must be free to do their jobs proficiently and properly. Like the House of Representatives the Senate will also determine their own rules and procedures. They need to have capability to decide who will lead them and the qualifications of such leadership. In turn the Senate will need to develop their own code of ethics and promote systems of realizing these goals.

Article 7, Section 4. Investigation and Review

The Senate will need the power to investigate and obtain information. Knowledge is an important part of the legislative process and such proceedings should not be discounted or restricted. It is understood that many times such Congressional inquests become political in nature, that the original goal of reviewing legislation or a governmental process may become overshadowed by personal or party interest. It is impossible to develop a Constitution that is unencumbered by politics, for it is the nature of the creature. The spirit of the Article is an honest one, that the Senate as a part of the legislative process requires the power to investigate and examine measures sent to them. Without this ability the process becomes superficial.

Though the power to conduct investigations was not an item listed in the American Constitution. it was implied. It has proved to be an effective and forceful tool of the Legislative branch. The power to investigate is one of the reasons the national government has become a dominant feature in American society and has superseded the states. In many ways the ability to investigate is a more powerful mechanism than the capability to legislate.

What is equally important is not just the investigation of issues or bills, but the publishing of all consequential findings. In any investigation there are many blind alleys, issues that later prove to have no merit. The media may focus on those subordinate topics and committees may spend considerable time with them, in the end the findings need to be published. It is the divulging of the information obtained that has the most value. Here all such investigations need to be honest and straightforward.

Article 7, Section 5. Treaty Ratification

A part of the Proposed Constitution that is identical to the American Constitution is the ratification of treaties. The Senate will still be expected to review such documents and pass them by a vote of two-thirds. If a treaty is rejected by the Senate it may be resubmitted by the Prime Minister but the House of Representatives can take no action to pass such an item. The Prime Minister may negotiate such items but the only way they become valid is through the Senate.

Article 7, Section 6. Ambassadorship Ratification

The Senate has the responsibility to review and confirm all appointments to government. Ambassadors are but one of many types of governmental positions that the Senate must review and vote on. They are able to hold hearings, investigate back rounds, and reject a nominee if they choose to do so, all of which is done by a fifty-percent majority vote.

Article 7, Section 7. Court Ratification

The original concept of the American Constitution was that the people would actually vote for only one of our four controlling bodies of government. The House of Representatives was directly elected by the masses. Even with the changes in the election procedures for the Senate it still leaves a gap between the people, and our form of self-government, and those that have dominion over our power structure. The two chief problems are the Electoral College and the appointment process of the Federal Court System. There are those that have argued that Federal judges and members of the Supreme Court should be elected positions. There have also been those that feel the offices should not be confirmed for life.

Without going into detail, these are honest arguments and there is a place for this type of discussion. Yet, at some point one of two position must be accepted—either Federal judges are directly elected or they are appointed. Both systems have their advantages and their protractors. The current system of appointing judges is also a political process and it becomes elitist in design. If Federal judges were elected by the people the process would become personalized to the point where judicial actions would become campaign promises. There would be an expectation to perform in a given social direction.

The one single advantage to the current system of appointing Federal judges and members of the Supreme Court is that the undertaking can be designed as an examination into the expertise of the candidates. It is the view that the Senate can better arbitrate and understand the legal skills of an individual appointed to these high offices than the average citizen. While it is still a political process, qualifications are still required. In the Proposed Constitution the Senate would be required to oversee the appointment process and their input into this matter would be considerable.

Article 7, Section 8. Cabinet And Administrative Ratification

The review of appointments and assignments of governmental posts become the responsibility of the Senate. The issue of Cabinet Members is but one more. The Prime Minister would nominate an individual to the position and the Senate would need to confirm. The expectation is that such ratifications would occur in a timely manner within the same time frame as passing legislation. Situations may occur where Cabinet officers have been placed in a department and have been doing their jobs for a considerable period of time before they are confirmed by the Senate.

Article 7, Section 9. Sanctioned Territory Ratification

This one area of the Proposed Constitution may be controversial. It may have the feel that the United States is attempting to project its political, economic, and military will on other nations. The goal is something else, the Sanctioned Territory sections of this Proposed Constitution are designed to protect democracy, and to a lesser degree to project democracy, as an international element. There is a risk to this concept. It is possible that this honestly intended Article could be used in the most corrupt fashion. It is possible that foreign nations may attempt to use this Article as a defense for the status quo rather than the securing of democracy.

Regardless, there has to be a body or a group of individuals that will oversee the process. The Senate is the most appropriate body to accomplish this act. If a sovereign state wishes the protection of the United States and they wish to become a Sanctioned Territory it will be the Senate that will determine the merits of the case. As it is with other elements of government, the Senate becomes the custodian of altruistic power.

Article 7, Section 10. Senate Immunity

Members of Congress need to have some level of assurance that they will be able to do their jobs without unacceptable outside behaviors. This does not mean that Senators are beyond wrongdoing, it is more a matter of pursuing such issues in the correct format. A Senator should be able to say what ever he feels is appropriate without fear of reprisal. It is hoped that honesty, good taste, and moral conduct are always the rule. Freedom of Speech should have an even greater regard on the floor of the Senate.

The Senate should also be seen as a sanctuary. It should not be possible to arrest, detain, or serve a member of Congress with a warrant while they are in that body. There are places where warrants can be dispensed, the Senate should not be one of them. The reason for such events would be more of an act of ridicule than of justice.

One of the questions that can be asked in drafting a Constitution is whether there are legislative crimes. Currently under the structure of the American government it is possible for a group of three hundred people properly placed to have complete control of the Federal government. Millions of people would be subject to the exigency of these few people. Their needs and wants could be instantaneously fulfilled, but it would be at the expense of all others in society. In time their self-interest and selfishness would became too oppressive. The people would simply vote them out of office. In this scenario the new representatives would look back at the abuse of governmental power committed by their predecessors and they may attempt to prosecute them.

This type of situation is very possible. Examples in history may be found and there may even be an outcry from the public to pursue those individuals that abused their public trust, but there are limits to what can be accomplished. One person's abuse of power is another person's civic duty. The three hundred or so individuals may be nothing more than a political party. They may have been pursuing their perceived mandate, which was counter to the new group in power. Politics creates odd behaviors and interactions, but regardless there should not be legislative crimes. Such processes will destroy a democratic state.

Article 7, Section 11. Governmental Community

Unlike the House of Representatives the Senate would have a permanent structure. The reasons are not well defined or explicit. A Senator still would not be able to interact with the people at anything representing an exclusive level even if they were stationed in their home state. State governments would not be any better served as well. A Senator's home may be hundreds of miles from their own state capitals. For a person to live in a state capital would not be any more desirable than simply having them at the national capital.

No matter how government is designed there still is a need for a national capital. The Prime Minister and the departments of government need established residences. The Supreme Court needs a forum from which to operate. The nation-state will receive and credit ambassadors, while other nations will need embassies. A national capital does have utility and purpose. It is difficult or even impossible to operate a large modern Federal state without permanent structures. If this interpretation is correct it is also justified to have the Senate at the national capital.

The reality is that government, especially at the international level, has parts to it that are ceremonial. The Senate will be able to serve these sentiments. This does not mean that the Senate will not have real work to do within the framework of government, but there are many levels of need and responsibility. One of which is the protocols of government.

One of the reasons why there is a need for a new Constitution deals with the growth of government and the related concept of architecture. Congress moved into the capital in 1800. While full of tradition, the building by both use and design, has become antiquated. These are issues seeping with emotion, but looking beyond such sentiment the reality is that a new structure would not only serve the people better but also those individuals elected to office. It would represent an opportunity to modernize the structure of government.

While there is nothing within this Proposal that would dictate the construction of new Federal buildings and it must also be understood that most of these commentaries are a matter of conjecture, opinion, and contemplation. There is an image that a new Senate building would be needed. Ideally it would be a huge complex supporting both the Library of Congress and the Senate. In the center would be the upper house. It would include modern conveniences, telecommunication equipment, offices, and support staff. Within this complex there could also be sections where specific House committees could meet to hear concealed information. Even so, the majority of the building would be taken up by the Library of Congress. If a person's imagination would be allowed to wonder even further there is the possibility of connecting such a complex to a university. It would definitely place the Senate on a different plane.

Article 8, Section 1. The Prime Minister as Executive Officer

One of the changes in this Proposed Constitutions is the switch to a government more closely aligned to the parliamentary system. It is really not involved or complex. The chief difference is between the Prime Minister and the President. As the system currently stands the President is the executive officer of the government. From the view of the nation's founders the President is the administrator of governmental functions and operations. Over the years those powers have been expanded. Even so, the Prime Minister will also be able to wield considerable power. In fact the Prime Minister will have greater capability of following up with the party agenda than the President of the United States. The chief difference is that the Prime Minister is able to direct and create legislation. The issue and the comparison at some point becomes meager. It is a rare President who is unable to have their views heard and acted upon. The only real question is whether we want the power structure to be accountable to the direction in which they take us.

With a parliamentary system enough power is given to act. When the processes have been completed it is clear to everyone concerned who is responsible and what political party has taken us to that point. There is something more honest about this approach that makes hiding behind confusion and distractions more difficult.

Under a parliamentary system the political parties take on greater importance. To some degree the Prime Minister is an extension of the political parties. The majority of the members of the House of Representatives elect the Prime Minister. While not directly stated, the majority will be the majority party. At any time the preponderance of the House membership wants to vote on a new Prime Minister such a vote would be held. If a new Prime Minister is elected a week's transition will be given. The process is expedient and disciplined. It allows for problems to be corrected quickly and with the minimum of convulsion for government.

But a wide range of advantages to electing a Prime Minister can be shown over the current presidential system. One of these is the simple changing of the position or office. Unlike the presidential system, it is not a drawn out affair. The concern of governmental paralysis becomes less of a fact with the parliamentary model. It is by far more efficient. It is not represented by a political campaign that is waged for two years, with its drain on time and money. Government is not placed on hold while Presidential behaviors or actions are interrogated by the media, the opposition parties, and the masses.

Impeachment becomes a non-issue under this system. If a Prime Minister has committed a crime, or has given even the implication of illegal activities, the individual in the position can be voted out. The point at which a Prime Minister became a political liability is the time that a party vote would be held, regardless of whether there is any criminal activity or not. While it may be a personal tragedy for the Prime Minister who is removed, government would not suffer by having an ongoing scandal.

The American Constitution has spent a considerable amount of time reviewing the line of succession for the Presidency and what would occur if a chief executive were unable to complete a term or became gravely ill. Again, for the parliamentary system this becomes a non-issue. If the Prime Minister dies or becomes too ill to perform the duties of office, the position is filled by a simple vote of the House of Representatives. The whole issue of a Vice-President becomes moot.

Article 8, Section 2. Election of Prime Minister

The replacement of a Prime Minister can occur even when illness or illicit behavior is not a factor. If the Prime Minister is nothing more than ineffective or has poor leadership skills, the party may choose to supersede the officeholder with another. In the end the job takes on a different preconception. Prime Ministers were elected to office by local districts, they know that regardless what happens they will retain this position, at least until the next election. Prime Ministers are also tied to their districts; even as the executive officer and head of government, they still must maintain this connection to the home district. In the case of the American President the office becomes imperial. To become a President a person must have spent a considerable amount of time in party politics and in the various governmental positions. The process is apt to detach the person from the people. Many Presidents have a collection of home states. It is a position that does not associate itself very well with any other body or group. The American Presidency is an entity that truly does stand alone.

The only real concern with the process of electing a Prime Minister is during the holiday break. The House would not be meeting during this time. If the Prime Minister would become seriously ill, more than likely action on such a vote might be delayed. The issue should be a minor one. The house leadership would still be in place; if an election vote would be needed the membership could still be contacted and a vote could be made.

One advantage in the use of a parliamentary government or a Prime Minister is that this is not a new system. The British and most of the democratic nations of the world have been using the system for extended periods of time. Most of the issues and problems have been worked out; it is a long way from experimental. We should be able to tap into this wisdom and experience that has already been obtained.

While debates are not required in the election of a Prime Minister this does not mean that such events would not occur. Generally within the parliamentary system the party has already determined who their designee will be, but this is not to say that such discussions or debates could not still take place. In fact opposition political parties will also field candidates. It is just that these votes fall along party lines.

The one item that is lost with the Prime Minister that is found in the presidential system is the direct vote. Even understanding that the American President is not elected directly but through the Electoral College, there remains still a structure connecting the President to the electorate. This should not be discounted. To have the people vote for their leaders is an important part of a democracy. The problem is simply a matter of proficiency. Regardless of the system employed trade-offs are to be expected. With the parliamentary system the direct vote is the one concept that is lost.

Article 8, Section 3. Head of Government

The statement that really should be noted is not that the Prime Minister is head of government, but that the Prime Minister is not head of state. This Proposed Constitution lists no head of state. In American government the President has taken on that dual responsibility. This represents an odd set of circumstances. Most democratic governments around the world have found some way to divide these obligations. Some separate the two concepts between a Prime Minister and a President, others do it by use of a Prime Minister and the Monarchy. It does give an unfair advantage to a political party or even a Prime Minister to allow the officer to speak for the nation-state when in truth all they are speaking for is the government or the regime. There are no easy solutions, and this represents a major flaw in this Proposed Constitution. Nevertheless, in this Proposed Constitution there is no head of state. In the most symbolic of ways the true head of state is the people.

Article 8, Section 4. Foreign Relationships

This issue of course returns to the ideas related to being head of government. The Prime Minister becomes responsible for all the interactions that the Union has with other nations. In fact the Prime Minister will become the chief focus of such interactions, conversations, and correspondence. As much as anyone it is the executive officer that will need to see that international law is followed and that the nation-state responds to other nations in a civilized manner. It becomes the Prime Minister's job to negotiate treaties and to determine what is in the best interest of the country, then submit the treaties to the Senate. While the Senate will need to ratify the treaty, the Prime Minister will surely have to defend the direction and the need. It will also be the executive officer who will have to receive and accept ambassadors and envoys. All of those items that represent being the Head of Government become the responsibility of the Prime Minister.

Article 8, Section 5. Appointment to the Cabinet

The Prime Minister is responsible to appoint to Cabinet posts capable and competent people. Cabinet and departmental heads are extremely important to the proper functioning of the government. The Prime Minister will need to find conscientious people to fill these positions. Once that has been done then the Senate will need to confirm and ratify the choices.

Article 8, Section 6. Prime Minister Status

While clearly the executive officer of the government, the Prime Minister also is a member of Parliament and has been elected by her or his district. The advantage is that the Prime Minister is able to submit bills directly to the legislature and is able to vote. The Prime Minister is not seen as an outsider, an individual from a different branch of government; rather, the Prime Minister is a member of the Legislative body and operates accordingly.

The one problem is that the district from which the Prime Minister was elected will still need representation. In this case the Prime Minister when in office will appoint an individual to represent him or her in that district. This appointee will be a nonvoting member of the House of Representatives and will function as a staff member and as an overseer of the needs of the Prime Minister's district. This district administrator will be responsible to keep the executive office informed of events of the district, the concerns of the electorate, and their individual needs.

The last point is simply that the Prime Minister will be paid at a higher level than the other members of the House. There is always the possibility, and even likelihood that the House leadership would be paid at a higher level than the other Congresspersons, commensurate with her or his responsibilities. It is not an unlawful concept but is related to the pay structure of any large organization.

Article 8, Section 7. Commander in Chief

While this article represents only one line it is an extremely complex issue. Traditionally the President of the United States has been the Commander in Chief of the armed forces. This is an excellent concept and has readily been accepted as an important philosophy of democracy. The importance of civilian rule over the military should not be minimized. The only other options would be to allow the Cabinet member that is head of the Department of Defense to be Commander in Chief or to allow the top military officer of the nation to hold that position. The difficulty is ultimately that the Prime Minister is still responsible for what occurs within the military. While the difference between Commander in Chief and the chief administrative officer is subtle, it is too important a job to leave outside of the elective process. In the end the Prime Minister is the best individual to hold this position and have control over the armed forces.

This Proposed Constitution does recognize that ongoing conflicts have arisen between the Executive branch of government in the United States and Congress over the power to wage war. Ideally that issue would be determined by a Declaration of War. If the nation-state is at war then the total resources and force of the country should be directed at that task. The problem is that war seems to come in different levels. It is also possible to be involved in a military conflict that was actually originated by a third party, by a treaty, or even a world organization such as the United Nations. These are issues that are ongoing. Each situation will have a little different slant on what represents war and power found within the Constitution.

The Proposed Constitution does have designs within it that make war more deliberate, one of which is a balanced budget. War by its very nature is an expensive process and requires large amounts of revenue. To wage a military conflict and fit it inside a peacetime budget would be incredibility difficult. The use of a no-confidence vote would also be a tool by which such a national controversy could be placed before the people.

War is a very conscious act. If that step is taken it should be total and complete. It should be done with the support of the people and of Congress, and the goal should be absolute. If the citizens of the nation are to die in a military conflict, let us make sure the cause is just and that it is crystal-clear who is responsible for this action. In this case it will be the Prime Minister, who will be the Commander in Chief.

Article 8, Section 8. Executive Functions

The question that is asked in this Article is, "What office is responsible for the Federal bureaucracy?" The answer is the Prime Minister. The Prime Minister to some degree will be accountable for the size of the government. The executive office will be expected to review and mandate the direction of the regulatory process and to make sure that proposed regulations are moved through the legislature so that they become law.

Governmental regulations are not intrinsically evil. Two concepts predominate. One is that governmental regulations lessen the ability of business and related entities to function effectively in the marketplace. That governmental paperwork and system creates a drag upon the commerce of the nation. It limits and stifles new ideas and concepts. On the opposite side of the debate is the public good and safety. By regulating various enterprises it creates a fair playing field and ensures the well being of the public. These are pendulum-type issues that swing back across the political spectrum depending upon the doctrine of the times. The issue for a Constitution is simply to allow for governmental regulations and oversight. Someone must be answerable to the process. There still may be items that are not brought before the Legislative branch and at some level represent regulations. By accepting the post of Prime Minister a person must acknowledge the full level of responsibility.

In any case as executive officer the Prime Minister becomes the chief administrator of all the Federal departments and agencies.

Article 8, Section 9. Question-and-Answer Period

To be accountable, the party in power must address the opposition party's concerns in a straightforward manner. In the parliamentary system power to govern is clearly given to the majority party. This ruling party must be able to explain the given path of government and society. The opposition parties need to remain visible. They need to assert themselves and to make sure that the management of government by the ruling party is consistent with the goals of the people.

One tenet that is critical to the well-being of a democracy yet rarely discussed is the importance of a *loyal opposition*. Democracy cannot survive unless this idea is firmly in place. Minority parties are entitled to express their views and ideas. One of the ways this can be done is through the use of a question-and-answer period.

Rules and procedures must be hashed out. While this is a system that the British have used pragmatically and effectively in the House of Commons, this is not to say that the rules need to be the same as British rules. Each nation needs to create its own set of rules and develop their own traditions.

Clearly this Article must designate the leadership of the House of Representatives to stand in for the Prime Minister. If the Prime Minister was out of the country engaged in the affairs of state or at a leadership conference, the question-and-answer activity could be suspended. On the other side is the concern that the Prime Minister may not wish to face the opposition parties. The chief executive may find a reason to leave the country. Without addressing that concern directly, the spirit of this item is for the Prime Minister to take that responsibility of encountering the questions generated by the contrasting political parties.

The goal with this item is to allow the difficult questions to be asked and the answers not to be hidden. The reply can be revealing, even to those that respond.

Article 8, Section 10. Pardons

Inevitably unseen or unexpected issues and circumstances will arise. Not every circumstance or future event can be predicted or anticipated. Therefore a fail-safe factor must be built into the system that allows us to correct wrongs, to forgive, and to end suffering. To allow the Prime Minister the power to pardon and grant reprieves is well within the scope of the duties of this office.

Article 8, Section 11. Residence

In the Proposed Constitution the House of Representatives does not have permanent structure; a democracy does not require buildings. This, however, is not a point of totality. An established residence might be desirable for many reasons and offer many advantages, especially for the Prime Minister. The first point is one of utility and convenience. The Prime Minister will meet with eminent people and dignitaries from around the world. A place will be needed to discuss the affairs of state and the inter-workings of government and to conduct the many meeting of democratic government. A permanent structure allows for entertainment and socialization by the chief executive. A building provides a forum from which news conferences can be held and addresses given. It would also be more readily secured, but as much as anything a residence for the Prime Minister allows for a physical image of the executive office; a point of visibility and accessibility for the nation-state. Symbols do count, and they say a great deal about a nation. If one part of this visual governmental image is to be taken away by teleconferencing and electronics, part of it still needs to be maintained.

Article 8, Section 12. Authority during election periods

Much goes without saying; the powers of the Prime Minister would remain in force continuously, or at least until the Prime Minister is voted out. The problem is that as soon as there is not a confirmation of such a provision it comes into question. The office of the executive will remain in force and service throughout a general election or the holiday break.

Article 8, Section 13. Immunity

This issue of forcing a Prime Minister into litigation because of a governmental policy or a decision made in office seems inappropriate. While the Prime Minister as a member of the House will have the same immunity as other Representatives, the office will need the added benefit of not being pursued by frivolous lawsuits. The court system has always been reluctant to review issues that are political in nature. This Article gives credence to the court's position. Also, the reality of governmental policy is that many times by giving to one person you are taking away from someone else. This should not be a legal issue.

Article 9, Section 1. Proposition and Initiatives

If the goal of a new Constitution is to increase democracy, to develop systems that improve and enhance democracy, it becomes a matter of course that a system of Referendums, Propositions, or Initiatives should be developed. There is nothing more fundamental to democracy than allowing the people to write, advocate, debate, and vote on their own legislation. It is truly an extraordinary and marvelous concept, that the people have the power to govern themselves. When Referendums and Initiatives are allowed in a community it brings that society to a new level of self government.

The people are able to directly influence the process of public affairs and the making of laws. Voting becomes not just a matter of electing a politician to an office, but the people are also voting on ideas and philosophies as well. The system requires greater input and an association from the electorate. Referendums require discussion, review, and debate—which is the essence of the political system.

This is by no means a new idea. These are ideas that were found within the framework of the republican governments of ancient Greece and there were forms of Propositions in the Germanic tribes of two millennium ago. These are the type of concepts found in the town meetings or the early colonial governments. Currently modern Switzerland has developed a system of Referendums as a part of their democracy. In the United States there are twenty-two states that have systems by which Initiatives can be placed on the ballot. They are Alaska, Arizona, Arkansas, California, Colorado, Idaho, Maine, Maryland, Massachusetts, Michigan, Missouri, Montana, Nebraska, New Mexico, Nevada, North Dakota, Ohio, Oklahoma, Oregon, South Dakota, Utah, and Washington. There are other states that have systems in place that allow the electorate to vote on issues but they are highly controlled by the legislative system.

The intention here is for Propositions to be generated by a petition drive. The goal would be to obtain the signatures of fifteen percent of the registered voters in a state. Most Referendums in the states run about ten percent, some even as low as five percent. The issue is not so much with how supportive a person is on any given question, but more a matter of allowing a vote on the subject. The petitions would be submitted to the Attorney General of the respective states for validation. It would be important for all the petitions to say the same thing with identical wording. Not all the states would need to be polled. Once the petitions were certified they would be presented to the Administrative Clerk in Congress. For the next two general elections, unless it was defeated in the first round, the electorate of the country would have an opportunity to vote on the legislation. If it was successful then it would become law.

The system is not set up to be easy. Any organization that begins the process of placing a Referendum before the people, regardless how just that cause may be, is facing a major task. The United States is an extremely large country, with a great diversity. Such Initiatives will be an arduous, time consuming, and a painful process. For those that are successful it will be a triumph as much for the human spirit and a sheer sense of will as much as the cause from which it was spawned.

The Proposition becomes another part of the *Checks and Balances* which were so important to the Founding Fathers. In the most real sense it is the truest of all the forms of *Checks and Balances*. It allows for a system where the last say in the legislative process is absolutely the people. Under the current processes of the American Constitution the last say is the Congress.

One issue remains. Congress like any other organization or body in the world has issues which are special or unique unto themselves. No matter how many restrictions or *Checks and Balances* are placed in the system, government still has a separate interest. It is possible to have total agreement by all the branches of government and yet that issue not be in the best interest of the people. Propositions allow society to have a semblance of democratic equilibrium. It allows for the people to pilot a course of action.

It should be noted that the use of a Referendum is not perfect. Most states that have Initiatives can attest to the fact that rarely does a Referendum go unchallenged in the court system. It has become one more step in the Proposition process. Some have argued that Referendums do more for keeping attorneys practicing than any other set of proceedings. It could also be contended that there is nothing within a Referendum that would stop the House of Representatives from simply rewriting a new law and passing it. Laws do change. An Initiative is but one more piece of legislation. Even conceding these points, nothing empowers the electorate as much as the ability to generate a Proposition. It hands the people a tool that is the ultimate weapon in democracy.

Article 10, Section 1. Function of the Cabinet.

The Cabinet is a significant part of government representing the system of administration. Both the American presidential system and the parliamentary system use the Cabinet effectively and it is an important component of representative government. The Cabinet is more than a body of individuals appointed by a head of government or executive officer, these are the administrators and advisers to the government.

Cabinets are designed with two types of direction and structure. One is the American model and the other the form favored by the British. In both cases one of the functions of the Cabinet is that of advisers. The other part of the operation deals with administration of various departments. Most European Cabinets follow the British archetype while most Latin American countries are aligned more closely to the United States system.

In the European paradigm the Cabinets are connected to the legislature, most of which still hold position in that body. The Cabinet is made up of Ministers who are head of a given department, but not always. Sometimes Ministers will have what is known as Cabinet Rank. These are individuals who are given specific responsibilities within the government or operate within the Cabinet as advisers. It is possible within this European system for some of the Cabinet members to be from outside the ruling party. If a majority could not be obtained by one party, a coalition would be formed and the Cabinet could be divided accordingly.

The British seem rarely to have problems with a coalition government. A combination of legislative and executive power is nestled within the Cabinet. The British have their *Cabinet Ministers* and then a second group that parallel appointed positions. These are called the *Shadow Cabinet,* and they are made up of civil servants who hold permanent posts as heads of various departments. It allows for greater continuity of service and action. The British Cabinet also have greater responsibility to the legislative process and in setting policy. It is through the Cabinet, with the support of the Prime Minister, that the majority of new bills are introduced. It is common for opposition political parties to have formed Cabinets even through they are out of power.

The Canadian Cabinet functions very much like the British. It is formed by the Prime Minister from the members of their own party. Most of the ministers serve as heads of departments within the Federal Government. When the government "falls" the ministers will resign en masse.

The United States Cabinet does have a little different feel to it. While the President appoints the members of the Cabinet and they too serve as administrative heads, they must also be approved by the Senate. The Cabinet has advisory and consultative roles that move beyond their specific departments. It is common to have members of the Cabinet meet to do brainstorming on various issues, some of which are purely matters of foreign policy. In the American system the Cabinet has no formal power and wields no executive authority.

The American Constitution does not provide for a Cabinet. In one case it even places a barrier to the process by not allowing members of the legislation to hold federal offices. What occurs is that Cabinet members have considerably less say in the legislative process, and most of their involvement deals with giving testimony before Congressional committees and hearings. The lack of legislative capability of the American Cabinet is the chief reason that the American government creates regulations instead of legislation.

At the beginning of the twenty-first century the United States Federal Government had fourteen Cabinet posts. They included:

Secretary of State
Secretary of the Treasury
Secretary of Defense
Secretary of the Interior
Secretary of Agriculture
Secretary of Commerce
Secretary of Labor
Secretary of Health and Human Services
Secretary of Housing and Urban Development
Secretary of Transportation
Secretary of Energy
Secretary of Education
Secretary of Veterans Affairs
Attorney General

The list does show how our nation has changed over the years. When George Washington took office there were four Cabinet posts, the Secretary of War, the Secretary of State, the Secretary of the Treasury, and the Attorney General.

The issue for this Proposed Constitution is not so much to outline the activities of the Cabinet as it is recognizing the Cabinet as a Constitutional entity. Cabinet officers are extremely important. The size of government and the pure nature of governmental bureaucracies require guidance. This responsibility falls onto the Cabinet and the Prime Minister. As to which type or structure will be used for the Cabinet, this will deal in part with the character and personality of the Prime Ministers. Just like every President has used the Cabinet differently so will future generations of executive officers of the Union.

At some point the idea of who may discharge an appointed government official or a member of the Cabinet will surface. Traditionally the President of the United States has had this privilege. Even so, it has never been a perfectly defined power. Throughout American history there has been confusion at times as to what represents an appointed position and what represents a civil service job. Part of this controversy can be traced back to 1801. When Thomas Jefferson became President of the United States he found that his predecessor John Adams had given commissions to a large number of newly created positions of Justices of the Peace. Jefferson was incensed. He did not feel these positions were needed or wanted. The greater issue dealt with the fact the new appointments were all Adams' supporters and part of the Federalist Party. Only by using the court system was Jefferson able to reverse this process and even then it had mixed results.

There has been the argument that appears occasionally that if the President appoints and the Senate must ratify, then why should not the Senate also be required to ratify the dismissal? After all it is an equal process. This was the issue over which Congress attempted to remove President Andrew Johnson from office. He was impeached because he had removed Edwin Stanton, his Secretary of War. Congress had passed the Tenure of Office Act of 1867 purely as an effort to control the membership of the executive branch of government. For Johnson it was a matter of policy and the President had the right to determine the course of action within his own administration. Congress at the time felt differently and this was the issue used to try Johnson. In 1887 Congress repealed this Act, but with provisions.

The direction of this proposed Constitution is that the Prime Ministers may dismiss at their discretion any appointed office holder. Within the Parliamentary system the issue is not as pronounced as it is within the American Presidential system, but it needs to be addressed and reviewed. When there is a change in government, the government needs to change. This Article will allow that process to occur.

Article 10, Section 2. Appointments

It needs to be noted that a Cabinet position is a different job. It is unfair to the people to expect the same service and representation from an individual that is employed at two jobs, the example here would be working in the Congress and being a Cabinet officer. If an individual became a secretary of one of the departments they will need to resign their position in either the House of Representatives or the Senate. The normal process of replacing them would occur. There is no requirement that the Cabinet officers even have to be from the ruling party. It is the Prime Minister that will choose the Cabinet, and the nomination would be sent to the Senate.

Article 10, Section 3. Ratification

As it is with all governmental appointments the Senate will need to review and confirm the appointment. It will be the responsibility of the senate to examine the background and credentials of these Cabinet nominations. This overseeing capability is an important part of the current American government, as it would be for future configurations of government.

While there is no time limit on when the Senate must either approve or reject a nominee, it will be possible for a person to work as head of the department once they are appointed. If the Senate finds the person objectionable they will need to move forward with their hearings and the floor vote. In the same text if the Senate becomes sluggish over confirming the individual at least the department and people would not be penalized. In the case of ambassadors and judges they will need to be confirmed before they can fill their position.

If a person has been rejected by the Senate there is nothing that would curtail the executive from reappointing the same individual. They would face the same process of ratification. Such a situation would become a political dispute and one in which the people would need to address during the next election as they looked at the personalities involved.

Article 10, Section 4. Change of Executive Office

The issue is a simple one—the Cabinet serves at the discretion of the Prime Minister. If the Prime Minister wishes to discharge a Cabinet officer that is their prerogative. It is nothing more than an item of pragmatism. Ideally Prime Ministers needs to surround themselves with individuals that have similar philosophies and points of view concerning government. These ideas are connected to both administration and ideology. It creates a system of cohesion and proper succession. Even if there is a change in the Prime Minister, but not the political party, the executive officer needs to have the option of picking their own people. Of course during these periods of transition the Cabinet officers would continue to serve until replaced.

Article 11. Regulations

One of the advantages of the parliamentary system over the American presidential system is the ability to direct legislation to the Congress. Within the American form of government regulation is more common than legislation. It may seem minor in its operation, but if the goal is increased democracy, the people are better aligned to the legislative process than the regulatory one.

The goal is for items that would have been regulated in the past to now become legislation. Though some level of regulations may still exist, it is hoped that procedures would be the determining factors rather than directives to different institutions. Cabinet officers, and ultimately the Prime Minister, will be responsible for these acts. If a piece of legislation supported by a Cabinet officer moves through Congress and the item is poorly written or mismanaged, the responsibility will fall to the Cabinet Minister.

While not outlined in this Proposed Constitution it is hoped that the dividing line between what is submitted to Congress for passage as legislation and what is simple regulation deals with financial obligations or more specifically, taxation. If a regulation is created that represents a form of taxation or requires that a person spend money, it seems proper to run that item through the Congress for review and enactment. The authority and power to tax is in the hands of Congress, and the people need an opportunity to address these issues as well. If a governmental department or agency produces a regulation that is a form of taxation, that defeats the purpose of the system and stands outside the framework of the democratic process.

Article 12. Priority

At first glance it looks as if this Article in the Proposed Constitution is superseding all of the states' rights. The reality is that what is being conceded is the status quo. This is the reality of our current relationship with the Federal government and its relationship to the states. The truth is that Federal law takes precedence over state law, at least in actuality if not in perception.

Of course this is not how it started out or the original intent of the Founding Fathers. When the American Constitution was written it listed the responsibility for the nation's government and equally declared that all provisions not hereby stated became the rights of the individual states. This was an honest system and for the next seventy years the United States functioned accordingly. The states in the Union had considerable power and authority. In fact it could be argued that most governmental power was nestled within the states. The shift occurred during the American Civil War or shortly thereafter. The United States government became in the most real sense a Federal system. The majority of all governmental power was invested in the Federal government. While the American Constitution is unchanged in its inventory of governmental power and its relationship to the states, the point is that supreme authority in fact is now vested with the national government.

This is neither inherently good nor evil. In every situation or set of circumstances someone must have the last word. In the case of our government the last word is the American Congress. In this case it is little more than stating the obvious.

While some issues will be delegated to the states by the Federal government, on other topics the national government will choose not to become involved. Certain issues and problems are clearly state affairs and have importance only to an individual state. The importance of state governments should not be undermined; it is the states that create the Union and determine the nature of our Federalist system. The states still have considerable authority and this should continue.

The issue can be more clearly recognized by looking at the court system. Each state has a hierarchy of courts including an appeals court and a supreme court, but the end of any appeal process is with the United States Supreme Court. It is the final interpretation of the Constitution and the review of court proceedings. A great deal of activity is found in a state's court system. In fact most criminal and civil activity is addressed in these forums. Yet, it is understood that the U.S. Supreme Court is the last court of appeal and legal recourse; so it must be with the other branches of government.

If a system is developed that would not allow for Federal law to take precedence, or if the system attempts to divide power equally among the states and national government, what would occur is not a Federal System but a Confederation. There may be those who argue for such a system, but the United States has attempted that type of government in the past and it failed. The first government the United States had was a Confederation and it was established under the *Articles of Confederation*. The central government was subordinate to the states and Congress was dependent on the states, almost to the point of needing their good will to operate. Laws could not be generated unless the states supported the law and its usage. The national government had little ability to generate funds or to tax. The whole process was inherently weak and to some degree dangerous. The states began to operate as independent sovereign countries. The solution that was found was to create a stronger centralized government through the American Constitution, which in turn has become a Federalist system.

Article 13, Section 1. War Powers

War ranks with the most disturbing activities of humankind. Nothing shoulders with it a greater promise of absolute destruction. Human aggression is more than an antiquated feeling of self-preservation; it is entrenched in the whole nature of humanity. In truth it deals with some hidden instinct of our species. Without saying more it is human beings who create war, and human beings who must take responsibility for its perpetuation. It must also be said that the moment war no longer exists is the time that mankind will have evolved into a different creature and will have emerged as a different species.

It is committed only when all other options have ceased and all other institutions have conceded failure, but to believe that war has come to an end, that there will be no future wars is to ignore history. Institutional violence is part of the chronicle of every nation-state. It is not a point of glory, but part of the commission of government for it is government that may legally commit acts of violence either against their own citizens, or in this case, against the citizens of another country through war.

These very issues return to the primary reason for government. One of the chief responsibilities of a supreme authority is security. This issue cannot be underestimated. It is one of most important reasons why governments exist. The people give up their right to do whatever they wish in return for security and protection. If a government is to attend to this question, then they must have the power to defend, and in the most real sense to wage war.

If that issue is conceded then the power to declare war needs to be addressed within a Constitution. The next question is why does a declaration of war need to be a provision? After all, scores of wars are being fought around the world in any given year. The United States has been involved in numerous wars and military conflicts without a declaration of war. The point is twofold. War should not be easy, and, second, if the nation is to commit its armed forces to battle, then the people need to support those actions. It is only through a declaration of war that the process be validated. We have heard the old adage that "war is too important to be left in the hands of the generals." It also needs to be said that "war is too important to be left in the hands of the politicians." It is no different than any other issue; the path needs to return to the people.

The method of declaring war is fairly straightforward. The Prime Minister will submit the resolution to both Houses of Congress. They will vote it up or down. Both Houses would need a vote of fifty percent. One concern is that if the national government is to enter into a war it needs to be with another nation-state. Again, that sounds obvious, but there is a concern. Within the Proposed Constitution the only way that the budget does not have to be balanced is under a declaration of war. It is not in the best interest of the constitutional process if a politician were able to declare war on the economy just so that increased spending could occur.

There is another problem. War is not something that happens overnight. Most wars are begun in small steps. International hostilities sometimes have been raging for a substantial period of time before they are even acknowledged as wars. The Prime Minister must be able to have the power to command the armed forces and even commit the nation's military to a conflict while the Congress reviews the issues involved.

Article 13, Section 2. Military Conflicts

The nation's founders in developing the American Constitution created a dual capability of involving the nation in a war. On one side the Constitution stated that only Congress could declare war and on the opposite side the President was made Commander in Chief. Outwardly that would not look like a conflict, but in practice it has proved to be a considerable problem. Part of the difficulty is that war, or military conflicts, come in many sizes. There are wars like World War II that required the total resources and human skills of the nation to obtain success, and on the other end of the spectrum are military struggles such as Grenada in 1983, which are completed in a few days. Timing of such operations may not lend itself well to complete consultation with other bodies, and the Prime Minister, as it has been with the President, must be given freedom to act. Yet, at some point the question remains, what body has the last word in the nature of military conflicts. In this case, as with the American Constitution, it is Congress.

One of the advantages of the Parliamentary system is that the division between the Executive office and the Legislative branch is no longer distinct. Conflicts may still occur between Congress and the Prime Minister over the use of military forces but such disagreements should be lessened. A consensus within the leadership of the ruling party would be obtained before armed forces would be committed.

This article of the Proposed Constitution represents the core concept of the War Powers Resolution passed by the United States Congress after the Vietnam War. This was a valid piece of legislation. There is an effort to allow the President the ability to conduct foreign affairs and to use the nation's military forces, but still develop systems by which Congress would be kept involved. In the end the issue deals with Congress. They are the direct link to the people. The reality is that wars do occur, but if the military resources of the nation are to be committed to battle, it should be done with the support and permission of the people, especially in protracted conflicts that take extended periods of time. If we are to be a representative government the last word in whether a war is to be fought should rest with Congress.

Article 13, Section 3. Means of Production

In World War I the United States government was granted exceptional administrative powers to control the nation. Many of these powers bordered on abuse or operated beyond the Constitutional limits that we currently believe exist. Some of these authoritarian powers can be found in the Espionage and the Sedition Acts. These are not events that need to be duplicated and represent a very dark period of American Constitutional history. A specific definition of what represents Emergency War Powers needs to be set forth. In the case of the Proposed Constitution it is possible for government to pass an Emergency War Powers Act, but only under a declaration of war and only directed at resources. The government can control both the production and the financial resources needed to wage war, but civil liberties must remain intact.

There is also a concern that government may choose to declare a nonmilitary emergency and attempt to manage the economy. This cannot be done under this Proposed Constitution. It is not in the best interest of the other institutions of our society for the government to dictate their roles. In the same context during a time of war the government may need to have just such control. The argument is that only with a declaration of war may the government be allowed special emergency war powers. It should be permitted during a war and such powers should be discontinued at the cessation of hostilities.

Article 14, Section 1. Balanced Budget

One of the issues that has hounded the United States government in the last half of the twentieth century is a balanced budget. This is one of the simplest of ideas. The government through its various forms of revenue gathering and taxation spends money on those goods and services that the nation state needs. Congress, through the support of the people, determine what those needs will be. The government should not be spending money that they do not have. Regardless of the situation the budget needs to be balanced.

Every citizen in this country is held to the same set of conditions. We earn money, spend that money on things that we need or want, and we are held accountable if we do not stay within our budgets. This level of accountability is not only mandated by legal requirements, but also points of ethics. As children we are taught that we stay within our budgets and pay back what we borrow. It becomes a moral principle and a point of honor. Our government needs to be no different. The budget must be clearly defined and it needs to be balanced.

The problem is that there always seems to be some type of emergency. Things that were not budgeted, crises not imagined, or department over runs not expected. The reality is that there is always crisis, but that does not mean that they can not be managed. Each year regardless on how well we plan there will be a weather related national disaster. Each of these represent a human tragedy. If we are going to assist with the process of personal recovery then we need to anticipate the need. Most of this deals with little more than administration and management of our financial resources. It is something the nation state needs to do, just like it is something every individual needs to do.

There is also a hope of building into the system some type of structure that insures compliance. This is not perfect. One reason is that the all the parties concerned exist within the governmental sphere. Another reason is that Federal budgets are complex and huge. It sometimes takes years to determine if the budget actually was balanced. Even so, an effort is being made to find such a method.

Article 14, Section 2. Budget Exception

There is one area in which a balanced budget seems meaningless. If the nation is at war then every resource that the country has needs to be available to the government and the armed forces. To allow for future generations to assist with the payment of a national debt under these contingencies seems appropriate and fair. After all if the nation state does not survive then a need for a budget is irrelevant.

Article 14, Section 3. General Accounting Office

The budgetary system requires that some type of method be developed to scrutinize the process. It is not considered in the best interest to all the parties concerned to have the House of Representatives declare when a budget is balanced. The two groups that will have overseeing capabilities will be the Senate and the General Accounting Office.

The problem with the Senate is that it is a political body. If history is the judge it is not clear how responsible the Senate will be in keeping a watchful eye on the budget. How the Senate relates to the House of Representatives may have more to do with party alignment than actual budgetary authenticity. How sympathetic the Senate may become or how aggressive they pursue budgetary investigations may say more about politics than it does fiscal responsibility.

The more important issue is the General Accounting Office. This is the governmental agency that does most of the Federal budget reviews, estimates, and forecasts. While many other departments and agencies have budgetary responsibility, the General Accounting Office is made up of civil servants empowered to perform these oversight duties. It is hoped that they would be the best organization to monitor the Federal budgets and make sure they are properly balanced.

If the General Accounting Office is to do their job in overseeing the budgetary process they need to have the freedom to do it. This changes the nature of the work done in the GAO. They need to become a Constitutional entity. This will be one governmental agency or department that Congress will not be able to curtail. The GAO will have considerable power, but once saying this it will be Constitutional power designed for a specific area of government.

In actuality there will be two budgets created by the Federal government. One from Congress as they go through the deliberation and drafting process, and a second budget from the General Accounting Office. The budget from the GAO will represent the terminated budget or the official accounting. What currently occurs with the Federal budget is the true amount spent on any given year is not known until some time later. In most cases years later. It is hoped that the GAO will be able to speed up this process of public accounting.

There is one area that some discretion will be allowed. There are always programs or projects that require levels of secrecy or concealment. These programs will be coded with a number and budgeted accordingly. They do not fall outside of the Federal expenditure and budgetary listings, only that the names of such programs and their purpose may be hidden even from the GAO. The responsibility of the General Accounting Office is not so much to reveal the budgetary process or even what is in the budget, but only that it is balanced at the end.

The General Accounting Office will have the power to trigger elections. If at the end of the budgetary process the estimated expenditures do not balance or at the end of the year the current budget did not balance, the General Accounting Office must step forward and make such a declaration. While there is the possibility that the United States could have a general election every year, the issue is not elections but balancing the budget. If it is not balanced we need to return the issue to the people. There needs to be some system or structure to penalize or discipline our Representatives for not operating in the public interest. The only real reprimand is to face the people. It is the view of this Proposed Constitution that good government requires a balanced budget.

Article 15. Redistricting

Currently individual states are responsible for adjusting and changing the Congressional districts when needed. Historically they have done a poor job of this task. While the Federal government has become involved in the process, their efforts as well have been unsatisfactory, to say nothing about whether such engagements are even constitutional. As of late the Federal courts have been involved and have set guidelines for redistricting. It is still not a good system and lacks uniformity. The courts are not an appropriate entity to be setting up district lines. The problem has been that the process evolves into a political struggle between the two major parties. While judges are removed from the center of political activities, they are still appointed within a political atmosphere and have generally served in the political arena in the past.

The past problems with redistricting are so numerous it is difficult to list them. Two chief problems prevail—gerrymandering and inaction. The first is an attempt to gain political advantages by setting up Congressional districts to the benefit of one party over another. It is possible to obtain a majority vote in a given state by slicing the districts injudiciously even if the representatives are from the minority party. Hence, what occurs most often is no action. The states simply do not redistrict. It is a difficult and time-consuming process with individuals arguing over a city block or a county road. To do nothing is far easier.

A number of political groups in the United States have advocated that a separate commission be set up to be responsible for redistricting. The idea found within this proposed Constitution is an extension of that concept. In this situation the General Accounting Office is given the capability of changing district lines and making sure that the proper ratio is achieved in the House. After each census a survey would be made and the GAO would adjust the districts within a state. The goal would be to complete such a process within one year.

Article 16. Language

The United States has a tremendous advantage over other large nations; it has, for the most part, one dominant language. This reduces the dimensions in which government must operate and creates benefits for every institution. It is a point of utmost productiveness and benefit to have one language predominating within a nation-state. Whether the issue becomes business, education, the military, or in this case, government, it becomes a unifying force and bonds the nation-state together.

The trap of course is in becoming ethnocentric. The English language is not inherently better than others. Language is a tool, one of many forms of communications. It expresses our needs, our wants, and it helps us move through our daily activities. While each of us has a collection of loyalties and language may be one of them, it is not a point of philosophy, it is not art, it is not the hopes and dreams of a people. It is fortuitous that in America one major language transcends the others, but this is not an issue of superiority. It is little more than good fortune.

The other trap is to believe that somehow language is culture. They are not the same. While there is a connection between language and culture, these are different concepts. It is as if language is the core of culture, a cylinder that runs through the center, but culture is hardly attached. Culture deals more with some agreed-upon level of comfort. It is one of the most difficult items to define. It is like looking at an ocean when you are standing on the shore. You can see that it has substance and body, but it is possible to describe it. You can see the enormity of it and you know that it has significance, yet when you attempt to hold it in your hands it runs through your fingers and falls away. The point is simple. Language and culture are different. Stating that the official language of a nation will be English deals only with how we are to comprehend our government.

The only point that this Proposed Constitution is making is that for the Federal government the language in which they will do business will be English. It implies nothing else. It recognizes advantages when a society and a government operate from one communication base. It should be remembered that language is but a form of expression; it has nothing to do with intelligence. Regardless of which language our representatives use, their actions will require foresight, common sense, and aptitude. This is far more important than the jargon, phraseology, dialect, idioms, or more likely, the rhetoric used.

Article 17. Taxation

One of the ideas that is propagated in this work deals with why we have governments. One of the tasks of government is to do those things for us that we are unable, or unwilling, to do for ourselves. Government maintains the infrastructure of society. It helps and supports the education of our children; it creates safe conditions from which we can live and protects us from menacing outside forces, it expands our body of knowledge; and maintains our environment. It performs scores of such services, all of which are unlisted in these pages. The reality is that every governmental action carries a price tag.

There is no government without taxation. If we agree that we need a government, and that we want one, then there is a price that must be paid. This does not mean that we do not want our government to be cost effective. The idea is that we need to be taxed fairly. We need a return on our investment. When we enter into this contract with government, part of the compact is that we allow ourselves to be taxed.

It also should be remembered that the money involved still remains that of the people. Government procession does not mean governmental ownership.

For a Constitution the issue should not be a point of great precision or even one of degree. Government either can tax, or it cannot. The details can be worked out by legislation and interaction with the people, but the power to tax remains. Government may tax us by our income, property, or the goods we produce. It is only a matter of working through the distinct parts.

Article 18. Freedom of Information

Of course this article is derived from the Freedom of Information Act. The argument is that government should not be hidden from the view of the people, that it is a process that needs to be observed and understood by the masses. When government becomes concealed it takes on a clandestine nature.

Some would say that certain inter-workings of government require exemption from this concept. If the issue of national security is being reviewed by a governmental agency or a committee of Congress, they should be allowed to review such issues openly and freely. This may require such hearings to be closed. It is not that such conferences are hidden from the people as much as they are reserved. At times it is not in the best interest of the nation-state to make all of their business public, especially as it relates to national defense. Also the problem of an individual's right to privacy needs to be considered. The government through its law enforcement agencies keeps records on many individuals. Every file should not be a matter of public record. People do have a right to privacy and it is not the place of government to deny that claim. Another issue that borders on this concept is the inter-workings and management of a given agency or department. There is a difference between the public's need to know the actions of an agency, and that agency's interactions with their employees. If a department reprimands an employee for poor attendance, that should not be a matter of public knowledge.

The point is that there are exceptions. They need to be spelled out and made specific. The spirit of this Article is to have an open government, one in which information is available to the people.

While employment records would not have to be kept long, a suitable time should be specified for how long a government document can be kept from public view. The most appropriate time limit seems to be fifty years. Nothing that the government may become involved with will supersede that time. Even patents and copyrights have set lifespans. The concern is the reverse situation; that some issue that may be embarrassing to government is buried forever. There needs to be a restriction on how long a document can be held.

It is a credit to the American government that such a law is in place. The

Sunshine Laws of the 1960s created a different atmosphere for government and also how the people viewed the act of governing. It is not power that is the great evil, it is how that power is used. Power needs to be supervised. If we are to have self-government it becomes the responsibility of the people to oversee how authority is maintained and practiced.

Article 19: International Treaties

The issue with international treaties is that they countermand a Constitution. This should be seen as a concern, but not a fear. The United States Constitution is subject to this same procedure and condition. Generally these types of issues are not in conflict. The scope and direction of a treaty is ordinarily not the same as a Constitution, but there can be contradictions. If that does occur, the treaty must be followed. The key for the people is that they need to examine all international agreements closely. They need to recognize how powerful treaties can be and study such documents.

The length of time that a treaty is enforceable seems to generate some confusion. There are those who argue that all such agreements are only valid for ninety-nine years. Yet, Great Britain has had commercial treaties in place for more than three hundred years. One such item with Sweden was signed in 1654 and it is still active today. The direction of this Article is to set a time limit on treaties and to inform all parties concerned of any limitations that are being placed on these documents. Another sovereign state negotiating a treaty with the United States will have to recognize that the treaty will be valid for ninety-nine years. Provisions for termination of these treaties will need to be set. If both parties are interested in continuing the agreement, they will have to renegotiate the document at that time.

The one exception to this rule would be an Act of Union. The United States has twice entered into an agreement with another foreign power for purposes of creating a union. This occurred with both Texas and Hawaii. A specific document was generated in both of these cases that brought about these unions It would not be appropriate to expect a renegotiation of an Act of Union every ninety-nine years. The world is changing. The future may offer our nation opportunities that may need to be considered. It is not the place of this document to restrict such deliberations.

Treaties negotiated with numerous Native American tribes are also a concern. Many of these treaties are no longer enforceable because the United States government has disconnected itself from that process. Yet, it seems that the only way to bring about a uniformity to our democracy is to reestablish a treaty-making process with Native Americans. Such negotiations seem far more workable if set time limits are placed on these documents. There is a difference between allowing inequities and injustices to exist, and setting markers in place that will correct the dilemma, then leaving the status quo in position indefinitely.

This issue may be a Pandora's Box. Diverse and unforeseen problems may be related to this issue, which would surely change the economic and political relationship of the Federal government and Indian reservations. It is not clear how such negotiation would change the system. Some groups may choose not to continue the Reservation system, or wish to change the total nature of their relationship with the Federal government. The government may even wish to offer compensation to various tribes for different concessions. Other groups may argue for ever-increasing levels of independence. If the American Constitution is to be modernized, all these issues need to be addressed, even those that are extremely difficult. The reservation system is a scheme that this nation created, and we did so by treaty. If the idea of treaties is to have merit, we need to face these issues and change what needs to be changed. If we function within an environment of mutual support, all things become possible.

Article 20. Census

There was a reason why the nation's founders had included in the Constitution a section on a census. It is connected to the *representation ratio*. The nation's founders had set it at one to thirty thousand. It was understood that as the population grew the number of districts and Representatives would change. The only way to find out the true number of Representatives needed for Congress is by taking a census. In the Proposed Constitution it is acknowledged that a set ratio is more desirable then an ever-increasing representation level. The ratio was set at one to seventy-seven thousand. The only way of knowing when new districts are needed and the population has changed is by taking a census.

There are other advantages in taking the census. The Federal government, as well as state governments, have numerous programs based on local population.

Moneys are returned to the municipal governments to administer a wide range of programs and services. These revenues are important to the survival of these local organizations and municipal governments.

Article 21, Section 1. Commerce and Regulation of Trade

In the American Constitution the Federal government was given power over the commerce of the nation, which included the coining of money and regulating of trade. This regulating of trade is done not only at the international level, but between states as well. In turn the Federal government conceded back to the states all those issues not listed in the Constitution. While that may sound equitable, the truth is that the "biggest plum" is commerce. Everything originates out of commerce and it controls many of the other concepts within our society—at least most of the important items within the nation are connected to revenue generating entities.

What is actually most significant is not the placing of the power into the hands of government, because in the end someone or some institution must have that authority; rather, it is making sure that government uses that power when needed. Institutions are powerful entities. Most move with a similar purpose, designed to access a single goal. Business as an institution is set up to create profit. Not an organization of great benevolence, business per se is not naturally inclined toward fair play, virtue, or altruism. Business exists purely and simply to create profit for the principals involved. It is not entirely negative; that dimension is only the "nature of the beast." An individual may start a business for a collection of reasons. Business owners may like the kinds of people who are involved in the enterprise, may believe that their businesses will help their fellow citizens, may like what they do, but when a business no longer makes money it will cease. An unprofitable business can continue only if it becomes a hobby or is supported by some level of volunteerism. Profit is the force that moves business.

The obligation of government is to make sure that business does play fairly, that the rules of the game are the same for everyone. This needs to be done in such a way that business cannot only survive, but prosper. Yet, the growth and expansion of business activities cannot be done at the expense of the many so that only a few can benefit. The only institution that has the power to equal that of business is government. Government must regulate commerce, and commerce needs to be regulated energetically and effectively.

Monopolies tend toward invalidation. One sees a mental picture of an entity stripped of its competitive vitality, repeating the same sequence over and over. Picture a process trapped in the past, unable to move forward, unable to compete, and using its accumulated power to defend a stagnant market. Without debating the issue, there may be some truth to this view, but exceptions always seem to arise. In some cases government may need to grant monopolies. A balance may need to be reached between the public good and the economic stability required by such a step.

Take the United States Postal Service with its delivery of first-class letters as an example. Our technology has not reached the level where the elimination of the letter is either required or needed. The post still connects each individual to all other persons regardless of where they live in the world. If a monopoly did not exist on the delivery of an individual letter, and true competition were allowed to exist on this service, it could rightfully be argued that delivery in profitable large urban areas would be solicited, leaving rural communities with restricted service. The whole arrangement would suffer. A monopoly on the program remains, even with the implied understanding that some parts of the nation are paying for the service of others.

In some cases monopolies may be necessary evils. While every situation cannot be determined, the Congress needs the power to grant monopolies. The huge advantage is that if government declares a company or organization a monopoly, it is then documented and debated. If the situation would change, the charter should change accordingly.

The last issue deals with the operation of profit-directed companies that the government has either seized or obtained through lawful action. It is not always in the best interest of the government, the people, or the company in question simply to let these businesses close. Lost revenue would result, not only in wages but also taxes. The community may lose earning power or related vendors may be forced into receivership as well. The government may be compelled to manage these firms while adjustments and buyers are located. If this issue is conceded then there should also be a time limit on how long the company would be operated.

The issue is that institutions should do what they do best. Business should be free to do those activities at which they are most accomplished and skilled. In turn business should not attempt to manipulate government. It would be no different than talking about the church as an institution. It is not the place of government to work toward the salvation of the soul. This is the function and place of the church. Each institution has a primary function and the Constitution should direct each toward its respective goals.

Article 21, Section 2. Bankruptcy Laws

The issue of bankruptcy laws has always been open to debate. The nation's founders discussed the issue at length, as did the Anti-Federalists. The problem was that each state had a different view of what represented bankruptcy and the validity of the concept. At the time of the creation of the American Constitution the issue was focused on repayment of the Revolutionary War debt. For the nation's founders it was agreed that the Federal government should determine what the bankruptcy laws should be.

In modern times criticism still can be leveled at the scope and direction of bankruptcy law. Many will find such judicial procedures too accommodating, yet, workable alternatives to bankruptcy are few. The idea of risk is coupled with concepts of growth and progress, but with risk also comes the potential of failure. If it is agreed that bankruptcy should be allowed, especially because of the nature of our economic system, then it seems proper to have one set of laws governing the process. In this case it is the Federal government that will be able to determine the bankruptcy laws.

Article 21, Section 3. Copyrights, Patents, and Trademarks

The Federal government has accepted the responsibility of setting up a system of copyrights, patents, and trademarks for the nation. These are important concepts in business and human development. Some level of regulation is required. It seems only proper and fair for government to perform this obligation.

Article 21, Section 4. Weights and Measures

Equally important is the idea of weights and measures. One unified system for the whole country is helpful and advantageous to the operation of the nation.

Article 22, Section 1. Political Parties

The nation's founders understood character and the disposition of political parties. This was by no means a new concept. Political parties were a functional part of Great Britain. Not including a structure for political parties in the American Constitution was therefore a deliberate act. Instead of viewing them as a viable political entity, they were perceived as a point of considerable distrust. Their concern was based on a fear that political "factions" would take control of the government. This view was shared by most of the nation's founders; in fact when George Washington became President he made an asserted effort to develop a Cabinet from many different political points of view and philosophies. The problem of course is that political parties and the democratic process do go hand-in-hand. They are a functional part of government by the people.

Ideally a political party would represent an established set of views and concepts. The party would develop core concepts, and individuals who supported those fundamental ideas would gravitate toward those organizations. This does not mean that periphery issues could not be addressed or even changed, but there would be a center-most concept, almost metaphysical in design. Those who could not accept that essence of the party would drift off to join other political organizations or create their own.

This ideal approach would apply to how the party membership would choose their candidate. They would find an individual who embodied the spirit and essential qualities of the party. That, person would be experienced, have effective leadership skills, be charismatic, and be able to communicate the important sentiment of the party to the masses. The candidate would also be loyal to the party and its platform. The party in return would work toward their collective success, as one point of solidarity and unity.

While the idealized version may be true in part, it is more myth than reality. The reality is that while democratic governments cannot properly exist without the use and performance of political parties, in the United States they are more of a shell than an essential component. An individual running for a political office is not chosen. It is more a matter of a candidate choosing to run. They must bring to the party their own organization, money, and status. The political party becomes more of a shell from which to operate within; a rented stage. This does not mean that core ideas do not exist. Individuals will move toward those parties that best represent their views, but political parties become secondary entities, little more than vehicles of conveyance.

Within the government political parties operate much more in the traditional sense. They become voting blocks. It is generally in the best interest of the elected official to perform within accepted party guidelines. There are exceptions such as votes of conscience, but self-preservation is a powerful instrument within the Legislative process. It is generally in the best interest of the representatives to follow the party leadership. Parties in Congress are also more likely to set acceptable levels of behavior. They become a stabilizing force. In turn opposition parties become the "watch dog" of the political party in power, reviewing and examining the conduct of the government.

What must be understood is that political parties are not destructive or sinister associations. They are but one part of the total macrocosm from which election and government take place. The nation's founders in all of their wisdom were simply wrong. Not only do political parties belong in a Constitution, they are an essential part of the overall process. It is more damaging, or even amazing, to believe that democracy can exist without them.

Two questions need to be asked. The first is how disciplined do we want political parties to be? After all if political parties become the most dominating creature on the political landscape, will it restrict independent political thought? In the same context the parliamentary system by its very nature will create greater levels of party discipline. It is not clear how these issues will develop within the American mind-set. Traditionally Americans pride themselves on their autonomy and freedom of thought. Yet, this is a system that requires greater animation and focus from the political parties.

Under this Proposed Constitution political parties will be more active in the home districts than Americans have experienced in the past. Since it is never apparent when elections are going to be held, parties must remain far more dynamic than what is currently found in the American political system. Also, since general elections are compressed into six weeks, the parties must be ready to go at any moment. They must determine their candidates, promote their programs, and wage a campaign within a considerably short period of time. This whole process will require substantial party discipline.

Within the House of Representatives the role of the political parties will be different because only one party will be able to set the agenda. Nothing will destroy the ability of the party to move forward on their agenda faster than the lack of party unity. It would be a matter of squandering the opportunity. The goals of the party would be understood by the electorate and generally it would be in their interest to move forward on the party platform.

The second issue concerns the effect of money and wealth upon the system. It is hoped the assets required to seek a political office will be reduced, especially at the Federal level. There are two advantages from within the parliamentary system. Since the districts have been reduced in size, the need for large amounts of revenue to stage a political campaign is no longer warranted. The most efficient way to run a political campaign will be to personally interact with the voters. Money of course will help, but the candidates only have six weeks. There are only so many hours in the day and only so many commercial spots that can be obtained in the media.

The Senators will be able to solicit votes over a longer period of time. Their electioneering would represent more of conventional American political campaigns. The money spent may not be as beneficial to a special interest group since the root of political power has changed to the House of Representatives. Even so, the need for larger financial resources for the Senators may still be in order. Regardless of how a political system is designed, wealth will play a part; the hope is to diminish the effect. No matter how many times it is denied, the truth is that money will buy influence and open doors.

Political parties are important parts of the governmental process at work and it is also believed they will be even more important under the restructured parliamentary system. A procedure must develop by which parties develop and evolve. One of the problems in the American scheme is that each state determines how candidates place their names on the ballot and what new political parties are created. In each state that process is different and in some the system is so exhausting that the possibility of success is marginal. The argument is simply that if political parties are meaningful to a healthy democratic society, a consistent system is needed for their creation and use. In this case a new political party would appear on the ballot if three percent of the registered voters signed such a petition.

A third political party faces a difficult process and because of it they are generally unsuccessful as political entities. The first reason is that most new political parties are created because of one secular idea. They are operating from a base and it generally deals with one concept. If that idea takes form and the masses agree with the rationale behind the issue, one of the major political parties will absorb the political concept, taking it as their own.

The second reason deals with attainment. Individuals are willing to work toward a goal, sacrifice, and commit to the cause as long as there is some degree of progress. In the case of a political party if the votes secured from the public never reach beyond ten percent, appeal and enthusiasm begin to wane. At that point a decline of their fortune is assured. There are reasons why the two-party system exists, it is doubtful that anything within this Proposed Constitution's formula will change that design.

The issue that will have to be worked out is the way the candidate is chosen in the Primary. Primary elections will have a considerably different feel from what the United States has experienced in the past. While state and senatorial races should not fundamentally change, the general elections for the House will be distinct. For one reason, the time will be shortened. Individuals interested in running for office will have to "stand in the wings" waiting for the opportunity, though they may still be chosen by a convention, a caucus, or an open election.

This would have to take place in a week preceding general elections. An abundance of political activity will surface in a very short time. Part of it deals with how the parliamentary system operates. Of course the reverse of the system is the current American election process where years separate the declaration of a nominee and the actual election. In any case the states and the political parties will need to work out the details of how primaries will function.

What is being proposed in this new Constitution deals purely with the general elections. The states are well within their rights to develop a different system or collection of criteria for their elections. The senatorial races will be tied to the states and their processes. The selection of senators will mirror those elections found in the particular states of the Union. Equally, the states will be free to determine under what conditions state political campaigns will function. This is no different than what we currently experience.

Article 22, Section 2. Public Accounting

This Proposed Constitution indicates changes in how political parties operate and are perceived. Political parties become Constitutional entities. They have a right to exist, for no other reason than because they are Constitutional. This represents a change in formation. With that change comes responsibility and culpability. Like office-seekers, political parties must be held to some level of public accounting. How they obtain their funds and from what sources must be a matter of public record. Balance sheets will be provided to the people, not only on how funds were received, but also how money was spent.

Nothing is wrong or improper in expecting from our political institutions levels of accountability, especially in dealings with money. It is hard to determine which corrupts faster, money or absolute power, but we must always be aware of this problem. Only through sound policy and vigilance will we be able to keep our democracy open.

Article 22, Section 3. Party Platform

Political parties need to stand for well-thought-out philosophies, issues that make them different from other parties or groups. Since this set of fundamental principles would be found in the party platforms, one hopes that such platforms would be points of detail rather than rhetoric, but that may be too high an expectation. The issue is a larger one. What is important is not individual candidates but ideas. Political processes should be fueled by the strength of a party's vision for the future and how such goals can be reached. These beliefs and opinions are paramount. Those who stand back and simply pay homage to the nation's traditions or icons need to be cast in a very negative light. Political parties have a responsibility to openly declare their belief system and debate these issues.

Article 22, Section 4. Party Interplay

This issue is not complicated. If it is agreed that political parties are a consequential part of a democracy and the political process, then they need to be an animated part of the system. Artificial barriers should not be created either to reduce the effectiveness of political organizations and their ability to establish themselves or conduct business. It is possible that political parties may represent a set of ideas not commonly held. The majority may disagree with their views, but they still need to be heard. Parties can represent an asylum for ideas. It is more important to let them stand on their own merit than be restricted by law.

These issues may sound trivial, especially from the perspective of established democratic nations. The problem is that in many countries in the world the ruling regime or party will use the legislative process to curtail and abridge the views of other political parties. This is not democracy; it is authoritarianism. If we are to validate our own democracy we must make sure that we operate from a position, and a set of rules, where this is not possible. Conflicting ideas are as important to the system as the views of the majority.

Article 22, Section 5. Party Access

We are all political creatures. Even those of us who do not vote are still aware of political models and have stated political views. Political participation takes place at many levels. Since the minimum active level is voting, persons who do not vote waste the major part of their political will. Zero interaction in the political process means that persons have subjugated themselves to the caprices, influences, and intercourse of others.

Many of us may choose to be activists, becoming involved in political parties or affiliated groups. Those of us who support special interest groups or pay our dues to various politically sensitive associations can be seen as activists. At some point along this sequence, political activism becomes political candidacy. The shift can be seen in the use of time and administration. At this level the passage becomes far more competitive. It becomes corporate in structure. Now an individual must not only challenge policies and political direction, but politics also becomes a career choice. There will be rivals. For many individuals finding themselves in this environment it is not just the party nomination, but it is a matter of validating their views. It becomes proof that they are right, and another is wrong. This is a process that requires rules. Political parties need to set the system by which candidates are declared and under what condition. The terms need to be enforced and uniform.

Political parties, especially at the local level, may not be the most friendly of places. Every organization or group in the country has elitists. These are the people who believe most strongly in the cause, have served the longest, worked the hardest, have held the most offices, and been there regardless of the conflicts. There are politics within politics. Sometimes this issue deals with little more than individual personality; some people feel a need to do more. They may come to believe that they are entitled to a degree of ownership of the structure. What can occur is that people may come to believe that because they do most of the work in maintaining the organization, they should be able to make most of the decisions. As a rule it generally works out that way, but the political process must be such that all individuals have an opportunity to participate at whatever level they wish. Their candidacy may not be successful. They may be defeated within the party or in the general elections, but the process should not deter a person. The process needs to be open and free, even within the party structure.

Article 23, Section 1. Elections

Elections and voting must be maintained in the purest of forms. The fewer restrictions and impediments the better. This has not always been the case in American history. Poll taxes and literacy tests have been devised to reduce the size and nature of the electorate. Efforts have even been devised to restrict voting groups by intimation or violence. The issue is not who should be allowed to vote. Every citizen should be allowed to vote. The only restriction is whether an individual is eighteen years of age or older. The concept, the process, needs to be seen as unchangeable. Voting comes with citizenship. It is a point of honor.

It is a two-edged sword. While government must take every action to see that voting and elections are genuine and honest, the people have an equal responsibility. They must not dissipate the value of their ballot by nonuse. If government by the people is to exist, if democracy is to germinate and take root, it can only be done by having the people participate. Nothing should be more communally sacred.

Article 23, Section 2. General Elections

Currently in the American Federal elections four offices are being voted on and filled. These offices are the President, the two Senatorial positions, and a member of the House of Representatives. Within this Proposed Constitution this is adjusted to three. The people will vote for their Senators and House Representative, but not the executive office. In this case the Prime Minister, would be voted on by the House. What will be left is two types of elections, each functioning differently, each having a different feel.

The first will be the *conventional election.* Traditionally this has been held on the first Tuesday of November. The term of office would determine how often a nominee would have to run for these elected positions. The time is clearly set and everyone knows when the election is to be held. Individuals seeking such an office can begin their campaigns anytime they wish. It is not uncommon for such declarations to be made a year in advance, sometimes longer.

These offices will be state directed. It will be the responsibility of the state governments to determine the characteristics of these elections. The state governments may also set the nature of primaries and how they are to be held. By composition these offices will either be state or local. The one exception is the Senatorial races that are aligned to the state governor's contests. In any case these elections are rigid. The date of the elections are clearly set and understood.

The second type of election is the *general election.* This is held only for the House of Representatives. Elections are called by the Prime Minister or they occur because of a *no-confidence vote* in Congress. Elections must be held within five years of the last time such a vote was held. The states and the related political organizations will determine how Representatives will be chosen from within the political parties—whether by primary, caucus, or local convention. The process should not be too difficult because the districts represent only 77,000 citizens. Of these many are under the age of eighteen, some people do not vote, and some are involved in other parties. What will make the process difficult is time. The parties will have to develop a system by which the candidates have been chosen well in advance or this primary election process will need to occur within the first few weeks of the general election. The completion of the general election must be held within six weeks. Time will be a very valuable commodity.

The general elections would be held the first Saturday after a measurement of six weeks from which the no-confidence motion was passed or the application was submitted. The change from Saturday to Tuesday has been an idea that has been debated for some time. The argument has been that more people would be able to vote on a Saturday than a Tuesday. While the difference seems minor, the idea of a Saturday election seems to be the stronger argument. A Saturday election would also help the local party leadership obtain workers and volunteers for voting precincts.

Article 23, Section 3. Election Disputes

This Article asks the question of who, or what body, settles disputed elections. Rare as it may be, an election might end with a tied vote. What organization gets to break the tie? In the American Constitution that issue falls to the assemblage for which the office seeker is running. This Proposed Constitution is no different. These issues need to end somewhere; some group needs to have the last word in a disputed election. It seems appropriate to let the respective body work through the issues involved.

The political reality is that these types of votes in the assemblage will generally break down along party lines. Though fair play and justice would be considerations, party loyalty is a powerful force. It may be too optimistic to believe that such issues could be overcome by a need to be impartial, but in the end some system needs to be in place in case just some such problem arises. In both Constitutions the body in question that makes the final decision is the one sought by the candidate.

Article 23, Section 4. Parallel Elections

As has been noted in different parts of this document, the Senators will be elected parallel to the governors of the state governments. The goal of course is to attempt to reconnect the Senate as a body to that of the states. It is reasoned that the state governments have issues and concerns that need to be correlated with the Federal Government. The Senators will still be elected by the people, but a slate would be created by having the governor and Senators run at the same time.

Each party would be able to have two senatorial candidates run for election at the same time. The two individuals that receive the most votes would be elected and would serve in that office. The process would not be complex, but it would have a different appearance. The theory in the past has been that by staggering the election of the Senators it maintained a higher level of experience. At least one official from the upper chamber from each state would have a working knowledge of the assembly. This is a valid concept, but it has been overstated. Senators would be facing elections every four years rather than six. The adjustment in the length of the term of office are hoped to bring greater familiarity with local issues as well.

Article 23, Section 5. Election Financial Responsibility

As it is with any program or model someone will step forward and ask who is going to pay for this item. In this case the discussion is on elections. At some point it must be determined who will pay for the elections held in the country. The proposition represented here seems to be fair. The states will pay for the state elections, which would include the Senatorial races, and the Federal Government would pay for the general elections.

Article 24, Section 1. Voting

The goal is to bring the idea of voting up to the point of reverence, that the whole idea of a person's vote would be sanctified. If that is a valid goal, then it needs to be total. If a person is a citizen of this nation and over the age of eighteen, they should be allowed to vote. No one or no institution can take that vote away. It is yours by right.

If it is agreed that voting is a right, and not a privilege, a number of things are set in motion. The most disconcerting is that everyone will be able to vote, regardless of their mental disabilities or crimes against humankind. The first group is far easier to acknowledge. It should be noted that just because an individual has a mental illness does not mean that the person is unable to make logical and rational decisions as part of the electorate. Mental illness has nothing to do with intelligence. Even those individuals with thought disorders are able to make prudent decisions about their own situation and environment.

While an informed electorate is the aspiration of any democratic society, knowledge about the issues and active involvement in the political process are not mandatory. Intelligence is not a prerequisite to voting. If a median is established for mental aptitude and an average is determined, half the people voting will have a below-average intelligence. It is irrelevant. If government is to be by the people, all the people then get to govern, and in turn all the people get the vote. The problem is whether individuals who are profoundly mentally disabled with severe mental retardation should also be allowed to vote. If voting is a right, they should be allowed.

Of course voting requires some propensity for the act. Individuals with extremely low levels of functioning will not vote because they lack the ability to work through the complexity of the process. Voting is a conscious act. It requires a number of steps and a knowledge of why the exercise is taking place. There is the reality of the situation and the spirit of the concept. While the essence of the argument is that voting is a right and that all citizens may vote, the reality is that the process may be beyond the capacity of some individuals to master. While there may be a right to vote, there is no right to have someone lead you through the system.

The last group may be more controversial. Does an individual who had been tried in a court of law and found guilty of a crime have a right to vote? Many individuals vote by mail. Many times because of their occupation, military service, disability, or for no other reason than a vacation, a person may cast their ballot by mail. Should an individual who is incarcerated have that same right? If voting is a right, even those individuals who have committed truly wicked crimes would still be able to vote. If that is not allowed then what is being conceded is that the state has the power to strip a person of their citizenship. If that is the case then those situations and circumstances should be listed. They become Constitutional elements.

The political reality of this issue may be more pronounced. If convicts were allowed to cast a ballot, they could become a voting block. At any one time the United States has about 1.3 million people in jails, prisons, or correctional facilities. Even if half choose to vote it could affect the election process. What could be even more profound is that in some cases where a large penitentiary is in a district it could have a sizable impression on the political issues. The constituents may be extremely interested in concepts related to prison reform.

This should not be seen as a negative. An argument could be made that to allow representation at all levels of American society would benefit the total community. There are individuals that have been convicted of malicious crimes. Clearly there are punishments involved, but that does not mean they should exist without citizenship or representation. They are not stateless. It returns to the chief issue. Is voting a right? The Proposed Constitution clearly believes that it is and should not be abridged in any form.

Article 24, Section 2. Secret Ballot

Elections are an elaborate and involved process. They require the commitment of a large number of individuals most of whom are volunteers. They come together at a ward or precinct to assist with the process of democracy. Polling is a fundamental consequence of democracy. It is even more important than the election campaign, because what is really significant is not who is running for office, or even what they said, but the collective judgement of the people.

Balloting has had a checkered past. Voting fraud has come in many forms: unlawful registration policies, allowing people to vote more than once, maintaining deceased voters on the roles, stuffing the ballot boxes, and dishonest counts all have existed in the American voting system. Yet, the most debased of all fraudulent voting practice is intimidation. If one person can see your hand go up, or hear you say yes, or watch you place a marble into a can it inhibits the process. Voting is a self-serving act, calculated and uncensored. If en employer, a member of the clergy, teacher, or even your spouse can see your vote, it could affect the nature of your relationship. More importantly, it could affect your vote. Politics brings to the surface great passions. Yet, a vote is a very singular act and personal. A person does not have to make excuses, or explain why, and voters do not have to outline their intentions. There are no wrong votes when it comes to the ballot. There is only one way to ensure the veracity of the vote and that is by having it secret.

This is a difficult process and does require many steps. Elections cost money, and a secret ballot is more costly than any other system. It is government, and especially local governments, that must maintain the equipment, obtain the supplies, and support the staff. It is to their credit that as a rule the American election process is more just than not. Even so, democracy requires a vote that is veiled from all but from whom it was cast.

Article 24, Section 3. Special Elections

For many reasons individuals do not complete their term of office. They become ill, they decide on a career change, they are forced out because of improper conduct, they resolve that it is time to retire, or they simply die. For whatever reason a system must be in place so that when an individual does leave office how succession will occur is clearly understood.

In the case of the Senate, the governor of the state will appoint an individual to fill the office. They will hold that office until the next election. It is the same system in use within the current Constitution. It is practical. A state-wide election to fill a Senator's vacant seat would be unrealistic, especially if the time till the next election was short. The governor is the most logical person to choose the replacement Senator.

A member of the House of Representatives is a different matter. If a person vacates a seat in the House an election would be possible, and even desirable. Under the parliamentary system the political parties in the districts should be ardent in their ability to stage a campaign quickly. Even allowing for the six weeks to manage the campaign it is still within range to allow the electorate to determine their own representative.

The last office at the federal level that would ever have to be replaced would be the Prime Minister. This issue has been covered in detail, but the process is rather simple. The membership of the House of Representatives vote on a new leader. A new Prime Minister can be chosen expediently and the changeover can occur with a minimum of difficulties.

The other issue is a recall. Some built-in system needs to be in place whereby the people under their own initiatives can remove an elected official from office. All the states have some system for recall. Under this Proposed Constitution the people are able to introduce a petition requesting that an individual be removed from office. It is a difficult process and they would need fifty percent of the registered voters. For a Senator that would be fifty percent of the registered voters. If it is confirmed by the Attorney General of the state, the person would be replaced in the case of a Senator. With a House member new elections would be held.

Article 25, Section 1. Judicial Review

Regardless of the time and effort taken to outline and draft a Constitution, some points of confusion, technicality, or unexpected problems will arise. Humans are not perfect; any document written by man will have imperfections. Someone or some group will have to interpret the text. Judicial Review was not originally established in the United States Constitution; rather, it came about by necessity. When a need arose the Supreme Court took on the responsibility to interpret the

Constitution.

When the nation's founders wrote about *freedom of the press,* they meant just that or, more exactly, *freedom to print.* They had no working knowledge of the broadcast media. It is possible to argue that these two terms do not have the same meaning, but someone has to make that decision. Someone needs to interpret, explain, and clarify. This function falls back to the court system and, more specifically, the Supreme Court.

When the nation's founders developed the American Constitution, they recognized the importance of a conclusive court system. Doubtless the Federal Court system is far more immense than the nation's founders had envisioned, if for no other reason than that our population has grown to eighty-three times what it was at the birth of our nation. Today the Federal court system includes tax courts, Federal circuit courts of appeals, claims courts, courts of military appeals, bankruptcy courts, United States district courts, United States courts of appeal, and the Supreme Court. All of these can interact with state courts and their operations. For better or worse the court system maintains our stability and guarantees our rights. The courts represent the consistency in our society.

Forces are at play in other branches of government that can move them to behave in ways that will restrict democracy. There are always crises-events that overwhelm our mental impression of moral behavior, events so insidious, so cruel that no level of rationale can justify the act. The public will demand retribution or retaliation in kind. Laws will be created to hinder such exploits in the future; this will be done in haste without regard to the structure of our democracy or the rights we enjoy. It may be the minority that suffers, or it may be only one person, but it would be done nonetheless. Government by the people should not supersede the contract we have agreed upon. No event, no situation, no evil force should have the power to break our commitment to Constitutional government. In the end it is the court system that brings order to this chaos; the courts ensure that we do not destroy what is good while we work against that which is pernicious.

The Supreme Court is most important—not because of any grand design, but for no other reason than that it is the final stop, the end of the judicial path. Chiefly its mandate deals with the interpretation of the Constitution, but the power of the Supreme Court runs beyond that single task. The Supreme Court has complete authority over all United States courts; even those within the states ultimately are responsible to the Supreme Court. The high court by appeal or by *writ of certiorari* has jurisdiction over these lower courts. All issues representing a public minister, ambassador, or foreign consul are subjects of the Supreme Court. The power of the high court extends to any legal issue in which the United States has become involved or issues between the different states. It is more than simply Constitutional law; all laws and treaties could be subject to review by the Supreme Court.

The issue is not the power of the Supreme Court or any of the Federal courts, but of Judicial Review. Few concepts in democracy are as important. It is the fundamental method through which the people address grievances against their government. Judicial Review is the pathway, the link between governmental heavy-handedness and justice. Without this tool there would be no democracy. Without Judicial Review we would all be slaves.

That statement may seem harsh or fictitious, but imagine a world wherein dwelt political and social Darwinism, where those of phlegmatic or stoic philosophies dictated the conditions of the human existence. Even though a progressive Constitution was in place, even though points of fair play and equity were understood and accepted, there would be no way to request compliance. No way to demand justice. The document would be meaningless; in small but deliberate steps the needs of the few would replace the needs of the many until servitude became the reality.

The major problem the Supreme Court has faced in its history has been whether to rigidly interpret the American Constitution to the strict written word or to interpret the document at a level of implied admonition. Both have their traps. If the words have no meaning and can be interpreted liberally, what is the point of having a Constitution? Equally, growth requires some level of change; we do not want to entrap ourselves in situations with no options. As an example a strict constructionist would argue that the principal power of government still rests with the states. This was the original philosophy of the American Constitution. Since the state concedes power to the Federal government, the national government should be seen by a constructionist as a secondary authority. The opposite concept would be held by the Federalists. They would hold that the American Constitution allows for implied powers. From a broader perspective and through court interpretation the Federal government has expansive powers. A true Federalist would argue that the central government is able to critique anything found within its scope of interest.

The Constitution needs to account for these adjustments and reflect the changes that have occurred in our society and government. If the court is to interpret the Constitution and the attributes of the nation-state, the people need to empower the court to perform this function. It is unjust to ask them to interpret a document that has evolved into something else. At this point what the high court is interpreting is not the Constitution but a developmental process. It is far better to state who we are today, rather than let a group, or in this case a set of judges, declare who we are and what we have become. Within the framework of this Proposed Constitution we are a Federalist state and the courts are sanctioned to interpret the document from that perspective.

Article 25, Section 2. Jurisdiction

The Supreme Court is not only the highest judicial forum within the national court system, but also the highest court in the land. It possesses authority over all appellate and appeals courts, not only within the Federal system but the states as well. Again, this is not something new. Currently in the United States the Supreme Court is the ultimate court of appeals. It has created enough precedents to establish supremacy over most issues. The article simply is a statement of the contemporary level of authority of the highest court in the land.

One of the difficulties with the existing Constitution is that jurisdiction for the Supreme Court is actually determined by the United States Congress. While currently almost total jurisdiction has been conceded to the Court, Congress still determines the nature of what cases can be heard. The change in the Proposed Constitution is that the Supreme Court can determine its own jurisdiction, which is granted without restrictions by any other body.

Article 25, Section 3. Appointment

In recent times the Supreme Court has had nine members, but the American Constitution does not set an optimal number. During the course of its history the number of justices has fluctuated from five to ten with the total number generally determined by Congress.

In 1789 the Supreme Court was set at five associate justices and one chief justice, a number that changed to five in 1801. By 1807 Congress again changed the number to seven, and by 1837 the number was increased to nine. During the American Civil War the court's membership increased to ten, but by 1869 the more accepted level of nine was restored. The greatest crisis over the number of sitting justices came during the Franklin Roosevelt administration. Roosevelt was disgruntled over the conservative Supreme Court's rulings on his New Deal programs. Without directly engaging the court the administration implied that the Court was unable to do its business because of their advanced age and heavy workload. Roosevelt had suggested increasing the number of justices to fifteen and a formula was developed to implement the plan. Because it was never forged into a complete program, the idea disappeared as the high court began to reverse many of its earlier decisions.

The only real point of maintaining a set number of justices on the Supreme Court involves creating an acceptable level of equilibrium. The fluctuating of the number of justices is not in the best interest of the court or the people. With nine comes the advantage of being able to break a tie; furthermore, it is the traditional number for the court. This should maintain a level of stability and allow for an appropriate number of justices to do their jobs. Also, a set number will help reduce some of the problems that have occurred in the past.

The system of appointment remains constant. The chief executive nominates a person to fill a position on the Supreme Court who in turn will have to be confirmed through the Senate's hearing process. The process allows for review and evaluation and is consistent with the democratic process.

The last item is merely the method by which decisions are made. Court decisions will be confirmed by a majority vote. Though not unduly complex a process, the issue needs to be understood and stated within a Constitution.

Article 25, Section 4. Affiliation and Impeachment

If an individual is appointed to a position for life it becomes more than a career choice or a characteristic of the job; it becomes a fundamental principle of government. A person who obtains a position, especially a justice of the Supreme

Court, needs to function in an environment without restrictions or fear of retaliation. The loss of income, prestige, or reputation can influence people. The office of Supreme Court Justice is not a job where even a hint of coercion should be allowed. More important, the position requires reflection and thought. No matter how well a Constitution is designed there will still be issues that need interpretation.

This issue of interpretation needs some discussion. A solid argument could be made that a properly designed Constitution would not require interpretation. After all what is being done is only describing what has already been stated. It is like listening to a speech and then a second party comes along and explains what was said. It could be said that if a person were paying attention there would be no need for a second person to come along and reiterate the dialogue. The problem deals with the complexity of the law and to some degree the intricacy of human behavior. The infinite possibilities of various situations contrasted with human involvement in them and ways to contrast each situation with the law—this becomes endless. Each event may have more than one issue of the law in play since more than one Article of a Constitution may be at work. The conclusion and options may be many. Someone must interpret the law and in turn interpret the Constitution as it relates to the law. In our society the task falls to the judges.

For better or for worse humanity has created an increasingly complex world. We do that through our technology, our social interactions, the interplay with our institutions, and even how we choose to be governed. Interpretation is required for no other reason than the fact that we are still evolving, improving, and developing as a species. Whenever a court makes a ruling there will be winners and losers. It is part of the adversarial nature of the court system. The key is for these issues to be decided in the court and not within any other forum. The way to defend against this possibility is to appoint Federal judges for life.

Only impeachment will dislodge a Federal judge or a justice of the Supreme Court, a process that is difficult and time consuming. Grounds for impeachment would be criminal conduct or misdeeds. A judge may possibly become so feeble that he or she is unable to hear cases or correctly apply the law. Encouragement from peers or higher courts may be sufficient to maintain acceptable levels of performance. A more nefarious situation may arise if a judge abuses power for self-interest or gain. While the expectation is that a need for the impeachment process will not arise, our history teaches us differently.

Article 25, Section 5. Quorum

As with most bodies or organizations that have come together to conduct business or to complete a task, a quorum is required. Under most circumstances the organization would be able to set their own rules of how they conduct business. What represented a quorum would easily be handled by their rules of order. The problem is that the Supreme Court is a distinctively powerful body that can affect the lives of every person in the country. Should one single Justice render a decision, this would not be in the interest of the nation-state. With the Supreme Court, a collective judgment is better than a singular one.

Article 25, Section 6. Counsel

While the separation of power in the American system of government does have some benefits, it also has many drawbacks. The different branches of government do not interact or even attempt to function at a reticulated level. The Executive branch has no ability to introduce laws into the Legislative branch., even through the President by virtue of being the chief administrator of the government may see valid areas of improvement. The Presidents must use the "back door" to promote legislative issues that he or she feels are important. The President has to approach a sympathetic member of Congress to introduce the legislation the executive office wants. The advantage to the current system is that power is dispersed; the disadvantage is that it reduces cohesion and continuity.

Nothing is wrong with the different branches of government interacting, reviewing, and verbalizing concerns about an issue before it comes into existence. It is a more dialectic approach. Not only should the different branches of government interact among themselves, but they should be encouraged to do so. Under the current system of government the involvement of the Supreme Court in the legislative process is marginal. While a brief discussion may occur between leaders of the different branches, there are no written reviews or understandings. Only after an issue is argued by attorneys before the Supreme Court are their views announced. Nothing would change concerning that item. In the end only after the Supreme Court has created a decision would the issue be settled, yet their participation would be helpful in the legislative process. It would save considerable amounts of time and money if the court would issue a brief or even state a concern about a piece of legislation before it was generated. This would be done in such a way that the opinion would not be binding.

This Article may seem disconnected to the normal workings of a Constitution, and by design it may not prove to be a benefit. The spirit of the item is directed elsewhere. The Supreme Court is as much a part of the government as any other branch. It has a tendency to be seen as aloof or above the mechanical workings of government. If this Article were used properly it would be a wonderful tool for government. It can maintain our rights and vitalize our democracy. The Supreme Court would not be seen as indifferent to the laws being created by Congress. It also has a stake in the process and their point of view, guidance, and encouragement is not only solicited, but required. The Supreme Court should be seen as an adviser, or even a mentor, to the Legislative branch. We need to find a way to tap into the experience and knowledge of the court on the nature of the law.

Of course this may be wishful thinking. The reality is that if the court counseled the Legislative branch that a law would be constitutional and then later it was found not to be, the credibility of the high court might be lost. It would be safer not to give an opinion. A piece of legislation may look different in the halls of Congress than it does in practice. The goal is an honest one. It is the simple idea of giving government a few more options.

Article 26. Order of Authority

This article represents one of the most perplexing items within the Proposed Constitution. To some degree it does represent the status quo. As an accepted rule of order this is the listing for which type of law takes precedence over another. The Constitution is considered to be the foundation for all laws and rules of conduct for the society, but as a nation-state, commitment to treaties must stand beyond the issue of a Constitution. This has little to do with rights, laws, or regulations, but more to the fact that if a nation makes assurances and promises these need to be kept. Treaties are the word of the nation and a pledge of its people. This is one of the reasons why the people need to be aware of treaties and what is constructed within them because they do supersede a Constitution.

The next level is Acts of Congress. Within the Federalist system laws of the central government are dominant over all other governmental law. An Act of Congress cannot supersede the Constitution, nor can it change a treaty; but it does have say over all other laws. In turn the state Constitutions have greater jurisdiction than state laws, but either have more authority than Federal statutes. The last two sections of law will generate the most resistance; at least in listing which takes precedence.

Nations employ two types of laws, each with their own history, each having their own advantages and disadvantages. The first is English Common Law. This appeared in medieval England where issues were presented to the monarch in the hope of obtaining justice. Many times the subjects petitioned the monarch to address various items or problems. The petition could be heard by the king, or more than likely they would be referred to the court of the Lord Chancellor or the chancery. Over a period of time this body grew into a set of royal courts of law. They would examine the questions, listen to concerns, review witnesses, and issue rulings. Again, over time these rulings grew into a body of precedents. At first all that mattered was the precedents. Judges were expected to follow the rulings set out by those who had preceded them. There were always special circumstances and judges were given some discretion in finding fairness in their decisions, but the key was the precedents.

Common law became a doctrine and set of principles where law originated and was based on court decisions. Most of it became a matter of custom and usage. Over time it became the main body of law for England, later Great Britain, and from the colonial period it developed in both the United States and Canada. Common law is a prominent part of the United States and the American Constitution. The Supreme Court in their interpretations and court decisions is but an extension of English Common Law.

The other form of jurisprudence is *codes*. These are a set of standard laws generally issued by a ruler in written form. Sometimes these codes are little more than a statement of duty or of custom that over time became law. The process was reinforced by other rulers or through various legislative bodies.

The first known codes were from Babylon and were called the Code of Hammurabi. They are believed to have been written in the eighteenth century B.C.

Most noted of the codes are those of Roman Emperor Justinian I. Variously named Codex Justinianus, Justinian Code, Corpus Juris Civillis, or some times just *The Code*. This Roman code covers a wide range of topics and categorizes various types of law. Many types of Roman codes and law exist today, especially in Latin America. Codes have also been used as points of national unity. One of the most renowned of all the codes is the Code Civil des Farancais, commonly called the Code Napoleon. This is one of the most important of the modern codes and is the basis for many legal systems within Europe, as well as the state of Louisiana. The most noted part of the Code Napoleon deals with issues representing Criminal Law. Other distinctive codes include the Danske Lov, Code Frederic, and the Code of Canon Law. Each has a valid content and has been influential in the body of law found around the world. The one area in which the United States has advanced the codification of law is within the military. The Uniform Code of Military Justice applies to all military personnel serving in the United States armed forces.

The advantage to a codified system of law is that it is developed from a logical and comprehensive statement. Many laws are generated from these fundamental charges. There is an accounting. The process of using codes brings about identical value and equity for each point of law, and to some degree how it is applied. Codes have been set up to include Civil Law, Public Law, Maritime Law, and Criminal Law. It can be argued that a codified system of laws is more stable and clear with changes occurring only through the Legislative process.

There are also supporters and defenders of the use of common law. They note that judges are able to depart from established systems and create new precedents. In turn other judges can use their decisions to create new rules. The system is more animated and dynamic. Change occurs at a far more profuse rate. They note the importance that experience plays upon the common law and the wisdom found within its usage.

The problem is not one of law as much as it is of creating law. As a people, or as a nation, do we want our judges creating new law? Under the common law system they will be free to do just that and create new precepts. There will be a dual system of lawmaking. The additional question is, "How important is it to solely empower our legislators with the ability to make laws?" Recalling that some of the most enlightened social enactments came about not from the legislative process but from judicial decision. These principles were founded on common law, but the reverse argument is that judges should not be lawmakers. They need to administer the law.

Common law lacks structure. It is built upon twists and turns. The logic may be sound, but the method of travel has been lost or blurred. It shifts, bends, turns, moves about the landscape in ways that seem unnatural. Full of redundancies and oddities, it is like going to work for a new company and finding a complex procedure that is confusing in its required steps. If you confront someone and ask them why it is done this way, their response will be, "We have always done it that way." It is part of the organizational culture of the company. You may resist at first, but within six months you find that you too are doing the procedure the same as those who have preceded you. It seems as natural and normal as sleep. The law need not be so elaborate. There is no reason why it cannot be understood and cataloged. It is in the best interest of the people to comprehend the law, or at least as much as possible.

The one single advantage to a codified system of laws is that it can be more focused. If there is an unjust law the masses are more aware of what needs to be changed and can work toward that goal. It is far more difficult for the people to work toward changing an unjust precedent. It is complex, arduous, time consuming, and expensive to continue to appear in court hoping a judge will change the ruling of a fellow jurist. The law needs to be clearly understood. This is a more complicated task when the nation is ruled by precedents.

In the Proposed Constitution a codified system of laws would take precedence over Common Law. This is a rather ambiguous point, especially considering that most of the American judicial procedures are set up on the ideas of English Common Law. There are American legal codes though. Many of the states have developed a systematic level of codes for issues relating to criminal procedures and Civil Law. More important, the direction of the American legal structure is toward a more codified system of laws. This process could be accelerated with the clearer understanding that Federal law had authority over state law. Even so, it would require a high degree of motivation on the part of our legislators to move toward a more codified system of laws. What is represented here is but an opportunity.

Article 27. Litigation

One of the realities of American life and to some degree modern society is that one person can sue another person. Regardless of how frivolous or foolish the issue may be, each of us may use the court system to pursue what we believe to be righteous and correct. If the issue of judicial review is to be accepted as an important part of democracy, it must equally be allowed that legal action is a part of such a process. The truth is that anyone can sue anyone else and a Constitution should not take that right away.

The courts are powerful tools within a democracy. The people need to have access to the judiciary. Without being ecstatic about the process of our court system being used for trivial disputes, it still must be open to the people. There is another related issue. If the courts are not available to the people, then they will become disenfranchised from the system. Other alternatives will increase in value, including the possibility of violence.

While it is important to allow people to bring litigation against other persons, it is equally consequential that government be able to use the legal system as well, regardless of whether a state government brings issues to bear against the Federal government or the reverse. It does not matter what combination of groups, governments, agencies, organizations, or individual parties are involved. The court system needs to be open to all. Obstacles that restrict, limit, or damage our society need to be judged.

Though under the current Constitution an individual cannot sue a state, many ways have been devised to get around this section of the Constitution. It is possible to sue an administrator of a state department or an agency, but not the state proper. This proposed Constitution would eliminate this absurdity. Besides, the ability to address grievances against your government, even a state government, is lessened if a person cannot bring the issue into court. For better or worse the courts are the forum where disputes are settled and they need to be open.

Article 28. Equal Protection under the Law

The Fourteenth Amendment to the American Constitution ensured *equal protection under the law*. The concept is simple: all people will be treated equally under the Constitution and the law. The government cannot make unreasonable distinctions between individuals or groups of people; the law needs to apply equally to all individuals.

Of all the rights enjoyed by a free people equal protection is the most important. It is the basis from which all other rights emerge. If this guarantee is not in place, if it is not supported by the courts and encouraged by the people, the other rights become meaningless. If the rights of one group, or even one person, are subverted the credibility of the whole nation-state and the total rights placed before the people are lost.

One of the reasons that equal protection under the law is so important concerns how we treat people. Though rules, or in the case of government laws, are essential to civilized living, these rules need to be evenly and fairly applied. Families need household rules. The specifics of those rules are not as important as that they be reasonably and consistently applied to each person. So it is with government. Though we must live by its laws, we may like some better than others. What is critical is not so much the law as the fact that it be fairly and objectively applied to all.

Equal protection under the law has two related clauses in the American Constitution. The first is Article 2, Section 1 which states that "The citizens of each State shall be entitled to all privileges and immunities of citizens in the several States." Of course the second clause is found within the Fourteenth Amendment. "No State shall make or enforce any law which shall abridge the privileges or immunities of citizens of the United States." Both of these statements enforce the same concept and point to the same issue: they represent equal protection under the law.

Equal protection has been a stormy issue throughout American history and one to which little pride can be attached. When asked about or confronted on the theory, the courts and nation's ruling bodies have always declared their endorsement of this section, but the policy of government has not been so inclined. The Fourteenth Amendment was created after the American Civil War to give slaves the same rights as other citizens. During Reconstruction groups of whites were developing tactics to continue the bondage of the large African American populations throughout the South. The tactic was to declare that blacks were not citizens. The Fourteenth Amendment was designed to correct this situation and give all people equal protection under the law. This Amendment must be considered a valid effort even though it was ignored for a hundred years. Still, in reality blacks were not given the protection this law afforded regardless of the nature or goals of this Constitutional Amendment. Once stating this and recognizing the history of our nation, we still must continue to strive for compliance. Without equal protection within the structure of American society, history will be re-lived and with the same horror and depravity that has been found in our past.

The problem of course is that there are exceptions to equal protection, most of which center around the rights of minor children in society. While this Article was meant to ensure that the government does not make unreasonable distinctions between groups of people, one group that has a distinction all their own is the young. They are not given the same rights and privileges as all other citizens. They are treated differently, both as a special class and within the law. Nothing within the concept of equal protection under the law should change that issue. The problem is that there are always exceptions that must be noted and worked through as points of law.

Article 29. Freedom of Expression

A question may be raised about whether freedom of speech differs from freedom of expression. While in the American Constitution we clearly have been given freedom of speech, freedom of expression also has been implied. The Supreme Court has conceded the related concept of freedom of expression as it correlates with free speech or in some cases actions. What is being done in the Proposed Constitution is more a matter of fine tuning. Though speech is connected to the thought processes as a form of expression, it is not the only form. Since other forms of expression exist besides speech, the Constitution should state that the written word and the use of pictures is also guaranteed. As with much within the American Constitution antiquated concepts simply need to be updated. Freedom of expression is one of these.

Some scholars have noted that the entire First Amendment to the American Constitution should be seen as an Article on freedom of expression. Others break it down into the five basic liberties: freedom of speech, freedom of the press, freedom of assembly, freedom of petition, and the freedom of religion. These five items would not be possible without an ability to express ourselves openly and freely. In fact the nature of civil liberties is connected to freedom of expression. It allows us the endowment to speak out on those issues that concern us and to challenge restrictive measures.

Freedom of expression is absolutely essential to a democratic state. Without this concept democracy cannot exist. If the people are to participate in their government, if the power of government is truly invested with the people, they need the ability to debate and review the issues of the day. Opinions need to be expressed. Whether those opinions are correct or not is unimportant. Many times they simply need to be aired. Only by bringing them forward can they be tested and critiqued. Democracy requires an informed public, and information does not always come from governmental sources or the established press.

If this view is accepted it is meaningful only if contrary ideas are allowed. What makes freedom of speech worth having is the ability to speak out on unpopular topics. When people become entrenched in their ideas and opinions, a minority may step forward and force them to look at a situation differently. These views of the minority need to be protected. The problem of course is that these views may make us feel uncomfortable. They may run counter to our own logic or deductions on how the world functions. It does not matter. If this one freedom is abridged or circumscribed, democracy is impossible.

Once saying this however, freedom of expression clearly does have its limits. Total unrestricted freedom of expression would infringe on other rights within our society and violate the rights of others. As has been said many times, freedom of speech does not give a person a right to shout "Fire" in a crowded theater. This is an issue of public safety. The same argument can be used during a time of war. Freedom of speech in its purest form may place the lives of our military personnel in jeopardy. Equally, a person should not incite a riot by demanding action through spoken words. With such freedoms come the realization that the conflict has not been so much over the issue of public safety as to unpopular ideas that have been labeled subversive. Hence, our institutions likely will be quickest in using that term when verbally attacked.

Other limitations also exist. Freedom of expression does not include the right to libel or slander someone. If a person maliciously defames or denigrates another with the goal of destroying the person's good name and reputation and to harm and hurt, that is not freedom of speech. Our freedom of expression should not be seen as a weapon but more an expansion of our knowledge and wisdom. We must be able to speak out and voice alternative views without denouncing or calumniating others.

A related issue is obscenity. Pornography does exist. The problem has been what separates pornography from accepted elements of expression. On the scale of values it becomes an issue of definition. It is even difficult to determine the nature of the harm. The struggle seems to be between the differences in how we would like to see society and the reality of our society. No definitive answers to such questions will be found in these pages, for the problem is truly a moral one and absolute answers will not be found in the political spectrum. What is important is that by championing freedom of speech and, in this case, freedom of expression, the issue will continue to be reviewed and discussed. What may be most important is not the outcome but the process.

These issues of lewd material may have little to do with freedom of expression, but more to do with protection of the young. As a nation, as a society, we do have much to say about the type of environment in which we wish our children to be raised. If we remove children from the equation, the problem becomes less fatiguing.

Some have argued that freedom of speech is an inalienable right, and certainly within the United States it has had enormous importance. Its history is reflected in one of the first state's Constitution—Virginia in 1776. A right to free speech was laid out in this Constitution. Massachusetts failed to adopt their Constitution of 1778 for the very reason that it did not have such a clause. When the American Constitution was first submitted to the states for ratification, the chief complaint dealt with the lack of guarantees on civil liberties, one of which was freedom of speech. Four states refused to accept the American Constitution unless a *bill of rights* was added. New York and Pennsylvania sided with Virginia and Massachusetts on this issue.

This item was referred to as the "Liberty of Utterance." Freedom of speech has been tested many times in the American courts. One of the first transactions of the new national government was to pass the Alien and Sedition Act of 1798. It stated that to foster opposition to the Federal government was a criminal offense.

Those who spoke out against the government or Federal law were seen as being in violation of the act. The battles for freedom of speech and expression have been fought. It is simply time to build upon what has already been won.

Like many concepts, freedom of expression is constantly being revised as new issues present themselves. What is significant for a Constitution is that our rights are outlined and one of the most important is freedom of expression.

Article 30. Freedom of the Press

Freedom of the press is another traditional item within the American Constitution. Considered a pillar of democracy, freedom of the press has been expanded over the years to include the broadcast media as well as the print media. With each new technology the court reviews the situations and circumstances. With each passing year new layers of media become part of that institution.

What the media is actually tied to is information. Information is power. Those who attempt to use their power in sinister ways will take every effort to control the information that the public receives. This issue runs even beyond the realm of politics. Every institution needs to exist within the exposed eye of the masses. Institutions need to be aware of the direction and intent of those who operate within them. Most failures within the media are not a matter of design. Sometimes an error in judgment or a course of action poorly conceived leads to faulty reporting, but the circumstances of human events need to be passed on to the public. The press is expected to perform this function.

The authentic right that the media possesses is not information that can be passed on to the people; it is the right to publish. No one can take away or abridge that right. People are still responsible for what they publish. If print or broadcast material is libelous, they may be brought before a court. If they ridicule or defame an individual, and they do so with malice, the press must defend the nature of their reporting. What must be kept in perspective is that what the press does is to pass on a collection of facts; it may not even be all the facts but at least those that have been found to that point. The goal may not even be the truth. Freedom of the press and truth do not go "hand in hand." Allowing this one function, this simplest of concepts, the right to publish, is a step toward maintaining our democracy. The media has little responsibility in enhancing democracy; it does not embellish it or even strengthen it. There are many trade-offs with individual privacy, but in maintenance of a democracy a free press is mandatory.

The media cannot change or correct the flaws within government. They lack both power and ability to complete such actions. That responsibility falls upon the people; they are the only ones who can adjust or change the nature of their government.

What the press can do, however, is observe. Though this may not sound like much, it is critically important. They become the eyes and ears of the masses, especially in understanding the type of government that a democracy represents. Before republican governments were in power the sovereign was the chief authority. They were the law. The existence and preservation of the society became the responsibility of the monarchy. The fundamental change that occurs in a democracy is that the leaders themselves and the government become restricted by law. No one is above the law. This is a major adjustment in thinking and theory. Governments have become bound by their own laws. Yet, the legal mechanisms of maintaining the law are still in the hands of the rulers. The police, the prosecuting attorneys, the courts and penal system—all are still under the governmental umbrella. It represents considerable control and power. If we are to bind the government to its own laws we need a body, or in this case an institution, designed to oversee the affairs of state.

This does not mean that the media cannot be manipulated; one institution can be used by another for purposes of obtaining advantages within the society. The media also functions from their own separate standards and rules, some of which can lead to a detached agenda—one representing their own interests. These issues to some degree are unimportant. What is important is balance, and one of the ways to create a balance is an open and free press.

There is one concern. As representation has expanded, and a single elected official is representing more people, our politicians have been forced to turn to the media to convey their message. It has become depicted in the "30 second sound byte." Directly this is not the fault of the media, but the information obtained by the masses becomes distorted. Within thirty seconds only quips, slogans, core statements, or brief diatribes can be offered. The system has created a dependency for both parties. News personnel are fearful of being expulsed from the information flow and our elected officials have become dependent upon the media to link themselves to their constituents.

The media does have a responsibility not generally understood. There is an expectation that the media will educate. It is not enough just to report. There are issues that may not be sensational, but critical to the health of the nation. The best that the media has to offer is when sincerity is coupled with wit and charm.

Article 31. Freedom to Exchange Ideas

The First Amendment to the American Constitution outlines four distinct concepts: freedom of speech, freedom of the press, freedom of religion, and freedom of assembly. Yet, a similar theme runs through each of these ideas. The bond that unites these four concepts deals with the exchange of ideas. One of the reasons people read newspapers, watch television, and listen to the radio is to hear what other people have to say. People congregate in one location to hear a speaker discuss an issue. What is important is not that people be allowed to meet in one spot—it is not the right to assemble that is significant—but rather that meeting in a group facilitates an interchange of views. Equally, it is not any particular speech that is so precious, but rather the idea that it can be shared. Regardless of how invested we are in a point of faith, the issue can never be empirical. Religion can be seen as an exchange of ideas. Religion must be accepted as a point of faith, as an idea. While some ideas have to be proved, others do not. What is important is that society give ideas an opportunity to be heard. The common thread that runs through the First Amendment to the American Constitution is the notion of ideas.

Ideas are as valuable as any commodity in our society. They are the essence that fuels business, education, science, foundations, and the media. Progress and development are but by-products of the optimism found in peoples' inspiration. Ideas are the movers of nations and institutions. Yet to be valid any idea must be tested, reviewed, and fielded. One individual advances an idea, sometimes in a written form, other times verbal, but it is placed before another. That person accepts the concept or adds to it or rejects it. It is then passed to another and then another. The idea either develops into volition or withers and slips away, lying dormant until perhaps it reemerges in another form.

What is important to an idea is not the hypothesis or the rationale, but rather the analysis. Is it able to withstand the light of day? An idea must be able to be tested and examined. It must be able to be compared to related concepts and investigated. This process occurs by an exchange of ideas. In a free society the exchange of ideas is not only allowed but encouraged. This represents one of the methods by which a healthy democracy can be judged. If new ideas and concepts are given a high level of exchange, if they are reviewed, discussed, evaluated, and if need be rejected, then the soundness of the democracy is assured.

An exchange of ideas should not be misinterpreted to run counter to copyright laws, trademarks, or patents. In these cases the creator has declared exclusive right to an idea as it appears in an established form. He or she requests little more than acceptance or rejection. While these ideas may spawn other beliefs or concepts, the connection becomes one of reshaping. An item that is copyrighted or is presented as a patent has a greater degree of permanence.

Freedom to exchange ideas is far more important to academia. When individuals attend colleges and universities it is not just a matter of learning the school stationery or uniform; rather, it is a matter of reviewing all ideas, philosophies, and theories. The educational process becomes a time for persons to express their own views and to interact with the knowledge that is being presented. Learning becomes not a point of acceptance but of exchange. A person may come to the same conclusions as those that have preceded them, but the information does need to be challenged. In fact it is the responsibility of each generation to challenge the ideas that precede them. To do this, the parties need to have the freedom to exchange ideas.

The greater problem is whether this same concept would be accepted by educational institutions in theology. The problem exists for both public and private schools, the question being whether such ideas can be discussed and reviewed not as points of creed or dogma but as ideas. The argument is that doctrines of faith would survive such reviews. People find comfort in their religious beliefs. They are important in how people see themselves and the world around them. The process would enrich the image, not subtract from it, but more rewarding for society would be the exchange of ideas and concepts.

Another issue needs to be reviewed within this Proposed Constitution. Does the freedom to exchange ideas represent a duplication of the Article on freedom of expression? There are modest differences, enough so that the two concepts need to be listed separately. Freedom of expression is a far more personal issue. It does not require interaction. What is actually being conceded is nonconformity. While it may not always be desirable, as a people we are saying that it is acceptable to be a nonconformist, as long as it does not curtail the rights of others. With the exchange of ideas the process becomes reciprocal, allowing for a free flow of information. Ideas can move about the society, be embraced or discharged as needed. If both of these concepts are allowed to endure, the possibility of suppression of any of our liberties becomes less.

One last argument concerning the freedom to exchange ideas. Regardless of the utility of this Article, there is a separate conclusion. A Constitution needs to be more than a listing of procedures or the management of governmental affairs. It needs to be a document stating what the nation and the society find to be important, either in actual or implied terms. An Article in the Constitution saying that the exchange of ideas is meaningful is also saying that an individual thought may well be momentous—that a person's beliefs and opinion do matter. We are a nation of ideals, or in this case, ideas.

Article 32. Freedom of Religion

Freedom of religion has been one of the pillars of American democracy and our Constitution. Though any individuals may take exception to the almost radical detachment this amendment has placed on governmental interaction with religion, it has proved, nevertheless, to be a most practical Article in the Constitution. The separation of Church and State has proved to be an astoundingly simple concept, one in which both institutions have benefited. When freedom of religion is allowed in its purest form, individuals may embrace whatever doctrine they choose without fear or concern about any other group or governmental intervention into these affairs.

Religion is always a matter of faith; it neither requires nor seeks corroboration or confirmation. People accept their points of faith because it brings them solace, addresses the future, and gives moralistic standards from which to operate. No other institution can attest to these concepts in the same way as religious ideology, but the reality is that no two people share precisely the same collection of beliefs. Variations in point of view and intensity of feelings over interpretation abound in a free society. Many of these differences can be found in a person's background and life experiences. To devise a system that allows all persons to be free to choose a personal religion, practice their faith as they wish, and worship their God as they want is to grant freedom of considerable integrity. This is especially true when the history and conflict between Church and State is examined.

Though countless battles have been fought in the name of religion and religious certainty, none have ever proven that one item of faith has greater credibility than another. Faith is not empirical. These battles have been waged with the support and assistance of all the other institutions. They have been done within the bizarre combination of reverent conviction and violent rage. Within this same context institutional discrimination took a toll on the fabric of human existence. People, in the name of God, harmed other people. The line between government and church was blurred. Justice could be found only from within the established set of dogma or religious point of view.

America's Founders were familiar with the nature of human history, but they were also concerned about two related issues. The first was the establishment of a state religion. The British monarch, starting with Henry VIII, in his skirmishes with the church in Rome had established the Anglican church as the dominant creed in England. Most, if not all, nations of Europe had governments that supported a given religious sect, a practice that created points of conflict. It even produced divisions within their own states. The second point is that the United States was not set up or created from only one religious group. Each of the colonies emerged from a specific set of divine teachings or leaders. The establishment of a particular point of theology would have been contemptible to all the others. For the nation's founders the compromise was to establish the concept of freedom of religion. It created a political doctrine that all religions are equally valid and that government has no say in their operation or tenets.

This issue has never been perfect. Religious groups in their desire to practice their creed have taken exception to government's refusal to partake at any level. This can be seen even in the simplest of terms and actions. Yet, all such actions have repercussions. To concede the one act means to concede the many. In the end each institution needs to do what it can do best. Government needs to govern and theology needs to engage moral standards as it relates to the soul.

To separate Church and State should not be seen as a negative; rather, it should be a point of great celebration. Representing for the first time in the history of humankind a statement of almost complete rectitude. While nourishing both parties, each institution benefits from the arrangement. It reduces the possibility that the state would become a theocracy and in turn eliminates the ample influence the government can muster in the support for a given doctrine. The separation of Church and State needs to be total, but it also needs to be seen as something marvelous within the field of political science and organized religion. It is a great step forward.

Article 33. Freedom of Assembly

One of the ways an oppressor subverts the masses and destroys civil liberties is by control of public meetings. If the people are able to unite, discuss, and interact among themselves, resistance can be formed. One of the most fundamental rights of a free people is the ability to assemble. Freedom of assembly has proven to be a valuable tool in the maintenance of a democracy. It allows people to meet and review an issue that they feel is important. Without such a guarantee the other rights within a Constitution become feeble and far easier to suppress.

Of the two typical types of gathering—indoor or outdoor, each has its own special problems. The first would occur *inside* a structure. If a handful of people are meeting to discuss or exchange ideas the inside location poses no difficulty. Within the Constitution people have a right to assemble; they may meet anywhere they like as long as the building or dwelling is safe. There is only a predicament if large numbers of people are present. While the freedom to assemble remains, large numbers of people create an atmosphere all their own. Regardless of the purpose of the gathering, public safety must be maintained. Laws considering fire safety, general security, and order must be upheld.

Outdoor assemblies represent a different kind of issue. Whether it is a large group or a small one, out-of-doors assemblies, protests, or demonstrations present special problems. It is always possible that opposition groups may appear, and conflict or even violence may result. Protection of all the parties concerned may force local authorities to invest in additional police or security units. The right of assembly stands without question. This does not mean that government cannot issue a permit and assist with the organizational process, especially if there is a possibility of colliding with another adversarial or counter group.

A balance must be found between freedom of assembly and the protection of personal safety. Protecting property is within the responsibility of government and its police powers. People need to meet lawfully and within the support of order. Yet, once saying this the power of the people to take to the streets, to be heard, and even to demand that their grievances be considered—this is all part of the democratic process. Protest is as much a part of a constitutional government as voting. To restrict it in any form would lessen the ability of the people to initiate change.

Article 34. Freedom of Association

While freedom of assembly gives people the right to meet, freedom of association gives them the right to form groups, some of which may exist for extended periods of time. We are all members of various groups and organizations. Many have little to do with political activities, but all relate to the society at large. People join. Our personalities are connected to the types of organizations we become associated with and from which we interact. Restriction on this basic and most fundamental of rights runs counter to all ideas of democracy.

Every institution is a product of organizations or associations. They grow into institutions by meeting for a common purpose and reviewing common goals and aims. Over time these groups developed formal structures. Leaders rise to the surface, elites emerge, and levels of rank are created. Each group develops traditions, customs, and rites. Competing groups form. They relate in purpose but with different goals and processes in obtaining those goals. Through these organizations institutions are established. Each institution develops separate rules, but lack a single, formal leader. Each is important to society. Without question or debate such institutions are the core of society for through association, institutions are formed.

While the old adage that birds of a feather flock together may be correct, the issue is more complex than that. No one has a right to tell another with whom the person may associate. We interact and associate with people and join associations because these activities fill a need. The most healthy of activities, stretch far beyond political issues. It is part of the very nature of being human; we are all social creatures.

Once saying this some exceptions must be allowed. If the purpose of the meeting is to originate a crime, if the goals of the organization are criminal in direction and intent, the law will restrict such gatherings. While conspiracies are difficult to prove, laws need to be in place that restrict or punish those who commit crimes as a collective group. People coming together for an unlawful reason should be treated differently than those that meet for reasons of fellowship or even mutual interest. If groups are designed to protest or demand change, however, no restrictions will be made in a free society. Groups are the most important bodies for democracy. They test the theories by which the society has been constructed.

Article 35. Right to Privacy

Though the American Constitution does not specifically verbalize a right to privacy, it implies such a right. The Fourth Amendment that deals with search and seizures states, "The right of the people to be secure in their person, houses, papers, and effects, against unreasonable searches and seizures shall not be violated." It continues by discussing the use of warrants and "probable cause." The Constitution is specific. If a search is to occur it needs to be particular to the situation. The exact items that the authorities will seek and what is to be seized must be listed in the warrant. It has also been argued that the Third Amendment implies a right to privacy by disallowing the quartering of soldiers in private homes, at least in peacetime and without consent.

This issue of implied rights runs throughout the American Constitution. While at times ambiguous and misleading, this is a fair doctrine. What is being said is that since not every possible violation can be anticipated and listed, as a point of precept the idea of implied rights is conceded. This gives the court considerable discretion. In turn the court has ruled consistently in favor of a right to privacy. An example would be *Griswold v. Connecticut* in 1965, which confirmed the right of marital privacy.

Privacy has become more than an implied right. It has become clearly understood and has become a stated right. The people have come to believe that they have a right to privacy. If that is the case this right needs to be articulated in the Constitution. Unwarranted intrusion by the government, the media, or other institutions into an individual's life is neither desirable nor Constitutional. Privacy becomes a protected right.

The chief problem with such an Article deals with defining what is private. Many of these issues seem to center around the home. What individuals are doing within their own homes, as long as they are law-abiding and not infringing on the rights of others, becomes a private matter. It must also be understood that all members of a household have protection from unlawful acts against their person. A right to privacy does not allow one person to commit a crime against another simply because it is within a person's residence.

The Article is better understood in a singular form. Each person standing alone has the right of privacy. If others live in the same dwelling, qualifications are placed on the right as it pertains to the rights of others. The right of privacy also implies that all the parties have the insight to understand the decisions being made in a household and what those decisions presuppose. A person with marginal mental capabilities should be entitled to degrees of protection from within the law and society in general. This would be equally true with children. Parental responsibilities must be tempered with the community's responsibility to insulate the young from the depravity that can also be found in the society.

The right of privacy can be best understood in personal thoughts, writings, and journals. A journal or a diary is a very private matter. While selected others may be allowed to pick up such a book and read a person's private thoughts or feelings on a given day, it is by no means public. To read another person's journal is unwelcomed. It is an intrusion into matters and effects beyond the right of another to see. Equally, letters sent to another person are confidential. If persons wish to divulge the correspondence, that is their right, but a third party should have no right of access without permission.

Privacy does have a connection to property and the related concept of property rights. If a person has established residency by contract, rent, or ownership, it implies that the individual may do what he or she wishes within these boundaries. This idea is false. An illegal act is an illegal act. If criminal behavior occurs it is illegitimate regardless of the location. In the simplest of terms the right of privacy does make encroachment on a person's solitude inappropriate.

The issue of the right of privacy may deal more with the state's ability to access, disclose, and obtain personal information than on the incursion into personal property. Financial records and personal histories should not be a matter of public record. We are entitled to privacy in our financial affairs and personal business. This is especially important since we find ourselves in the information age. Limits to what types of information can be obtained are essential. The government needs to recognize this issue and assist the citizenship in setting up systems that respect this right.

Article 36. Freedom to Petition

The right to petition is an important part of addressing grievances against government. The people have a right to make claims upon their leaders, to demand change, or adjust the direction in which the nation is going. Many methods have been used so that the citizenship can make their feelings known. The people are capable of protest en masse, they can write letters to specific individuals, they can form political organizations, become active in a given political party, or sign petitions. Each system reflects a different type of interplay; the effect is different with each response. A petition represents a large group of people, inconspicuous in personality, but equally burdened by the same issue. To sign your name on a petition means that you are at least willing to allow the issue to be heard. The greater the number of names, the greater the influence on the Representative.

A petition is a formal process. People are making a statement that they want redress on a given topic. The problem is that the government or Representative could ignore such petitions and in some situations may be forced to do just that. There are risks, however. The voters may use such petitions as rallying points. In the next election the petitions could again be proffered and the elected official would be forced to address the reason action was not taken. The petitions could be used as starting points for initiatives or propositions. If petitions sent to our government officials are ignored, the next step would be the formal process of creating a proposition.

While this right may not be as dynamic or as substantial as many of our individual rights, it is one of the requirements of a free society. Without the ability to petition government, a wide range of democratic maneuvers become unavailable. The right to petition becomes one of the pieces of democracy's total structure.

Article 37. Property Rights

The ownership of property is very much a part of human conduct and behavior. It exists as a goal, as one of the reasons behind the energy and activities of humankind. Human beings exhibit a drive to own, to acquire, to collect. People collect things, whether they be old coins, houses, tools, photographs, or books. The human need to own objects and commodities appears to be innate. It is far more pronounced than simply survival. It is a driving force and at times a consuming one. Yet, the right to own property is as fundamental as devotion or affection.

Of the two types of property, the first is *real property* or *real estate*. This would be land or anything connected to it and would cover items such as buildings, structures on the property, or minerals found within it. *Personal property* is everything else and this includes anything that can be owned that is not real estate. Personal property can be divided into two categories, one is *tangible* which is a physical item such as an automobile or a lamp. The second is *intangible* which would be a copyright or patent right. For the purposes of a Constitution all forms of property have the same weight and legitimacy. The people have a right to own both real and personal property. The reality is that both forms of property can be acquired by government through due process.

Every philosopher has had something to say about property. They seem to fall into two camps, for or against. One of the best negative views of the ownership of property comes from Rousseau:

> "The first man who, having enclosed a piece of ground, bethought himself of saying *This is mine,* and found people simple enough to believe him, was the real founder of civil society. From how many crimes, wars and murders, from how many horrors and misfortunes might not anyone have saved mankind, by pulling up the stakes, or filling up the ditch, and crying to his fellows, Beware of listening to this impostor; you are undone if you once forget that the fruits of the earth belong to us all, and the earth

itself to nobody."[1]

Of course Karl Marx saw the ownership of property as a great evil and a system for oppression.

There is an alternate view, one in which the ownership of property and government have similar interests. One of the reasons that we have government is to insure order in the exchange of property and the title of such items. This view would be expressed by John Locke, one of the individuals who had great influence on the nations founders. He said, "Government has no other end but the preservation of property."[2] There is a huge breach between these two philosophies. The truth is that while many may wish to restrict the property rights of others, none are eager to yield what they own.

Government does have a responsibility in the maintenance of property rights. The reality is that humans do create boundaries and seek to possess. Government does play a part in this process. It can bring about order and stability in the ownership of real estate, manufacturing of products, and the fair marketing of goods. It can enforce contracts and agreements. They can regulate arrangements, exchanges, and merchandising. Either through the judicial process or legislation, government helps determine what constitutes property or its ownership. Yet, before any of this can occur one must concede that the people have a right to own property. This issue must be confirmed.

The American Constitution does guarantee property rights in the Fifth Amendment to the Constitution. The view is that persons cannot be separated from their property. It is theirs by right. Only through the courts and due process are such acts allowed. Two court actions would make separation possible. The first is through forfeiture by a criminal act and civil action. There are scores of ways the court system can take a piece of property from an individual and hand it to another: Either through loss by default, claims for bad debt, breach of contract, divorce, and judgments of different diversity and size. People lose property because of criminal activity. They commit crimes and part of their punishment is the forfeiture of many of the possessions, especially those items that were purchased with illicit funds.

The second method of separation deals with *eminent domain*. Government does have the right to take private property for public use with just compensation to the owner. Eminent domain is a necessary part of the nature of government. Through this process roads, bridges, dams, and public projects are created—undertakings that benefit all the people. This is a part of all sovereign states, and both the Federal government and state governments have this power. Commonly the states entrust this issue to local authorities. The state may also delegate the issue of eminent domain to other parties as well. In the United States this right has been given to railroads, utility companies, and public service companies. Yet, a person's property cannot be taken from them without due process of law and appropriate compensation. What is most important is that the Constitution recognizes private property. If such property is to be taken for the public good, it needs to be a Constitutional process.

Government has a clearly defined role in the management of property rights. In fact most of what government does is in some way connected to issues related to property. It establishes ownership, keeps records, determines usage of such items, disciplines those who steal, and bases taxes on property. If the issue of property were removed from the theory of government as an entity it would become subordinate to most of the other institutions in our society.

If we concede this one issue that since property exists, an individual can own an item, then we must move one step beyond that statement and declare that these guarantees must exist within the Constitution. Ownership of property creates stability or order in society. It defines what physical appendages are part of people and to some degree who we are as persons. It also becomes clear to all the parties concerned what are the boundaries of necessity and the limits of cupidity. Ownership of property is a right, but with that ownership does come an obligation.

Article 38. Freedom of Movement

Freedom of movement is integral to a free society. The nation-state cannot restrict or retard in any way the movement of the people. Citizens may live where they choose within the confines on their own economic prerequisites and limits placed upon personal safety. The issue here is not one of a specific location but one of area or even state. Neither the national government nor the individual states may develop laws that restrict movement of its citizens or disallow them to live in one area of the country over another.

Mobility becomes a right. It represents the idea that a free people may move about their nation without undue restrictions on the part of the governmental authorities. Many of the rights within a Constitution deal with freedom of thought, but freedom of action is also essential. Mobility would be part of that type of response. It allows people to interact, to meet and discuss issues at a personal level. Freedom of movement allows people to experience the nation and to interact in ways that create a sense of one nation.

What is important to the idea of mobility is not just the individual, but for all of the institutions. They are unable to operate effectively if the individuals within those bodies are unable to move about the country. The chief example would be business. The nature of business requires managing and interacting on a personal basis. Without engaging both the buyer and seller there can be no business. While it is possible to do business from afar, it is most effective when contrasting of views and sharing of information is done in the same surroundings. All of the institutions benefit by having freedom of movement, and it is significant to a free society.

The United States has always enjoyed this right. While it was never specifically addressed in the American Constitution, it was implied as a normal function of an expanding, growing nation. For the nation's founders it was as natural as breathing. For them writing an Article stating that an individual had a right to breathe would have been just as idiotic, but the United States has changed. Today we rank third among the nations of the world in population. People by their sheer numbers create problems, and this is even more pronounced when they condense into small areas. If this is an important issue, it needs to be addressed in the Constitution. There is a risk in believing that because a right has been implied in the past it will exist equally in the future. Far better to write it down as clearly a right of a free people.

Nations that wish to control their populations restrict mobility. It diminishes the probability of a united action against the government in power. Such nations also place people wherever government wants them rather than where the individual wishes to live. Examine any totalitarian state and restrictions on the mobility of its citizens are inevitable. Democracy does require freedom of movement.

Once noting this there are exceptions. At times of natural disaster or epidemics the government needs to protect the populations from harm. To restrict travel at points of a specific emergency is a different matter. Again it returns to the issue of public safety. The problem differs from a short-term dilemma, to that of a definable long-term issue of personal mobility.

Article 39. Discrimination

An issue that the United States has been wrestling with is the problem of discrimination in our society. For the better part of the history of America, discrimination against one group or section of our own citizens has not only occurred, but has been sanctioned by the government. Every group or classification of Americans has experienced some form of discrimination. For a nation that is made up of as many different ethnic, religious, and social groups as the United States, it is hard to understand how it would be able to function with such bias. Yet, throughout our history discrimination has not only been commonplace, but encouraged by governmental bodies.

Nothing seems to erode democracy more rapidly than issues of discrimination. It eats away the concepts that are so important for a healthy society. It implies that one person's vote is not as valid as another. It insulates one group of people from another, reducing interaction and the exchange of ideas. Discrimination degrades all the parties involved, trivializes the process of democracy, taints the issues, and corrupts our national leaders. It leaves a trail of anger from generation to generation. It haunts the people and forces them to view their world in distorted ways, hiding the truth and igniting emotions. It is the tool of all great tyrants, and a curse of the human race.

If a nation, a people, believe in democracy, that belief must be total. It requires the defense of liberty. The issue is not your liberty, but the liberty of all. There is no liberty if you degrade another, if you live in a system of prejudice and bias. It must be resisted at every turn, every point, and every time. Though America has made considerable progress, we need to move to a new, higher level. The issue of discrimination should appear in the Constitution. The nation needs to clearly state that it is wrong and stands outside the framework of the nation's principles.

It is possible that an argument could be raised presenting discrimination as a social or moral issue, rather than a Constitutional issue. After all it deals with how people think, reason, and how they interact with others. Should a Constitution be dictating thought? The distinction may be a small one, especially considering discrimination's power in curtailing the influence of democracy. An equal argument can be made that a nation-state or the Constitution should outline the principles for which they stand.

The laws of the United States currently forbid discrimination. What is actually being done in the Proposed Constitution is to levitate the issue from a piece of legislation to a Constitutional right, that no one group or the members of that group be faced with bias or prejudice. Most important, government will not promote such prejudices by action, inaction, or policy.

This issue explicitly deals with tolerance. This is one of the chief concepts of democracy; without levels of tolerance the interplay between people is not possible. Each of us was raised in a separate family grouping, nurtured within the family belief system, with each member conforming to the whole. In the end we are more like our parents and our siblings than anyone else in the world. Yet, when we move beyond this nurturing environment into the sustaining environment where we must earn a living, we find ourselves interacting with a wide range of different people. Most will have different views from ourselves. They will see the world around them in a different perspective, and from a different set of experiences. If we believe the world should exist only at our own level of comfort, it will create a bias toward any who do not conform to our belief system. The only alternative is tolerance. If every person accepts others in a moderate and temperate way, the nature of society becomes far more benevolent. Tolerance becomes a point of unity.

The issue of freedom of religion is an extension of this idea—that the state, and the authority invested in government, would not discriminate against one religious group over another. It has proved to be of great value to the country and the political process. This is especially notable in looking at history and the degrees of discrimination that have existed within national bodies and governments.

In the Proposed Constitution a complete listing is attempted of the types of groups that have experienced discrimination in the past. The list would include race, creed, color, gender, age, national origin, economic status, physical capacity, handicaps, or sexual orientation. The one area in which there is a transgression from existing concepts of discrimination is the idea of handicaps. While mental and physical handicaps should be included, other forms of handicaps may not be categorized. The point is not to cover new ground or to expand existing understanding of discrimination, but to allow for clarification. The problem is that most people have some form of handicap. It may be more obvious when we recognize a blind person, but most people have something that holds them back. In those cases the true worth of an individual is how we deal with our handicaps. Nonetheless, discrimination in whatever form it takes is wrong. It limits human potential and nothing is more tragic.

Each of these different types of discrimination are tied together. Discrimination is destructive. It is impossible to justify prejudice. No form of rationalization or intellectualizing can make it work. To attack individuals, either verbally or physically, because they are homosexuals is to say that it is acceptable to defame an individual because they are black, or female, or Jewish. There is no difference. It is the act that is harmful, not the reason. As a people we must move beyond such issues, and government needs to defend the rights of those without influence and power.

Article 40. Emancipation

At what point does an individual receive the full rights of citizenship? At what point does an individual have a complete set of mental faculties including reliable life experiences to make judgments about moral and social issues? When does a person move from the safety of childhood to the demands of adulthood? Is there really such a point when a person crosses over such a line? Since every person is different and everyone matures at a different rate why set such a determinate marker? The main reasons are expectation and responsibility. At some point an individual must accept the responsibilities of citizenship. It is far better to make that time measurable so that it is clear to all the parties involved at what point full citizenship is granted.

This is important because expectations are different for children than of our adult population. Adults can be brought into the military and required to fight in wars. Military conflict carries with it the possibility of death. Persons may be killed in the defense of their nation. Adulthood also carries with it the franchise. At this point in a person's life they are able to vote; clearly that is a change from childhood. Currently, a person's life begins to change at age eighteen. At this time a person is able to hold a job and keep it independent of governmental regulations or family concerns. They can end their education. In most states they can do this even earlier, but after eighteen it is impossible to require a person to continue unwanted education. At eighteen a person may leave the family home and no authority will return them or charge them as a runaway. At this age a person may enter into contracts and sign legal documents. An individual who commits a crime is tried as an adult with its stiffer penalties, not as a child. Eighteen-year-olds are allowed to marry without consent from their parents. There is a true division between being eighteen years old and being less than that age.

At eighteen, people are treated differently and some of what is being argued is currently a matter of record. Some would say that if you want a person to act responsibly, you give them responsibility. If it is clearly defined and understood that at the age of eighteen a person is a full citizen, and with it come the responsibilities of citizenship, then we should expect an individual to act responsibly with that commission. If we do not have such an item in our social contract, then at what point are we simply attempting to control? Such control issues are counter-productive and exist outside of the framework of how we need to interact with one another.

Once saying this there is a reality to life within a family. A person is always a member of their family of origin, regardless if a person is emancipated or not. Healthy families will continue to care for and nurture its members. It is the nature of what is a family. As an institution this is what makes them so valuable. Most people have children but the reality is that they never leave the family of origin. Even when they leave the household and start their own family, they remain a member of the family from which they came. When they return they do not return as guests, but as members of the family. The reality is that children will always be children to the parent. No matter what the age, no matter if a person is emancipated or not, the relationship is always one of parent and child.

If a parent chooses to withdraw support of a child who is more than eighteen years old, while it may not be morally or socially proper, it would be Constitutionally allowable. To abandon a child regardless of their age is a failure of the family relationship, but degrees of disassociation do exist. A time may come when financial, social, and kindred responsibilities do end. It becomes a matter for the individual to seek her or his own way, one hopes, with the direction and affection of the family, but it can no longer be legitimized by law. This is clearly different for a child under eighteen years of age. The state does have a responsibility to ensure the welfare of a child, as does the parent. Financial, educational, and social obligations remain.

Society seems to place some restriction on age even beyond the right of citizenship. Laws may place qualifications on the young and the elderly in the driving of automobiles. Laws establish the legal age that alcohol can be consumed. All of this falls beyond the age of eighteen. Laws prohibit the young from entering movie theaters and watching certain films depending on their rating. These are not issues that limit rights. Without opening a Pandora's box, "Is drinking alcohol a right or a privilege?" Emancipation may have more to do with the family than the law. The issue that is being presented here is that a time does come in which a child becomes a man or a woman.

Emancipation is the time when we recognize the individual as an adult. At the age of eighteen a person will become something different; they will not be the same as they were before. An eighteen-year-old is now a citizen with obligations and responsibilities to the community to equally stand before others. They should be secure in their inheritance, that the rights found within the Constitution are genuine, and that they will exist from this time forward.

Article 41. Inherent Rights

One of the problems in looking at the rights of the people within a Constitution is that a complete list is impossible. Any such effort will leave something out, or one item will be incomplete. Time also changes how we look at our rights. What the drafters of the Bill of Rights saw as freedom of the press, twenty-first century United States citizens think of as freedom of the media. It is the same concept, established for the same reason, designed to cover the same ground, but the scope is different. We refine our rights; as a people we accept the ideas of freedom of speech, but we also know that slander is not free speech. Democracy is an ongoing, continuous process. Each generation adds to the image, each contributing to the philosophies that encase democratic government. A Constitution needs a catch-all phrase, one in which there is room to explore different rights and new concepts.

The American Constitution has been set up accordingly. The nation's founders included the topic of inherent rights or implied rights, or as the Declaration of Independence noted "inalienable rights." The Ninth Amendment to the American Constitution has been used to that effect. While not specific, and understanding that the best document would be one in which rights are clearly outlined, the reality is that all such rights cannot be properly listed.

The right to privacy was never categorized in the American Constitution directly but was always implied. The Supreme Court noted that the Fourth Amendment declared that the people would be "secure in their persons, houses, papers, and effects, against unreasonable searches and seizures." From this concept the courts have held that a right of privacy exists. It is a right that has evolved. Some issues need to be left to future generations. What needs to be allowed is a concept by which these rights can be examined.

This does not mean that every issue is an inherent right. As broad as the topics of happiness and liberty may be, some issues fall outside of these concepts. These issues always return to a similar theory. "One person's right should not infringe upon the rights of another." This is one of the chief reasons for a Supreme Court and why we must include an Article dealing with inherent rights.

Article 42. Search and Seizure

Rights can be assigned to two different categories. The first are rights that are maintained even though we accept the authority of government. These would be a collection of personal rights or "natural rights." The second group would be those rights directly connected to the legal process or the courts—a set of rules that both the government through the courts and the individual as a citizen must abide by and acknowledge.

One of the first such rights deals with *search and seizures.* The actual issue is not searches and seizures, but unreasonable searches and seizures. The authorities have the power to search a person's dwelling and seize evidence or illegal items, but there are qualifications. If the items are to be used in a court of law, they must be obtained by a warrant. Of course the issue is far more complex than that and with many exceptions. Items such as vehicles, boats, or other movable items function differently under the law. If there is a concern that the evidence may vanish before a warrant can be realized, a separate path of action is allowed. There is also the issue of "hot pursuit" and what occurs under those conditions. What needs to be asked is what will be done with the evidence that is obtained in an illegal search? It is clearly unconstitutional to use that evidence against a person in court.

Search warrants have to be specific, outlining the exact items to be looked for, the location, who will do the search, under what conditions the search takes place, and within what given time. All of this must be submitted under oath. *Probable cause* to expect wrongdoing must be present. The reasons behind this cause needs to be spelled out to the judge who issues the warrant. Authorities once in the home or location to be investigated have the authority to search, but not to destroy property.

Protection from unlawful search and seizure was an important issue for the nation's founders and the people during the Revolutionary period. Up until that time the British authorities were allowed to enter homes, search at will, and remove personal property at their discretion. Under British law *Writ of Assistance* could be issued. This allowed officials to enter any home, search any property at any time they chose, and under any conditions. It severely angered the citizens of colonial America. When the Bill of Rights was added to the Constitution such guarantees against unlawful search and seizures were consciously included.

Nothing within this Proposed Constitution would represent a change from the Fourth Amendment of the American Constitution. Law enforcement agencies need to be able to move forward on criminal investigations, but the people have an equally valid right to be free from unfounded harassment by such governmental bodies. The compromise is the search warrant issued by a judge and properly documented.

Article 43, Section 1. Due Process

Few concepts within the American Constitution, or any Constitution, are as consequential as *due process*. It is the basis by which the Constitution is derived— the starting point from which all other conceptions, ideas, and theories about our society and government emerge. Without due process there would be no democracy, no review of Constitutional issues, no interaction between the people and their government. Due process is by far the most important element of Constitutional law.

Once noting the magnitude of this concept, it is actually quite uncomplicated. Due process is nothing more than the establishment of court proceedings or a course of legal action set up by a judicial body. It is designed to safeguard the rights of the people. If action is to be taken against an individual, or the people in general, it cannot be done in an arbitrary and capricious manner. Specific procedures and rules must be followed.

If the government charges a man with a crime, it cannot simply incarcerate him or lynch him. A person is entitled to a fair trial with all the rules relating to a criminal court in place. Rules of evidence must apply. Regardless of a person's guilt or the nature of the crime he is allowed an impartial hearing.

The government wishing to obtain private property to build a structure for public use must either obtain the property by a properly negotiated contract or through the court process under *eminent domain*. In either case the government must fairly compensate the individual and the property has to be used for public purposes. It is not proper to acquire property from a citizen just to build a retreat for governmental officials. Due process is the system by which we use the courts to maintain our rights and institute legal sanctions within our society.

This is another instance of the concept that no one is above the law—not the leaders of government, not the administrators of governmental agencies, not the leaders of our institutions, not the officers charged with the duty of upholding the law, nor the people. The law should be seen as a point of pride. Individually there are bad laws that need to be resisted and changed, but the idea that we are governed by laws and we are all subject to the same laws should be seen as a point of great satisfaction. This is the concept behind due process.

Four Amendments to the American Constitution ensure due process under the law. The first is the Fifth Amendment. "No person shall... be deprived of life, liberty, or property, without due process of law." This clearly sets out the issue, but the Fourteenth Amendment was added in 1868 to include the states. From the view of twenty-first century logic it is difficult to understand why the issue needed to be restated a second time, but a number of items were in play after the American Civil War. Amendments Thirteen, Fourteen, and Fifteen to the Constitution were attempts to secure the rights and privileges of the newly freed slaves. Many of the Recontructionalist Republicans believed that the freed blacks in the American South would not receive due process under the law unless these Amendments were added, especially after the Dred Scott case of 1857 when the Supreme Court declared that blacks were not citizens.

A second factor also came into play. While the act may not have been conscious, nevertheless the United States was moving toward a purer form of Federalism. In fact an argument can be made that the beginnings of American Federalism occurred after the American Civil War. Regardless of the reasons, at this juncture due process is mandated at both the Federal and state levels.

Due process should be seen as a guarantee of civil liberties. The right that stems from due process is not a construct or right in itself. It is more connected and testifies to other rights. The government cannot reduce, limit, or abolish our rights without due process. The key is that the process cannot be hidden. It becomes part of an open forum, recorded and within stated reasons. While the courts bear the responsibility to ensure our rights, especially within the guidelines of the Constitution, the process must be open and exposed. This is part of the reason for due process. If this concept is in place, the people can assist in the defense of their rights; furthermore, the fear that, they might erode is lessened.

Article 43, Section 2. Legal Affirmation

Part of the backbone of judicial procedures is the concept that an individual does not have to be a witness against herself or himself. In colloquial terms it has been known as "Taking the Fifth" a right guaranteed by the Fifth Amendment to the American Constitution. The argument simply stated that an accused person cannot be called as a witness if she or he is accused in a criminal action. The burden of proof belongs to the prosecution. This would be done through evidence or by witnesses, but it cannot be done by having the accused take the stand. This does not mean that a person cannot be heard. The defense may feel that it is in the best interest of the accused to testify. If she chooses to testify she is allowed but will also be subjected to cross-examination. The issue is that the prosecution cannot compel an accused person to take the stand.

A related concept is that a person does not have to speak out on a topic that would incriminate him or her. If a man found himself in a courtroom as a witness he would not have to testify to any issue that would confirm a criminal act of which he could be charged. This would be equally so if confronted with an ongoing criminal investigation. The burden of proof remains with the prosecution and law enforcement agencies.

A distinction must be drawn between a criminal court and a civil court. In the pursuit of criminal charges the accused cannot be forced to take the stand. In a civil court that is a different matter. In a civil trial the two parties stand as equals. Both the petitioner and respondent need to meet on a balanced playing field. In this case criminal wrongdoing is not the issue. The issue becomes more a matter of pursuing justice through an impartial process.

Article 43, Section 3. Double jeopardy

Again, nothing in this section of the Proposed Constitution is new. The American Constitution guarantees that a person cannot be charged with a given offense or crime more than once. If the prosecution tries a person for a given crime and he is found not guilty, the person cannot be retried for the same offense. It is referred to as *double jeopardy*. The prosecution and the law enforcement agencies are given only one opportunity to try a person for a given criminal transgression. If they fail to obtain a conviction, then at least for that charge, the process comes to an end.

The second part of this concept deals with changing the degree of the crime for the purpose of retrying an individual. An example may be a person charged with first-degree murder who was found not guilty after a lengthy trial. To charge and retry him for second-degree murder would be improper and unconstitutional. In this scenario a person could face scores of indictments for each degree of murder, manslaughter, and negligence. The issue is not whether the individual committed the crime, but at what point the process become harassment. At what point does the process become an abuse of power by the authorities? They are able to continue to bring an individual in and out of court, exhausting a person's financial resources, destroying his reputation, ruining his ability to earn a living, and disrupting his family life. What is at stake is not the prosecution of criminal activity, but whether the government under the disguise of "crime" be allowed to persecute.

In recent years a problem has developed in Constitutional law. Individuals have been charged in state court with felonies of which a not guilty verdict has been returned. The case takes on a high profile and reaches national attention. The Federal government intervenes and the person is charged with crimes related to denying a person her civil rights. The second trial would occur in the Federal courts. In this case the individual is now charged with a different crime, but involving the same event. The Federal court system has ruled that this is not double jeopardy. While nothing within this Proposed Constitution would change this judicial tactic, this is an issue that requires examination. One of the purposes of a Constitution is to ensure justice. It becomes an odd situation when the Constitution is subverted so that justice can be obtained.

Article 43, Section 4. Rights of the Accused

The Supreme Court ruled in a landmark decision in 1966 that law enforcement agencies needed to inform an individual upon being arrested of their Constitutional rights. Most Americans are familiar with this process and it is commonly called "Mirandizing." It dealt with an Arizona case where an individual was arrested for a violent crime. In subsequent interrogation he confessed. The police questioning occurred without an attorney being present. When the case reached the Supreme Court they ruled that individuals must be informed of their Constitutional rights upon arrest or before they are questioned by the police.

The rights themselves are not something new. They emerge from the Constitution, and currently law enforcement agencies are following this procedure. Mirandizing has become a part of American legal policy and course of action. There are a collection of items connected to Miranda rights. A person may choose to speak to the police or to remain silent. If persons so chooses to submit to questioning by the police ideally they will be given a waiver to sign. An individual may have a lawyer present or can waive that right If a man or woman wants an attorney and cannot afford one, a public defender would be appointed. If at anytime during an interrogation the accused wishes to end the questioning, he or she may do so, regardless of whether an attorney is present or not.

The issue of silence is not total. When approached by a law enforcement officer an individual does have a responsibility to identify herself or himself,

Citizenship does carry certain obligations, one of which is to assist the police in the performance of their duties. Their job is going to be more difficult if a person refuses to answer even the most basic of questions.

The actual question that needs to be asked is not whether Miranda rights should be in a Constitution because currently they are in place, but whether or not the police have to tell an accused person of these rights. Reading of Miranda rights does make the process of law enforcement more cumbersome and it does influence the way the police are forced to do their jobs. The difference is between having a conversation or sharing information with an officer to that of being a suspect. When Miranda rights are read to a person, the nature of the relationship changes. Miranda has had an effect on how the police interact with the accused and victims alike. Interrogations have become far more formal, with specific policies covering this activity. In many cases waivers are given to suspects to sign. Miranda has also had an effect on the number of confessions obtained by the police. Confessions are an administrative process to police work and a functional part of this profession. The National Center for Policy Analysis believes that the number of confessions has dropped sixteen percent since Miranda rights have been read to accused persons.

Rights do represent a change of concept. These are issues fundamental to the relationship of the individual and their association with the state. Rights need to be constant, complete, and absolute. They need to be clearly understood by all the parties concerned. If a statement addressing a person's Constitutional rights is required at the beginning of a change in status, in this case an individual being held in police custody, then that change needs to be recognized. The goal is consistency. It deals with the idea of placing Constitutional rights at a higher plane.

Even if the point was conceded that Miranda rights need to continue to be stated by the authorities upon arrest, this would not mean that they have to be placed in the Constitution. It could be argued that if the rights are already present in the document, the act of stating them becomes redundant. Two concerns surface at this point. The first is that the rights are implied rights as they are perceived in the American Constitution. Nothing in the current Constitution directly declared that an individual has the right to remain tacit while in police custody. Nothing in the document notes that an attorney may be present during an interrogation or even that the state will pay for such services. In fact an argument could be made that the founding fathers would have been dumbfounded at the idea of the state paying for the legal services of a jailed person. That issue deals more with the progression of our democracy than with the letter of the document. Nonetheless, nothing in the American Constitution directly addresses these rights. If they exist, and the Supreme Court has ruled that they do, then they need to be clearly stated in the Constitution.

The second issue deals with whether the reading of Miranda rights is a good idea. The questions may be asked, are there any nations in the world that are experiencing an abuse of police powers? Has there ever been a time in American history when police powers have been abused? Unmistakably those issues have occurred in the past and currently exist in parts of the world. As a nation, as a democracy, and for the Constitution we need to be vigilant. Our rights should not be vague or diluted. They need to be understood, and there are times when we may need a reminder.

Article 43, Section 5. Writ of Habeas Corpus

Habeas corpus, which translates to "that you have the body," or "bring forth the body," is a system of judicial action that stands against unlawful imprisonment or lengthy imprisonment without a trial. The Writ of Habeas Corpus is a tool used by the courts, and established within the Constitution, to have a person brought before the magistrate or judge. At that time the reasons why a person is being held by the authorities is reviewed. The issue is that a person needs to be either arraigned or set free, and the Writ of Habeas Corpus is a system to ensure that a person is not held indefinitely without charges being filed.

The drafters of the American Constitution were supportive of the concept of habeas corpus. The British during the Revolutionary period had detained many people without charges being filed or trials being held. The British of course operated from the position of terminating the rebellion; this the colonials saw as an extreme form of despotism. This does not mean that Great Britain did not have a tradition of habeas corpus. The concept was generated by the abuses of the Privy Councils and Star Chambers. The concept developed and was enhanced both by common law practices of the British courts and Acts of Parliament. With the abolishing of the Star Chambers, the Writs of Habeas Corpus became more common as the court extended their jurisdiction over such legal matters. In 1679 an Act of Parliament placed penalties on judges who refused to issue writs for just causes and punishments for those refusing to comply with such writs. In any case the statutes dealt with criminal offenses and not until 1816 did the British extend the rights of habeas corpus to other issues.

The United States Constitution establishes the right of habeas corpus under Article I, Section 9: "The privilege of Writ of Habeas Corpus shall not be suspended, unless when in cases of rebellion or invasion the public safety may require it." The idea of habeas corpus is to ensure that an individual is given the rights of due process. It says nothing about a person's guilt or innocence. Habeas corpus is simply a matter of determining if a person is being held legally, or in some rare cases, discovery of a person's location.

The only real question is whether habeas corpus is a right or a privilege. The United States has operated as if it were a right. Fundamentally the American courts have practiced habeas corpus as an integral part of their procedures. What is being offered in this Proposed Constitution is the same concept as our current Constitution. It is one of those ideas that corresponds to our democratic traditions and it represents a defense against despotic practices.

One outstanding problem persists. Under what conditions can the Writ of Habeas Corpus be denied? The American Constitution felt it could be transgressed at times of revolt or invasion. During the American Civil War President Lincoln suspended the right of habeas corpus. This was done by proclamation and later Congress through the legislative process granted the power. At times in American history individual states have suspended the right of habeas corpus, generally when martial law has been declared. The argument for allowing a provision for the deferment of the Writ of Habeas Corpus has always dealt with public safety. If the protection of the public requires such a suspension then it has been recognized. It is a questionable argument at best, but one in which some maneuvering should be granted. There are always special situations unforeseen at the onset. More important, if the Writ of Habeas Corpus is to be suspended it needs to be a very deliberate act. A Prime Minister or a President must offer a specific reason to withhold this right. It needs to be documented, and it needs to be for a precisely specified time.

Article 43, Section 6. Trial by Jury

A jury trial is part of the strength of our democracy and a mainstay of our judicial system. It says that an accused person is not convicted by the government or the court, but by the people. A person is being judged by their fellow citizens who are charged to determine guilt or innocence.

No two states seem to have the same system of choosing jurors. Some states choose jurors from their lists of registered voters and others are selected from property tax rolls. States vary on age. Most want an individual more than twenty-one years old, but some courts will not take a person who is extremely elderly. Illiterate people, those with criminal records, or past history of bias may be rejected. Some states disallow civil servants, military personnel, and elected officials..

Juries in the United States are of two types. The first is the *grand jury*. A grand jury is convened to hear part of the evidence against a person. The jury will determine if enough evidence is found for a person to stand trial for the crime. It is a preliminary process. The system and usage of grand juries changes considerably from one state to another. The rules for presenting evidence and judicial rights are not the same in a grand jury as in a regular trial. The reasons for a grand jury are far more basic. The goal is only to see if enough evidence or information exists to bring in a *presentment* (accusation). The second type of jury is the *Petit*, These are juries that hear criminal cases. Generally the number is twelve, but in some states the number is less for civil trials or minor criminal cases. As a point of reference the judge decides the points of law and the jury tries the case. Disputed points of law always arise, and the judge is responsible to see that the proper principles are applied.

Many criticisms are made of the jury system. In fact no other part of the criminal justice system receives more criticism than the use of juries. One complaint is the idea of finding an impartial jury. The attorneys will screen possible jurors to make sure that none are familiar with the case or even overly knowledgeable about the law and community issues or are even too moralistic. This is counter to how the jury system developed. In medieval England when a dispute occurred it was believed that a person's neighbors would be acquainted with the facts of the case and would be able to make informed decisions. Currently the more knowledgeable a person is about a case, the less likely they would be chosen to sit on a jury.

Attorneys are looking for people ignorant of the facts, and to some degree the system in general.

Another criticism is that the most competent people, or the most intelligent people, are generally busy. An example could be made of individuals in business or professional pursuits. Both seem to find ways to avoid jury duty. It is common for a judge to excuse an individual who can show a professional obligation. It is rare for a doctor to serve on a jury. What occurs is that the better qualified individuals evade the system and the less qualified serve.

A greater problem is that the whole process of picking jurors is a time-consuming process. It is long, tedious, and exhausting. Judges are required to sit through the procedure and in turn they fall further behind on their docket. This is one of the major weaknesses of the jury system; much of the trial time is spent on issues outside of the indictment or hearing of evidence.

Some students of judicial procedures also feel that juries are more apt to hear appeals to their emotions rather than focus on the facts. It is difficult for any person not to become incensed by the brutality of many crimes. Equally, it is hard not to subtract the pain felt by all the parties concerned, both that of the guilty and of the victim. A criminal trial can be an extremely emotional proceeding. Discussion can turn to issues of immense depravity and human suffering. It would be difficult for any individual not to be drained by the experience.

Recommendations are many. Some reformers would like to see the size of juries reduced from the standard twelve to a more manageable six. The view is that a lesser number still would represent a cross-section of the community and be able to digest the material properly. Undoubtedly it might even be easier for a lesser number to reach a consensus, but working by committee also has its special kinds of problems. Some would like to change the system so that the unanimous requirement would be removed. It would be possible to reach a guilty verdict with something less than twelve votes. Other suggestions involve the elimination of the jury system entirely, noting that the judge would be the best person to determine the guilt or innocence of the accused. This is a common argument. In about a third of the states it is possible for the accused to waive their right to a jury trial. In all the states it is possible for misdemeanor and civil cases to be heard by a judge.

In designing this Proposed Constitution a position is not taken about the validity of the jury system. Each system has its supporters. Reform is needed, especially in jury selection and time utilization. The best system may be one in which a number of options exist, not only to the indicted but the judges as well. Nothing within the current American Constitution or this Proposed Constitution would disallow such reforms.

Once making this statement, the jury system has one overriding significance: it connects the people to the judicial process. No one item in a Constitution is a freestanding entity. Each part is connected to another. It is this nexus that creates democracy. We can no more delegate our vote than we can our responsibility to serve on a jury. Involving the people in the court process is the best way to ensure that we maintain our rights. More than any other body the courts oversee our liberties. It would be a grievous error to disconnect the people from this process.

Article 43, Section 7. Judicial Rights

Within the American Constitution is a collection of rights and procedures for the courtroom. In looking at a person's Constitutional rights as they relate to the judicial system, they do seem to represent different segments of the prosecution process. Rights apply to an individual upon arrest, while in custody, and during a trial. Those rights at the time of the trial include being confronted by the accusers, hearing the witnesses, and observing the evidence as it is being presented. Either the person indicted or their attorney is entitled to cross-examine the witnesses. Equally, an individual has a right to put on their own defense and bring forth their own witnesses and evidence. A defendant has the right to be represented by an attorney. Lastly, an individual standing trial needs to be aware of the events around them. If that requires an interpreter so that the accused can understand the information related to the affidavit, the court is required to supply such a person.

These items do imply that an individual is able to participate in their own defense. A person needs to be capable of understanding the nature of such proceedings and to assist with their own defense. The whole issue deals with competency. A trial requires a level of mental proficiency. The American court system has consistently ruled on the importance of these issues and it is part of our judicial processes.

One of the issues that seems to surface during such discussion of rights in the courtroom is the corresponding problem of cost. The reality is that trials are expensive; this is compounded if the accused person cannot pay for her or his own defense. The total cost of the trial is paid for by the state. These judicial rights add to the cost; they drain the system and place an additional burden on the taxpayers of the nation. These issues need to be noted and understood, but that is not a satisfactory response. A minimum level of operation is required in the judicial process to guarantee our Constitutional rights. They become unavoidable. It is one of the pledges of democracy and it become the standard by which the judiciary must function.

Article 43, Section 8. Arraignments and Bail

Within the United States, individuals who have been accused of a crime and have been arrested by a law enforcement agency are brought before a magistrate. This generally is done in a timely manner. These arraignments serve a number of purposes. General information on the nature of the crime may occur or even a review of probable cause. At this preliminary hearing charges may be dismissed or reduced or the person may plead guilty and sentencing may result. This is likely if the crime is a misdemeanor. Of the two major purposes for hearings, the first is to make sure a valid reason exists to hold the person and the second is to determine bail.

The drafters of the American Constitution through the Eighth Amendment covered the issue of bail in these words, "excessive bail shall not be required." An exorbitant amount of bail would be another way that an oppressive government could control the masses and imprison leaders of an opposition group. Even if all the other judicial rights were in place but excessive bail was allowed, an individual might spend an enormous amount of time in jail working through imaginary charges. The presumption of innocence plays a part in the usage of bail.

The purpose of bail is not to punish, but to make sure that the individual returns to face the charges presented against him or her. Generally the issue is money. If he does not return he will forfeit the bond. In some cases the court will allow securities or real estate. More times than not, it is the bail bondsman who puts up the bond in exchange for a fee.

In some situations an individual should be denied bail. If a person has no connection to the community in which she is charged, incentive to stay in the area may be low. The possibility of evasion is greater. If an individual has considerable criminal history, even to the point of being considered a professional criminal, a more restrictive bail would be appropriate. In the cases of capital offenses an extremely high bail still may not be significant to guarantee that the accused would not flee. In those cases bail should be denied. Currently this is the structure under which the current system functions and the same basic design is being advocated

Article 43, Section 9. Grand Jury

The nation's founders saw the grand jury system as an important part of the overall judicial system. Grand juries are far more loosely described. They are set up to review the evidence and consider whether a person should be held for a formal trial. The evidence has to be sufficient to justify pursuing the issue to the next level.

Grand juries can consist of as many as twenty-three jurors, but for many states it is less. Generally the states determine the law on such matters. As a rule twelve jurors must agree to bind the person over for trial; if the number is less than twenty-three it would change the ratio A few states have grand juries of as few as six; in those cases five jurors must agree. The issue for a grand jury is not guilt or innocence as much as feasibility. If there is a probability of guilty as indicated by the grand jury, the person charged will face a formal trial.

Grand juries are looking for a *true bill of indictment,* the formal charge against the person. If jurors believe that a person has violated a criminal code, they need to bring forth the indictment. The issue of reasonable doubt is not a factor in grand jury proceedings—this is in sharp contrast to a regular trial. The prosecuting attorney will bring in witnesses to testify against the accused. The person under indictment cannot cross-examine these witnesses, but the members of the grand jury may recall these witnesses and question them separately. At that time no one is allowed in the room except the jurors, the witness, the prosecuting attorney, and more times than not the stenographer.

The deliberation of grand juries is done privately. When they have competed their work and a consensus is found they will return to the courtroom where their bill of indictment is read. The court clerk will record the indictment. Grand juries meet over extended periods of time, six months is not uncommon. In rural communities a grand jury may meet only once; in some counties more than one grand jury may be operating at the same time. In any case there are terms for these bodies and they may be adjourned only to be called again as needed.

Article 43, Section 10. Prompt and Public Trial

The American Constitution in the Sixth Amendment declared, "In all criminal prosecutions, the accused shall enjoy the right to a speedy and public trial." Without being critical of the American judicial system, this issue has become blurred. The judicial system has become anything but "speedy." While most criminal trials may last between two days to two weeks, requiring a person to linger in jail for a year or more awaiting trial has become commonplace. This whole issue of what represents a speedy trial has been corrupted.

While this is not some judicially created conspiracy, it has occurred in small steps with each part of the criminal justice system contributing to the problem. If the issue is one of blame, and that is not implied in these pages, there is enough blame to go around for everyone. The police in an effort to be thorough retard the system. The process of determining true culpability requires time. Both the judicial system and law enforcement agencies are overwhelmed by paperwork requirements. Defense attorneys as a legal tactic attempt to slow the process so that memories are impaired or the anger of the community subsides. They can drown the judicial system in motions in the hope that the prosecution will accept a lesser plea as a method of bringing the proceeding to an end. The prosecuting attorneys embedded in the political processes of the community become protracted by public opinion. Overwhelmed by cases, a shortage of staff, and the need to allot meager financial resources, they find themselves slowing the process because of departmental needs. Judges equally are confounded by paperwork, the outside responsibilities of their positions, and the size of their caseload. All the parties have overseers and supervisors, each requiring great detail but not allowing the time to fulfill that requirement. The simple fear of making a mistake slows the process. The people as well must accept part of this blame. Crime in many cases is tolerated. We allow our institutions rather than the family to raise our children. When a criminal is brought to justice the public demands that the full measure of the law be applied, which leaves no room for error. The Constitution and its requirements of adhering to individual rights has an effect upon the system. It is not an environment that encourages a speedy process.

If it is agreed that the spirit of the American Constitution is not being followed, what remains are two options. We could drop the idea that a timely or prompt trial is possible. It may be argued that a speedy trial will lead to more mistakes and is not in the best interest of the judicial process. This view found in the American Constitution under Amendment Six would be abandoned and the judicial system would be able to drift toward their own level of swiftness, the goal being one of thoroughness rather than speed. The opposite view is that the boundaries of the Constitution could be reduced to dictate what represents a speedy trial. Specific time lines would be developed. After all the idea of a speedy trial is ambiguous. One person's speed may not be another's. In this view an allotment of days would be allowed to complete a case depending on the seriousness of the crime. The issue would become more measurable.

The problem is that both of these ideas are flawed. The goal should be one of being expeditious. Nothing is wrong with acting with the utmost speed and dispatch as long as the process is done within acceptable levels of efficiency. It is a difficult combination and one in which the judicial system would have to become more vigilant.

The problem is not the trial. By the time the defense and prosecuting attorneys have reached the point of a trial the process will move forward. The difficulty is the huge gap that exists between the time of the trial and the arraignment. Regardless of the guilt or innocence of a person, it seems incredibly calloused to place anyone in such a position for an extended period of time. It is not the outcome that is so distressing as the issue of not knowing. The more humane approach to this state of judicial oblivion is to allow such persons to get on with their lives, even if that happens to be in prison.

In an effort to find some common ground, the Proposed Constitution is attempting to assign measurable time frames to the process. The accused may ask for a "Speedy Trial." This would be set within two months. While not stated it would be hoped that all criminal proceedings should be discharged within one year. The clock would start upon a person's arrest and the trial must begin within one calendar year. If that does not occur, the individual needs to be released or the bond returned. This process should function as if a person had actually been to trial and double jeopardy should apply. If there was reason enough to apprehend a person, or indict them, there must be reason enough to go to trial. What is being asked is that this be accomplished in a set period of time. It could be debated that one year hardly represents a speedy process, but it is an effort to bring the limits and boundaries of this process into something more executable.

Article 44. Torture

For the nation's founders the issue of physical punishment or torture was not directly addressed. For them the issue was related to *cruel and unusual punishment,* and it was listed in the Constitution under the Eighth Amendment. As simple and honest as this statement may be, it has proved to be one of the most complicated and undeniably difficult provisions in the document. The diverse and various opinions on what represents punishment that is cruel and unusual is as assorted as the citizens in the nation. No two people seem to have the same view; furthermore the issue is multiplied by the enormous changes between colonial America and our contemporary society. While attempting to recognize the high ideals that the statement meant to ensure, it has proved to be one of the most confusing, nebulous, and deceptive items in the Constitution.

The Federal government has been hesitant to clarify the issue because the states have traditionally and Constitutionally determined their own limits of penal punishments. The states are more involved in criminal justice procedures than the Federal government. Yet, those incarcerated attempt to use the Federal court system to protest their treatment, generally under the *cruel and unusual punishment* clause. Likewise, all the state Constitutions have articles dealing with cruel and unusual punishments. In turn each state's supreme courts have over the years made rulings on the subject, many times based on conflicting or contradicting premises from other state courts.

The philosophy of the nation's founders is even difficult to determine on this topic. The idea of cruel and unusual came from the English Bill of Rights of 1689. Though it was designed to eliminate extremely barbarous acts, the effect of this document on the British penal system was marginal at best. Some scholars have stated that the issue of cruel and unusual punishment was strictly aimed at the government with the hope of curbing the abuse of power. This was intended as a notice to government about the general treatment of the people rather than a specific handling of individuals while in custody. Still others argue that the real issue is not "cruel and unusual" as much as "arbitrary and capricious." The goal was more of a guarantee of due process. In any case the drafters of the American Constitution left few signposts to follow.

The Supreme Court has not been overly helpful in defining this issue either. Of course most of these discussions of cruel and unusual punishment hinge on individuals who have been jailed and the conditions in which they find themselves. Rarely will the Supreme Court even hear a case on excessive prison terms and when they do, reversals of lower courts are practically unheard of. Only once in the twentieth century has the Supreme Court ruled that a prison sentence was excessive. In this one case the court was most focused on the dimensions of the penalty imposed rather then the type of punishment.

When attorneys have attempted to argue that the death penalty was cruel and unusual punishment the court has sidestepped the question and ruled on issues related to due process. The Supreme Court has refused to rule on whether the violence and savagery of prison life constitutes cruel and unusual punishment. In *Ingraham v. Wright* (1977) the court ruled that brutality in the prison system represented part of the punishment for the crime from which a person was convicted. It is the belief that the cruel and unusual punishment section of the Eighth Amendment is limited after incarcerations.[3]

As with its definition, the goals of cruel and unusual punishment are also difficult to grasp. If such an item is to be in the Constitution, it should serve a purpose and be related to a specific goal. Each item should have a standard by which it will function. The Supreme Court has been willing to listen to issues that it sees as representing unnecessary and wanton infliction of pain, but because the meaning of this is so unclear, consensus is rarely reached. There is no clear answer on what represents cruel and unusual punishment. The whole issue becomes conjecture. It is a statement without goals, poorly defined, and disconnected to the realities of our society.

The real issue is not cruel and unusual punishment but torture. This issue, while still not perfect in definition, becomes a better guidebook for action. In this case an act is committed by one person against another that is designed to cause severe physical pain and represents an entity outside the framework of punishment. Torture is not done to punish; it is done to wound, to inflict suffering, to demean. It is sadistic in nature, designed to show that one party has power over another party. Torture is also used as a method to project authority and power on specific groups. By torturing one of the members, even in a prison population, it sends a message that the power structure can function without restraint.

This should not be confused with all issues that cause physical pain. A poorly cooked piece of meat may cause an upset stomach, but it is not torture. Corporal punishment is different from torture. In the most honest sense it is wrong for one person to inflict pain upon another. Whether this is a slap or a kick does not matter; it is still wrong. These are social issues on how we interact with one another. These issues need to be addressed concerning what represents acceptable human behavior. The world is full of rewards and punishments. These punishments may result in pain. While they may be physical in nature, they are not torture; torture is surrounded rather by a totalitarian structure.

The bigger problem is determining what represents psychological torture. With physical torture methods of actions can be delineated, physical evidence can be left on the body, instruments of use can be fabricated, special locations used can be found, but psychological torture is far more subtle. In some ways it is more individualized. What represents psychological torture for one person may not be for another. An example could be of a person placed in a dark room for an extended period of time with no light allowed to penetrate into the chamber. Such an act would obstruct a person's senses, distort time, and leave a person devoid of even the most basic levels of social contact. Any review of the situation would classify it as harmful, but the event would have a different effect on different persons. For one individual it would be torture and for another it would not. It may be enough to note that psychological torture does exist and like physical torture it is an issue of great wickedness. As it is with so many other malignancies of humans, we may be forced to face them when they appear.

The position that is being taken in this Proposed Constitution is that the term cruel and unusual punishment is unqualified. It is neither manageable nor applicable, and a different terminology needs to be used. In this case it is torture. To be truthful this issue is more in line with the current direction of the Supreme Court. The position is one of interpreting cruel and unusual punishment as unnecessary and wanton infliction of pain. To use torture as the criteria better defines the goal. The idea is one in which cruel and barbaric acts would be removed from the penal system.

The issue raises a larger concern. In the world community the concept and practice of torture is used by some nations as an extension of governmental policy. At any given time some thirty nations of the world are involved in some type of military or police conflict. It may represent a foreign war, a civil war, a counter insurgency, a rebellion, or a coup d'état. It may be nothing more than a handful of malcontents fighting for personal gratification or perhaps a small collection of revolutionaries fighting for social justice. In any case the state believes that it has a responsibility to exist. In an effort to defend itself and secure its own power the governmental leaders will use whatever tool is at their disposal, including torture. These are issues that fall beyond investigation, self-defense, or punishment. It becomes a perverted sense of self-preservation that dwells outside of the right to govern, yet torture is commonplace in the world community. Placing such an item in our Constitution is a statement of certitude that such acts fall outside the accepted parameters of government. Whether our own government or those of others matters not; it is simply not acceptable.

Article 45. Capital Punishment

If one issue brings forth absolute feelings of emotion and passion it is *capital punishment.* Even within our own individual consciences there can be disharmony. A person may look at the information, see it in its entirety, and still be wracked by internal conflict. A person's heart may tell her that an individual who kills another, who stalks the helpless, the young, the defenseless, and takes their lives has no right to live among the principled in our society. Equally, our mind may tell us that the state has no more right to take a life than the depraved criminal convicted of such an offense.

Murder creates such conflict because it is a hideous crime. It takes everything. For those who have loved and cared for the victim it leaves an emotional breach that is never repaired. It is never justified, it is never honorable, it can never be rationalized.

Effort is made here to review the chief arguments on capital punishment. The longer list is on the side of those opposed to capital punishment. Whether they are the strongest arguments is debated, but the reasons to eliminate the death penalty are clearly more numerous.

The first issue is whether capital punishment is a *deterrent.* Some have argued that capital punishment is needed to deter those who would kill. The theory is the belief that execution as the penalty for killing someone will stop others from committing the act. The reality is that not one valid piece of research or study has shown that capital punishment deters murder in any way.

The difference between the murder rates in those states of the Union that use capital punishment and those that do not, has no statistical significance. In fact the numbers of murders are actually shown to be lower in those states with no death penalty. Equally, only in ten percent of the cases where an individual has been convicted of first-degree murder is the death sentence actually carried out, and of those ten percent most linger on death row with no immediate risk of execution. This can hardly be seen as functional deterrent. In those nations around the world that have eliminated capital punishment not one has had a statistically significant increase in their murder rate. In most cases the number has remained constant.[4]

Those who argue against the death penalty note that disproportionate numbers of black Americans are executed. Since the 1930s more than fifty percent of those put to death by the states were black, yet the black population presents less than half of all those convicted of murder in the United States. The concern is whether equal protection under the law is being applied. In addition the black population represents twelve percent of the total population but nearly half of the total prison population. It is the disadvantaged and minority groups who suffer the most under the provisions of capital punishment. Black inmates were less likely to have received competent legal services because of limited financial resources. A structural bias is built into the system against the poor, and it is compounded if the person is a poor black.[5]

There is also the argument of cost savings. If a trial is thought to result in the enforcement of the death penalty, it becomes considerably longer, more complex, and costly. Capital punishment cases are automatically appealed to Federal courts, which in turn adds to their cost. Clearly guilty individuals who would no doubt accept their condition within the prison system if a life sentence were imposed will resist the order of the death penalty aggressively, tying up the judicial system with endless motions and delays. Each of these represents an added expenditure for the state.

This issue of cost is used by those who support the death penalty. While they argue that the cost to execute a person is less than to house them, this issue is not sustainable. The days of prisoners sitting idly in cells have long since passed. In fact both state and Federal prison systems have extensive work programs. Everything from military hardware to office equipment is being manufactured in prison factories. The cost ratio has reached a point at which it has become cost effective to house inmates. Not only are convicts paying for their own keep, but, additional funds are being created so that victims of their crimes are receiving some compensation.

In the same context those given capital punishment sentences are housed in a different section of the prison facility as they wait execution. They are not productive and there is a cost in maintaining those on death row. Yet, there is no proximity to their execution. It is not uncommon for a person to spend twelve to fifteen years on death row as the case continues to work through the appeals process.

In any case cost is a poor argument for taking a human life. If that represented sound judgment, then mental hospitals would be equally susceptible as would many of the unproductive members of our society.

There is also the fear that individuals who have killed will kill again. The argument is that placing an individual in the general prison population increases the risk of violence and even death of other inmates, or if they were ever released they would repeat the crime. The problem with that, position is that while the penal system is full of murder convicts, those released back into the civilian population have one of the lowest rates of recidivism of any crime. The truth is that most people convicted of a homicide return to society. Those individuals who are the most violent do remain in the penal system. In the 1970s the state of California did a study of first-degree murderers released from prison. They noted that ninety percent completed their parole without any form of violation, and only 2.9 percent committed any type of new crime that returned them to jail.[6]

One of the weakest arguments for those opposing capital punishment is the concept that the death penalty is a primitive act that no longer has a place in modern society. When a healthy person is killed, regardless of the circumstances, it is an ugly, brutal process. An extreme measure is needed to force the body to succumb. Coupled to this view is the concept that the purpose of the judicial and penal systems is justice, not revenge, that modern man should be above such positions and attitudes. The fallacy is in perceiving that modern humans are really more civilized than archaic. In ancient Greece those who committed malignant crimes were not imprisoned, but were expected to do penance. Though there is a contention that ancient societies were more inclined to put an individual to death that may be false. The weakest part of this argument is not the higher ideals that are implied, but the reality of modern society. We do accept a form of vengeance against those who break our laws, and it is done at the extreme edge of ruthlessness and totality.

One of the issues that has become enmeshed with capital punishment is the American Constitution's issue of *cruel and unusual punishment* found in the Eighth Amendment. It is a rare homicide case when the death penalty has been applied that the issue of cruel and unusual punishment does not come into play. Defense attorneys will sincerely argue that the simple act of taking a life, regardless of the situation, is cruel. While the Supreme Court has never directly acknowledged that point, it has forced changes in the method of executions and the environments under which it can be done. The issue has become disconcerting and confusing, especially when taken in the context that not all first-degree murder cases end with a death sentence, and again defense lawyers will argue that is "unusual."

Another argument against the death penalty is the issue of mental illness. Even beyond the mind-set or emotional stability of a person at the time of a murder, specific mental illnesses are known to distort personality and emotional makeup. It is the nature of their mental health diagnosis that creates these compulsive behaviors. While society has a right to protect itself, should society destroy those with thought disorders or antisocial behaviors because of the characteristics of their mental illness? A person may be competent to stand trial, for this issue has nothing to do with intelligence, but are they competent to be executed?

The last assertion for those that oppose capital punishment is that there is no reprieve from death. If a person has been wrongly convicted, and is innocent, there is no way to reverse the decision. Numerous examples can be found of individuals who have been executed who were innocent of the crime for which they were convicted. Capital punishment is the only situation where the miscarriage of justice is immutable.

Those who argue in favor of capital punishment focus on retribution. It is the core concept for the justification of the death penalty and should not be discounted. While it may stand alone as the chief argument for state-supported executions it is nonetheless a strong one. There is a sense of equality in the forfeiting of a life in return for taking another. The value of a human life becomes set; a human life is equal to a human life. There is a parsimony of thought and one that can clearly be understood by all the parties concerned.[7]

If the goal is justice, then it can only be found in the symmetry within the death penalty. We cannot forget about the victims; those individuals that die appalling deaths, bludgeoned and left naked at the side of the road. They too had lives to live, and stories to tell. They too were loved and cared for by others. They were robbed of the most precious of our terrestrial gifts. Their lives were cut short, ended by the selfishness and cruelty of another. This horrendous wrong should not go unpunished and the only way to rebuke such an act as murder is through capital punishment. Retribution should not be seen as some form of evil, but little more than fairness.

Both Thomas Hobbs and John Locke talked about the "state of nature," how humans have created a society of laws and allowed themselves to be governed. In so doing the individual gave up total freedom, but what was gained in the process was security. The new world that was constructed was safer. If persons break the laws of the nation, refusing to accept the "social contract" that has been agreed upon, then they can not live in that society. They may choose to move, to find a different community, one in which their belief system is closer aligned. If no other society can be found, if no one else will have them, then the society is well within their rights to eliminate that person. It is no different than the rabid dog. Even if persons were placed in prison, they still exist within the society. No matter how rational this argument may be it cannot be more irrational than having sympathy for a murderer.

The reasons why this Proposed Constitution has abolished the death penalty is not structured around any of these arguments, either in support or opposition. The problem with the death penalty in the United States deals with *equal protection under the law.* The idea that surrounds "equal protection" is that everyone will be treated equally and face the same degree of punishment before the law. Fifteen states in the United States have no capital punishment and have passed laws forbidding it. Another dozen states have not had an execution since the moratorium of 1962. Even though they have such a law on the books they created a de facto restraint on capital punishment. This same problem is occurring in the military. Since the 1930s, more than 170 American servicemen have been executed, all from the Army and Air Force. The Navy has not executed anyone since 1849. What occurs is that an individual who commits such a crime in one state may die, but that same crime in another state will result in a life sentence. Legally this is unmanageable. Even recognizing that prison sentences may vary in murder cases, the punishment is the same; what is different is the degree or more properly the length of time. This is not the case with the death penalty. There is a marked difference in the punishments. If due process is to be followed, there must be a reasonable relationship between the crime and punishment in each state.

To see how unmanageable this issue has become, imagine attempting to force those states that have abandoned capital punishment into enforcing the sentence. If the goal is to keep the death penalty, there would be a need for a Federal mandate to enforce the law in all the states. If this argument was taken a step further, in some cases Federal law enforcement agencies would need to take control of some state penal systems to insure that executions were being carried out. Those states that resisted would turn to the Federal courts for relief. If a Federal judge sided with the state they would be subject to impeachment. It is possible to see where this argument is going. It would create considerable conflict in the nation as the public took sides and opinions were voiced. This is not the type of relationship that would endear the central government to the states or enhance our national reputation.

This returns to one simple idea. Within the framework of due process and equal protection under the law the death penalty is unworkable. At least at this point in time, it is not possible to have simultaneously equal protection under the law and capital punishment.

Article 46. Imprisonment for Debt

While imprisonment for a debt in contemporary American society is unheard of as a point of law, this was common throughout world history until fairly recent times. In Europe before the American Revolution prisons were full of individuals unable to pay their debts. One of the goals of the nation's founders was to correct this situation, and they made it impossible to incarcerate a person because of a bad debt. They also established bankruptcy court to assist with this legal problem.

Though some cases appear to exist where individuals are imprisoned for debt, these are situations that deal more with restitution for a crime. An individual who has not made such payments or refuses to do so is seen as being in contempt of court. A distinction is made between civil action and a criminal case.

Article 47. Victim's Rights

Most Constitutions spend a great deal of time outlining the rights of the accused for two reasons; the first is to ensure that an innocent person is not wrongly convicted of a crime. There is always the possibility of a rush to judgment. The public, incensed and fearful over a rather hideous crime, demands that the perpetrator be captured and punished. The law enforcement agencies, feeling the pressure of public opinion and submitting to the demands of the citizenship, arrest an individual. A case is developed, most of which is circumstantial. The prosecuting attorney and the judge, both elected officials, feel the pressure from the people. The prosecuting attorney presses the case and overlooks gaps in time, motive, and opportunity. The judge allows questionable evidence. The jury chosen from the community persists with their anger in a case that represents considerable emotion. In the end an unempowered member of society is found guilty and is sacrificed to the public need for closure. While this narrative may seem trite, every generation has at least one high profile case where just such an act is played out.

The second reason deals with the possibility of governmental abuse. While elected as public servants, government officials do enjoy financial rewards and status different from all other citizens. They immortalize a given political point of view or philosophy, and the fact that they have been elected indicates that the majority of the citizens support their beliefs and programs. Equally, since they operate for the betterment of the community, all who oppose their leadership must be evil. Those amoral people must be resisted at all costs. Friends on the police force, on the city council, within the bureaucracy, and in the court system will assist against these adversaries. Charges are filed and these individuals are pursued aggressively. It sounds like a grand conspiracy. It is hard to imagine that a democratic government, an American government, could be the product of the misapplication of governmental power until you remember *Jim Crow*.

While being aware of these concerns, the reality is something else. The vast majority of the individuals who are brought into the criminal justice system are there because they have broken a law. In turn the vast majority are found guilty because the evidence supports their culpability. These rights so meticulously stated and listed in the Constitution to defend against a miscarriage of justice are but half the issue. The other half of the question is the victim. In an effort to secure the rights of the accused, the rights of the victim become lost. They too have rights, and their cause is likely the more righteous of the two.

The objective is to assure that the victims are not repeatedly victimized. They need to feel empowered; after all, the event left them feeling helpless and powerless. There is a need to allow the victim some say, to allow them an opportunity to make some decisions concerning this event. The goal is to bring a sense of balance to the situation. When the woman was victimized she had no say, no control. It is no different when the victim is male. As these events move into the judicial system the victim's rights should be as well understood as those of the alleged perpetrator.

A movement has been emerging in the United States to recognize and to list the rights of the victim. Many of the state Constitutions have already incorporated Articles to that effect. Most of these rights evolve around the idea that the victim needs to be involved in the judicial and criminal process. They are not some secondary factor, an item of modest importance. In many ways they are the core issue, the reason why the criminal proceedings were started. Clearly, the victim also has rights, and such rights need to be stated explicitly in a Constitution, especially if that same Constitution has painstakingly listed the rights of the accused.

The rights of the victim should include being involved and present at all judicial hearings. The American Constitution and this Proposed Constitution noted that persons charged with a crime have a right to face their accusers. It seems only fair that the accuser has an equal right to face the assailant. A plea bargain may have been reached by the defense and prosecuting attorneys, but there is still the matter of sentencing. A hearing is scheduled for that part of the process allowing the victim an opportunity to speak. At some point it is appropriate to hear from the victim. In turn the victim needs to be kept informed of all such hearings and trials. Even if the victim is not going to testify she or he has a right to be there.

Victims of crime, regardless of whether it is violent or not, suffer losses. There are losses in time, in money, in self-esteem, in relationships, in future dreams. Crime takes things from people, things to which the transgressor was not entitled. Victims have a right to be compensated for their loss. In most cases criminals have no funds, but any and all future income should be taken into account. If a person works in a prison factory, part of the money generated needs to be returned to the victim. Compensation should be seen as a victim's right.

Likewise, if a convict comes before a parole board and they are considering releasing him back into the general population, the victims of his deeds should have an opportunity to speak at that hearing. It becomes the responsibility of the penal system to keep the victims informed of all parole hearings and schedule a time for them to be heard. The victim's rights do not end when an individual has been sent to jail. These rights end only when the perpetrator has completed his sentence, and that may have little to do with whether the person is in or out of prison.

The issue, and maybe the most important idea, deals with the victim being safe from the attacker. It matters not if a person is out on bail, waiting for a grand jury to meet, on work release, probation, or parole. The victim has a right to be safe from the accused and the convicted. Specific guidelines need to be set for those charged, and they need to understand the rights of the victim as well as understanding their own rights. The greatest fear that a victim has is to be constantly pursued or intimidated by their criminal antagonist in a continuous and ongoing way. The victim does have a right to be free from that burden. People have a right to be free from criminal intrusion, to be safe in their personal lives and within their own property. This may be an outstanding reason why certain prison sentences extend for greater lengths of time than others.

This issue also needs to extend to witnesses as much as victims. Persons who become witnesses are placing themselves in jeopardy as well. They too may be fearful of the possibility of retaliation from a miscreant of our society. Harm should not be the consequence for reporting what has been seen or heard.

Article 48. Awards and Titles

The nation's founders had an antipathy toward titles. This cannot be overstated. The British of the eighteenth century had created a society based on the prominence of the upper class that cut across the society as a point of identification. The government was a monarchy, and the nobility spread through the government and the military to touch every point of administration. Governors of the colonies, military officers, and magistrates were all part of the upper class. With this distinction came titles. Some were passed on from generation to generation, as part of the royal dynasty. Others were purchased as a sign that a person had arrived. Most titles were upheld not as signs of great deeds or actions, but for no other reason than heredity. Those of noble birth flaunted their pedigree and demeaned those of lesser birth.

As much as any reason it was the arrogance of the British nobility that created the American Revolution. The colonists were carving out a life in the American wilderness, living in wood and mud cabins, poorly educated, working the soil for a living. They lived by what they grew, what they made themselves, or what they could barter. The colonials were a far cry from the upper class of England. When the Revolution had ended this anger still remained. The drafters of the American Constitution envisioned a society without a class of nobility. Royalty was repugnant to the nature of the American Revolution and the type of democracy that our leaders wished to develop.

There are two types of titles. The one is earned and the other unearned. The problem is not the earned title. As we live our lives, remain productive, and are good at what we do, with some luck, awards and distinctions come our way. Part of human nature is to work toward some level of self-actualization. We need to see such awards, prizes, decorations, citations, and even titles for what they are—a point of achievement. As a people we should honor those who have worked and endeavored to reach the top of their professions. Such honors have been earned and there is nothing wrong with accepting this distinction.

The other side of the issue, however, are unearned titles; those titles of the nobility that have been passed on by birth. It is not the place of this document to say that they are wrong, only that unearned distinctions of rank are undemocratic. Unearned titles imply that one person through ancestry has greater honor than another and in addition that a privilege goes with these titles. This is simply wrong. Noble birth does not confer greater integrity or deserve greater respect. It is a concept invested in an expired part of history.

Even so, as a people we need to make peace with the past. We need to recognize that awards and distinctions come in many forms, and for those who are deserving they should be allowed. An example could be the British knighthood with the title *Sir*. A number of American Presidents have been made knights of the Order of the Garter, which is given for meritorious service. These titles were earned. They are justified by the years of public service. These are the individuals who have moved from politician to statesperson. It seems only appropriate to recognize the spirit in which these awards were given and to address these individuals as sir.

This may be one of the items that is not even needed in the Constitution. Americans no longer see the monarchy or royalty as an issue of superiority. An American who purchased a title would be seen as self-indulgent. In truth it is a matter of small concern, but it seems proper to allow people to use titles that they have earned.

Article 49. Education

Some statements have high-sounding ideals but represent points of great difficulty in implementation. Guaranteeing a person an education may be one such statement. It will take considerable effort and will require focus on the part of the nation, but education is important. Few issues are as important as educating our young. Yet, this is not something new; the United States has been working on universal education for some time and has made immense strides in doing so.

Conflicts are possible in implementing this Article. Stating that all children are guaranteed an education through the age of seventeen includes everyone. If individuals are profoundly mentally disabled they still are entitled to an education, at least to the best level of their aptitude and skills. As a rule this is an issue that has been conceded by both the state governments and the court system, even though some school boards have had problems with the cost of such specialized education. The goal nonetheless is to educate our young, excluding no one. This is important not only for the future well being of the nation, but also of our democracy. It represents equal treatment, even though it may not represent equal cost.

This type of Article while mundane in appearance does have the potential of creating conflict between Church and State. Most private and public schools work from the same agenda, their goal being to educate their students. While they may disagree with the nature of that education or even a few classes, both groups are operating from the same perspective. They see the importance of education and wish for their students to take their educational skills into society. Some communities limit education, withdrawing their children from school as soon as legally possible. This could be seen as a problem if the goal of the society were to educate a child through the age of seventeen. This Article in the Proposed Constitution is more a statement of priority. Nothing within this document changes the relationship of Church and State. What does remain is that most states still have laws that keep children in school until the age of sixteen. While in some states the age limit has been changing, the issue is more of government's responsibility to educate or at least assist with the cost of that education.

As a society and as a people we do have a responsibility to educate our young. To stretch at the boundaries of known knowledge and to teach them that education does have value. It becomes a virtue in itself.

Article 50. Academic Freedom

The fuel that runs our institutions is ideas. They change, are adjusted, reviewed, debated, and accepted, only to have the process start again. It is not that one idea is necessarily better than another. We all find our own truths. What is important is the freedom of ideas and the freedom of expression. Those concepts are never more meaningful than within the nation's colleges and universities. Powers are always at play, people who attempt to get their views heard over the views of others. We see reality through our own life experiences and what we see as significant comes from those experiences. It is but a half truth. No one person can know the whole truth; to do so would mean we were omnipotent. There needs to be one location where ideas come together, a place where all ideas can be heard. This place needs to be our institutions of higher education. Academic freedom needs to become a Constitutional right.

In American society when the name Karl Marx is heard it evokes a negative response. Marx in his writings and views stood outside the framework of democratic philosophies. He viewed the world as a struggle between the classes. This was the focus of his political thought. Marx encouraged and supported the destruction of the upper classes, believing that they were oppressive. From the teaching of Marx, Lenin brought totalitarian government to Russia and from Lenin emerged the suffocating effects of Joseph Stalin. These events and histories run counter to democracy, especially the experiences of American Constitutional government. A line can be drawn between the suffering of the people of Eastern Europe during parts of the twentieth century and Karl Marx. Still, does Marx have anything to add to political philosophy? Is there anything meaningful in his writings?

One of the most difficult questions for political philosophers to respond to is the question, "What is history?" Marx made an effort to examine this relationship between humanity and history. While Marx's ideas have fallen from favor, the quest is a valid one. It is no different than the case with Sigmund Freud. Many of Freud's views of human sexual motivations have fallen from favor. New psychotherapies have replaced those of Freud's psychoanalysis, and those that remain have been changed or expanded in ways he would find difficult to conceive. What is important is that Freud still has something to say. The situation is no different with Marx. It has nothing to do with either man's level of activism or the path their lives took. It deals only with academia. This Article says that academic freedom does exist. No one person has the right to shout down another and no one truth exists.

Education is also one of the institutions of our society. It is the view of this Proposed Constitution that a healthy society in one is which all the institutions are in balance. Education is an institution that is susceptible to the inclinations of the other institutions. The rules and purposes of this entity are different from its related bodies, the goal of education is the pursuit of knowledge. This very concept may run counter to the ideas of other institutions. Yet, funding for education must come from these bodies. If education as an institution is to survive it needs but one tool and that is academic freedom.

There is a difference between academic freedom at the university level and what is found at the elementary level. They should not be confused for they are not the same. In the elementary school the education that is being given is basic. A foundation is being laid. At this level education has to deal more with interacting and surviving in the larger community. Students arriving at the university level have already been taught how to think, and now they must do so. Academic freedom exists not only for the instructor, but the student as well. It becomes a right to contemplate.

John Locke influenced the thinking in this Proposed Constitution as he influenced the drafters of the American Constitution. While he may not have felt comfortable with total academic freedom, this English philosopher did support an environment where science and the general scholarly pursuits could take place. His writings demonstrated the need for an unrestrained capability to question. Many of these issues return to democracy. The very nature of democracy requires that a person question. Not only is the freedom to question needed, but also the actual desire to dispute and doubt. More than any other place that will occur in academia.

Article 51, Section 1. Federal Reserve

Few governmental related agencies or bodies seem to be as confusing or as overwhelming as the Federal Reserve. The misconceptions and half truths seem to be as limitless as dollars in the banking system. The Federal Reserve truly is an entity that functions behind a veil. This secrecy is based more on issues related to monetary markets and business activity than as a contradiction to democratic behavior. Congress has created this semi-governmental body, the Federal Reserve, to be powerful in the economic life of the nation. When the Fed commits an act as simple as adjusting an interest rate that single act can change the fortunes of many. Questions arise about their motives and system of operation. While problems and issues concerning the Federal Reserve need to be addressed, it still does not make the Fed a pernicious creature. In fact the Federal Reserve has functioned within its mandate and created a sound economy for the United States.

Nevertheless, a collection of reasons show why the Federal Reserve needs to be in the Constitution. The first deals with the discrepancies between the American Constitution and the realities of twenty-first century economics. When the nation's founders developed the Constitution, they accepted the obvious—gold and silver would be legal tender for the new nation. During the eighteenth century that was the only choice and option. Two hundred years later the nation-state and its economy has evolved into a different element. The economy of the United States is so large that not enough gold and silver can be obtained in the world to support the nation at the level the Founders envisioned. Any type of *gold standard* would require prorating it, which in itself would create problems. What has occurred is that the United States economy is based on the *value of the nation*. This represents the goods and services produced by its citizens. The Federal Reserve determines the nature of that level. Today for better or worse the United States, as all modern economies, is based on the value of the nation.

The next question is who determines this value of the nation? In the case of the United States it is the Federal Reserve. Again, for the prosperity of the nation the Federal Reserve has been assigned the responsibility of determining the money supply. They do this by the way they loan money to the member banks. Through this process the economy grows and develops.

This problem is twofold. If we leave the control of the economy and the generating of money in the hands of the politicians, there is always the possibility that personal motives or the desire to be reelected would overshadow responsible government. An example of this can be made of Congress's inability to balance the national budget. It does not take much of an imagination to envision a government printing more money in an ever-increasing attempt to supply services to a public that is demanding them. A scenario could be developed where the Federal Reserve was determined to force what they saw as a responsible fiscal policy, while the governors believed that the national government needs a balanced budget. The Fed conceivably might begin to hold the economy hostage to force the issue. These are the type of rhetorical questions that may not have valid answers, but one thing is certain the current system is not found in the American Constitution.

The gap is that the American Constitution has clearly given Congress the power to regulate the economy. Yet, Congress has delegated that responsibility to the Federal Reserve. Even in the simplest of concepts like the coining of money, it is actually the Federal Reserve that decides how much money is to be coined. The United States Mint fills the orders of the Federal Reserve banks. The chair of the

Board of Governors reports to Congress and will give testimony at various committees, but the actions of the Federal Reserve remain independent. The Congress could of course eliminate the Federal Reserve, but that is unlikely for there is not a valid alternative. Few people are eager to return to the economic conditions of the nineteenth century.

What is left are a number of basic items. The first is that an exceptionally powerful body is controlling our economy, but it exists outside of our Constitution. The Federal Reserve is too important, too influential, and too dominant a creature to be left outside of the basic document of our society. If we are to keep the Federal Reserve, and this Proposed Constitution believes that we should, it needs to be in the Constitution. The mandate for the Federal Reserve should be from the people and not just from Congress.

Even without a fundamental change in the Federal Reserve, by placing them in the Constitution they become a governmental element. Currently they are not. In fact a good definition may not exist. Yet this quasi-governmental body is responsible for the monetary policy of the nation. It can be described better as a governmental enterprise rather than an agency. The point is that the Federal Reserve needs to be placed squarely within the Constitution and the government. It needs to be seen as connected to the government. This may be little more than posturing, but democracy requires all departments, agencies, and bureaus exercising authority to fall within the jurisdiction of government. It can stand as a separate body, but like the military, the Federal Reserve needs to be filtered through the process of government.

There is one last issue. If it is conceded the Federal Reserve is responsible for the money supply of the nation, then the two governmental agencies responsible for producing money, whether it be coin or paper, should be nestled under the management of the Federal Reserve. If the Federal Reserve administers the Mint and the Bureau of Engraving, the operation becomes more efficient.

Article 51, Section 2. Ownership

If democracy is to exist in any nation a few basic elements need to be in place. One of the first and foremost is that the power of the government is invested in the people. An extension of this concept is that the ownership of the government, if that is a proper term, must be found within the people as well. There are always decisions to be made, direction decided upon, and goals to be reached, but government must do these acts with at least tacit consent by the people. The problem is that currently there is no such connection with the Federal Reserve and the people. There is a real difference between giving a body permission to have independent action and having that body disassociated from the whole.

The Federal Reserve is not a governmental body; it is a corporate one. Returning to these issues of institutions, the Federal Reserve is owned by business. While its board of governors is appointed by the Executive Administration, it is still owned by commercial interest. As an organization, as a body, it is housed squarely in the arena of business as an institution. The question is whether this is the proper location for this powerful entity. This is an extremely important discussion because both business and the government have an equal interest in the economy. Each participates, each can force changes in direction, each wishes to set standards, each can overwhelm and destroy. What hangs in the balance is the financial well being of the nation. The mere fact that the Federal Reserve exists is a statement that laissez-faire economics does not exist. We are not so much a Capitalist society as we are a mixed economy. This may be a struggle, not between competing ideas of economy, but purely a struggle between competing institutions. John Kenneth Galbraith noted, "The great dialectic in our time is not, as anciently and by some still supposed, between capital and labor; it is between economic enterprise and the state."[8]

The question remains, "What camp is the Federal Reserve placed in?" The argument in the Proposed Constitution is that it belongs in the government. The reason is basic and sincere. One of the responsibilities of government is to create a fair playing field for business where rules are equal and just for all. The Federal Reserve helps shape that playing field, and creates many of the rules; because of this they need to be lodged in government as an institution. This does not mean that membership in the Federal Reserve by banking concerns will not exist, but the ownership of the Federal Reserve will become the people's.

Article 51, Section 3. Appointment of Officers

If the Federal Reserve is to be a body within the central government, its primary leadership needs to be appointed by the same process as for all other governmental departments, ministries, and agencies. Serving on the Board of Governors or on the board of directors at the individual Federal Reserve banks needs to be arranged by elected officials. In the case of this Proposed Constitution the Prime Minister would appoint an individual to fill a vacancy. They would then be confirmed by the Senate and sworn into that position.

The difference is not with the Board of Governors of the Federal Reserve. This is the same system that is currently in place. The change is with the separate Federal Reserve banks. Currently the member banks are able to support particular board directors, and they can vote on individuals accordingly. In this situation that process comes to an end and the government appoints individuals to all director posts.

The real difference may be marginal. If the government is seeking individuals to fill these positions, they will be looking for people with finance experience and background. It will be the same people currently running for these offices. They may be more politically connected than the current system, but again this is marginal. To be elected to the board of the Federal Reserve, regardless of the position, is a political process. It requires the acquisition of votes. A few miles may change but not the spirit of the pursuit.

The time frame of the Board of Governors has been extended. If the goal is to create a stable economy, the decisions made by the board needs to be based on economic principles, not political. It becomes almost a contradiction. Individuals chosen by a political administration are put into place to make sure political decisions about the economy are not made. The longer the term, the more secure the officers will be in this mandate. The goal is a stable economy.

Article 51, Section 4. Economic Policy

A study of history will uncover a tendency of adventurous leaders or empire builders to debase the metal from which their coinage or economy is grounded. Foreign wars require capital and are expensive processes; a considerable amount of money is needed to wage an armed conflict. Even if the nation is successful it costs large amounts of money, and if you are unsuccessful it will cost everything. One of the prime tactics of such speculators in territorial supremacy is to debase the currency. It is nothing more than inflation. In times past it was common to put less silver and more copper into a coin in an effort to buy the same amount of goods and services for less money. The theory is that by the time the debasement reaches the lower classes military victory has been assured or through these military successes greater income will flow into the treasury. Of course it never quite works out that way. Wars become prolonged and stretch out for years. The regime is overthrown. Somewhere along the way the treasury is depleted, and less becomes none. The point is that debasement of the currency, regardless of the reason, is an invalidating process to the people and their government.

A strong economy deals with a uniformity of policy over a long period of time. The rules of acquiring wealth are the same for one generation as for another. Such rules should not be designed to benefit one individual over another, one class over another, or one group over another. The rules need only to be fair and constant. The goal is simple: maintain the money supply, keep inflation diminutive, encourage responsible spending by government, and preserve the economic base of the nation. Only by having a regulatory agency, like the Federal Reserve, operating outside of politics is it possible to have a stable economy.

Congress originally was given the responsibility of guiding the economy. Through many mishaps and errors, they proved not to be the best body to maintain the economy. The test of this statement can be found in the economic history of both the nineteenth and twentieth centuries. The leadership of both systems have had their setbacks. Overall the Federal Reserve has had the better record. Congress at some point has recognized this issue and this task has been given over to the Federal Reserve. If we expect them to continue to do this job properly they need the independence to follow through on it.

Article 51, Section 5. Expenses

While some practices made sense when they were first established, over time they prove awkward to explain; so it is with the ownership of the Federal Reserve. When the Federal Reserve was first created in 1913 it was more of a liaison between banking interest and the Federal government. Financial crises were common and they created convulsions both for the government and the financial institutions in the country. The Federal Reserve was set up to stabilize the system, especially in securities. It was to be a central bank that the government and banking community both would be able to use. Financing the Federal Reserve was not a major concern because it was allowed to charge fees for its services. It was a corporate entity and operated outside of the Federal Treasury. The Federal Reserve developed a system by which it became a self-financing body. As the nation's economy grew, the amount of money the Federal Reserve brought in began to increase to the point where billions of dollars in profits were being generated.

Within this Proposed Constitution the Federal Reserve becomes a governmental agency. If that is the case should this body be allowed to be a self-financing body or should the expenses of the agency appear in the Federal budget? As with all other agencies and concepts of good government, budgets need to be clearly defined. The Federal Reserve needs to be budgeted with an appropriate amount of money to administer the duties they have been assigned, but it seems amiss to allow any agency or department to propagate their own budget.

The argument is no different for any other governmental entity. Would it be appropriate for the Environmental Protection Agency (EPA), as an example, to generate their own budget? The money they obtained through fines and penalties would be the base of their allocated expenditures. In turn, services for testing and consultant work would add additional revenues. This same type of arrangement could be made for most governmental operations, but such processes stand apart from the nature of government. There must be an accepted level of public accounting. The money generated and spent by government needs to be inventoried, listed, and balanced.

This issue of income is magnified even to a greater degree when the idea of seigniorage is placed in the picture. This represents the difference between the face value of a coin and the actual cost of the material and its production. The variance can be considerable and the government uses seigniorage as an acquisition of the budget. It represents billions of dollars. If the Federal Reserve is to have managerial authority over the manufacturing of money, this income is so great that the Treasury Department is needed as a counterbalance. It represents a form of *checks and balances.*

Article 52. Subordinate Power

The United States has been amazingly fortunate at times. As a nation-state we never had to endure foreign military occupation or face counterrevolutions. The worst of our civil unrest has been riots in the largest of our cities. Even considering the American Civil War as an armed conflict, the basic rights of our society remained intact. Great movements have occurred within our nation, with sweeping changes to our society, yet through all of these events the armed forces have stayed firm. Even when our military has been used as an extension of political thought, it has been little more than to assist small children in entering schools. As a nation there has been violence and anger in our streets with some causes more just than others, but it was the police, not the military that stepped forward. It is something this nation should be proud of, for the truth of the matter is that we are the exception to the rule, not the norm.

If the twentieth century is to be a judge, only a handful of nations had governments that stayed in place with the consent of the people. All the others either have been occupied by a foreign military force, had their own military take power in a coup d'état, or the military has been used by authoritarian regimes to intimidate the masses and stay in power. It is a sad commentary on human existence. The military, while designed to defend the nation-state and its principles, can also be the product of its destruction. The world has yet to see a military regime that was a democracy.

Once noting this concern, the issue has as much to do with tradition than any other factor. During the 1930s Stalin purged the Soviet military. Large numbers of Soviet military officers were put to death, but no effort was ever recorded of the army attempting a takeover. In the 1990s that same military body, now formed into the Russian army was called upon by its commanders to squelch governmental reforms. The army proved to be inept in that role. Russia, like the United States and Great Britain, has no history, no tradition of military involvement in politics or government. The military is used and seen in the role of the defender of the nation, not the developer of governmental regimes.

Even so, when a Constitution is designed, the nature of the armed forces of that country needs to be reviewed. The role of the military needs to be included. Most of those issues are rather basic, but critical to a free people. The primary of all such issues, the armed forces of that nation, must be subordinate to the civilian government. While the military may be a separate institution, it is government that tempers the character of this exclusive body.

Each of the institutions have different focuses; each is grounded differently. No matter how it is sugar-coated the military is designed for one activity—to kill. It is trained to do so proficiently, competently, and totally. It is intended to harm. A military body that is not capable of completing this single most important task is profoundly sterile. Those who serve our nation through the armed forces should be honored and respected. They perform a duty to this nation, they maintain our freedoms, but this esteem should not be confused with the reality of this profession. There is an unyielding brutality that goes with the military. It needs to be balanced and that equilibrium is found within its relationship with the institution of government.

The military operates from within a slightly different perspective than any other institution, and because of the nature of the armed forces it has developed a distinctive system of operation. Such systems are known as Standard Operational Procedures. They are used in a wide range of different situations; sometimes they represent rules of engagements and other times levels of readiness. These Standard Operational Procedures set certain events into motion. They tell field commands what is expected of them in certain situation or conditions. It centers with how they are to respond. It keeps the decision-making process simple. With military forces scattered around the world it gives units a base from which to operate. The dubious part of such systems is that it can put events into motion that become difficult to correct. The main concern is armed conflicts. It is against the temperament of the military to withdraw from a fight once it has begun, but the interest of the nation-state may require other options or at least the total view.

An example of how Standard Operational Procedures work can be seen in the Cuban Missile Crisis of 1962. Both the United States and Soviet Union armed forces were functioning within their Standard Operational Procedures. If these systems had not been superseded by the civilian governments of both nations, a nuclear war would have occurred. The processes were laid out and had been set into motion. Only through the intervention of the civil authorities was war averted.

It is far better to have the military subordinate to civil control. This system allows for the civil government to be the focal point. It also allows the people a say through their representatives about the nature of military activities.

Article 53. Military Conscription

Most of this Proposed Constitution is not something new. It is more a matter of stating the current stage of political and social development of the nation. The United States at present has an all-voluntary standing army. While both a professional military and communal military have their supporters, the view here is that a professional army is better. To be able to maintain a professional military is an item of exceptional achievement. It creates a body embedded in professional conduct, proficient in operation, and experienced in the arts of warfare. Few nations are able to accomplish this task. By far the majority of the nations in the world have conscription. If the military draft is in place, at least during peacetime, it creates an environment where democracy is diminished. Without being critical of the military, the armed services are not democratic. To place an individual into the military who does not want to be there is to compound a problem, and it nullifies the best that the society has to offer.

The argument is simple. It is far better to have an individual in the military who wants to be there than one who does not. This same argument can be used in education. By the time individuals reach institutions of higher learning they are there because they wish to be. Students in college are more apt to work through their subjects because of self-motivation, and personal needs rather than outside dictates. This argument can also be used for the armed forces. It is better served by having someone who volunteered for the service that chose this career, than one forced under penalty to serve. What is important for a democracy is not so much who is in the military, but that the people support the institution. The public needs to see the members of their armed forces as their neighbors and friends. If a gap appears between the views of the people and that of the military, if the view of "us and them" begins to surface, it will create a rupture in the society.

Many individuals are concerned that the military is populated by members of the lower classes. This is hardly a concern; it is the nature of the armed services. This is part of the history of the American armed forces and consistent with this institution. As long as there is a military, and as long as there are classes, some of those who are poor, without social advantage, or exist without privilege, will use the services as a method of advancement. None of this is important. What is consequential is that the average citizen on the street and the average person in the military see themselves as the same. This can be done within the concepts of an all-volunteer army. The United States has proved that such a component is possible. America has the third largest military force in the world and it is all voluntary. What is being asked is not eccentric but the current gauge of the system.

The concern that some may have is that the needs of the military must be recognized and their needs supersede the needs of all other bodies. The counterargument is that the defense of the nation is so important that we should not handicap this institution by declaring that conscription should not be allowed during peacetime. Placing such a statement in the Constitution reduces options and choices for the military. It can be reasoned that there is always the possibility that a crisis may develop that does not represent a declared war, and a need may arise for a military draft. Though the argument that is heard most frequently is, "What happens if no one joins?" none of these issues should be a concern. If the military mirrors the society, if we are one and the same, there will always be those who choose a career in the armed services. Again, in the end the right kind of person for the military is one who wishes to be there, not one who has been forced. As for the argument of what happens if no one enlists, if that occurs then we may have reached a point where war is no longer an option in resolving disputes.

Regardless how an individual wishes to see the military, conscription does have parallels to other activities. Is it proper, or desirable, for government to conscript the general population to work on roads and highways during the course of the year? The infrastructure of the nation is important. We all benefit from the existence of bridges, roads, water systems, tunnels, and a collection of other mass usage structures. Would it not be a civic duty to help with such maintenance? Four or five days of labor each year would go far in reducing our tax burden and every citizen would be able to participate. If the answer to this question is yes then a military draft in peace-time may be proper, if the answer is a negative it becomes harder to justify.

The issue changes considerably if the discussion turns to a declared war. Here the issue becomes more a matter of proficiency. In fact it is not the military that goes to war, or that wages war; it is the nation. Every institution must contribute. The draft becomes a method by which the war can be managed. Instead of wasting resources on recruitment that same money can be spent on training. War is a total phenomenon. Each person in the nation needs to be committed. There should be one goal; anything else represents destruction of the society.

Making the distinction between how the draft can be used is also making a distinction between war and peace. This whole issue becomes far more transparent. If our sons and daughters are to die fighting a foreign power, let it be by a declared war. If they are to die fighting in a war that was not declared, let it be by their choice. The reality of death may be the same; we still will need to grieve the death of our young, but the conscience of the nation is at least one degree clearer.

The last issue is whether an individual can refuse military service. The position of this proposed Constitution is that a person can refuse military involvement but not service. The concept of conscientious objectors should exist. For those who make that type of declaration, a different type of national responsibility would be required.

As a nation we should not be overly critical of those who refuse to serve in the military. There are many different types of courage. In some ways courage is an extremely common entity. Shelby Foote has talked about Pickett's Division at Gettysburg when that long, gray Confederate line started up the center toward Cemetery Ridge. These Confederate troops were veterans. They knew what that half-mile charge across the grassy field represented, but they moved out when the order was given. He noted that no one had sufficient courage to stay behind.[9] At times of great crisis, when the nation requires the mettle of each person, to say that you will not fight takes considerable courage. In many ways it takes more courage to stay behind, to be a conscientious objector, than it does to go and fight. In any case, the individual who wishes not to serve in uniform should be given that right without question or belittlement, but their obligation to the nation-state is the same, and alternative service would be substituted.

Article 54, Section 1. Military Judicial System

The United States military employs a separate judicial system, one that does not correlate very well with the civilian or established judicial system. The system and process is much more codified and grants the officer's corps throughout the armed forces judicial responsibility. Even in the use of military discipline there is a judicious feel to the interplay. The point is that the United States has developed a duplicate judicial system of justice, one for the civilian population and one for the exigencies of military life. What is being said in this Article is only a recognition of this duality. The rules are simply different.

The goal of both is not the same. Regardless of the judicial system the goal is still one of justice. It should not be to defend the institution or the organization. Each person who stands in a courtroom, despite the system that underlines the procedures, should expect the same level of justice. Yet once noting this the nature of the military is different. The goals and direction of this institution are distinct. The judicial process in the military not only has a different system of operation but in some cases serves a different purpose. What is being noted here is that the methods of justice in the armed forces is modified from what is found in the civilian court and that difference is being allowed.

Article 54, Section 2. Restriction of Freedom

A Constitution is not simply the listing of an individual's rights or the structure of government, in part it is also a listing of some of the basic beliefs of the society. Some of these ideas do permeate as rights, but others are little more than arrangement of ideas. There needs to be a listing which outlines under what conditions rights can be restricted. This is important because rights are not total entities; in many cases there are restrictions or exceptions even to those we hold most dear. The most common example is the one on freedom of speech. Despite a person's bravado or mastery of the spoken word they still do not have a right to incite a riot. The reality is that the military does operate by a different standard. What is most important is not the rules, but that they are understood by all.

In this case the issue deals with freedom of expression and the right of mobility. The military operates from a different perspective, to be effective the armed forces needs a unity of thought. If a person were actually given freedom of expression many situations or concepts found within the armed services would be challenged. The military is not an organization that functions well when direction is disputed. In the field of tactics many forms of deceptions, feints, probing attacks, and reconnaissance in force are used to mislead an enemy. The unit used in these operations may suffer casualties, but for the greater good or in this case a military advantage, such tactics are used. For the military unit in question the advantage may seem nonessential or minimal, especially for those who lose their lives. Given an opportunity they may wish to speak up and put forth an alternative plan. The point is that freedom of action in the case of the military is more important than the individual freedom of expression. The nature of the armed services is such that questioning orders or the unity of command is not a fundamental part of that organization.

The bulk of this concern deals with security. Information is a powerful force when dealing with military matters. Restricting information is critical. If the military is to be given the power to limit knowledge about its methods of warfare, equipment, strength, and objectives, it needs that same power to control the individuals within their operations. After all they are the key; most information that is obtained by a potential enemy has been achieved through our own military personnel. These types of issues have little to do with trust, they deal more with being prudent.

The freedom of mobility, while it may be a security concern for the military, more directly deals with service-related needs. Crisis at times may develop quickly. It is far easier and efficient to mobilize troops if they are located in a given area, rather than scattered across a larger region. With a modern transportation system it is possible, even with a short pass, to travel great distances. Yet, that same transportation system may become congested at a time of crisis making immediate travel impossible.

Nevertheless individuals in the military are still citizens. The rights they enjoy should be the same, and it is equally important that they view themselves as part of the larger whole. Membership in the armed forces does not mean that a person has given up their citizenship or their rights. Yet, in these two cases individual Constitutional rights are being restricted. As with so many topics in this document, the military finds ways to abridge these issues now. The methods are simply not very enlightened or even upfront.

Article 54, Section 3. Rite of Enlistment

It is agreed that of all the Articles in this Proposed Constitution the weakest one may be this item. This Article represents little more than orientation. It could be argued that a Constitution should not be involved in either the process or the advocacy of something as negligible as orientation. Yet once saying this, the concept of listing our Miranda Rights in a Constitution may fall into this same category. It could be argued that giving a person their Miranda Rights is a form of orientation. In the case of the military, this same type of process is taking place. A person is moving from one location or environment to another. There is considerable difference between being free in the community and then being held by the authorities. Equally there is considerable difference between being in the community and then finding yourself in a branch of the military.

The armed forces of a country are a two-sided sword. In the one area the defense of the nation and the rights found within the nation-state require a strong military. When the military is called upon to perform its duty it must be successful; failure represents destruction of the society and the government. In this case the discussion deals with the destruction of a democratic government. On the other side, the military is one of the forces that can invalidate democracy. As an organization, as a body, it is not a democracy. It teaches not democracy, but submission, order, and control. Persons need to recognize that they are no longer functioning in the same environment as they were as civilians. While some of their rights are intact, others are not.

Article 55. Quartering of Soldiers

The quartering of troops in private residences has become somewhat of a non-issue. Throughout the history of the United States service personnel have been housed at their posts, forts, or bases. The military has always seen it as a method of coordination of its forces to have the soldiers stationed in the same general location. Even during the American Civil War when large numbers of troops were in the field the quartering of troops in private homes was never contemplated. The oddity with the concept of quartering troops in individual houses is that during World War II American troops were systematically placed in the homes of the citizens of Great Britain. This must be seen as a peculiar twist of fate for it was the British system of housing troops in Colonial American that brought about this Amendment to the Constitution.

The Third Amendment to the American Constitution states that troops will not be housed in private homes. Under certain conditions this Amendment can be breached, but transgressions have been few. Of all the issues in the Constitution this has been one with which the court system has had little interplay. The main reason is that it has never proved to be an issue. It is not in the best interest of the either the people or the military to house troops in private homes.

The question of why such an Article even needs to appear in this Proposed Constitution may be raised. Why list something that is a non-factor? In this case the reason dealt with heritage. More than any other part of the Constitution this one Article ties us to our past. This was a major concern and issue for our forebears. They found the idea of housing troops in their own homes as repugnant as anything government could do. They had experienced having British troops garrisoned in their towns and cities. British troops were housed in private residences both during Colonial times and during the American Revolution. In both cases the system was obnoxious and offensive. If there ever was an issue where a people "walked backwards into the future" this was it. When they wrote the Bill of Rights its supporters wanted this issue represented in the document. They saw it as much a part of our basic rights as freedom of speech.

Mirroring this Article in the Proposed Constitution is a way of connecting ourselves to the past. No one document is a free standing item. The American Constitution is connected to the English Bill of Rights and the English Bill of Rights is connected to the Magna Carta. Both the American Constitution and the Rights of Man were inspired by the Declaration of Independence. In turn all the state Constitutions, and those Constitutions found in other democratic countries around the world are connected to concepts found within the American Constitution. The idea of government by the people, of democracy, is not one item, not one document but must be seen as a process. As strange as it may sound, keeping this one item in the Proposed Constitution is a way of commemorating the past and expressing gratitude to those who have preceded us.

Article 56. State Legitimacy

Over the last two hundred years of American political history a shift in preeminence has taken place. Regardless of the view that a person may take, the reality is that the Federal government is dominant over the state governments. The Supremacy Clause and the American Civil War ended any alternative view on this political entity. Both within the United States Constitution and this proposed Constitution the states are subordinate to the Federal government. The question that has to be asked is, "Which body has the last word?" If that issue is not predetermined society could experience considerable disorder and chaos. Even among equals one party seems to be more equal than another.

What is the place of the states? The states could not be discounted. They are extremely important entities within the total governmental structure, and without them there would be no Federalism. The states more than any other body represent a check on the Federal government. It should also be noted that the state governments have more supportive policies and public services programs than the Federal government. It is the states that give patronage to the masses.

The point is that the states have a right to exist. They have a right to established borders and they have a right to do those basic components found within all governments. States are able to exercise authority over the people living within their borders. They can tax and they have police powers. The states are able to maintain a separate court system and laws. They are and will remain political entities. The simple fact that they exist will enhance and improve democracy. The states understand the nature of government as well as any body and their collective interest will preserve a balance. States are legitimate and they need to be maintained without fear of being expunged from the greater whole.

Article 57. Militias

The great trap of the American Constitution, the one in which invested interest, emotion, and counterclaims abound is the Second Amendment. For some the Second Amendment and the right to bear arms is the standard by which the Constitution has been built. It is their focus, their obligation, and their defense of this document. Without being critical of this position, it has become a compulsion, an item that must be challenged at every turn and under every circumstance. The problem, or the issue, is a complex one. It is the one single issue that critiques the differences between eighteenth century life and twenty-first century America.

A discussion of the Second Amendment involves two issues. They are not related to each other as well as some may believe. They have a relationship but not necessarily a common purpose. Each will need to be covered in detail and an effort made to find common ground. The one issue is militias and the other is the right to keep firearms.

When the framers of the Constitution wrote this document America's frontier was never far away. The chief conflict dealt with Native Americans. Without examining in detail the cause of this antagonism, most of these issues can be found within concepts related to land speculation, creed, xenophobia, and culture. It is safe to say that the United States was established in a very hostile world. The Native Americans saw the white population as interlopers on their lands and territory. Equally the Americans saw the Indians as adversaries. The majority of the Indian tribes had sided with the British during the Revolution and hostilities were ongoing. Americans were continuing to press the native populations into extinction. The history of Colonial America can be read within the confines of this aggression and it was found within both parties. Even so, there is not one native tribe that did not experience some level or act of violence against them by the white settlers moving west.

Regardless of the outcome of this epic conflict between the Indian Nations and this new country, one point is noteworthy. At the end of the American Revolution the native tribes were in control of the majority of lands conceded by Great Britain to the United States. Also, during the war the Indians had successfully defended this territory and they had fought very effectively. The Indian inhabitants of the frontier represented an imposing force. An example can be made of the fact that in the 1790s two entire American armies were devastated by the Miami Indians, and they were not even considered to be the most dominant military tribes in the Ohio Valley region. This was left to the Iroquois and Mohawk.

Moreover, at the end of the American Revolution the British still controlled forts and sections of the United States. While after signing the Treaty of Paris in 1783, the British withdrew from the original thirteen colonies, they still held on to many of the forts in the interior of the nation. Only after the War of 1812 did the British army finally withdraw. The British had a number of reasons for their conduct, but at the very least it should be viewed as an antagonistic act.

During the American Revolution, Spain and the Netherlands along with France aided the colonists. Yet their governments were monarchies similar to Great Britain. This could be said about all the nations of Europe. The divine rights of kings was the standard for world governments. The United States stood alone as a democracy and it is not much of an argument to state that the majority of the world powers were not eager to see this new nation succeed. Clearly it was not to their benefit for a government by the people to prosper. These European nations were eminently powerful, dwarfing anything the United States could muster, especially in the military arena. Nor was economic America any match for these European powers. The nation was in debt because of the Revolution. It was not even coining its own money, and at best the United States was a remote agricultural nation.

The United States did originate in a very hostile environment. The only real advantage this new nation had was in its people, and so in turn the defense of the nation became the responsibility of the average citizen. For the United States this was found in the use of militias.

To the nation's founders militias were highly significant. In actuality the militias carried the war. The British troops at Lexington and Concord faced an armed citizenry organized into local militias. At Saratoga, which is one of the most important battles fought during the Revolutionary War, it is generally agreed that Burgoyne "drowned in a sea of militia." American militia from all over New England halted General Burgoyne's advance and forced him to surrender. France decided to enter the war on the side of the colonists chiefly because of this one battle more than any other event. Four years later, and with considerable help from the French, the British were defeated at Yorktown. Hardly a battle was fought in the American Revolution in which militia did not play a part.

Militia units never were believed to have great staying power or military prowess. Generally the opposite was true. It dealt with the advantages of a civilian military force that could be called upon at a point of crisis. These military units would be responsible for their own equipment, weapons, and training. The deterrent could be seen in the numbers. A sizable force could be assembled in a short period of time to impede the advance of any possible foe, whether it be a foreign military power or the Indian tribes.

When the nation's founders added the Second Amendment to the Constitution they saw militias as an important part of the nation's defense. For them it was "a well regulated militia, being necessary to the security of a free state." The goal was for Americans to form militia units to defend their own homes and property. As for the right to bear arms this was connected to the idea of a community defense. For the nation's founders a firearm was a fact of life, a tool no different than a plow or an ax. The idea of banning or restricting the use of firearms was as foolish as restricting the use of an ax. A musket was neither good nor evil. On the frontier is was a necessary part of life.

These ideas of militias, a hostile frontier environment, and the use of weapons are now placed two hundred years later into a modern world. The United States is now one of the dominant players on the world stage, a setting where the citizen soldier is now connected to the military reserves or the National Guard, and the term militias is seen as a negative. We live in a world where the true hostility within our environment comes from our fellow citizens. There are two spheres here. One is found in the eighteenth century in a place and at a time few of us can imagine, and the other is the beginning of the twenty-first century. Each has its own special problems and issues, each require different solutions. To believe that the Second Amendment to the Constitution is as valid today as it was two hundred years ago is like saying churning butter by hand is more desirable than the processed product. It is simply not the same.

These ideas do swirl around where it is difficult to determine the head from the tail. The Second Amendment reads, "A well regulated militia, being necessary to the security of a free state, the right of the people to keep and bear arms, shall not be infringed." The Supreme Court has ruled that this amendment represents one supposition and that is the maintenance of militias. Yet, the First Amendment has four distinct concepts, the Fifth Amendment at least five, and Sixth Amendment seven. The Constitution was written so that many ideas and rights were placed in the same clause. It is possible that the Second Amendment represents two enunciated ideas—one being the usage of militias and the other being the right to bear arms. The vexing part of this topic is that the Second Amendment is within the Bill of Rights. It implies a listing of rights, one of which is the right to bear arms.

The whole issue of society's use of firearms is paradoxical. On one side are individuals who enjoy the use, trade, and activities that these implements represent. There are people who shoot skeet and collect weaponry. They do so with reverence toward the activity and the nature of the pastime. Others are taught as small children the connection our society has toward firearms and the history involved. Most are instructed in the safety of such items. Yet, on the other side of this issue is the fact that some 25,000 Americans are killed each year in the United States by handguns and rifles. Still others use firearms to wound, to steal, and to intimidate. These two concepts are incompatible. What is actually being offered is an opportunity to do something different, to find a middle ground. The issue cannot be total. Each camp must recognize the needs and the valid concerns of the other. Each situation needs to be viewed as distinctive and laws need to be passed that represent these differences.

The adjustment that is being offered in this Proposed Constitution is to change the concept from a Federal issue to a state issue. This is being done both for the organization of militias and the use of firearms. Nothing is inherently wrong with allowing the state governors to determine what represents a militia unit and how to charter such units. The states could decide what resources they wish to make available, if any, to such groups and under what conditions they can maintain their charter. Some individuals may enjoy the nature and vigor of military life for many reasons but others may stand outside the enlistment process of the regular army. Such militias would give them an opportunity to fulfill a need.

In the Proposed Constitution the National Guard would continue as it has in the past. It is both military and compassionate. At times of great crisis the National Guard is there to assist the citizenship. It has helped both with the defense of the nation and the safety of the masses during natural disasters. It fills a void that no other organization can. In many ways it represents the ultimate concept of a citizen soldier.

In the same context the states, not the Federal government, would control and regulate the use of weapons. Currently there are fifty states in the Union. Each state is unique, each has its own interests and needs. To believe that the use of firearms is the same for Connecticut as it is for Montana is unrealistic. Each state needs to determine the laws and use of weapons within their borders. This is not a point of radicalism, it is simply more pragmatic. In this case the states are probably better at defining the laws on this issue than the Federal government. What is being advocated is allowing the states the power to determine their own regulations and laws on the use of firearms. The Federal government would still be able to manage interstate commerce.

Article 58. Legal Counselors

Two concepts clash in the framework of American society. The economic structure of the nation is such that each person is entitled to demand their own fee schedule for goods and services. Prices are determined by what the market will bear. It is the essence and nature of the free enterprise system. Lawyers are connected to this system through their separate practices or through a law firm. In either case they operate as companies supplying a service to their clients. Like any other company the cost of their service is determined by what they are able to charge. On the other side of the issue is the fact that democracy is tied to the court system. No matter how this issue is adjusted or altered it returns to one basic concept—it is the courts that dispense justice. If persons believe they have been treated unfairly, if they have been charged with a crime, if some level of recounting is required, or if restitution is demanded in some form, the courts ascertain what is just.

Democracy is a system of fair play and justice, one in which all the members of the society are treated equally and evenhandedly by the laws of the nation. It is a system by which government is seen as the protector of individual rights. An arrangement is developed between the people and their government so that inconsistencies in the society can be addressed, reviewed, and corrected within a forum designed specifically to accommodate these issues. The courts determine what is fair and proper. They interpret our rights and certify the results. There is no other valid option. The courts become the custodians of justice. In any other choice the system of government breaks down and anarchy prevails.

Invading this system of justice is the free enterprise system. Each attorney is able to charge clients whatever the market will bear and consequently a huge gap develops in the price lawyers charge. The system implies that justice is determined by the ability of a person to pay, that an attorney who charges four hundred dollars an hour is better then an attorney who charges one hundred dollars an hour. After all, if the system were totally objective why would a person pay four times as much money for the same service? Again it implies that the greater amount of money will benefit the consumer, that justice is not a point of law or impartiality, but of financial resources. This system is incompatible with democracy. It suggests that justice can be purchased.

The only way to adjust this controversy is by state regulation of the prices that an attorney can charge. Each state would set the standard. A listing of services generated by lawyers and the cost of each service would be listed. This could be done either by documents created for the courts, a set program fee, charges per hour, or some combination of these cost arrangements. In any case it would be the responsibility of the states to regulate the fees attorneys would charge.

While many will argue that restricting or limiting the amount of money an attorney can charge a client represents a restraint of trade, a lawyer is an "officer of the court." This is a very special relationship. It connects the attorney to the court system in ways unknown in any other profession. In many ways an attorney is an extension of the court system. Ethically and through rules of conduct she or he is required to behave within a given set of standards. They are required to pass on to the court pieces of evidence and information when uncovered. The state's power to regulation the cost is but a dilatation of the concept of officer of the court.

This system would not be perfect. It is possible to perceive of scores of ways that such a system could be subverted. Individuals with wealth and influence will find methods of adjusting to the new format, even conceding that such methods would be within the framework of legitimate activities and this Proposed Constitution. This system could be by-passed fairly effortlessly, if by no other way than a large corporation hiring a lawyer as an employee. Such an application would alter the design. Individuals with aptitude will find ways to legally increase their income, even working within this system. The goal is simply to bring the boundaries of congruent legal action into line with democratic ideals.

Article 59. Privileges and Immunities

When the nation's founders sat down in Philadelphia in 1787 to discuss the problems of the Articles of Confederation, one of the chief difficulties was that the separate states were starting to drift apart. If a correction had not been made in the structure of the national government there is little doubt that the United States would have evolved not as a unified nation but as separate nations. As the Constitution was created the issue of unattached citizenship became relevant. In Article IV, Section 2, the issue is plainly noted. An individual becomes a citizen of the United States and not just one of the states. A person traveling from one state to another is entitled to the same rights and privileges as an individual living in that state.

This is not the same as residency. States do distinguish between persons living in the state and others that are transient. The states supply services to their citizens and they tax their people accordingly. It is unjust to allow a person services who does not permanently live in that state. In the same context it is improper to discriminate against persons because they are from another location within the country. States have an obligation to treat all the people the same.

This issue has one more component. It deals with reciprocity. While an individual needs to be treated the same in all the states, a person has an equal responsibility to citizenship of the whole. If a person commits a crime in one state and is captured in another, the state from which the individual fled can demand extradition. While it is hoped that some discretion is allowed, each state has a responsibility to assist another state with the legitimate exercise of its law.

Article 60. Rite of Passage

If there is one item that seems out of place in this Proposed Constitution it is the issue of Rite of Passage. This is a contrived Article that stands outside the concepts of most Constitutions, but the goal is a sincere one. There are two parts to this theory. The first, and probably the more important, is social, with the second part being political. In any case nothing like this has ever appeared in a Constitution before and may be too peculiar for many to accept. Yet, the idea is put forth with the most honest intent. From the social perspective the question that is being asked is, "What makes a woman or a man?" From the political perspective the issue is, "What makes a citizen?" Such a system also allows the population to recognize and accept the idea of a social contract. It becomes more than tacit consent, but a true agreement.

From the social rationale this Article is set up for both young men and women, and with the belief that both sexes would benefit by such programs, but the major concern lies with the male population, for it is the male who commits the vast majority of violent crime; it is generally the male who stalks, probes, and harms. The anger and rage that can be found in our society is neither normal, nor natural; it is a learned behavior passed on from generation to generation. It is a belief that a

Person's power, prowess, and strength should be used to control the behaviors of another. All of these ideas are false. Manhood does represent a different level in a person's life. It should represent a point of equality with all other men, a passage from one point to another, when a person accepts the rights of manhood and the responsibilities of our society. Yet, within our culture there is little to mark this passage. Nothing points to the fact that we have changed, that we have become something else, and what this new level represents.

We should not underestimate the part that rituals and rites of passage play in our lives. There are ceremonies that mark the passage of time or the movement from one role in society to another. Rituals are important. They are important for the society and they are equally significant for the individual. It becomes a clear-cut point between what had come before and what came afterwards; in this case the difference between childhood and adulthood. Rituals are very much a part of our daily lives and our growth as individuals. They present an opportunity to pass on information to the person about the nature of this new role and what it portrays. The person entering the new role is given a sense of membership and of belonging. Within this new role are duties and obligations. The older members pass on information to the younger ones regarding what this new responsibility represents, how they are to act, and the renewed insight into their own presence. In turn a bond is developed with the whole.

These concepts are common throughout many societies and the rites come in many forms: rituals at birth, puberty, adulthood, marriage, menopause, and death. In other cultures rites are performed as individuals move throughout the different institutions. In some cultures a ceremony occurs when an individual takes ups arms as part of the defense of the nation. Still in other cases it is religious in nature. In the Jewish community the ceremony surrounding bar mitzvah and bat mitzvah represents the bringing of a young person into the center of religious participation within the community. The Navajo have a ritual for young women as they enter puberty. It notes the changes in maturity and the new place the young woman has in society. In fact the African and Native American cultures are the most engaging in their developments of rites of passage.

In the United States we are not without our rites and rituals, though many of these cannot be viewed as totally positive experiences. The first time the family offers us an alcoholic beverage or biological changes in our body that require adjustments in our dress are a few examples. Registering for the draft is a milestone. Obtaining a driver's license is considered a major modification in the adolescent's life. The mobility alone changes the definition of the person. Yet, throughout these teen years nothing formally denotes the changes in a person's existence.

What is being offered in this Article is a formal process by which individuals participate in a rite of passage, a system by which our young are allowed, even expected, to participate in observances and ceremonies noting their passage into manhood and womanhood. These ideas should not be discounted. They represent a powerful tool for the society. Such a rite connects the child with the larger society and both of their parents. In turn it concedes what adolescents universally work toward: greater independence.

A few basic facts need to be remembered about teenagers. Even in the best of families adolescents will challenge the rules of the household. It does not matter what the rules are; in fact it is unimportant. Creating conflict cuts the bond with the family. Up until this time in their lives their identity was aligned to the family. Who they are as a person was connected to the family. From the view of the adolescent, the only way to gain independence is to break with the family unit. In the same context where the teenager obtains identity is with the peer group. From a parent's point of view if the child connects to a good social peer group it is a positive; if they connect with a "bad crowd" there are problems for the family. The last idea to understand about teenagers is that they believe that they are immortal. This is the most dangerous of all concerns. It creates situations in which the adolescent is clearly not operating in her or his own best interest.

In time the adolescent turns back to the family. In the end a child will be more like his or her parents than any other person. It is the family that teaches social values and proper behavior. It is the family that defines a person's character and it is the family that gives us our personal legacy. It is also the family that gives us the greatest gift of all, a sense of belonging and love. By designing rituals that note the passage from one point in our lives to another we will assist families in the promotion of our children. It will help with the complexity and obtrusive parts of the adolescent years.

The idea that is presented here is that over a period of a couple of years instruction is given to the adolescent. Classes would be offered in which the adolescents are given information about what is expected of them as adults and to outline some of the rules of our society. Even ideas surrounding marriage and sexual behavior could be covered. Rites and ceremonies could be designed along the way. Special gifts and pins could denote the stages of the process. Somewhere near a person's eighteenth birthday a final ceremony would be held to mark their passage into adulthood. Along with this rite could be titles such as Mister, Miss, Ms, or Sir.

The system needs to be designed in such a way that the stages and mobility through the process can be noted, but not so rigid as not to allow individuals to engage in the rite even after their adolescent period. There are individuals who drop out of high school only to return years later to obtain their diplomas. Some will choose to complete the rites at a later time. The system needs to be accommodating and flexible.

Not everyone will wish to participate. Some will see it as an extension of some governmental authority; other will resist the regimentation or discipline required by the process. As a whole the rite should be viewed as a positive. It is not designed to control as much as to assist. For those who choose to participate it will represent a monumental point in their life, a passage into adulthood.

Article 61. Public School Districts

While both the Federal government and the state governments assist with public education, the body with the most accredited authority on the secondary educational institutions in the country is the local school districts. Consistently they do a good job. These individuals are focused on education and work toward the goal of educating our children, but there is one single problem. These school districts are autonomous units. While they may be subject to state standards and rules of conduct, financially each school district operates separately.

As a rule school districts receive money through property taxes. If a secondary school operates out of an affluent school system, these property taxes will generate greater funds. Likewise, if a school district is found within a poorer district or inner city, fewer funds may be available. The current system creates a disparity of options with discrimination and bias built into the process. Within the public school system each child should have the same educational opportunity. Money simply needs to be evenly divided, and the states are the best body to create a more uniform and equitable system.

This does not mean that individual school districts should not exist. School boards, teachers, parents, students, and the community at large need to be involved in local education. Our future requires it, but the bias on how money is generated and returned to the school districts needs to be fair. Currently this is not the case. There is a wide financial disparity even between connecting school districts. The states will be able to manage this process.

Article 62. Reciprocity

In the United States Constitution under Article IV there is a section called the "full faith and credit" clause. It is one of the most basic of all the sections of the Constitution, yet one of the most confusing to the layperson. It says that if a court in one state makes a ruling or creates a judgment against a person in another state, that decision will be accepted in all the other states. Once liability is determined others states will acknowledge the rulings of the first court.

An example can be made of an individual who does damage to an automobile in a motor vehicle accident. This person is taken to court and a judgment is obtained. If that person moves to another state, he or she does not have to be sued again. The second state will honor the verdict in the first state. If such an item did not exist in the Constitution, economic, social, and legal interaction between the different states would be extremely difficult. Even the simplest of legal judgments would be trapped in a mire of legal problems.

This is still not a perfect system. The issue of jurisdiction within the various states can still be called into question. There can also be problems with contracts generated by large business enterprises. If a company does not have a facility or employees in a state, but their products are sold in that state by a third party, does the state have jurisdiction in a case dealing with the manufacturing company? These issues can be complex and many have been worked out by existing law and conventions. What is being offered in the Proposed Constitution is a continuation of the "full faith and credit" clause. If we are to be one nation, some effort must be made to support the legal understandings found in other states.

Article 63. Responsibility to the Young

In the final analysis it is the responsibility of the family to care for, nurture, teach, and cherish the young. It is the nature of that institution. The family must provide for and sustain the children within the unit. The human animal, more than any other species, requires an extended period of time for growth and development, and it needs to be done appropriately. It is the family that maintains this support. It is what families do best.

Once saying this, there is a larger community. A nation-state is a community. We collectively band together to do those tasks that would be impossible to do separately. We have a responsibility toward one another. If a person is blind and unable to feed herself, we have an obligation to help sustain her. This is not a revolutionary socialistic concept; rather it is part of the reason we have government, and it exists within the scope of our current government. It carries those that cannot walk, guides those that cannot see, and it speaks for those who cannot talk. As a people we want a thoughtful, benevolent, amicable government. This has nothing to do with being overly generous or overly absorbed into the lives of the people. Government is not a philanthropic entity. Government needs to protect and create a balance between those forces that would serve purely their own needs and those unempowered in our society.

This bring us to our children. One of the purposes of families is to pass information, knowledge, and insight onto our offspring. As adults we give guidance and direction. In turn the children accept this guardianship and the security it offers. The problem is that not all households are healthy families. There are dysfunctional families, trapped by mental illness or addictions. There are adults who have never learned what represents a healthy family. They in turn pass on to their children mixed messages about society and personal relationships. There are families that instead of nurturing, actively hurt and inflict pain. There are also families who abuse the weakest of its members. While it is clearly the responsibility of the family to raise children, to teach them ethical values, and to interact properly with others, the government has an equal responsibility to oversee this process.

Article 64. Educational Diversity

Regardless of how the system is developed or implemented, families are still responsible for the education of the young. In fact children learn more from their parents than from the school system. Families are not only responsible for the education of their children; they also have a right to educate. If parents wish to instruct their own children within the framework of their own homes, that should be allowed. There is never only one way to accomplish the same objective. As a nation and as people we need to give our citizens choices.

The people have a right for their children to be educated with virtuous views, even if that represents a denominational education. The type of education a person receives is not so important as teaching her or him an enthusiasm for learning. If we teach children to think, they will educate themselves. What is hoped for from the parents is to encourage and promote a child's education. A parent needs to become involved in a child's education. It does not matter the form it takes—just that parents are actively involved.

Parents also need to be involved in the school system. If a child is not being educated at home, it becomes the responsibility of the parent to assist the school system with their goals. It is an equal partnership. We cannot expect the schools to educate our children without help from the community, and in turn the parents cannot escort the child through the system without direction from the schools. It is a dual effort requiring the interactions of many people.

Article 65. Child Information

Parents need to know what is going on with their children. As a child moves through life, a wide range of tests, reports, charts, and documents are created for that person. This should not be secret information. The parents need to be informed to make proper judgments about the upbringing of their children. In fact the more information parents have, the better they are at making appropriate decisions about the care of their young.

This issue represents more than just the educational system. This same argument can be made with mental health professionals, medical doctors, counselors, insurance companies, credit bureaus, or specialized trainers. Any organization which keeps individual files about a child should have some method in place by which that information or data can be made available to the parent. The family unit will benefit the most from that material. To keep it from them seems self-defeating, and the question can be raised, whom is it designed to benefit?

There are always exceptions. If services were being generated by a psychiatrist and the treatment was ongoing, it may not be in the best interest of the individual or the family to be privileged to all the details of the activity. Some treatments are paradoxical in nature and actually would be detrimental to the interest of the patient if the treatment information were made available. In the same context agreements in medical circles are sometimes made with the patient in clinical trials. If legal action is also being considered or pursued, such charts and information may not be accessible, at least not immediately. The scope of this Article is to note that parents are entitled to information on their child that has been created by professionals in the community. It should not be kept a secret and to do so is not in the best interest of the child. At times certain exceptions and conditions may require that some of that information be restricted, but it should not be kept from a parent indefinitely.

Again, most states have laws that govern this process. If a parent is looking for information or wishes to review a chart generated by a professional or the schools, it is possible for them to see these records. The process may be a formal one, noting that the parent may read the progress notes and test results, but not remove any documents from the charts. A staff member may have to be present while the chart is reviewed. *Releases of Information* may have to be signed in some cases, but the process is currently available. Placing such items in the Constitution makes a statement about how important it is for parents to be involved in their children's lives and that the state supports such concepts.

Article 66. The Right to Labor Representation

Each institution in our society must be seen for what it does right, not purely for what it does wrong. It is impossible to talk about labor without discussing business; they are as connected as the brain is to the hand. Through labor the vision of business is constructed and takes form through the sweat and toil of each person. By this process economy is created. No matter how ingenious or brilliant an idea, it can never come into volition unless that idea is worked. It must be nudged, jabbed, and twisted until it becomes a point of reality. Business contemplates while labor fabricates. They are a part of the same body; it is the same conception and together they become enterprise.

Business is the great esotericism of society. In many ways it is the lifeblood of the nation. It alone produces revenue. Without a healthy thriving business community all of the other institutions wither and become shallow remnants of their true aspirations. All of the institutions feed off the funds produced by business. It matters not if the discussion is the family, the church, education, or the media. Neither the church, the media, nor educational institutions can feed our families; only business has that ability. Government would be unable to collect taxes if business did not produce the revenue in the first place. As for foundations they are an outgrowth of business interest. In many ways business is the "golden goose." It must be allowed to grow and produce. Through business and the marketplace flow ideas, products, and money.

Business also has a dark side. It is set up for one reason. A company, a firm, a corporation has one purpose—to make money. Profit is the single most powerful element in business. Nothing else matters. Nothing else moves, stimulates, or motivates people the way that money does. It is both the master and slave of business. Profit is the only reason business exists. No matter how charitable a company may appear, it can never sacrifice profit. To do so would represent its own demise, for a company that does not maintain a profit will die. That bare truth creates a ruthlessness found in no other institution.

Entering into this mix is labor. Business needs labor to fuel the engines of production. Each employee adds to the value of the company. Each employee supplements the company with energy, resourcefulness, intelligence, skills, and drive. Each employee adds to the profit of the greater whole. It is inconsistent, and beyond the nature of business to keep personnel who do not in some way contribute. Each of us must be productive; it exists at the heart of human nature. In the same context employees benefit from the relationship through their wages and the improvement in self-esteem. They remain loyal to the firm that employs them. Each in her or his own way serves the needs of the company and embraces the goals that have been outlined by the employers.

The commitment to the general health of the enterprise needs to be the same regardless of the position that a person holds within the company. Yet, a division many times is drawn between the interest of the elites of a company and the workers. If the upper levels of management believe that there is no such thing as too much profit and that the issue is determined only by what the market will bear, then the employee will become nothing more than a part of the accounting. A person's labor will appear on the balance sheet and be viewed in the same way as copper wire, plastic tubing, and light fixtures. In those cases where a company begins to treat their employees not as associates, but as commodities, a defense is needed.

The recourse is labor representation. Employees need to have the power to organize and bring a labor union into the workplace. What is needed is a point of refuge from avaricious and self-seeking management. Labor organizations can represent a balance against the purely predatory part of American capitalism. Even if a union does not exist within a company, but only its possibility, that concept will temper management actions and behaviors. Labor unions should not be seen as an unfortunate part of the industrial age; they need to be seen as a fail-safe device against corporate absolutism and intolerance.

This same process should work in both directions. There are times and conditions when labor unions are needed and when they are not. The process of organizing and bringing about labor representation should be just as easy to do away with as it is to certify a union. If a company develops programs that incorporate their employees, solicit their opinions, are equitable with the finances, and are sincere in their treatment of staff, there is little need for a labor organization. There should be times when unions would be decertified.

In the most idealistic form a partnership needs to be forged between labor and business. The interests of both are the same. A successful, profitable company is as much in the best interests of labor as business. Ideally labor organizations should not see themselves as a form of opposition to management, but a complement to the corporation. Members of the rank and file have as much to offer in their intellect and common sense as their muscles. Both sides need to tap into this resource. There is nothing written that says that the relationship between labor and business has to be an adversarial one.

While an alliance between these two institutions is desirable, the nature of these entities must also be noted. Business is not a democracy. In fact labor is structured far more democratically than business. The rules of business are far more finite. Any organization, body, or group that restricts the nature of business will be seen as being hostile. It is the unity that labor represents that makes it a viable force.

A fundamental question is at play in this Article. Is the ability of organizing a labor union a right or a privilege? The issue is fairly basic. If the claim is that organizing into labor unions is a privilege, it should not be in a Constitution. If organizing is believed to be a right, it should be in such a document. In the Proposed Constitution the belief is that such an act is a right. The primary reason is that it deals with the people—not even democracy, but just the people. We are all involved in labor. In fact the worth of individuals is in their labor. We must bring value to what we produce and create. Placing labor unions where they are needed is saying that labor does count. It is the belief that labor is not simply a commodity. To take this idea one step further, it also implies that people count. The production of goods and services are not the only goal; wages earned and the self-respect gained by the process also have merit.

The last question is whether employees of the Federal government should be allowed to organize into labor unions. The state, provincial, and city governments around the country deal with labor organizations. It is part of the operations of these bodies, but the Federal Government has disallowed such organizations. A built-in prejudice seems to imply that the Federal government is too important to have to deal with such issues and that it is more important than the state governments. The argument being put forth here is that this is false. The Federal government supplies services to the people as do the state governments; each is equally important in relationship with the people. The central government is entitled only to whatever endowment the other governments receive as well. The system needs to be as universally fair as possible. Everyone needs to operate with the same set of rules.

Article 67. Child Labor

The United States has had a spotty history on the issue of child labor. Throughout most of our existence the use of child labor has not only been allowed but to some degree expected. Within most of eighteenth and nineteenth century America the philosophical belief was that children were nothing more than small adults. They were as capable of working as any other individual. They simply were not as productive. By the twentieth century sociologists were taking a different position. They noted the importance of allowing children the opportunity to be children. They pressed the view that play and social interaction with other children was a healthy process of human development. Our society has evolved and all the states have prohibitions on the use of child labor.

As a rule, children exist without the same Constitutional rights as other citizens. They are far more an extension of the rights enjoyed by their parents. In many ways they do not have the right to assembly, the right of mobility, or the right of association. They cannot freely express their ideas. Few academic or religious freedoms are protected. It is the parent who has the say on what type of medical services a child will receive, what kind of school they attend, and what church they will frequent. Children are instructed, taught, and guided. Through most of their early years they have little say in the direction of their lives. If there is one right that a child should have, it is not to be exploited for purely commercial interest.

The reason that the child labor article appears in the Proposed Constitution has little to do with the United States. We have come to grips with this issue and as a rule our laws are fair and just. We have developed standards on the use of individuals under the age of eighteen in the labor pool. The real problem is the world community. Child labor is still commonplace throughout this planet. It is a disruptive entity that destroys a person's childhood. It is a harsh component of many places in the world and the reality of undeveloped nations. Constitutions do not exist in a vacuum. Parts of the United States Constitution have been used by many nations as they have created new governments. Stating that this issue is a concern and that immutable child labor is wrong notes to the world our position. Our hope is that when other nations review their society and the nature of their laws, the concept of child labor would be addressed.

Article 68. District of Columbia

Perhaps the vision of an American capital prompted the nation's founders to include the District of Columbia in the Constitution. The capital was to be a place where legislators and members of the government met to review the issues of the day, debate the concerns of the nation, and deliberate the future of our country. It would be a place where the mandate of the people met with the confidence of a new land. America was something fresh and new. Our capital needed to represent this spirit. An image arose of the American capital being set out in an orderly fashion, tree-lined streets wide in berth, and majestic buildings. A place where our legislators moved freely about the boulevards and structures, each adding a voice to the chorus that is representative government.

Something happened in the process. What occurred was that the District of Columbia became Washington, D.C., a metropolitan city. Washington has become the same as any other large urban city in America. It has a population of hundreds of thousands of people with the same needs as any other city of its size. Yet, something is very wrong with the way the district turned out. It became a contradiction to everything the Founders had hoped for in their capital. It became not a campus or a seat of government, but a city.

Two fundamental problems are apparent. The first deals with democracy and the other with administration. If the nature of our government is that of a representative democracy, the people need to be represented. That assertion may seem so obvious it is hardly worth stating, but reality is that not all of our population is receiving the same level of democracy. It represents hypocrisy at the best and tyranny at worst. If we deny any group of people the same rights as others in our society, it defames our republican form of government. The people of Washington do not have representation. Registered voters throughout the country elect Representatives and Senators to represent their interests. Though it is part of the American process and the nature of our democracy, we are refusing to give these same rights to others. The only way we can call ourselves a democracy is by allowing all the people to experience the same level of representative government.

The other problem is administration. Cities and states work in tandem to cover the basic governmental services of urban populations. Money generated by our tax dollars is filtered by the Federal government and returned to the states in various forms. Cities add their own tax revenues to the money they receive from the states. In the case of Washington, D.C., the Federal government supports the needs of the city. Its own tax structure is negligible. Though the city finds itself constantly attempting to negotiate with the Federal government for funds, the arrangement is not one of equals. The central government sees the city of Washington as an extension of its own domain. The issue becomes more a matter of control than of operating funds. What occurs in the end is that the people of the district suffer. They receive fewer services and governmental support than an equivalent city anywhere else in the country.

Part of this problem is the makeup of the capital's population. On one side is a large portion of the population that is not invested in the city. These residents are connected in some way to the government. After all, the largest employer in the city is the Federal bureaucracy. Many individuals, especially those in power, do not see themselves as permanent residents of the area. The other portion of the population is unempowered and without a voice in government. It creates an atmosphere of neglect.

This leaves five basic choices. The District of Columbia could become a state. A Constitutional Amendment was passed by Congress and sent to the states with implications to that effect. Due to a lack of leadership and disinterest on the part of the states, the measure has not been passed. Even so, the issue is more complex than creating a state. The main problem is that even if it became a state, the district would still be locked into a continuous struggle with the Federal government over funds, even more than it is now. While the central government is the chief employer in the area, the new state would certainly make additional demands upon the national government. Few would feel comfortable with this arrangement. This new state would be rather small in size, and because of the nature of its population, it would not have the same ability to raise revenue. Since the national government is the chief employer, how untroubled would the overall population be in allowing only one state to tax the Federal government? Additional financial demands would surely be placed on transient political citizenry. This first option is not seen as feasible.

The second choice is the status quo. This still leaves the problems of a counterfeit democracy, poor administration of resources, and neglect. Even if a system were developed where representation for the district was allowed and they were given Senators and Representatives, the question has to be asked. Who would these representatives represent? Would they represent the interest of the migratory political populace or the core of Washington's citizens? A battle of political will could develop between these two groups.

There is a third option, we could simply try it again. There is the possibility of moving the capital to another location and seeing if we can keep people from moving into the ten square miles allotted in the Constitution. As an example, the

Federal government owns most of the state of Nevada, it should not be difficult to find the land. A new capital would be built and laws would be passed so that citizens could not live in the district.

One possibility is for the Federal government to buy all the land and property in the District of Columbia. They could then force all the residents out of the city. These sections of Washington would then be leveled. All property in the city would be owned by the Federal government. While this option needs to be listed it is also the least desirable. It would be expensive and dispassionate. Not all the property in Washington is single dwelling housing. Motels, office complexes, and apartments also dot the area. Both the powerful and the politically weak would resist the loss of their property. Many of the poor would be forced to move to other cities or states, placing a strain on them. This idea is simply not very workable.

What it comes down to is that the whole idea of a district turned out differently than our leaders had expected. The United States became a large nation. To accommodate the size of the country and the ever-increasing size of the population, our government grew. As the number of agencies and departments increased so did the size of the Federal bureaucracy. It is not the same system or conditions that were found in 1787 when the idea of a district was proposed. What seems to be the only viable option is to return the district back to the states that granted the land in the first place. This has already been done for Virginia. It would require only an understanding or agreement with Maryland. They could help administer the city and supply state services. Most of the countries around the world have national capitals that do not function within a district. While there are some advantages to having a district, it should not be at the expense of civil liberty or good government. The District of Columbia needs to be abolished.

Article 69, Section 1. Union

Constitutions need to be structured in such a way that changes in political thought can be accommodated or adapted within its pages. Of the many political theorists today, most are well intentioned, most have something to say. A Constitution should not restrict ideas from maturing or developing an audience. An example can be made by the fact that the United States is a mixed economy. Our political and economic theory drifts back and forth across the spectrum between pure capitalism and socialism. Nothing within the American Constitution or this Proposed Constitution would disallow the times to dictate the conditions of our political thought. Yet, this Proposed Constitution does make a few political statements. This is a Constitution embedded in democracy and government by the people. It cannot work or function if any form of authoritarian or totalitarian government is attempted within its pages. This is designed as a democratic Constitution for a democratic government.

The second issue is political integration. One of the most basic concepts found within the United States is Union. It is as important as any theory in the well being of the American society. Union is so universally accepted as a political element that it is rarely discussed or reviewed. The United States is a product of political integration or Union. The power of the national government is enhanced and increased by this one substantial concept. Union is so important that it exists unchallenged. To destroy the nature of our Union is to destroy the United States. This Proposed Constitution simply notes the significance of Union and the defense it represents to democracy.

While this Proposed Constitution notes that the United States has become a Federalist state certain responsibilities and powers still remain with the individual states. Certain ideas have been specifically assigned to the states within the Constitution, others have been the traditional rights of the states to maintain. The prime example is criminal law. While the Federal government has a separate court system and statute relating to criminal behavior this is not the main responsibility of the central government. Rather, the states are left to determine the nature of flagitious and unlawful behavior within their borders.

The state systems offer numerous advantages. Historically it has been the states that have brought forth new thesis about government and were the first to establish progressive ideas. In the late 1800s many of the western states began to pass laws that conceded suffrage to women. Throughout the west women were voting in state elections long before the franchise was passed by the Federal government. The states, rather than the Federal government, are the most active in the education of our children. New ideas and concepts are constantly being tried by the states to find better ways to educate our populace. Likewise, the states are most active in welfare programs, mental health, care of the elderly, and child protection.

Far more than the Federal government, the state governments supply services to our communities. If we accept the argument that one of the chief responsibilities of government is to supply services to the population, the states do a far better job of it than the national government. Not only is there a place for the states within a Federalist system, there is a basic necessity for them.

Article 69, Section 2. State Autonomy

The boundaries of states need to be as eternal as any part of the political landscape. This matter cannot be a point of discussion or debate. One state cannot annex another state's territory or population. These are concerns that must be set in stone. A Union requires that this single issue be above question or compromise.

A very similar cause and concept is found within the American Constitution. Article IV, Section 3, reads in part, "no new states shall be formed or erected within the jurisdiction of any other state; nor any state be formed by the junction of two or more states, or parts of states." Of course the problem is West Virginia. Somewhere along our history that theory was ignored. West Virginia became a state in 1863 during the American Civil War and was carved out of the state of Virginia.

The logic at the time seems contradictory and incomplete. While Virginia had seceded from the Union and had joined the Confederacy, a majority of the people in northwestern Virginia wanted to stay with the Union. Traditionally there had been a gap between these two groups of people. The population of the hill country of western Virginia had seen themselves as different from the settlements along the eastern coast of the state for a long time. Disagreements over policies were common. Congress was petitioned and West Virginia was granted membership in the Union as the thirty-fifth state. The problem is that the United States never acknowledged the right of the Southern states to secede from the Union. The core of this great conflict dealt with the Constitution. While Virginia may have been in revolt, they were still part of the Union and the Constitution was still in effect. If that was true, West Virginia should not have been allowed membership in the Union under Article IV.

Of course the issue had nothing to do with the American Constitution, but political considerations of the times. Congress wanted to be accommodating to a group of people who supported the Union and were willing to assist in the struggle.

It was more of a political necessity, and maybe even a military one in allowing West Virginia to become a state. The Constitution was easy to overlook when the Union was coming apart at the seams. In retrospect the problem remains more profound. The Constitution is not something that can be disregarded simply because it is not politically prudent.

Nothing within these pages is requesting or demanding a change in the status of West Virginia. While it may be the "Bastard Child" of the Constitution, it is also family. It is currently an accepted part of the Union, an integrated part of the whole. The point is only that the borders of the states should be established and firm. It should not be subject to adjustment, transition, or change.

The last issue in this Proposed Constitution may be one of the most intensive, penetrating questions found within the document. Under what conditions can a state leave the Union? This was the major question that surrounded the American Civil War. While many underlying issues are presented when examining this great conflict such as slavery and state rights, they are subordinate to this single issue of Union.

The argument that the American South made was that they joined the Union openly and freely, and as a state they should be entitled to leave the Union equally as freely. The rights of the central government are actually derived from the states. The states created the Federal government and gave it life. Since the states determined the nature of the Union they thought that if the states wished to terminate their membership they had that right. The Unionist had a different position. They argued that the American Constitution gave each person specific rights. When a state seceded from the Union it was in essence denying people their rights under the Constitution. Even if a new Constitution were created, perfect in detail to the original document, it was still not the same one, nor would it be administered in the same way. To disallow the process all that is needed is one person who would not support the secession of the state and believed that his or her rights were being tampered with. For the Federalist the Constitution, and the pledge found within its pages, was the main focus of the rebellion. In the end the Union won, not half so much because of the strength of their argument, but because of force of arms.

Regardless of which view is the more applicable, the question remains, under what conditions can a state leave the Union, or is it possible for a state ever to leave the Union? Both of the above arguments can lead to the same place. The Southern argument of the 1860s would be that under certain conditions a state can leave the Union; the Northern position held they could not for such action would jeopardize individual right under the Constitution. But what happens if there is no Constitution? What happens at the indeterminate time between Constitutions? If a new Constitution is agreed upon and ratified by two-thirds of the states, what happens if a state refuses to accept the new Constitution? If the Constitution holds the Union—and the position taken in this document is that this is true—at what point does a state become an independent sovereign nation? It is at the point of ratifying a new Constitution that the Union is dissolved. The risk for the country is the greatest at that point. It is the right of the people of each individual state to choose whether they wish to accept a new Constitution, and even if they wish to become part of the Union.

This is a powerful statement. At some point the people of each state get to choose whether they wish to be part of the Union. There is the risk that one or a few of the states would refuse to ratify a new Constitution. If that would occur they would be free to form their own union or exist independently. Membership does come with responsibility and that needs to be done with a sense of commitment. In the end you cannot hold a state any more that you can hold an individual. At some point the state must choose. Under this Proposed Constitution every two hundred years the states get to make that decision.

Once that decision has been made, and the people have agreed to a new Constitution, then that state is a part of the Union. They will remain so until the next time a new Constitution is ratified or instituted. At that point the Union and Constitution become one.

Article 69, Section 3. The Commonwealth

The issue of course is that the Union is not a stagnant entity. It is changing and evolving like any other body or association. It changes for no other reason than the fact that our population is growing. Our institutions change and how we see ourselves changes. From time to time individual territories may wish to join our Union. It is a great compliment to our society and our nation to have others who wish to be part of it. As a people we need to be equally gracious to those who wish to join. A structure and system needs to be developed so that such a process becomes comfortable to all the parties involved.

Several types of territories are attached to the Union. While the core of the Union is the individual states and their state governments, there are also commonwealths. This is a specific relationship and level of involvement with the national state. A commonwealth would have its own government—as independent as any of the state governments—a Constitution, and a separate commonalty. A commonwealth would not be allowed its own foreign policy or to coin its own money. Central governmental services and police agencies would function the same within the commonwealths as they would in the states. Federal law would apply. All the people of the commonwealth would have citizenship in the Union and would be able to move freely within the general society. The territory itself would not have national representation and while residing in that territory the citizens would not be able to vote at the national level.

This needs to be seen as a transition category. A commonwealth is an evolving entity that will either choose to become a state or move away from the Union. The people of a commonwealth can elect to become an independent, sovereign nation. This is well within their rights and the choice must be left to the people within that community.

One of the current examples is Puerto Rico. The people of this area are considering their options and the nature of our Union. They are a commonwealth. They are also citizens of the United States and equally Puerto Ricans. It is no different than those from any other state. We all have many different loyalties. As a people we need to accept our differences and rejoice in that diversity.

Article 69, Section 4. The Protectorate

A *protectorate* becomes another type of territory found within the United States. In many cases this may be territory with little or no population. It is possible that such protectorates could be administrated by a governmental agency or by one of the branches of the military. A protectorate may be a territory in transition, one that requires limited supervision while traditional services or government are established. The United States was the protectorate of a number of islands in the

Pacific Ocean after World War II. Some have become independent nations, others have remained protectorates.

Two examples of protectorates would be Wake and Midway Islands. They have very small populations and are administrated by the Department of Defense—Wake by the United States Air Force and Midway by the Navy. These areas are so small it is unlikely they will change their status. Even so, the nature of protectorates needs to be understood and placed in the Constitution. If the national government is to administrate territory, and even if one person lives in that region, that person's status must be realized. Each person living under the Constitution must understand their rights and the nature of their citizenship. Regardless of where a person lives, or within what section of the overall country, the classification of their citizenship needs to be found within the Constitution.

One of the issues that is most confusing, troublesome, and poorly designed is the system of reservations for Native Americans. Reservations were not created for the benefit of the indigenous population. They were designed to separate the Native Americans from the majority of the population and settle the land from which they had come. While the Bureau of Indian Affairs was set up to manage these reservations, historically they have been inadequately governed. Originally they were under the jurisdiction of the Department of War and later transferred to the Department of the Interior. Indian reservations may have made sense to concepts of Manifest Destiny of the eighteenth century, but they are practically impossible to justify within the framework of a Constitutional document.

Many Native American today see the reservations not as a negative, but as a connection to their tribe and culture. As a people we need to assist the Native American in preserving their past and their heritage. The only argument that is being made here is that if reservations are to exist they need to be included in the Constitution. The only way that can be done appropriately is by declaring Indian reservations as protectorates.

It is hoped that a solution can be found for the reservation system. They stand in opposition to American representative government. What is created is a dual system with an effort to maintain the concept of *Equal but Separate.* While this proposed Constitution allows for reservations to become protectorates a better outcome may be in their elimination. There is no reason why this process could not be accommodating to all the parties involved.

Article 69, Section 5. Sanctioned Territory

If there is one topic on which this Proposed Constitution transgresses from the norm it is with the Article on *sanctioned territory*. As a rule Constitutions are strictly internal matters outlining the rules of the nations and the structure of the government, but that is not the case with this Article. It is external in nature and represents a commitment to a political concept. Of course that political concept is democracy and the question that is being asked is, "What are we willing to do as a nation-state to enhance democracy around the world?"

At first glance this item may seem like some form of American hegemony. Unlike the world in which the nation's founders lived, the United States is a major military-industrial-economic power. As a nation we do represent considerable political and economic will. As a world power our government does have sway in the world arena. The issue here is not dominance, but protection and development. What are we willing to do as a nation to help democracy as a political concept grow and survive? Is it enough simply to be concerned about our own nation or can we make a commitment to this idea on the world stage as well?

It is common for many nations of the world to change their government by force of arms. Regardless of the outcome, violence or the threat of violence proved to be the deciding element in the adjustment of the government. Governmental power connected to the military can be a disintegrating blow to the political will of the people. Democracy can be a very fragile image, especially for a nation wrestling with the concept for the first time. Time is required for democracy to develop and to allow the tradition of a republican government to take hold.

The United States of the nineteenth century had an advantage in the development of their democratic institutions. Some referred to the Turner Principle. It states that one of the reasons America was able to mature and develop a democratic tradition was the westward expansion of the country. Those disgruntled or unhappy with the interactions of government could find relief by moving west beyond the reach and control of the state. This process allowed the concept of self-government to take root. Despite the reason, tradition and a general inclination toward self-government is the basis from which democracy can grow.

Of course the major concern for any fledgling democracy is its own military. Democracy requires a military that is subordinate to the civilian government. This may be counter to the customs of the country. Likewise, the expenditures for the military may be checked if a civilian government attempted to reduce the role of the armed forces. Friction is possible on many issues. In the worst-case scenario the military may attempt a coup d'état. Even if the issue of civil wars and revolutions are added to the mix, a nation may have experienced substantial political and social upheaval. If a foreign nation is looking for stability few solid options are at hand.

This Article is only an attempt to assist the ideas of democracy. As a people we need to make a commitment to this philosophy and this may require action at many different levels. We need to be true to our beliefs. As a nation we need to lead by example. If another nation wishes for us to assist with their process of developing a democratic state we should help.

This type of situation would happen very rarely. For a foreign nation to ask to be sanctioned would require considerable determination from their leadership. This foreign state would be in a high level of turmoil and insecurity. The goal has nothing to do with economics. Monetarily the nation would still be expected to develop it own economic resources. The responsibility of the United States would be toward only the idea of stability.

The Senate would also be expected to approve such a sanctioned state. The oddity is that it is actually the Senate, not the House of Representatives, that would make the determination if a nation was to be sanctioned. The leadership of that country must take the first step; they would have to petition the Senate for review. If the Senate agreed and accepted the nation as a sanctioned territory, the House would have to accept the issue. The Prime Minister would assist with the appropriate resources and work collaterally with the foreign assembly. Historically the Senate has been more active in foreign affairs; this is designed accordingly. If the sanctioned territory wished to move beyond that status to commonwealth status, that would be a different matter and would require the vote of both Houses of Congress.

This issue has nothing to do with meddling or even attempting to manage their affairs. Our experience with democracy will not be the same as others, and each nation will need to find its own way. The issue is more a matter of making sure no one else meddles in the affairs of those attempting to establish their own democratic government. There are risks in having a government by the people, and if the United States can assist in such systems, we should help.

Article 70. Amendments

All Constitutions are a product of the human mind. It is impossible for one person or one group of people to consider all the hazards and problems that can result from any one document. People change, behaviors change, and societies change. Systems are essential within a Constitution that allow for the adjustment that will assuredly occur. The system that has been proposed for amending the Constitution is within range of the current structure.

The United States Constitution has twenty-seven amendments. Actually the first ten represent the Bill of Rights, which could be considered as part of the initial ratification process. While a few represent an appeal of existing amendments or articles; most of them are but fine-tuning of the document. All the major political parties in the United States have advocated various Constitutional amendments. Many political organizations are set up purely as lobbying groups to promote specific amendments. Regardless whether a new Constitution is enacted or we maintain the current one, amendments will continue to be offered and debated. It is part of a Constitutional government.

In this proposed Constitution is the idea that an amendment must be ratified by the states within seven years. Most of the contemporary amendments that have been sent to the states for ratification have included this provision. The scope is to include it in the Constitution so that this part of the process becomes automatic. The states will have seven years to validate an amendment or it dies.

Article 71. Constitutional Conventions

More than one way is needed to amend the Constitution. Situations or circumstances may arise that require an adjustment or change in the Constitution at a time when Congress is unable or unwilling to address the issue. If Congress is unable to rectify the situation, the states or the people may have to step forward. A system needs to be in place that allows the states to demand redress, change, or correction of the document outside the framework of Congress.

There is always the possibility that Congress itself may become the miscreant. Imagine a scenario where the members of the House of Representatives and the Senate were unable to balance the budget. In turn, they ignored the rules and Articles of the Constitution presently in place. The states would then be responsible to address the issue. They may be forced to call a Constitutional Convention to remedy such abuses. As with all organizations, unwritten rules go along with every assemblage or body. The organization becomes a fraternity. As a group there is loyalty to that body. Individuals begin to work toward the interest of that organization, which may not be in the best interest of the nation as a whole. The states need the power to call a Convention as a balance to the process of government. It represents one more of the checks and balances that help keep government responsive to the people.

While one issue might force the states to call for a Constitutional Convention, it should not be limited only by that one item. If the states are going through the trouble of organizing a convention, no limits should be placed on what can be discussed. A Constitutional Convention needs an open forum with procedural rules set up accordingly.

Article 72. Ratification of the Constitution

When the nation's founders had completed the American Constitution, they submitted it to the states for ratification. There was a great debate. Throughout the country newspapers printed articles and opinions. The American Constitution may have been written in Philadelphia by fifty-five people, but it was conceived in the debate that followed. Mostly the elites of society determined the new Constitution. They helped draft the document, they demanded a Bill of Rights, and they formed the state conventions or were part of the state legislatures. While the discussion was animated, and everyone had an opinion, the people never voted on the document. The American Constitution is seen as the premier monument to government by the people, but the people had no direct say. It was the states that ratified the document.

A Constitution is too important to be placed purely in the hands of the politicians; the people themselves need to ratify the Constitution. It is unjust and improper that others settle the issue. A Constitution needs to be placed before the people and each person needs to be given an opportunity to cast a vote.

During the Revolutionary period most of the colonies began to develop state

Constitutions. All had different views of what was the best democratic model. To its credit, Massachusetts did one of the best jobs. They had elected delegates to a constitutional convention. They drafted a written constitution and submitted it to the people for ratification. It is impossible to formulate a more basic and fundamental process. If sovereignty rests with the people, only they can approve the nature of their social compact. Constitutions are important. It is a statement of who we are as a people. In time we will have to explain to our grandchildren how we voted and why. They will learn about the ratification process, their teachers will tell them about the time when a new constitution was drafted. We will try to explain to our children what the event meant to us and the kinds of conversations that were held around the kitchen table. Regardless how we viewed the process and regardless how we voted, we need to be able to say, "Oh yes, I voted that day."

Article 73. Abatement

The greatest gift we can give future generations is an opportunity to review the character of their government.

Part Six: An Overview

Chapter 34

Items Not Included in the Proposed Constitution

There are five concepts found in the United States Constitution that are not included in this Proposed Constitution. They are executive veto power, succession to the executive office, listing of federal powers, State of the Union address, and impeachment of the chief executive. Either these are not needed or they are irrelevant because the Proposed Constitution advocates the parliamentary system used in most other democratic societies.

Veto power. An example would be the veto power of the Executive office. The Prime Minister would not need veto power because that office will have influence and direction over the legislative process. The parliamentary system requires leadership on the part of the chief executive, but not necessarily procedural or implementation control. While the Prime Minister is still responsible, the Cabinet will in fact be administrative in nature. In this proposed Constitution if there is a veto power it rests with the Senate.

Succession to the executive office. Similarly, nothing in the proposed Constitution bears on the succession to the Executive office. The American Constitution has spent considerable time reviewing and discussing changes in leadership. This is true not only for succession of standing Presidents, but also the election process. For the Parliamentary system the process is far less complex and the listing of possible combinations is no longer needed. Succession has been a difficult issue within the American Constitution. It appears in a collection of different forms. Everything from when the Vice-President can become President to how a standing President can be removed from office. For all practical purposes the Parliamentary system corrects all of these issues.

Federal powers. The American Constitution also attempted to be exact in the listing of Federal powers, detailing these in Article I, Section 8. This very deliberate act on the part of the nation's founders reflected the view of many that the states held separate sovereignty. An argument can be made that the United States was a Confederation at the time the Constitution was drafted. Once the

Articles of Confederation were in place, the sovereignty of the nation actually rested with the states as the following excerpt from these Articles states:

> Each state retains its sovereignty, freedom, and independence and every Power, Jurisdiction, and Right, which is not by this Confederation expressly delegated to the United States, in Congress assembled.

Under the Articles of Confederation, few rights were given to the national government. When the nation's founders wrote the Constitution they knew that if the states were to pass the document they would have to be specific in outlining Federal power—and they were. Eighteen rights of the Federal government are listed in Article 1, Section 8. The original idea was that all items not listed were still under state control. The problem of course is that two hundred years later we have become a true Federalist state. The listing of individual Federal rights is nonsensical at this time in our history because the central government transcends the rights of the states.

State of the Union Address. The United States Constitution declares that the duty of the President is to report to Congress about the state of the government (Article II, Section 3):

> [The President] shall, from time to time, give to the Congress information of the state of the Union, and recommend to their consideration such measures as he shall judge necessary and expedient.

Without being overly critical of the State of the Union Address it has become little more then political rhetoric. Presidents use the opportunity to paint broad pictures of their administration. Goals that are defined are done so in the largest dimensions with little substance. If the executive office wishes to report on the State of the Union, nothing within the proposed Constitution would disallow such actions, but neither are they required.

Impeachment. An issue that becomes less of a factor with a parliamentary system is the need to impeach the chief executive. The procedure for impeachment never was very clear; the Constitution lists only "treason, bribery, or other high crimes and misdemeanors." Since some confusion remains over exactly what these represent, it is a matter of some interpretation. Under the parliamentary system this becomes less of a factor. As soon as there is a hint of wrongdoing, the political party will discharge the Prime Minister and the courts will be able to work through the issue without the added political baggage. Most political parties recognize that if the chief executives are heavily invested in defending themselves against criminal charges of any kind, this will detract not only from the work that needs to be done in government, but will also reflect back on the party. In these cases the party will remove the person long before an impeachment trial could be completed. Such a prosecution within the government is equally unlikely because the majority party appoints the Prime Minister and a majority would be needed to impeach. An article outlining an impeachment process for the executive office is simply not needed in a parliamentary system.

Chapter 35

Is a New American Constitution Needed?

The problem that the American Constitution faces is not one of utility or practice. It has a sense of adequacy. Each day throughout the United States parts of the American Constitution touch every community and the lives of all the members of our society. The Constitution has influence and application to scores of interactions. A person cannot be a citizen of this country and be exempt from its puissance. It is found in how institutions function among one another, how contracts are developed, the way laws are passed, the use of authority, and the protection of our rights. It is a thread that runs through society and a defining force of our democracy. The American Constitution is the supreme document of the land and the most powerful tool that a free people possess. The problem is that after two centuries the American Constitution is outdated.

Not an eternal document. This work is a rejection of the idea that the American Constitution is eternal. Others may argue that the Constitution is a living document, one with the potential to evolve and grow, to change and adapt to new situations and environments. In part this is true. Systems are in place to incorporate new ideas and programs into the United States Constitution, this is a laborious process and one rarely used. By far the majority of time when the Constitution changes it is through interpretation by the court system. Issues that were unimaginable to the nation's founders become renderings of the court. As human imagination, technology, and social topics evolve so does our interpretation of these issues. This is not inherently wrong or evil. One of the purposes of the court system is to review issues presented to them and to address questions of change. Over extended periods of time a body of legal renderings are created. The problem is that it is not the Constitution that is being interpreted. What is being interpreted is the interpretations. There is a layering effect. Obsolete parts of the Constitution take on a different frock and move the nation in ways unintended by the original design. The issue becomes little more than Common Law.

Common misunderstandings. Scores of ideas and concepts that the general population believes to be explicitly part of the United States Constitution in reality are not. The courts over the years have declared that these concepts have emerged from the document. A partial list would include concepts such as the following:

1. A fair trial	2. Beyond reasonable doubt
3. Executive agreement	4. Spending powers
5. Cross-examination	6. War powers
7. Separation of Church and State	8. Exigent circumstance
9. Interstate commerce	10. Public purpose
11. Strict scrutiny	12. Separate but equal
13. Right to privacy	14. Presumption of innocence
15. Discrete and insular minorities	16. Liberty of contract
17. Right to silence	18. Equal justice
19. Right to travel	20. Fair return
21. Community standards	22. Police powers
23. Exclusionary rule	24. Right against self-incrimination

The court has declared numerous concepts as part of the Constitution that in reality are not written therein. This is not to say that a new Constitution would be immune from such a process, but there would be an opportunity to clarify many of these issues.

Dated, ignored, ambiguous, irrelevant parts. The point is that time does take a toll on all living things as well as human-made objects. There is such a notion as *Conceptual Decay.* Laws or articles of individual rights that made sense two hundred years ago become dated or ignored. A constitution is like no other document, it needs to be a clear, precise link between the people and their government. The rights and responsibilities of both parties must be explicitly outlined. They need to be written in such a way that even the youngest of our society can read and understand their meaning. A constitution represents the fundamental principles of a society and its government. It is not something that is implied or suggested. A Constitution is basic and axiomatic.

The problem that the American people face is that our Constitution has become in part ambiguous or in some cases no longer pertinent. Articles and clauses are found within this document that no longer apply to our society. They were founded on an eighteenth century bias or are clearly vague. In some cases they are no longer being followed. At times in our history the Constitution has simply been ignored in favor of a new program or process of government—and this was done for no other reason than expediency.

The issue may return to the concept of an inherent abstraction. The real question may not be if we are to keep the current Constitution or advance a new one. The question may really lie between whether we will have a new Constitution or an uncodified one.

Chapter 36

Is a New Constitution Realistic?

This book is by no means the first work that has outlined a need for a new American Constitution. A few individuals have actually taken the time to write a new Constitution, while others have only voiced an opinion. Of the scholars, writers, jurists, academicians, and journalists who ponder such topics, no one group or profession seems more critical of the current document than another. Each offers a slightly different view. Anyone who has ever advocated the incorporation of a new amendment to the Constitution has recognized that some level of adjustment is needed. Even so, there is a difference between drafting a new Constitution and simply revising the old one. The real question though is whether to do so is realistic. Is such a process even possible?

The argument for a new Constitution. The problem falls into two categories. The first is how strong an argument can be made for a new Constitution, and the second asks whether there is enough political will to move forward on such a project. The former is far easier than the latter. The United States Constitution has many flaws and has been weathered. Logically it is possible to make a strong argument that the document needs to be revised and modernized. The issue of political will is far more vexing.

Voices echo from the past. Many people speak to us from the past. They have advocated periodic alteration in our social contract. The first and foremost was Thomas Jefferson:

> "Some men look at constitutions with sanctimonious reverence, and deem them like the arc of the covenant, too sacred to be touched. They ascribe to the men of the preceding age a wisdom more than human, and suppose what they did to be beyond amendment. I knew that age well; I belonged to it, and labored with it. It deserved well of its country. It was very like the present, but without the experience of the present; and forty years of experience in government is worth a century of book-reading; and

this they would say themselves, were they to rise from the dead."[1]

Jefferson did believe that a Constitution needed to be current. He even supported changing the Constitution every generation. It becomes a matter of defining our responsibility to the past. Is old always better? Must we keep systems in place only because that is the way they were done in the past? In each era of American history, some have felt that a new Constitution was needed.

Nevertheless there is a difference between believing that a new Constitution is needed and referencing this view with the political reality of the nation. At some time the question has to be asked if any of this is realistic. What are the chances that the United States would adopt a new Constitution? A collection of ideas float about, many of which are disconnected. The chances of our political leaders within the United States stepping forward and conceding the need for a new social contract are small indeed. Change is infested with uncertainty. Regardless of what a document looks like at its completion, regardless how sincere the drafters may be or how in tune to detail, change will still involve unknowns. While there may be many successes and conditions that move democracy forward, some deficiencies are bound to surface as well. The single most important goal for the nation's founders was to enhance and maintain the Union. Despite everything else, the American Constitution was able to achieve that central purpose and has done it well. Political integration is very much a part of the American psyche, but seeds of disunion were also found with the Constitution. This issue of union proved to be the document's greatest success. It is connected to one of the most horrid of all events in our history, the American Civil War. This issue was both a success and a failure. Change represents this same type of risk. For our political leaders to acknowledge the need and to actively work toward such a goal would be beyond their nature. The easiest path is the one well traveled.

Changing rules changes players. While the old adage "Change some of the rules and you change some of the players" may seem nonsensical, in reality it is true. Many, perhaps most, of the politicians within the Federal government would not be eager to see a new Constitution drafted. If they had been critical of the process and the new document proved to be a major achievement, they would find themselves on the wrong side of the proceedings. If they agreed that time had come to address the issue and reform proved to be misconceived, again, they would be on the wrong side of the question. Changing a Constitution represents many intangibles. For politicians used to orchestrating events and situations this would be a nightmare. Outcomes could not be controlled and many leaders of our current system of government would not survive politically.

Power. There is also the issue of power. This is a concern. Individuals in political office hold considerable power. It is found in the laws they make, the influence they have, the people they know, and the budgets they manage. They manipulate a vast network of supporters and staff. Their power can be magnified by the skill they possess in moving these forces and surviving within this medium. Power taints the psyche and changes the sense of self. It can be as addictive as any drug and as alluring as any mistress. Persons who hold sway over the lives of others are altered by the process. They are forever changed, and to give up that power, even a small part of it, is as difficult as jumping into the center of the sun.

Democracies are robust and stalwart political bodies. They develop an inner strength not found in any other form of government, but as a rule they are more reactionary than proactive bodies. Even when something is broken, fixing it may be a matter of considerable compromise. The end result can look like a patchwork of procedures, policies, and systems with a complexity far greater than what is really needed. Fundamental change is not apt to come from the system itself. Those operating from within the existing political parties, the governmental bureaucracy, or the status quo have little motivation to support such a major modification in our government or society. People reach a comfort level. Even when a better system is available, the prospect of change can be very disconcerting.

Democracies do need an aggregation of political will to move forward on an issue. Change occurs because the masses have demanded it and the political elite simply cannot avoid the issue, or more likely, because of crisis. Some part of the total structure no longer works. The problem is inescapable and requires some level of action. Crisis brings about change in ways no other phenomenon can, and the changes that come about will be more than simply reaction to the problem. Over-reaction is always a problem. The risk is that democracy itself could be in jeopardy. The people may come to believe that the dilemma that has brought about the crisis may not be a matter of Constitutional stricture but of the system itself. The result may be far more pronounced than the establishment of just a new social contract.

The great peril is that crisis will occur. It is as automatic as a person's next breath. No matter what we do, no matter how we function, no matter how we insulate ourselves crises will arise. They represent one of the conspirators to life and the test of our true character can be found in how well we deal with these crises. The fact is that there will be Constitutional crises. They will happen regardless of whether or not we adopt a new Constitution. The question is how we can best divert such urgencies. Is it better to address the inaccuracies in the Constitution during a time of stability, or do we wait until a crisis develops and there is no longer an option?

There is a difference between needing to draft a new social contract, or even having a desire to work on such a project, to the position that it is now essential. When a Constitutional crisis occurs there will be no choice; the issue will have to be resolved. Time may not permit the luxury of debate or reflection, only action. A crisis will adjust, change, and correct just the immediate issue. It will leave a scar. In fact the American Constitution was born out of crisis and every crisis in the two centuries of our history has pockmarked the document. In the end the Constitution will be changed, and more than likely it will be a point of enormous exigency.

The question is not whether the United States Constitution will ever be replaced, but more a matter of when. If a person agrees that fifty years or a hundred years or even a thousand into the future we will have a new Constitution, then what is actually being discussed is degree. If we do not act then it becomes something we pass on to our children and grandchildren to accomplish. The only criticism that can be leveled at persons who advocate change in the Constitution is that they are ahead of their time. In the end the issue may not be whether it is realistic, but whether we have reached that time when the process must be instituted.

Ways to create a new Constitution. A new Constitution could be created in scores of ways. Two such methods exist within the current document. The states could call for a Constitutional Convention, a process not dissimilar to the process that occurred in 1787. Delegates would be elected from the individual state assemblages and sent to an agreed-upon location. Rules of order would be determined and the process of piecing together a new Constitution could occur. Upon completion the document would be sent to the state legislatures or state conventions for ratification. The people would interact with their state-elected officials supporting the new document or demanding the old Constitution be kept intact. The broadcast media and newspapers would run stories of the new document, interviewing those that embraced the new Constitution and balancing it with those who did not. Editorials would appear, debates would transpire, and each citizen would be forced to compare the new with the old.

Such a process must be viewed as the most logical of any approach to the creation of a new Constitution. After all it is how most Constitutions come into existence and is the general method by which the United States Constitution was generated. It is also the method allowed within the current document. Like the United States Constitution it would have to be produced in an environment of secrecy. There would be blind alleys, points of compromise, miscues, arguments, and simple miscommunication between parties. Each deliberation could not be reported to the press. There would be a misrepresentation of the process to the public. The process of creating a Constitution should be one that occurs on the floor of the convention and not the airwaves of the country. The document would need to be viewed in its entirety rather than piecemeal. Certainly that level of secrecy would be extremely difficult to maintain. If each state supplied only three delegates, that would mean 150 members to the convention, in addition to staff and security. Even if one person rebelled against the direction of the convention and quit, the information the person passed on to the public could harm the process. People would obtain a misconception of what is being produced.

For example in an assembly with a base of 150 delegates, some of those would champion a private agenda. Likewise a collection of individuals might unite in attempting to move the convention in a given direction. They would be totally focused on one topic with everything else revolving around that one single item. It is possible to envision such a scenario where the convention would come to a halt because of the disruptive nature of those with a single issue. To some degree this is what happened over the issue of slavery at the Constitutional Convention in 1787. This runs to the heart of the risk in changing a Constitution. There would be those who would accept the total inequities of the status quo rather than endanger even a part of their own doctrine on a social issue.

Constitutional change by amendment. A second method within the

United States Constitution that could be used to change the document is the amendment process. Generally this process is seen as a surgical method to correct peculiar problems in the document, either some point of social justice or improvement in flexibility. The entire document could be rewritten by the United States Congress in special committee and submitted to the states for ratification. It would represent one colossal amendment. The advantage is that security could be better managed. The same subterfuge used by the nation's founders could be used. The purpose of the committee would be to evaluate the United States Constitution and to determine if any structural changes were needed. In the interim a new Constitution would be drafted. Like our current social contract some would be disgruntled over the use of guile or the lack of a mandate. They would complain bitterly and declare the process illegitimate, but this new Constitution would be sent to the states. They would have an opportunity to appraise the work and determine if it met the needs of the nation.

Problems with the amendment method. The negative with this process in changing the Constitution deals with disposition of the parties themselves. The United States Congress is an association with interests and opinions specific to this group. It would be unimaginable for such a body to eliminate or reduce their own privileges. While in the end such a document created by this conference would mirror the views of the ruling elites, this should not be seen as fundamentally wrong. The United States Constitution was created in this fashion, but it would represent a form of criticism that would be leveled at the new document.

Another problem arises with changing the Constitution by amendment. The system that the nation's founders set up to amend the American Constitution is actually a very laborious, obtuse process. It is not designed to be easy. Nearly total agreement is needed to get anything passed. While twenty-seven amendments have been ratified to the Constitution each came about by way of almost complete congruity of thought. To amend the United States Constitution requires a two-thirds vote of both Houses of Congress. It is then sent to the states where those legislatures must also pass the amendment by two-thirds vote, and this must be done by three-fourths of all the states. This means that even when the states get an amendment, if twenty-four out of ninety-nine legislative bodies are unable to pass the measure, it dies.

The chief problem with either one of these methods of initiating a new Constitution is that it eliminates two of the most important players from the process, the people and the Supreme Court. If a Constitution is the ultimate law of the land, and the Supreme Court is invested with the responsibility of interpreting and maintaining the homogeneity of the document, then it seems only proper that they should be involved in the process of drafting a new Constitution. Besides, what group knows more about the United States Constitution than the Supreme Court? They work with Constitutional law everyday. They are as aware of both the shortfalls of the current document, as well as the marvels of the Constitution, as anyone in government or our society. To exclude such a group seems incomprehensible.

An argument could be made that it is the responsibility of the Supreme Court to move forward with such a project. To their detraction, it is surprising that members of the Supreme Court have not stepped forward with greater admonishment for our current social contract. The clear duty of the Court would seem to be to sound a warning when our current Constitution has become unmanageable or when it is time to move democracy to a higher plane. In any case, a requirement that the Supreme Court make up the core of any body assigned the task of drafting a new Constitution would make sense.

The other group that at some point or at some level needs to be involved is the people. When the United States Constitution was drafted and came into existence the entire process occurred without one vote, or prerequisite from the masses. In the end they had only marginal say. Ideally, if a new Constitution was to be created it should flow from the people. If a system could be devised where one gigantic convention could be held, each citizen with one vote, then that would be the perfect situation. Of course that is the most unrealistic of all.

How the process could occur. There is a way in which such a process could occur. It would be complex and would require considerable time and furthermore would involve the people. While Constitutions necessitate substantial amounts of thought, they are not beyond the ability of the average person or group to write. Many different associations or organizations could compose a Constitution. When the United States Constitution was drafted, not only were whole groups of people excluded from the process, but many from cultural, racial, social, and gender groups were suppressed outright. One wonders what a Constitution would look like that emerged from these political, civil, and cultural groups today. A procedure could be developed in which an organization or governmental agency would accept the responsibility of being a clearing-house for various Constitutions. Political parties, social organizations, civil groups, fellowships, and foundations, even educational and religious institutions could write a new Constitution and submit it to this agency. They in turn would compare all these documents and group them. Some would be rejected as unworkable or undemocratic, others may lose various articles or sections, but five general categories could be created. The five new Constitutions, along with our current document, could be submitted for a plebiscite. The people would vote. The top two Constitutions, and our present one, would be offered for a second set of balloting. At the conclusion of this process a Constitution would emerge. It may be the one we have now or something more innovative, but in any case it would be an extraordinary process. The people for the first time in recorded history would determine the nature of their government and the attributes of their social contract.

Such a system would take years to work through. At times it would be belligerent, undignified, and self-seeking. There would be others times that it would not seem to be worth the effort, and there would be those that see the process as a point of great frustration rather than an item of self discovery. Yet, in the end we would learn and we would find out what is important to us. The process would educate us about our government and our civilization. As a people we would grow from the experience.

There would be those strict constructionists who would argue that any form of changing the United States Constitution, which did not include Congress or the states, would be illegal. Such a position is only partly true, but changing a Constitution is like no other activity. While some liberties must be allowed, what is most important is that the process is orderly and fair. When the Founding Fathers wrote the American Constitution they were clearly outside of the framework of the Articles of Confederation. In some ways that issue of legitimacy was disregarded and they moved forward. Such a project would require some freedom of action. Even if a new Constitution was drafted by the Supreme Court, and it could be argued they would be a knowledgeable and a competent body to do such a task, that in itself would be outside of the normal structure of changing the document.

When discussing the issue of how realistic any of these possibilities may be there are two stories that must be told. The first deals with the Dorr Rebellion. During or shortly after the War of Independence most of the original thirteen states developed new Constitutions. It was a process that represented the changing times and the new positions in which the former colonies found themselves. As much as any procedure it allowed the states to address the concept of Liberty. This was not true with Rhode Island, they continued to function under the royal charter that had been issued by Charles II in 1663. Many efforts at reform were attempted, all of which proved to be unsuccessful. It led to ever increasing frustration on the part of the Progressives in that state. Those in power in Rhode Island were well entrenched and few democratic ideas existed within the royal charter.

In October of 1841, Thomas W. Dorr, a reformer in the state called for a Constitutional Convention. The goal was to draft a new Constitution for the State of Rhode Island and by the Spring of the next year that process was completed. The state officials declared that Dorr's actions were illegal and extraneous. He ignored this assertion and established a parallel state government. By this time considerable national attention was being focused on the situation. Dorr, believing he represented the legitimate state government, attempted to seize the arsenal at Providence. The effort failed and he was arrested. The Federal government refused to support the actions of Dorr and the rebellion collapsed. The State of Rhode Island tried him for treason and sentenced him to life in prison. The rebellion did have a positive impact though; within two years democratic reforms were instituted and a new Constitution was drafted for the State.[2]

The other story deals with Vatican II. The Roman Catholic Church over hundreds of years, and even thousands, had developed systems of stewardship and doctrine that were badly in need of review and restoration. Many individuals were skeptical that fundamental change could occur within the church, the task was too large, and there also was a vested interest in the status quo. Still others were critical of such a process. They saw it as representing heresy and a divergence from established doctrine.

The first effort at reform occurred in 1869. A Vatican Council was called, church leaders and scholars attended. A number of topics were covered. During this period Council papers were submitted that helped clarify issues related to papal infallibility, faith and reason, and supernatural revelation. In the end Vatican I was forced to disband prematurely and most issues were left unresolved.

In 1962 the Catholic church made a second effort at reform under the title of Vatican II. The goal was to review church dogma, discipline, and the scope of canonical matters. The Bishops and their mentors reviewed and discussed these issues for years. They neither condemned nor defined a new level of dogma, but what emerged was a cultivation of church doctrine. A new commission was established. Vatican II generated 16 canonical documents and four constitutions. What occurred was a review of social, cultural, political, and economic problems that occur within the framework of Christian teachings. As a result of Vatican II changes in administration of the church, activities of the priests, renewal of religious life, education, moral functions, religious freedom, and the view toward non-Christian religions changed. The Roman Catholic Church is a considerably different entity and institution than it was before the council met.[3]

Notwithstanding the above discussion, the real question remains, is any of it practical? Is there enough political leadership to encourage Constitutional change because it is needed, is there enough appeal in Constitutional reform for the people to react? Without a Constitutional crisis it is doubtful. It would require participation in the political process far in excess of what has been shown in the past by the electorate. Even so, there is one hope. One concept remains, or maybe more correctly, a subtle challenge. It must be remembered that great nations do great things.

Part Seven: Appendix

The Constitution of the United States of America

Preamble

We the people of the United States, in order to form a more perfect union, establish justice, insure domestic tranquility, provide for the common defense, promote the general welfare, and secure the blessings of liberty to ourselves and our posterity, do ordain and establish this Constitution for the United States of America.

Article I

Section 1.

All legislative powers herein granted shall be vested in a Congress of the United States, which shall consist of a Senate and House of Representatives.

Section 2.

The House of Representatives shall be composed of members chosen every second year by the people of the several states, and the electors in each state shall have the qualifications requisite for electors of the most numerous branch of the state legislature.

No person shall be a Representative who shall not have attained to the age of twenty five years, and been seven years a citizen of the United States, and who shall not, when elected, be an inhabitant of that state in which he shall be chosen.

Representatives and direct taxes shall be apportioned among the several states which may be included within this union, according to their respective numbers, which shall be determined by adding to the whole number of free persons, including those bound to service for a term of years, and excluding Indians not taxed, three fifths of all other persons. The actual enumeration shall be made within three years after the first meeting of the Congress of the United States, and within every subsequent term of ten years, in such manner as they shall by law direct. The number of Representatives shall not exceed one for every thirty thousand, but each state shall have at least one Representative; and until such enumeration shall be made, the state of New Hampshire shall be entitled to choose three, Massachusetts eight, Rhode Island and Providence Plantations one, Connecticut five, New York six, New Jersey four, Pennsylvania eight, Delaware one, Maryland six, Virginia ten, North Carolina five, South Carolina five, and Georgia three.

When vacancies happen in the Representation from any state, the executive authority hereof shall issue writs of election to fill such vacancies.

The House of Representatives shall choose their speaker and other officers; and shall have the sole power of impeachment.

Section 3.

The Senate of the United States shall be composed of two Senators from each state, chosen by the legislature thereof, for six years; and each Senator shall have one vote.

Immediately after they shall be assembled in consequence of the first election, they shall be divided as equally as may be into three classes. The seats of the Senators of the first class shall be vacated at the expiration of the second year, of the second class at the expiration of the fourth year, and the third class at the expiration of the sixth year, so that one third may be chosen every second year; and if vacancies happen by resignation, or otherwise, during the recess of the legislature of any state, the executive thereof may make temporary appointments until the next meeting of the legislature, which shall then fill such vacancies.

No person shall be a Senator who shall not have attained to the age of thirty years, and been nine years a citizen of the United States and who shall not, when elected, be an inhabitant of that state for which he shall be chosen.

The Vice President of the United States shall be President of the Senate, but shall have no vote, unless they be equally divided.

The Senate shall choose their other officers, and also a President pro tempore, in the absence of the Vice President, or when he shall exercise the office of President of the United States.

The Senate shall have the sole power to try all impeachments. When sitting for that purpose, they shall be on oath or affirmation. When the President of the United States is tried, the Chief Justice shall preside: And no person shall be convicted without the concurrence of two thirds of the members present.

Judgment in cases of impeachment shall not extend further than to removal from office, and disqualification to hold and enjoy any office of honor, trust or profit under the United States: but the party convicted shall nevertheless be liable and subject to indictment, trial, judgment and punishment, according to law.

Section 4.

The times, place and manner of holding elections for Senators and Representatives, shall be prescribed in each state by the legislature thereof; but the Congress may at any time by law make or alter such regulations, except as to the places of choosing Senators.

The Congress shall assemble at least once in every year, and such meeting shall be on the first Monday in December, unless they shall by law appoint a different day.

Section 5.

Each House shall be the judge of the elections, returns, and qualifications of its own members, and a majority of each shall constitute a quorum to do business; but a smaller number may adjourn from day to day, and may be authorized to compel the attendance of absent members, in such manner, and under such penalties as each House may provide.

Each House shall keep a journal of its proceedings, and from time to time publish the same, excepting such parts as may in their judgment require secrecy; and the yeas and nays of the members of either House on any question shall, at the desire of one fifth of those present, be entered on the journal.

Neither House, during the session of Congress, shall without the consent of the other, adjourn for more than three days, nor to any other place than that in which the two Houses shall be sitting.

Section 6.

The Senators and Representatives shall receive a compensation for their services, to be ascertained by law, and paid out of the treasury of the United States. They shall in all cases, except treason, felony and breach of the peace, be privileged from arrest during their attendance at the session of their respective Houses, and in going to and returning from the same; and for any speech or debate in either House, they shall not be questioned in any other places.

No Senator or Representative shall, during the time for which he was elected, be appointed to any civil office under the authority of the United States, which shall have been created, or the emoluments whereof shall have been increased during such times; and no person holding any office under the United

States, shall be a member of either House during his continuance in office.

Section 7.

All bills for raising revenue shall originate in the House of Representatives; but the Senate may propose or concur with amendments as on other Bills.

Every bill which shall have passed the House of Representatives and the Senate, shall before it become a law, be presented to the President of the United States; if he approve he shall sign it, but if not he shall return it, with his objections to that House in which it shall have originated, who shall enter the objections at large on their journal, and proceed to reconsider it. If after such reconsideration two thirds of that House shall agree to pass the bill, it shall be sent, together with the objections, to the other House, by which it shall likewise be reconsidered, and if approved by two thirds of that House, it shall become a law. But in all such cases the votes of both Houses shall be determined by yeas and nays, and the names of the persons voting for and against the bill shall be entered on the journal of each House respectively. If any bill shall not be returned by the President within ten days (Sundays excepted) after it shall have been presented to him, the same shall be a law, in like manner as if the had signed it, unless the Congress by their adjournment prevents its return, in which case it shall not be a law.

Every order, resolution, or vote to which the concurrence of the Senate and House of Representatives may be necessary (except on a question of adjournment) shall be presented to the President of the United States; and before the same shall take effect, shall be approved by him, or being disapproved by him, shall be repassed by two thirds of the Senate and House of Representatives, according to the rules and limitations prescribed n the case of a bill.

Section 8.

The Congress shall have power to lay and collect taxes, duties, imposts and excises, to pay the debts and provide for the common defense and general welfare of the United States; but all duties, imposts and excises shall be uniform throughout the United States.

To borrow money on the credit of the United States;

To regulate commerce with foreign nations, and among the several states, and with the Indian tribes;

To establish a uniform rule of naturalization, and uniform laws on the subject of bankruptcies throughout the United States;

To coin money, regulate the value thereof, and of foreign coin, and fix the standard of weights and measures;

To provide for the punishment of counterfeiting the securities and current coin of the United States;

To establish post offices and post roads;

To promote the progress of science and useful arts, by securing for limited times to authors and inventors the exclusive right to their respective writings and discoveries;

To constitute tribunals inferior to the Supreme Court;

To define and punish piracies and felonies committed on the high seas, and offenses against the law of nations;

To declare war, grant letters of marque and reprisal, and make rules concerning captures on land and water;

To raise and support armies, but no appropriation of money to that use shall be for a longer term than two years;

To provide and maintain a navy;

To make rules for the government and regulation of the land and naval forces;

To provide for calling forth the militia to execute the laws of the Union, suppress insurrections and repel invasions;

To provide for organizing, arming, and disciplining, the militia, and for governing such part of them as may be employed in the service of the United States, reserving to the states respectively, the appointment of the officers, and the authority of training the militia according to the discipline prescribed by Congress;

To exercise exclusive legislation in all cases whatsoever, over such district (not exceeding ten miles square) as may, by cession of particular states, and the acceptance of Congress, become the seat of the government of the United States, and to exercise like authority over all places purchased by the consent of the legislature of the state in which the same shall be, for the erection of forts, magazines, arsenals, dockyards, and other needful buildings; And

To make all laws which shall be necessary and proper for carrying into execution the foregoing powers, and all other powers vested by this Constitution in the government of the United States, or in any department of officer thereof.

Section 9.

The migration or importation of such persons as any of the states now existing shall think proper to admit, shall not be prohibited by the Congress prior to the year one thousand eight hundred and eight, but a tax or duty may be imposed on such importation, not exceeding ten dollars for each person.

The privilege of the writ of habeas corpus shall not be suspended, unless when in cases of rebellion or invasion the public safety may require it.

No bill of attainder or ex post facto Law shall be passed.

No capitation, or other direct, tax shall be laid, unless in proportion to the census or enumeration herein before directed to be taken.

No tax or duty shall be laid on articles exported from any state. No preference shall be given by any regulation of commerce or revenue to the ports or one state over those of another: nor shall vessels bound to, or from, one state, be obliged to enter, clear or pay duties in another.

No money shall be drawn from the treasury, but in consequence of appropriations made by law; and a regular statement and account of receipts and expenditures of all public money shall be published from time to time.

No title of nobility shall be granted by the United States: and no person holding any office of profit or trust under them shall, without the consent of the Congress, accept of any present, emolument, office, or title, of any kind whatever, from any king, prince, or foreign state.

Section 10.

No state shall enter into any treaty, alliance, or confederation; grant letters of marque and reprisal; coin money; emit bills of credit; make anything but gold and silver coin a tender in payment of debts; pass any bill of attainder, ex post facto law, or law impairing the obligation of contracts, or grant any title of nobility.

No state shall, without the consent of the Congress, lay any imposts or duties on imports or exports, except what may be absolutely necessary for executing its inspection laws: and the net produce of all duties and imposts, laid by any state on imports and exports, shall be for the use of the Treasury of the United States; and all such laws shall be subject to the revision and control of the Congress.

No state shall without the consent of Congress, lay any duty of tonnage, keep troops, or ships of war in time of peace, enter into any agreement or compact with another state, or with a foreign power, or engage in war, unless actually invaded, or in such imminent danger as will not admit of delay.

Article II
Section 1.

The executive power shall be vested in a President of the United States of America. He shall hold his office during the term of four years, and, together with the Vice President, chosen for the same term, be elected, as follows:

Each state shall appoint, in such manner as the Legislature thereof may direct, a number of electors, equal to the whole number of Senators and Representatives to which the State may be entitled in the Congress: but no Senator or Representative, or person holding an office of trust or profit under the United States, shall be appointed an elector. The electors shall meet in their respective states, and vote by ballot for two persons, of whom one at least shall not be an inhabitant of the same state with themselves. And they shall make a list of all the persons voted for, and of the number of votes for each; which list they shall sign and certify, and transmit sealed to the seat of the government of the United States, directed to the President of the Senate. The President of the Senate shall, in the presence of the Senate and House of Representatives, open all the certificates, and the votes shall then be counted. The person having the greatest number of votes shall be the President, if such number be a majority of the whole number of electors appointed; and if there be more than one who have such majority, and have an equal number of votes, then the House of Representatives shall immediately choose by ballot one of them for President; and if no person have a majority, then from the five highest on the list the said House shall in like manner choose the President. But in choosing the President, the votes shall be taken by States, the representation from each state having one vote; a quorum for this purpose shall consist of a member or members form two thirds of the states, and a majority of all the states shall be necessary to a choice. In every case, after the choice of the President, the person having the greatest number of votes of the electors shall be the Vice President. But if there should remain two or more who have equal votes, the Senate shall choose from them by ballot the Vice President.

The Congress may determine the time of choosing the electors, and the day on which they shall give their votes; which day shall be the same throughout the United States.

No person except a natural born citizen, or a citizen of the United States, at the time of the adoption of this Constitution, shall be eligible to the office of President; neither shall any person be eligible to that office who shall not have attained to the age of thirty five years, and been fourteen years a resident within the United States.

In case of the removal of the President from office, or of his death, resignation, or inability to discharge the powers and duties of the said office, the same shall devolve on the Vice President, and the Congress may by law provide for the case of removal, death, resignation or inability, both of the President and Vice President, declaring what officer shall then act as President, and such officer shall act accordingly, until the disability be removed, or a President shall be elected.

The President shall, at stated times, receive for his services, a compensation, which shall neither be increased nor diminished during the period for which he shall have been elected, and he shall not receive within that period any other emolument from the United States, or any of them.

Before he enter on the execution of his office, he shall take the following oath or affirmation: "I do solemnly swear (or affirm) that I will faithfully execute the office of President of the United States, and will to the best of my ability, preserve, protect and defend the Constitution of the United States."

Section 2.

The President shall be Commander in Chief of the Army and Navy of the United States, and of the militia of the several states, when called into the actual service of the United States; he may require the opinion, in writing, of the principal officer in each of the executive departments, upon any subject relating to the duties of their respective offices, and he shall have power to grant reprieves and pardons of offenses against the United States, except in cases of impeachment.

He shall have power, by and with the advice and consent of the Senate, to make treaties, provided two thirds of the Senators present concur; and he shall nominate, and by and with the advice and consent of the Senate, shall appoint ambassadors, other public ministers and consuls, judges of the Supreme Court, and all other officers of the United States whose appointments are not herein otherwise provided for, and which shall be established by law: but the Congress may by law vest the appointment of such inferior officers, as they think proper, in the President alone, in the courts of law, or in the heads of departments.

The President shall have power to fill up all vacancies that may happen during the recess of the Senate, by granting commissions which shall expire at the end of their next session.

Section 3.

He shall from time to time give to the Congress information of the state of the Union, and recommend to their consideration such measures as he shall judge necessary and expedient; he may, on extraordinary occasions, convene both Houses, or either of them, and in case of disagreement between them, with respect to the time of adjournment, he may adjourn them to such time as he shall think proper; he shall receive ambassadors and other public ministers; he shall take care that the laws be faithfully executed, and shall commission all the officers of the United States.

Section 4.

The President, Vice President and all civil officers of the United States, shall be removed from office on impeachment for and conviction of, treason, bribery, or other high crimes and misdemeanors.

Article III

Section 1.

The judicial power of the United States, shall be vested in one Supreme Court, and in such inferior courts as the Congress may from time to time ordain and establish. The judges, both of the supreme and inferior courts, shall hold their offices during good behavior, and shall, at stated times, receive for their services, a compensation, which shall not be diminished during their continuance in office.

Section 2.

The judicial power shall extend to all cases, in law and equity, arising under this Constitution, the laws of the United States, and treaties made, or which shall be made, under their authority; to all cases affecting ambassadors, other public ministers and consuls; to all cases of admiralty and maritime jurisdiction; to controversies to which the United States shall be a party; to controversies between two or more states; between a state and citizens of another state; between citizens of different states; between citizens of the same state claiming lands under grants of different states, and between a state, or the citizens thereof, and foreign states, citizens or subjects.

In all cases affecting ambassadors, other public ministers and consuls, and those in which a state shall be party, the Supreme Court shall have original jurisdiction. In all the other cases before mentioned, the Supreme Court shall have appellate jurisdiction, both as to law and fact, with such exceptions, and under such regulations as the Congress shall make.

The trial of all crimes, except in cases of impeachment, shall be by jury; and such trial shall be held in the state where the said crimes shall have been committed; but when not committed within any state, the trial shall be at such place or places as the Congress may by law have directed.

Section 3.

Treason against the United States, shall consist only in levying war against them, or in adhering to their enemies, giving them aid and comfort. No person shall be convicted of treason unless on the testimony of two witnesses to the same overt act, or on confession in open court.

The Congress shall have power to declare the punishment of treason, but no attainder of treason shall work corruption of blood, or forfeiture except during the life of the person attainted.

Article IV

Section 1.

Full faith and credit shall be given in each state to the public acts, records, and judicial proceedings of every other state. And the Congress may be general laws prescribe the manner in which such acts, records, and proceedings shall be proved, and the effect thereof.

Section 2.

The citizens of each state shall be entitled to all privileges and immunities of citizens in the several states.

A person charged in any state with treason, felony, or other crime, who shall flee from justice, and be found in another state, shall on demand of the Executive authority of the state from which he fled, be delivered up, to be removed to the state having jurisdiction of the crime.

No person held to service or in one state, under the laws thereof, escaping into another, shall, in consequence of any law or regulation therein, be discharged from such service or labor, but shall be delivered up on claim of the party to whom such service or labor may be due.

Section 3.

New states may be admitted by the Congress into this Union; but no new states shall be formed or erected within the jurisdiction of any other state; nor any state be formed by the junction of two or more states, or parts of states, without the consent of the legislatures of the states concerned as well as of the Congress.

The Congress shall have power to dispose of and make all needful rules and regulations respecting the territory or other property belonging to the United States; and nothing in this Constitution shall be so construed as to prejudice any claims of the United States, or of any particular state.

Section 4.

The United States shall guarantee to every state in this union a republican form of government, and shall protect each of them against invasion; and on application of the legislature, or of the Executive (when the Legislature cannot be convened) against domestic violence.

Article V

The Congress, whenever two thirds of both houses shall deem it necessary, shall propose amendments to this Constitution, or, on the application of the legislatures of two thirds of the several states, shall call a convention for proposing amendments, which, in either case, shall be valid to all intents and purposes, as part of this Constitution, when ratified by the legislatures of three fourths of the several states, or by conventions in three fourths thereof, as the one or the other mode of ratification may be proposed by the Congress; provided that no amendment which may be made prior to the year one thousand eight hundred and eight shall in any manner affect the first and fourth clauses in the Ninth Section of the First Article; and that no state, without its consent, shall be deprived of its equal suffrage in the

Senate.

Article VI

All debts contracted and engagements entered into, before the adoption of this Constitution, shall be as valid against the United States under this Constitution, as under the Confederation.

This Constitution, and the laws of the United States which shall be made in pursuance thereof; and all treaties made, or which shall be made, under the authority of the United States, shall be the supreme law of the land; and the judges in every state shall be bound thereby, anything in the Constitution or laws of any State to the contrary notwithstanding.

The Senators and Representatives before mentioned, and the members of the several state legislatures, and all executive and judicial officers, both of the United States and of the several states, shall be bound by oath or affirmation, to support this Constitution, but no religious test shall ever be required as a qualification to any office or public trust under the United States.

Article VII

The ratification of the Conventions of nine states, shall be sufficient for the establishment of this Constitution between the states so ratifying the same.

Done in convention by the unanimous consent of the states present the seventeenth day of September in the year of our Lord one thousand seven hundred and eighty seven and of the independence of the United States of America the Twelfth. In witness whereof we have hereunto subscribed our names,

G. Washington - Presidt. and deputy from Virginia
New Hampshire: John Langdon, Nicholas Gilman
Massachusetts: Nathaniel Gorham, Rufus King
Connecticut: Wm: Saml. Johnson, Roger Sherman
New York: Alexander Hamilton
New Jersey: Wil. Livingston, David Brearly, Wm. Paterson, Jona. Dayton
Pennsylvania: B. Franklin, Thomas Mifflin, Robt. Morris, Geo. Clymer,

Thos. FitzSimons, Jared Ingersoll, James Wilson, Gouv Morris

Delaware: Geo. Read, Gunning Bedford Jr, John Dickinson, Richard Bassett, Jaco.
Broom

Maryland: James McHenry, Dan of St Thos. Jenifer, Danl Carroll

Virginia: John Blair, James Madison Jr.

North Carolina: Wm. Blount, Richd. Dobbs Spaight, Hu Williamson

South Carolina: J. Rutledge, Charles Cotesworth Pinckney, Charles Pinckney,
Pierce Butler

Georgia: William Few, Abr Baldwin

Attest: William Jackson, Secretary.

Amendments to the Constitution of the United States

Amendment I (1791)

Congress shall make no law respecting an establishment of religion, or prohibiting the free exercise thereof; or abridging the freedom of speech, or of the press; or the right of the people peaceably to assemble, and to petition the government for a redress of grievances.

Amendment II (1791)

A well regulated militia, being necessary to the security of a free state, the right of the people to keep and bear arms, shall not be infringed.

Amendment III (1791)

No soldier shall, in time of peace be quartered in any house, without the consent of the owner, nor in time of war, but in a manner to be prescribed by law.

Amendment IV (1791)

The right of the people to be secure in their persons, papers, houses and effects, against unreasonable searches and seizures, shall not be violated, and no warrants shall issue, but upon probable cause, supported by oath or affirmation, and particularly describing the place to be searched, and the persons or things to be seized.

Amendment V (1791)

No person shall be held to answer for a capital, or otherwise infamous crime, unless on a presentment or indictment of a Grand Jury, except in cases arising in the land or naval forces, or in the militia, when in actual service in time of war or public danger; nor shall any person be subject for the same offense to be twice put in jeopardy of life or limb; nor shall be compelled in any criminal case to be a witness against himself, nor be deprived of life, liberty, or property, without due process of law; nor shall private property be taken for public use, without just compensation.

Amendment VI (1791)

In all criminal prosecutions, the accused shall enjoy the right to a speedy and public trial, by an impartial jury of the state and district wherein the crime shall have been committed, which district shall have been previously ascertained by law, and to be informed of the nature and cause of the accusation; to be confronted with the witnesses against him; to have compulsory process for obtaining witnesses in his favor, and to have the assistance of counsel for his defense.

Amendment VII (1791)

In suits at common law, where the value in controversy shall exceed twenty dollars, the right of trial by jury shall be preserved, and no fact tried by a jury, shall be otherwise reexamined in any court of the United States, than according to the rules of the common law.

Amendment VIII (1791)

Excessive bail shall not be required, nor excessive fines imposed, nor cruel and unusual punishment inflicted.

Amendment IX (1791)

The enumeration in the Constitution, of certain rights, shall not be construed to deny or disparage others retained by the people.

Amendment X (1791)

The powers not delegated to the United States by the Constitution, nor prohibited by it to the states, are reserved to the states respectively, or to the people.

Amendment XI (1798)

The judicial power of the United States shall not be construed to extend to any suit in law or equity, commenced or prosecuted against one of the United States by citizens of another state, or by citizens or subjects of any foreign state.

Amendment XII (1804)

The electors shall meet in their respective states and vote by ballot for President and Vice-President, one of whom, at least, shall not be an inhabitant of the same state with themselves; they shall name in their ballots the person voted for as President, and in distinct ballots the person voted for a Vice-President, and they shall make distinct lists of all persons voted for as President, and of all persons voted for as Vice-President, and of the number of votes for each, which lists they shall sign and certify, and transmit sealed to the seat of the Government of the United States, directed to the President of the Senate; The President of the Senate shall, in the presence of the Senate and House of Representatives, open all the certificates and the votes shall then be counted; the person having the greatest number of votes for President, shall be the President, if such number be a majority of the whole number of Electors appointed; and if no person have such majority, then from the persons having the highest numbers not exceeding three on the list of those voted for as President, the House of Representatives shall choose immediately, by ballot, the President. But in choosing the President, the votes shall be taken by states, the representation from each state having one vote; a quorum for this purpose shall consist of a member or members from two-thirds of the states, and a majority of all the states shall be necessary to a choice. And if the House of Representatives shall not choose a President whenever the right of choice shall devolve upon them, before the fourth day of March next following, then the Vice-President shall act as President, as in the case of the death or other constitutional disability of the President. The person having the greatest number of votes as Vice-President, shall be the Vice-President, if such number be a majority of the whole number of electors appointed, and if no person have a majority, then from the two highest numbers on the list, the Senate shall choose the Vice-President; a quorum for the purpose shall consist of two-thirds of the whole number of Senators, and a majority of the whole number shall be necessary to a choice. But no person constitutionally ineligible to the office of President shall be eligible to that of Vice-President of the United States.

Amendment XIII (1865)
Section 1.

Neither slavery nor involuntary servitude, except as a punishment for crime whereof the party shall have been duly convicted, shall exist within the United States, or any place subject to their jurisdiction.

Section 2.

Congress shall have power to enforce this article by appropriate legislation.

Amendment XIV (1868)
Section 1.

All persons born or naturalized in the United States, and subject to the jurisdiction thereof, are citizens of the United States and of the state wherein they reside. No state shall make or enforce any law which shall abridge the privileges or immunities of citizens of the United States; nor shall any state deprive any person of life, liberty, or property, without due process of law; nor deny to any person within its jurisdiction the equal protection of the laws.

Section 2.

Representatives shall be apportioned among the several states according to their respective numbers, counting the whole number of persons in each state, excluding Indians not taxed. But when the right to vote at any election for the choice of Electors for President and Vice-President of the United States, Representatives in Congress, the executive and judicial officers of a state, or the members of the legislature thereof, is denied to any of the male inhabitants of such state, being twenty-one years of age, and citizens of the United States, or in any way abridged, except for participation in rebellion, or other crime, the basis of representation therein shall be reduced in the proportion which the number of such male citizens shall bear to the whole number of male citizens twenty-one years of age in such state.

Section 3.

No person shall be a Senator or Representative in Congress, or Elector of President and Vice-President, or hold any office, civil or military, under the United States, or under any state, who, having previously taken an oath, as a member of Congress, or as an officer of the United States, or as a member of any state legislature, or as an executive or judicial officer of any state, to support the Constitution of the United States, shall have engaged in insurrection or rebellion against the same, or given aid or comfort to the enemies thereof. But Congress may by a vote of two-thirds of each House, remove such disability.

Section 4.

The validity of the public debt of the United States, authorized by law, including debts incurred for payment of pensions and bounties for services in suppressing insurrection or rebellion, shall not be questioned. But neither the United States nor any state shall assume or pay any debt or obligation incurred in aid of insurrection or rebellion against the United States, or any claim for the loss or emancipation of any slave; but all such debts, obligations and claims shall be held illegal and void.

Section 5.

The Congress shall have power to enforce by appropriate legislation, the provisions of this article.

Amendment XV (1870)

Section 1.

The rights of citizens of the United States to vote shall not be denied or abridged by the United States or by any state on account of race, color, or previous condition of servitude.

Section 2.

The Congress shall have power to enforce this article by appropriate legislation.

Amendment XVI (1913)

The Congress shall have power to lay and collect taxes on incomes, from whatever source derived, without apportionment among the several states, and without regard to any census of enumeration.

Amendment XVII (1913)

The Senate of the United States shall be composed of two Senators from each state, elected by the people thereof, for six years; and each Senator shall have one vote. The electors in each state shall have the qualifications requisite for electors of the most numerous branch of the state legislatures.

When vacancies happen in the representation of any state in the Senate, the executive authority of such state shall issue writs of election to fill such vacancies: Provided, that the legislature of any state may empower the executive thereof to make temporary appointments until the people fill the vacancies by election as the legislature may direct.

This amendment shall not be so construed as to affect the election or term of any Senator chosen before it becomes valid as part of the Constitution.

Amendment XVIII (1919)
Section 1.

After one year from the ratification of this article the manufacture, sale, or transportation of intoxicating liquors within, the importation thereof into, or the exportation thereof from the United States and all territory subject to the jurisdiction thereof for beverage purposes is hereby prohibited.
Section 2.

The Congress and the several states shall have concurrent power to enforce this article by appropriate legislation.
Section 3.

The article shall be inoperative unless it shall have been ratified as an amendment to the Constitution by the legislatures of the several states, as provided in the Constitution, within seven years from the date of the submission hereof to the states by the Congress.

Amendment XIX (1920)

The right of citizens of the United States to vote shall not be denied or abridged by the United States or by any state on account of sex.

Congress shall have the power to enforce this Article by appropriate legislation.

Amendment XX (1933)
Section 1.

The terms of the President and Vice President shall end at noon on the 20th day of January, and the terms of Senators and Representatives at noon on the 3d day of January, of the years in which such terms would have ended if this article had not been ratified; and the terms of their successors shall then begin.

Section 2.

The Congress shall assemble at least once in every year, and such meeting shall begin at noon on the 3d day of January, unless they shall by law appoint a different day.

Section 3.

If, at the time fixed for the beginning of the term of the President, the President elect shall have died, the Vice President elect shall become President. If a President shall not have been chosen before the time fixed for the beginning of his term, or if the President elect shall have failed to qualify, then the Vice President elect shall act as President until a President shall have qualified; and the Congress may by law provide for the case wherein neither a President elect nor a Vice President elect shall have qualified, declaring who shall then act as President, or the manner in which one who is to act shall be selected, and such person shall act accordingly until a President or Vice President shall have qualified.

Section 4.

The Congress may by law provide for the case of the death of any of the person from whom the House of Representatives may choose a President whenever the right of choice shall have devolved upon them, and for the case of the death of any of the persons from whom the Senate may choose a Vice President whenever the right of choice shall have devolved upon them.

Section 5.

Sections 1 and 2 shall take effect on the 15th day of October following the ratification of this article.

Section 6.

This article shall be inoperative unless it shall have been ratified as an amendment to the Constitution by the legislatures of three-fourths of the several states within seven years from the date of its submission.

Amendment XXI (1933)

Section 1.

The eighteenth article of amendment to the Constitution of the United States is hereby repealed.

Section 2.

The transportation or importation into any state, territory, or possession of the United States for delivery or use therein of intoxicating liquors, in violation of the laws thereof, is hereby prohibited.

Section 3.

This article shall be inoperative unless it shall have been ratified as an amendment to the Constitution by conventions in the several states, as provided in the Constitution, within seven years from the date of the submission hereof to the states by the Congress.

Amendment XXII (1951)

Section 1.

No person shall be elected to the office of the President more than twice, and no person who has held the office of President, or acted as president, for more than two years of a term to which some other person was elected President shall be elected to the office of the President more than once. But this article shall not apply to any person holding the office of President when this article was proposed by the Congress, and shall not prevent any person who may be holding the office of President, or acting as President, during the term within which this article becomes operative from holding the office of President or acting as President during the remainder of such term.

Section 2.

This article shall be inoperative unless it shall have been ratified as an amendment to the Constitution by the legislatures of three-fourths of the several states within seven years from the date of its submission to the states by the Congress.

Amendment XXIII (1961)
Section 1.

The District constituting the seat of government of the United States shall appoint in such manner as the Congress may direct.

A number of electors of President and Vice President equal to the whole number of Senators and Representatives in Congress to which the District would be entitled if it were a state, but in no event more than the least populous state; they shall be in addition to those appointed by the states, but they shall be considered, for the purposes of the election of President and Vice President, to be electors appointed by a state; and they shall meet in the District and perform such duties as provided by the twelfth article of amendment.

Section 2.

The Congress shall have power to enforce this article by appropriate legislation.

Amendment XXIV (1964)
Section 1.

The right of citizens of the United States to vote in any primary or other election for President or Vice President, for electors for President or Vice President, or for Senator or Representative in Congress, shall not be denied or abridged by the United States or any state by reason of failure to pay any poll tax or other tax.

Section 2.

The Congress shall have power to enforce this article by appropriate legislation.

Amendment XXV (1967)
Section 1.

In case of the removal of the President from office or of his death or resignation, the Vice President shall become President.

Section 2.

Whenever there is a vacancy in the office of the Vice President, the President shall nominate a Vice President who shall take office upon confirmation by a majority vote of both Houses of Congress.

Section 3.

Whenever the President transmits to the President pro tempore of the Senate and the Speaker of the House of Representatives his written declaration that he is unable to discharge the powers and duties of his office, and until he transmits to them a written declaration to the contrary, such powers and duties shall be discharged by the Vice President as Acting President.

Section 4.

Whenever the Vice President and a majority of either the principal officers of the executive departments or of such other body as Congress may by law provide, transmit to the President pro tempore of the Senate and the Speaker of the House of Representatives their written declaration that the President is unable to discharge the powers and duties of his office, the Vice President shall immediately assume the powers and duties of the office as Acting President.

Thereafter, when the President transmits to the President pro tempore of the Senate and the Speaker of the House of Representatives his written declaration that no inability exists, he shall resume the powers and duties of his office unless the Vice President and a majority of either the principal officers of the executive department or of such other body as Congress may by law provide, transmit within four days to the President pro tempore of the Senate and the Speaker of the House of Representatives their written declaration that the President is unable to discharge the powers and duties of his office. Thereupon Congress shall decide the issue, assembling within forty-eight hours for that purpose if not in session. If the Congress, within twenty-one days after receipt of the latter written declaration, or, if Congress is not in session, within twenty-one days after Congress is required to assemble, determines, determines by two-thirds vote of both Houses that the President is unable to discharge the powers and duties of his office, the Vice President shall continue to discharge the same as Acting President; otherwise, the President shall resume the powers and duties of his office.

Amendment XXVI (1971)

Section 1.

The right of citizens of the United States, who are 18 years of age or older, to vote, shall not be denied or abridged by the United States or any state on account of age.

Section 2.

The Congress shall have the power to enforce this article by appropriate legislation.

Amendment XXVII (1992)

No law varying the compensation for the services of the Senators and Representatives shall take effect until an election of Representatives shall have intervened.

The Articles of Confederation

Agreed to by Congress November 15, 1777; ratified and in force, March 1, 1781.

Preamble

To all to whom these Presents shall come, we the undersigned Delegates of the States affixed to our Names send greeting. Whereas the Delegates of the United States of America in Congress assembled did on the fifteenth day of November in the Year of our Lord One Thousand Seven Hundred and Seventy Seven, and in the Second Year of the Independence of America agree to certain articles of Confederation and perpetual Union between the States of New Hampshire, Massachusetts bay, Rhode Island and Providence Plantations, Connecticut, New York, New Jersey, Pennsylvania, Delaware, Maryland, Virginia, North Carolina, South Carolina and Georgia in the Words following, viz. "Articles of Confederation and perpetual Union between the States of New Hampshire, Massachusetts bay, Rhode Island and Providence Plantations, Connecticut, New York, New Jersey, Pennsylvania, Delaware, Maryland, Virginia, North Carolina, South Carolina and Georgia."

Article I. The Style of this confederacy shall be "The United States of America."

Article II. Each state retains its sovereignty, freedom and independence, and every power, jurisdiction and right, which is not by this Confederation expressly delegated to the United States, in Congress assembled.

Article III. The said States hereby severally enter into a firm league of friendship with each other, for their common defense, the security of their liberties, and their mutual and general welfare, binding themselves to assist each other, against all force offered to, or attacks made upon them, or any of them, on account of religion, sovereignty, trade, or any other pretence whatever.

Article IV. The better to secure and perpetuate mutual friendship and intercourse among the people of the different States in this Union, the free inhabitants of each of these States, paupers, vagabonds and fugitives from justice excepted, shall be entitled to all privileges and immunities of free citizens in the several States; and the people of each state shall have free ingress and regress to and from any other State, and shall enjoy therein all the privileges of trade and commerce, subject to the same duties, impositions and restrictions as the inhabitants thereof respectively, provided that such restriction shall not extend so far as to prevent the removal of property imported into any state, to any other state of which the Owner is an inhabitant; provided also that no imposition, duties or restriction shall be laid by any state, on the property of the United States, or either of them.

If any person guilty of or charged with treason, felony, or other high misdemeanor in any state, shall flee from Justice, and be found in any of the United States, he shall upon demand of the governor or executive power of the state from which he fled, be delivered up and removed to the State having jurisdiction of his offence.

Full faith and credit shall be given in each of these States to the records, acts and judicial proceedings of the courts and magistrates of every other state.

Article V. For the more convenient management of the general interests of the United States, delegates shall be annually appointed in such manner as the legislature of each state shall direct, to meet in Congress on the first Monday in November, in every year, with a power reserved to each state, to recall its delegates, or any of them, at any time within the year, and to send others in their stead, for the remainder of the year.

No state shall be represented in Congress by less than two, nor by more than seven Members; and no person shall be capable of being a delegate for more than three years in any term of six years; nor shall any person, being a delegate, be capable of holding any office under the United States, for which he, or another for his benefit receives any salary, fees or emolument of any kind.

Each state shall maintain its own delegates in a meeting of the States, and while they act as members of the committee of the States.

In determining questions in the United States, in Congress assembled, each State shall have one vote.

Freedom of speech and debate in Congress shall not be impeached or questioned in any Court, or place out of Congress, and the members of Congress shall be protected in their persons from arrests and imprisonments, during the time of their going to and from, and attendance on Congress, except for treason, felony, or breach of the peace.

Article VI. No state without the Consent of the United States in Congress assembled, shall send any embassy to, or receive any embassy from, or enter into any conference, agreement, or alliance or treaty with any king, prince or state; nor shall any person holding any office of profit or trust under the United States, or any of them, accept of any present, emolument, office or title of any kind whatever from any king, prince or foreign state; nor shall the United States in Congress assembled, or any of them, grant any title of nobility.

No two or more States shall enter into any treaty, confederation or alliance whatever between them, without the consent of the United States in Congress assembled, specifying accurately the purposes for which the same is to be entered into, and how long it shall continue.

No state shall lay any imposts or duties, which may interfere with any stipulations in treaties, entered into by the United States in Congress assembled, with any king, prince or state, in pursuance of any treaties already proposed by Congress, to the courts of France and Spain.

No vessels of war shall be kept up in time of peace by any State, except such number only, as shall be deemed necessary by the United States in Congress assembled, for the defense of such State or its trade; nor shall any body of forces be kept up by any State, in time of peace, except such number only, as in the judgment of the United States in Congress assembled, shall be deemed requisite to garrison the forts necessary for the defense of such State; but every State shall always keep up a well regulated and disciplined militia, sufficiently armed and accoutered, and shall provide and constantly have ready for use, in public stores, a due number of field pieces and tents, and a proper quantity of arms, ammunition and camp equipage.

No state shall engage in any war without the consent of the United States in Congress assembled, unless such state be actually invaded by enemies, or shall have received certain advice of a resolution being formed by some nation of Indians to invade such State, and the danger is so imminent as not to admit of a delay, till the United States in Congress assembled can be consulted: nor shall any state grant commissions to any ships or vessels of war, nor letters of marque or reprisal, except it be after a declaration of war by the United States in Congress assembled, and then only against the kingdom or State and the subjects thereof, against which war has been so declared, and under such regulations as shall be established by the United States in Congress assembled, unless such state be infested by pirates, in which case vessels of war may be fitted out for that occasion, and kept so long as the danger shall continue, or until the United States in Congress assembled shall determine otherwise.

Article VII. When land forces are raised by any state for the common defense, all officers of or under the rank of colonel, shall be appointed by the legislature of each state respectively by whom such forces shall be raised, or in such manner as such state shall direct, and all vacancies shall be filled up by the state which first made the appointment.

Article VIII. All charges of war, and all other expenses that shall be incurred for the common defense or general welfare, and allowed by the United States in Congress assembled, shall be defrayed out of a common treasury, which shall be supplied by the several States, in proportion to the value of all land within each state, granted to or surveyed for any person, as such land and the buildings and improvements thereon shall be estimated according to such mode as the United States in Congress assembled, shall from time to time direct and appoint. The taxes for paying that proportion shall be laid and levied by the authority and direction of the legislatures of the several States within the time agreed upon by the United States in Congress assembled.

Article IX. The United States in Congress assembled, shall have the sole and exclusive right and power of determining on peace and war, except in the cases mentioned in the sixth article of sending and receiving ambassadors entering into treaties and alliances, provided that no treaty of commerce shall be made whereby the legislative power of the respective States shall be restrained from imposing such imposts and duties on foreigners, as their own people are subjected to, or from prohibiting the exportation or importation of any species of goods or commodities whatsoever of establishing rules for deciding in all cases, what captures on land or water shall be legal, and in what manner prizes taken by land or naval forces in the service of the United States shall be divided or appropriated of granting letters of marque and reprisal in times of peace appointing courts for the trial of piracies and felonies committed on the high seas and establishing courts for receiving and determining finally appeals in all cases of captures, provided that no member of Congress shall be appointed a judge of any of the said courts.

The United States in Congress assembled shall also be the last resort on appeal in all disputes and differences now subsisting or that hereafter may arise between two or more States concerning boundary, jurisdiction or any other cause whatever; which authority shall always be exercised in the manner following: Whenever the legislative or executive authority or lawful agent State in controversy with another shall present a petition to Congress, stating the matter in question and praying for a hearing, notice thereof shall be given by order of Congress to the legislative or executive authority of the other State in controversy, and a day assigned for the appearance of the parties by their lawful agents, who shall then be directed to appoint by joint consent, commissioners or judges to constitute a court for hearing and determining the matter in question; but if they cannot agree, Congress shall name three persons out of each of the United States, and from the list of such persons each party shall alternately strike out one, the petitioners beginning, until the number shall be reduced to thirteen; and from that number not less than seven, nor more than nine names as Congress shall direct, shall in the presence of Congress be drawn out by lot, and the persons whose names shall be so drawn or any five of them, shall be commissioners or judges, to hear and finally determine the controversy, so always as a major part of the judges who shall hear the cause shall agree in the determination: and if either party shall neglect to attend at the day appointed, without showing reasons, which Congress shall judge sufficient, or being present shall refuse to strike, the Congress shall proceed to nominate three persons out of each State, and the Secretary of Congress shall strike in behalf of such party absent or refusing; and the judgment and sentence of the court to be appointed, in the manner before prescribed, shall be final and conclusive; and if any of the parties shall refuse to submit to the authority of such court, or to appear to defend their claim or cause, the court shall nevertheless proceed to pronounce sentence, or judgment, which shall in like manner be final and decisive, the judgment or sentence and other proceedings being in either case transmitted to Congress, and lodged among the acts of Congress for the security of the parties concerned: provided that every commissioner, before he sits in judgment, shall take an oath to be administered by one of the judges of the supreme or superior court of the state, where the cause shall be tried, "well and truly to hear and determine the matter in question, according to the best of his judgment, without favor, affection or hope of reward;" provided also that no State shall be deprived of territory for the benefit of the United States.

All controversies concerning the private right of soil claimed under different grants of two or more States, whose jurisdictions as they may respect such lands, and the States which passed such grants are adjusted, the said grants or either of them being at the same time claimed to have originated antecedent to such settlement of jurisdiction, shall on the petition of either party to the Congress of the United States, be finally determined as near as may be in the same manner as is before prescribed for deciding disputes respecting territorial jurisdiction between different States.

The United States in Congress assembled shall also have the sole and exclusive right and power of regulating the alloy and value of coin struck by their own authority, or by that of the respective States fixing the standard of weights and measures throughout the United States, regulating the trade and managing all affairs with the Indians, not members of any of the States, provided that the legislative right of any state within its own limits be not infringed or violated establishing and regulating post offices from one State to another, throughout all the United States, and exacting such postage on the papers passing through the same as may be requisite to defray the expenses of the said office appointing all officers of the land forces, in the service of the United States, excepting regimental officers appointing all the officers of the naval forces, and commissioning all officers whatever in the service of the United States making rules for the government and regulation of the said land and naval forces, and directing their operations.

The United States in Congress assembled shall have authority to appoint a committee, to sit in the recess of Congress, to be denominated "A Committee of the

States," and to consist of one delegate from each state; and to appoint such other committees and civil officers as may be necessary for managing the general affairs of the United States under their direction to appoint one of their number to preside, provided that no person be allowed to serve in the office of president more than one year in any term of three years; to ascertain the necessary sums of Money to be raised for the service of the United States, and to appropriate and apply the same for defraying the public expenses to borrow money, or emit bills on the credit of the United States, transmitting every half year to the respective States an account of the sums of money so borrowed or emitted, to build and equip a navy to agree upon the number of land forces, and to make requisitions from each state for its quota, in proportion to the number of white inhabitants in such state; which requisition shall be binding, and thereupon the legislature of each State shall appoint the regimental officers, raise the men and clothe, arm and equip them in a soldier like manner, at the expense of the United States, and the officers and men so clothed, armed and equipped shall march to the place appointed, and within the time agreed on by the United States in Congress assembled. But if the United States in Congress assembled shall, on consideration of circumstances judge proper that any State should not raise men, or should raise a smaller number than its quota, and that any other state should raise a greater number of men than the quota thereof, such extra number shall be raised, officered, clothed, armed and equipped in the same manner as the quota of such State, unless the legislature of such state shall judge that such extra number cannot be safely spared out of the same, in which case they shall raise officer, clothe, arm and equip as many of such extra number as they judge can be safely spared. And the officers and men so clothed, armed and equipped, shall march to the place appointed, and within the time agreed on by the United States in Congress assembled.

The United States in Congress assembled shall never engage in a war, nor grant letters of marque and reprisal in time of peace, nor enter into any treaties or alliances, nor coin money, nor regulate the value thereof, nor ascertain the sums and expenses necessary for the defense and welfare of the United States, or any of them, nor emit bills, nor borrow money on the credit of the United States, nor appropriate money, nor agree upon the number of vessels of war, to be built or purchased, or the number of land or sea forces to be raised, nor appoint a commander-in-chief of the army or navy, unless nine States assent to the same: nor shall a question on any other point, except for adjourning from day to day be determined, unless by the votes of a majority of the United States in Congress assembled.

The Congress of the United States shall have power to adjourn to any time within the year, and to any place within the United States, so that no period of adjournment be for a longer duration than the space of six months, and shall publish the journal of their proceedings monthly, except such parts thereof relating to treaties, alliances or military operations as in their judgment require secrecy; and the yeas and nays of the delegates of each state on any question shall be entered on the journal, when it is desired by any delegate; and the delegates of a State, or any of them, at his or their request shall be furnished with a transcript of the said journal, except such parts as are above excepted, to lay before the legislatures of the several States.

Article X. The Committee of the States, or any nine of them, shall be authorized to execute, in the recess of Congress, such of the powers of Congress as the United States in Congress assembled, by the consent of nine States, shall from time to time think expedient to vest them with; provided that no power be delegated to the said Committee, for the exercise of which, by the Articles of Confederation, the voice of nine States in the Congress of the United States assembled is requisite.

Article XI. Canada acceding to this Confederation, and joining in the measures of the United States, shall be admitted into, and entitled to all the advantages of this Union: but no other colony shall be admitted into the same, unless such admission be agreed to by nine States.

Article XII. All bills of credit emitted, monies borrowed and debts contracted by, or under the authority of Congress, before the assembling of the United States, in pursuance of the present Confederation, shall be deemed and considered as a charge against the United States, for payment and satisfaction whereof the said United States, and the public faith are hereby solemnly pledged.

Article XIII. Every State shall abide by the determinations of the United States in

Congress assembled, on all questions which by this Confederation are submitted to them. And the Articles of this Confederation shall be inviolably observed by every state, and the union shall be perpetual; nor shall any alteration at any time hereafter be made in any of them; unless such alteration be agreed to in a Congress of the United States, and be afterwards confirmed by the legislatures of every State.

And whereas it hath pleased the Great Governor of the World to incline the hearts of the legislatures we respectively represent in Congress, to approve of, and to authorize us to ratify the said Articles of Confederation and perpetual Union, KNOW YE that we the undersigned delegates, by virtue of the power and authority to us given for that purpose, do by these presents, in the name and in behalf of our respective constituents, fully and entirely ratify and confirm each and every of the said Articles of Confederation and perpetual Union, and all and singular the matters and things therein contained: And we do further solemnly plight and engage the faith of our respective constituents, that they shall abide by the determinations of the United States in Congress assembled, on all questions, which by the said Confederation are submitted to them. And that the Articles thereof shall be inviolably observed by the States we respectively represent, and that the Union shall be perpetual.

In Witness whereof we have hereunto set our hands in Congress. Done at Philadelphia in the state of Pennsylvania the ninth Day of July in the Year of our Lord One Thousand Seven Hundred and Seventy-eight, and in the third year of the Independence of America.

The Virginia Plan

1. Resolved that the Articles of Confederation ought to be so corrected and enlarged as to accomplish the objects proposed by their institution; namely. "Common defense, security of liberty and general welfare."

2. Resolved therefore that the rights of suffrage in the National Legislature ought to be proportioned to the Quotas of contribution, or to the number of free inhabitants, as the one or the other rule may seem best in different cases.

3. Resolved that the National Legislature ought to consist of two branches.

4. Resolved that the members of the first branch of the National Legislature ought to be elected by the people of the several States every _____ for the term of _____; to be of the age of _____ years at least, to receive liberal stipends by which they may be compensated for the devotion of their time to public service; to be ineligible to any office established by a particular State, or under the authority of the United States, except those peculiarly belonging to the functions of the first branch, during the term of service and for the space of _____ after its expiration; to be incapable of re-election for the space of _____ after the expiration of their term of service, and to be subject to recall.

5. Resolved that the members of the second branch of the National Legislature ought to be elected by those of the first, out of a proper number of persons nominated by the individual Legislatures, to be of the age of _____ years at least; to hold their offices for a term sufficient to ensure their independency, to received liberal stipends, by which they may be compensated for the devotion of their time to public service; and to be ineligible to any office established by a particular State, or under the authority of the United States, except those peculiarly belonging to the functions of the second branch, during the term of service, and for the space of _____ after the expiration thereof.

6. Resolved that each branch ought to possess the right of originating Acts; that the National Legislative ought to be empowered to enjoy the Legislative Rights vested in Congress by the Confederation and moreover to legislate in all cases to which the separate States are incompetent, or in which the harmony of the United States may be interrupted by the exercise of individual Legislation; to negative all laws passed by the several States, contravening in the opinion of the National Legislature the

articles of Union; and to call forth the force of the Union against any member of the Union failing to fulfill its duty under the articles thereof.

7. Resolved that a National Executive be instituted; to be chosen by the National Legislature for the term of years, to receive punctually at stated times, a fixed compensation for the services rendered, in which no increase or diminution shall be made so as to affect the Magistracy, existing at the time of increase or diminution, and to be ineligible a second time; and that besides a general authority to execute the National laws, it ought to enjoy the Executive rights vested in Congress by the Confederation.

8. Resolved that the Executive and a convenient number of the National Judiciary, ought to compose a council of revision with authority to examine every act of the National Legislature before it shall operate, and every act of a particular Legislature before a Negative thereon shall be final; and that the dissent of the said Council shall amount to a rejection, unless the Act of the National Legislature be again passed, or that of a particular Legislature be again negative by _____ of the members of each branch.

9. Resolved that a National Judiciary be established to consist of one or more supreme tribunals, and of inferior tribunals to be chosen by the National Legislature, to hold their offices during good behavior; and to receive punctually at stated times fixed compensation for their services, in which no increase or diminution shall be made so as to affect the persons actually in office at the time of such increase or diminution. That the jurisdiction of the inferior tribunals shall be to hear and determine in the first instance, and of the supreme tribunal to hear and determine in the dernier resort, all piracies and felonies on the high seas, captures from an enemy; cases in which foreigners or citizens of other States applying to such jurisdictions may be interested, or which respect the collection of the National revenue; impeachments of any National officers, and questions which may involve the national peace and harmony.

10. Resolved that provision ought to be made for the admission of States lawfully arising within the limits of the United States, whether from a voluntary junction of Government and Territory or otherwise, with the consent of a number of voices in the National Legislature less than the whole.

11. Resolved that a Republican Government and the territory of each State, except

in the instance of a voluntary junction of Government and territory, ought to be guaranteed by the United States to each State.

12. Resolved that provision ought to be made for the continuance of Congress and their authorities and privileges, until a given day after the reform of the articles of Union shall be adopted, and for the completion of all their engagements.

13. Resolved that provision ought to be made for the amendment of the Articles of Union whensoever it shall seem necessary, and that the assent of the National Legislature ought not to be required thereto.

14. Resolved that the Legislative Executive and Judiciary powers within the several States ought to be bound by oath to support the articles of Union.

15. Resolved that the amendments which shall be offered to the Confederation, by the Convention ought at a proper time, or times, after the approbation of Congress to be submitted to an assembly or assemblies of Representatives, recommended by the Several Legislatures to be expressly chosen by the people, to consider and decide thereon.

Part Eight: References and Notes

References and Notes

Chapter 1 Notes: Introduction

1. W. Lance Bennett, *The Governing Crisis: Media, Money, and Marketing in American Elections* (New York, n.p., 1992).

2. *Citizens against Rent Control v. Berkeley* 450 U.S. 908 (1981) and *First National Bank of Boston v. Bellotti* 435 U.S. 765 (1978).

Chapter 2 Notes: How Did We Get to This Point?

1. Bailyn Bernard, *The Ideological Origins of the American Revolution* (Cambridge, n.p., 1967), 66-67.

2. "Congress and the States: Operating under the Articles of Confederation" by Richard Morris in *The Forging of the Union 1781-1789* (New York n.p.) 80-110.

3. http://www.csusm.edu/A_S/History/docs/artcon.html

4. Merrill Jensen, *The New Nation: A History of the United States during the Confederation 1781-1789* (New York, n.p., 1950). Seen as a positive view of the era.

5. Ralph Ketcham, *James Madison: A Biography* (New York, n.p., 1971), 185.

6. Melvin Urofsky, *A March of Liberty, A Constitutional History of the United States* (New York, n.p., 1988), 91.

7. Richard Bernstein, *Are We to Be a Nation: The Making of the Constitution* (Cambridge, n.p. 1987), 174-175.

8. William Peters, *A More Perfect Union* (New York, n.p., 1987) 37-49.

9. John Lewis, Ed., *Anti-Federalists versus Federalists* (San Francisco, n.p. 1967), 4-10.

10. Herbert Storing, *What the Anti-Federalists Were For* (Chicago, n.p. 1981), 7-14, 22-23.

11. William Wallace, *Our Obsolete Constitution* (New York, n.p., 1932), 46-47.

12. Leonard Levy, *Original Intent and the Framers' Constitution* (New

York, n.p.,1988).

13. Francis N. Stites, *John Marshall: Defender of the Constitution* (Boston, n.p.1981), 80.

14. Melvin Urofsky, *A March of Liberty: A Constitutional History of the United States* (New York, n.p.1988), 111.

15. Arthur Schlesinger, *The Imperial Presidency* (Boston, n.p. 1988).

16. *Marbury v. Madison,* 1 Cr. 137 (1803).

17. "No. 78" in Alexander Hamilton, *The Federalist Papers,* Clinton Rossiter, Ed., (New York, n.p.,1961), 464.

18. *McCullock v. Maryland,* 4 Wheat, 316 (1819).

19. *Gibbons v. Ogden,* 9 Wheat. 1 (1824).

20. *Dred Scott v. Sanford,* 19 How. 393 (1857); *Plessy v. Ferguson,* 163 U.S. 537 (1896); *Northern Securities v. the United States,* 193 U.S. 197 (1904); *Schenck v. the United States,* 249 U.S. 47 (1919); *Gitlow v. New York,* 268 U.S. 562 (1925); *Schechter Poultry Corporation v. the United States,* 295 U.S. 495 (1935); *Dennis et al. v. the United States,* 341 U.S. 494 (1951); *Brown v. Board of Education of Topeka,* 349 U.S. 294 (1955), *Mapp v. Ohio,* 367 U.S. 643 (1961); *Giswold v. Connecticut* 381 U.S. 479 (1965), *Miranda v. Arizona;* 384 U.S. 436 (1966), *Roe v. Wade,* 410 U.S. 113 (1973); and the *United States v. Nixon,* 418 U.S. 683 (1974).

Chapter 3 Notes: The Paradoxes to the American Constitution

1. Page Smith, *The Constitution: A Documentary and Narrative History* (New York, n.p.,1980), 248.

2. John Alexander, *The Selling of the Constitution: A History of News Coverage* (Madison, n.p., 1990), *188.* Many Anti-Federalist took exception to the "Well Born" status of the drafters of the United States Constitution.

3. Edward Dumbauld, *The Bill of Rights and What It Means Today* (Norman, 1957), 174-183.

4. John Lewis, Ed., *Anti-Federalists Versus Federalists* (San Francisco, n.p., 1967), 24, 28, 128-130.

5. Robert Rutland, *The Birth of the Bill of Rights 1776-1791* (New York, n.p. 1955, 1962). Elementary and basic review of the main issues related to the time

period.

6. Louis Hartz, *The Liberal Tradition in America* (New York, Harcourt Brace Jovanovich, Inc., 1962).

7. Larry Tise, Proslavery: *A History of the Defense of Slavery in America* 1701-1840 (Athens, n.p., 1987) 193-203.

8. William Wiecek, *The Guarantee Clause of the United States Constitution* (New York, n.p., 1972). This work covers Article IV, Section 4, at length.

Chapter 4 Notes: Federalism

1. P. Allan Dionisopoulos, *The Government of the United States* (New York, n.d., 1970), 136. Dionisopoulos noted that the current Federalist system does not even match the type in place in 1900.

2. Wiliam Wallace, *Our Obsolete Constitution (New York, 1932),* 41.

3. Garrett Sheldon, *The Political Philosophy of Thomas Jefferson* (Baltimore, n .p.,1991), 4.

4. Robert Bowie and Carl Friedrich, Eds., *Studies in Federalism* (Boston, n.p., 1954) and Jane Clark, *The Rise of the New Federalism* (New York, n.p., 1938).

5. Ronald Clark, *Benjamin Franklin* (New York, n.p., 1983) 102-107, or Thomas Fleming, Ed., *The Founding Fathers: Benjamin Franklin, a Biography in His Own Words* (New York, n. p., 1972),136-140.

6. Edmund Burnett, The *Continental Congress* (New York, n.d., 1941).

7. Irving Brant, *Storm over the Constitution* (Indianapolis, n.p., 1936), 180-183.

8. Raoul Berger, Federalism, *The Founders' Design* (Norman, n.p., 1987), 21-23. A review of how the drafters of the United States Constitution attempted to set up American Federalism.

9. Alexander Hamilton, James Madison, and John Jay, *The Federalist Papers,* Clinton Rossiter, Ed. (New York, n .p., 1961).

10. Raoul Berger, Federalism, *The Founders' Design* (Norman, 1987), 33.

11. Donald Lutz, *A Preface to American Political Theory* (Lawrence, n.d., 1992), 53.

12. Daniel Elazar, *American Federalism: A View from the States* (New

York, n.p., 1972) 36-42. Elazar also noted how over the years changing state Constitutions have conceded sovereignty to the Federal government.

13. Jack Rokove, *Original Meanings: Politics and Ideas in the Making of the Constitution* (New York, n.p., 1996), 191-197.

14. *McCulloch v. Maryland,* 4 Wheat 316 (1819) and *Gibbons v. Ogden,* 9 Wheat. 1 (1824).

15. Wiliam Wallace, *Our Obsolete Constitution* (New York, n.p., 1932), 51.

16. Raoul Berger, *Federalism, The Founders' Design* (Norman, n.p., 1987), 178-192. Berger argues that the United States Constitution needs to be revised simply on the issue of Federalism alone.

Chapter 5 Notes: The Living Document

1. Alexis de Tocqueville, *Democracy in America,* Ed. Richard Heffner (New York, n.p., 1956).

2. "The Constitution: What the Judges Say It Is" in Ralph Ketcham, *Framed for Posterity: The Enduring Philosophy of the Constitution* (Lawrence, n.p., 1993), 156-164.

3. Robert Bork, *The Tempting of America* (New York, n.p., 1990). Note the writings of both jurists Robert Bork and William Rehnquist concerning the original intent of the argument.

Chapter 6 Notes: The Contract

1. Martin Edelman, *Democratic Theories and the Constitution* (Albany, n.p., 1984), 212-215.

2. Patrick Riley, *Will and Political Legitimacy* (Cambridge, n.p., 1982).

3. Christian Bay, "From Contract to Community: Thoughts on Liberalism and Postindustrial Society," from *Contract to Community: Political Theory at the Crossroads,* Fred Dallmyr, Ed. (West Lafayette, n.p., 1978), 34-35

4. Walter Berns, *Taking the Constitution Seriously* (New York, n.p., 1987), 134.

5. William Graham Sumner, "What Social Classes Owe to Each Other," in *American Political Thought,* Kenneth Dolbeare, Ed. (Chatham, n.p., 1981), 345. For

further readings of Sumner's reviews on the social compact note *Essays of William Graham Sumner,* Albert Keller and Maurice Davie, Eds. (New Haven, n.p., 1934), 86, 285.

6. Frank Donovan, *The Mayflower Compact* (New York, n.p., 1968), 95-124. For the text of the Mayflower Compact note George Grant, *The Patriot's Handbook* (Nashville, 1996), 4.

7. William Swindler, Magna Carta: Legend and Legacy (Indianapolis, n.p., 1965), 228-238, and Faith Thompson, *Magna Carta: Its Role in Making of the English Constitution 1300-1629* (London, n.p.,1948).

8. "The American and British Constitutions Are Two Entirely Different Things" in Michael Kammen, *A Machine That Would Go of Itself: The Constitution in American Culture* (New York, n.p., 1987), 156-184.

Chapter 7 Notes: The Electoral College

1. Henry Mayo, *An Introduction to Democratic Theory* (New York, n.p., 1960.

2. George Grant, *The Patriot's Handbook* (Nashville, n.p., 1996), 202.

3. Alexander Hamilton, *The Federalist Papers, No. 68,* Clinton Rossiter, Ed. (New York, n.p., 1961), 412.

4. James Cleaser, *Presidential Selection: Theory and Development* (Princeton, n.p., 1979).

5. Michael Glennon, *When No Majority Rules: The Electoral College and Presidential Succession* (Washington, n.p., 1992), 20.

6. Lawrence Longley and Neal Peirce, *The Electoral College Primer* (New Haven, n.p., 1996). Detailed information on how the Electoral College functions and its many flaws.

7. _____, 108-109.

8. Michael Glennon, *When No Majority Rules: The Electoral College and Presidential Succession* (Washington, n.p., 1992), 37-39.

9. Roger MacBride, *The American Electoral College* (Caldwell, n.p., 1963), 45.

10. Neal Peirce, *The People's President: The Electoral College in American History and the Direct-Vote Alternative* (New York , n.p., 1968), 82-86.

11. Michael Glennon, *When No Majority Rules: The Electoral College and Presidential Succession* (Washington, n.p., 1992), 14.

12. For statistic information note Dean Burnham, *Presidential Ballots 1836-1892* (Baltimore, n.p., 1955), 118-120. For a history note Paul Buck, *The Road to Reunion 1865-1900* (Boston, n.p., 1937), 97-101, or a more complete text James Blaine, *Twenty Years of Congress: From Lincoln to Garfield*, Vol. II (Norwich, n.p., 1886), 567-592.

13. Neal Peirce, *The People's President: The Electoral College in American History and the Direct-Vote Alternative* (New York, n.p., 1968), 92-93.

14. _____, *Congressional Quarterly's Guide to U.S. Elections* (Washington, n.p., 1985).

15. Seymour Sudman, "Do Exit Polls Influence Voting Behavior?" in *Public Opinion Quarterly,* Fall Vol. 50 (1986), 331. Also note Edwin Diamond, "Too Much Too Soon," *New Yorker,* November 21, Vol 21, No. 46 (1988), 26.

16. This problem has been profound enough that an amendment to the United States Constitution has been introduced. "TV Networks Again Support Poll Closing Amendments," *Broadcasting,* May 16, Vol.114, No.20 (1988), 38.

Chapter 8 Notes: One Person, One Vote

1. Ward Elliott, *The Rise of Guardian Democracy: The Supreme Court's Role in Voting Rights Disputes 1845-1969* (Cambridge, n.d., 1975).

2. "Apportionment in the Nineteen Sixties" in *Documents of the National Municipal League* (August, 1967), part II, a.

3. *Wesberry v. Sanders,* 376 U.S. 1 (1964). The Supreme Court confirmed that Article I of the Constitution required one person, one vote districts.

4. *Reynolds v. Sims,* 377 U.S. 533 (1964). The high court declared that one person, one vote was a "fundamental principle" of the United States Constitution.

5. Not until *Baker v. Carr,* 369 U.S. 186 (1962) that the court declared that the people had standing in such issues as redistricting. In the past the Federal courts had deflected it as a "political issue" and would not hear cases on the subject.

6. Source: United States Bureau of the Census – 1990 Census

7. Source: Morgan Quitno Press using data from the United States Bureau of Census unpublished data reported in Statistical Abstract of the United States

1995. Calculated by multiplying voting age population by percent registered.

    8. Source: U.S. Bureau of the Census

Chapter 9 Notes: What Represents Economy?

    1. Jonas Prager, *Fundamentals of Money, Banking, and Financial Institutions* (New York, n.p., 1987), 30.

    2. Beth Deisher, Ed., *Coin World Almanac* (New York, n.p., 1987), 197-198.

    3. Leland Yeager, *International Monetary Relations: Theory, History, and Policy* (New York, n.p., 1976), 13-34.

    4. Lewis Solomon, *Rethinking Our Centralized Monetary System: The Case for a System of Local Currencies* (Westport, n.p., 1996), 22-25.

    5. Milton Friedman and Anna Schwartz, *A Monetary History of the United States 1867-1960* (Princeton, n.p., 1963), 152

    6. Lawrence Goodwyn, *Democratic Promise: The Populist Moment in America* (New York, n.p., 1976), 518.

    7. Milton Friedman and Anna Schwartz, *A Monetary History of the United States* 1867-1960 (Princeton, n.p., 1963), 189-196.

    8. Eustace Mullins, *Secrets of the Federal Reserve: The London Connection* (Staunton, 1991), 159. The work represents a detailed but critical view of the Federal Reserve.

    9. Jonas Prager, *Fundamentals of Money, Banking, and Financial Institutions* (New York, n.p., 1987), 353-361.

    10. William Elliot, *The Need for Constitutional Reform* (New York, n.p., 1935), 41-62. A look at some of the New Deal economic problems.

    11. Andrew Bartels "Volcker's Revolution at the Fed" in Harold Vatter and John Walker, Eds., *History of the U.S. Economy since World War II* (New York, n.p., 1996), 418-423.

    12. Theodore Thoren and Richard Warner, *The Truth in Money Book* (Chagrin Falls, n.p., 1989), 261-268.

    13. Milton Friedman and Anna Schwartz, *A Monetary History of the United States 1867-1960* (Princeton, n.p., 1963), 131-134.

    14. Richard Timberlake, *Monetary Policy in the United States: An*

Intellectual and Institutional History (Chicago, n.p., 1993). An excellent work on United States monetary policy and history.

15. Richard Timberlake, *Gold, Greenbacks, and the Constitution* (Berryville, n.p., 1991), 13.

16. *Hepburn v. Griswold*, 8 Wall, 603 (1870).

17. *Parker v. Davis*, 12 Wall 457 (1871), and *Knox v. Lee*, 12 Wall 457 (1871).

Chapter 10 Notes: Delegation

1. Laurence Tribe, *Constitutional Choices* (Cambridge, n.p., 1985), 79-83.

2. David Schoenbrod, *Power without Responsibility: How Congress Abuses the People through Delegation* (New Haven, n.p., 1993).

3. David Schoenbrod, *Power without Responsibility: How Congress Abuses the People through Delegation* (New Haven, n.p., 1993), 12-13.

4. *Field v. Clark*, 143 U.S. 649 (1892).

5. *Schechter v. United States* 295 U.S. 495 (1935), *Louisville Joint Stock Land Bank v. Radford* 295 U.S. 555 (1935) and *Humphrey's Executor v. United States* 295 U.S. 602 (1935). Within a couple of years the Supreme Court came to retreat from their earlier position; note *Wright V. Vinton Brank Bank* 300 U.S. 441 (1937).

6. *Panama Refining Company v. Ryan U.S.* 388 (1935), *Schechter Poultry Corp. v. United States* 295 U.S. 495 (1935), and *Carter v. Carter* 298 U.S. 238 (1936).

7. Two of the more notable books on the story behind the Supreme Court and the New Deal are Robert Jackson, *The Struggle for Judicial Supremacy* (New York, n.p., 1941) and Arthur Schlesinger, Jr., *The Politics of Upheaval* (Boston, n.p., 1960).

8. Sotirios Barber, *The Constitution and the Delegation of Congressional Power* (Chicago, n.p., 1975), 11, 26.

For definition note http://www.lia.org/duct-d, htm.

9. Mark Raszkowski, *Business Law: Principles, Cases, and Policy* (Glenview, n.p., 1989), 289-296.

10. John Locke, *Two Treatises of Government*, Thomas Cook, Ed. (New

York, 1947), 193.

11. Robert Corley and Peter Shedd, *Fundamentals of Business Law* (Englewood Cliffs, 1990), 250-252.

12. Mark Raszkowski, *Business Law: Principles, Cases and Policy* (Glenview, 1989), 154-166. An introduction to contract law.

13. Sotirios Barber, *The Constitution and the Delegation of Congressional Power* (Chicago, n.p., 1975), 24.

Chapter 11 Notes: What Congress Has Given Away

1. Paul Bator, Paul Mishkin, David Shapiro, and Herbert Wechsler, Eds., Hart & Wechsler's *The Federal Court and the Federal System* (Mineola, n.p., 1973), also, Henry Friendly, *Federal Jurisdiction: A General View* (New York, n.p., 1973).

2. Charles Warren, *The Supreme Court in United States* (Boston, n .p., 1935), 8-9.

3. Sometimes the legislation is called the Judiciary Act of 1925. Melvin Urofsky, *A March of Liberty: A Constitutional History of the United States* (New York, n.p., 1988), 619.

4. *Milligan, Ex parte,* 4 Wall, 2 (1866), 463-64, 470, 727, and *McCardle, Ex parte,* 6 Wall, 318 (1868), 467-68.

5. Laurence Tribe, "Silencing the Oracle: Carving Disfavored Rights Out of the Jurisdiction of Federal Courts." in *Constitutional Choices* (Cambridge, n.p., 1985),

6. *Cooper v. Aaron,* 358 U.S. 1 (1958), 778-79, 783. What emerged from this case was the idea that the Constitution is whatever the Supreme Court determines it to be. The original issue centered on segregation of public schools.

7. Alexander Bickel, *The Least Dangerous Branch* (Indianapolis, n.p., 1962), 16-23.

8. Louis Fisher, *Constitutional Conflicts between Congress and the President* (Princeton, n.p., 1985), 128-134.

9. Melvin Urofsky, *A March of Liberty, A Constitutional History of the United States* (New York, n.p., 1988), 123-125.

10. Maeva Marcus, *Truman and the Steel Seizure Case* (New York, n.p.,

1977).

11. Note *Dames & Moore v. Regan,* 453 U.S. 654 (1981), 944. The problem with this issue was that the Supreme Court was trapped in the center of an international and political dispute with Iran. A ruling on either side had far reaching international ramifications.

12. Winston Churchill, *Their Finest Hour* (Cambridge, n.p., 1949), 398-416.

13. John Terrell, *The United States Post Office Department: A Story of Letters, Postage, and Mail Fraud* (New York, n.p., 1968), 19-23.

14. Ross McReynolds, *History of the United States Post Office, 1607-1931* (Chicago, n.p., 1935). When the nation's founders began to operate the Post Office they thought it would be a money-making operation.

15. "Postal Reform" http://www.usps.gov/history/his3.htm.

16. Joel Fleishman, *Future of the Postal Service* (New York, n.p., 1983).

Chapter 12 Notes: How Important Is Efficiency?

1. Walter Oleszek, *Congressional Procedures and the Policy Process* (Washington, n.p., 1996), 75.

2. _____, 69.

3. Edward Nell, *Prosperity and Public Spending: Transformational Growth and the Role of Government* (Boston, n.p., 1988), 5.

4. Sarah Binder and Steven Smith, *Politics or Principle?: Filibustering in the United States Senate* (Washington, n.p., 1997), 11.

5._____.

Chapter 13 Notes: The Ratio of Elected and Citizenry

1. Christopher Wolfe, *How to Read the Constitution: Originalism, Constitutional Interpretation, and Judicial Power* (Lanham, 1996), 95-96.

2. James Madison, *The Federalist Papers,* Clinton Rossiter, Ed., No. 55 (New York, n.p., 1961), 343.

3. "Congressional Districts in the 1990s: A Portrait of America" in *Congressional Quarterly*, Washington, 1993), 4.

4. "Congress A to Z" in *Congressional Quarterly,* (Washington, 1993),

321.

5. "Congress A to Z" in *Congressional Quarterly,* (Washington, 1993),
322.

6. "Congressional Districts in the 1990s: A Portrait of America" in *Congressional Quarterly,* (Washington, 1993), 8.

7. Edward Schneier and Bertram Gross, *Congress Today* (New York, n.p., 1993), 32-33.

8. "How Congress Works" in *Congressional Quarterly,* Washington, 1991) 101-110.

9. Burdett Loomis, *The Contemporary Congress* (New York, 1996), 60-67. Many of these issues are connected to how members of Congress get elected.

Chapter 14 Notes: The Art of Ignoring the Constitution

1. Sedition Act of 1918, 40 Stat. 553 1918. 2.

2. Paul L. Murphy, *World War I and the Origin of Civil Liberties,* (NewYork, 1979), 80.

3. _____, 81.

4. *Debs v. United States,* 249 U.S. 211 (1919).

5. *Abrams v. the U.S.,* 250 U.S. 616 (1919).

6. John Morton Blum, *Liberty, Justice, Order* (New York, 1993), 111-122.

7. *Hirabayashi v. United States,* 320 U.S. 81 (1943), *Yasui v. United States,* 320 U.S. 115 (1943), and *Korematsu v. United States,* 323 U.S. 214 (1944). For a look at Japanese Americans note Paul Spickard, *Japanese Americans: The Formation and Transformation of an Ethnic Group* (New York, 1996).

8. Richard Timberlake, *Monetary Policy in the United States: An intellectual and Institutional History* (Chicago, n.p., 1993), 187.

Chapter 15 Notes: The District of Columbia

1. Judith Best, *National Representation for the District of Columbia* (Frederick, n.p., 1984), 15. Also note James Madison's position on a District in the *Federalist Papers* (No. 43).

2. Sterling Young, *The Washington Community 1800-1828* (New York,

n.p., 1966).

3. David Lewis, *District of Columbia* (New York, n.p., 1976), 70.

4. Note the District of Columbia Government Reorganization and Self-Governing Act of 1974. Public Law 93-395, 793.

5. Harry Jaffe and Tom Sherwood, *Dream City: Race, Power, and the Decline of Washington, D.C.* (New York, n.p., 1994).

6. _____, "Abolish D.C.," *The New Republic,* Dec. 5 (1946), 7.

7. Nancy Beiles and Michael Mayo, "Police Protection in D.C.: Separate and Unequal," *Washington Monthly,* (March, 1995), v 27, n 3, 15.

8. Judith Best, *National Representation for the District of Columbia* (Frederick, n.p., 1984), 7.

9. James Madison, *The Federalist Papers,* (43), Clinton Rossiter, Ed. (New York, n.p., 1961), 272.

10. John Vile, *Encyclopedia of Constitutional Amendments, Proposed Amendments, and Amending Issues, 1789-1995* (Santa Barbara, n.p., 1996), 98-99.

11. Judith Best, *National Representation for the District of Columbia* (Frederick, n.p., 1984), 37.

12. Erik Wemple, "Democracy's Discontent: Death of Home Rule," *The New Republic,* Jan. 20 (1997), 20-22.

Chapter 16 Notes: Native Americans

1. Henry Woodhead, Series Editor, Time-Life Books, *The Reservations,* (Alexandria, n.p., 1995), 26-27.

2. Thomas Abernethy, *Western Lands and the American Revolution* (New York, n.p., 1938, reprint 1958). A detailed look at early American interest in western expansion.

3. Alexander Hamilton, *The Federalist Papers,* Clinton Rossiter, Ed. (New York, n.p., 1961),157-162.

4. James Madison, *The Federalist Papers,* Clinton Rossiter, Ed. (New York, n.p., 1961), 268.

5. Walter Berns, *Taking the Constitution Seriously* (New York, n.p., 1987), 34-35. Also note Arnold McNair, *The Law of Treaties* (Oxford, n.p., 1961), 465, especially those areas of "good faith."

6. Felix Cohen, *Handbook of Federal Indian Law* (Washington, n.p., 1945), 55-56. Note the Indian Removal Act.

7. *Cherokee Nation v Georgia*, 5 Pet. 1 (1831).

8. *Hauenstein v. Lynham* 100 U.S. 483 (1880).

9. Arnold McNair, *The Law of Treaties* (Oxford, n.p., 1961), 512, 746-749. Note what represents a Breach of Treaty. The problem is one of territory; once given in exchange for Treaty considerations it is difficult to disallow the agreement.

10. Curtis Jackson and Marcia Galli, *A History of the Bureau of Indian Affairs and its Activities among Indians* (San Francisco, n.p., 1977), 88-90.

11. Charles Wilkinson, *American Indians, Time, and the Law: Native Societies in a Modern Constitutional Democracy* (New Haven, n.p., 1987), 8-9.

12. Curtis Jackson and Marcia Galli, *A History of the Bureau of Indian Affairs and its Activities among Indians* (San Francisco, n.p., 1977), 99-100.

13. Charles Wilkinson, *American Indians, Time, and the Law: Native Societies in a Modern Constitutional Democracy* (New Haven, n.p., 1987), 21-23.

14. "Federal Indian Reservations and Trust Lands" in Robert Famighetti, Ed., *The World Almanac and Book of Facts 1994* (Mahwah, n.p., 1993), 434. Data from the Bureau of Indian Affairs, United States Department of Interior, 1990.

15. Charles Wilkinson, *American Indians, Time, and the Law: Native Societies in a Modern Constitutional Democracy* (New Haven, n.p., 1987), 10-13, 117-119.

16. Walter Berns, *Taking the Constitution Seriously* (New York, n.p., 1987), 36.

17. "United States History," Robert Famighetti, Ed., in *The World Almanac and Book of Facts 1994* (Mahwah, 1993), 441.

18. *Moe v. Confed.* Salish and Kootenai Tribes, 425 U.S. 463 (1976). The states cannot exercise legal jurisdiction over Native Americans on reservations.

19. *Brown v. Board of Education of Topeka*, 349 U.S. 294 (1955) and related documents.

20. Charles Wilkinson, *American Indians, Time, and the Law: Native Societies in a Modern Constitutional Democracy* (New Haven, n.p., 1987), 99. Combination of Federal statutes, Federal regulatory agencies, Bureau of Indian

Affairs, and the Supremacy Clause keeps state governments at a distance.

21. Charles Wilkinson, *American Indians, Time, and the Law: Native Societies in a Modern Constitutional Democracy* (New Haven, 1987), 87-96. The issue continues to evolve around the idea of what represents "Legitimate Tribal Interest."

Chapter 17 Notes: The Vice-Presidency

1. _____, Congressional Quarterly staff, *Congress A to Z: CQ Ready Reference Encyclopedia* (Washington, n.p., 1988), 437.

2. James Madison, *Notes of Debates in the Federal Convention of 1787*, (New York, 1966), 596.

3. Jules Witcover, *From Adams and Jefferson to Truman and Quayle: Crapshoot: Rolling the Dice on the Vice Presidency*, (New York, 1992), 36.

4. Chester J. Pack, Jr. and Elmo Richardson, *The Presidency of Dwight D. Eisenhower*, (Lawrence, n.p., 1991), 175.

5. _____, *The United States Budget 1997*, http://access.gpo.gov/omb. Part of the Federal Budget listing is estimated.

Chapter 18 Notes: Sections Not Being Followed

1. *Kentucky v. Dennison*, 65 U.S. 24 Howard-66 (1861).

2. Esmond Wright, *The Search for Liberty: from Origins to Independence*, Vol. 1, 1995, 72-74.

3. Leland Lovette, *Naval Customs, Traditions and Usage*,1939, n.p., 284.

4. William Bishop, Jr., *International Law: Cases and Materials*, 1971, 1035. Declaration of Paris, 7 Moore, Digest of International Law 562 (1906). Some sources refer to it as the Treaty of Paris of 1856 or for related material note the Congress of Paris.

5. George Anastaplo, *The Amendments to the Constitution: A Commentary*, 1995, n.p., 173-185.

6. _____,179.

Chapter 19 Notes: Sections No Longer Needed in the Constitution

1. Leonard Levy, *Original Intent and the Framers' Constitution* (New

York, n.p., 1988) 127-130.

2. Charles Warren, *The Supreme Court in United States History* (Boston, n.p., 1935).

3. Wiliam Wallace, *Our Obsolete Constitution* (New York, n.p., 1932), 50. The nation's founders believed strongly in the sanctity of private property and contracts. This is so well established in American society it is nearly cultural.

4. *Fletcher v. Peck*, 6 Cranch 87 (1810).

5. Leonard Levy, *Original Intent and the Framers' Constitution* (New York, n.p., 1988) 130.

6. *Dartmouth College v. Woodward*, 4 Wheat, 518 (1819).

7. *New Jersey v. Wilson*, 7 Cranch 164 (1812).

8. *Sturgis v. Crowinshield*, 4 Wheat, 122 (1819).

9. *Northwestern Fertilizer Company v. Hyde Park* 97 U.S. 659 (1878).

10. *Home Building and Loan Association v. Glaisdell*, 290 U.S. 398 (1934).

11. Benjamin Wright, *The Contract Clause of the Constitution* (Cambridge, n.p., 1938). Also, Wallace Mendelson, *Supreme Court Statecraft: The Rules of Law and Men* (Ames, n.p., 1985), 337-349.

12. *Chisholm v. Georgia*, 2 Dall. 419 (1793).

13. Clyde Jacobs, *The Eleventh Amendment and Sovereign Immunity* (Westport, n.p., 1972).

14. Leonard Levy, *Original Intent and the Framers' Constitution* (New York, 1988), 59.

15. Louis Henkins, *Foreign Affairs and the Constitution* (Mineola, n.p., 1972), 189, 203-205. While foreign citizens may have a far more restricted set of individual rights and protections in Federal Court, the basic concepts of the United States Constitution apply.

16. Carl Van Doren, *Secret History of the American Revolution* (New York, n.p., 1941), 277.

17. Paul Finkelman "Manufacturing Martyrdom: The Antislavery Response to John Brown's Raid" in *His Soul Goes Marching On: Response to John Brown and the Harper's Ferry Raid*, Paul Finkelman, Ed. (Charlottesville, n.p., 1995), 41-66. Also, Jeffery Rossbach, *Ambivalent Conspirators: John Brown the*

Secret Six, and a Theory of Slave Violence (Philadelphia, n.p., 1982).

18. Nathaniel Weyl, *Treason: The Story of Disloyalty and Betrayal in American History* (Washington, n.p., 1950), 10-17.

19. Bradley Chapin, *The American Law of Treason: Revolutionary and Early National Origins* (Seattle, n.p., 1964).

20. J.G.A. Pocock, *The Machiavellian Moment: Florentine Political Thought and the Atlantic Republican Tradition* (Princeton, n.p., 1975), 528.

21. Alexander Hamilton, *The Federalist Papers*, Clinton Rossiter, Ed. (New York, n.p., 1961), 171.

22. William Gregory, *The Defense Procurement Mess* (Lexington, n.p., 1989).

23. Jacques Gansler, *The Defense Industry* (Cambridge, n.p., 1980).

Chapter 20 Notes: Sections That Are Confusing or Contradictory

1. Raoul Berger, *Impeachment—the Constitution Problem* (Cambridge, n.p., 1973), 7-49. Found within the concept of impeachment is *retrospective treason.*

2. Charles Black, Impeachment: A Handbook (New Haven, n.p., 1974), 49.

3. Raoul Berger, *Impeachment—the Constitution Problem* (Cambridge, n.p., 1973), 53.

4. John Labovity, *Presidential Impeachment* (New Haven, n.p., 1978), 57-62.

5. Wayne LaFave and Jedd Israel, *Criminal Procedure* (St. Paul, n.p., 1985).

6. *Barker v. Wingo*, 407 U.S. 514 (1972).

7. *Strunk v. United States* 412 U.S. 434 (1973).

8. Through most of United States history a public trial was easily defined, but in recent years the Supreme Court has been forced to look at this issue from a different perspective. *Gannett Company, Inc. v. DePasquale* 443 U.S. 368 (1979) and *Richmond Newspapers, Inc. v. Virginia* 448 U.S. 555 (1980).

9. Walter Berns, *For Capital Punishment: Crime and the Morality of the Death Penalty* (New York, n.p., 1979) and Thomas Massey, Healing the Wounds that Divide Us (San Diego, 1995), 134-138.

10. *Ingraham v. Wright* 430 U.S. 651 (1977), *Youngberg v. Romero* 457 U.S. 307 (1982), and *Bell v. Wolfish* 441 U.S. 520 (1979).

Chapter 21 Notes: Is the American Constitution Discriminatory?

1. Charles Simmons and Harry Morris, Eds., *Afro-American History* (Columbus, 1972). For a humanist view of black social issues and struggle note John Egerton, *Speak Now against the Day: The Generation before the Civil Rights Movement in the South* (New York, n.p., 1994).

2. Wiliam Wallace, *Our Obsolete Constitution* (New York, 1932), 74-76.

3. Nancy Woloch, *Women and the American Experience* (New York, n.p., 1994).

4. For an overview note Sara Evans, *Born for Liberty: A History of Women in America* (New York, n.p., 1989).

Chapter 22 Notes: Militias

1. William Riker, *Soldiers of the States: The Role of the National Guard in American Democracy* (Washington, n.p., 1957), 12.

2. _____, 84.

3. _____, 2.

4. A distinction must be made between the American militia movement and organized hate groups. While firearms and weaponry may be a part of both entities, the organizational structure is different. For hate groups note James Coates, *Armed and Dangerous: The Rise of the Survivalist Right* (New York, n.p.,1987). For another view of modern American militias note J. Harry Jones, *The Minutemen* (Garden City, n.p., 1968).

Chapter 23 Notes: Primaries

1. Lyn Ragsdale, *Vital Statistics on the Presidency* (Washington, n.p., 1996), 62. Also note the *Congressional Quarterly*, "Guide to the 1992 Democratic National Convention" (Washington, n.p., 1992), 70.

2. _____, 64.

3. _____, 46.

4. John Haskell, *Fundamentally Flawed: Understanding and Reforming*

Presidential Primaries (Lanhan, n.p., 1996), 68.

     5. Arthur Hadley, *The Invisible Primary* (Englewood Cliffs, n.p., 1976).

     6. John Haskell, *Fundamentally Flawed: Understanding and Reforming Presidential Primaries* (Lanhan, n.p., 1996), 73-74.

     7. _____, 76-78.

Chapter 24 Notes: How Readable Should a Constitution Be?

     1. Michael Kammen, *A Machine That Would Go of Itself: The Constitution in American Culture* (New York, n.p., 1987), 27.

     2. Leonard Levy, *Original Intent and the Framers' Constitution* (New York, n.p., 1988), 61.

     3. _____, 61-62.

     4. *Hylton v. United States,* 3 Dall. 171 (1796).

     5. J.A. Simpson and E.S.C. Weiner, Ed., *The Oxford English Dictionary* (Oxford, 1989), 956. It was noted that the "expression intended to refer inclusively to all the bodily faculties." The term appeared in Middle English text around 1205 or 1275.

Chapter 25 Notes: The Process of Interpreting

     1. Donald Lutz, *A Preface to American Political Theory* (Lawrence, n.p., 1992), 52-55.

     2. Christopher Wolfe, *How to Read the Constitution: Originalism, Constitution, Interpretation, and Judicial Power* (Lanham, n.p., 1996), 175-191.

     3. *Plessy v. Ferguson,* 163 U.S. 537 (1896).

     4. *Brown v. Board of Education of Topeka,* 349 U.S. 294 (1954).

     5. Melvin Urofsky, *A March of Liberty: A Constitutional History of the United States* (New York, 1988), 770.

     6. *Bolling v. Sharpe,* 347 U.S. 497 (1954).

     7. *Swift v. Tyson,* 16 Pet. 1 (1842).

     8. *Erie Railroad Company v. Tompkins,* 304 U.S. 64 (1938).

     9. Melvin Urofsky, *A March of Liberty: A Constitutional History of the United States* (New York, n.p., 1988), 301.

     10. *Griswold v. Penniman,* 2 Conn. 564 (1818).

11. Melvin Urofsky, *A March of Liberty: A Constitutional History of the United States* (New York, n.p.,1988), 698

12. *Goesaert v. Cleary*, 335 U.S. 464 (1948).

13. *Reed v. Reed*, 404 U.S. 71 (1971).

14. *Stanton v. Stanton*, 421 U.S. 7 (1975).

15. *Craig v. Boren*, 429 U.S. 190 (1976).

16. *Kirchberg v. Feenstra*, 450 U.S. 455 (1981).

17. *Flast v. Cohen* 392 U.S. 83 (1968).

18. *Valley Forge Christian College v. Americans United for Separation of Church and State* 454 U.S. 464 (1982).

Chapter 26 Notes: How Nations Decline

1. Will Durant and Ariel Durant, "XII. Growth and Decay"in *The Lessons of History* (New York, n.p., 1968), 87-94.

2. *The Richmond Recorder*, September 1, 1802, noting the Sally Hermings affair.

3. Willard Randall, *Thomas Jefferson: A Life*, (New York, n.p., 1993), 555; also see Thomas Jefferson's own work *The Philosophy of Jesus* later expanded into *The Life and Morals of Jesus.*

4. Garrett Sheldon, *The Political Philosophy of Thomas Jefferson*, (Baltimore, n.p., 1991) 129,

5. Thomas Jefferson, *Notes on the State of Virginia: The Writings of Thomas Jefferson*, Albert Bergh, Ed. (Washington, D.C., n.p., 1904), Vol. 8, 382-86

6. David Lowenthal, "The Purpose of Heritage," in *Possessed by the Past* (New York, n.p., 1996) 132.

7. David Lowenthal, "The Practice of Heritage" in *Possessed by the Past* (New York, n.p., 1996) 148.

8. Michael Kammen, *Selvages and Biases: The Fabric of History in American Culture* (Ithaca, n.p., 1987), 19.

9. Jocob Weisberg, *In Defense of Government: The Fall and Rise of Public Trust* (New York, n.p., 1996), 49. Weisberg noted that polls of the 1940s listed American trust in their government at 76 percent; by the 1990s it was 14 percent.

10. Bailyn Bernard, *The Ideological Origins of the American Revolution*,

(Cambridge, n.p., 1967), 66-67. Also note the writings of James Otis, *Rights of the British Colonies Asserted and Proved*, (Boston, n.p., 1764).

Chapter 27 Notes: Periodic Assessment

1. Michael Kammen, *A Machine That Would Go of Itself: The Constitution in American Culture* (New York, n.p., 1987), 394.

2. _____, 382.

Chapter 28 Notes: Philosophy and Perspectives

1. Lance Banning, *The Jeffersonian Persuasion* (Ithaca, 1978) 93. The United States Constitution must be seen as a liberal document especially considering the related national governments of the 18th Century plus the Puritan and Calvinist influences of the times.

2. Bernard Bailyn, *The Ideological Origins of the American Revolution,* (Cambridge, 1967), 18-19.

3. Edward Erler, "The Political Philosophy of the Constitution," in Herman Belz, Ronald Hoffman, and Peter Albert, Ed., *To Form a More Perfect Union: Critical Ideas of the Constitution,* (Charlottesville, 1992), 137.

4. Natural Rights is a specific term in political philosophy noting rights that a person has upon birth or in a primitive state. It was discussed freely in the works of Edmund Burke, David Hume, John Locke, Jeremy Bentham, and many others. Of the revolutionary theorist John Adams, Thomas Jefferson, and Thomas Paine wrote on the topic as well. The best overview of the period can be found in Thomas Paine's work *Let Them Call Me Rebel.* Moncure Conway, Ed. *The Writings of Thomas Paine* (New York, 1894) "Rights of Man, Part One" (1791).

5. Garrett Sheldon, *The Political Philosophy of Thomas Jefferson,* (Baltimore, 1993) 76. A similar theme can be seen in Jefferson's celebrated writings on "earth belongs to the living" and his correspondence with James Madison in 1787.

6. Morton White, *Philosophy, The Federalist, and the Constitution,* (New York, 1987), 22.

7. _____, 28.

8. Robert Hendrickson, *The Rise and Fall of Alexander Hamilton,* (New

York, 1981), 232.

9. Walter Berns, *Taking the Constitution Seriously,* (New York, 1987), 165.

10. John Locke, *Of Civil Government Second Treatise,* (South Bend, 1955). Also, Locke, *Two Treatises of Government,* Thomas Cook, Ed. (New York, 1947). More to the point, John Locke, *A Letter Concerning Toleration* (Indianapolis, 1955), 52.

11. Walter Berns, *Taking the Constitution Seriously,* (New York, 1987), 134

12. Melvin Urofsky, *A March of Liberty, A Constitutional History of the United States,* (New York, 1988), 94-96.

13. Edward Erler, "The Constitution and the Separation of Powers," in Leonard W. Levy and Dennis Mahoney, Eds., *The Framing and Ratification of the Constitution,* (New York, 1987), 151-166.

14. Pluralism is the doctrine where governmental authority is distributed among many different groups and interest. One of the earlier works is by Earl Latham, *The Group Basis of Politics* (Ithaca, 1952). Also see, Robert Dahl, *Who Governs?* (New Haven, 1961) and Edward Banfield, *Political Influence* (New York, 1961).

15. George Sabine, *A History of Political Theory* (New York, 1961) 54.

16. James Madison, *The Federalist Papers,* "No. 47" Clinton Rossiter, Ed. (New York, 1961) 300.

17. J.G.A. Pocock, *The Machiavellian Moment,* (Princeton, 1975) 527-28. Pocock does support the view that Machiavellian concepts of virtue and corruption did shape early American thought.

Chapter 29 Notes: Past Efforts at Constitutional Reform

1. John Vile, *Encyclopedia of Constitutional Amendments, Proposed Amendments, and Amending Issues 1789-1995* (Santa Barbara, n.p., 1996), xi.

2. Akil Amar, "The Bill of Rights as a Constitution," *Yale Law Journal* (Winter, 1992), 1137-45.

3. Melvin Urofsky, *A March of Liberty: A Constitutional History of the United States* (New York, n.p., 1988), 298.

4. Keogh Stephen, "Formal and Informal Constitutional Lawmaking in the United States in the Winter of 1860-1861," *Journal of Legal History* (December 1987), 275-99.

5. John Vile, *Encyclopedia of Constitutional Amendments, Proposed Amendments, and Amending Issues 1789-1995.* (Santa Barbara, n.p., 1996), 119.

6. Judith Best, *National Representation for the District of Columbia* (Maryland, n.p., 1984).

7. Ronald Rotunda and Stephen Safranek, *Amending the Constitution by a Call for a Constitutional Convention,* http://www.termlimits.org.

8. Ronald Rotunda and Stephen Safranek, *Amending the Constitution by a Call for a Constitutional Convention,* http://www.termlimits.org.

9. John Vile, *Rewriting the United States Constitution: An Examination of Proposals from Reconstruction to the Present* (New York, n.p., 1991).

10. John Vile, *Encyclopedia of Constitutional Amendments, Proposed Amendments, and Amending Issues 1789-1995* (Santa Barbara, n.p., 1996).

11. August Heckscher, *Woodrow Wilson* (New York, n.p., 1991).

12. John Vile, *Encyclopedia of Constitutional Amendments, Proposed Amendments, and Amending Issues 1789-1995* (Santa Barbara, n.p., 1996).

13. Steven Boyd, *Alternative Constitutions for the United States: A Documentary History* (Westport, n.p., 1992), 25.

14. James West, *A Proposed New Constitution for the United States* (Springfield, n.p., 1890).

15. Frederick Adams, *President John Smith: The Story of a Peaceful Revolution* (Chicago, n.p., 1896).

16. Henry Morris, *Waiting for the Signal* (Chicago, n.p., 1989).

17. Steven Boyd, *Alternative Constitutions for the United States,:A Documentary History* (Westport, n.p., 1992), 129.

18. _____, 151.

19. _____, 178.

20. Rexford Tugwell, *Total Democracy: The New Constitution for the United States: A Democratic Ideal for the World* (New York, n.p., 1941) .

21. Leland Baldwin, *Reframing the Constitution: An Imperative for Modern America* (Santa Barbara, n.p., 1972).

22. Steven Boyd, *Alternative Constitutions for the United States, A Documentary History* (Westport, n.p., 1992), 15.

23. Plaque from the Jefferson Memorial in Washington, D.C., 22.

Chapter 31 Notes:

1. Eric Hoffer, *The Passionate State of Mind and Other Aphorisms*, (New York, n.p., 1955), 50.

Chapter 36 Notes: Is This New Constitution Realistic?

1. Thomas Jefferson, *Writings/Thomas Jefferson*, Merrill Peterson, Ed., (New York, 1984).

2. Marvin Gettleman, *The Dorr Rebellion: A Study in American Radicalism 1833-1849* (Huntington, 1980). Also Dan King, *The Life and Times of Thomas Wilson Dorr with Outlines of the Political History of Rhode Island* (Freeport, 1859, reprint 1969), 34-54. For a related court case note *Luther v. Border,* 7 Howard 48 U.S. 1 (1849).

3. Matthew Bunson, *Our Sunday Visitor's Encyclopedia of Catholic History*, (Huntington, n.p., 1995), 884-886.

Selected Bibliography

Anastaplo, George. *The Amendments to the Constitution.* Baltimore: Johns Hopkins University Press, 1995.

Arkes, Hadley. *Beyond the Constitution.* Princeton: Princeton University Press, 1990.

Bailyn, Bernard. *The Ideological Origins of the American Revolution.* Cambridge: Belknap Press of Harvard University, 1967.

Bailyn, Bernard, Ed. *The Debate on the Constitution: Federalist and Antifederalist: Speeches, Articles, and Letters during the Struggle over Ratification.* Vols. I-II. Library of America, 1993.

Barber, Sotirios A. *The Constitution and the Delegation of Congressional Power.* Chicago: University of Chicago Press, 1975.

Beard, Charles A. *An Economic Interpretation of the Constitution of the United States.* New York: Free Press, 1986.

Berger, Raoul. *Federalism: The Founders' Design.* Norman: University of Oklahoma Press, 1987.

Best, Judith. *National Representation for the District of Columbia.* Frederick: University Publications of America, 1984.

Binder, Sarah A., and Steven S. Smith. *Politics or Principles: Filibustering in the United States Senate.* Washington: Brookings Institution Press, 1997.

Bishop, William W., Jr. *International Law: Cases and Materials.* Boston: Little, Brown, and Company, 1953.

Boorstin, Daniel, Ed. *An American Primer.* Chicago: University of Chicago Press, 1966.

Boyd, Julian P., Ed. *The Papers of Thomas Jefferson.* Princeton, New Jersey: Princeton University Press, 1950.

Boyd, Steven. *Alternative Constitutions for the United States: A Documentary History.* Westport, Connecticut: Greenwood Press, 1992.

Brant, Irving. *Storm over the Constitution.* Indianapolis, Indiana: Bobbs-Merrill, 1936.

Brown, Bernard E., Ed. *Great American Political Thinkers: Creating America from Settlements to Mass Democracy.* Vol. I-II. New York: Avon Books, 1983.

Bryce, James. D.C.I. *Studies in History and Jurisprudence.* Vol.I-II. Freeport, New York: Books for Libraries Press, 1901.

Congress A to Z, CQ:A Ready Reference Encyclopedia, Washington, D.C.: Congressional Quarterly, 1988.

Cohen, Sanford. *Labor in the United States.* Columbus: Charles E. Merrill Publishing, 1970.

Conlan, Roberta, Ed. *The Reservations.* Alexandria, Virginia: Time-Life Books, 1995.

Corley, Robert N., and Peter J. Shedd. *Fundamentals of Business Law.* Englewood Cliffs: Prentice Hall, 1990.

De Tocqueville, Alexis. *Democracy in America.* Richard D. Heffner, Ed. New York: New American Library, 1956.

Deisher, Beth, Ed. *Coin World Almanac.* Sidney, Ohio: Amos Press, 1987.

Dolbeare, Kenneth M. *American Political Thought.* Chatham, New Jersey: Chatham House Publishers, 1981.

Domhoff, G. William. *Who Rules America.* Englewood Cliffs, New Jersey: Prentice-Hall, 1967.

Dworkin, Ronald. *Freedom's Law: The Moral Reading of the American Constitution.* Cambridge: Harvard University Press, 1996.

Dye, Thomas R., and L. Harmon Zeigler. *The Irony of Democracy: An Uncommon Introduction to American Politics.* Belmont, California: Wadsworth Publishing Company, 1970.

Edelman, Martin. *Democratic Theories and the Constitution.* Albany: State University of New York Press, 1984.

Elazar, Daniel J. *American Federalism: A View from the States.* New York: Thomas Y. Crowell Company, 1972.

Famighetti, Robert, Ed. *The World Almanac and Book of Facts.* Mahwah, New Jersey: St. Martin's Press, 1994.

Fisher, Roger. *International Conflict for Beginners.* New York: Harper Colophon Books, 1969.

Foner, Philip S., Ed. *Basic Writings of Thomas Jefferson*. Garden City, New York: Halcyon House, 1944.

Friedrich, Carl J., and Zbigniew K. Brzezinski. *Totalitarian Dictatorship and Autocracy*. New York: Frederick A. Praeger, 1956.

Galbraith, John Kenneth. *Economics in Perspective: A Critical History*. Boston: Houghton Mifflin, 1987.

Glennon, Michael J. *When No Majority Rules: The Electoral College and Presidential Succession*. Washington, D.C.: Congressional Quarterly, 1992.

Goodwyn, Lawrence. *Democratic Promise: The Populist Moment in America*. New York: Oxford University Press, 1976.

Hanson, A.H. *Governing Britain*. London: Fontana Press, 1970.

Hawkesworth, Mary, and Maurice, Kogan, Eds. *Encyclopedia of Government and Politics*. London: Routledge, 1992.

Ibadan, Peter Boe. "Circumcision: The Rites of Manhood in the Bille Tribe." In *Traditional Religion in West Africa*, Adegbola, E. A. Ade, Ed. Nigeria: Daystar Press, 1983.

Jacobsen, G. A. and Lipman, M.H. *Political Science*. New York: Barnes and Noble Books, 1965.

Jefferson, Thomas. *Writings/thomas Jefferson*. New York: Viking Press, 1984.

Jensen, Merrill. *The American Constitution*. Malabar: Krieger Publishing, 1979.

Kammen, Michael. *Selvages and Biases: The Fabric of History in American Culture*. Ithaca: Cornell University Press, 1987.

Ketcham, Ralph. *James Madison: A Biography*. New York: Macmillan, 1971.

Lazare, Daniel. *The Frozen Republic: How the Constitution Is Paralyzing Democracy*. New York: Harcourt Brace and Company, 1996.

Levy, Leonard W. *Original Intent and the Framers' Constitution*. New York: Macmillan, 1988.

Levy, Leonard. *Seasoned Judgements: The American Constitution, Rights, and History*. New Brunswich: Transaction Publishers, 1995.

Lewis, John D., Ed. *Anti-Federalists versus Federalists*. San Francisco: Chandler Publishing, 1967.

Lieberman, Jethro K. *The Enduring Constitution: A Bicentennial Perspective.* Saint Paul: West Publishing, 1987.

Locke, John. *Two Treatises of Government.* Thomas Cook, Ed. NewYork: Hafner Press, 1947.

Longley, Lawrence D. and Neal R. Peirce. *The Electoral College Primer.* New Haven: Yale University Press, 1996.

Lowenthal, David. *Possessed by the Past: The Heritage Crusade and the Spoils of History.* New York: Free Press, 1996.

Lutz, Donald S. *A Preface to American Political Theory.* Lawrence: University Press of Kansas, 1992.

Lutz, Donald S. *The Origins of American Constitutionalism.* Baton Rouge: Louisiana State University Press, 1988.

Notes of Debates in the Federal Convention of 1787. New York: W.W. Norton and Company, 1987.

McClenaghan, William A. *American Government.* Boston: Allyn and Bacon, 1964.

McDonald, Forrest. *A Constitutional History of the United States.* Malabor: Robert E. Krieger Publishing, 1982.

McNair, Arnold D. *The Law of Treaties.* Oxford: Clarendon Press, 1961.

Miller, Arthur, S. *The Secret Constitution and the Need for Constitutional Change.* New York: Greenwood Press, 1987.

Mogi, Sobei. *The Problem of Federalism: A Study in the History of Political Theory.* New York: Macmillan,1931.

Morgan, Edmund S. *The Genius of George Washington.* New York: W.W. Norton and Company, 1977.

Morgan, Kathleen O'Leary, Scott Morgan, and Neal Quitno, Eds. *State Rankings 1996: A Statistical View of the Fifty United States.* Lawrence, Kansas: Morgan Quitno Press, 1996.

Morgan, Robert, J. *A Whig Embattled: The Presidency under John Tyler.* Lincoln: University of Nebraska Press, 1954.

Oleszek, Walter J. *Congressional Procedures and the Policy Process.* Congressional Quarterly, 1996.

Parenti, Michael. *Democracy for the Few.* New York: St. Martin's Press, 1980.

Peirce, Neal R. *The People's President: The Electoral College in American History and the Direct Vote Alternative.* New York: Simon and Schuster, 1968.

Plato, *The Republic of Plato,* translated by Allan Bloom. New York: Basic Books, 1968.

The Presidency A to Z, CQ:A Ready Reference Encyclopedia. Washington, D. C.: Congressional Quarterly, 1992.

Presidential Elections Since 1789. Fifth Edition. Washington, D.C.: Congressional Quarterly, 1991.

Rachels, James, Ed. *Moral Problems: A Collection of Philosophical Essays.* New York: Harper and Row, 1979.

Ragsdale, Lyn. *Vital Statistics on the Presidency: Washington to Clinton.* Washington, D.C: Congressional Quarterly, 1996.

Randall, Sterne Willard. *Thomas Jefferson: A Life.* New York: Henry Holt and Company, 1993.

Reid, John Phillip. *The Concept of Representation in the Age of the American Revolution.* Chicago: University of Chicago Press, 1989.

Riker, William H. *Soldiers of the States: The Role of the National Guard in American Democracy.* Washington, D.C.: Public Affairs Press, 1957.

Roszkowski, Mark E. *Business Law: Principles, Cases, and Policy.* Glenview, Illinois: Scott, Foresman and Company, 1989.

Schattschneider, E. E. *The Semisovereign People: A Realist's View of Democracy in America.* Holt, Rinehart and Winston, 1960.

Schoenbrod, David. *Power without Responsibility: How Congress Abuses the People through Delegation.* New Haven: Yale University Press, 1993.

Shanor, Charles A. and Lynn L. Hogue. *Military Law in a Nutshell.* St. Paul: West Publishing Company, 1996.

Sheldon, Garrett Ward. *The Political Philosophy of Thomas Jefferson.* Baltimore: Johns Hopkins University Press, 1993.

Simmons, Charles W. and Harry W. Morris, Eds. *Afro-American History.* Columbus: Charles E. Merrill Publishing, 1972.

Spero, Robert. *The Duping of the American Voter: Dishonesty and Deception in Presidential Television Advertising.* New York: Lippincott and Crowell, 1980.

Stites, Francis N. *John Marshall: Defender of the Constitution.* Boston: Little, Brown, and Company, 1981.

Storing, Herbert J. *What the Anti-Federalists Were For.* Chicago: University of Chicago Press, 1981.

Story, Joseph. *Commentaries on the Constitution of the United States.* Durham: Carolina Academic Press, 1987.

Sundquist, James L. *Constitutional Reform and Effective Government.* Washington, D.C.: Brookings Institution, 1986.

The Supreme Court A to Z: A Ready Reference Encyclopedia. Washington, D. C: Congressional Quarterly, 1993.

Timberlake, Richard H. *Gold, Greenbacks, and the Constitution.* Berryville: The George Edward Durell Foundation, 1991.

Tribe, Laurence H. and Michael C. Dorf. *On Reading the Constitution.* Cambridge: Harvard University Press, 1991.

Urofsky, Melvin I. *A March of Liberty: A Constitutional History of the United States.* New York: Alfred A. Knopf, 1988.

Vile, John R. *Encyclopedia of Constitutional Amendments, Proposed Amendments, and Amending Issues 1789-1995.* Santa Barbara: ABC-CLIO, 1996.

Vile, John R. *Rewriting the United States Constitution: An Examination of Proposals from Reconstruction to the Present.* New York: Praeger Publishers, 1991.

Weisberg, Jacob. *In Defense of Government: The Fall and Rise of Public Trust.* Scribner, 1996.

Wilkinson, Charles F. *American Indians, Time, and the Law: Native Societies in a Modern Constitutional Democracy.* New Haven: Yale University Press, 1987.

Wilson, Woodrow. *Congressional Government; a Study in American Politics.* Cleveland: Meridian Books, 1965.

Index

Index